The Family on Trial
in Revolutionary France

SUZANNE DESAN

D1453607

University of California Press

BERKELEY   LOS ANGELES   LONDON

*The publisher gratefully acknowledges the generous contribution
to this book provided by the Ahmanson Foundation Humanities Fund
of the University of California Press Associates.*

University of California Press
Berkeley and Los Angeles, California

University of California Press, Ltd.
London, England

First paperback printing 2006
© 2004 by the Regents of the University of California

Library of Congress Cataloging-in-Publication Data

Desan, Suzanne, 1957–.
  The family on trial in revolutionary France / by Suzanne Desan.
    p.   cm. — (Studies on the history of society and culture ; 51)
  Includes bibliographical references and index.
  ISBN 0-520-24816-3 (pbk : alk. paper)
    1. Family—France—History—18th century. 2. Family—Political
aspects—France 3. Domestic relations—France—History—18th
century. 4. France—History—Revolution, 1789–1799—Women.
5. France—History—Revolution, 1789–1799. I. Title. II. Series.

HQ623.D45 2004
306.85'0944'09033—dc21   2003014269

Manufactured in the United States of America

14 13 12 11 10 09 08 07 06
10 9 8 7 6 5 4 3 2 1

The paper used in this publication meets the minimum requirements of
ANSI/ NISO Z39.48-1992 (R 1997) (*Permanence of Paper*). ⊚

Parts of chapter 4 appeared in "War between Brothers and Sisters: Inheritance Law and Gender Politics in Revolutionary France," *French
Historical Studies* 20 (1997): 597–634, and are used here by permission
of Duke University Press. Parts of chapter 6 were first published in
French as "Qu'est-ce qui fait un père? Illégitimité et paternité de l'an II
au Code civil," *Annales: Histoire, Sciences sociales* 57, no. 4 (2002):
935–64, © Éditions de l'EHESS. Parts of chapter 7 appeared in "Reconstituting the Social after the Terror: Family, Property, and the Law in
Popular Politics," *Past and Present* 164 (1999): 81–121, reprinted by permission of Oxford University Press.

The Family on Trial in Revolutionary France

STUDIES ON THE HISTORY OF SOCIETY AND CULTURE

Victoria E. Bonnell and Lynn Hunt, Editors

For Barbara

Contents

Illustrations

Acknowledgments

I am profoundly grateful to the many people and institutions who have helped me with this project. For putting me in touch with the French revolutionaries, I thank the staffs of the Archives nationales, the Bibliothèque nationale, the Bibliothèque Marguerite Durand, the Bibliothèque Cujas, various departmental archives, the Bibliothèque municipale de Caen, and the Archives départementales du Calvados. Gilbert Lauvergne gave me invaluable assistance in working with the unclassified L Series in the Calvados. The librarians at the Newberry Library, the University of Wisconsin at Madison, the Houghton Library, the Harvard Law School, and the University of Maryland at College Park also have my gratitude. David Warrington kindly braved the construction at Harvard Law School to satisfy my quest for obscure French legal pamphlets, and Allan Rough at the University of Maryland resurrected an almost defunct videodisc system so that I could examine revolutionary images.

I could never have written this book without help from many colleagues and friends. For their constructive observations about various portions of this manuscript, I am grateful to Julia Adams, Gail Bederman, Lenard Berlanstein, Joshua Cole, Margaret Darrow, Paul Hanson, Steven Kaplan, Michael Kwass, Darline Gay Levy, Martyn Lyons, Laura Mason, Cynthia Milton, Roderick Phillips, Zoe Schneider, and Isser Woloch. André Burguière and Françoise Fortunet inspired me with their excellent work on French families. Corinne Bléry shared her knowledge of the Norman custom. Dialogue with Betsy Colwill, Natalie Zemon Davis, Dirk Hartog, Gary Kates, Sarah Maza, and Jeffrey Merrick has invigorated and influenced me. Megan Ballard, Carol Blum, Anthony Crubaugh, Jeffrey Ford, Rene Marion, and Becky Rassier generously supplied me with crucial information.

Sheryl Kroen read the entire manuscript at a key moment and enabled me to articulate its most central arguments. Tip Ragan's zest for intellectual exchange, his love of fine food, and shared passion for the French Revolution have made him a treasured friend and critic forever. Like me, Julie Hardwick, Jennifer Heuer, Janine Lanza, and Matthew Gerber have developed a quirky addiction to the intricacies of French family law; their conversation and criticism have been essential. Lucid commentary from Rachel Fuchs informed my final revisions. I thank Dena Goodman for her intellectual companionship and perceptive reading. I am grateful to Elinor Accampo, Jo Burr Margadant, Karen Offen, Sylvia Schafer, and Whitney Walton for providing comments and sharing their knowledge of the nineteenth century when I was trying to imagine France after the Revolution. Lynn Hunt taught me to embrace French history as an adventure. She has listened insightfully, critiqued my work with skill and grace, and encouraged me time and again. I offer her my heartfelt thanks for her kindness, inspiration, and counsel.

At the University of Wisconsin, I am surrounded by the stimulating scholarship, friendship, and encouragement of many colleagues and friends. For more than a decade, Jeanne Boydston and I have carried on a conversation about gender and revolution in the transatlantic world. Her probing questions and critiques, always delivered with humor and warmth, have helped me rethink this book in so many ways. I thank David Sorkin for his discerning comments and ideas about structure. Tom Broman's enthusiasm and critical acumen have always sent me back to my manuscript with renewed zeal. If Laird Boswell, *cher camarade*, still does not believe that the French Revolution was the most significant era in French history, it is not for lack of reading many, many pages about the all-important impact of the Revolution on the family. He has showered with me suggestions great and small, helped me with my French, and made me laugh since we were students together twenty years ago. Linda Gordon's broad-ranging intellect has been a welcome source of new perspectives always. Only Jane Schulenburg—with her unique combination of personal zaniness and scholarly expertise in medieval women's history—was able to supply me with the name of the patron saint of unhappily married wives (Sainte Livrade, of course).

I thank Colleen Dunlavy for her expertise and her reassuring soul. I am grateful to Nan Enstad, Robert Kingdon, Florencia Mallon, Domenico Sella, Steve Stern, and Anne Vila for exchanging ideas with me and providing models of engaged scholarship. Lou Roberts arrived in Madison just in time to energize the final stages of this project with her critical reading skills and lively spirit. Lunch buddy Steve Kantrowitz, writing buddy Ron Radano, and everybody's buddy Tim Tyson commiserated with me as we all wrote our books together; in their different ways, they each inspired me with their inimitable approaches to the written word. Mike Lynn and David Ciarlo not only offered stimulating dialogue and criticism, but also kept me sane with many games of racquetball and squash. I have benefited from Franca Barricelli's kindheartedness and carefully considered comments. Louise Robbins has shared her editorial, ornithological, and historical expertise. For their support, I thank Joy Newmann, Judith Allen, Severino Albuquerque, and Perri Morgan, kindred, restless spirit. My gratitude also goes to all the members of the Madison Area French History Group—now revived and expanded as the Wisconsin French History Group—for reading my work, drinking my wine, and cheering me on.

My graduate students at the University of Wisconsin have aided me more than they realize. Working through ideas with them in seminar has helped shape me as a historian. Research assistants Tom Campbell and Heather Hales helped me read through reel after reel of the *état civil* searching for divorces. The Church of Jesus Christ of Latter-day Saints generously made these records available. I am beholden to Jamie Lee for building the divorce database and giving me many useful suggestions. Thanks go to Susan Nelson and Lisa Cline for tracking down engravings at the Bibliothèque nationale.

The Fulbright Foundation, the University of Wisconsin Graduate School, and the Société des Professeurs français et francophones d'Amérique supported the original research for this book. Assistance from the John Simon Guggenheim Foundation and the Humanities Institute of the University of Wisconsin at Madison made it possible for me to complete it. Erik Rundell of the University of Wisconsin Cartography Lab drew the maps. Sheila Levine, Rose Vekony, Nancy Evans, and the staff at the University of California Press have edited and shepherded this work with care.

My far-flung family of Forrests and Dolaras, Hussons and Desans, Backuses and Huys, stretching from the Big Horn Mountains to the Flanders to Tuscany, has entertained me, fed me, and watched my progress with puzzlement and love. My brother Paul's wit and clarity have given me perspective always. By different twists of fate, my sister Christine and I both became historians of the late eighteenth century. Her brilliant suggestions have saved this book many times, but most of all I am grateful for the undying friendship and mutual understanding that began the day she was born. My mother Elizabeth Desan has animated my life with her intellectual curiosity, compassion, and wry sense of humor. My father Wilfrid Desan, philosopher and revolutionary, passed away while I was completing this work. He embodied generosity, passionate intellectual engagement, and keen appreciation of the complexities of European culture. I miss him always and I hope this book reflects his inspiring example. Finally, my deepest thanks go to my soul mate Barbara Forrest. Her creativity, warm spirit, and *joie de vivre* have sustained me through this project and sustain me always.

Introduction

"The family is a small state, just as the State is a large family," declared the "Younger Sons of Provence" in 1789 as they denounced the inequalities and internal "privileges" that tore Old Regime families apart. These petitioners urged the new legislature to curtail the authority of despotic fathers, secure equal inheritance for all sons and daughters, and foster "mutual esteem" within the family. "The names father, mother, brother, and sister will no longer be insignificant words. . . . Moral affection, purified at its very source, will spread like a torrent in society. . . . The Provençal will become a good friend, good citizen, good subject, and the regeneration of the laws will also rebuild social morality."[1] These younger sons of the Midi formed just one voice in a louder chorus urging fundamental changes in domestic relationships. The outbreak of the French Revolution created a potent space for questioning the customs, laws, emotions, power relations, and gender assumptions that informed family life.

During the 1790s the French Revolution radically redefined the family, its internal dynamics, and its relationship to the state. As part of an all-embracing attempt to liberate individuals, recreate citizens from within, and build a more egalitarian social structure, the revolutionaries challenged long-standing domestic practices and infused politics into the most intimate relationships. From 1789, citizens across France—jurists and deputies, pamphleteers and moralists, sons and daughters, illegitimate children and unhappily married spouses, lawyers and judges—all disputed how the family should be reformed to remake the new France. They debated how revolutionary ideals and institutions should transform the emotional bonds, gender dynamics, legal customs, and economic arrangements that structured the family. They asked how to bring the principles of liberty, equality, and regeneration into the home. And as French sisters and brothers, wives and husbands confronted one another in the home, in court, and in print, they gradually, wrenchingly, negotiated new domestic practices which balanced Old Regime customs with revolutionary innovations in law and culture. This book explores these struggles to envision and put into practice a new set of familial relationships. It examines the family as an arena of social and political contestation during the French Revolution and asks how citizens both reimagined and experienced family life.

The French revolutionaries were ambitious in their attempts to transform the family, for they saw how profoundly politics and the gendered matters of daily life were intertwined. In 1789, when the "Younger Sons of Provence" drew an analogy between family and state, they articulated a commonly held Old Regime concept: the internal dynamics of family and the politics of state paralleled and reinforced each other. Political theorists from Jean Bodin to Jacques-Bénigne Bossuet had justified absolutism by posing a correlation between the patriarchal rule of the monarch over his kingdom and the father's empire over his family. According to belief at the time, this hierarchy within state and household rested neither on contract nor on the choice or consent of the governed. Rather, it was ordained by nature and God. Countless discussions in "myth and sermon, science and philosophy" naturalized these notions about the superiority of male over female, parent over child, and wove these assumptions into the cultural fabric of everyday life.[2]

Royal policies and social practices within families lent added strength to these ways of perceiving gender and the political order. From the mid sixteenth century, as they laid the foundations of absolutism, monarchs and magistrates also pursued certain laws and policies that explicitly reinforced the authority of fathers and the stability of families, especially the lineage families of the king's elite allies. Royal decrees and jurisprudence strengthened parental control over marriage, defended the indissolubility of marriage, criminalized female adultery and infanticide, fostered the exclusion of illegitimate children from inheritance and civil status, and facilitated the imprisonment of rebellious children and adulterous wives with *lettres de cachet* (royal arrest warrants for summary incarceration).[3] These Old Regime patriarchal practices and ideologies contained spaces for negotiation: notions of sexual difference were continually being disputed and remolded. As Julie Hardwick has argued for early modern Nantes, the "practice of patriarchy" emerged as a process rather than simply as an ideology or set of laws imposed from above. Women and adult children in many cases exercised more power over property or decision-making than the letter of the law allowed, and family patterns differed immensely from region to region.[4]

Nonetheless, by and large patriarchal household politics and the broader political system of absolutism were integrally interconnected and mutually reinforcing. Old Regime family critics—such as litigating wives, Enlightenment philosophes, reform-minded lawyers, and feminist novelists—did not hesitate to condemn "domestic despotism" in language at once familial and political.[5] When the Revolution toppled the absolutist monarchy and attacked the hierarchical structure of society, many citizens from Lille to Languedoc believed that a new form of politics and state demanded the remaking of the family as well. "If we finally accept as an organizing principle that the strong will no longer impose laws on the weak in the great family of the State, why would we allow it in our own families?" asked two women from Rouen in 1789 in their *Remonstrances by Norman Mothers and Daughters of the Third Estate.*[6]

This book follows the lead suggested by these "Mothers and Daughters" of Normandy and by the "Younger Sons of Provence." It takes as its central question: What was the relationship between family, politics, and state during the French Revolution? In addressing this question, I analyze the continual interaction between family members and revolutionary politics and state-building. On the one hand, I argue that the Revolution transformed the most intimate relationships and challenged the patriarchal structure of Old Regime families. Revolutionary social reforms enabled—or sometimes required—various citizens to make concrete changes in their domestic situations. Women in certain positions in the family were especially able to benefit from innovations in civil law. Moreover, family members across France saw personal applications for the bold principles of revolutionary politics. As they struggled to reshape and reimagine their domestic worlds, they tapped into the social ideology of the Revolution to demand more egalitarian or affectionate relationships at home, to pressure the new state to recast domestic practices and policies, or, in some cases, to defend age-old customs from new angles.

On the other hand, I also argue that remaking the family and gender relationships was integral to forging the revolutionary state and politics. The family became a practical terrain for wrestling with the most fundamental questions of the French Revolution: how to invent the rights-bearing, legal individual within a newly secularized state; how to refashion subjects into citizens and political participants in the nation; how to remold social bonds and practices to promote equality, liberty, and unity. The revolutionaries had high hopes and deep criticism for the family because they recognized its centrality and potential: as the legal frame for defining citizenship, as a promising site of patriotic conversion, as the elemental building block of society and the gender order, as a testing ground where the ideals of personal liberty and equality could take shape in workaday life. The revolutionaries could not accomplish their essential legal, politico-cultural, and social goals without reforming domestic relationships, but reconstructing the family was neither a top-down nor an abstract process. Family members themselves—as litigants, petitioners, activists, pamphleteers, arbiters, and judges—influenced the generation of social policies and hammered out the practical meanings of citizenship and revolutionary principles in home, courtroom, and legislature. By asking how domestic and public contestation over familial matters interacted with revolutionary politics, this work places the day-to-day practices, gender negotiations, and political activism of ordinary men and women at the heart of the revolutionary attempt to build a new social and political order.

To probe the Revolution within the family offers the opportunity to address basic questions about social change, politics, and gender during this pivotal era. I argue that many individuals experienced the tumult of the 1790s as a social revolution as well as a political one. I use this phrase not in the classic sense of class transformation, although there were distinct class differences in the experience of family reform. Rather, the 1790s witnessed profound transformations in the expectations and practices within families and in the relationships between women and men, between siblings, between parents and children. Mistrustful of prerevolutionary customs that promoted domestic hierarchy, revolutionary leaders responded to vocal, popular appeals for change and passed controversial new laws, intended to dismantle the traditional family and to guarantee liberty and civil rights to individual family members. Divorce; the redefinition of marriage as a freely chosen, civil contract; egalitarian inheritance among daughters and sons alike; the reduction of paternal authority; adoption; the lowering of the age of majority; the gradual abolition of paternity suits by unwed mothers; the incorporation of illegitimate offspring into the family; the secularization of marriage and of civil record-keeping. These ambitious reforms pleased many people and resonated with the new politics, yet they inevitably provoked opposition and conflict, for they left almost no aspect of private life untouched. They struck at the core of property relations, kinship structures, and agrarian customs. They challenged complex webs of long-standing mutual obligation, built on gendered and generational lines. Despite resistance to change, many families were wrenched away from their customary means of negotiating intimacy and distributing resources and authority within households.

Revolutionary culture, institutions, and laws created opportunities for various women and men to carve out new roles and positions within the home. The outbreak of Revolution unleashed potent reform ideologies. Individuals who chafed against the constraints and hierarchies of families appropriated concepts such as "liberty," "natural right," or "equality" and forged a vehement critique of family customs. Miserable or abused wives, stigmatized "bastards" who were denied rights and civil status, defiant adult daughters or sons seeking to marry against their parents' wishes, abandoned husbands hoping to remarry, sisters and younger brothers angered by family strategies favoring eldest sons—discontent family members such as these invoked revolutionary ideals both in their personal attempts to recast their relationships and in their appeals to the state to reform domestic laws and policies. In the process, they articulated new models of intimate relationships that favored affection over purely pragmatic arrangements, individual liberty over sacrifice for the family line, and egalitarian relationships over domestic hierarchies.

In analyzing the social revolution within the home, I make the methodological assumption that one can understand the relationship between family and Revolution, between gender and politics, only by continually exploring the interactions between social practices and cultural construction. More specifically, I draw in part on the methodological insights of historians of gender and historians of political culture who have highlighted how powerfully language and imagery influence, shape, at times limit, at times make possible the perceptions and actions of men and women.[7] But rather than focusing solely on lawmakers or the most renowned culture-makers, on men such as Robespierre or Rousseau, I argue that women and men at all levels of society generated new social norms and gender ideologies. As the French struggled to create the revolutionary family, they took part in ongoing debate over the cultural meanings of femininity and masculinity and over the interpretation of politically loaded principles, such as "natural law" or "equality." This study traces these discursive controversies and strategies across multiple arenas: in households, print culture, legislatures, festivals, speeches at Jacobin clubs, petitions, and courtrooms. A wide range of sources, from judicial briefs to feminist grievance lists *(cahiers)*, even notarized property donations, provide access to citizen opinion close to the ground and enable me to demonstrate how profoundly revolutionary politics incited the social imagination and stirred up society-wide debate over the ideal interactions and relationships between genders and generations.

But I also explore the family as a socioeconomic institution, as a network of social relationships, as a group of individuals engaged in negotiation and conflict over resources, gender roles, legal identity, and domestic authority.

Every citizen was keenly aware of the family as a legal and economic institution that conferred legitimacy and status, demarcated boundaries, organized the distribution of property, delineated juridical relationships and obligations, and enabled individuals to exercise control according to their domestic position. If my work takes inspiration from cultural approaches, it also reacts against the tendency of revolutionary historians of gender and of political culture to ignore questions about social dynamics and legal and economic structures. In conjunction with a nationwide examination of how the family was imagined, I use a local case study of the family court cases in the department of the Calvados in Normandy to probe domestic disputes and ask how the Revolution facilitated the redistribution of power and goods within households. Drawing on social and legal history methods also makes it possible to analyze how various factors—such as family position, geography, occupation, or exposure to revolutionary political culture—influenced individuals' opportunities to reshape their personal lives.[8] Above all, I seek to intertwine these cultural and social approaches. For just as new political concepts and gender thinking informed social interactions, contestations over meaning—the meanings, for example, of affection, fatherhood, domestic liberty, or illegitimacy—were also influenced by social and legal negotiations over resources and relationships, as well as by the twists and turns of revolutionary politics.

The combination of cultural, social, and legal history is especially necessary and promising for the 1790s because French revolutionary leaders altered legal institutions and overhauled family law as a key part of building the secular republic and forwarding the politics of regeneration. In an attempt to make justice more accessible, affordable, and democratic, the National Assembly in 1790 established new institutions to deal with family disputes: notably, it set up temporary, local arbitration courts known as "family tribunals" or "family courts" (tribunaux de famille). Family members in conflict each chose two arbiters—ideally family members or friends—to adjudicate their disagreements and make rulings on matters such as divorce, division of inheritance, parent-child altercations, and so forth. Temporary and appointed by the litigants themselves, these family courts made justice seem especially malleable, relatively affordable, and close to home.[9]

At the same time, a growing list of innovative laws offered new rights to divorce, marry without parental consent, or inherit unexpected legacies. Citizens entered litigation in large numbers. Four chapters of this book draw on court cases to peer into households and assess the contours of this revolution within the home. For example, Chapter 3 focuses on divorce in the

Calvados: urban women of artisanal or professional classes initiated divorce more than any other group, while rural resistance to divorce ran especially high. This new practice challenged the given of male dominance and also increased male and female expectations for compatibility between spouses, even as feuding spouses, their families, and arbiters disputed the multiple meanings of companionship and reciprocity in marriage. Chapter 4 investigates legal conflicts between Norman brothers and sisters over the new egalitarian inheritance laws and illustrates that sisters in this region won unprecedented legacies, lobbied for a more affectionate and equitable model of parent-child relations, and made political claims on both family and state to increase women's stature within conjugal families. In Chapter 5, I use a case study of paternity suits, petitions, and government policy in the early 1790s to examine the changed rules of courtship, the legal struggles of unwed mothers, and the escalating rates of illegitimacy. I also show how gendered expectations about the "natural" responsibilities of mothers and the freedom of alleged fathers prompted revolutionary lawmakers to abolish women's rights to paternity suits, although they offered illegitimate children new rights and civil status. In the wake of these legal innovations, Chapter 6 looks at the redefinition of fatherhood, motherhood, and family in a series of controversial court cases over paternity and the legacies of natural children. In the late 1790s and early 1800s as the political mood shifted rightward, the courts and judicial opinion once again tightened the boundaries of legitimate families, curtailed revolutionary promises to illegitimate children, and invented a new form of fatherhood that would underpin the Civil Code.

In conjunction with exploring social transformation within the home, this book also advances several points about revolutionary politics. I highlight the remarkable power of politics to inform intimacy. I also want to demonstrate the centrality of gender, family matters, and social change to the invention of revolutionary politics, state, and citizenship. Succinctly put, family and state shaped each other mutually, and remaking family and gender played a pivotal role in constructing the new state and politics.[10] The intimate habits, rights, and relationships of parent and child, husband and wife, became politically contested terrain during the Revolution precisely because the family acted as the crucial matrix—natural, moral, and legal—that linked each individual to the new nation-state. For the deputies, to create juridical citizens equal before the law seemed impossible without considering the position of individuals within the family: the legal stature of each Old Regime subject had been determined in part by his or her familial status as illegitimate daughter, married woman, younger son, widow, father, primary heir, and so on. To invent the rights-bearing citizen raised knotty questions about the contractual rights of women and the liberties of adult children. Likewise, to ignite the moral and emotional fires of citizenship, the French revolutionaries believed they could tap into the power of familial bonds. Yet, for example, when they romanticized the natural love of parents for their offspring born inside or outside of marriage, republican leaders imagined the affective attributes of mothers and fathers very differently. In short, the family defined essential aspects of law and culture—two realms that the Revolution fervently sought to reform. As they strove to found the republic on uniform law and regenerated citizens, the revolutionaries inevitably found themselves wrestling with gender-loaded questions about power differentials and practices within households. To make Revolution and Republic demanded the recreation of the family.

At every turn, this attempt to define rights and cultural ideals within homes—in effect, to invent citizenship and refashion the family in the process—took place as a dialogue, an interchange among lawmakers and citizens. In examining this dialogue, I embrace a particular model of revolutionary politics. The energetic potential of the French Revolution to enact change stemmed from the intersection of three forces: a vibrant new ideology and political culture; the legal act of forging a new state; and unprecedented popular participation in politics by citizens across France. In the 1790s French women and men became politically galvanized around family matters. Old Regime actors had certainly recognized the centrality of families to politics, but the Revolution produced dynamic new political languages, injected a new intensity and legitimacy into politics at the grassroots level, and loaded myriad everyday questions, from dress to religion to marriage, with political controversy.

Politicization around issues such as paternity, sibling rights, or illegitimacy sprang out of the routine texture of family life, as citizens interpreted their personal desires, customary obligations, and economic prerogatives through the prism of a new political culture and a new relationship to the state. Family members did not hesitate to bombard legislature, newspapers, and local officials with their opinions and demand that their personal experiences be brought to bear in the broader arena of the state. As one group of petitioners to the Convention asserted in 1795 as they defended egalitarian inheritance reform: "This sublime law does not belong to you, legislators, it is from nature; she alone has dictated it, you have only been her mouthpiece."[11] At this moment of intense political ferment and heightened anxiety over social issues, lawmakers responded intently to vocal outcries from citizens and local government officials. As revolutionary leaders crafted laws and cultural programs to reform familial practices, these in turn provoked nationwide responses. Negotiation within households, discussion in print and the public arena, and formal debate in the legislature all interacted to craft the republican family and citizenship.

This book is organized thematically around the issues of marriage and divorce, inheritance, and paternity and illegitimacy. At the same time, it traces the chronology of the Revolution and shows how each major turning point of the Revolution generated different gender models to underpin each new vision of the state and political order.[12] Chapter 1 examines how marriage came under political criticism from male and female revolutionaries, while Chapter 2 argues that the reform of marriage and gender relations played an integral role in defining citizenship and forging the new nation-state. After the outbreak of Revolution, as citizens unleashed vehement calls for family reform and as lawmakers first struggled to extract state and civil law from the hands of the Church, the Constituent and Legislative Assemblies repeatedly deliberated the nature of marriage and the secularization of civil record-keeping (the *état civil*) in 1790–92. But the overthrow of the monarchy and founding of the Republic in August and September 1792 made it urgent to refashion social relationships that would match and sustain a secular and antipatriarchal political order. Within the space of a few weeks, the representatives moved swiftly to curtail arranged marriages, reduce parental authority, laicize civil records, and legalize divorce. Meanwhile, journalists, festival-planners, club members, petitioners, and local officials all intently debated what particular feminine and masculine behaviors would best cultivate morality and patriotism in the new Republic. Like the creation of the Republic, the Thermidorian reaction and the crafting of the Napoleonic regime marked salient moments for rethinking gender and family-state relations. As Chapter 7 shows, the Thermidorian and Directorial backlash against innovations in family law emerged from the joint concerns of angry family members and legislators anxious to secure social stability in a property-based republic. But only during the patriarchal politics of Napoleon's Consulate would this reaction against republican family laws reach its fullest extent in the Civil Code, just at the moment when the new state most distanced itself from popular political input and abandoned the goals of political regeneration and individual liberty. Chapter 8 explores the genesis of the Code.

By analyzing family and politics, my work also challenges prevalent assumptions about the impact of the Revolution on gender and on women in particular. The dominant hypothesis, most forcefully articulated by Joan Landes, holds that the Revolution laid the foundations for domesticity by excluding women from politics and mandating a "private" role for them. Proponents of this interpretation emphasize that Jacobin imagery, festivals, speeches, literature, press, and political theory constructed a powerful discourse urging women toward republican motherhood and familial duties. Furthermore, male revolutionary leaders gradually took steps to circumscribe women's public role: for example, the Convention closed down women's political clubs in October 1793 and later foreclosed female activism in the streets of Paris and the galleries of the Convention.[13] As it emerged, this emphasis on female political exclusion during the Revolution coincided powerfully with other work in feminist scholarship. Lynn Hunt argued that male revolutionaries supported female domesticity because they feared social disorder and sexual dedifferentiation after the patriarchal model of politics and family had been overthrown. While literary specialists focused on eighteenth-century representations of domesticity, other prominent scholars theorized the links between liberalism and patriarchy more generally: influentially, Carole Pateman contended that liberalism rested on a sexual contract subordinating women, and Joan Scott analyzed the exclusions built into liberal universalism.[14]

One should not exaggerate the unity of viewpoints nor of method, but it seems clear that an interpretive conjuncture occurred by the early 1990s. Work coming out of diverse fields—including political theory, literary criticism, philosophy, intellectual and social history—coalesced to support a set of shared assumptions about the centrality of the Revolution in defining public politics as a male domain and domesticity as a female one. This interpretation is so dominant that historians who dissect nineteenth-century gender dynamics with great nuance often take as a given the domesticating and exclusionary legacy of 1789. In addition, this set of ideas about French republicanism holds all the more power because historians working on other regions, such as England, the United States, Central Europe, and Latin America, have also argued that republican or liberal politics, depending on the geography, reinforced the domestic subordination of women.[15] Although historians have questioned the public-private dichotomy and investigated the diverse nature of women's political engagement during the French Revolution, the thesis that republicanism played an integral role in channeling women toward the home still frames current understandings of the gendered impact of the Revolution.[16]

My research proposes a new interpretation. First, analyzing social practices and cultural attitudes within households in the 1790s does not reveal a new domesticity. On the contrary, it shows how frequently women in certain positions in the family made use of republican ideology, new laws, and new access to the state to challenge their former positions of domestic inferiority. Notably, the laws on divorce, egalitarian inheritance, and parental authority not only allowed individual women to ameliorate their familial standing, but they also called into question ambient assumptions about the subordination of wives and daughters in general. I do not want, however, to argue that the Revolution was "good" rather than "bad" for women as an undifferentiated whole.[17] Rather than painting a uniform portrait of the gender impact of the Revolution, I ask how diverse elements, such as urban-rural differences, regional cultures and customs, social class, and family position, all affected women's experiences within the household differently.[18] To give but one important example, the example of class, by and large women of middle or lower middle class, those with at least a small amount of property, were most able to take advantage of changes in family law. The harshest domestic policy of the 1790s—the abolition of paternity suits—landed hardest on a group of women who were often poor: unwed mothers.

Second, I also want to illustrate how revolutionary ideas and debates led to diverse claims about gender ideals within households. The argument that the Revolution fostered domesticity rests primarily on the discursive analysis of various texts that called upon women to embrace their household duties and to nourish patriotism as republican mothers. Without a doubt, a strong strand within revolutionary discourse encouraged a Rousseauian vision of gender roles: in this model, women should strive to please men and inculcate republican morality in their children while husbands displayed their patriotism as soldiers and public citizens. But at the same time, the Revolution kicked up alternate and intersecting gender models of femininity and masculinity. I analyze the construction of masculine and feminine ideals in tandem.[19] Everyone imagined distinct and complementary roles for men and women within the Republic and, as I argue in Chapter 2, male and female revolutionaries alike believed that marriage, heterosexual love, and gender complementarity held the political power to underpin patriotism.

Yet, the Rousseauian emphasis on docile republican mothers and wives competed with arguments advocating equality between spouses and greater independence, power, and control over property by women. Moreover, Rousseau's idealization of domestic submission held no sway over women like Marie-Françoise Godefroy, who demanded a divorce before a family court in rural Normandy in 1795 and declared that she could no longer "sacrifice her liberty" and remain "in slavery" to her adulterous husband.[20] The Revolution produced competing discourses that both advocated and undercut domesticity. It was not republican ideology, but rather the Civil Code of 1804—whose family laws were primarily written *in reaction* to the social revolution within the home—that most encouraged the nineteenth-century trend toward domesticity.

Furthermore, this work resists framing women's relationship to politics primarily in dichotomous terms, such as inclusion/exclusion or public/private. Revolutionary definitions and practices of citizenship did exclude women from essential aspects of political participation, including the right to vote, to hold political club meetings after October 1793, and to serve as officials, such as arbiters on family tribunals or deputies in Paris. Without in any way denying the fundamental importance of these exclusions, I nonetheless want to reframe the question by defining politics broadly, examining the political intertwining of personal and public matters, and illustrating how extensively women took part in a diverse array of political activities. Many of these actions, such as publishing or petitioning the state, had been expanded or opened up by revolutionary changes in law, commerce, or political structures.[21]

If historians in general have been working to rethink the relationship between women and politics, this reconceptualization seems doubly necessary for the French Revolution.[22] Undoubtedly, the revolutionaries recast democratic politics by producing new public institutions and formal modes of representation. But the political innovation and transformative energy of the Revolution also lay in generating new forms of power, injecting politics into every aspect of daily life, and rooting citizenship in the deeply intimate regeneration of each man and woman. As Lynn Hunt has argued, "by politicizing the everyday, the Revolution enormously increased the points from which power could be exercised."[23] I ask how women participated in inventing these new forms of power and how the new politics transformed gender relations.

To analyze these issues, this study draws on nationwide sources, but certain sections focus on the department of Calvados in Normandy. Given the immense diversity and regional particularity of Old Regime France, no one region can stand for all, let alone encompass the geographical variations of the Revolution within households. But only by in-depth study of specific areas can we uncover changes in domestic relations and attitudes and gradually build a portrait of the whole. Local analysis is integral to my argument: provincial activism influenced lawmakers, and local practices built the republican family on the ground, in constant negotiation with policies and political culture that spanned the nation.

I chose to examine Normandy because it presents promising comparative and analytical problems, especially regarding gender, inheritance, marriage, and the civil rights of women. This area had a tradition of dynamic participation by women as litigants in court and as businesswomen in the crafts and small commerce.[24] At the same time, the prerevolutionary custom of Normandy had a very explicit gender bias against women: by customary law and practice, families favored sons over daughters. Parents had no obligation to dower their daughters. "A father can dower his daughter with a hat of roses," ran one local proverb. In fact, if sons were present, all the daughters combined could inherit no more than one-third of their parents' patrimony. These factors make the Calvados a particularly important and accessible place to analyze the gendered impact of the inheritance law and to explore female litigation and political activism in general. Moreover, Normandy combines various family features from both the Midi and the North. As in the South, Norman families placed great emphasis on furthering the lineage and often chose to sacrifice the rights and opportunities of younger siblings. Once married, spouses did not merge their goods into community property, and they remained in many ways tied to their families of origin. But, as in other regions of the North, Normans more often formed nuclear rather than stem families, especially in cities. This household structure reinforced the strength and independence of the conjugal couple and encouraged them to forge social and economic bonds with neighbors, rather than relying primarily on kin.[25] In interesting ways, Normandy encompassed elements of the conjugal model that the revolutionary reformers advocated and the lineage mentality they sought to eradicate.

In addition, the Calvados has a relatively good run of sources, including état civil, district court, and family tribunal records. The department is not dominated by a huge city, as is, for example, the neighboring Seine-Inférieure by Rouen. Rather, the Calvados provides a good urban-rural balance, with several notable small cities, including the textile towns of Bayeux and Lisieux, and the larger city of Caen, a growing commercial and administrative center of 35,000 people. Politically, the area spanned the gamut of views from ardent republicanism to federalism to counterrevolutionary *chouannerie*. Although the department more often voted to the right, relatively high literacy rates, political clubs in fifty communes, and exposure to press and revolutionary leaders from Rouen, Paris, and Caen all brought access to revolutionary laws and ideas.[26] I intend inquiry into the Calvados to lend depth to this study, but I frame this examination as much as possible within a comparative national context. By weaving together local and national sources, I hope to offer a new history of the revolutionary family that both demonstrates the impact of politics on domestic practices and integrates the history of family and gender into the making of the revolutionary state, politics, and citizenship.

1. Freedom of the Heart

Men and Women Critique Marriage

When revolution broke out in 1789, the Comte d'Antraigues had marriage on his mind. "A nation, for so long oppressed by despotism and its laws, all of a sudden becoming mistress of its own destiny, aspires for liberty. . . . Who would not tremble with horror to think that in this nation paternal authority nonetheless disposes of the hearts of young people for the sake of convenience; . . . that sentiment and love are not even heard. . . . It is not a marriage; it is a sacrifice, a sacrilege," he fumed in 1789.[1] As the French revolutionaries set out to rid France of "despotism" and build a new society and state, rethinking marriage became an indispensable part of their project. Many citizens, like the Comte d'Antraigues, drew tight connections between public and intimate politics: if the state was now to be rooted in a contract, freely chosen by the people, then marriage, too, should rest on the free choice and contract of individuals.

Although the legislators would turn only gradually to reforming this institution, the outbreak of the Revolution provoked a groundswell of debate about the reform and role of marriage. Already in 1789, women's cahiers, journalists, moralists, clergymen, and divorce pamphleteers clamored to be heard. By 1790–91, political societies, especially provincial women's clubs and the influential Cercle Social, debated how the relations between men and women might be culturally and legally recast by the Revolution. From the provinces, petitioners began to pour forth personal visions and pleas for transforming conjugal practices, as well as remodeling the laws governing inheritance, illegitimacy, paternity, and other family matters. The indissolubility of marriage, clerical celibacy, parental authority over nuptial choices, arranged unions, the hierarchical nature of gendered conjugal relations, the dowry system, and the unjust laws governing non-Catholic marriages—all these became matters of public scrutiny. The moral qualities of men and women, the very texture of their interpersonal relations, fueled avid debate.

This public ferment over marriage joined with the logic of building the revolutionary state to push the issue of marriage into the foreground for the National and Legislative Assemblies. For decades the Old Regime monarchy had been whittling away at ecclesiastical jurisdiction over familial matters. The Revolution more than intensified this trend. As they strove to build a secular state that would guarantee individual rights and a uniform rule of law, legislators took marital matters out of the hands of the Church, redefined marriage as a civil contract that could be broken, and foregrounded the rights of individuals and of the conjugal couple over the expectations of the lineage family. By September 1792, the assembly had passed laws laicizing the *état civil* (civil records), legalizing divorce, lowering the age of majority, and drastically reducing parental control over nuptial choices.

These legislative actions took place in dialogue with the vigorous public debate over marriage. Critique of marriage was not new in France in 1789. Old Regime novelists, philosophes, jurists, lawyers, and moralists had scrutinized and censured marital practices from many angles.[2] But the Revolution energized and transformed the attempt to remake the conjugal system. Not only did the volume of pamphlet literature and public talk about marriage escalate, but also the Revolution weakened the Church, produced ideologies that focused unprecedented attention on individual rights and liberties, and created legislative institutions bent on rewriting civil law as an integral part of defining the juridical citizen and the secular state. Above all, the revolutionary thrust toward reinventing the nation and the individual charged marriage with new political resonance. A wide-ranging assortment of pamphleteers, petitioners, and lobbyists argued that marriage was the site for constructing new meanings of the individual, social cohesion, and power relations—of the most intimate and gendered kind. Certain of the intersection between personal life and public politics, male and female marriage critics asserted again and again that the French people could not be politically free if they remained domestically enslaved. In the words of one polemicist, it was "above all by the reform of our marital customs" that the new nation could rebuild morals and "assure the political regeneration of France."[3]

If the French revolutionaries thought about politics through the prism of the family,[4] marriage held a peculiarly important place: it came to be imagined as the social contract in miniature, ideally tying each citizen to the state and integrating individual liberty and free choice with a profound commitment to society as a whole. As a cultural institution, marriage provided a frame for conceptualizing and acting out the gender order that secured each man or woman a place within the social whole. As a legal institution, marriage served as an essential matrix defining the status, identity, and rights of each citizen: for the couple and their offspring, marriage legally determined nationality, filiation, and the right to inherit, as well as one's relationship to taxation, conscription (for men), and command over property, or (for women) the incapacity to manage various forms of property.[5]

How did this pivotal position of marriage—for both conceiving the gendered social order and defining the individual's relationship to state and society—make marriage particularly open to critique during the Revolution? This chapter works in tandem with the next one to examine how the revolutionaries forged interconnections between marriage and public politics. Here, I focus on the early writings of marriage critics to argue that the new politics enabled and encouraged certain French women and men to reimagine conjugal relationships, to question family strategies built around personal sacrifice and marital indissolubility, and, in some cases, to challenge male authority within households and propose alternate gender dynamics. A crucial purpose of this chapter is to suggest the volume, variety, and interconnectedness of demands for reform. The diverse pamphleteers, moralists, satirists, journalists, feminists, petitioners, and club members held varying goals, styles, and viewpoints. They did not form a neat and coordinated chorus, but they nonetheless sketched out repeated motifs in common and, in their motley combination, proposed a wholesale reshaping of marriage, its internal dynamics, and its role within the social system.

THE CHORUS OF MARRIAGE CRITICS

When Louis XVI agreed to calling the Estates-General in 1789, he inadvertently provoked an outpouring of discussion in print and in every public venue from the intellectual academies of the provinces to the bustling arcade of the Palais Royal in Paris. When the French Revolution transformed public politics and created a whirlwind of popular debate, it built on the Old Regime development of a public sphere of expression. In the decades before the Revolution, growing literacy rates, commercial opportunities, and the excitement of Enlightenment ideas had stimulated the dynamic growth of print culture. By 1789, almost half of French men and 27 percent of women were literate enough to sign their names and perhaps also to read. For inspiration, edification, and entertainment, they could choose among a vast repertoire of works, including novels, cheap chapbooks, political pornography, philosophical treatises, works of popular science, and melodramatic legal briefs—to name but a few possibilities. At the same time, unfolding forums of public sociability—from cafés to Freemason clubs to reading societies— had emerged in tandem with the Enlightenment as a cultural movement.[6]

Building on and beyond this Old Regime expansion of literacy and debate, the French Revolution more than redoubled the possibilities for noisy contestation and public talk. As censorship relaxed and politics heated up, the Revolution let loose a veritable torrent of pamphlets, widened the floodgates of discussion about myriad issues, and stimulated the founding of hundreds of political clubs, as many as two thousand by 1793. The number of newspapers in Paris rose from 4 in 1788 to 184 in 1789 to 335 in 1790, while the annual production of plays skyrocketed from just a handful each year in the late Old Regime to more than fifteen hundred between 1789 and 1799.[7]

This section will introduce the genres and venues of marriage critics within this burgeoning public sphere and save the analysis of their thematic content for later in the chapter. Although the official cahiers (grievance lists) of parishes and bailliages paid comparatively little attention to familial matters,[8] hundreds of pamphleteers, journalists, club members, and petitioners voiced opinions that both influenced lawmakers and helped to define evolving ideals about marital reform and male and female gender roles in the new nation.

Lobbyists calling for divorce formed one vibrant chorus. "Opinion waits impatiently" for the legalization of divorce, observed the aptly named *Il est temps de donner aux époux qui ne peuvent vivre ensemble la liberté de former des nouveaux liens* (It is time to allow spouses who cannot live together the freedom to form new bonds).[9] In the two years between the summer of 1789 and the summer of 1791, close to fifty pamphlets dedicated themselves to this cause, while many others mentioned it in passing or made divorce part of their satirical repertory.

Polemicists conducted an ongoing, lively dialogue: they wrote to refute or satirize, refine or support each other's arguments. Some authors strove for an erudite and authoritative stance: they demonstrated the "philosophical, theological, and political" validity of divorce, to use Hubert de Matigny's illustrative title. Others aimed at a more popular audience and chose the cahiers genre that had become a prevalent means of calling attention to the manifold problems of state and society, as individuals, corporate groups, and satirists all showered the deputies with their thoughts on everything from serfdom to the price of bread.[10] Some set up their critique of marriage as an exchange of fictional letters or as a personalized narrative of woe and possible redemption through divorce. A handful demanded clarification of the Protestant right to divorce according to their own religious tradition.[11] In many cases, divorce proponents indicted other aspects of marital customs, such as the dowry system, arranged marriages, the dearth of conjugal affection, or the "marital tyranny" of heedless husbands. The most fortunate pamphleteers succeeded in presenting their work to the national legislature.

To give one prominent example, Albert-Joseph Hennet set off a furor of responses with his 148-page work, entitled simply *Du divorce* (On Divorce). Reviewed in the press and eventually commended with an "honorable mention" by the legislature, his polemic had gone through two editions by late 1789 and a third within another fourteen months.[12] At least eight pamphlets reacted to his with detailed refutation, anxious tempering, or unstinted praise. Several clerical writers sought to dismantle his historical and theological arguments point-by-point. Notably, the Abbés Barruel and de Chapt de Rastignac devoted more than five hundred pamphlet pages between them to counter his demonstrations and prove the irreligious, immoral, and unnatural status of divorce. In contrast, the anonymous author of *L'homme mal marié, ou questions à l'auteur "Du divorce"* (The unhappily married man, or questions for the author of "On Divorce") placed his trust in Hennet by pouring forth his marital anguish, begging him for specific advice, and asking in desperate tones what form the divorce law would take. Infatuated with Hennet as the savior of marital bliss and justice, this unhappy husband wrote to him as eagerly and intimately as earlier readers had addressed the novelist Rousseau.[13]

Meanwhile, a network of press reviews and letters spread their central points further abroad, or even inspired further pamphlets in reply. The *Moniteur universel* and the *Spectateur national*, for example, both published a series of reviews and exchanges of letters for and against divorce beginning in the winter of 1790.[14] Likewise, in July 1791 the *Journal de Paris* reviewed Charles Demoustier's play *Le divorce* with great aplomb.[15] Divorce has become the battle cry of a "crowd of scoundrels . . . a long rigmarole of citations," groused the *Lettre du Marquis de C—— au Comte de F——* (Letter from the Marquis de C—— to the Count of F——), which supported divorce by pretending to oppose it. Serious opponents of divorce had reason to complain of press and pamphlet "propagation of this dangerous opinion," for the defenders of marital indissolubility were outnumbered in print by about five to one. The cranky author of *Appel au bon sens contre le divorce en réponse au Paradoxe de M. Hennet* (Appeal to good sense against divorce in response to the paradox of M. Hennet) grumbled that he had become so disturbed by these subversive "posters of all colors" that he wasted 40 sous and six hours reading pro-divorce literature—only to refute it in a 94-page treatise.[16]

Some of these divorce pamphlets remained anonymous, although an increasing number of writers willingly acknowledged authorship of their visions of reform. The relaxation of censorship, the political climate, the prominence and publicity of leading works such as Hennet's, and the upsurge of pamphleteering in general combined to make authors more bold than in the Old Regime. A few writers, such as the deputy Bouchotte from Bar-sur-Seine, were prominent men. Most of the anonymous divorce tracts appear to have been written by men of middle or upper class background. But a few were penned by women, and some female authors no doubt used male pseudonyms.

In any event, the male or female narrative stance taken in any given pamphlet does not necessarily clarify the gender of the anonymous author. Madame Fumelh, who published her *Mémoire sur le divorce* anonymously, wrote from a male stance in her work, perhaps hoping her arguments would be taken more seriously. Conversely, despite her female self-positioning, Madame Cailly, the anonymous author of the widely read *Griefs et plaintes des femmes mal mariées* (Grievances and complaints of unhappily married wives) was taken to be a man by her fellow advocate of divorce, Monsieur Tapin. In his own lamentation as an unhappy husband, he jokingly invited the presumably male author of *Griefs et plaintes* to take his place and marry the unbearable Madame Tapin![17]

Intersecting with the tracts directly devoted to divorce was a second substantial body of pamphlet literature addressing marriage as well: from 1789 to 1791, roughly fifty pamphlets explicitly exposed clerical celibacy as an unnatural and unhealthy state. Often remaining anonymous, most of the authors seem to have been priests weary of abstinence. (Lay moralists advocating clerical marriage tended to combine this appeal with other commentary, such as the demand for divorce or a tax on bachelors.)[18] In contrast, clerical opponents of celibacy—converted to revolutionary reforms and anxious to challenge the ecclesiastical hierarchy—focused primarily on laying forth their personal sagas, historical exegesis, and utilitarian logic in favor of allowing priests to marry. Like the divorce pamphlets, these tracts varied in length and style from brief pleas to episodic satire to quite long, carefully argued treatises.[19] The works ranged in price from several sous to the more prohibitive price of almost four livres for a re-edition of Jacques Gaudin's influential *Les inconvéniens du célibat* (The disadvantages of celibacy), originally published in Geneva in 1781.[20]

These clerical polemicists could draw on Enlightenment writings that had ridiculed clerical celibacy as useless and unnatural.[21] But the philosophes—unlike these early revolutionary proponents of clerical marriage—had generally written out of a profound anticlericalism. In some cases, as part of the pervasive assault on sacerdotal power, their critique of celibacy incorporated humorous or pornographic mockery of clerical libido and sexual transgression. Before the Revolution, few priests had seriously engaged in castigating clerical celibacy from within the Church. Gaudin's censored 1781 text stood out as the only model, engendering comment and imitation in the early 1790s. The early Revolution witnessed both the continuation of anticlerical satire and an unprecedented outburst of politicized appeals from priests themselves who hoped to embrace both marriage and the Church. As key organizers of this movement, a group of pro-revolutionary, pro-marriage clergy met formally at the parish of Saint-Etienne-du-Mont in Paris and began generating various motions, petitions, and pamphlets in the fall of 1789. Several participants in this assembly became leading pamphleteers against celibacy and were among the first priests to marry.[22] In the emerging dialogue on the virtues of clerical marriage, only a handful of writers defended clerical celibacy at this early date.[23]

A third set of voices clamored for remaking marriage: the women's cahiers and broadsides and the feminine press. The cahiers genre of 1789–90 encompassed dozens of grievance pamphlets that claimed female authorship and addressed the National Assembly or the king on behalf of women. With a few exceptions these cahiers did not focus solely on marriage or divorce, but rather ranged widely in subject matter and stance. Topics included women's work conditions, prostitution, poverty, the cloistering of girls or women in convents, and the failure to offer women political participation and representation in the new nation. A few articulated the corporate interests of a specific group, such as the flower-sellers of Paris, and had little or nothing to say on marital matters. But most claimed to represent the collective concerns of the whole female sex and imitated official cahiers by stringing together multiple different grievances. Alongside the appeal for better education, the amelioration of women's position within the family and marriage topped the list of demands.[24]

While the pro-divorce and anti-celibacy tracts have their roots in Old Regime treatises or philosophical texts, the women's cahiers built upon the feminist writing of the Old Regime. Many of the authors grafted the new format of cahiers onto an older narrative style of works dedicated to the "defense of the sex."[25] But at the same time, these pamphlets moved beyond the old "*querelle des femmes*," the stylized, Old Regime debate over female nature and capability. They underwent a distinct metamorphosis in the emerging context of national representative politics. Although the writers built upon old arguments about the moral fiber, rational capabilities, and worthiness of the female sex, they incorporated revolutionary political ideals and demanded specific legal and political reforms of women's status. They proposed a new relationship between woman, family, and nation. To give but one example, Madame B—— B—— relegated her woman worthies to a footnote as she moved impatiently to demand female representation at the Estates-General, linked the woman question to debates over African slavery, and called on Norman women to lobby for legal reform of the dotal system.[26]

It is difficult to be certain of the authorship and audience of the women's cahiers, not only because they more often remained anonymous but also because they were imitated by pseudofeminist cahiers. These *poissard* works, presumably written by men claiming to be women, mingled licentious material or political lampoons with purportedly sincere feminist demands. The *Requête des femmes pour leur admission aux Etats-Généraux* (Request of women for their admission to the Estates-General), for example, subverted any real demand for female political participation with suggestive language about women's politico-sexual powers.[27] Historians have classified these texts in contradictory ways, for they sit on the hinge between the satirical and the serious. Perhaps they defied simple reading at the time as well.[28] Their very presence suggests that the more serious feminist claims were pervasive enough to strike a nerve and incite satire. Even as the satires lampooned a gender order turned upside down by the new politics, they exude anxiety: even defenders of the old order nervously acknowledged that remaking the nation and inventing citizenship demanded changes in the most intimate relations.

If one sets aside the poissard cahiers, these women's pamphlets seem to be written by educated, urban women from Paris or the provinces. The cahiers format may have been an especially easy genre for female authors to embrace. Since these cahiers were essentially petitions, a woman who was timid about taking up the pen could still remain in a traditional position of deference. Or she could appear deferential while making quite radical and broad political demands. In fact, over the course of the Revolution as a whole, Carla Hesse found the petition to be the most common form of printed writing by women.[29] Moreover, the grievance list format made it easy for an inexperienced or poorly trained writer to offer her thoughts in an informal fashion or to borrow from others' ideas. When Marie de Vuignerias published her *Cahier des doléances et réclamations des femmes de la Charente* (Petition of grievances and claims of women from the Charente) she copied Madame B——— B———'s pamphlet virtually word for word, misspelling "symbole" as "Saint-Bole" and "est tout" as "étout," and then adding her own personal supplication to the National Assembly in June 1790.[30] Finally, as they globalized their demands on behalf of "le sexe," authors of cahiers could easily remain anonymous and attempt to draw on the authority that anonymity could sometimes convey.[31] Anonymity also emboldened the authors of posted grievance lists. Among the sundry posters plastered on Parisian walls in the early Revolution, a few notable ones embraced the cause of marital reform on women's behalf. Olympe de Gouges, for example, used this anonymous genre to call for legal equality between spouses, the right to divorce, and married women's control over property.[32]

The ephemeral women's press also became a forum for discussion of the conjugal bond. Like the cahiers, newspapers directed at women could mix or span styles of expression. For example, the *Observateur féminin*, renamed *L'Etoile du matin, ou Les petits mots de Madame de Verte Allure, exreligieuse* (The morning star, or The witticisms of Madame de Verte Allure, ex-nun) undercut its pseudofeminist appeals with a licentious tone. By contrast, in the spring of 1791, the biweekly *Courrier de l'Hymen, ou Journal des Dames* (Messenger of marriage, or the Ladies' journal) veered between play and seriousness, but nonetheless contributed substantively to the debate over marriage. This journal joked around with its audience and material as it offered advice on suitable matches, spun tales about political divisions between married couples, and printed letters of complaint from young women cooped up in convents. Yet side-by-side with personal ads and lighthearted gossip, virtually every number raised issues of marital reform, female education, or women's rights. It debated divorce, the dotal system, married women's property, and the participation of women on courtroom juries. The journal printed reviews or commentary on authors such as the deputy Bouchotte on divorce, Madame Brulart on education, and Jean-Antoine-Nicolas Caritat de Condorcet on women's public role and rights. These sets of interlocking references operated within the women's press and pamphlet literature in general: for example, Madame Mouret's journal, the *Annales de l'éducation du sexe* promoted Madame Bastille's *Cahier*. Finally, although the *Courrier de l'Hymen* stood out for its dedication to marital questions, a cluster of other women's journals produced reflections on marriage and morals, and a variety of revolutionary newspapers published personal laments, particularly by women trapped in unhappy marriages.[33]

The growing network of political clubs formed another arena where marriage and gender relations came up for debate. As Gary Kates has demonstrated, the Cercle Social dedicated its co-ed club (the Confédération des Amis de la Vérité), as well as its newspaper *(La Bouche de fer)* to pushing for divorce and egalitarian inheritance laws.[34] This influential club included prominent journalists and politicians, many of whom would become leading Girondins, including Claude Fauchet, Jacques-Pierre Brissot, Jeanne-Marie Roland, and Condorcet. Most vocally, the Dutch feminist and Cercle Social member Etta Palm d'Aelders used the society as a launching pad to lobby other clubs and the legislature on behalf of civil law reforms and a transformation in the texture of male-female relations. Promoting conjugal reform, she gave several speeches at the Cercle Social; the Friends of the Constitution in Caen endorsed her 30 December 1790 speech and printed one thousand copies for distribution to local women. She also spoke at the Municipality of Creil-sur-Oise, published her speeches in pamphlet form, and petitioned the legislature at least twice. On 1 April 1792 she led a delegation of women to the bar of the Legislative Assembly to demand divorce, education, and equal civil and political rights for women. She also founded a women's club, the Parisian Société des Amies de la Vérité, and appealed for the creation of a nationwide network of women's clubs.[35]

The women's clubs that sprang up in close to sixty towns across France often wrestled extensively with the political meanings and reform of marriage. Their speeches, festivals, and debates frequently focused on how to reform gender relations in the service of the nation.[36] Male political societies devoted less time and attention to conjugal matters. Provincial men's clubs nonetheless debated divorce in 1791–92 without achieving consensus on the issue until it became law. More unified in their support of clerical marriage, some clubs lobbied in favor of its legalization and then proudly endorsed the marriages of local Constitutional priests after 1792. In some cases, male Jacobin clubs provided a forum for female speakers to address their sisters and brothers on family matters.[37]

The vibrant debate in press, pamphlet literature, and political clubs—combined with the greater political awareness and expectations of the Revolution—in effect encouraged individual citizens across France to begin petitioning the legislature for marital reforms, such as divorce or the loosening of parental control over youthful marriage. The first trickle of petitions on these issues began as early as 1790, grew slowly from 1791 to 1792, and escalated greatly after divorce became law in September 1792, as citizens imagined further improvements in the law and struggled to work out its practical implications in their own lives. The early petitions lobbying for divorce were primarily written by unhappily married men, although women also offered their comments. A few legal figures sent more erudite reflections, while other appeals are marred by bad spelling or rough penmanship. Usually handwritten, these petitions often combined political arguments with personal stories. Some burned with anger at the frustrating process of *séparations de corps* (judicial separation of persons), while others cited the promises of the new Constitution or introduced legal reasoning about marriage as a civil contract. No doubt some of these petitioners had read the divorce pamphleteers, for they spoke the same language. Some petitioners managed to present their work at the bar of the Constituent and Legislative Assemblies.[38]

In sum, in the years between 1789 and 1792, the press, popular societies, women's cahiers, petitioners, satirists, divorce pamphleteers, and lay and clerical moralists increasingly pushed marital reform into the arena of national debate. They focused the consciousness of ordinary citizens on these issues. As they responded to the shifting currents of revolutionary politics, they also put pressure on the legislature to deal directly with legal reforms.

LIBERTY AND NATURE: THE POLITICS OF EARLY MARRIAGE CRITICS

The diverse men and women who advocated marital reform were far from unanimous in their claims. For example, some hoped to reconcile divorce with Christianity, while others were markedly anticlerical. Some attacked women's position of inferiority within marriage, while others believed that women's self-sacrifice and willingness to please men formed the basis of conjugal companionship. The authors' styles also ranged widely, from biting satire to personal appeals for empathy to more restrained or philosophical modes of analysis. Yet, across these variations in form and content, these reformers repeatedly sounded many of the same themes. Among the many motifs and arguments, three stood out: individual liberty, the fulfillment of natural rights and law, and the pursuit of affection.

In the effervescent mood of the early Revolution, the tide-swell of liberty seemed to carry all difficulties before it effortlessly. Abstract and universal as a concept, yet peculiarly tangible and personal, "liberty" gripped the imagination of pamphleteers, petitioners, deputies, and reformers of the early Revolution. Because of its juridical grounding in rights newly guaranteed by law, liberty carried legal force, combined with tremendous psychological appeal. Rooted in natural law, liberty, whether political or civil, had a forceful, universal claim to validity. Because it referred powerfully to both individual freedom and national politics, it served as a bond between the person and the nation, between sentiment and the law. The quest for individual liberty lay at the core of the revolutionary revisioning of marriage. With virtually sanctified status, liberty had room for many meanings and, above all, conveyed intense emotional power. "Legislators! . . . Grant liberty to a million men, chained in iron . . . bent down like lowly slaves by the cruel and terrible chains of Hymen," urged one anonymous petitioner from Caen as he begged for the legalization of divorce.[39]

Crucially, early attempts to reconceptualize marriage referred both to freedom of contract and to freedom of the heart. Free citizens would have both legal and affective rights. First, the polemicists solicited a reinterpretation of marriage as a civil contract and demanded the legal right of each individual to make or break that contract at will. Women and men should both have this juridical prerogative. "Divorce must necessarily result from the wise constitution that a people, recently liberated, has granted itself," commented one pamphleteer.[40] Individual nuptial choices and practices must be freed from the Church, the prerogatives of the family line, and the corrosive power of financial arrangements. Second, the reformers' appeals foregrounded the notion that citizenship included the promise of personal contentment and a certain freedom of the emotions. Although they did not agree on the ideal roles for men and women within marriage, they held up companionate marriage based on love and gender complementarity as an ultimate personal and political ideal. On some level, these pamphleteers held the state—albeit vaguely—responsible for guaranteeing emotional fulfillment of its citizens, whether male or female. In turn, they asserted that the health of the nation was dependent on citizens' compatibility and personal well-being within marriage.

In appealing for legal liberty within marriage, the reformers built explicitly upon an Old Regime discourse about marriage as a civil contract. This contract was governed by *droit naturel,* meaning both natural law and natural right. Jurists and Enlightenment authors in prerevolutionary France had developed this discourse in tandem.[41] In the mid eighteenth century, civil law specialists, such as Pierre Le Ridant, François Bourjon, and Robert-Joseph Pothier, drew on the seventeenth-century natural law theorists Samuel von Pufendorf and Hugo Grotius to emphasize the contractual nature of marriage. They wielded this interpretation primarily in order to combat Church control and to assert royal domain over conjugal matters. In the words of Pothier, the premier late-eighteenth-century jurist of civil law, "There are two components in marriage, the civil contract between the man and the woman, and the sacrament that is added to the civil contract."[42]

Neither Pothier nor most other legal specialists took the more radical step of claiming that this contract could be broken.[43]

In contrast, a whole series of *philosophes*,[44] bolder and more brazen than the jurists, combined eclectic use of natural law theory with arguments based on social utility, history, and moral necessity to call for legalizing divorce and reducing both parental and ecclesiastical authority over marriage. Montesquieu and Morelly, and, in a less direct way, Voltaire, Diderot, Helvétius, d'Holbach, and Condorcet had all endorsed—though sometimes rather vaguely—the need for divorce. Less well-known figures, such as Cerfvol, Jacques Le Scène Desmaisons, and Philibert, had framed more explicit critiques of marriage, fusing natural law theory and the language of liberty and contract with a whole gamut of arguments based on utility, population, personal happiness and sentiment, and a repertoire of historical, geographical, and religious examples.[45] In the late Old Regime, arguments about natural law and natural right also permeated the ongoing debate about whether to grant Protestants and Jews the full civil right to marry. The 1787 Edict of Toleration would grant Calvinists this right, "constantly claimed by nature," but it excluded Alsatian Lutherans and Jews.[46]

The Revolution charged the interconnected concepts of liberty, natural law, and natural rights with even greater potency. This power grew not simply from the public fervor and fascination with liberty, but also from the specific context of revolutionary state building. Even as pamphleteers poured forth their ideas of marriage reform, lawmakers set out step-by-step to legislate the implications of the Declaration of the Rights of Man and Citizen. More specifically, in the case of marriage law, they strove to clarify the marital rights of non-Catholics and actors, who, like executioners, were deprived of certain civil rights because they exercised a disreputable profession. Above all, the legislators sought to expand state control over marriage at the expense of the Church. By late 1790 the deputy Durand de Maillane would put forth his controversial proposal: since marriage was a civil contract, then the civil state should replace the Church as regulator and recorder of the marriages of all its citizens, regardless of religion. Marriage should become a secular matter and the état civil should be laicized.[47] In the complex religious politics of the early Revolution, his idea would not become law until September 1792, although the Constitution of 1791 took the tentative but crucial step of defining marriage as a civil contract.

The deputies moved haltingly in articulating the relationship between civil marriage and the new rights of citizenship, for, as I will discuss in Chapter 2, their work involved the complex act of extricating the state-under-construction from its centuries-old entanglement with the Catholic Church. In contrast, for marriage theorists with no such limits, the language of natural right and liberty grew ever broader in its articulation and increasingly extended beyond the realm of learned authors, deputies, or legal scholars. Erudite pamphleteers, such as Hubert de Matigny, Bouchotte, and Hennet, explicitly cited Pufendorf or Enlightenment theorists to support divorce and clerical marriage; these polemicists sought to illustrate that *both* divine and natural law bolstered their recasting of marriage. Bouchotte's title says it well: *Observations sur l'accord de la raison et de la religion pour le rétablissement du Divorce, l'anéantissement des séparations entre les époux, et la réformation des loix relatives à l'adultère* (Observation on the agreement of reason and religion for reestablishing divorce, abolishing conjugal separations, and reforming the adultery laws).[48] Hennet was especially successful at popularizing philosophical arguments: "I claim the rights of nature," he stated. "Nature is the mother of all that exists, and like all mothers, wants her children to be happy. . . . What does nature prescribe [for unhappy or infertile couples]? To remain in sorrow and sterility? No, her voice calls them to happiness, to reproduction." Hennet's opponents—defenders of indissoluble marriage—also invoked nature, but they either simply equated it with God's will or used it to expose the inherent inconstancy of human passion.[49]

As the Revolution took a more anticlerical turn by 1790, many marriage reformers gradually moved away from contending that divorce was essentially compatible with Christianity. Instead, evocations of the "natural right" to individual liberty targeted the tyrannical family, the power-mongering Church, and the pope, "this wholesale merchant of indulgences," for confining individuals within indissoluble marriage and for preventing freedom of conjugal choice in the first place.[50] The Church seemed implicated in the flawed system of Old Regime marriage in myriad ways. Its sacramental dogma supported marital indissolubility and enforced clerical celibacy. Through their power to register and therefore approve marriages, its priests held inordinate power over lay people's personal lives. Its convents imprisoned wives accused of adultery and young girls too poor to marry; monasteries might do the same with younger brothers. The misuse of convents embodied the complicity between royal justice, the Church, and the family system. By the time she wrote her second divorce pamphlet in 1790, Madame Cailly impugned clerical dominion over the "civil contract" of marriage: "Indissoluble marriage is slavery; it goes against justice, reason, the intentions of Nature and of God. It is a yoke imposed by ultramontane despotism." Indicting the system that allowed husbands to imprison their wayward wives, she asked pointedly why lay women, especially separated women, continued to be held captive in the convents that the revolutionaries had begun dismantling. Why, she asked further, did the marriage vow still confine lay women and men once religious vows had been obliterated?[51]

In the increasingly anticlerical climate, a growing number of marriage reformers invoked droit naturel to trump or brush aside the claims of religion over marital matters. While some, like Madame Cailly, indicted "the chains of sacramental tyranny," others suggested that nature dictated law, and religion necessarily had to comply. For example, in 1790 one anonymous author promised to look at divorce from the point of view of "natural law." "I will not stop trying to discover whether religion allows divorce. But I will examine whether divorce is a useful law; because, if it is useful, it is authorized by religion." By 1792, Nicolas de Bonneville simply equated conjugal law with natural law, promoted civil marriage as a patriotic act, and claimed that religious marriages should only be legitimate if the couple had first conducted a civil marriage.[52]

In the tumultuous and varied writings of the early Revolution, many authors cared little for the erudite origins and complexities of natural law theory. Petitioners and authors of shorter, cheaper broadsides or pamphlets integrated references to natural rights into a more populist and dramatic style, trumpeting the benefits of liberty. By one pamphleteer's account, "Nature said to man: I want you to be free; and man replied: I want to be a slave." This anonymous address boldly declared that both nature and religion supported divorce, and if they disagreed, "religion would be wrong." The Revolution offered the chance to undo such absurdities.[53]

As this example suggests, when references to droit naturel became incorporated into everyday language, the nuances of political and legal theory gave way to imagery that was tangible and emotionally fraught with either anger or celebration. The legal language of natural rights fused with exultant calls for personal freedom. One anonymous "citizen philosopher" disparaged existing marriage as a "tomb of love," but applauded the brief definition of marriage in the Constitution of 1791 as a "civil contract." He urged the legislature to take the next logical step and obliterate marital indissolubility, "the only slavery that survives from the ruins of the Old Regime, the harshest form of slavery, and the one most contrary to the natural rights of man." Petitioners for divorce strove to rouse the legislators to follow their own commitment to droit naturel: the new state should discover and implement laws to mirror those written in nature.[54]

If proponents of divorce cited liberty and the natural right to loosen the marital bond, many lobbyists drew on the same language to argue in the complementary but opposite direction: couples should be free to marry at will. Clergy anxious to marry, separated couples intent on remarrying, lay critics of arranged marriages, and feminists who specifically indicted the sacrifice of daughters—these groups each pursued different goals. Yet they drew on the same repertoire of liberty, rights, and dramatic imagery to lambast an interlocking system of family strategies and religious celibacy. As the historian Jacqueline Hecht has argued, as part of their overall strategies, Old Regime families not only urged their children toward appropriate marriages, but also counted on placing some sons and daughters within the enforced celibacy of the cloister or priesthood. Old Regime novels, plays, and legal briefs had satirized and dramatized this system for decades. Even as they indicted the complicity of mercenary fathers and conniving churchmen, some of these works also evoked anti-aristocratic sentiments, for they associated the nobility with familial greed and the adulterous results of "marriages of convenience."[55]

Revolutionary politics made the old constraints on marriage seem all the more intolerable, and the anticlerical, anti-aristocratic, and antipatriarchal mood of the Revolution gave new life to this attack. Some nobles were critical of their own peers' investment in arranged marriage. The Comte d'Antraigues characterized "marriage among the higher classes of the State" as "an infamous contract dictated by greed: the cadaverous soul of a father sells the living heart of a young girl for its weight in gold." He argued compellingly for youthful and voluntary marriage. On behalf of enslaved daughters, victimized sons, frustrated priests and nuns, or desperate couples locked in miserable marriages, authors denounced the tyranny of family interest and religion over personal liberty from every angle and viewpoint. Some polemicists inculpated the system as a whole and agitated simultaneously for divorce and the end to arranged marriages and clerical celibacy. The epistolary novel *Emilie de Varmont, ou le divorce nécessaire et les amours du curé Sevin* (Emilie de Varmont, or The necessity of divorce and the loves of the Curé Sevin, 1791) told the tragic tale of three women trapped in devastating marriages and one clergyman pining away for his unattainable love. Marriage (or remarriage) was the "natural destiny" of human beings.[56]

This discourse on marital liberty encompassed a rough-and-tumble combination of styles and views. Legalistic arguments shared the stage with humor, sentimentalism, indignation, or even rage. Marriage theorists proposed all kinds of measures, most of them serious but some satirical. An early petitioner in 1790 argued that any unhappy and childless couples who had been forced into arranged marriage should be allowed to separate without legal costs by making a simple municipal declaration. The serious legal solution of this dejected petitioner contrasted with the satirical lewdness of another who portrayed lusty Parisian nuns clamoring for marriage and proffering their virgin "jewels" as a "patriotic gift." Another petitioner asserted merrily that marital freedom supported his right to polygamy. Late in 1790, the Père Duchesne most colorfully expressed his "indignation against the 'indissolubricité' [a pun: indissol-lust-ibility] of marriage." After describing several stormy marriages ending in bizarre murders, he called for legalizing divorce and ending arranged marriages: "Here's what our fucking marriage is . . . it's held together only by chains; it was okay when we were fucking slaves. But now we are free: it's not money, fuck, which should make marriages; it's no longer fathers' authority, it's inclination and taste." The abrasive and independent Père Duchesne captured the anger as well as the essence of the logic that linked the political freedom of citizenship to the emancipation of the heart.[57]

Freedom to choose a wife and marry would become a key element within revolutionary definitions of manhood (as I discuss in Chapter 2), but plenty of plays and pamphlets, especially some striking ones by female authors, turned their spotlight on the particular sacrifice of daughters. In 1789 the anonymous authors of *Pétition des femmes du Tiers-Etat au Roi* (Petition to the king from women of the Third Estate) uttered a simple protest that some girls "are obliged to throw themselves into cloisters which only demand a mediocre dowry." Taking a more vibrant approach, Olympe de Gouges' most performed drama of the decade was entitled *Le Couvent, ou les vœux forcés* (The Convent, or forced vows); it joined several similar plays in exposing the cruel fate of a lovesick young woman, forced to take religious vows by a parental figure, in this case her uncle. In 1791 the irrepressible Etta Palm d'Aelders called on the "imprescriptible rights of nature" to assure women that they would no longer be sent off to convents or sacrificed because of their parents' pride or their brothers' greed. The *Griefs et plaintes des femmes mal mariées* (Grievances and complaints of unhappily married wives) proffered endless depictions of women victimized by mismatched marriages. With typical drama, it lamented the fate of a young woman, "another victim dragged to the altar. . . . Bound forever, not to a spouse . . . , but to a master, an owner of her person and her goods, an avaricious tyrant who will demand and refuse everything imperiously."[58]

Priests, too, jumped on the bandwagon and linked the new public politics to personal freedoms. "Since the freedom to marry is a natural right, who can think that any earthly authority has the right to destroy it?" wrote one angry cleric in 1790. The Parisian priests who drafted an anti-celibacy

Motion at the church of Saint-Etienne-du-Mont in December 1789 asserted that the "natural goal" of men in society was to bond together and fulfill the "duties common to all citizens." Deprived of the right to marry, clergy had no "état civil," no personal, civil status. "You say I am a citizen, and you forbid me to use my civil right [*droit de cité*], and you dare to prohibit me from undertaking that sacred bond, without which society itself dissolves! Barbarous ones! . . . You allow even slaves to follow the leanings of their hearts." Only by guaranteeing their natural right to marry could the emerging revolutionary state transform clergy into citizens with full civil and moral status.[59]

Part of the power of the language of natural law and natural rights lay in its very malleability. Ever an ambiguous source of authority, "nature" could be summoned in support of universalizing claims about "natural" human behavior. In some polemicists' hands, "droit naturel" slid easily into proclamations about human nature and need: for example, it was manifestly unnatural to deny priests or separated couples the right to marry or remarry. The unnatural repression of sexual desire made the deprivation of personal liberty all the worse. Some pamphleteers uttered outrageous and entertaining (especially to our modern ears) depictions of the nefarious impact of celibacy on male and female bodies. In women it provoked fluid build-up, hemorrhaging, and fibrous tumors in the ever-problematic, ever-influential uterus. How strongly the peacefulness of a tender mother contrasted with the convulsions, vapors, and bitter tears of imprisoned young nuns, who "cursed the fatal moment when they had made the murderous vow to betray nature." For men, the effects were even worse: Matigny wrote graphically that abstinence provoked clerical hernias so frightful that many "priests could not even celebrate Divine Offices. . . . One way to alleviate this disastrous obstruction was to give in to the pleasures of the table." Denouncing this unseemly binge-eating, discomfort, and melancholy among the clergy, Matigny playfully theorized that perhaps celibacy had even provoked the Dominican Jacques Clément to assassinate Henri III back in 1589.[60]

The language of liberty and nature also sustained the concerted attack on the current system of *séparations de corps et d'habitation*. Old Regime law permitted two different forms of separation. By civil separation or *séparation de biens* (separation of goods), the courts allowed couples to legally separate their property. A wife could use this mechanism to shelter her goods from her husband's creditors if his dissipation or poor management had put the household at risk. Often, the couple continued to live together; sometimes a husband and wife jointly turned to civil separation as a strategy when they stood on the brink of financial disaster.

In contrast, séparation de corps et d'habitation inevitably stemmed from profound marital conflict: it literally meant that a couple legally separated their "bodies and places of residence." Although men had the legal capacity to request separation in some regions of France, demands came overwhelmingly from women. If a wife committed adultery, her husband had the right to imprison her in a convent for two years, and for a lifetime with the approval of a family council. Husbands also had other less formal and less drastic means of pressuring or disciplining their spouses. With fewer options and less power, wives in desperate straits could seek séparations de corps only for rigorous and specific grounds that varied slightly from region to region: severe cruelty or mistreatment; attempted murder by the husband; bigamy; exceptional cases of insanity; adultery accompanied by aggravating factors, such as debauchery, defamation, or supporting the mistress within the household. Battery headed the list of successful grounds in every region studied so far: séparation de corps frequently served as a last resort for a wife whose husband's brutality literally put her life in danger. In any event, legal separations were both rare and difficult to obtain.[61] Significantly, neither husband nor wife had the right to remarry.

Séparation de corps seized the imagination of the authors of cahiers, divorce pamphlets, and petitions, for it seemed to epitomize the need for marital reform. Like the lettres de cachet, which allowed certain individuals to imprison members of their own families, séparation de corps became an emblem of the inequities within families and the arbitrariness of the justice system. Like arranged marriage and enforced celibacy, it dramatized the collusion of Church and state against personal happiness.

In the free-form pamphlet world of the early Revolution, some critics of séparation de corps blended satire or comic tales with the political language of rights and liberty. According to Hennet, one divorce pamphlet carried the provocative title: *Evénement arrivé dans la rue Saint-Martin, Mort tragique d'un mari qui plaidait contre sa femme et qui voulait tuer sa belle-mère* (Event in St-Martin's street, Tragic death of a husband who was pleading against his wife and wanted to kill his mother-in-law). In one humorous indictment of séparation de corps, one Monsieur Tapin, an "unhappily married man," bemoaned the legal impossibility of getting a divorce and claimed that only women could bring separation proceedings under prerevolutionary law. On his lawyer's advice, he decided to provoke his insufferable wife with an act of public, witnessed cruelty. So, Monsieur Tapin recounts, at a dinner party, he picked a fight, slapped his wife twice in front of their scandalized guests, only to have her retaliate by hurling a half-full bottle of wine at his face. While he waited in vain for her to begin separation procedures, and for his face to heal, his vengeful and smirking wife tortured him by staying by his side, drinking his valuable wine, and merrily flinging the last thousand bottles at him. Monsieur Tapin finished off his comical tale with a suddenly serious appeal to the new constitution to guarantee his inalienable right to liberty: "The first right of man is the right to liberty. . . . Indissoluble marriage, of all life's acts the most detrimental to liberty, cannot be an exception to a rule so important to the happiness of man and society, and cannot spoil a constitution by which all evil should be transformed into good."[62]

Polemicists frequently stacked up piles of reasons upon reasons for overturning the separation system: "Break, break these hated bonds, contrary to natural law, good morals, propagation, individual happiness, the peace of families, and the veritable spirit of religion," commented the *Réflexions d'un bon citoyen en faveur du divorce* (Reflections of a good citizen in favor of divorce). Social utility, morality, and happiness all received repeated emphasis. Like this "good citizen," some lobbyists echoed the Old Regime argument that the conjugal system curtailed population growth: by outlawing remarriage, it compelled fertile men and women to remain celibate. This enforced celibacy and infertility fostered moral license. As Charles Rousseau complained, separation without remarriage "condemns people to become libertines or nonentities." The impact on female mores elicited special concern: if a separated woman could not remarry, she could not help but embrace promiscuity and engage in "illegitimate pleasures." The procedures also victimized woman by requiring her to take part in "scandalous" trials and to "lift the veil that decency had draped over the marriage bed." At the same time, by seeming to condone male adultery, such a system virtually promoted the libertine culture associated with the corrupt, privileged classes.[63]

As they listed the flaws of the system of *séparations de corps*, some authors highlighted the system's abuse of women. An undertone of national pride laced some of the milder feminist appeals by men; they echoed the Enlightenment notion that cruelty to women was a blemish on the civilization of Europe, which ought to stand above the harems of the Orient. How was it possible that a civilized country such as France would subject unhappily married women to such domestic torment and even incarcerate them, demanded Simon Linguet. Others focused more graphically on the harshness of the current law. As *Le divorce, ou l'art de rendre les ménages heureux* (Divorce, or the art of making households happy) pointed out in 1790, only the most outrageous defamation of character or the most severe beatings, performed before witnesses, would give an abused wife the possibility of bringing about a separation. A husband's private cruelty went unnoticed and unpunished. And if she could bring him to court, the process was costly, complex, and mortifying for the woman, who might well spend the rest of her days destitute or secluded in a convent.[64]

With its expansion of publishing and its medley of political languages and styles, the early Revolution had created a context for polemicists to hurl their varied weapons against the conjugal system of the Old Regime. Personal tales of woe, reasoned argumentation, sentimental scenes, historical examples, satirical barbs, and comic anecdotes all tumbled from the pamphleteers' pens. These disparate voices wove a rich tapestry of arguments: marital reform would promote population growth, personal morality, happiness, and the civilized treatment of women. Above all, the new politics demanded the remaking of intimacy: marriage should become an arena for testing and shaping the first meanings of individual liberty and natural rights. As the divorce advocate Bouchotte pronounced, "What difference does it make to me to have the right to make war and peace, to preserve the frontiers [of the nation], if in the interior of my own home I cannot avoid it [war]; if, as wife, subject to unequal laws, I risk my life at every moment, surrendered to a brutal man; . . . if, as husband, I cannot obtain peace in my own household, due to a wife who takes advantage of the Law to make my unhappiness eternal." Like fellow polemicists, he defined "domestic liberty" as the "first of all liberties" and argued that citizens' political rights were rooted in their familial rights.[65]

CONJUGAL COMPANIONSHIP AND EARLY CRITIQUES OF GENDER DYNAMICS

In their pursuit of a freer version of marriage, these critics idealized conjugal affection. They worked hard to argue that greater liberty would not splinter families: on the contrary, marriage should be a source of cohesion, love, and shared well-being. Revolutionary commentators embedded a political concept of liberty into their notion of affection and their psychology of the passions. Freedom—of the heart as well as the contract—was the precondition of marital happiness.

Yet marriage critics did not all agree on the ideal dynamics for fostering conjugal harmony. How did the discourses on rights, liberty, and idealized companionship open up debate over gender roles and the internal dynamics of marriage? While some polemicists embraced a Rousseauian model of marriages built on women's willingness to please men, others—especially a group of female authors—argued strongly that wives should have greater autonomy and economic and legal power within marriage. The new politics and the public vocalism of the Revolution fostered feminist demands for improving women's stature and rights.

Prerevolutionary novels, plays, and even legal briefs in causes célèbres stimulated the growing belief that freely chosen marriages should lead to personal fulfillment. More specifically, in the Old Regime, some authors, such as Montesquieu, had noted that freedom of choice strengthened love.[66] The outbreak of Revolution endowed the argument fusing liberty and conjugal happiness with new resonances and intensity: passion itself could be revolutionized by being emancipated. Many asserted that an initial freedom in the choice of partners would make love last longer, and, paradoxically, the knowledge that one could break the conjugal contract in fact would tighten the ties between husband and wife. Once divorce is legalized, argued the *Loi du divorce*, "Spouses will no longer stop being lovers and each will treat the other with the most delicate attention. They will find more sweetness in a bond that is always voluntary." It is the chains of marriage that embitter the emotions of desire and attachment, added one self-proclaimed "best friend of women."[67] While the opponents of divorce continued to inveigh against the instability of the passions and to argue that natural human inconstancy made marital indissolubility a moral and social necessity,[68] promoters of divorce relied upon "liberty" to temper the wayward passions and encourage enduring bonds.

Naïvely perhaps, divorce polemicists and critics of arranged marriages believed that structural liberty within marriage would keep kindling the flames of ardor. Even as the years passed and the fires of love burned low, the knowledge of freedom would join with the quieter pleasures of child-rearing to strengthen the emotional bond between husband and wife. One author promised, "Liberty elevates all the sentiments. . . . All the caresses will be like the first one, confirming their mutual choice: 'I love you' in their language will continue to mean, 'You are my favorite'; and for them, marriage will be a treaty agreed upon anew every day." For this anonymous pamphleteer, the imagery of liberty and affect had not made him forget that marriage was a contract, and one in need of continual consent.[69] Greater conjugal liberty would also offer *political* benefits to state and society. "Public liberty . . . will be cemented by happy marriages," avowed one author, while another petitioner commented, "Now it is a question of assuring liberty through regenerating it by love."[70]

As they embraced and idealized conjugal affection as a source of personal contentment and spousal unity, reformers differed in their assessment of what affection meant and how husband and wife should each work to achieve it. Some commentators sidestepped the gendered makeup of companionship, but proposed that if individual choice blended with careful matches, happiness would result. Both of the entrepreneurs who proposed "marriage bureaux" in Paris in 1790 and 1791 assumed that the model engagement would unite potential spouses of similar "age, birth, status, and fortune," and would merge family interests with the "penchants of the heart." But many authors had more specific notions of how each gender had certain qualities that could cultivate "an analogous taste for one another."[71]

In the view of some polemicists, companionate marriage rested on women's ability to charm and please men. Usurping the "Duc d'Orléans" as his pen name, Hubert de Matigny declared jubilantly, "Love governs everything." He indicted marriages devoid of love, proclaimed that wives should not be enslaved to husbands against their will, and then proceeded to define marital love as women's willing servitude: "If, on the contrary, love has formed the spouses' union, then the wife is legally and fully under the yoke, and remarkable thing, she likes it! . . . She loves the slavery of love." For Matigny, male dominance was both natural and God-given. He urged men to be gentle and to "cover their authority with flowers." He made the Rousseauian assumption that each wife should gratify her husband and bend her will to his. A wife should be allowed to divorce for adultery, but never for incompatibility. Only man should have this right since "he is not narrowly obliged to subordinate his character and temperament."[72]

Many other authors echoed—sometimes in more nuanced terms—this Rousseauian belief that women's sacrifice and devotion formed the underpinning of sentimental marriage. M. P. Juge de Brives (erroneously) claimed that Jean-Jacques Rousseau himself had supported divorce. According to Brives, the "fear of divorce" not only bound the couple "more tightly than all the knots of indissoluble marriage," but also encouraged wives to be better mothers who sought to please their husbands by bringing up patriotic children. Another supporter of divorce announced that nature had given women to men to make them happy. Like Jean-Jacques, Charles Rousseau (no relation) celebrated women's capacity for charm and unending devotion: "Feeling with ardor is her first attribute; loving with enthusiasm is her first need." Like 1790s versions of "women who love too much," they could become virtually obsessed with the object of their devotion: "Fortune, honors, high rank, they sacrifice everything to the adored object." In contrast, men were not quite as capable of pure sacrifice for love. "Man, busy with so many interests, plaything of ambition, victim of diverse tastes, is not so entirely devoted to the object of his tenderness."[73]

Virtually all authors shared the idea that men and women had different gender characteristics and hence should play complementary roles. Most of them also made the assumption, rooted in the thought of Jean-Jacques Rousseau, that wives should use their particular moral powers to foster male patriotism both for greater happiness within marriage and for the good of the new nation. But it is important to recognize that many polemicists ignored Rousseau, while others accepted certain aspects of his gender ideology and rejected others. Rousseau's influence on the marital debate was markedly uneven: his stress on women's moral power was often more influential than his embrace of female dependence and docility. In the hands of many authors, the new politics emphasizing equality or individual rights trumped Rousseauian ideologies of submission and supplied an explicit language for attacking Rousseauian support for male authority. As the petitioner William Williams stated before the Legislative Assembly in 1792, "To disregard equality, the principle that conserves all domestic unions; to claim to dominate one over the other . . . is to demonstrate the symptoms of incompatibility; this provokes the dissolution of a contract, signed too lightly."[74]

The escalating attack on Old Regime marriage opened the space for some pamphleteers and petitioners to explicitly challenge female subservience as the basis for affectionate marriage. Although both men and women criticized female servility, female authors—or at least those claiming to be female—were more likely to raise the issue of women's rights within marriage and to argue for companionship based on mutual respect rather than on wifely charm or seduction. These authors advocated women's control of property and protection before the law, and repeatedly used the phrase "marital despotism" to indict the legal, affective, and economic disparities that endowed husbands with disproportionate power. Whether male or female, these polemicists took a feminist stance: that is, they engaged in a substantive critique of the gender dynamics, cultural expectations, economic structures, and laws that reinforced women's inferiority.[75]

Indissoluble marriages dominated by men curtailed conjugal as well as filial affection, claimed these critics. Laws assuring women's legal rights within marriage would help revitalize domestic mores and build more equitable relations between men and women. As the petitioners femme Berlin and Anne Catherine Bagot argued vibrantly in 1792, legalizing divorce would make husbands more tender and egalitarian toward their wives. "A man who knows that his wife can demand a divorce will not treat her like a slave and will not think of himself as the great lord [*grand seigneur*]," promised femme Berlin.[76]

In Old Regime pamphlet literature and feminist discourse, words such as "despotism," "slavery," and "tyranny" had long been used to critique marital inequities.[77] This language gained greater power in 1789 as the Revolution lent legal and political force to the attack on social inequality. One pro-divorce letter from Madame la M. de M—— to the women's newspaper, *Etrennes nationales des Dames,* denounced husbands for being too "aristocratic" and demanded female emancipation within marriage and representation in public politics. After all, the "spirit of reason, justice, and equality . . . has destroyed the slavery of the French, the serfdom of the mountain-dwellers of the Jura, and will break the chains of Africans." What about women, thundered the letter writer: "Let's not allow them [men] with their systems of liberty and equality, with their declarations of rights, to leave us in a state of inferiority; or, let's call a spade a spade, in a state of slavery."[78]

Beyond generalized denunciations of husbands' dominance, some pamphleteers engaged in more specific refutation of the gendered expectations within the conjugal system of the Old Regime: indissolubility and parental control of marriage relied on the tractability and passivity of women. Like Mary Wollstonecraft, these authors wrestled explicitly with Rousseau's emphasis on women's natural duty of pleasing men. These commentators altered his vision by suggesting that greater power and civil rights within marriage would lift women above frivolity, deception, and inferiority. As *Lettre d'une citoyenne à son amie sur les avantages que procurerait à la Nation le patriotisme des dames* (Letter from a citizenness to her friend on the advantages that ladies' patriotism would bring to the Nation) complained, "In reducing a great part of [women's] talents to the art and means of being pleasing, we are given no idea of serious matters, important duties." As several cahiers remarked, if marriage was to become more companionate and less oppressive to women, they should no longer exist "solely to please" men and wield influence "only by the secret means of ruse and seduction."[79]

In her *Vues législatives pour les femmes, adressées à l'Assemblée nationale* (Legislative visions for women, addressed to the National Assembly), Mademoiselle Jodin praised Rousseau for perceiving women's moral force but drew quite different conclusions from this observation. Far from being confined to household duties, women should use their moral powers to exercise public judgment over the internal workings of marriage by running two official, female tribunals. The fifty-member *Chamber of Conciliation* would act as a civil court, with jurisdiction over marital separations, sibling conflicts, broken nuptial promises, and parent-child disputes over arranged marriages. Article VI even suggested vaguely that "all discussions raised between the two sexes will be submitted to the Tribunal." In addition, the eighty female magistrates of a separate *Civil Chamber* would have jurisdiction over various moral matters, including certain forms of gambling, prostitution, fraud, and, last but not least, the behavior of all actresses. Jodin further urged the king to call a female Assembly, made up of elite women, to write laws governing women alongside the male National Assembly.[80]

Madame de Cambis, a member of the Cercle Social, concentrated on women's civil rights within household and state. She commented that Rousseau had not fully recognized how women needed to be "rehabilitated" and lifted above the level of degrading superficialities, and that had not become possible until the current "salutary crisis." She pointed out that marriage and motherhood—the very acts that fulfilled woman's duty to society—deprived her of the right to property and left her "without rights, without property, without status [*état*], without power." She demanded the restoration of this right, not out of pity for women's unhappiness, but because it was a natural, inherent right.[81]

Just as Cambis embraced rights ideology, some women's cahiers, as well as other feminist writings in the early 1790s, expressly rejected the notion that since wives had potent, seductive sway over their husbands, they had no need for legal rights within marriage. "In vain shall one try to persuade [women] that their captivity is only apparent, and that they exercise a real empire through the force of their charms," proclaimed the poster the "Avis aux Mères" angrily. This anonymous author assailed marriage as an unequal contract and insisted upon the right to divorce, better education, and shared administration of communal property. Likewise, the *Griefs et plaintes des femmes mal mariées* inveighed against the notion that women should continually use their "sweetness and modesty" to manipulate men and enable indissoluble, arranged marriages to work.[82]

With its systematic reinforcement of female subservience and airiness, Old Regime marriage had turned women into childish and resentful rivals of men, claimed Madame Fumelh. In her *Mémoire sur le divorce*, she protested that forming women as light-headed nothings converted them into slaves who resented their despotic husbands. As a result most marriages became riddled with "internecine warfare, hatred, scorn, and intrigue." For men's own good, they should do away with this emphasis on women's seductive charm, suppleness, and sacrifice, and offer them an education that would make them worthier and more well prepared for companionate marriage. This upbringing and education would foster women's inherent moral capabilities, emotional sensitivity, intellectual delicacy, and vivacious imagination. In 1790 when Madame Mouret launched her moderate *Annales de l'éducation du sexe,* a woman's journal devoted to lobbying for female schooling and moral formation, she began with a lengthy and detailed letter to the National Assembly. In a veritable rant about the moral dangers of luxury, frivolity, and libertinage, she hung the fate of the nation, family, marriage, and "the happiness of men on the education of *le sexe.*"[83]

Keenly aware that they wrote at a moment when the state was being redefined, feminist advocates of marital reform began to invoke specific legal structures and statutes to ameliorate women's position within marriage. Like many during the early Revolution, they expressed Enlightenment optimism about the possibility that new laws could influence ethical and affective behavior, but they were also quick to demand that the laws offer concrete protection and recourse. Several pamphleteers and placard-writers asserted that feminine wiles gave a wife but a poor defense against the ferocity or anger of a brutal husband; laws must punish his abuses or allow the woman to liberate herself from him. Madame Cailly proposed that the new laws "oversee women's interests with more attention, and that a council or the public minister intervene" at moments of sale and contract-making to help women manage property within marriage.[84]

Indeed, control over property stood at the crux of the matter. Feminist marriage theorists drew on the classic argument that marriage was a civil contract, but insisted that contractual marriage formed "a society in which the condition of both contractors must be equal." For the contract to be mutual and equitable, the woman must have the power to administer her goods and have an equal voice within a communal marital property system. Likewise, as an unmarried woman, her fate should not be decided solely by the force of dowries and interfamilial property arrangements. One anonymous male proponent of divorce asserted that marriage constituted bondage for both husband and wife, but more so for woman since man "had claimed absolute dominion over [woman] . . . and her property as if it were his conquest." Even her name was taken from her "to remind her that she is no longer anything. . . . One stipulates, contracts, acquires, sells: she is a witness to everything, but takes part in nothing. Her person, her will, everything has passed into the hands of a new owner."[85]

In the Old Regime, marital property regimes varied according to region.

Nowhere in France did married women share control of their property equitably with their husbands.[86] Some of the more knowledgeable authors contrasted the different marital property systems of Normandy, the Midi, and Paris. They indicted the dotal structures of Normandy and the Midi in particular and disparaged families in these areas for favoring sons over daughters, but also noted that the communal marital property system of Paris was far from perfect, for the wife had virtually no control over the shared products of the couple's labor. By and large, the feminist critics faulted marital property systems for depriving women of economic independence and for sacrificing their rights both before and during marriage. Proclaiming that marriage was "a continual state of war," Madame Fumelh proposed that conjugal relations would be vastly improved if men's and women's property within marriage was separated from the outset *and* each partner shared in the control of their respective goods.[87]

Critics of dowries suggested that this financial transaction reinforced the arbitrary authority of husbands and fathers, corrupted romance, and made companionate marriage impossible. The *Doléances des femmes de Franche-Comté* (Grievances of the women of the Franche-Comté) faulted parents for forcing their daughters to marry "repugnant" candidates "without other consideration than their property or their names." Invoking the ideal of the sentimental marriage based on a "perfect equality . . . exclusive of any notion of authority," Madame Bastille suggested in her cahier that a new law should "oblige men to marry women who have no dowries."[88]

It is worth noting that the assault on the dowry as a barrier to companionate marriage could come from those who hoped to improve women's status and autonomy within marriage, as well as from men who hoped to find wives more anxious to please their husbands. Some male authors in 1789 reiterated the Old Regime argument that dowries made rich wives too independent and too disinterested in cultivating wifely social skills. If dowries were eliminated, bachelors would be free to choose fiancées based on personal charm rather than wealth, and then wives would work harder to hold their husbands' love and attention. Marital compatibility, rooted in female compliance, would increase accordingly.[89] Companionate marriage and its ideal gender dynamics had no single definition in the early 1790s.

Olympe de Gouges is most well known as the revolutionary feminist who drew up a declaration of women's rights and boldly demanded a public, political role for women. Yet, integral to her feminism was a scathing critique of familial and marital inequities and an indictment of the marital property system. She wrote plays, pamphlets, and posters addressing divorce, arranged marriage, and the harsh fate of illegitimate children.[90] For de

Gouges, woman's political and civil rights were intertwined. In her famous declaration, *Les droits de la femme*, she sustains her articles enumerating women's rights with a proposed marriage contract. This voluntary contract would give both husband and wife control over their communal property, guarantee them an equal right to inherit their shared goods, and oblige both to recognize as legitimate any child of either partner. Once woman was on an equal standing with man in the home and in the "administration of their property," she would no longer engage in the dissimulation and immoral manipulation of men and power that characterized female behavior in the Old Regime. Only by refurbishing the emotional and legal relationship between man and woman could woman gain the equality promised by nature.

> I offer a foolproof way to elevate the soul of women; it is to join them to all the activities of men; if man persists in finding this means impractical, let him share his fortune with woman, not at his caprice, but by the wisdom of the laws. Prejudice falls away, morals are purified, and the rights of nature are restored. Add the marriage of priests; the King will be strengthened on his throne, and the French government cannot fail.[91]

For all of her radicalness, Olympe de Gouges wrote in dialogue with other authors who, like her, saw a fundamental connection between the reform of public politics, the remaking of gender relations, and an increase in women's economic and legal status.

Male and female members of the Cercle Social took a leading role in lobbying for restructuring familial property arrangements. Not only were some members directly involved in pressing for more egalitarian inheritance laws, but their calls for conjugal reform also tied the question of property to the moral regeneration of male-female relations. In April 1792 Etta Palm d'Aelders led a group of fellow women to the bar of the Assembly to call for divorce, civil rights, and the lowering of women's age of majority. Her demand in action invoked her earlier speeches that appealed for "equal and separate" powers for husbands and wives. As noted earlier, Cercle Social member Madame de Cambis lobbied for married women's property rights. She may well have joined Etta Palm d'Aelders to influence the drafting of an unsigned Cercle Social petition that exposed how easily a woman could become impoverished during the séparation de corps process. Since her husband alone had legal control over their joint property, he could conceal its true value or seem to go broke just before the final separation. In the absence of divorce, the petition outlined a proposed law requiring an inventory of communal goods as soon as separation procedures began. This accountability would at least partially protect women's property rights.[92]

As early revolutionary feminists clamored for the legal and affective reform of marriage, they gradually cultivated the view that familial reform was critical for securing women's loyalty to the Revolution. "It seems that the Revolution has done nothing for women. . . . The time has come to give you the rights that nature owes you," declared the poster "Avis aux mères de familles" across the streets of Paris late in 1789 as it demanded divorce, civil equality within marriage, and property rights for married women. With her typical directness, Etta Palm d'Aelders put the issue squarely to the Confédération des Amis de la Vérité in December 1790: "If you want us to zealously embrace that happy Constitution which gives men their rights, then begin by being just towards us; from now on let us be your voluntary companions and not your slaves."[93]

Female pamphleteers were more likely than male ones to point out gender inequities within marriage. But a striking number of male pamphleteers—or at least authors writing from a male stance—advocated marital reform and improvement in women's status before the law and within the home *as a means of gaining women's support for the Revolution.* They presented divorce, and civil reform more generally, as causes that particularly interested women. Several men dedicated their pro-divorce works to women or appealed to them as an interest group consciously invested in conjugal matters. Eighteenth-century authors sometimes addressed their works to women as a signal that their work was accessible to everyone. Moreover, the female reader in some sense authorized the male writer to express his opinions.[94]

Clearly, male divorce pamphleteers could have been following the same policy, but they also wrote out of the assumption that familial issues were pivotal in defining female citizenship. Women, as wives and mothers, had a fundamental role of advancing the Constitution and garnering support for it. Yet how could they be expected to perform their political duty of upholding the state, if the Revolution disdained all interest in their institutions, wondered the author of *Un mot sur le divorce* (A word on divorce)? No, the Constitution must focus also on civic matters, such as divorce, which specifically earned the enthusiasm of women. When M. P. Juge de Brives advertised his pamphlet as "destined mainly to be read by sensitive and unhappy women," he maintained that the possibility of divorce would make women more respected as mothers and wives. One light-hearted pamphleteer reported to the king that he had seen a group of delightful young women seized with "transports of joy" at the notion that the king would legalize divorce. But if our wives can divorce us and take back their dowries, "What will we use to pay our mistresses?" joked another anonymous observer. In other words, in humorous pamphlets as in serious ones, the conviction arose that divorce would endow women with more power and independence within the marriage pact and help to win their moral support for the nation. Some men argued that they had to lighten their hold over women to assure their wives' attachment to the Revolution and to obtain greater liberty and love themselves.[95] Their arguments would influence the revolutionary deputies who turned to debate marriage and divorce in 1792.

. . .

The outbreak of Revolution sparked a lively dialogue about marriage reform as a wide range of revolutionaries—from frustrated clergymen to vocal feminists to provincial petitioners—argued that revolutionary politics and state-building had direct meaning for personal relationships. Marriage, like the state, should be built on a freely chosen contract and should cultivate both individual and collective happiness. Among the arguments for conjugal reform, the politically loaded concepts of individual liberty and natural rights held particular potency, and marriage theorists stressed both the legal and the emotional significance of these concepts. As they began to tease out possible meanings of free and affectionate marriage, these revolutionary pamphleteers and petitioners launched a fervent appeal for specific reforms, such as divorce, the reduction of parental control over marriage, and an end to clerical celibacy.

These early debates also created opportunities for rethinking the power relations between husband and wife. Within the broader agitation over marriage, a small but significant group of feminist critics wielded revolutionary language to demand greater legal and economic rights for married women. Even as they embraced women's moral capacity, they often attacked the Rousseauian assumption that successful companionship was rooted in women's subservience and attempts to please men. During the Revolution, this early agitation in pamphlets and press contributed to politicizing women far from Paris around family matters and also challenged male revolutionaries and lawmakers to address women's rights and the issue of household gender politics. Over the longer term, this 1790s combination of rights ideology with a moral discourse on the family would inform French feminist thinking in the nineteenth century.[96]

As the Revolution progressed, these early claims about men's and women's rights and affection within marriage took on greater urgency and concreteness for two reasons. When the lawmakers struggled to build a state free from religious control and to articulate the legal rights of the juridical individual, they necessarily turned to debate and delineate the status of individuals within marriage. Moreover, as the Revolution increasingly assaulted Old Regime sources of social cohesion—from Church to crown to myriad corporate bodies—marriage and the conjugal family emerged in the revolutionary imagination as a "natural" force for social unity, built on affection and the gender complementarity of man and woman. Reformed and refurbished, revolutionary marriage should provide a fundamental glue to the social structure and work morally and culturally for the new nation-state. As Nicolas de Bonneville stated in his *Le nouveau code conjugal* (The new conjugal code) in 1792, "Marriage is the social bond that unites the citizen to the *patrie* [fatherland] and the *patrie* to the citizen."[97] The next chapter will explore the deputies' redefinition of legal marriage and analyze the revolutionaries' emerging conviction that love and gender complementarity within marriage could help to regenerate the nation from within.

2. The Political Power of Love

Marriage, Regeneration, and Citizenship

In 1791, the *Courrier de l'Hymen,* the "Marriage Gazette," offered an unusual format: side-by-side with political news summaries and witty editorials critiquing marriage practices, it featured what could only be called personal ads, quite detailed paid announcements by individuals who hoped to engage in that matrimonial institution that the rest of the journal seemed bent on reforming. Among the hottest candidates were deputies, members of the National Assembly. One representative from the Antilles advertised for a fiancée in Paris: he hoped she would have "a gentle character and a pleasant face," and concluded, "Although I am a member of the legislative body, I don't need her to have strong opinions on politics and would even prefer that she lean neither to the right nor to the left but rather maintain a judicious moderation." A later issue printed a scathing reply from one woman who declared that there could be no marriage without politics and that even though she was twenty-five, "forgotten for seven years in an Ursuline Convent" (in other words, even though she was desperate), she "would not take him even though he was a deputy and even if he owned all the 660,000 unhappy beings who paid with their liberty and their blood for the wealth and pleasure of 40,000 Europeans. I hate tyrants and executioners. . . . And I don't want anything to do with someone who does not cherish with his whole heart this happy revolution which has restored the rights of man and replaced the destructive regime of oppression and despotism with the benevolent reign of national liberty and equality."[1] Soundly rebuked, the deputy probably slunk off to find a less vocal wife from a procolonial town like Nantes or Bordeaux.

Perhaps with her fervent antislavery opinions, this anonymous young woman was especially politicized, but on a broader scale, she gives an inkling of that revolutionary moment when the most private and personal ties took on profound political resonance. She was not alone in seeing politics within intimacy. This chapter will ask how husbands and wives, legislative deputies, moralists, unhappy clergymen, and club members together imagined that marriage—reformed along revolutionary lines—could help to regenerate citizens and promote the new politics.

While the last chapter focused on how revolutionary ideology facilitated the critique of marriage, this one argues that the reform of marriage was integral to inventing and negotiating the gendered meaning of citizenship in revolutionary France. Among the multiple meanings of "citizenship," two were most crucial to rethinking marriage.[2] First, citizenship meant that the state guaranteed each legal individual, each member of the French nation, certain civil rights—such as the right to the freedoms of expression, the legal right to fair treatment before the law, and the personal rights to marry, inherit, work, own property, or make contracts. The corollary to these legal rights was a set of obligations, including the duty to pay taxes and participate in the military efforts of the nation. Crucially, the new secular state grounded its legitimacy in guaranteeing the juridical rights of all individuals within a uniform system of law. Because marriage played such a central role in defining the status of the citizen, inevitably the legal and cultural contours of marriage and the rights of husband and wife as individuals came up for debate. The very act of inventing the secular state and juridical citizenship was inextricably bound up with refashioning marriage and its gender dynamics.

Second, citizenship also had a profound moral and cultural meaning. To really become a citizen, one must remake oneself into a virtuous and patriotic being dedicated to the new nation and its core values of liberty, equality, and fraternity. Only then could the citizen, at least the male citizen, truly take full advantage of the third quintessential element of citizenship: the formal right to participate in public politics, to be a full member of the sovereignty. In constructing the cultural and moral meanings of citizenship, the revolutionaries demanded that politics permeate the most ordinary acts and the most intimate emotions. In the process, they generated and dispersed new forms of power for women as well as men, and they opened up contestation over gender relationships and the nature of masculinity and femininity. Marriage and the possibilities of heterosexual love became a particular point of focus for the revolutionaries. They placed tremendous faith in marriage: not only would the affectionate and natural bonds between husband and wife help to forge the social unity of the Republic, but also, ideally, the intersecting gender characteristics of woman and man would transform marriage into a site of political transformation and moral regeneration.

The bond between citizenship and marriage did not emerge seamlessly in the 1790s, nor did it have the same ramifications for women and men. Rather, the gendered definitions of citizenship and visions for conjugal reform were hammered out in give and take, in the public arenas of debate, in the halls of the legislature, and in local assemblies, political clubs, judicial courts, armies, and families across France. This chapter explores those negotiations. How, according to the revolutionaries, would the legal and cultural reconstruction of marriage underpin revolutionary politics, regeneration, and state-building? And how did this reform of marriage contribute to configuring masculinity and femininity differently? To answer these questions, I will first examine the deputies' early reform of marriage and then analyze public expectations of the regenerative power of conjugal love.

MARRIAGE AND THE SECULAR STATE

In the Constitution of 1791, the National Assembly defined marriage as a "civil contract." A year later, soon after the fall of the monarchy, the Legislative Assembly legalized divorce, reduced paternal authority over marriage choices, lowered the age of majority, removed all nuptial matters from clerical control, and established a secular état civil for recording births, marriages, divorces, and deaths. These decrees distinctly recast the nature of marriage in France. With the passage of these laws, the deputies attempted to situate marriage as a secular civil contract, voluntarily agreed upon by two individuals acting freely. No longer eternal, no longer necessarily sanctioned by the divine, this contract could be broken. Lawmakers omitted the stipulation, omnipresent in Old Regime law, that had defined the relationship between husband and wife as a feudal one: the wife owed fidelity and obedience to her husband, who in turn owed her protection, assistance, and a home. Not until the Napoleonic Civil Code would such language of vassalage reemerge.[3] Marriage had officially become a site of individual liberty, as had been so vibrantly demanded by lonely clergymen, divorce pamphleteers and petitioners, feminist cahiers, and various moralists.

But at the same time, these laws made clear how intently the new republican state counted upon marriage to define the status of individuals and to tie each man and woman to the new republican state and nation. As the Old Regime jurist Bourjon had written, "Almost all civil rights flow from the legitimacy of marriage." As in the Old Regime, marriage would serve as a fundamental legal mechanism for defining rights, identity, and status. But now the republic—unencumbered by Church or clergy—would oversee this crucial ability of marriage to determine each citizen's nationality, filiation and legitimacy, right to inherit and to control—or in women's case, not to control—certain forms of property. Civil obligations, most notably taxation and conscription, varied according to marital status. The state's relationship to marriage would only grow in importance: especially as the Revolution entered its most radical and xenophobic phase in 1793–94, the conjugal status of foreigners, émigrés, nobles, and former priests and nuns could definitively alter their legal standing and political claim to citizenship.[4]

As the deputies debated and devised the changing legal contours of marriage, they gradually elaborated on a vision of marriage as a microcosm of the social contract. They anticipated that this institution would tie the individual to the social whole, the citizen to the state, the patriot to the nation. In their eyes, marriage held unique power because of its apparent standing as a practice at once universal and natural. Although freely chosen and based on mutual consent, marriage also marked the quintessential and natural union between man and woman: this most elemental social bond, grounded in the natural complementarity of the genders, should enable virtually everyone to contribute to the nation. By forming a useful and even virtuous bridge from the state of nature to civil society, and from civil society to the state, marriage took on political importance at this moment when revolutionaries strove to unite the civil and natural man in service of the new nation and to draw on the distinct, but socially useful qualities of each citizen, female or male.

When the Legislative Assembly attempted to reform marriage according to this vision, their lawmaking stemmed from a complex interplay of factors. First, the extensive popular lobbying for greater liberty, happiness, and affection within marriage gradually made its mark on the deputies. Second, at the same time, the logic and process of secular state-building pushed the deputies toward grappling with the definition of marriage over the course of 1790–92. Intent on demarcating the legal parameters of the new state, enacting natural law, and guaranteeing juridical uniformity and individual freedom of conscience, the deputies gradually disengaged marriage from the hands of the Church and sought to define it as a civil, secular contract between two rights-bearing individuals. Inevitably, this process raised loaded questions about paternal authority, marital indissolubility, women's civil rights, and the legal parameters of this institution that so profoundly defined the status of citizens and their property. Finally, particularly by the spring and summer of 1792, the deputies' debates over marriage would be informed by the escalating emphasis in political culture on forging patriotic citizens, regenerated from within and dedicated unquestioningly to the patrie. In sum, public opinion, the building of the secular state, and the evolution of political culture all intersected to influence the lawmakers.

Proponents of divorce made their voices heard in the legislature in the early 1790s.[5] From the first broaching of the topic in the National Assembly in August 1790, the deputies were keenly aware of the discussion of marriage in petitions, pamphlets, and the press. "The public voice calls out for your empathy, . . . Fifty works, all the newspapers, all the social circles call upon your justice," proclaimed the deputy Pierre-François Gossin as he indicted indissoluble marriage as a tyrannical prison.[6] Gossin's invocation of the pervasive cry for divorce fell on deaf ears within the assembly, but, over the next two years, multiple supporters of marital reform appeared at the bar of the successive legislatures: Alsatian Lutherans hoping to follow their traditional social customs, individual authors presenting their pamphlets or petitions, and delegations of lobbying citizens, including two groups of Parisian women with marital despotism on their minds.[7]

The Committee of Petitions and the Committee of Legislation received a slow stream of pro-divorce petitions between them in 1791 and 1792, with a distinct increase in the winter-spring of 1792. In the fall of 1791, so struck was the Committee of Petitions by the heartbreaking tale of a battered wife in the Sarthe who had hung herself in despair that they sent a report to the Committee of Legislation, urging them to clarify the right to divorce: "If the constitutional act allows divorce, we need explicit laws regulating its effects." By June 1792, the citizen-petitioner Roche and thirty-nine supporters declared, "Legislators! Almost all citizens wait impatiently to learn that you have created and sanctioned that wise law that abolishes the indissolubility of marriage." In August 1792, a petition read at the bar would help to turn the legislators' attention more definitively toward divorce.[8]

The voices of pamphleteers, petitioners, and occasional delegations at the bar chipped away at the deputies' consciousness, but the Committee of Legislation and the Legislative Assembly were slow to embrace the highly controversial issue of divorce. The politico-religious context and the social conservatism of many leading jurists caused them to postpone open debate about the topic. Instead, the seemingly mundane matter of how to record and regulate marriages in parish registers placed the matter of marriage squarely onto the agenda of the National and Legislative Assemblies. In the Old Regime, parish priests had kept the official registers of births, marriages, and deaths—a responsibility made official by the 1579 Ordinance of Blois. This bureaucratic task actually left considerable power in the hands of priests, for they could, for example, refuse marriage to those deemed unworthy. The system also left in limbo the official registration of the civil status of non-Catholics, despite the attempt of the 1787 Edict of Toleration to develop a form of civil marriage for Protestants.[9]

One notorious incident captured the attention of the Assembly. In 1790 the curé of Saint-Sulpice in Paris refused to publish banns and bless the marriage of the well-known actor François-Joseph Talma. While the National Assembly had officially recognized the civil rights of actors on 23 December 1789, canon law still condemned the "immorality" of their lifestyle. On the basis of this authority, the curé suggested that Talma repudiate his acting career. Outraged by this treatment, the actor succeeded in having an angry denunciation read at the bar of the National Assembly. Talma made a perfect figure for this test case of civil rights versus the traditional power of the Church over matters of morals and marriage. He was an actor of some renown: late in 1789 he had made his name by playing the leading role in Marie-Joseph Chénier's provocative play, *Charles IX*. Moreover, as a member of the Cordélier Club, he had ties to Georges-Jacques Danton and Honoré-Gabriel Riqueti de Mirabeau. In his petition to the Assembly, he invoked the "rights of the constitutional law" and "the rights of the citizen" which did not "exclude those who embrace a career in the theater." On hearing Talma's case, the deputy Guillaume Goupil immediately demanded that the matter be considered by the Ecclesiastical and Constitutional Committees, for the case encompassed not just the rights of actors, but also the question of ecclesiastical authority and the uniformity of civil law. The right of actors to marry freely, like that of Protestants and Jews, tested the meaning of universal citizenship before the law. Moreover, the Ecclesiastical Committee was already reviewing the system of marital impediments and dispensations, which lay under episcopal control.[10]

Talma eventually resolved his personal dilemma by renouncing his profession for eleven days—just long enough to get his marriage blessed and his twins legitimized and baptized during his theater's Easter break in 1791![11] But the tough task of the Ecclesiastical Committee was not so easily resolved in the complex politico-religious climate of 1790–91. Pierre-Toussaint Durand de Maillane, the head of the Ecclesiastical Committee and a prominent canon lawyer, had difficulty even bringing his report on marriage and the état civil to the floor for debate and his plan faced vigorous attack.[12] In February 1792, Honoré Muraire, on behalf of the Committee of Legislation, would once again propose laicizing the état civil, but only after repeated and drawn-out debate would the Legislative Assembly take action in September 1792.

From 1790 to 1792, the legislators, especially members of the Ecclesiastical

Committee, heard recurrent complaints from individuals who had difficulty winning the right to marry. Some sought redress against bishops reluctant to grant routine dispensations; in other cases, actors or couples of mixed religious background complained about opposition from local curés. In 1790 when the Assembly drafted the Civil Constitution of the Clergy to restructure the French Church, the ensuing conflict only intensified the debate about who had control over the approval and registration of marriage. The legislature demanded that all priests take an oath of loyalty to the new nation and Civil Constitution; the French clergy became divided between the oath-taking "constitutionals" and the "nonjurors," who were soon to be replaced by constitutional colleagues in parishes across France. Many underground nonjuror priests continued to baptize, marry, and bury loyal parishioners. But were their clandestine parish registers valid, especially when their constitutional rivals kept official registers as well? Parishioners worried and "distressing scenes" ensued: in Strasbourg a set of unhappy parents could not convince the constitutional bishop to bury their two dead children who had been baptized by a nonjuror. The Conseil du Bas-Rhin faced so many incidents of conflict that they ordered priests throughout the department to deposit the civil records at local municipalities. By May 1791 Jean-Sylvain Bailly, the mayor of Paris, appeared at the bar of the Assembly with a petition imploring the deputies to end this confusion by appointing civil officials, rather than priests, to keep official records of birth, marriage, and death of all citizens under one homogeneous civil law, regardless of creed.[13]

This pressure from below to clarify questions of civil status and the right to marry dovetailed neatly with the desire of leading jurists to promote religious toleration, strengthen the new state's jurisdiction, and create uniform laws guaranteeing the civil rights of all citizens. The deputy Jean-Denis Lanjuinais used the complaints of Mayor Bailly to turn debate toward the report on marriage and the état civil by the Ecclesiastical and Constitutional Committees. In this report, Durand de Maillane proposed that government officials maintain the état civil and have jurisdiction over marital matters. Delicately defending the notion that marriage could remain a sacrament under the spiritual aegis of the clergy for Catholics, he nonetheless insisted that marriage was first and foremost a civil "contract formed by the free and mutual consent of the parties." He also called for lowering the age of consent and reducing paternal authority over marriage and disinheritance. His proposal could not become law in 1791 because his opponents feared further alienating certain Catholics in the tense aftermath of the Civil Constitution. But his report paved the way for the crucial formula in the Constitution of 1791, stating that "the law considers marriage only as a civil contract."[14]

Durand de Maillane certainly built upon Old Regime jurists' definition of marriage as a civil contract, and his appeal followed from the long-standing trend toward asserting royal power over familial matters.[15] Within the revolutionary context, however, his proposal differed from these Old Regime precedents in several key ways. As he set forth the mechanism of a lay état civil, he moved beyond simply increasing state authority over marriage: in essence he grounded the legitimacy of state and society in the juridical act of guaranteeing rights equally to all citizens. By wholly governing the intimate domain of marriage, the new state would simultaneously defend its legal unity and begin to define and protect the rights-bearing citizen. "As it recovers its liberty, the nation has the greatest interest in removing anything that can cause it to lose this liberty." The "false prejudices of religion" posed exactly that threat. Despite his careful dance on the sacramental nature of marriage as a "mystery," Durand de Maillane came close to declaring what later orators would make explicit: uniform law and the family must replace religion as a force of cultural and institutional cohesion.[16]

For Durand de Maillane, the key questions were how to guarantee juridical equality and how to free marriage and civil rights from clerical dominion. He did not yet fully postulate a different role for marriage within the relationship between the individual and the state or between the individual and society. But between February and September 1792, as republican sentiment, patriotic fervor, and anticlericalism all grew stronger, certain legislators gradually envisioned an increasingly central role for marriage in the constitution of citizenship. In their recurrent debates over the état civil, the registration of birth and death spurred little discussion, but to redefine marriage solely as a civil contract under the aegis of the state stirred up endless controversy. For in the eyes of opponents, this move broke the Catholic threads woven into the cultural cloth of France and opened up dangerous challenges to paternal authority and marital stability. Conversely, in the eyes of proponents, regenerated marriage would become the natural, social, legal, and moral bond that tied the individual citizen to society and to the patrie.

As he proposed laicizing the état civil in February 1792, Muraire promised that the Committee of Legislation had "established [their proposed law] on two bases: liberty and the good of the State." The état civil implicitly cemented a new reciprocal relationship—a relationship of rights and duties—between the free individual and the state. The state was now to become the sole guarantor of the legal status of the citizen. "The citizen is born in the bosom of the municipality," declared Muraire in February 1792; thus the state "should assure each citizen his most precious property: his *état* [status]." As careful recorders of birth, marriage, and death, the official representatives of the civil government then would safeguard each individual from (religious) prejudice, facilitate the transfer of familial property and name, and guard the uniformity of the law. The state also became the protector of individual liberty. As Louis-Jérôme Gohier stated in the ongoing debate, "Slaves have no état civil. Only the free man has a *cité*, a patrie; he alone is born, lives, and dies as a citizen." Muraire stressed that marriage—of all civil acts—most demanded liberty: "Liberty, having become our principal element, holds a claim above all in marriages." Attacking paternal authority and conjugal impediments, he echoed the language so prominent in pamphlets and petitions: "It is happiness that must be assured in marriage. Therefore, if you want marriages to be happy, grant them [fiancés] the freedom of choice."[17]

According to Muraire, if the state protected the marital liberty and état of individuals, citizens also owed the state and should marry. The interests of state and citizen were inextricably intertwined and marriage constituted a bridge between the two. "The citizen lives and dies for the patrie," he announced. If marriage was a site of liberty and juridical identity, it was also a political act and a social duty. "Marriage belongs to the political order," asserted Muraire. Tellingly, he spoke of the nuptial act as that "interesting moment when, recognizing that his duties toward society are not limited to personal devotion, [the citizen] engages in a contract to reproduce himself."[18]

In envisioning marriage as a social obligation, Muraire embraced the ambient discussion in pamphlets and press alike that men and women should marry and reproduce in order to be useful citizens. On the most basic level, this idea developed out of utilitarian and populationist Old Regime discourse, enhanced by mercantile state theorists, physiocrats, and various philosophes: marriage was a useful, natural duty of subjects, who should produce population for state and society. Drawing on this logic, for example, divorce proponents in the Old Regime and the New had argued that divorce would benefit the state by allowing couples from broken households to remarry and multiply.[19] The pronatalist goals of the enthusiastic new nation reinforced the tendency to represent marriage as productive and to penalize celibacy as sterile and selfish. Already in 1791, festivals celebrated fertility: in Rouen a mother who had given birth to twenty-five children was given the honorary role of flag-bearer in a special ceremony. In the sale of *biens nationaux* (nationalized lands), married men with children were privileged over bachelors. Likewise, the 13 January 1791 law placed bachelors over thirty-six into the highest tax bracket and established a descending tax scale for families who produced three or more children. To be celibate was to be a social parasite: "Bachelors form a useless weight on the earth that nourishes them," rang one slogan. The outbreak of war in 1792 would only further ignite the attack on celibacy and the glorification of fertile marriage.[20]

The language of social parasitism burgeoned with the growing anticlerical fervor of the early Revolution. The celibacy of religious and secular clergy marked and indicted them as leeches on the body politic. All too aware of this opinion, patriotic priests, especially those who hoped to marry, insisted that the right to marry would redeem them in the public eye, render them more useful, enable them to "work together for the common good," and tie them to the body social. Anxious to illustrate the potential utility of clerical marriage for the secular state, one priest calculated that if France's 100,000 clergymen married, they might well father 10,000 well-educated children per year. Yet another contended that married priests could perform socially beneficial functions as surgeons, justices of the peace, police commissioners, or lawyers. Many others denounced the vows and institutions that rendered them egotistical, "anti-social," "anti-moral," "anti-natural." With good reason did the Old Regime equate entering the religious life and taking vows of chastity with "civil death," noted one clergyman, who likened his status to that of a condemned man, cut off from the finer sentiments and true purpose of humanity. At death, each man would be measured by his utility to society, concluded this patriot priest.[21] Little wonder, then, that by 1793–94 marriage would become the ultimate litmus test of clerical allegiance to the Republic: by rejecting church-ordained celibacy, married priests embraced the social whole, rejoined the body politic, and became fully useful citizens.

When Muraire tapped into this broader discourse that defined marriage as civil obligation, he also pointed toward the linkage between citizenship and marriage that his fellow deputies would theorize about more fully in the coming months. Because the revolutionaries believed that they were founding society anew and because they envisioned the family and especially the conjugal bond between men and women as the original social contract, marriage took on a palpable importance in constructing ties not only between the individual and the collectivity, but also between nature as intimate and human, and society and the state as collective and institutional. Because of its legal and official structure and because of its basis in mutual contract as well as nature, the conjugal relationship had a moral and political power that sexual liaison or love alone did not possess in the eyes of the revolutionaries. It civilized male and female sexuality, legitimized offspring, and harnessed sexuality to the state and social good. As the deputy Pierre-Victurnien Vergniaud commented in 1792:

> Marriage is the first social convention. . . . Only the mutual consent of the spouses forms its essence. Nonetheless, in the state of civilization, a distinction is made between the two sexes simply coming together because of need or momentary caprice and the will to unite one's whole existence with the loved one, to give and receive happiness constantly, and to transmit life to children. . . . Among all civilized [policés] people, the instinct of modesty has provoked opprobrium toward the first of these unions; in contrast, they have honored the second with the name of marriage, surrounded it with pomp and solemnity, and regarded it as a contract worthy of the keenest interest and all their solicitude, because it has individual happiness as its goal and also influences the power and splendor of Empires.[22]

Vergniaud argued that marriage could fill goals near and dear to the hearts of the revolutionaries. As they struggled to "unite the social order so much with the natural order that they make only one," no other institution could so fully tie the biological, natural realm to the social and the civilized. Crucially, it purified morals en route even as it produced new life for society and the state and happiness for the individual—at least in its ideal form.[23]

As Vergniaud also suggested, the *public* in all its "pomp and solemnity" must bear witness to the union. Public and official approval enabled marriage to play its moral role; the public purified the conjugal bond by elevating it above mere sexual caprice and certifying the couple's responsibility to the social whole. In the reforming jurists' view, the Catholic Church and congregation could no longer serve as the public witnesses legitimating marriage. The new France would turn to "society," the "social body," and the "state" to sanction the conjugal union. These words became almost interchangeable elements in this discourse, for the deputies imagined social practices and identity to be tightly bound with the newly created institutions, laws, and ideology of the state. The law had infinite power to mold human morals and to "tie one to society without making [this bond] be a burden." The patrie, the law, and society itself would replace religion in offering public sanction.[24]

Indeed, by the summer of 1792, Gohier proposed that marriage and all other civil acts, such as birth, death, and inscription into the national guard, be celebrated on a newly constructed Altar of the Patrie. He distinguished marriage from all other contracts because it involved the interest of society as a whole. Society, according to Gohier, should stand witness to the couple's mutual promise of love and, perhaps more important, to the legitimacy of their child, whose cradle would be "surrounded by all the protection, all the force of the law." All the more important then, that the contract be public and imbued with liberty, and that marriage be "one of the *first duties of the citizen*" (his emphasis). Since spouses should remember that they belonged to the patrie even before they belonged to each other, the civil marriage vow would be sealed with the exultant cry of "Live free or die!"[25]

By the time Gohier pushed his plan, some citizens had already engaged in rituals of civil marriage and the concept had begun to spread through imagery and pamphlet literature (see Figure 1). In 1792, former deputy and Cercle Social member Nicolas de Bonneville proposed an alternate civic ritual to replace religious weddings. Each fiancé would declare publicly out loud: "I declare, as a free man and good citizen, that I take ___ as my friend and my wife." Likewise, each fiancée, "as a free woman and good citoyenne [citizen]," declared that she took her fiancé "as my friend and as my husband." Highlighting citizenship and freely chosen companionship, Bonneville soon made explicit that the patriotic act of marriage naturally encompassed both love and friendship: "The Constitution *has wanted* that the law on marriages be all love and all friendship, like the law of nature" (his emphasis).[26]

Gohier argued that the turning points of life, especially birth, marriage, and death, opened the human heart to passion and affective influence. Civic ceremonies at these touching moments would tap into powerful human emotions and encourage citizens to intertwine their most personal feelings with the higher sentiment of loyalty to the public good. "Let us imbue them [these turning points] with a civic hue; let us profit from that moment when the soul is agitated to fill it with elevating virtues," he urged. He gestured toward a belief that would become increasingly explicit: marriage had the emotional possibility of regenerating citizens for the new nation. In this same vein, knitting marriage ever closer to patriotism, the deputy Jean-Baptiste Jollivet proposed that loyalty to the nation be part of the legal definition of marriage: it would be a freely chosen contract in which couples pledged "to live together and to *raise their children with love of the patrie and respect for its laws*" (my emphasis).[27] Within its very definition, marriage now implied a political as well as a personal commitment.

In sum, by August–September 1792, the deputies had gradually created a new imaginative and legal space for marriage. This voluntary contract of love took on ever more resonance and responsibility within citizenship. Because it stood at the juncture between nature and social convention, it elevated sex to the level of social utility and civilized morality. At the nexus between affect and law, it united sentiment with the state and fully embodied the revolutionaries' dream of rooting society in natural law. In the ideal

Figure 1.   Civil marriage before the Supreme Being (1792).
Courtesy of the Bibliothèque nationale de France.

marriage, a free individual made a choice that simultaneously benefited himself or herself, society, and the state. Joining freedom of choice with social stability, marriage exemplified the reconciliation of the individual with the general good.

LAICIZING MARRIAGE, LEGALIZING DIVORCE, AND CHALLENGING MARITAL AND PATERNAL AUTHORITY

Yet for marriage to fulfill such an idealized role, it needed to be regenerated. As the deputies debated the relationship between marriage and the état civil, they inevitably also raised various issues about how internal conjugal and familial dynamics should be reconfigured. If marriage was a voluntary contract rooted in individual liberty, all sorts of other reforms swirled unspoken—and then spoken—in these debates. Paternal authority over arranged marriages and disinheritance, divorce, adoption, marital impediments, paternity suits, trial marriages, "private" informal marriages, the size of dowries, women's control over marital property, the rights of illegitimate offspring: all of these sensitive issues would rear their heads, despite the prudent reluctance of many members of the Assembly to address them. Notably, for the moment, the deputies set aside passionate appeals by Claude Pastoret, Charles-François Oudot, and Pierre-Edouard Lemontey to legalize adoption, abolish paternity searches, and endow illegitimate offspring with rights.[28]

In fact, the legislators drew the état civil debate out over so many months not only because they were wary of offending rural religiosity and challenging traditional clerical authority, but also because they knew that to laicize the état civil and define marriage as a voluntary, reciprocal contract opened the floodgates to myriad other issues. "The people are not yet *philosophes,*" pronounced François de Neufchâteau in March 1792. They were hardly ready to conceive of marriage as anything other than a sacrament, let alone to entertain the notion of divorce implicit in this legislation. Even some supporters of secularizing the état civil, heedful of the contentious implications of the new practice, tried repeatedly and without success to separate the discussion of record-keeping from consideration of the nature of marriage itself.[29]

Paternal authority over marriage was the first controversial issue broached in conjunction with the état civil, attacked initially by Durand de Maillane in 1791. Paternal authority in general was already under assault from pamphleteers and feminist cahiers opposed to arranged marriage, as well as from proponents of inheritance reform. In particular, from 1789 on, petitions and pamphlets from the daughters of Normandy and the younger sons and daughters of the Midi poured into the Assembly. Daughters from Normandy and the Midi decried tyrannical fathers who unjustly favored sons over daughters, while younger sons denounced the father's power under Roman law to privilege one son over other offspring, to disinherit wayward ones, and to delay emancipating their sons until far into adulthood.[30] Moreover, the legislature had already begun to whittle away at the father's command over the family: they had abolished lettres de cachet in March 1790, established family arbitration courts in August 1790, and decreed equal division of intestate estates in April 1791.

The issue of inheritance had especially unleashed bitter, legislative polemics over *puissance paternelle* (paternal authority). While deputies from Normandy and the Midi, most notably Jacques-Antoine de Cazalès, defended fathers' power as a historically rooted force of morality and a natural source of order, left-wing deputies argued that the "vicious social system" of puissance paternelle corrupted the instinctive love of equality within the family and distorted filial love into a base and dissimulating competition built on self-interest. Pétion de Villeneuve, Robespierre, and a posthumously read speech by Mirabeau presented the "denatured despotism" of fathers as a threat to morality and to the social equality that underpinned the fragile political and civil equality of the fledgling nation. They spoke the language of rights, reason, and law, but their speeches also vibrated with the impatient and impassioned desire to overthrow the father that Lynn Hunt has targeted at the heart of the revolutionary imagination.[31]

By 1792 in the état civil debates, critics of puissance paternelle implicitly argued that the citizen, imagined male, could not stand as a free adult in full possession of his manhood as long as he bore the crippling and constraining weight of his father's authority. Furthermore, the deputy Marie-David Lasource suggested that liberty was a better safeguard against moral corruption than all the wisdom of fathers: "When a man cannot have command of himself and his property, nor be a citizen, he surrenders himself to all the turmoil of his passions." He might well become a seducer or a profligate. For his part, Gohier situated the demise of patriarchal power within the broader social turn toward egalitarianism: the father's ability to arrange marriage had lost its importance in a world where social orders had broken down and France had become one "grande famille." Spouses should now be free to choose each other for virtue and affection rather than rank and economic interest.[32] These arguments drew distinctly on the imagery and logic so prevalent in pamphlets and plays of the early Revolution.

The fall of the monarchy in August 1792 brought about a political climate in which the challenge to paternal authority and the laicization of the état civil could be realized in law. In a burst of activity, the lawmakers did away with various marital impediments and emancipated both men and women from paternal control at the new, lower age of majority, twenty-one. They further reduced the father's power by abolishing *substitution* (entailment), the testamentary procedure allowing parents to ensure that their legacies would descend within the lineage, often by disqualifying immediate heirs and substituting their grandchildren. Then, after months of foot-dragging, on 20 September, the Legislative Assembly definitively placed the état civil in the hands of state officials rather than priests.[33]

In late August and September, the deputies acted with sudden urgency for several reasons. In the waning days of the Legislative Assembly, they were anxious not to leave the long-debated reform of the état civil undone. Moreover, the initiative in the Committee of Legislation had gradually shifted toward Jacobin reformers.[34] For months it had been absorbing the pressure of public opinion as an ever-stronger flow of petitioners demanded all sorts of family law reform. Crucially, the overthrow of the monarchy on 10 August created a political space in which this pressure could reach fruition: the event unleashed a decisive leftward movement, a pressing need to rid France of the vestiges of feudalism, and an increase in anticlerical sentiment and policies. In addition, the overthrow of the king, the father of the nation, encouraged the French revolutionaries to envision a less patriarchal social and political order.[35] Overturning the monarchy and inventing the republic led to more than killing the father/king: the deputies now counted on constructing a new familial structure to mirror and promote the new political structure. Just as the republic replaced the monarchy, so too, the conjugal family rooted in freely chosen, companionate marriage should replace the lineage family built on puissance paternelle and arranged, indissoluble marriage. Then marriage could perform its political duty as a secular, civil contract linking male and female citizens to each other and to the new nation.

In fact, on that same final day of its session, the Legislative Assembly also took the bold step of legalizing divorce. The new law would allow either men or women to sue for divorce based on seven different grounds, as well as "incompatibility" or "mutual consent." By relying on family tribunals to handle divorce litigation, the law would make the new practice remarkably accessible to both women and men.[36] Despite its far-reaching consequences, divorce became law with relatively little debate. In late August 1792, while debating marriage registration, the legislators turned their attention toward divorce because yet another petitioner at the bar exhorted the deputies to put an end to marital indissolubility. The deputy Jean-Baptiste Aubert-Dubayet took up this challenge. In defining marriage as a civil contract, he demanded, why haven't we considered how the conjugal contract might be broken? Strikingly, he also called upon his colleagues to consider the happiness and rights of women: "The contract that ties spouses is made in common: indubitably they should both enjoy the same rights, and the woman should not be the slave of man." Pierre-Joseph Cambon immediately seconded this appeal for divorce, prompting a flurry of debate and a resolution that the Committee of Legislation write a proposal.[37] Within a week Léonard Robin had presented a draft of the new law, and within three weeks France had done away with indissoluble marriage.

Since so many other historians have recounted these divorce debates in detail, I will highlight only a few points.[38] First, undoubtedly, the deputies were centrally motivated by the ideology of individual liberty and their commitment to defining marriage as a voluntary, civil contract, undergirded by natural law. As Jacques Mulliez has noted, the juridical reasoning that led from individual liberty and contractual marriage to divorce was already present in Gossin's initial appeal for divorce in August 1790; what remained was for the political and religious situation to change.[39]

Second, the outpouring of public demand for divorce played a crucial role in urging the deputies on and, ultimately, in legitimizing their decision to carry legal reasoning through to action. Cambon first invoked "long-standing public opinion" before asserting that divorce was an inherent and necessary consequence of the Declaration of the Rights of Man and Citizen. And, as Aubert-Dubayet's comments suggest, even the feminist arguments had made their mark. The presence of women in the galleries may have influenced the debate, as the legal historian Jean-Louis Halpérin has noted. On 13 September, when Mathurin Sédillez introduced an alternate proposal for divorce, he framed his presentation by claiming that Robin's project left women too open to desertion. He proposed that in cases of repudiation, a jury of women should judge divorces demanded by husbands, while male juries assessed female demands. Sédillez's recommendation echoed arguments made by feminists such as Mademoiselle Jodin and Elisabeth Lafaurie that women should have a public, judicial role in family matters. More pervasive among legislators was the tacit recognition of women's civil, private rights and the awareness that their support of the Revolution was important but fragile.[40]

Last but not least, the deputies legalized divorce because it was a crucial component in their overall vision of regenerated marriage as a linchpin of citizenship. For marriage to encompass both individual liberty and the social good, this bond should be free, harmonious, and morally virtuous. Indissoluble marriage not only violated personal freedom, but also sapped marriage of its moral and regenerative power. Even as he invoked marriage's roots in natural liberty, Robin reminded his colleagues that marriage was "a political institution" and "an important social institution." Constraints—such as paternal authority, economic familial interest, religious impediments, and, above all, indissolubility—deprived marriage of the spontaneity and emotional vibrancy so critical for the new moral and social order. Marriage without love could not sustain the mutual sensitivity that underlay personal happiness and opened hearts to patriotic sentiment and moral responsibility. "Society has no interest in preventing mismatched beings from separating and going elsewhere to find the sweetness and consolation so necessary to the human condition," commented Sédillez. Divorce cemented and even fortified marriage by guaranteeing the freedom and emotional well-being so necessary for marriage to play its moral role.[41]

Laicizing marriage, legalizing divorce, reducing parental authority, and lowering the age of majority would have the most decisive impact on social practices in the 1790s, but the deputies of the National Convention turned once again to alter marriage in a striking fashion in the summer and fall of 1793. The first version of a unified Civil Code, proposed by Jean-Jacques Cambacérès and the Committee of Legislation on 9 August 1793, included controversial provisions. This Code stipulated that if a couple made no marriage contract, communal marital property would become their default marital property regime, and, most notably, *husband and wife would have equal control over their shared goods.* The proposed Code further attacked traditional conjugal arrangements by declaring that if the couple chose to follow a dotal regime, the husband who wanted to use or invest his wife's dowry would no longer have to guarantee repayment as a mortgage—in effect removing the protection of the wife's goods that underpinned the dowry system so prevalent in the Midi and Normandy. While the Code sought to abolish the customary incapacity of married women in the communal system, conversely it deprived wives under dotal regimes of this crucial safeguard to their property. In any event, the crafters of the Code were confident that the communal system would carry the day.[42]

As Cambacérès first presented these stunning proposals, he argued that the communal property system "most conformed to this intimate union" of marriage, and that joint administration by husband and wife was rooted "in the principle of equality that must regulate all the acts of our social organization." Speaking on behalf of the Committee of Legislation, the deputy Jean-Etienne Bar of Moselle seconded Cambacérès's points and assured his listeners that nature dictated liberty and reciprocal rights to both spouses. After a bitter denunciation of the dowry system for allowing couples to fool their creditors, he praised the communal system as more equitable and streamlined, asserting, with exaggeration, that it made it easier to settle property disputes should the couple divorce. In addition, he roundly attacked the "ridiculous conjugal authority [*puissance maritale*]" of husbands as a holdover from despotic days, hardly acceptable "in the time of liberty." The customary practice of masculine control had incited marital discord, had failed to recognize women's true abilities, and had allowed wayward husbands to dissipate the spouses' joint property.[43]

Inevitably, such radical propositions for overhauling marital practices across both the dotal and communal systems provoked anxious debate. Despite objections, the Convention made choices that favored wives in both traditional and innovative ways: they would reiterate certain dowry protections and also vote to give women shared control of communal property unless their marriage contracts stipulated otherwise. Before taking action, the Convention returned twice, on 23 August and 27 October 1793, to discuss these issues. Jean-Joseph Génissieux succeeded in justifying the inalienability of the wife's goods in dotal regimes. The Convention reasserted the long-standing principle that a husband had to offer a mortgage as a guarantee if he invested or alienated his wife's dowry. Deputies Jacques-Alexis Thuriot and Philippe-Antoine Merlin de Douai ultimately met with less success in their attempt to champion masculine prerogative over financial decisions. They attacked the joint administration of communal goods as impractical, "absurd," and "unjust." Both men decried women's ability to manage property and asserted that shared decision-making would sow discord and "perpetual dissension" within the household. Merlin de Douai countered Bar's insistence that the law of nature ordained conjugal collaboration and joint control with the observation, "Woman is generally incapable of administering [goods], and man, having a *natural superiority* over her, should conserve it" (my emphasis).[44]

These two conservative jurists faced a series of short but vibrant retorts from deputies who favored the Code's new egalitarian provisions. At the crux of their logic in favor of joint administration lay three key points. First, several lawmakers emphasized the defense of women's rights. "In a free country, we cannot hold women any longer in a position of slavery," fired off Jean-François Delacroix in an opening salvo. Likewise, Georges Couthon invoked nature as he declared that "woman was born with as much capacity as man." Danton commented that "nothing is more natural" than shared management, while both Camille Desmoulins and Michel Lecointe-Puyraveau denounced puissance maritale as a creation of despotism. Second, in a more pragmatic vein, these last two deputies also stressed a "political consideration, that it is important to make women love the Revolution," as Desmoulins put it. In this fall of 1793, as the dechristianization campaign heated up across France, left-wing deputies nervously worried about winning women away from "fanaticism." Also, echoing the logic of pro-divorce pamphleteers, Lecointe-Puyraveau noted that women would surely influence the fate of liberty: to make them happy would help them to love liberty. Last but not least, several deputies suggested that equality was a crucial element of marriage. Philippe Pons de Verdun argued that most wives managed property already and concluded that the Convention "exhorts you to re-establish the equality of rights in such an intimate society; without it [this equality of rights], there is no real society." "Aren't women half of ourselves?" asked Lecointe-Puyraveau. "Why wouldn't they have the same rights that we do?"[45]

On 27 October 1793—three days before closing the Jacobin women's clubs[46]—the Convention approved the Code's proposed articles in favor of shared administration of communal marital property: "The spouses have and exercise an equal right to administer the goods of their community. No act bringing about a mortgage on the goods of the community is valid unless one and the other spouses both consent. Acts intended to conserve or ameliorate their goods likewise must be agreed upon by the two spouses." Thuriot succeeded in tempering the radicalism of this act by immediately convincing the Convention to allow couples to use marriage contracts to stipulate various marital property regimes and to renege on communal administration. Moreover, the first Civil Code was soon abandoned in the complex politics of November 1793 and the act never became law.[47] But the salient point remains that in October 1793, the National Convention adopted the principle that husbands and wives shared an equal right to administer their communal property. Not until 1985 would French women finally gain equal control over marital property.[48]

This step-by-step transformation of marriage was integral to the construction of the secular state. By 20 September 1792, the Legislative Assembly had already altered marriage along many of the lines demanded by the eager pamphleteers of the early Revolution. The deputies strove to enact a form of marriage that mirrored as closely as possible its origins in natural law and preserved the individual liberty of men and women. But marriage should also embed the citizen within society and define his or her civil status and relationship to the state. The lawmakers built civil marriage as part of their bulwark against Catholicism. The official keepers of état civil traced the legal stature of citizens; with each pen stroke, they inscribed marriage as the legal underpinning of society and the secular nation. No longer sacramental, but still sacred, marriage was now "drawn from the constitutional act," ideally as a free and mutual contract between two citizens.[49] At the height of the radical Revolution, the National Convention even briefly affirmed equal control over this contract and the shared administration of goods by both husband and wife.

REGENERATION, GENDER, AND CONJUGAL LOVE

When the deputies redefined marriage as a civil contract that could be broken, they took a step that was in some ways filled with danger for the new state. In 1792–93, as the revolutionaries stripped away the legal indissolubility of marriage, they were keenly aware that their actions made property arrangements uncertain. Within the escalating war on Christianity, the lawmakers also knew that secular, contractual marriage lacked the sacral glue, the moral force of unity that characterized Old Regime sacramental marriage. To create the juridical individual, to count on his or her free choice as the foundation of marriage—these acts were loaded with anxiety. The deputies imagined that the public validation of marriage by the new state would endow the institution with a new sacrality, but they also relied on other forces of cohesion. Repeatedly, they expressed their perennial confidence in the regenerative power of the law: their newly crafted laws would transform the social and moral practices of marriage and citizenship. For example, to legalize divorce and abolish arranged marriages would reduce adultery and illegitimacy.

But above all, the jurists, like many other revolutionaries, invoked the affective power of marriage and the potent force of gender complementarity. Conjugal love was central to the revolutionary project of refashioning marriage as a linchpin of citizenship: the bonds of sentiment and the "natural" force of heterosexual love could unite the family and even underpin the new politics. As Gohier suggested, so powerful were the emotions connecting man and woman that the nation should tap into the affective power of conjugal love in order to foment patriotic fervor.[50] Outside the halls of the legislature, various revolutionaries argued more extensively that nuptial love had a political and ethical role to play in the Revolution. In the late Old Regime, novels, plays, treatises, and even legal briefs had fostered an image of marriage as a socially useful site of true affection between husband and wife.[51] Embracing and building upon this imagery, the revolutionaries demanded even more of marriage: it should facilitate moral regeneration and patriotic conversion.

As the historian James Traer has argued, the revolutionaries hoped to cultivate emotional bonds between husband and wife, parent and child. Traer situates this emphasis on sentiment within a broader "modernization" of the family. His interpretation usefully highlights how strongly the revolutionaries espoused the ideal of familial affection but fails to probe several crucial matters. Like other proponents of the modern family thesis, he pays little attention to how power dynamics might operate within "companionate marriage," nor does he ask how the revolutionaries imagined that gender differences would sustain intimacy.[52] Although various male and female club members, pamphleteers, deputies, clergymen, and family members did not agree on the ideal characteristics of male and female nature, they all shared the assumption that men and women had different but complementary roles to play in forging conjugal affection as well as political unity. As I will explore, these assumptions often demanded that women dedicate themselves to converting men and children and to expressing their patriotism primarily through familial roles. Moreover, in contrast to Traer, I will argue that the revolutionaries believed that conjugal affection had distinctly political resonances and purposes.

This political role of companionate marriage depended on a particular vision of gender complementarity that grew out of Old Regime thinking and underwent metamorphosis in the revolutionary context. The revolutionaries envisioned gendered characteristics as fundamentally interdependent but distinct. They saw no contradiction between asserting civil equality between men and women and portraying their personal characteristics and roles as profoundly different. Male and female qualities naturally and necessarily worked in direct relationship to each other. Nowhere did this synergy work with greater emotional power than in marriage, that institution that tied the intimate self to the broader nation. As the first social contract with profound moral and political significance, marriage—suspended between individual right and collective need—became an arena for negotiating how politics transformed gender and how gender complementarity could work for politics. Discussion over female and male characteristics and their complementarity intensified and took on urgent political significance. Male and female revolutionaries participated in this negotiation in pamphlets, political club meetings, newspapers, images, and civic festivals. As they debated how to reform marriage and its internal gender dynamics, they asserted and expanded upon its crucial role in constructing citizenship. They also profoundly politicized the realm of intimacy and tied the realm of the family tightly to the practice of public politics.

Refurbished marriage could bring about two forms of regeneration: it could elevate the different but complementary virtues of husband and wife and simultaneously stimulate patriotic allegiance. If intimate relations could be transformed, men would become less tyrannical, more sensitive, more attentive to women and children but also freer and stronger. Women would rein in their wilder passions, curtail their vulnerability to seduction and deceit, and use their moral sensitivity and empire over men for cultural and political reform. "Each one will follow the role nature has assigned," and a stronger nuptial bond and happiness would result. According to some, the legalization of divorce would help to produce these emotional and moral benefits. M. J. Lequinio, a Breton deputy and divorce advocate, offered an archetypal vision of the impact of the divorce law on men and women: "The same law will necessarily produce contrary effects in the two sexes: to men it will give gentleness (douceur), to women energy (énergie); the first will stop being insensitive, unjust, and dissipated; and women will be less languid, or less coquettish and frivolous; equilibrium will be established in the spouses' dispositions and wills."[53]

Lequinio's opinion is illustrative, not only for its confidence in the regenerative power of the divorce law, but also for its underlying vision of gender strengths and weaknesses. He and others tapped into the Old Regime belief that women by nature possessed a feminine *sensibilité*, a certain moral and emotional sensitivity, compassion, and impressionability. As a result, women were believed to be morally powerful and to have a special ability to touch and evoke the emotions of others, especially their husbands and children. "The morals of men are more depraved than women's," commented the Comte d'Antraigues in 1790. "Nature still speaks to their hearts, and sensibilité never is entirely extinguished there." Revolutionaries across a political spectrum sought to appropriate and define feminine sensibilité in the service of the new nation. "Oh French women! Recognize your empire and the sacred duty that the patrie imposes upon you. . . . You should breathe patriotism into the souls of the French," declared the anonymous author of the *Influence des femmes dans l'ordre civil et politique* (Women's influence in the civil and political order) in 1789.[54] Women held in their hands the power to convert men to the nation. At least as important as the republican motherhood more often mentioned by historians,[55] republican marriage endowed—and burdened—women with the politico-moral act of regenerating men.

The journalist Jean-Louis Carra sought to clarify the political implications and possibilities of gender characteristics when he advocated a nationwide network of patriotic women's clubs in October 1791. In his *Annales patriotiques et littéraires de la France,* he contended that women needed to be recruited and to organize for the Revolution precisely because they had the moral and mental capacity to inspire male virtue, liberty, and commitment. Drawing on prerevolutionary assumptions about the neurological and psychological differences between men and women, he argued that male patriotism and advancement drew sustenance from women and the "progress of their public spirit." Male and female moral faculties were different but interdependent:

> The difference between them [man and woman], would be perhaps that man has a greater capacity, a natural disposition more well suited for encompassing a large spectrum of knowledge and of subjects; but this difference is well compensated for in woman; she has a greater aptitude for grasping all the relationships of the object in question; this skill is truly precious for judgment, and gives women a real right to speculate about morals and politics, not just to conceptualize them, but also to perfect them.[56]

A new form of politics called for new uses of male and female strengths. According to Carra, despotism had invested in the political debasement of women, but male revolutionaries should encourage the political education of women, for only women could free men from the cultural bondage of the Old Regime: "It is up to women to pull us from that degradation of ideas and language, and raise us finally to the height and dignity of men who are really free and really philosophes." Women could console and shape men in the home, even as they contributed publicly to political "progress, the advancement of virtue and social prosperity." He praised the new women's clubs from Grasse to Nancy, and lauded Elisabeth Lafaurie's pamphlet demanding political rights and organization for women.[57]

Within the intimate framework of home and marriage, women and men would be most able to use their different sensibilities to cultivate mutual patriotism and moral growth, but, as Carra suggests, women as well as men should use their gendered capabilities to influence each other in public as well as domestic settings. Although woman's patriotic and sensitizing influence took quintessential form within the family, public events, such as festivals or club meetings, should reinforce the stimulation of private, conjugal virtues.

Certain women, like Jodin and de Gouges, seized a more radical stance and argued that both natural rights ideology and women's moral qualities justified endowing women with a more formal, public political role. For example, the anonymous author of *Lettre d'une dame aux dames de son département* lamented women's failure to have created their own national assembly and asserted that women's moral qualities and sensitivity to family affairs made them supremely qualified to become justices of the peace, jury-members, and arbiters in newly formed family tribunals and bureaux of conciliation. Likewise, Elisabeth Lafaurie insisted that women—at least married ones—should participate fully in men's clubs. Women should vote in the primary assemblies and take part in making family law: "[L]et us agree that we should collaborate on those laws that govern private law; for everything that concerns marriage, maternal authority, guardianship, contracts, wills—in a word, everything that relates directly to individuals, and to keeping peace and unity among Citizens—all these matters, I say, interest us just as much as they do men; hence, we have an incontestable right to take part in making laws of this sort at least."[58] With their explicit claims for official, public female power, these authors pushed at the edges of mainstream republican discourse. Yet their bold claims suggest that the discourse on female moral capacity provoked further debate on the extent of woman's public power and its relationship to her familial role.

Etta Palm d'Aelders also endorsed a division of political labor based on complementary male and female qualities; and she, too, thought these gendered skills should be put to use across the span from public to conjugal spheres. Advocating a proactive role for women, she supported a France-wide network of women's clubs. If men had created clubs across France to defend the Constitution with force and vigor, women should initiate societies to make that same Constitution "loved." Or, as she stated on behalf of the "Amies de la Vérité" to the men of the 48th Section of Paris several months later, it was up to women to "revive morals" and "make this Revolution cherished and blessed." She championed equitable and companionate marriage as one arena of women's politico-moral power. Like Carra, Palm d'Aelders had an explicit awareness of women's persuasive skills, derived from nature and fortifed by education. She specifically cited women's "moral force," their "vivacity of imagination, delicacy of feeling, resignation against setbacks, firmness and patience in time of suffering and pain, and finally, generosity of the soul and patriotic zeal." Like other female club members and feminist pamphleteers, Palm d'Aelders warned male politicians that they in turn must support female education and equity within marriage so as to promote these feminine skills.[59]

Women's charge to convert men to patriotism was not couched in terms of conveying specific ideas, forms of knowledge, or ideology. Even the discussions of their education of children contained relatively little about the explicit content of learning. Rather, their mandate was both more intangible and more profound. They were to "regenerate social morality [*mœurs*]," to mold character, customs, and behavior, for this was a politics of passion and the personal rather than of dogma or doctrine. Above all, women were to guide the act of humanity being born anew, the act of regeneration. Before the Revolution, "regeneration" had both theological and medical meanings: to be regenerated was to be spiritually engendered anew or to regrow lost tissue. "It is the act by which one is reborn for a new life" stated the *Encyclopédie*, depicting both spiritual and surgical regeneration.[60]

The revolutionaries appropriated regeneration to imagine the political rebirth and new growth that defined the "new man" of 1789. As Antoine de Baecque has cogently argued, this regenerated man, born of rupture and destruction, needed also to be integrated into the new community and to imagine himself within a newly defined political order. The patriots set forth the Declaration of the Rights of Man as a foundation for regeneration. Rabaut Saint-Etienne characterized this declaration as "an alphabet for children, to be taught in the schools. With such a patriotic education a strong and vigorous race of men can be born, and know well how to defend the liberty that we have won for them: always armed with reason, they will know how to resist despotism."[61]

But for this regeneration to occur deep within the souls of children and adult men, women must tend this "new growth" within young and old, and act as unifying forces tying male energy, independence, and fervor to the patrie by marriage and family. Marital and familial bonds reintegrated the regenerated man and his offspring within the newly forged society. As "domestic apostles of liberty," women should ignite and sustain a fundamental affective commitment to liberty and the patrie, and nourish a moral reservoir of virtue from birth until death. "We promise that our children will imbibe the love of liberty with our breast-milk," commented Catherine Larrieu, president of the women's club of Pau.[62]

The patriotic motherhood central to this reintegration could take myriad forms. A republican mother should be fertile and ever-willing to sacrifice her sons as soldiers for the patrie, as the play *Barra, ou la mère républicaine* dramatically demanded in the year II (1793–94). Above all, mothers should promote revolutionary ideology and patriotism by inspiring their children to be "useful to the patrie" and by "teaching them at a young age to speak the male language of liberty," in the gendered language of one male speaker in Orléans.[63] Women's clubs often adopted the secular reform of schools as one of their central lobbying and local organizational efforts. In addition, their festivals often incorporated pedagogical or familial themes. In their exclusively female initiation ceremony, the citoyennes of Marseille embraced their maternal role with oaths and the solemn baptism of newborns—one young girl was to be named "Bienvenue Désirée Liberté." In a ritual reiterated across France, the "Amies de la Liberté et de l'Egalité" of Lyon bestowed awards on their patriotic offspring for reciting the Declaration of the Rights of Man, the seventh chapter of Rousseau's *Social Contract*, and a longer series of revolutionary prayers, oaths, and songs.[64]

But more striking (and less noticed by modern historians) was the call to women to politicize their relationships with their husbands and fiancés, to bring political judgment as well as moral lessons to the most intimate relationships. For all of their stress on educating and shaping the next generation, male and female revolutionaries returned repeatedly to the political responsibilities of wives. Speaking at the male Jacobin society of Caen in 1791, Françoise Sanson denounced counterrevolution and the insidious power of nonjuring clergy. She urged her fellow women to inspire their children with the love of liberty, but to exert influence on their husbands as well: "The power of women is in their sensibilité; let us use this valuable arm that we gain from nature or education, to bring back our husbands who may be led astray or cravenly seduced by metaphysical subtleties."[65]

Swept up in the zeal of the early Revolution, both male and female revolutionaries called on women to put their peculiarly powerful influence on men to work for patriotism within the bedroom. The "Société des dames citoyennes" promised to "double our tenderness in order to heighten our husbands' civism." Likewise, the women of Ruffec took an oath "to be loyal to nation and laws, to maintain the Constitution"—nothing surprising—but the unmarried women also swore "to give hand and heart only to him who conforms to the true principles of the Constitution." This same women's club heard an exhortation from one of their male colleagues: "If it is necessary, let a prudent and friendly refusal of your caresses be the punishment of traitors [to the cause]; use the irresistible force of your insinuations to weaken the heart of stone [bronze] which the sweet name of liberty cannot move." He comments, "Sisters and friends, you form opinion. . . . It is before your tribunal that politics must submit its operations and the warrior his triumphs." At a meeting of the Parisian Society of Revolutionary Republican Women, Olympe de Gouges urged women to "reject the desires of a man who is useless to his country. . . . Nothing can resist the power of our seductive organ." At outdoor festivals and club meetings from Nantes to Nîmes, young women pledged to shun aristocrats and lend their hearts only to republicans and soldiers. Women songwriters echoed these same themes:

"Let us swear fidelity to the brave defenders // They alone can claim to capture our hearts," rang out the verses of citoyenne Allain.[66]

Male patriots frequently prevailed upon their female colleagues to sway their husbands toward the Revolution. The *Adresse au beau sexe* assured women that the Revolution would restore their dignity, trampled by Old Regime despotism, but urged them in turn to charm men into patriotism and to heap scorn or ridicule onto proud or useless men. In 1791, Grosjean, the future president of the department of the Doubs, reminded the women of Baume that each one had a "heart made for sentiment and all its inspiring eloquence." They should put this quality to work to "enchant" men on behalf of the patrie: "Loving is one of your first needs and your first talent is to please. If the patrie is dear to your affections, you will seduce us by defending its rights." This discourse transformed the civilizing and seductive capacity attributed to Old Regime women into a peculiarly political power and a positive force.[67]

WOMEN'S CULTIVATION OF MASCULINE SENSIBILITÉ: ENERGY AND HUMANE SENSITIVITY

Within marriage, women ideally should foster two sets of male personal qualities: male action, energy, and bravery on the one hand and male sensitivity to politics and people on the other. Although these characteristics could be in tension with one another, according to the medical notions of the moral anthropologists, the male body's inherent sensibilité fostered both sets of qualities: men's moral qualities found physical roots in the makeup of their nerves, tissues, and organs. During the Revolution, men were typically seen as fundamentally more energetic and independent than women; perennially restless, they were virtually bursting with the desire for liberty and independence. While women's innate modesty and timidity reined in their actions, men had no comparable need to curtail their own vigor. Action and vitality characterized depictions of male citizens. In his analysis of caricatures from 1789 to 1790, Antoine de Baecque discovers male citizens first shedding their status as subject-slaves: as working peasants, they cast aside the privileged classes and then purged the body politic of these diseased or fatted members. From this act of purging emerges the new citizen: peasant, worker, or member of the National Guard, he stands surrounded by emblems of virility and sexual potency.[68]

In 1792, with the coming of war and the creation of the Republic, the masculine ideal of activity and the restless quest for liberty and independence gradually encompassed more emphasis on stoic, single-minded devotion to the patrie. Jacobin ideology particularly defined masculinity in terms of military loyalty, and worked to fuse a classical model of Spartan and stoic soldierhood, drawn from antiquity, with the rough-and-tumble image of the pike-bearing sansculotte, drawn from the streets of Paris. Allegiance to one's fellow soldiers was central, and revolutionary men incited one another's militant patriotism. Ceremonies and prints promoted an image of soldiers as virile brothers, united by fraternal ties and marching off to defend each other's honor. This male image could take the classical form of an austere Brutus placing loyalty to the nation above family ties, as in Jacques-Louis David's well-known painting. As this painting implies, true revolutionaries might be called upon to transfer their Old Regime honorable defense of family to a higher defense of the patrie.[69]

But for all of their homosocial emphasis on fraternal male loyalty to the patrie, the revolutionaries fervently believed that patriotism was rooted in family honor and also in female approval. They hoped to reincorporate the patriotic Brutus within the conjugal family. Loyalty to family and nation should reinforce each other: as one republican father wrote to his soldier son, "When you suffer, know that it is for your parents and for your Patrie. When you march into combat, never forget that it is for your father, your mother, your brothers and sisters, and choose even death over disgrace." The acts of marrying and fathering children aroused the honor, vigor, and patriotism of men, even priests. As one clerical pamphleteer promised, their marriage would bring "more energy to national character and more nerve to patriotism."[70]

Spartan masculinity and fraternity drew strength from heterosexual love. By emphasizing the power and naturalness of the conjugal bond, the revolutionaries protected the homosocial, male bond from association with effeminacy or homosexuality. Elizabeth Colwill has argued that Marie-Antoinette's depiction as a lesbian "warned citoyens and citoyennes to police the 'natural' boundaries of desire." Likewise, fraternal bonds and patriotism were defined in contrast to the purported homosexuality and feminine weakness of priests and aristocrats, portrayed as sodomites in pornographic pamphlets and caricatures.[71] Revolutionaries depicted male strength, fortitude, and even love of nation as a "natural" outgrowth and corollary to love of women. As François Chabot proclaimed, "Unhappy the man who doesn't love women! He who resists this most holy, sweet, and sacred inclination in Nature, *he will never be a good republican*" (his emphasis).[72]

Within the world of festivals, this balancing act between the natural con-

FÊTE CÉLEBRÉE EN L'HONNEUR DE L'ÊTRE SUPRÊME.
Le 20 Prairiale l'an 2ᵐ de la Rep

Figure 2.   Family at the festival of the Supreme Being (June 1794). Courtesy of the Bibliothèque nationale de France.

jugal bond and same-sex sociability also appears. Revolutionary festivals celebrated the family as the biological unit underpinning society, yet often divided the participants into sex-segregated age groups based on stage of life. Battalions of young boys or youths, schoolgirls with their teachers, young women in virginal white, wives and mothers holding babies, husbands and fathers of families, and the old often formed separate ranks even as they represented familial complementarity and unity. For example, the procession to the Supreme Being included sex-segregated groups, but prints

Figure 3. Wedding announcement of a civil marriage (1797). Courtesy of the Bibliothèque nationale de France.

celebrated the family's worship of the Supreme Being (see Figure 2). As Mona Ozouf notes about festivals in general, only the unmarried citizen was left out in the cold.[73]

Moreover, from 1792 on, various deputies and pamphleteers proposed rituals to surround civil marriages or to celebrate the value of conjugal love. They expanded upon the early imaginings of those lawmakers, discussed above, who laicized the état civil and set the stage for civil marriages. Depictions of civil unions idealized romantic attachment, upheld by the Republic (see Figure 3). Conjugal love was one of thirty-seven festivals *(fêtes décadaires)* for the republican calendar advocated by Robespierre, based on the work of the Committee of Public Instruction in the spring of 1794. Likewise, François-Antoine Boissy d'Anglas envisioned the marriage festival as a rustic, springtime event, featuring sweet-smelling flowers, dances and games, reciprocal vows at an outdoor altar, and the sage advice of an old man to the young couple. He waxed lyrical: "The festival of marriage among free and equal men, whose morals are pure and whose souls are sensitive should be the most beautiful of festivals, the festival of love and sensual delight."[74]

As the deputies debated the cycle of *fêtes décadaires* in the year II (1793–94), communes across France began to incorporate conjugal love into their wide repertoire of revolutionary rituals. In La Rochelle one ceremony in the spring of 1794 featured an older couple renewing their nuptial vows after fifty years, a young mother adopting an abandoned orphan, and a soldier marrying the citoyenne of his dreams. Poverty-stricken but in love, "the two had no fortune, other than the love of virtue and the love of their country." Fortunately, the "people" of La Rochelle generously provided a "civic dowry." Likewise, the popular society of Firminy in the Lyonnais dowered the lucky wife of a "good sans-culotte" and celebrated their union with much panache. After planting a Tree of Fraternity, the national guard led a parade of all age groups toward an outdoor banquet table, laden with bread, wine, and cornucopias of fruit and vegetables.[75]

Festivals organized by women's clubs often made more explicit the idea that women could spark and sustain the virility and virtue of husbands and sons. "Do you want to recover the force of soul, the energy of character that makes a nation great and superior? Then address that sex which appears to be the weakest. . . . Women are men's teachers. They inspire [in men] love and virtue, patriotism and courage. Their gaze animates men and sustains them in the most difficult efforts." The ideas of this male Cercle Social member found ample expression in the activities of the women's societies as they admonished their husbands, brothers, and sons to fight without fear and as they staged balls and banquets to launch the nation's volunteers. These festivals repeatedly proclaimed the capacity of women to inspire male valor and physical bravery. Solemn send-offs of volunteers by women's clubs invariably included reminders that their wives' praise and love would be the reward of fearless struggle on behalf of the *patrie en danger*. Caresses and domestic intimacy would welcome them home if they fought honorably. "One never sees men retreat in the field of honor, when they sense women behind them," pronounced the "Amies de la Constitution" of Dijon, who soon orchestrated an elaborate song ceremony to inspire the newly recruited soldiers in the summer of 1792. For their part, male patriots echoed this view. As one self-proclaimed "nephew of the Père Duchesne" wrote to the *Vedette* in Besançon in the war-crazed summer of 1792, "Women, women, know that your ascendance over us, it's inconceivable. As you please, you can turn our emotions toward heroism or cowardice." As he urged each woman to send "letters burning with patriotism" to her soldier-lover, he invoked an ardor in which love of woman and of patrie blurred.[76]

The notion that women should spur men to action pervaded revolutionary politics from its outbreak and informed thinking about popular uprisings as well as war. Emphasizing the reciprocity and mutual reinforcement of masculine and feminine political practice, Dominique Godineau has shown that in Paris female revolutionaries and members of the "Citoyennes

Figure 4.   Altar of Liberty: A bourgeoise from Paris instills her children with military spirit (c. 1789–92). Courtesy of the Bibliothèque nationale de France.

républicaines révolutionnaires" repeatedly roused their husbands to political insurrection or derided them as "faint-hearted" or "cowardly" when they failed to take to the streets or march on the Convention.[77] The militant speeches and festivals that urged and shamed men to defend family and patrie combined populist expressions of bravado and anger with constant allusions to the austerity and military dedication of classical times. Members of women's clubs routinely took oaths, even before the war began, to raise sons and daughters as young Spartans (see Figure 4). Reformulating a Spartan slogan, citoyenne Blandin-Desmoulins proclaimed in 1793: "When their brothers in arms left for the frontiers, the citoyennes exhorted them with all the energy of free women not to reappear in their homes without having destroyed the despots. Oh! what lofty actions our sex inspires when it speaks to Frenchmen in the language of glory and virtue!"[78]

Female club members and other prorevolutionary women at times volunteered to take up arms and fight for the patrie. Steeped in military rhetoric, Madame Peutat of Avallon warned that women's sensibilité and gentleness would only be weakness if it prevented them from taking up swords to defend France. In the most well-known case, in March 1792 Pauline Léon and a delegation of armed women carried a petition to the Legislative Assembly to volunteer their military services.[79] But both male and female revolutionaries more often positioned women as sustainers and inspirers of male bravery.

The intersections between love, marriage, gender, and valor could take unexpected turns, especially at the height of the radical revolution. In 1793–94, citoyenne Desmoulins wrote a play, *L'héroïne républicaine*, that glorified conjugal love as a spur to military daring. Despite his father's plan that Valcour marry a wealthy young woman, this soldier had fallen head over heels in love with Zélime, the republican heroine. Remarkably, she herself had become a soldier within his same army, making his admiration for her bravery and beauty only redouble. As Valcour's closest male friend stated: "Love causes courage to grow rather than diminish. It animates, it invigorates him; the amorous soldier fights with more ardor to return victorious." By its end, the play not only had celebrated passionate love and affectionate marriage over marriage for money, but also had validated male friendship and reconciled father and son, as the chastened father blessed his son's wedding with the words: "Let us celebrate Mars with Love."[80]

At the same time, within marriage women should also encourage the other side of masculine patriotism, its humane and sensitive side, so crucial for the new politics. Although they celebrated male energy and activity, the revolutionaries remained equivocal about associating male patriotism solely with physical strength and militant courage. Notably, even in wartime, festivals, paintings, and speeches sometimes represented the young heroes of the Republic, such as Bara, as androgynous or romanticized figures. As Figure 5 suggests, the imagery of "virility" could incorporate both military motifs and a gentler, contemplative stance. Likewise, ambivalence about equating popular sovereignty primarily with the brute force and strength of Hercules caused the Convention first to tone down his image and ultimately to choose Marianne to represent the Republic instead. Class-based anxiety about popular uprisings and force informed the Convention's decision and built upon competing images of patriotic maleness.[81]

For side by side with the image of the energetic, fearless, or stoic man stood the ideal of male sensitivity. Building on Old Regime notions, moralists and marriage pamphleteers throughout the Revolution noted that men possessed the humane and perceptive side of sensibilité just as

Figure 5.   To Virility, from the *Manuel des autorités constituées de la République française* (1797). Courtesy of the Bibliothèque nationale de France.

women did, but in men it needed more nurturing and development. Over the course of the 1790s, male sensitivity would become increasingly valued in both the intimate and public political realms. A prospective fiancée "wants a virtuous man, sensitive and kind, who thinks and acts according to his heart," editorialized one moralist in 1790.[82] Both within and beyond the conjugal bond, this attribute implied moral and political acuity and responsiveness, rooted in natural emotions and the moral senses; ideally, each man would experience fraternal and benevolent feelings and act "according to his heart."

It is crucial to recognize that the revolutionaries believed that male sensitivity had political significance. According to prevalent conceptions of political participation, (male) citizens absolutely required these traits in order to read or intuit the general will and act as part of the sovereign nation. Republican ideology in particular drew on the Rousseauian ideal of "transparency" and emphasized its centrality: only by maintaining a sincerely open heart could each citizen honestly and directly sense the general will and participate in a form of politics that could transcend factionalism.[83] Expressing one's emotions and intuitions candidly seemed to guarantee open politics and formed an essential contrast to the manipulative and se- cretive politics of the corrupt Old Regime court and monarchy. This aspect of male sensibilité in some sense protected revolutionaries from the artifice and egotism of the Old Regime in a way that neither reason nor abstract loyalty to nation could.

Revolutionaries valued sincere affect and expression from 1789 at least through 1794. Especially during the Terror, fear of deception and the quest for personal virtue would only accentuate the extent to which political va- lidity was measured on the register of personal sensitivity and interior feel- ing. In the pressure-cooker of the Terror, intensity of patriotic expression might help to prove innocence. The revolutionary judiciary in 1793–94 trusted personal letters as the most intimate and direct proof of revolution- ary sentiment and loyalty. Only those who spoke from the wellspring of the human heart could truly be patriots.[84]

In addition to guaranteeing open politics, responsive sensibilité tied the individual citizen to the social and the public good. The legal act of marriage bound the individual citizen to the body social and the state, but the affec- tive benefit of marriage completed and deepened this bond. For the compas- sion awakened by conjugal love had universal political and humanitarian ramifications. During the Revolution, Brissot voiced the same confidence in natural feeling that he had articulated in 1782: "Reason shows me only shadows, where the moral sense enlightens and directs me. I leave reason behind, therefore, and follow only my moral instinct, the voice of happiness. I am happy when I work for the good of my fellow humans, when I do good for them." As this quotation from Brissot suggests, the revolutionaries thought that sensibilité enabled the citizen to move from empathy or com- passion about individual need or suffering toward the universal goal of hu- manitarianism and benevolence. For example, as David Denby has shown, revolutionary orators and authors, including Brissot, Henri Grégoire, Mirabeau, and de Gouges played masterfully on the sentiments in their anti-slavery campaign. They believed that evoking the spectacle of cruelty and injustice would induce a humanitarian reaction, as potent an argument against slavery as the more abstract reasoning of universal human rights.[85] Humanitarianism and fraternity, that least studied of the revolutionary tri- partite slogan, found roots in sensibilité.

In short, the revolutionaries believed that moral intuition and humani- tarian feeling were integral qualities of male citizenship. But they also nervously believed that these crucial characteristics drew their strength from the intimate realm of the family and from the interactions between men and women. Marriage, that first and most natural bond, infused men with the nuances of sensibilité, for this quality needed to be nurtured by social practices, and above all by women. The deputies debating marriage reform in the legislature shared this view. As Oudot commented, ideally marriage stimulated virtuous feelings and mutual kindness. Men had a particular need for developing these characteristics. For, just as female sensitivity and softness opened women to excess passion, flightiness, or physical weakness, the male constitution, with all its natural strengths and energies, nonetheless made men susceptible to certain corollary faults as well: too easily they might engage in the tyrannical abuse of power, become hard-hearted, or slide toward dissolution or corruption. Some commentators blamed Old Regime institutions and especially the imbalance of power within marriage for encouraging these gendered flaws. Madame de Cambis of the Cercle Social claimed that "our former tyrants . . . have led woman through an excess of sensibilité to find merit and happiness in slavish dependency. And with this same purpose, they have made man hard and proud, by giving him inordinate power." The inegalitarian marriages of the Old Regime had morally corrupted both men and women. Only regenerated, companionate marriage could soften men and strengthen women.[86]

Madame de Cambis was not alone in believing that improved male-female relations and a refurbished institution of marriage would underpin citizenship by reforming the morals and correcting the flaws of both men and women. Clergymen appealing for the right to marry repeatedly celebrated the power of marriage to make men humane and indicted celibate men as callous and egotistical. "My heart froze," lamented one. Without wives to awaken their humanity, warned another, ministers "are less sensitive to your suffering. . . . The hardening of the heart is an almost inevitable effect of celibacy, and the supernatural graces of religion, as heavenly as it is, cannot replace this active and profound sensibilité, that is poured into our hearts by natural means." The clerical proponents of marriage wrote out of their individual anguish, but they invariably linked their appeals for the softening powers of female companionship to its greater social good. Suggesting that marriage was the "first bond," the "base of social conventions," they argued that their emotional and moral amelioration through companionate marriage would make them more responsive as priests and more productive and socially minded as citizens. The tenderness of conjugal love encouraged "sentiments of humility and universal goodwill, and ties us to society by relations that we cannot break nor forget." Only married men could transcend individual interest and work for the "general good."[87]

The political societies, revolutionary moralists, and marriage commentators shared the idea that "mutual assistance," "reciprocal love," and "intimate liaison" would strengthen both men and women morally. Men's and women's separate aptitudes in loving would foster interdependence and mutual well-being. Husbands would grow solicitous toward their wives and considerate toward their children. The anonymous "best friend of women" expressed confidence that the divorce law would make husbands less domineering and corruption-prone: "They will be passionately fond of [their wives]; they will repay with tenderness and care all the pleasures which their wives help them to rediscover in the bosom of the family." Revolutionary commentators on marriage and citizenship built an image of the attentive husband to complement the ideal of the sentimental father. The self-proclaimed *Homme mal marié* (Unhappily married man) covered the page with tear-drenched ink depicting his surprise at how domesticity tamed his dissolute rake's soul, marriage offered him "the most tender love," and fatherhood awakened unexpected compassion and kindness in his soul. Now that his heartless wife had cast him aside like dirt, he fought tooth and nail for the right to divorce and to gain sole custody of his daughter. His angry demand to break the bonds of marriage competed loudly with his self-portrayal as tender and broken-hearted.[88]

Marriage cultivated paternal sensitivity because a wife's fidelity reassured the husband that their offspring were indubitably his own. This certainty of paternity made it possible for the republican father to truly love his children. As Etienne Lenglet argued in his 1792 *Essai sur la législation du mariage* (Essay on marriage legislation), rivalries and jealousies among men made marriage necessary in society: it reassured fathers of their paternity, and mutual faithfulness and confidence were bolstered because all of society bore witness to this union on behalf of future generations. For marriage to transform the hearts of fathers and husbands, female sexuality must be contained and stable.[89]

In fact, although pamphleteers devoted far more attention to woman's power to reform her husband, they also depicted the husband's ability to instill seriousness and stability into his wife's habits and psyche. In 1790 the author of the *Histoire de l'établissement du célibat ecclésiastique* claimed with great aplomb that priests, if allowed to marry, would generate models of conjugal harmony and egalitarianism. Unlike the many husbands who treated their wives in a condescending, dismissive, or jealous fashion, newly married priests will make their wives happier, and will see them as companions ánd equals. Instructed to think soundly by their thinking husbands [*maris penseurs*], . . . these judicious wives will use the gift of speech sensibly and never abuse it . . . They will not daub themselves with white and red [makeup]. . . . Modesty will embellish their natural graces; amiable, sweet simplicity will form their character and will be a model for others.

He also promised that priests and their well-educated wives together would raise their children as patriots, disposed toward "serious ideas and noble sentiments." In his depiction of wifely qualities, this optimistic priest countered point by point the negative attributes most commonly ascribed to female sensibilité: intellectual frothiness, the tendency toward babbling and frivolity, immodesty, and flightiness—all these would be banished within this model marriage of restored "dignity" and "the sweet metaphysics of love."[90]

FEMALE SENSIBILITÉ, SEDUCTION, AND CLASS

If the discourse on revolutionary masculinity championed both aggressive vigor and humanitarian sensitivity, the discourse on femininity within marriage also contained room for evolving and competing conceptions of sensibilité. As I mentioned in the previous chapter, the early revolutionary discourse on individual rights and companionship generated debate over what feminine qualities would best sustain affectionate, contractual marriage. The politicization of women's moral influence only intensified this discussion. Although most commentators agreed that marriage must be reformed for the political power of love to work most effectively, they did not fully agree on what women's politico-moral qualities meant for an intimacy traditionally built on women's submission. Moreover, the revolutionary ferment over marriage would gradually change the class associations of sensibilité and seduction.

In the most Rousseauian vein, some commentators contended that regenerated marriage would help wives to channel their natural generosity and self-sacrifice toward their husbands and children. To become better companions and patriots, women should embrace female selflessness and stimulate patriotism while remaining deferential to their husbands. In his 1793 sermon on the benefits of divorce and the new form of marriage, the Constitutional Curé Dominique Lacombe argued that divorce would make each husband less tyrannical, but also make each wife more attentive to her duties, as well as "gentle, modest, considerate, mindful of her reputation, eager to win over her husband rather than defy his authority."[91]

This stress on docile wives coexisted with a discourse that explicitly championed equality and power-sharing between spouses. In his 1793 *Déclaration des droits des amants* (Declaration of the rights of lovers), Plaisant de La Houssaye offered a point-by-point defense of perfect reciprocity and equality between the couple: he advocated communal property, equal rights, and shared sovereignty. Nor should either one be master over the other, for love was governed only by "their gentle, constant, and mutual will."[92] The ideal marriage would establish the independence of each spouse and restore reason and self-governance to women through education, argued Lequinio in *Les préjugés détruits* (Prejudice destroyed). Writing in 1792 as the battle against the Church began to heat up, he made the crucial point that strengthening women's minds within marriage would help to free them from religious prejudice.[93]

In fact, by embracing a role as intimate crusaders for the Revolution, female revolutionaries legitimized their appeal for increasing women's stature within marriage. Certain club members and feminist pamphleteers argued that women could not exert patriotic influence without themselves being educated, treated with greater respect, and endowed with equal rights within marriage. "To form free men, it is necessary to know liberty," commented Etta Palm d'Aelders. Throughout the early 1790s, the lobbyists for marital reform infused their rights-based appeals with arguments about women's power to shape citizenship through their intimate relations. Madame de Cambis offered a crystallization of this combination in her 1791 plea for women's control over property. Without this right, women could not be citizens, nor could they adequately perform their crucial role of molding men's morals and raising the nation's children. "If we want morals, then women have to respect themselves [*s'honorer*]; and if we want them to respect themselves, then we have to give them back their rights, their property; all of these are as holy, as sacred as the rights and property of men."[94]

As many commentators asserted, if women were to exercise charm on behalf of the patrie, they must be freed from the flirtatious and degrading task of pleasing men with coquettish behavior. They should raise themselves above the most superficial and frivolous forms of political seduction. A leading Jacobin woman in Dijon demanded: "Do you wish to hold women forever in a state of childhood or frivolity? . . . It is time to bring about a revolution in the customs of women; it is time to reestablish their natural dignity." Although men were more likely to refer, even obliquely, to the sexualized aspect of women's political power, male Jacobins too urged female revolutionaries to set aside the ways of a "frivolous century" while they turned their homes into "schools of patriotism."[95]

In a 1792 speech to the "Amies de la Constitution" of Bordeaux, Marie Dorbe denounced the Old Regime when women were "forgotten, reduced to housework and the education of our children; deprived of the benefits of the law, we lived in abject obscurity, painfully enduring our degradation." She then urged the unmarried members "to form ties only with those men who have shown the most ardor for the defense of liberty and the most love for this dear patrie. . . . Tell them that the *language of flattery and romance (langue romanesque) no longer pleases you,* and that now you only love frankness and truth" (my emphasis). Citoyenne Dorbe suggested that if women were to exercise intimate political persuasion, male-female companionship must now rest on transparency and truth. Moreover, the revolutionary context and reformed marriage transformed women in a striking fashion: they would no longer be so gullible and easily duped by pretty words with no meaning. Their public, political allegiances informed and revolutionized their private ties. As the citoyenne Maugras laid forth the Besançon women's plan to enlighten feeble consciences and propagate liberty, she stated simply, "Raised to the heights of the Revolution, we prefer liberty and equality to all the platitudes of love."[96] In a nutshell, the newly envisioned relationship between politics and marriage—the politicization of sensibilité—gave added strength to calls for conjugal reform and provoked a critique of reducing women to superficial seductresses.

By rejecting frivolity and arguing that female sensibilité within marriage had transparent, transformative power, the revolutionary vision of companionate marriage also altered the class associations of the discourse on seduction and sensibilité in a noteworthy fashion. Proponents of patriotic marriage strove to cleanse political seduction of its aristocratic resonances and to universalize sensibilité as a female characteristic. They deliberatively distinguished the influence of republican wives from the devious or duplicitous forms of seduction that might be associated with the aristocracy. In press and caricature, the early revolutionaries had ever more virulently denounced the aristocracy not only for their luxurious and wasteful lifestyle, but also for seduction, feminine artifice, and backroom politics. This imagery built upon the Old Regime literary and judicial discourse that had depicted adultery primarily as a noble offense and had accused noble and monarchical mistresses of abusing their sexual power to influence high politics.[97] This double discourse effeminized and degraded noble men, and conversely, opened up all women, including patriotic women, to the possible accusation of aristocratic duplicity, promiscuity, or profligacy.

By envisioning the feminine practice of patriotic sexuality and seduction *within the institution of marriage*, revolutionaries intended to purify this form of influence, purge it of aristocratic, adulterous, or duplicitous resonance, and emphasize its equalizing and transparent elements. Clearly, the revolutionaries believed that the heterosexual attraction between men and women could operate politically in public arenas as well as intimate ones. Yet by often surrounding public female influence—in festivals for example—within virginal or familial symbolism, the revolutionaries cast the feminine influence within a moralized realm. Despite the implicitly sexual nature of feminine patriotic persuasion, club members spoke continually of each other as "brothers," "sisters," and "companions." Familial and conjugal imagery contained female influence in part because revolutionaries believed that marriage channeled sexuality for the good of the state and society. As a site of social utility and regeneration, marriage incorporated both legitimate reproduction and patriotic conversion. The deputy Gohier argued that the chief goal of marriage was "to put into the service of morals the same principle which corrupts them, and to perpetuate society by refining the softest sentiments of nature."[98] As Gohier implied, marriage as a fundamental social contract transformed natural human instincts and practices into social ones with moral and political ramifications.

Just as revolutionary marriage contained seduction in the service of the state, it recast the usage and meaning of sensibilité. Old Regime novelists and educational theorists had imagined sensibilité, vibrant imagination, and moral intuition largely as traits of elite or at least middle-class women. Initially, club members echoed some of these assumptions, particularly in organizing and depicting bourgeois women's benevolent work toward poorer women or prostitutes.[99] Likewise, the divorce pamphlets of 1789–90 reflected a pervasive assumption that the upper and lower classes had different kinds of marital relations; pamphleteers virtually always used elite women to illustrate the profound heartbreak that could be remedied only by divorce. Authors implied that emotional distance within marriage was primarily a problem for the sensitive middle and upper classes, while poorer couples had other, perhaps more violent marital problems. Simon Linguet compared the "moral torture" of upper class women with the physical hardship of poorer women's lives.[100]

But as Jacobin women's clubs and revolutionary pamphleteers and journalists endowed female sensibilité with political resonance, they also broadened its class associations. Especially by the spring of 1791, political societies across France had begun to recognize the crucial role that any prorevolutionary woman might play in the cultural battle against the nonjuring clergy.[101] Within Paris in particular, the emerging Jacobin left grew intent on winning the allegiance of the women of the people and countering the populist propaganda campaign of the right.[102] Women of all classes should exert persuasion for the patrie, and patriotic female wiles must be decoupled from the coquetry and seduction so linked with the aristocracy. The anti-aristocratic and deliberately coarse *Lettres bougrement patriotique de la Mère Duchêne* aimed at winning over *sans-jupons* (female sansculottes) in 1791. The journal was equally quick to revile noble luxury and to applaud women's "imagination, penetration . . . fertile in resources and expedients." "Take my coiffure, my petticoat, and my cotillion dances, cowardly devil; and me, I will take up a helmet, sabre, and musket," proclaimed the spirited Mère Duchêne. Praising female strength, stubbornness, and persuasive powers, she asserted that even "if women make motions only in the interior of their houses, the ideas they communicate can contribute greatly to developing [the ideas] of men."[103]

Like the Mère Duchêne, the women's club members imagined political influence as a universal female characteristic, transcending class boundaries. In their speeches, festivals, and benevolent works, the leading women repeatedly invited all their "tender sisters," especially those led astray by the fanaticism of nonjurors, to join them in the crusade to win over hearts for the patrie. Speaking on behalf of the women of Meulan, Madame Challan promised that they would set aside frivolity, make the Constitution loved, and partake in that "moment when equality brings men of all classes into fraternal unity."[104] Although often led by bourgeois women, the clubs included many women of shopkeeping or artisanal classes. In Ruffec, for example, the 236 members of the Friends of the True Friends of the Constitution ("Amies des vrais amis de la Constitution") had a wide range of occupations and identities: they included a schoolteacher, a curé's sister, a midwife, a baker, several seamstresses and laundresses, two cabaret owners, two wigmakers, as well as the wife of the *procureur syndic* (a local district official). In Pau, a laundress founded the club, and the women of one club in Bordeaux emphasized their lack of wealth, describing themselves as "seven hundred to eight hundred citoyennes peu fortunées."[105] Purged of elite resonances, feminine sensibilité could hold forth and convert men to patriotism across the universal Republic. At least, this political use of gender complementarity stood out as a revolutionary ideal.

. . .

The revolutionaries infused marriage with political, legal, and cultural importance in constructing citizenship. Forging the link between citizenship and marriage took place both in the realm of law and state-building and in the realm of political culture. In the process of building the secular state and defining the rights-bearing individual, lawmakers in the Legislative Assembly redefined marriage as a civil contract binding individuals to each other and to the nation-state. Public agitation and the ideology of natural rights encouraged them to imagine this contract as one that could be broken and had to be freely chosen; perhaps its control should even be equally shared by husband and wife. In 1792–93, as the deputies struggled to find a form of marriage built on both legal individualism and state cohesion, they undermined lineage practices, curtailed parental authority over marriage choice, grounded the nuptial contract fully in state rather than church law, made divorce accessible to both men and women, and even passed the principle that women and men should have equal administration over their communal marital property.

At the same time, outside the halls of the legislature, the revolutionaries invested marriage with great political and moral responsibility in the refashioning of revolutionary citizenship. Building on and beyond the Old Regime valorization of sentimental marriage, they glorified and politicized the power of heterosexual love. Revolutionaries hoped it would integrate the splintering force of juridical individualism. In addition, as the Revolution radicalized, it increasingly degraded traditional sources of cultural authority and unity, including religion, monarchy, corporate bodies of myriad sorts, the lineage family, and paternal authority. As these Old Regime sources of certainty and structure tumbled, the natural bonds of conjugal love and family unity assumed ever greater importance as an imagined source of political transformation as well as social cohesion. Divisions between a private realm and a public one became unimaginable, as deputies in Paris, male and female moralists, and women's club members from Pau to Besançon all argued in varying ways for building politics out of intimacy.

The revolutionaries demanded that the institution of marriage perform a crucial act of integration: like citizenship, this relationship should simultaneously embody individual freedom and attachment to the social whole. In this sense, expectations for the miniature social contract of marriage mirrored and undergirded the tension built into the broader republican goal of harmonizing individual rights and liberty on the one hand with political regeneration and social unity on the other. After the Terror, when fears of social disintegration increasingly outweighed the republican commitment to individual rights and equality, revolutionary leaders would redouble emphasis on marriage and the conjugal family as sources of moral cohesion, even as they abandoned their earlier confidence that the family could also encompass individual liberty and equality. For example, only in 1795 did the legislature finally officially promote the *Fête des époux* (festival of spouses) as one of the seven national holidays to be celebrated as a *fête décadaire*. The years between Thermidor and the Civil Code would also reveal how the malleable notion of gender complementarity could be redefined to increasingly emphasize female domesticity at the expense of women's rights within marriage.

This exploration of marriage should also contribute to our understanding of revolutionary notions of maleness and femaleness. The idea that intimate relationships could contribute to making citizens was based on widespread assumptions about the distinct and complementary gender contributions of wives and husbands. Although its impact on practice was uneven, this confidence in the power of gender complementarity held tremendous staying power in the French imagination of gender into the nineteenth and twentieth centuries.[106] In the shorter term, it contributed to crafting certain ideals of revolutionary masculinity and femininity. The Revolution marked an especially striking shift in ideals of maleness. In the 1790s, republican gender ideology did not root men's identity and stature in their position as commanding husbands or patriarchs within the home. Rather, republican masculinity should encompass both energetic, unflinching dedication to the nation and humane sensibilité both inside and outside the household. The new politics required fraternal bonds and stoic valor, but also a kind of moral acuity and sensitivity that could only come from intimate relationships and companionship with women. The true patriot married as a companion, for marriage joined this individual to the social whole, allowed him to embrace fraternity while protecting him from the effeminizing overtones of homosexuality, and provided a space for the politicized love of a woman to foster his moral qualities.

This image of maleness left room for debating what the nature of femininity and male-female relations should be. Within the contestation over gender ideals, virtually all conjugal models called upon wives to be exceptionally dedicated to the social whole via the family and to cultivate their husbands' sensibilité, strength, and political allegiance to the Revolution. Likewise, virtually all commentators on revolutionary womanhood suggested that wives should be morally sensitive, sexually loyal, and patriotic rather than fanatic. But these commentators did not uniformly and simply embrace Rousseauian visions of marriage based on sweetly submissive wives. Rather, this model competed with others and often faced ardent criticism for turning husbands into tyrants and reducing wives to subservience, silliness, and seduction. As I have suggested over these last two chapters, female and male marriage reformers painted alternate scenarios of companionate marriages in which wives shared contractual rights, affection, education, and control over property with their husbands. Some commentators embraced independence, political criticism, and equal power within marriage as crucial components of revolutionary femininity.

At the same time, changes in law offered women as well as men new status as civil individuals within this institution: although the state did not overturn male authority within marriage, women nonetheless gained the crucial rights to choose their own nuptial partners, break the conjugal bond, and make demands on the state as juridical individuals. My purpose here is not to idealize revolutionary marriage or its possibilities for women, but rather to emphasize that constructing citizenship opened up cultural and legal contestation over gender dynamics and domestic roles in distinct ways. The Revolution simultaneously endowed women with new civil rights within family and state, encouraged a moralizing, domestic role for women, and fostered vibrant debate over the nature of that role and over the nature of male-female relations.[107]

Finally, these attempts to reimagine marriage had a direct impact on familial practices. Law and political culture alike abruptly changed the terrain for negotiating intimacy as they placed great emphasis on the validity and stature of the conjugal unit at the expense of the lineage family. Family strategy—based on sacrificing male or female individuals for the greater good of the group—lost its legal scaffolding. Paternal authority, arranged marriage, enforced celibacy of certain offspring, and the indissoluble conjugal bond together had formed the framework for family thinking and family strategizing for centuries. As it dismantled this frame, the Revolution suddenly altered both the personal expectations and the legal possibilities of individual men and women. These marital reforms no doubt heightened prerevolutionary hopes for conjugal affection, even as they created a means for escaping unhappy marriages. The political glorification of conjugal influence and attachment only redoubled this desire for a different kind of marriage, now made more accessible by the new state and its laws. How did individuals far from Paris seize upon, appropriate, or reject the openings created by these structural and imaginative changes in the family? Only by peering inside families can we assess how revolutionary reforms affected the texture of individual lives. For this reason, this book now develops a local focus to complement the national one. Over the next four chapters, I will examine how revolutionary redrafting of civil laws—governing divorce, inheritance, paternity suits, and illegitimacy—altered possibilities for women and men within the family.

3. Broken Bonds

The Revolutionary Practice of Divorce

In the full flush of the new Republic, the keepers of the état civil in the town of Caen marked New Year's Day 1793 somewhat soberly: they recorded the department's first divorce. As they converted the 1787 séparation de corps of Pierre Hommais and Anne Delaville into a more permanent disunion, they pronounced the couple "personally free [*libres de leurs personnes*] as they had been before contracting marriage." For all the liberating language, the divorce had been hard won, as the family tribunal struggled over the meaning of the new law. Reluctant to surrender his advantageous control of the couple's property, Pierre protested, and his arbiters demanded that Anne demonstrate once again that her husband had abused her back in the 1780s. Finally, after several meetings, a tie-breaking arbiter tipped the scales in Anne's favor: not only did the couple already live miles apart—she in Nantes, he in Caen—but also the existing separation proved "the couple's clearly articulated will that they could not live together."[1] The mutual contract had been broken.

Just before adjourning on 20 September 1792, the Legislative Assembly passed the first nationwide divorce law, and the most liberal one France would witness until 1975. In late 1792 and early 1793, like Pierre Hommais and Anne Delaville, the first mismatched couples made their way desperately or tentatively to family courts and municipal officers. Even before the 20 September 1792 law, a few hardy souls had convinced local authorities to grant them a quasi-official divorce on the grounds that the Constitution of 1791 defined marriage as a civil contract.[2] What began as a trickle of divorce requests soon became a river, as family tribunals worked out interpretations of the new law. Remarking on this "torrent" of divorces, the *Journal et affiches du département de l'Oise* commented in August 1793, "You would think that a dam had been holding back all those who hoped to break their chains." According to the best synthetic estimates, some 38,000 to 50,000 divorces took place during the eleven years from 1792 through 1803, when Napoleonic legislation restricted access to divorce.[3] Until that moment, the 20 September 1792 law and earlier judicial reforms made the divorce procedure relatively inexpensive and accessible.

For marriage to fulfill revolutionary expectations as a site of regeneration and liberty, both husband and wife must be free to break the conjugal bond. As Arlette Farge and Michel Foucault have commented, "the conjugal bond is a place," a site of negotiating economic well-being as well as emotional and sexual understanding.[4] Eighteenth-century couples moved within that space according to a deep and often unspoken set of rules and practices. As they navigated the marital domain, they were also profoundly influenced by their position vis-à-vis the land or workshop and by their understandings with kin about duty, property, and familial rapport. When the revolutionaries legalized divorce, they altered the terrain of marriage and abruptly increased the space for individual spouses to wrestle with the revolutionary ideals of individual liberty, equality, and companionate marriage in the home. The possibility of divorce not only loosened the hierarchical bond between husband and wife; it also stretched the ties between the couple and the extended family. For the very fact that a couple could choose to dissolve their contract recast the position of marriage within the broader arena of family strategies. Divorce validated the growing expectation that the couple share a loving or affectionate relationship. It enabled the unhappiest wives to question their lifelong submission to brutal or tyrannical husbands and empowered husbands as well as wives to free themselves from desolate or burdensome matches. It also transformed the relationship between spouses and the state: men or women could turn to new legal venues, procedures, and laws to completely redefine their civil status and personal lives.

But even as divorce allowed couples to imagine marriage differently, rupturing the conjugal unit was not a routine or easy choice precisely because marriage was so deeply embedded within familial strategies, cultural expectations, and property systems. Spouses threaded their way between new opportunities and time-honored practices and expectations. Although the drafters of the new divorce law intended to offer access to everyone, certain sectors of the population more eagerly or easily took advantage of the new system. When thirty-two-year-old Angélique Poignaut divorced her woodworker husband for incompatibility in Caen in the spring of 1794, the couple fit the profile of a typical divorcing couple, at least in statistical terms.[5] More often initiated by women than men, divorce was also primarily an urban phenomenon, used most readily by couples from artisanal, commercial, or bourgeois backgrounds.

This chapter will examine the texture and experience of divorce by combining two elements: a nationwide exploration of popular petitions on divorce policy sent to the legislatures and a regional study of 468 divorce cases within the department of the Calvados.[6] Historians have focused thus far on urban divorce, especially in the large cities of Paris, Lyon, and Rouen.[7] To complement and broaden their findings, I look at divorce between 1792 and 1804 in the rural areas and smaller cities of the Calvados. I have examined the état civil, or civil records, for seventy-eight communes, including all those that were heads of cantons, as well as some smaller communes: they range in size from the small village of Pont with only 89 inhabitants to the vibrant city of Caen with some 35,000. For the city of Caen, I also trace divorce rates through the Napoleonic period. Court records from family, district, and civil tribunals yield richer but more varied information than the formal registrations of the 422 divorces in the état civil. My portrait of divorce also draws on petitions sent to the national legislature from across France. Some of these requests, particularly before September 1792, lobbied for the legalization of divorce, but most were written by individuals engaged in divorce litigation. Enmeshed in the struggle to work out the law in practice, these husbands, wives, and arbiters often proposed changes in policy. Their personal stories, demands, observations, and modes of argument offer insights into attitudes toward marriage, gender, and revolutionary politics.

How did revolutionary social policies and political ideas dramatically transform certain women's and men's lives, challenge long-standing gender practices, and awaken reflection and conflict about conjugal dynamics? After setting out the basic parameters of the divorce process, I will examine how men and women approached divorce differently and argue that the new marriage laws politicized men and women in distinctive ways around personal matters. I also seek to show how delicately spouses in conflict steered their way between revolutionary ruptures and the long-standing practices that ensconced marriage within systems of property, expectation, and family. Finally, examining the geographic and class contours of divorce reveals variations in the impact of civil legislation. Given the prevalence of women as initiators of divorce, close analysis of access to family legislation helps to assess how the Revolution affected women—in this case unhappily married women—very unevenly in different parts of the Republic.

THE BASIC PROCESS OF DIVORCE

Strikingly flexible and far-ranging, the 20 September 1792 law abolished séparation de corps and allowed husbands or wives to file jointly for a divorce of "mutual consent" or to demand a unilateral divorce, on grounds ranging from abuse to abandonment to incompatibility. Notably, the law awarded both women and men equal access to all divorce grounds, though women faced the disadvantage of having to initiate proceedings in their husband's place of residence. Unlike couples separated under Old Regime law, divorced spouses were free to remarry after a one-year wait. Moreover, as part of the settlement, they divided their property according to their marriage contract provisions or local marital property law. However, if the husband had divorced his wife on specific grounds *(cause déterminée)* other than mental illness, she lost out on her share of communal goods. The family court could also negotiate various property and custody arrangements, such as requiring the wealthier spouse to pay food pensions or child support. According to the new law, the mother normally took charge of all girls and boys under the age of seven; fathers retained custody of boys over the age of seven. With a few minor changes, this liberal revolutionary divorce law held sway until 1803, when it was replaced by much more restrictive Napoleonic legislation.[8] For fifteen months, the law of 4 floréal an II (23 April 1794) made divorce even easier to obtain, granted on proof of six months of de facto separation.

Revolutionary divorce law outlined a relatively straightforward and economical process. In laying out the judicial procedures, the deputies sought to strike a balance between facilitating easy access and encouraging couples to reflect and consider reconciliation. Easiest to come by were divorces by mutual consent or by incompatibility. In the first case, if both husband and wife agreed to separate, they convoked one meeting of a family assembly *(assemblée de famille)*, made up of six relatives or friends. If this attempt to reconcile the spouses failed, everyone present signed an "act of nonreconciliation." Between one and six months later, the couple then presented this act to the registrar of the état civil, who duly recorded and decreed their divorce (see Figure 6). In the case of divorce for "incompatibility of temperament and character," the family assembly met three times over the space of six months to allow ample time for reconsideration, since the divorce was initiated by just one spouse. If the petitioner persisted, she or he could formalize the divorce between one week and six months later.[9] Although the defendant spouse might present obstacles or pursue a countersuit, divorce by incompatibility was procedurally simple and moderate in

Figure 6. Republican divorce (c. 1793). Courtesy of the Bibliothèque nationale de France.

cost. Mutual consent and incompatibility became the two most popular, and most controversial, forms of divorce. Across France divorces by mutual consent made up somewhere between 15–25 percent of marital separations, while unhappy couples chose the incompatibility motive even more frequently, particularly in the later years of the Revolution.[10] In the Calvados, about 18 percent (74 of 422) of divorcing couples did so by mutual consent, and divorce for incompatibility topped the list of unilateral motives at 35 percent of all divorces.

These two modes of divorce marked radical departures from Old Regime practice: nowhere had séparation de corps—let alone divorce—been allowed without specific fault being proven. Strikingly, by legalizing these two forms of divorce, the Legislative Assembly validated the growing expectation that marriage should be more than a pragmatic union: it should encompass intimate companionship as well. Admittedly, spouses might choose these routes to divorce because they were comparatively easy to obtain or because, as one anonymous petitioner observed, incompatibility allowed the couple "to avoid being forced to reveal disagreeable scenes that took place within the household; recounting these scenes risked making the arbiters blush with embarrassment."[11]

At the same time, the widespread use of mutual consent and divorce for incompatibility bears testimony to the assumption that marriage should encompass mutual tenderness and cultivate personal happiness. Both men and women expressed sorrow at failed intimacy. "I could not live with her," confessed the citizen Manuel to the arbiters, as he acquiesced to his wife's request for a divorce. Stunned by his wife's act of divorcing him, one merchant-manufacturer, Beauvais of Rouen, proclaimed his timeless devotion dramatically, "I will never marry anyone else as long as she is alive." In yet another scenario, Emilie reported that she had been "young and unhappy" in her arranged marriage with Jérôme, until she fell in love with Gabriel "who made her forget the miseries of her first marriage." The divorce lawyer François Belloc of Tonneins stated the case more globally: "Now more than ever, marriages should be the union of hearts, and not the poorly matched union of two beings who usually marry for money, without either love or mutual esteem."[12]

Beyond mutual consent and incompatibility, the law stipulated seven causes déterminées for divorce: insanity; the condemnation to an infamous punishment; cruelty or serious injury; notorious disorder of morals; abandonment for at least two years; absence without news for at least five years; or emigration. Several of these motives were drawn directly from Old Regime grounds for separation, and indeed, existing séparations de corps could also be converted into divorce. Spouses soliciting divorce by absence or desertion simply procured an official act certifying absence, and then registered the divorce in the état civil.[13] A new judicial institution, the family court (*tribunal de famille*), handled the other forms of divorce based on specific grounds. Family tribunals also negotiated divorce settlements by determining the division of property, allocation of alimony, and custody of children.

Family tribunals had been created in August 1790 by the National Assembly to arbitrate disputes within the family.[14] Originally envisioned as a means of avoiding expensive, public, and time-consuming legal procedures, the family court dealt with conflicts between parent and child, husband and wife, brother and sister. Its jurisdiction gradually encompassed a wide range of matters, including marital separation, inheritance, guardianship and custody, detention of unruly children, approval of marriages by minors, and altercations over family property. The family tribunal was essentially a temporary arbitration court: opposing parties each chose two arbiters, ideally relatives or friends, to represent their interests and come to a mutually agreed-upon resolution. If the four arbiters could not agree, they would in turn name a fifth arbiter *(surarbitre)* to break the deadlock. Losing petitioners could appeal their cases to the local district court. The revolutionaries conceived of this system as a family council that would replace the arbitrary decisions of despotic fathers and the costly procedures of corrupt lawyers. It was meant to encourage mutual respect, democratic decision-making, and affection within the family. Falling a bit short of this ideal, family tribunals rarely succeeded in reconciling divorcing couples, and litigating spouses turned increasingly to lawyers rather than family members to arbitrate their cases. But crucially, the family courts nonetheless provided accessible justice and placed divorce within reach of all but the poorest members of society.[15]

Some 76, 000 to 100,000 individuals experienced divorce from 1792 to 1803, and several hundred thousand more served as witnesses or arbiters. Everywhere in France, divorce rates peaked in the years II and III (1793–95) as couples ended marriages that had already fallen apart long ago, often because one spouse had abandoned the other years earlier. In the Calvados, over 70 percent of spouses who used the grounds of desertion, absence, pre-existing séparations de corps, or six months de facto separation divorced in the first three years of the Revolution. Specific regional conditions, such as the sieges against counterrevolution in Lyon and Toulon, temporarily slowed the rush to divorce locally, but the nationwide pattern was clear. Divorce rates leveled off during the late 1790s, albeit with a slight dip after the repeal of the 4 floréal law in the summer of 1795 and again in the fall of 1797, when the legislature made divorce for incompatibility slightly more difficult to obtain.[16] At the end of the Revolution, divorce rose slightly again around years VIII (1799–1800), IX (1800–01), and especially years X and XI (1801–03) as very real rumors circulated that divorce would soon become more difficult to obtain. After the institution of the Napoleonic Code, divorce rates plummeted everywhere.[17]

GENDER AND MARITAL CONFLICT

The recourse to divorce followed a distinct and striking gender pattern. Sometimes, husband and wife both agreed to put an end to their marriage. For either sex, divorce could bring relief, bitter anger, or the welcome opportunity to remarry and regularize a "free union" formed with a new partner. But, in the case of unilateral divorces, women were more likely to initiate divorce than were husbands in every region studied so far. Wives began the procedures about two-thirds to three-quarters of the time. They requested 63–64 percent of unilateral divorces in Metz and Montpellier, 66 percent in Lyon and Toulouse, 71 percent in Rouen and Nancy, 72 percent in Le Havre, 74 percent in Paris, 75 percent in Bordeaux, and 76 percent in Rennes.[18] In the Calvados the pattern was no different: women petitioned for 250 (72 percent) of the 348 unilateral divorces department-wide, 68 percent within the city of Caen, and some 64 percent of divorces in villages under 2,500 people. In the smaller cities of the Calvados, women seemed especially likely to dominate unilateral separation demands, requesting 92 percent in Vire, 85 percent in Honfleur, 77 percent in Bayeux, and 70 percent in Lisieux.

Such statistics raise questions. Why did women initiate divorce more frequently than men? Did wives and husbands seek divorce for the same reasons? How did divorce—or divorce and the context of revolutionary politics—alter the nature of gender dynamics within marriage and within the extended family more generally? Clearly, the possibility of divorce offered new forms of independence to both sexes and encouraged all spouses to think about intimacy in newly politicized ways, but, as I will suggest, men and women used divorce differently and they diverged in their interpretations of "liberty" and "companionate marriage."

Petitions from husbands and wives offer an initial clue to these commonalities and contrasts. The language of liberty pervaded both male and female pro-divorce rhetoric. While both male and female pro-divorce petitioners imagined divorce as a form of liberation from loveless or problematic marriages, they portrayed the promised freedom rather differently. In men's petitions the rhetoric of emancipation tended to be more abstract. "A day of slavery is a day of mourning and a day of death for the patriot," proclaimed Gauthier as he appealed for a shorter wait time before remarrying. Male petitioners used the imagery of "chains" or "irons" binding them "as slaves to Hymen," forcing them into arranged unions, or forbidding them from remarrying. The citizen Robin, infuriated with his devious wife, lamented that he lived "in a sort of slavery" and commented that, but for divorce, "We would be two beings who would be forever anti-social, to say nothing of eternally unhappy." Male petitioners were more likely to cite the notion that marriage was a "contract that could be dissolved by the will of the two parties," and to emphasize the need for freedom *from* marriage more than the need to reform the internal dynamics of marriage.[19]

In contrast, female petitioners were more likely to speak explicitly about tyranny *within* marriage and to finger male domination or specific forms of abuse to justify their desire for divorce or divorce reform. Individual female petitioners echoed the candid critiques of "marital despotism" made in the early Revolution by feminist authors of pamphlets, cahiers, and moral treatises. For example, in a 1792 petition femme Berlin presented herself as a tender mother, deceived by a despotic and malicious husband. Then she appealed to the President of the brand-new Convention:

> I have entered into these details . . . because I am convinced that the Convention intends to recognize woman for something, and to remind certain men (what they have forgotten) that woman is not their slave, but rather their companion, and she should not be the victim of their tempers and bad treatment. . . . I hope that you will take my appeal into consideration, all the more so because a large number of unfortunate women, like me, wait for you to pronounce on their fate.[20]

As femme Berlin suggests, many women shared with men the hope for companionate marriage, but more explicitly denounced the conjugal hierarchy that jeopardized that harmony. In October 1793 as the citoyenne Gavot offered her wedding ring, "symbol of my slavery" to the National Convention in gratitude for the "holy law of divorce," she announced that she had "trembled under the empire of a despotic husband. . . . Today, restored to dignity as an independent woman, I adore this benevolent law that breaks badly matched bonds, gives us back our hearts, and restores them to nature and to divine liberty as well."[21]

Although both men and women sought relief from unhappy marriages, women suffered more directly from the imbalance of power within marriage. Certainly, in day-to-day life, the balance between a husband's authority and a wife's submission was under constant negotiation. Wives at times exerted surprising power and individual men compromised their authority as they developed mutual esteem and patterns of interdependence.[22] However, law, popular culture, economic structures, and family strategy all reinforced male dominance within the household. It functioned as a given within family dynamics and would weigh especially heavily on a wife in a conflictual marriage. Structured into the institutional fabric of eighteenth-century society, the husband's conjugal and paternal control did not end if he left home. An abandoned or separated wife found herself curtailed by her legal inability to perform property transactions or make decisions about her children's welfare without the permission of her husband or a family council. When the citizen Duboulay advocated greater female administration of property in 1793, he commented, "According to the former province of Normandy, women under coverture could not dispose of anything, they could neither buy nor sell any part of their goods, even with the consent of their husbands."[23]

TABLE 1. Divorce Motives and Gender, Department of the Calvados (1792–1804)

Divorce Motives[a]	Divorces Initiated by Wives (n)	Divorces Initiated by Husbands (n)	All Divorces N	%
Incompatibility	107	40	147	35
Six-Month Separation (4 floréal an II law)	29	21	50	12
Prerevolutionary Separation	7	2	9	2
Criminal Condemnation	9	0	9	2
Abuse/Cruelty	18	2	20	5
Immoral Behavior	4	5	9	2
Absence/Abandonment	51	21	72	17
Emigration	10	0	10	2
Unspecified Grounds (any of 7 causes déterminées)	12	4	16	4
Motive unknown	3	3	6	1
TOTAL UNILATERAL DIVORCES	250	98	348	82
Mutual Consent			74	18
TOTAL DIVORCES			422	100

SOURCE: Etat civil records from 78 communes within the Calvados, 1792–1804. See Appendix I for complete list of communes and sources.

[a]Unilateral motives for divorce included incompatibility, six-months de facto separation (an additional motive introduced by the law of 4 floréal an II [23 Apr. 1794]), prerevolutionary séparation de corps, and seven specific grounds (causes déterminées). Couples could also divorce by mutual consent. Among the seven specific grounds, no spouse in my sample used the first ground (insanity). I have combined "abandonment for two years" (fifth) with "absence for five years without news" (sixth) because these grounds both indicate desertion.

A woman ensconced in a troubled marriage had fewer options than did her husband. Divorcés of both sexes expressed longing for happiness within marriage and bemoaned the failure of intimate emotional connections, but wives' petitions to the legislature and to the courts more often paired the failure of affection with other marital difficulties, especially abandonment, impoverishment, and domestic abuse. Interestingly, female petitioners tended to paint pragmatic, rather than romantic, depictions of their husbands' failings. Anxious to extricate herself from "slavery to despotism," the citoyenne Van Houten decried her arranged marriage to a "quick-tempered, vexatious, stupid, dirty, and lazy husband . . . with *the most absolute inability in business matters*" (my emphasis).[24]

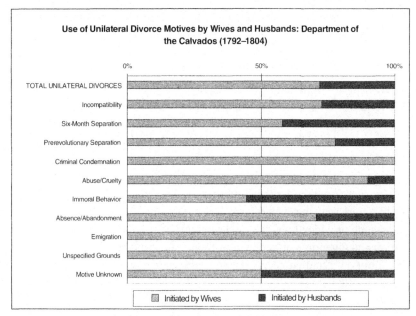

Use of Unilateral Divorce Motives by Wives and Husbands: Department of the Calvados (1792–1804)

SOURCE: Etat civil records from 78 communes within the Calvados, 1792–1804. See Appendix I for complete list of communes and sources.

Total N=348 unilateral divorces. The first line shows the distribution of all unilateral divorces (wives initiating 72%; husbands 28%) and helps gauge whether wives or husbands were more or less likely to use a given motive.

A statistical examination of husbands' and wives' varied use of divorce motives bears out the impression that women turned to divorce for a wider gamut of marital problems. When men initiated divorce in the Calvados and elsewhere, they relied most heavily on two divorce causes: most often, they cited incompatibility of temperament, followed by various forms of desertion or absence. Women also used these categories most often: in Lower Normandy, women filed close to 73 percent of the incompatibility cases and 71 percent of the cases of desertion or absence. But other than desertion/absence and a few accusations of immoral behavior, men rarely invoked specific grounds for divorce. In contrast, women dominated unilateral claims filed on every ground, except immoral conduct. (See Table 1 and Graph.) Similar patterns of gender behavior existed in Lyon, Paris, Rouen, and Metz.[25] In 1795, the citoyenne Jacquette of the commune of Fervaques dramatically laid out the range of problems that could provoke a woman to divorce:

> To save my life from the fury of my spouse; to keep me from sharing his infamy when he is condemned for a criminal act; to shield me from his cruelty, crimes, and harsh insults; to avoid witnessing his derangement;

to punish him for his ingratitude when he has been cruel enough to abandon me; finally, to keep me from being blamed as the accomplice of his emigration or tyrannized when his crime is turned against me, I find salvation only in the law of divorce.[26]

Particularly in the early years, women often turned to divorce because a husband was long gone. Among divorces initiated by women, only incompatibility topped absence/desertion as a motive for divorce in the Calvados. Women also filed all nineteen of the divorces based on either emigration or the condemnation of one's spouse to infamous punishment.[27] Many of these women left behind viewed their status as abandoned women as permanent. When the citoyenne LeBlanc queried the National Convention about the right to remarry, she even referred to her life since her husband's departure as "a state of widowhood for the last eight years." By emphasizing the duration and givenness of her "widowhood," she implicitly voiced her entitlement not only to divorce but also to swift remarriage.[28]

A deserted spouse of either sex might want to divorce in order to remarry. But for a forsaken woman, even one without plans to remarry, divorce would be especially crucial for two reasons. A woman who took up with another man while still married could be subject to losing her good name. Although neighbors might well be sympathetic toward the plight of an abandoned wife, her honor was nonetheless more rooted in her own sexual fidelity than was a man's. Above all, divorce would enable her to rescue whatever property she might have from the limbo status of her absent husband's control. Jacques Hue apparently locked up all the couple's goods, including his wife's own clothes and bedsheets, before he left the village of Cresserons. Surviving only because of her mother's kindness, his wife Anne Picard managed to convince the family tribunal to allow her at least to take back her meager, but crucial movable property while awaiting a decision about divorce. For wealthier women, control over substantial sums could be at stake. In an innovative twist, in 1794 the former noblewoman Marie-Adelaide Turgot argued that it was in the national interest to allow her to return to Caen and divorce her long-absent husband in his place of residence. (Nobles had been barred from port cities in April 1794.) Once divorced, she argued, she would win back key goods from her husband and spend them on a piece of nationalized land confiscated from an émigré: the nation would directly benefit from her personal freedom and wealth![29]

As this former noblewoman suggested, one obstacle facing deserted women was the stipulation that they divorce in their husband's place of residence. Municipal officials seem to have enforced this onerous requirement somewhat unevenly, and the état civil does not record the location of the wandering spouse. In any event, the requirement touched a chord of pragmatic and political anger among women who could not afford the journey to a distant town or who had young children to care for or jobs, land, or shops to maintain. Or perhaps they had no idea where their husband's domicile was or felt themselves unable to divorce far from home without the support of family and neighbors. The wives of foreigners or women whose husbands were in the Caribbean faced particular difficulty with the residence requirement.

Within the revolutionary context promising equality, female petitioners were quick to cite the gendered inequities of this "despotic" law. Femme Girard praised the National Convention for legalizing divorce and for striving to offer the poor access to "citizen's rights" and "justice" just as easily as the rich. But she berated the legislators for failing to recognize the plight of unfortunate women who could not displace themselves, and outlined some basic amendments to favor abandoned or separated women with clear domiciles. Other women suggested that the residence requirement might privilege counterrevolutionary men over republican women. Jeanne Hellequin attacked the law for failing to meet the test of expressing the general will, accessible to all, and noted that her husband from Nantes had most likely joined the rebels and died. Another citoyenne complained that her German husband had returned to Aachen, making it impossible for her to divorce him. Just because her husband had "become a slave of despots," was she also forced to become one? Wasn't she "a citoyenne and a citoyenne independent of the slave who had forsaken her?"[30]

As I will discuss below, the largest segment of divorcing women overall came from artisanal and middle-class backgrounds. But poor urban women, those married to unskilled or unemployed men, divorced on the grounds of desertion far more than did rural women or more well-off urban women.[31] Day laborers, domestic servants, diverse service workers from launderers to water-carriers, and the very poor "without profession"—this group made up only 14 percent of the divorcing couples whose occupations can be known, but they filed a quarter of the divorces for absence or desertion. Among women initiating unilateral divorces, the class basis of this pattern is clearer: 14 percent of women with bourgeois standing claimed absence/abandonment, compared to 19 percent of wives in the artisanal/small commerce group and a more substantial 30 percent of divorcées married to unskilled or unemployed men.

Both city and countryside in late eighteenth-century Lower Normandy experienced the ebb and flow of migration as a crucial component in the "makeshift economy" of the poor. While some migrants left home for good, many left for seasonal work or temporary employment as young workers. As Jean-Claude Perrot notes, the Paris Basin, especially the city of Paris, exerted a subtle but constant draw on Norman migrants in the later eighteenth century, and Caen itself also exercised a constant push and pull, particularly on nearby rural areas. More specifically, more than half, 66 of the 122 departmental divorces for absence/desertion or six-months de facto separation, occurred in Caen. Caen's population had swelled with itinerant workers in the expansive economy of the mid 1700s, but declined as the varied textile sectors contracted in the fifteen years before the Revolution. The political upheavals of the 1790s encouraged further population decline until 1793. Outward migration, rather than increasing mortality, was responsible for the descent from nearly 41,000 inhabitants in 1775 to 34,996 by 1793. Notably, emigration away from Caen peaked in the early 1790s, with roughly 1,500 inhabitants leaving annually from 1790 through 1793. Moreover, although men and women journeyed to Caen in roughly equal numbers, once there, men were more likely than women to displace themselves and migrate a second time. Women were more likely to move when young and unmarried.[32]

These macro patterns, so carefully traced by Perrot, made themselves felt within the day-to-day struggles of families to survive. Husbands, especially laborers, took to the road for many reasons: to escape a loveless marriage, to seek better work elsewhere, to perform a job as a peddler or sailor, to avoid shouldering the burden of yet another newborn child, to join the revolutionary armies or the *chouans* (counterrevolutionary rebels). In contrast, wives, particularly those with children, were far less likely to leave home. The limited sources on divorce for desertion offer no information on the couples' children, but most women filing for abandonment or six-months separation had been married for more than ten years.[33] (By and large, couples with children were less likely to divorce in the Calvados or elsewhere, but these statistics come primarily from the mutual consent divorces.)[34] Couples divorcing for absence/abandonment were more likely to be already migratory than the average divorcing couple. In Caen overall, just over three-quarters of divorcing couples had originally married in Caen. In contrast, among those who divorced for desertion or absence, only 58 percent had celebrated their wedding day in the city.

For women left behind—whether due to economic pressures, the vagaries of their husband's personal choices, or some combination of both—the legalization of divorce by the new republican state offered the opportunity to regularize their status, restore their own honor and independence, and move ahead. Anne Catherine Bagot, who had been "abandoned twelve years ago by a barbarous and faithless husband," stated the case concisely: "It is for the sex that is commonly called the weaker sex but that has nonetheless shown itself the most ardent in support of the Revolution, it is for this sex, until now subservient to the arbitrary will of the other, that divorce is most necessary."[35] Clearly, in her mind the Revolution marked a watershed in gender relations: the new politics demanded new domestic dynamics.

If divorce for abandonment was dominated by female initiators, this pattern was even more true for divorces for mistreatment or serious insult. Within the Calvados, women requested 90 percent (18 out of 20) of the divorces granted on the grounds of physical or verbal cruelty. In other regions, women also used this motive far more often than men did, initiating 72 percent of the cases in Toulouse, 87 percent in Paris, 93 percent in Lyon, 96 percent in Rouen, and 98 percent in Bordeaux.[36] In addition, wives in the Calvados also filed twelve of the sixteen divorces based on unstated "causes déterminées," which no doubt included cases of spousal abuse. (Registrars of the état civil in villages or smaller towns used this catchall phrase either to avoid clarifying the exact nature of spousal conflict or to indicate multiple specific grounds at work.)

Early in the winter of 1793 Marie-Françoise Faucon recounted her heart-wrenching tale of seven years of abusive marriage to Etienne Feron. The troubles began when she first got pregnant, which infuriated Etienne and launched him into a cycle of violence, desertion, and infidelity. When their first daughter was born, the curé of Amayé could barely get the father to return home to wife and child or to invite friends or family members to be the godparents of the newborn. So frightening were his beatings that Marie sometimes left home or barricaded herself in her room, only to have him climb a ladder and crawl in through the window. He mistreated their daughters as well, so much so that "a respectable neighbor" told Etienne that he would call the police since he couldn't keep order in his own household. Feron rebuked the neighbor and continued his violent and neglectful ways. He stole Marie's bedclothes, took up with their serving girl, and apparently paid their servants to insult his wife. If she spoke back even to the servants, Etienne threatened to rain punches down upon her. To add insult to injury, he gave his wife and children only cheap dark bread and offered the domestics white bread. For the last four years, he had left home entirely, although he came to the second family court meeting to deny all these accusations. Even his witnesses could only uphold the wife's tragic tale, however, and the local official of Amayé-sur-Seulles duly recorded the official divorce early in the spring of 1793.[37]

Implicit in the tribunal discussion between wives, husbands, neighbors, and arbiters was the presumption that the husband's mistreatment had to be excessive and to compound other failings to merit breaking the strong contract of marriage. Women like Marie-Françoise Faucon depicted their abuse within a broader culture of marital violence and breakdown.[38] The repertoire of curses, threats, and blows with every imaginable object at hand rarely encompassed the whole story. Wives almost invariably reported that their husbands had also dissipated the couple's goods, denied bread to their children, had an affair with a neighbor or servant, or had disappeared for a time only to reappear drunk and penniless. Moreover, arbiters often posed questions to witnesses to elicit information on whether the husband had become brutal and overstepped the bounds of "acceptable correction" by a husband. At issue was not just the level, frequency, or cause of his violence, but above all whether husband or wife had violated their reciprocal responsibilities within marriage. If neighbors testified that the wife had carried out her duties and the husband had neglected his, the arbiters granted the divorce. If neighbors had felt compelled to intercede in a household dispute, their very intervention in effect made a judgment.

While generally straightforward and succinct, witness testimonies revealed that neighbors shared a set of assumptions about marital conflict, honor, gender roles, and public versus private behavior. In November 1794 Catherine David of Lisieux filed for divorce against André LaFosse on the grounds of mistreatment and immoral conduct. The baker Charlotte Coquère testified that when she went to their house to tell LaFosse that she could no longer supply his wife bread without payment, she also reprimanded him for insulting his "honest wife *in public*" as "a damned buggeress, a slut, a whore." Another witness, Marguerite Armond, the wife of the justice of the peace, reported that the couple had repeatedly sought out her husband to conciliate them. Once when André insisted that his wife had threatened to kill him, she had assured him that Catherine was incapable of doing that, returned home with him, and found everything very peaceful. Even though his wife had served him supper, he flew into a rage and called in the guard with no reason. On another day, yet a third witness, the neighbor and weaver Augustin Hébert, had taken the enraged LaFosse by the arm and led him upstairs to show him that his wife had supper ready, but even this had not stopped André from hurling insults and threats. Catherine went to sleep elsewhere for fear. The arbiters granted divorce without debate, for to slander one's wife in public, to berate her even as she fulfilled her duties, and to abuse her without cause went beyond the bounds of acceptable behavior.[39]

In some cases, the husband attempted to justify his behavior by pointing out that his wife had fought back, that she had exaggerated his beating, or that she in some way deserved this treatment, perhaps because she herself was having an affair or had fallen down in her duties as the household manager. "Sometimes I am not the master," commented Jacques Carrey in explanation. Interestingly, no husbands accused their wives of being poor mothers, although to be a bad household manager might imply that failing. These excuses rarely convinced the arbiters, although the husband's arbiters might stall; often the husband's defense ended in anger. When Jean-Baptiste Perrier continued to "vomit insults" at his wife, the arbiters dutifully recorded their failure to reconcile the couple and granted the divorce. Other husbands acknowledged their fault, but announced that they had "repented" and would welcome their wives back. "I only want to . . . treat her as a husband should and live with her as a faithful husband," promised one. Some men, like Jean Poisson, a *rentier* (independent investor) of Caen, claimed that their wives had in effect forgiven them by agreeing to come back home more than once in the past: why would divorce be an acceptable alternative now? In another case, Marie Catherine Sonnet refused her husband's plea that she return home, claiming she no longer wanted to expose herself and her children to his furies. All hope of companionship had vanished: she added succinctly, "He no longer has the friendship for me that he had at the beginning of our union."[40]

Some men immediately began a countersuit for another motive, such as immoral behavior or incompatibility, in hopes of winning their own divorce and salvaging their honor and more of the couple's property.[41] Others later attempted to overturn the divorce at the appeal level of the district tribunal.[42] Overall, husbands resisted being divorced far more often than wives did. The lawyers or family members who served as the husbands' arbiters could become complicit in this process of delay or opposition, sometimes forcing the decision into the hands of a fifth arbiter. Individual men developed various strategies, including lost marriage contracts, written memoires opposing the divorce, sudden illnesses, procedural runarounds, and attacks on the witnesses' credibility. Angélique Fouque's violent husband had used "endless trickery" to suspend their marriage in procedural limbo even though he already lived with a lover in another village in the plaine de Caen. A petition sent on Angélique's behalf to the National Convention cut to the heart of the matter, and in fact encapsulated the dynamic of many other cases as well: "He is opposed to the divorce . . . in order to protect his usage of his wife's goods." On occasion, a husband's creditors could even contest a divorce, just as they had sought to block separations of property in the Old

Regime, for they feared losing out to the ex-wife in the division of marital and dotal property.[43]

Most men's opposition to their wives' divorces smacked of opportunism. Property and reputation were at stake, particularly in divorces based on grounds such as mistreatment. Yet at the same time, husbands expressed a sense of injustice and even bewilderment at the new rules of the game. Exposing his own "immortal mortification" that his wife was divorcing him, the soldier Vuillerment asked how it was possible to allow divorce when both parties did not agree to it. Calling himself "your brother in arms," he explicitly called upon the male legislators' fraternal understanding of his plight as a wronged husband. The citoyen Sullot, angry and befuddled in turn, had succeeded in overturning his wife's attempt to divorce him for causes déterminées; he had since divorced her for incompatibility and now was engrossed in a battle over some 12,000 francs of marital property that his wife had placed under seals. He demanded that the legislature clarify the rules of these new disputes and protect men's traditional prerogative over marital property: "Experience tells us that every day a woman—because seven-eighths of divorces are provoked by women—takes everything she wants, provokes and obtains her divorce, and then still takes her share from what is left of communal goods."[44]

This disillusioned husband put his finger on the palpable new reality within marriage: the legalization of divorce altered the nature of this complex negotiation of intimacy between husband and wife. It made the state a greater player within the marital dynamic and a possible ally of the unhappy or abused spouse. Given the hierarchical nature of marriage, this possible leverage proved more important for women. The sources on family life and divorce generally reveal the most about those marriages that broke down entirely; it is difficult to know how the *possibility* of divorce affected marital dynamics. Perhaps a third or more of the time, couples abandoned divorce procedures that were under way.[45]

Some spouses no doubt initiated proceedings as a bargaining chip within the complex and tenuous negotiations between husband and wife. More broadly, the awareness that marriage could be dissolved entered the popular imagination and became an element in interactions between troubled couples. One Norman man who had already had his heart broken by divorce had nonetheless remarried, but complained vehemently that the very possibility of divorce had changed the texture of his relationship. He emphasized that his new wife had brought no money to the marriage—he had even paid for her wedding clothes—but now she wanted half of what he earned. "She threatens me constantly with divorce," he grumbled, "whenever I don't satisfy all her caprices and whenever I allow myself to make the smallest reprimand." Divorce had called into question his assumption that a wife owed her husband submission in exchange for economic support.[46]

Wives clearly sometimes used divorce proceedings to put pressure on their husbands. Undertaking legal action could provoke a husband's wrath and end all hope of resolution, or it could pave the way for a new round of struggles and compromises. In the village of Amayé-sur-Seulles, Marie-Françoise Godefroy, weary of putting up with her husband's affair with their servant, returned home to her parents and began to file for divorce based on immoral conduct. Anxious to avoid divorce, Jacques Gournay quickly promised to send away his young mistress and their newborn illegitimate son if only his wife would come back and tend the household for him. She duly returned home and their reconciliation nearly came about despite his delays in expelling his mistress; but one day Marie-Françoise saw Jacques "holding in his arms the young woman Poidevin's child and caressing him to show his paternal love." Once she had discovered that Jacques had hired a wet-nurse for the child and promised 5,000 livres worth of goods to the servant, Marie-Françoise renewed her divorce proceedings. Embracing the ambient revolutionary language, she commented to the family court that "from then on she could not convince herself to sacrifice her liberty and put herself into slavery." Torn between his responsibilities to two women, Jacques denied fathering the child, and his arbiters argued that since he had invited Marie-Françoise to return home, she should do so. Finally a tie-breaking arbiter tipped the scale in favor of divorce, yet the proposed divorce apparently never took place and we enter the gray area of historical speculation. Probably, within the small rural community of Amayé-sur-Seulles, the prospect of imminent divorce encouraged the couple to attempt once again to harmonize their differences.[47]

By enabling wives to challenge the long-held acceptance of male dominance within marriage, the revolutionary legalization of divorce had changed the nature of the contractual agreement between husband and wife. It gave wives leverage that they had not had before, even though it did not entirely overturn old patterns of male authority. Wives initiated divorce more often than men did because they had so much less freedom to negotiate viable lives within a broken, miserable, or alienated marriage. Some women became intently aware of the political as well as the personal implications of the divorce law. As the citoyenne LeMachais commented to the Convention when engaged in a bitter divorce struggle with a husband determined not to let her go, "You have promised us liberty; you have not foreseen all the methods that our former masters would employ to preserve their despotic empire. Make it possible for us to enjoy our rights."[48]

Divorce escalated many women's expectations that the republican state owed them support as individuals with civil rights. Not all divorcing women were as articulate or as explicitly politically conscious as the citoyenne LeMachais. Nor did they all experience divorce as a process of liberation. But for many women, the divorce law provoked them to think concretely about the meaning of revolutionary politics for their intimate lives. Above all, the legalization of divorce offered them the very real possibility of ending unhappy alliances, winning control of their goods, or lending legitimacy to a new marriage freely chosen.

The centrality of divorce for miserable wives should not obscure the fact that the new law also offered husbands an unprecedented opportunity to remake their conjugal lives. Men initiated only 28 percent of the unilateral divorces of the Calvados. Yet if men filed for divorce much less often than women did, this percentage also forms a stark contrast with Old Regime separation practices. Before 1792, although they had the legal right to request separation in some regions of France, men had obtained a very small percentage of séparations de corps, roughly 2 percent.[49] Husbands had requested few separations largely because they had a wider variety of formal and informal means of exercising authority over their spouses. In extreme circumstances, a man could use a family council or a lettre de cachet to imprison an adulterous wife in a convent. He might punish her harshly at home or have the priest read shameful warnings to her from the pulpit. A frustrated husband could more easily abandon his wife. In any event, he maintained control over household goods. Although men certainly had more options and power within marriage, they had no greater guarantee to conjugal companionship or happiness. Nor did they have the right to remarry.[50]

In short, if divorce was especially crucial for desperate wives, it also marked a sea change in the lives of distressed husbands. Overwhelmingly, they used the motives of incompatibility (41 percent of male-initiated unilateral divorces), followed by absence (21 percent) and six-months de facto separation (21 percent) to justify these marriage dissolutions. Incompatibility and abandonment were very real factors underlying husbands' decisions to divorce, but these categories suggest only part of the story. Male-initiated divorce reveals an interesting fusion of changing and traditional attitudes. On the one hand, divorcing husbands counted on the new republican state to guarantee their "individual liberty"—a catch-all phrase implying the right to escape the web of obligations of extended family or to disentangle oneself from personal unhappiness. Yet, on the other hand, husbands also divorced their wives when they seemed to have violated strongly held, long-standing expectations of female obedience, household management, or faithfulness.

Given the interwoven connections between the conjugal couple and kin, men who sought divorce time and again vented anger at their wives' families of origin. Declaring their disillusionment with in-laws, they made clear their expectation that marriage should bring a fruitful kinship alliance, but without curtailing the son-in-law's independence. In addition to enkindling new expectations of conjugal liberty, revolutionary politics could add new layers to the resentment of sons-in-law: political divisions complicated or overlaid traditional disputes over property. Before the Revolution citizen Fortin had married the daughter of the "ci-devant Chevalier de Trévigny de Falaise." "I want to wash myself endlessly in the baptismal font of divorce," he declared colorfully in 1794 as he denounced his in-laws, an entire family filled with émigrés and palace guards of the king. Conflict with his wife long outdated his new repulsion at the aristocracy, however, for she had been imprisoned in a convent in the Old Regime, presumably by him! "The Revolution brought her liberty, but not virtue," he remarked acidly. Likewise, the customs officer Noé had left his "vicious and corrupt wife" with her family in Bayonne ten years earlier; now in 1793 he indicted the superstitious fanaticism of her family for preventing his divorce and forcing him "to languish forever in the bonds of a marriage that I hate and that has made me spend the most beautiful days of my life in sorrow." Counting on the new republican state to develop a more "expeditious" form of divorce, Noé argued that only by "intervening in sexual relations," could the law form excellent citizens.[51]

Just as this customs officer equated indissoluble marriage with grief and the loss of liberty, the citizen Sentix called upon the National Convention and the Mountain in particular to guarantee "the entire liberty" of citizens and release spouses from the "continual hell of living with a being who made their very life insupportable." He demanded more rapid forms of divorce and the right for men to remarry immediately. In October 1793, one Norman citizen echoed this call for prompt remarriage to fill "the wretched emptiness, in which I have languished for so long." He lamented his arranged marriage to a woman with whom, by his own admission, he could build no bonds of sympathy, nor "even barely communicate together." Interestingly, the National Convention soon satisfied these petitioners' expectations that the new state should facilitate their speedy search for emotional fulfillment in new marriages. In late December 1793, it modified the law to enable men to remarry immediately, though women must wait ten months; and that spring the 4 floréal law fostered exceptionally easy access to divorce based on six-months de facto separation.[52]

Even as male divorcés expressed their desire for companionable marriages and greater independence, they mingled these feelings with entrenched notions of gender roles within marriage. First, wives owed their husbands faithfulness and obedience in exchange for whatever financial support the men could offer. Husbands felt that wives who violated this trust brought dishonor to the couple; grave violations of this contractual vision of conjugal reciprocity might merit divorce. When his wife moved in with a neighboring villager, Martin Guérard reported to the arbiters, "She has shaken off the yoke of marital authority; unfortunately, this is only too well known and public in this parish of Bavent and in the whole canton." He needed to advance no further proof and Marie Anne Beaudoit said nothing in her own defense. Conversely, a few husbands berated themselves for falling down on their side of the bargain. In the famine year of 1795 citizen Guérin, a Norman schoolteacher, bemoaned the harsh economic times that had "forced [him] to separate from [his] beloved wife." Since he could not care for her, she returned to her paternal household. "Sentiments of affection and humanity tore her from my heart, and my hand shook as I signed her permit" to return to her parents' home. By his account, she still loved him and had even sent him a letter "written in the most tender and friendly way." But then her family turned her against him and she inexplicably divorced him for incompatibility.[53]

Family tribunals shared Guérin's expectation that husbands should provide for their wives and children. By their actions they echoed the argument made by jurists, such as Robert-Joseph Pothier and the Norman David Houard, that husbands were responsible for supporting their wives in exchange for fidelity, obedience, and assistance. Family courts continued to allow a wife to demand a "separation of goods," as in the Old Regime, if the husband had ravaged the family finances. In divorce cases, arbiters took a husband's mismanagement into consideration and routinely awarded food pensions to divorced wives and children. Yet they expressed hesitation at requiring wealthier wives to pay annuities to their ex-husbands. When Jean-Philippe Costard of Honfleur implored a family court to grant him a pension from his former wife, the arbiters nervously and repeatedly debated the law's stipulation that the poorer spouse be granted alimony. Ultimately, they compelled Marie Anne Lamosnier to pay her ex-husband an annual sum of 450 livres and justified their decision by emphasizing that he was after all very old, infirm, and had only 150 livres in revenue in contrast to the 2,000 livres a year earned by his wife.[54]

The sexual fidelity of wives stood as the quintessential form of conjugal obedience and loyalty. Divorce could at least partly repair the dishonor brought by an adulterous wife. Citizen Tardy, a health official in Rochefort, filed for divorce because his wife had been seduced by a married man. Tardy complained of being left dishonored and disheartened, "like so many other unfortunate souls in the most cruel despair."[55] Very few—only 9 out of 422 (2 percent)—of the divorces in the Calvados were explicitly based on the specific grounds of "immoral conduct." Using the grounds of immorality was by no means an easy way to sever the marriage bond: the plaintiff had to produce ample proof of promiscuity or infidelity, generally by calling fifteen to twenty neighbors as witnesses to the defendant's misconduct. More frequently, accusations of adultery figured alongside other complaints in family tribunal cases. In addition, many jilted husbands had recourse to more accessible and less invasive forms of divorce. Men's frequent use of the grounds of incompatibility, desertion, and six-months separation no doubt saved husbands and arbiters from many a tale of cuckoldry and resentment, to say nothing of court costs.

By a narrow margin, husbands were more likely than wives to accuse their spouses of dissolute behavior in the Calvados; the same pattern took hold in other parts of France, although in some areas the gender imbalance was more marked. In Lyon men filed almost 90 percent of the divorces based on immoral conduct.[56] The 20 September 1792 law technically made men and women equally accountable for marital infidelity. The law legally deprived husbands of their prerevolutionary power to imprison adulterous wives, but could do little to undercut the double standard that prevailed in popular assumptions about fidelity. Not only did family tribunals turn down women's attempts to press charges of notorious conduct more often, especially in rural areas,[57] but the arbiters also more frequently tried to dissuade women from pursuing divorce on this grounds. When Séraphine Saint-Pierre of Caen accused her husband Pierre Bertault of serious insults and adultery, the arbiters stalled with the admonition, "It would be more genial for her to live together with her husband who can provide her a tranquil life with his fortune and his reflections." Insisting that she "had not taken this action without reflection and absolutely intended to divorce him," Séraphine nonetheless persevered and won a substantial annual pension of 15,000 livres from her wealthy businessman husband.[58]

Men accused of adultery generally dismissed their infidelities as dalliances. One male petitioner went so far as to argue that revolutionary liberty and new morals justified male promiscuity: legalizing polygamy would secure [male] liberty, promote fertility, and guarantee that fewer women would be abandoned! In the less fantastic realm of court cases, men accused of infidelity protested their innocence more loudly than women did. Despite being presented with lines of witnesses or even an illegitimate child, many husbands persisted in denying or justifying their extramarital liaisons. After the damning testimony of sixteen witnesses, Jacques Aubey of the village of Abenon disavowed having fathered the child of their domestic servant, but undercut his own disclaimer with the comment "that if he had gone astray in this way, it was only because of the proximity between himself and the girl . . . and because [his wife] often refused to share the marriage bed with him." To justify his actions further, he noted that he was not the one who had invited the servant into their home; that had been his wife's idea. Equally unremorseful, Simon Ch—— of the district of Montpellier far to the south candidly admitted "that he publicly supported another woman, that he intended to live with her always, that it was not a crime to have a mistress, that it was a *fairly common form of gallantry*, and that his wife should not have paid any attention to it" (my emphasis). He argued that he had fulfilled his conjugal duties by sending money home to her while he was in the army. Behind Simon's cocky words lay the assumption that a husband owed his wife financial support more than fidelity. The arbiters apparently shared elements of this notion, for, notwithstanding Simon's acknowledgment, they insisted on interviewing witnesses to be sure that his "moral profligacy was notorious" before granting his wife Anne the divorce.[59]

Despite the assumption that female adultery was more egregious, women could also be defiant when accused of straying from the marriage bed. The historian Roderick Phillips has found perhaps the most entertaining excuse: when asked how she produced three children during her husband's prolonged absence, Marie Gruchy of Rouen reportedly declared, "My husband who is off serving the Republic sends them to me in a letter." More often than not, in the Calvados women accused of adultery were not present at family tribunal cases. In fact, while adulterous husbands brought a mistress into the home surprisingly often or became involved with a servant or lodger within their own household, wives developed liaisons only outside the home and were more likely to feel compelled to leave entirely if the relationship became serious. In 1795 when the gardener/soldier Thomas Dumesnil accused his wife Marie Anne Lemoine of Lisieux of "carrying the fruit of her debauchery in her womb," he claimed that since leaving Lisieux back in 1792, she had since been spotted in Paris, Chinon, Saumur, the Morbihan, Laval, Cholet, La Rochelle, the Île-de-Ré, and Paris—a formidable and doubtless exaggerated trajectory.[60]

Husbands sometimes sought to divorce wives for immoral conduct because a woman divorced on specific grounds could keep only her dowry and lineage goods *(propres)*. She lost her share of communal property or goods acquired jointly during the marriage *(acquets)*. No parallel penalty applied to the goods of a husband divorced for grounds, although the law directed family tribunals to grant pensions to either spouse who won such a divorce.[61] In divorces between those with property, a husband could benefit substantially from winning the correct kind of divorce. Family tribunals seemed keenly aware of the gravity of their decisions and tried to prevent abuses. In cases where both spouses sought divorce for cause, courts sometimes proposed a more neutral divorce based on incompatibility or mutual consent. They rarely validated the "secondary demands" of husbands who tried to turn the tables by pressing charges against wives who had just begun proceedings against them. Arbiters also filtered out flimsy divorce charges. In 1793 when the rentier André Brunville of Caen tried to divorce his wife for immoral conduct or desertion, the family court turned him down. He could produce only the vaguest of allegations about her misconduct and he himself had apparently done the abandoning: he had moved to Caen without inviting his wife but promised to pay her living expenses as long as she stayed behind. A year later the couple agreed to divorce based on mutual consent and his wife won back her dowry of 40,000 livres as well as retroactive payments on an annual pension of 400 livres.[62]

Divorcing husbands whose wives became pregnant with another man's baby were particularly virulent in condemning female infidelity. After the Terror when the more conservative Thermidorian social climate encouraged critiques of divorce, petitioners and pamphleteers alike came to associate easy divorce with female licentiousness and with the illicit introduction of illegitimate children into the family.[63] Even earlier, several male petitioners recounted tales of woe, in which a long-absent wife reappeared just as her husband was inscribing their divorce into the état civil. She presented the unsuspecting husband with children, "issued from her debauchery and . . . born of scandal in secrecy," and demanded that he recognize these illegitimate offspring as his own. Perhaps this "criminal conduct . . . could find some support in the Old Regime given the indissolubility of marriage . . . , but now it is entirely contrary to the principle of divorce and to our constitution," wrote one deceived husband. Family tribunals should not force such men to become fathers on false pretenses. In short, even some men who supported divorce worried that it could be misused and "become the triumph of dissolute women."[64] If divorce were truly meant to liberate men, it should also free them from false presumptions of fatherhood and from the age-old subterfuges of female sexuality.

Indeed, this husband's words hint at the ambiguous meaning of divorce for husbands in the 1790s. If divorce offered some men the welcome opportunity to carve out new private lives, it played this role even more so for women. On a fundamental level, the new practice called into question the givenness of male superiority within the household. The very possibility of divorce produced a potent disruption in how men and women imagined and practiced gender within marriage.

THE IMPACT OF DIVORCE ON CHILD CUSTODY AND PROPERTY

To divorce was an act with far-reaching ramifications. In the realm of everyday, once couples had obtained a divorce, they needed to sort out their material goods and decide on the fate of their children. The family courts made decisions about child custody and support. Childless couples were more likely to divorce,[65] but how did divorce affect those with offspring? Unfortunately, the arbitration records contain few decisions regarding child custody. Although children are mentioned in various contexts, couples must have usually agreed upon their children's placement without the help of family courts, for I found only nine cases that specifically clarified the allotment of custody and food pensions. The law provided that both spouses should contribute to the expense of upbringing, directed the family court to resolve disputes over custody and costs, and stipulated that in divorces for incompatibility or mutual consent, the mother should have custody of all children under seven as well as older girls; the father should have charge of sons seven or older.[66]

In fact, the nine cases in the Calvados, taken together with other mentions of children in arbitration sessions and petitions, suggest a few patterns. Although several petitioners to the national legislature recommended that the least "aristocratic" and most "morally pure" parent be granted the child, in practice the courts rarely made decisions based on parents' perceived morality or responsibility for the divorce. By and large, most arbiters and parents assumed by default that the mother should bring up the offspring, especially younger children. As Dominique Dessertine observes for Lyon, "Conjugal culpability did not deprive women of their maternal rights."[67] Out of the nine clear custody cases, only twice did the courts assign children—boys over seven—to their fathers' care; in one of these cases, they overrode the mother's protests that the boys had refused to return to their father's home. Like the lawmakers, arbiters and spouses alike assumed that a father would have greater interest and responsibility toward a son than a daughter. In one instance the divorce occurred during the wife's pregnancy and her husband demanded custody over their soon-to-be-born child only if he were a son. The mother wanted the child regardless of sex, leaving the family tribunal in a quandary over what to do.[68]

Family courts believed that fathers shared responsibility for sustenance and upbringing. When mothers appealed for child support, in all but one case family tribunals held fathers financially responsible for contributing what they could. When Louis François Pipard protested that he "owed nothing to his son, and that he is old enough to earn his own living and go into service for the Republic," the arbiters calmly overrode this premature judgment and conferred on the mother three-quarters of the pension granted to the family because of the death of an older son in the Republic's army.[69]

Tellingly, when children were mentioned in contexts outside of the nine custody cases, almost invariably they were in their mother's charge. Not only did divorcing wives request and receive child custody more often, but they also peppered other aspects of their court pleas with tacit or explicit assumptions about maternal bonds. With understatement, Marie Catherine Sonnet told the tribunal that she could not renege on her intent to divorce her husband for physical cruelty, "not only for her own happiness, but also that of her children."[70] Female pro-divorce petitioners voiced the view that mothers had a particularly strong affective and moral bond with their offspring. For example, as she appealed for a clarified law on child custody and alimony, one mother professed that her "children are as dear to me as they are not to their father." Another asserted that divorce with fair pensions for mothers would save children from the unhappiness and dissipation of broken homes. Like others, she reinforced the validation of the maternal, moral role, so prized by revolutionary culture. In a third case, Félicité Desrogues struggled to win her daughter back with the claim: "Wife and mother, my titles are sacred."[71]

Since they focused primarily on the pragmatic question of financial support, family court cases reveal very little about the affective relations between children and parents, especially fathers. But as I will discuss in

Chapter 7, petitions from the mid and later 1790s make clear that the practice of divorce ignited tremendous anxiety about the disruption of emotional bonds between parent and child. While various individual petitioners worried about "the torn hearts" of children severed from one parent or another, the Committee of Legislation produced a "Projet de Loi" suggesting that divorcing couples should be required to pass their small children back and forth between mother and father, so as to think harder about the impact of their divorce on children.[72]

The division of marital property was also a subject fraught with complexity and contestation. In fact, the economic impact of divorce varied greatly. Since most households relied on the intertwined efforts and income of husband and wife, to sever this economic unit could weaken their financial status or even impoverish them. For some women especially, divorce brought personal liberty at the expense of financial hardship; as one journalist in favor of wives' pensions commented, "the husband can supplement his [income] with work and industry, . . . but a wife does not have the same resources to lift herself out of need."[73] The divorce law specified that the couple divide their marital property according to local customary law or their marriage contract, although any mutual donations, dowry augmentations, and *gains de survie* (certain goods due to widows or widowers) would be abolished. In addition, a woman lost her share of communal goods if her husband divorced her on specific grounds. The law left considerable latitude to local family tribunals to allot alimony and to sort out complex property arrangements.

Property issues often arose even as arbitration sessions began. During the divorce process, a particularly angry or Machiavellian husband could use his continued control over the couple's possessions to defraud his wife of her share. As early as July 1793, the Minister of Justice pointed out to the Committee of Legislation that the divorce law failed to protect the divorcing wife's property adequately from the "plunder," "scandalous means," and "fraudulence" of her husband. Women "escaping the yoke" of marriage sent him continual complaints about the new law, for "even as it delivered them from marital tyranny, it plunged them headlong into poverty and need." In fact, family tribunals did their best to guard against this form of abuse. They often received petitions from women who had left home—or had been ousted—with few goods and little means of subsistence. These wives sought a food pension for themselves and their children as well as access to their clothes, linens, beds, and other furnishings. For their part, some husbands also claimed that their wives had stolen money, bedclothes, or other movable property during the litigation. Although family courts routinely acknowledged that a husband "should have the right to administer his goods and those of his wife," they almost invariably granted the petitioning wife a pension and access to necessary goods during the arbitration process.[74]

Most hotly contested was the final division of property. Since married men controlled assets by default, wives initiated most contests over property; some husbands pressed countersuits. In the majority of the cases, women succeeded in winning at least the minimum amount of goods, as designated by the divorce law and the Norman custom. Given the complexity of property provisions, currency fluctuations, and the combinations of land, income, movable goods, and pensions, it is not possible to come up with an "average" marital settlement. At one end of the scale, one unfortunate woman won back little more than her child's bed and a "few skirts wrapped in a sheet," while Louise Lemarchand regained her dowry of 40,000 livres.[75] Typically, the family court granted the wife her initial dowry, the return of her personal material possessions, and the dower she would have obtained as a widow. More well-off women sometimes won back inheritance *(propres)* or income from their own family line, although this was a frequent point of contestation. In cases where marriage contracts had been lost, arbiters allowed wives to reconstruct content "from memory" combined with the testimony of extended family members. The tribunals also assessed alimony and some minimal child support according to the ability of the husband (or on rare occasions, the wife) to pay. As the court cases reveal, both wives and husbands worked hard to negotiate the open spaces within the 20 September 1792 law to their own advantage. One inventive and litigious wife even tried, without success, to sue her lover for palimony, even as she negotiated a divorce with her husband![76]

Because Norman law outlawed communal marital property, divorcées in the Calvados ran the risk of losing out on their share of conjugal equity, built up by the joint efforts of the couple. In the attempt to be fair, family courts generally ignored the article abolishing *gains de survie*, such as dower rights, and worked hard to retain the intention of the Norman custom to protect the widow—or in this case the divorcée—from poverty and her husband's business failures. At the moment of divorce, as at the moment of widowhood in the Old Regime, different marital property systems varied in their advantages and disadvantages. While the community system directed husband and wife to separate their joint acquisitions since marriage more equitably, Norman law enabled divorcées to more successfully protect their dowries and lineage goods from their husbands' creditors and from their husbands' own claims.[77]

Even as family tribunals relied on Norman law, the relative wealth and moral claims of each spouse also weighed heavily in the arbiters' assessments. Upholding the traditional notion that a hard-working and loyal wife should be rewarded for her contributions of work and dowry, they listened closely to wives who emphasized their key role in household maintenance and came down hardest on husbands who had violated their marital responsibilities. Catherine Fessard asserted that she had "never failed [her husband] whose children from a first marriage she had brought up and fed for seventeen years." Husband Claude Germain's argument that he now had to use his 1,200 livres of annual revenue to support two new illegitimate children fell on deaf ears. "An aged, virtuous, and penniless wife can not be the victim of her husband's unregulated passions," pronounced the arbiters as they awarded Catherine a small but crucial pension of 200 livres. Likewise, in the commune of Cormeille, when Nicolas Brunet tried to evade his wife's claims for her dower, dowry, and some other goods by contending that she generated her own income as a *femme commerçante*, Marie Anne Convenant pulled out all the stops. She pointed out that her small business earned very little (100–200 livres a year) and that she was nonetheless a "wife under coverture" who could not have the financial independence nor the administrative ease that her husband attributed to her. But in deciding in her favor, the court found most compelling her upbringing of their children, as well as her care and feeding of her mother-in-law Brunet for nine years.[78]

While some women petitioned the national legislature about difficulties recovering their dowries or other possessions,[79] male petitioners' complaints about divorce and property fell into two main categories. Men who had been married to wealthier women lamented their loss of income when their wives divorced them.[80] Second, others expressed astonishment and indignation that (formerly) married women could gain access and control over property. One citizen proposed in 1796 that divorced wives should only be able to sell their goods with the consent of their ex-husbands, while another argued in 1794 that it was more egalitarian for both spouses to come from the same income level and "for no women ever to have any fortune of her own beyond her temporary share in her husband's [wealth]." In practice women were not necessarily advantaged by the nature of marital property divisions. But in the post-Thermidorian period, resentment at the loss of male property right was one factor fueling the conservative backlash against divorce and against the attempt to ensure greater individual liberty and equality within the family.[81]

THE LANDSCAPE OF DIVORCE

The legalization of divorce enabled both women and men to escape unhappy marriages. But this possibility—with all its complex pros and cons—was not equally accessible to all members of the French nation. As this final section will show, the turn toward divorce in the Calvados, as in the rest of France, had distinct social, geographic, and occupational contours. By looking more closely at which groups of women and men could divorce, I aim not only to contribute to the social history of divorce, but also to illustrate why this revolutionary reform affected women's and men's lives and civil rights unevenly in different settings of France.

Divorce was overwhelmingly an urban phenomenon in the Calvados as in the rest of France. As Jacques Dupâquier highlights in his survey of divorce in France overall, France's largest cities exhibited a higher rate of divorce than did smaller cities between 1793 and 1803. With an estimated 12,148 divorces for its population of 641,000, Paris topped the list by a long shot. To measure the rate of divorce, historians often divide the number of divorces by the number of new marriages to determine a divorce/marriage ratio. In Paris this ratio from 1793 to 1802 reached 22.6, or almost one case of marital breakdown for every four or five new marriages celebrated. While other large cities did not experience this explosion of divorce, the resort to divorce remained substantial. Rouen had 953 divorces, second only to Paris. Dupâquier suggests a ratio of 22.6 percent for Paris, 7.4 percent for the nine next-largest cities with over 50,000 inhabitants in 1801, 6 percent for the medium-large cities of 10,000 to 50,000, and 2 percent for small cities under 10,000.[82] As Table 2 shows, although divorce rates dropped with the size of the town, no simple correlation existed between population size and divorce. Local circumstances, such as emigration patterns from towns like Versailles or Strasbourg, could escalate the trend toward divorce.

In the Calvados, Caen, with a population of close to 35,000, witnessed the highest number of divorces: 181 between 1793 and 1803 under the revolutionary law, a divorce/marriage ratio of 5.2 percent. But notably, divorce within the smaller cities and rural areas varied widely. The next-largest city, Falaise with 14,000 people, recorded only 14, while the smaller cities of Bayeux, Honfleur, and Lisieux, with populations in the 9,000 to 10,600

TABLE 2. Cities with the Highest Number of Divorces in France, 1793–
An X (1801–02)

City	Population	Divorces[a]	Marriages	Divorce : Marriage Ratio (%)
Paris	641,000	12,148	53,650	22.6
Rouen	84,000	953	7,543	12.6
Lyon	102,000	884	9,614	9.2
Marseille	108,000	795	8,866	9
Strasbourg	47,000	617	10,183	6.1
Bordeaux	105,000	517	8,649	6
Versailles	35,000	401	3,042	13.2
Toulouse	53,000	355	4,648	7.6

SOURCES: Divorce statistics: Jacques Dupâquier, "Vers une statistique nationale des divorces sous la première République," *Populations et cultures: Etudes réunies en l'honneur de François Lebrun* (Rennes, 1989), 31–37; Dominique Dessertine, *Divorcer à Lyon sous la Révolution et l'Empire* (Lyon, 1981), 107; Roderick Phillips, *Family Breakdown in Late Eighteenth-Century France* (Oxford, 1980), 3–4. Population statistics: *Atlas de la Révolution française*, vol. 8, *Population*, ed. Bernard Lepetit and Maroula Sinarellis (Paris, 1995), 74.

[a]Following Dupâquier, I have limited the number of divorces to those completed by the year X (1801–02). In fact, divorces by revolutionary law continued into years XI and early XII, so the divorces are slightly undercounted here.

range, experienced 39, 38, and 51 revolutionary divorces respectively. Orbec, a town of 3,086 people in the Pays d'Auge, had 24 divorces and a remarkably high divorce/marriage ratio of 9.7. In contrast, the comparably sized town of Vassy in the Bocage Virois did not register a single divorce during the revolutionary epoch.

Divorce rates dropped sharply in rural areas across France and in the Calvados. Of the 422 divorces in 78 communes between 1792 and early 1804, only 54 divorces took place in the 69 communes with less than 2,500 souls, and only 4 occurred in the 19 villages in my sample with fewer than 500 souls. Forty communes out of the 78 analyzed recorded no divorces whatsoever. In villages with fewer than 500 inhabitants, the divorce/marriage ratio came to a mere 0.8 percent, and only attained 1.5 percent for communes of 500 to 1,000 souls.[83] In smaller communes, not only did fewer couples resort to divorce, but those that did were less quick to take advantage of the law. In the cities with more than 8,000 people, about half of all divorces occurred in the first three years, compared to 39 percent of the divorces in smaller communes. Rural areas in other parts of France also witnessed a low resort to divorce, but much more analysis of rural practices

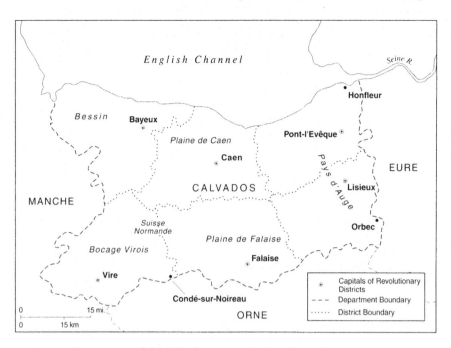

Map 1.   Department of the Calvados during the French Revolution

is needed.[84] For, as I will discuss below, access to divorce in specific regions of the countryside also varied. Within the Calvados, the extreme scarcity of divorce in the Bocage Virois or the Plaine de Falaise contrasted sharply with more prevalence in the Pays d'Auge or the Plaine de Caen, for example (see Map 1).

Within these varied geographies, divorcés came from the same social backgrounds. Any attempt to assess social behavior according to occupational categories in revolutionary France is fraught with hazards: data is often uneven and some occupations inevitably seem to overlap categories.[85] Yet Jean-Claude Perrot's masterful study of eighteenth-century Caen offers a model for classifying social complexity and also provides a point of comparison between divorcés and the population at large, at least for that city. Given the weakness of data on wives' professions, husbands' professions form the basis of these classifications.

Succinctly put, compared to their relative numbers within the city's population overall, divorcés came disproportionately from artisanal, commercial, or liberal professional backgrounds (see Table 3). For example, artisans and small shopkeepers *(commerçants)* made up 50 percent of divorcés but only about 29 percent of Perrot's count of the adult male population of

TABLE 3. Divorces by Husbands' Occupations,
Department of the Calvados (1792–1804)

Occupational Category	N	%
Artisans/Small Commerce	166	50
Administrators/Liberal Professions	34	10
Bourgeois (Vivant de son bien)	29	9
Businessmen (Négociants)/Merchants	29	9
Unskilled Laborers	29	9
Unemployed	18	5
Army	16	5
Agriculture	11	3
TOTAL	332	100

In 90 additional cases, occupations remain unknown.

SOURCE: Etat civil records from 78 communes within the Calvados,
1792–1804. See Appendix I for complete list.

Caen. Certain groups of shopkeepers and artisans—those working in the
food trades, clothing manufacture, and leather work—divorced proportionately more than those in woodworking, construction, or textile manufacture. Divorces among the three middling groups—liberal professionals,
businessmen *(négociants* and *gros marchands)*, and rentiers—all out-
stripped their proportion of the population. These groups made up 28 percent of divorcés and about 16 percent of the adult male population at large.[86]
Liberal professionals in particular contributed twice "their share" of divorces. Other cities of the Calvados revealed similar socioeconomic patterns,
with slight variations. Artisans made up an even larger segment (56 percent)
of the divorcing population in mid-size cities; and divorce among businessmen surpassed that among rentiers, while the reverse was true for Caen.

Unfortunately, rural local officials were less zealous in recording professions in the divorce acts than were the urban registrars. For the 54 divorces in
rural areas, I was able to discover the husband's occupation in only 25 cases.
Only three husbands clearly were involved in agricultural work as *cultivateurs*. Only two conclusively came from the lower tier of society, one day laborer and one individual without a profession. Assorted artisans, small commerçants such as innkeepers, and low-level administrative figures dominated
the divorce acts. As in urban areas, divorce remained most popular among the
commercial, artisanal, and middling sectors of the population. Slower to have
recourse to the new law everywhere in the department were the very rich,

the laboring or dependent poor, and anyone engaged in agriculture across the social spectrum from large landowners down to day laborers. The poorer sectors of the population apparently made up an even smaller portion of those who divorced in the countryside than they did in the cities.[87]

The uneven distribution of divorce among geographical and occupational groups says little about relative levels of marital conflict. Rather, couples in certain socioeconomic and geographic sectors turned more frequently to divorce because certain local conditions made it at least possible. Several crucial factors made it easier to sever the marital bond: knowledge about revolutionary laws, ideas, and innovations; the presence of *hommes de loi* (legal practitioners) and a legally aware culture; and socioeconomic and familial conditions allowing couples to break apart. Conversely, high levels of religious practice and the presence of strong counterrevolutionary sentiment and chouan warfare mitigated against divorce. These factors point to disparity between urban and rural divorce patterns across the board, and also to variations *within* divorce levels in *different regions* of the department.

Central to making divorce possible was exposure to revolutionary political culture. Particularly in the cities of Caen, Falaise, Honfleur, Lisieux, Vire, Condé-sur-Noireau, and Orbec, support for the Revolution rose early and strong. As the Revolution progressed and political alignments grew more complex, the Calvados did not stand out for sustained support for the Revolution. Sixty-one percent of the department's clergy refused to take the oath of the Civil Constitution. Leading revolutionaries in the department's largest cities—Caen, Bayeux, Lisieux, Honfleur, and Falaise—all supported the Federalist movement until its suppression in the summer of 1793.[88] More crucial than loyal alignment with the Jacobin cause was the pervasive debate over republicanism and social reform.

Divorce ran high in cities in part because inhabitants had more access to the revolutionary press, political clubs, and legal knowledge. To divorce, individual couples needed first to be able to imagine the act and to be aware of the new law. News of the decree spread by rumor, official announcement, and the printed word. Even playing cards carried female images, representing "Liberty of Marriage" and wielding the word "Divorce" (see Figure 7). Women and men who wrote petitions to the national legislatures about their conjugal plights occasionally revealed the source of their knowledge. "I read in a newspaper that any divorced woman was free to remarry after ten months," commented the citoyenne LeBlanc. Angélique Fouque reported that she had learned from the press about the 4 floréal an II law allowing divorce based on six-months separation; this news prompted her to abandon

Figure 7.   Playing card of the French
Republic: Liberty of Marriage (1793).
Courtesy of the Bibliothèque nationale
de France.

seeking a divorce based on cause and encouraged her to pursue this simpler
and swifter format.[89]

Within the Calvados, especially in the cities, citizens had access both to
newspapers from Rouen and Paris and to local pro-revolutionary journalists. For example, from Caen came the anti-clerical *Courrier du département
du Calvados* and the more moderate *Journal patriotique de Basse-
Normandie*. In the smaller, but vibrantly pro-revolutionary city of Vire, the
journalist Jacques Malo produced the *Courrier des Campagnes*, which sold
for only a sou and was explicitly written in an accessible style.[90] In addition
to bearing news of the actual laws, these papers carried other material per-
taining to familial reform. For example, the *Courrier du Calvados* printed a
letter from "Julie" who demanded the legalization of divorce to free women
from their status as "children and dolls." When Claude Fauchet, the
Constitutional Bishop of the Calvados, wrote a pastoral letter in November
1792 condemning divorce and the new practice of clerical marriage, local papers as well as Fauchet's own *Journal des Amis* avidly followed the conflict

pitting the bishop against local municipalities and political clubs in the winter of 1793.[91]

Both husbands and wives who divorced had higher than average literacy rates, regardless of whether they came from urban or rural settings. In Caen on the eve of the Revolution, Perrot found that about 86 percent of the men overall and 73 percent of women could sign their marriage declarations in the parish registers. Among divorcing couples in the 1790s, literacy rates were higher: 98 percent of husbands within the department as a whole and 99 percent in Caen could at least scribble their names on the état civil at the moment of divorce. Among women, 89 percent department-wide and 92 percent in Caen signed, however poorly. As Perrot suggests, those who could sign legibly used the written word more frequently and were more likely to be able to read than were those who painstakingly scratched down their names. In the Calvados as a whole, 85 percent of the divorcés and 77 percent of the divorcées could sign well, suggesting their ability to truly take part in print culture. Perhaps they could gain access to the handbook, written by citoyen Garnier in 1792, to guide couples and arbiters through the basic process of divorce. In addition, women initiating divorce were slightly more literate than those being divorced.[92] Although access to the law was more difficult for illiterate citizens, they too might gain knowledge through hearing newspapers read aloud or through public announcements of laws by local officials. Justices of the peace in rural as well as urban communes were supposed to receive free copies of the *Bulletin de la Convention*, so as to spread up-to-date information on the latest laws of the land. However, the outbreak of the Federalist revolt, chouan activism, transport expenses, and the lack of rural post offices prevented rural areas from having the same degree of access to this bulletin and other newspapers.[93]

Within the department as whole, couples were more likely to divorce in towns with political clubs.[94] Political societies had sprung up in fifty different communes by the year II (1793–94). Clubs acted as purveyors of revolutionary laws and ideas and sometimes sent proponents of various republican reforms into the countryside as well. The clubs subscribed to both the Parisian and Norman press, and occasionally produced their own papers, such as the *Journal des débats de la société patriotique de Caen*. While the debate over Fauchet's condemnation of the divorce law particularly focused the clubs' attention on the issues of divorce and clerical marriage, some of these societies had discussed and debated civil law issues from the early 1790s on.[95] Although not at all the most important factor in facilitating divorce, the presence of clubs went hand-in-hand with the broader emergence of republican consciousness and could be especially influential in rural areas. The turn to divorce in the Calvados was lowest in the districts of Vire and Falaise, areas with the fewest Jacobin clubs, as well as other socioeconomic and political characteristics that made divorce difficult. The choice to divorce did not necessarily depend on pro-revolutionary sentiment. But the salient point here is that access to revolutionary political culture not only conveyed basic knowledge about divorce but also fostered a climate in which unhappy couples could reimagine their domestic relationships through the lens of revolutionary politics.

Moreover, in the larger cities, a corps of legal professionals, from notaries to hommes de loi, provided expertise about legal change and increasingly staffed the informal arbitration courts that validated divorce. In fact, the small town of Orbec, with only 3,086 inhabitants and the highest divorce/marriage ratio in the department, had been a bailliage seat in the Old Regime; its lawyers facilitated the local population's disproportionate proclivity to divorce. In cities and certain rural areas with a strongly litigious culture, ordinary citizens themselves were likely to be more knowledgeable about Norman customary law as well as revolutionary innovations. Not only had the basic tenets of Norman law long circulated within oral culture, but cheap paper copies of the custom could be purchased in the eighteenth century from Rouen printers for less than a livre, roughly the same price as an almanac or a pamphlet of the *bibliothèque bleue* (chapbooks). In 1795 in the midst of an arbitration session over one divorcée's goods in Caen, her brother and supporter ran home to find "a book in which the jurists decided the question in favor of [his sister]."[96] Since family courts sorted out matters such as divorce property according to a combination of revolutionary and customary law, familiarity with both forms of law aided divorcing couples.

If revolutionary and legal cultures increased access to the new practice, the cities of Caen, Lisieux, Bayeux, and Honfleur also all experienced higher rates of divorce than other parts of the department because their more fluid and complex socioeconomic milieux enabled couples to disband more easily. The socioeconomic characteristics of these cities varied somewhat. Although smaller than the neighboring port Le Havre, Honfleur was a premier port of Lower Normandy, a fishing and maritime center whose volume of commerce ranked it seventh among the coastal port towns of France in 1792. Bayeux falls into Bernard Lepetit's categories of "Old Regime towns" and "wealthy towns." Although it had a textile sector, it drew its wealth from its long-standing position as a diocesan seat and royal administrative and judicial center. In comparison, Lisieux, although also the seat of a bishopric, lacked a bailliage court; but two-thirds of its population found employment in textile production; agricultural trading was another substantial source of weatlh. The largest city, Caen, seat of the généralité of Lower Normandy, was home to fiscal and judicial administration, a diversified textile sector, a significant port and agrarian marketing center, and a university.[97]

Within the socially and economically complex world of the larger cities, family bonds were already being transformed before the Revolution. Patterns of immigration weakened ties to the extended family, and couples forged bonds of solidarity with neighbors and fellow workers or business partners. Within Caen, couples were marrying later; more individuals remained single their entire lives; and family size was already on the decline, especially among more well-off families. Moreover, by the revolutionary era, particularly in artisanal sectors of the city, the conjugal unit had become the norm. Households with three generations all living under one roof had become rare, making up less than 3 percent of the total. While slightly over half the households encompassed parents and children, a substantial 44–46 percent counted only members of the same generation. These patterns already encouraged broader acknowledgment, or even acceptance, of a diversified family structure and may also mark a decline in the influence of the lineage family on the decisions and daily lives of the conjugal couple. The emphasis of the Norman custom on the family line stood in tension with these demographic changes.[98]

Furthermore, just as Roderick Phillips has suggested for Rouen, the growth and modification of urban industry in some ways facilitated divorce by transforming the household economy. Households in both urban and rural areas operated as intertwined units, dependent on the labor of husband and wife. But in urban areas, the family economy diversified its makeup in the late eighteenth century. Notably, textile production outside the home meant that husbands and wives could both be working separately outside the household and then pooling their resources.[99] Cities offered a range of possible employment, making the family economy less intertwined and more flexible in urban areas. As Perrot has written about pre-revolutionary Caen:

> Before industrialization, purely urban modalities of the economy already favored the destruction of this extended group [the extended family]. The confirmation of success was much more individual than in the agrarian world. The city often attracted single men and women. . . . Once constituted, the restricted family possessed more liberty in its lifestyle, its choice of homes, its use of capital; it was tempted to take more risks. . . . In brief, the compartmentalizing of tasks in the city provoked the fracturing of the family, and then nourished itself from this fracturing. Urban life paved the way for the solitary workers of the industrial age well before the Le Chapelier law.[100]

Perrot may exaggerate the individualism of workers in the urban world. He nonetheless suggests a crucial urban tendency toward greater economic and familial fluidity. Although both urban and rural couples needed to function as an interlocking economic unit in order to survive or prosper, on balance this familial economy was even more critical for the survival of rural families. Among those working the land, couples could not easily divide land, leases, or sharecropping contracts. Even in rural areas, those engaged in agriculture made up only a small proportion, 12 percent, of divorcing couples. An urban couple with property could divide its mobile urban capital, although that too would be wrenching and difficult. But nonetheless, psychologically as well economically, this transformation of the urban family economy made divorce more possible in the cities than in the countryside.

The cities also had a labor market outside the home for women—a crucial factor considering that urban women initiated divorce so much more often than did either rural women or men in any locale.[101] In Bayeux, for example, where women initiated 77 percent of the unilateral divorces, the lace-making industry "made a large proportion of the female population relatively independent." So prominent a role did lace-making play in Bayeux's manufacturing economy that women outnumbered men in this town. Admittedly, the revolutionary crisis in the luxury trades would have made matters especially precarious for lace-makers in the 1790s. And in any era, if a woman worked as a lace-maker, seamstress, or laundress to support herself and her children single-handedly, she lived close to the margin of subsistence.[102] But at least the possibility of economic independence existed.

I have data on the occupations of divorcing wives in only 74 cases, 71 of these in the cities. Of these divorcées, the largest proportion, 35 percent, come from artisanal or small commerce backgrounds, predominantly skilled textile workers or seamstresses; 32 percent from the ranks of the unemployed or unskilled laborers; 26 percent from the class of merchants and rentiers; only 7 percent listed agrarian occupations. Unemployed or unskilled workers are more strongly represented among the divorcées than in the data based on husbands' occupations. This observation needs to be taken with caution: poorer or artisanal women were more likely to list employment than were the wives of professional men.[103] But the presence of women with skilled jobs nonetheless stands out. The predominance of midwives, seamstresses, lace-makers, dress-makers, and clothes merchants among the divorcées illustrates the crucial role of female employment in making divorce possible. Moreover, another noteworthy pattern appears in the data based on husbands' occupations: among artisans and shopkeepers, divorce levels were highest in the food and clothing trades. Several of these guilds were among those most likely to allow widows the full legal right to continue their husbands' masterships; in sum, these occupations were most open to female participation and management. Since they tended to be small enterprises with low levels of capital intensity, a fortunate divorcée could conceivably maintain her position in these trades if she could set herself up on her own, albeit with the help of male family members or journeymen.[104]

Urban women also were more likely than their rural counterparts to benefit from another essential factor: local networks of support. When the lace-maker Marie Anne Coigny of Caen tried to divorce Nicolas Bourse for mistreatment, their arbiters were all family members who deadlocked, each in support of their own. Marie Anne ultimately won her divorce; her husband boycotted the act of registering the divorce in the état civil, but Marie Anne showed up to sign her name, surrounded by two brothers-in-law, a cousin, and a neighbor/button-maker as witnesses to her act.[105] Their presence highlights a crucial point: to take the bold and risky step of severing the marriage contract, a woman needed backing from a web of family members and/or neighbors. Within this urban, artisanal milieu, women were more likely to find solidarity from neighbors who stood behind their right to escape an abusive marriage. Also, Marie Anne Coigny had a profession of her own. As a lace-maker, she could earn a living, albeit a marginal one.

When the Legislative Assembly established the procedures for recording the état civil, in contrast to the Old Regime, they allowed women as well as men to serve as witnesses. These signatures within the état civil, especially in Caen, attest to the centrality of urban networks of female support for women who initiated divorce. Seventy-three women served as witnesses within my sample of divorces in the Calvados. Only one of these women bore testimony to a rural divorce; fifteen came from mid-size cities, and the remaining fifty-seven of them all signed divorce records in Caen. Female witnesses were overwhelmingly selected by women who initiated divorce. Everyone, male or female, was more likely to choose male witnesses; but only seven divorcing husbands opted to have a woman sign on their behalf. Moreover, twelve female witnesses did not even know how to sign, suggesting that the divorcées who solicited their help implicitly valued their closeness or friendship over the official value of literacy. Interestingly, women served as witnesses primarily in the years II–IV (1793–96), and almost entirely disappeared from the civil records during the more socially conservative Directory and Consulate. Finally, divorcing wives were more likely than husbands were to choose their own relatives or friends as witnesses. For example, after winning a hard-fought divorce for physical cruelty, Marguerite Paulmier recorded her decisive act accompanied by her own mother and three friends, including another woman, the wife of a day laborer. Again and again, these witnesses to urban women's divorces bore testimony to these crucial webs of local support.[106]

In rural areas, more forces combined to keep couples united and to discourage divorce. Kin groups in rural areas were quicker to exert pressure on the couple to remain united. For example, in Abenon Catherine Aubey initiated divorce proceedings against her husband Jacques Aubey on the grounds of mistreatment and immoral conduct. It quickly became clear that they were also feuding over his misuse of her lineage property. Yet despite the son-in-law's abrasive character and philandering ways, Catherine's own father was anxious to prevent a divorce. He offered "for the love of peace" to allow his son-in-law to continue using his cider press without recompense, as long as he agreed to contribute to its repair and upkeep. The arbiters, all cultivateurs and relatives, reported that numerous other friends and family members came to the arbitration meeting in the attempt to reconcile the couple. Despite this family pressure, the strong-willed Catherine was fed up; she refused her father's proposition and called sixteen witnesses for the next family tribunal meeting. Because of a deadlock between arbiters, Jacques' persistent resistance, and his initially successful appeal at the District Tribunal of Lisieux, it took her a full additional year to win her final divorce, ultimately for incompatibility rather than mistreatment. Her husband and extended family worked the wheels of justice to prevent, or in the end, delay her divorce.[107]

Within the Norman countryside, divorce became a more makeshift procedure than in the big cities. Family tribunals were more likely to be made up of family members rather than hommes de loi. More closely resembling the family councils of the Old Regime, they sometimes worked to develop a viable alternative to divorce. In the village of Mouen, the relatives of Philippe Saint-Martin and Anne Pigache recognized the incompatible temperaments of the couple, but rather than "follow the rigorous route of divorce that repulsed their hearts" the family court drew up an informal but very specific separation arrangement. Anne would go where she liked; Philippe would pay her 200 livres a year on a quarterly basis and would raise the amount once he received his inheritance from M. Decoudrelles. The arbiters listed in detail the linens, clothing, and armoire that the husband had to return to Anne and her brother.[108] In effect, the legalization of divorce and the creation of the family tribunal system created space for family tribunals to negotiate settlements and to mediate between local attitudes and revolutionary changes. While divorce in Caen and other cities fell largely into the hands of hommes de loi as arbiters who followed the revolutionary law more closely, rural family tribunals were more likely to develop alternate arrangements and to discourage wives from pursuing suits against their husbands.

Another aspect of rural divorce highlights differences between the rural and urban contexts: divorces by mutual consent formed a higher proportion of divorces in rural areas than in the cities of Lower Normandy. In the department as a whole, divorce by mutual consent made up 18 percent of the total (74 of 422). But in Caen, the rate was even lower: only 12 percent (21 of 181), compared to 22 percent (12 of 54) in rural areas. Within a village milieu resistant to divorce overall, if the both husband and wife agreed to end the marriage, the divorce was more likely to occur.

As the historian André Burguière has suggested, differences in family structures influenced the impact of revolutionary civil reform in different parts of France.[109] On the question of family structure and access to divorce, rural Normandy combined various features of the Midi and the North. In Normandy as in other parts of the North, the stem-family structure (three-generation households) was not as prevalent as in the Midi. But Norman customary law and practice nonetheless promoted attachment to lineage as in the South, rather than encouraging the communal merging of the couple's goods and interests, as was prevalent in much of the North. Especially in the countryside, this strong Norman emphasis on lineage mitigated against divorce, even as the tendency of couples to set up independent households lightened the influence of the extended family on the couple.

Across France as a whole, divorces were no doubt fewest and farthest between in those rural areas where couples were most ensconced within extended families, for example among in-marrying daughters-in-law of rural stem-families in the Midi or among the couples living in the communitarian families of the Bourbonnais or Basse-Auvergne. At the opposite end of the spectrum, the Parisian world in some sense facilitated divorce not only because of the high levels of social and geographic mobility, ample exposure to revolutionary and legal culture, economic opportunities for women, and networks of neighborhood solidarity, but also because of the conjugal family structure and communal marital property system that made divorce more possible and more acceptable.

Finally, emphasizing the low resort to divorce in rural regions should not conceal the fact that considerable variation existed in divorce levels from one part of the countryside to the next. Within the Calvados, very few peasants divorced in the Plaine de Falaise or Bocage Virois in the southern and southwestern regions of the department. In this entire area, only four divorces occurred in the twenty small communes studied; and even in the cities of Vire, Falaise, and Condé-sur-Noireau, divorce remained relatively rare, totaling only 36 cases in these towns. In contrast, especially in the Pays d'Auge and to a lesser extent the Plaine de Caen, rural divorce surfaced more frequently. Within the seventeen rural communes examined in the two districts comprising the Pays d'Auge, twenty-nine couples divorced. Urban divorce was also higher in this region.[110]

Although these numbers of rural divorces are too low to carry intensive study, they nonetheless suggest patterns and prompt reflection about why one part of the countryside might be more open to divorce than another. In the Pays d'Auge, an economy of dairy and cider production had led to the development of complex, rural hierarchies and the growth of a substantial rural middle class. This area included the wealthiest agrarian regions of the department, especially in the district of Pont-l'Evêque. The Pays d'Auge was nonetheless riven with internal conflicts. The livestock raisers and merchants took offense at the privileges of the nobility. In turn, both well-off peasants *(laboureurs)* and poorer ones resented the new wealth of the livestock producers. Tension ran high between urban and rural areas. In addition, the Pays d'Auge was marked by relatively low levels of religiosity. In his study of political allegiances within the Calvados, Jean Lethuillier has suggested that these social and cultural characteristics encouraged the Pays d'Auge to welcome the Revolution. At least in the early 1790s, the revolutionary abolition of privileges and the forward-looking rhetoric of equality seemed to offer promise to various sub-groups within this complex rural society. Arguably, the same factors—the presence of a considerable rural middle class, comparatively wealthy peasantry, lower levels of religious practice, and lower clerical density—contributed to making divorce at least a little more possible in this area. In addition, in the Old Regime the litigious "Pays d'Auge was the paradise of notaries, process-servers, attorneys, and barristers of all types." Higher divorce levels and economic opportunities in the cities of Lisieux, Honfleur, and Orbec may well have influenced couples in surrounding areas. Finally, revolutionary culture made its presence more distinctly felt in the rural Pays d'Auge, even though pro-republican sentiment declined in the later 1790s. The district of Lisieux, for example, had the highest concentration of rural political societies within the Calvados.[111]

Contrasting characteristics help to explain the paucity of divorce in the districts of Vire and Falaise. The Bocage Virois stood out for rural poverty, high degrees of religious practice and clerical density, and a homogenous social structure rather closed to outside influences. Lethuillier explictly contrasts the "in-group," tightly knit society of the bocage with the more fluid and multi-layered social dynamics of the Pays d'Auge. Chouannerie took hold strongly in this southwestern region of the department and the towns of Condé-sur-Noireau and Vire remained isolated in their support of the Revolution. The chouan activity of the Bocage Virois extended into the hilly Suisse Normande west of Falaise. Within the grain-producing area of the Plaine de Falaise, the disparity between peasant poverty and noble or ecclesiastical wealth stood at the highest level of the Calvados and contributed to greater support for the early Revolution. But in contrast to the more complex and litigious social world of the Pays d'Auge, the lack of a rural middle class and the agrarian poverty of the district of Falaise helped to discourage divorce in this region.[112]

In sum, rural divorce remained a relatively rare and easily discouraged phenomenon, but this new practice nonetheless made inroads in some parts of the countryside. Divorce became more viable in the presence of various factors, such as lower rates of religious practice, a relatively wealthy peasantry, greater exposure to revolutionary ideology, proximity to urban culture, and access to legal practitioners.

. . .

In March 1803 the Napoleonic Conseil d'Etat promulgated a new divorce law that would become part of the Civil Code in 1804. Severely restricting revolutionary reforms, the new law allowed couples to divorce by mutual consent with their parents' permission, providing they had been married for between two and twenty years and that the man was over twenty-five and the woman between twenty-one and forty-five years of age. Only three unilateral grounds remained: criminal condemnation of one's spouse, abuse or severe injury, and adultery. A woman could accuse her husband of adultery and divorce him only if he supported his mistress within the couple's home. In contrast, a husband had greater latitude in accusing his wife; if she were found guilty of adultery, she would not just be divorced, but also imprisoned for a period of three months to two years. The Code also reinstated séparation de corps.

Not surprisingly, divorce rates plummeted across France during the Empire. Caen had witnessed 181 divorces by early 1804, but only 13 occurred between late 1804 and 1816, when divorce was abolished until 1884. Divorce under the Empire was restricted to a handful of more well-established families in Caen. Unfortunately, the état civil offers but little indication of motive: in four cases, the couple divorced by mutual consent; seven wives and two husbands initiated the remaining nine divorces on unknown grounds. A small flurry of divorces in late 1809 and 1810 suggests that Napoleon's own divorce temporarily encouraged a few desperate couples to sever their marriage bonds, but divorce was by no means a common aspect of marital culture anywhere in France.[113]

The revolutionary experiment with divorce had been relatively short-lived and in many ways fragile. Hardly routine, hardly easy, the act of divorce during the Revolution tore at the interwoven fabric of family expectations, religious beliefs, and lineage practices. To divorce was a delicate move, fraught with danger and uncertainty. In many regions, such an act was barely thinkable, and this practice, like many other revolutionary innovations, affected France unevenly. Couples were most likely to divorce if they came from artisanal or middle-class backgrounds and lived in urban areas where certain conditions seemed to make divorce, if never easy, at least more viable: social and geographic mobility; familial and socioeconomic conditions allowing women in particular to break away; the prevalence of revolutionary political culture; the presence of legal experts; and, most difficult to measure, a cultural willingness to imagine that marriage should be built on individual consent, as well as companionship and economic complementarity. Just as important in making divorce an option would be the lack of curtailing factors, such as intense religiosity, pervasive chouan activity, and above all, family and property structures that made it inordinately difficult for an individual to set out on her or his own.

Recognizing the difficulty and unevenness of divorce should not obscure its importance. Divorce did more than transform the lives of individual couples: it also revealed the personal implications of revolutionary politics and called into question older conceptions of the character of marriage and gender relations. Admittedly, it is tricky to assess what the practice of divorce signaled about attitudes toward marriage and its internal dynamics. For some, this choice grew out of pragmatic necessity. In the Calvados, close to a third of divorcés took this path because they faced long-term abandonment, had won an Old Regime séparation de corps, or chose to sever their ties with a spouse who had emigrated or been condemned for criminal acts. Doubtless these official classifications of "grounds" paper over the complexity of these individuals' motives and emotions, but by and large they divorced at least in part to regularize lives already disrupted. Divorce offered these women and men—already separated from their spouses—the chance to free themselves from encumbering legal ties and to move on.

But the revolutionary climate and the possibility of divorce also kindled expectations among both wives and husbands that marriage should be rooted in conviviality, individual liberty, and personal happiness as well as pragmatism. This opinion was hardly new in the 1790s, but only with the

Revolution would it become legally possible to act on this notion, escape a miserable marriage, and seek a new spouse. Furthermore, revolutionary politics provided a framework, a legitimacy for decrying conjugal inequities or unhappiness. In the Calvados in the 1790s, almost one-fifth of divorcing couples (18 percent) made a reciprocal agreement to end their partnership and divorce by mutual consent. Another 35 percent of spouses chose "incompatibility" as their grounds for divorce. This easily accessible, catch-all category could conceal a host of motives, but its very existence as well as its frequent use put directly into practice the controversial idea that marriage should be based on mutual accord and reciprocal choice. In ending their unions, many divorcés acted on the pamphleteers' idealized proclamations that only a freely chosen, affectionate marriage could tie individuals to each other and to the social contract. As one unhappily married petitioner from Caen promised the legislators in September 1792, he would be the first to give an example "of liberty by breaking these cruel chains and living forever free in the bosom of loving friendship and happiness, invaluable for the life of every good French patriot."[114]

For abused, heartbroken, or abandoned wives, this transformation in the realm of marital practice and imagination proved especially crucial. Since men held greater authority and economic autonomy within marriage, unhappily married husbands were far less likely to initiate divorce than their wives were. For many women, particularly those who had been mistreated or deserted, divorce offered the only opportunity to gain control over their lives and property and to make a new start. The struggle to divorce also galvanized many women's relationship with politics and the republican state. Elisabeth Clay of Reims, for example, pushed her divorce property case all the way to the Committee of Legislation in 1794 and succeeded in convincing its members that it would not "be just for a wife, often brought to divorce by the errors of her husband, to lose her recompense . . . the just compensation for her participation in their common work."[115] The possibility of divorce encouraged wives to challenge the dominance of husbands within marriage and to ask most directly what equality meant within the conjugal frame. However, this opportunity was most possible for urban women of artisanal or middle-class backgrounds. To note how profoundly geography, class, and urban-rural differences affected access to divorce highlights how various women had disparate opportunities and experiences during the Revolution and helps us begin to build a portrait of those differences.

As the Revolution took a more conservative turn after Thermidor, divorce, especially divorce for incompatibility, became symbolic of the radicalism of revolutionary family reform. Perhaps more than any other aspect of family policy, it wrenched traditional expectations about gender, hierarchy, and family unity away from their Old Regime moorings. By stressing the freedom of the individual—male or female—to break the conjugal tie, it questioned the naturalness, inevitability, and strength of the family in general and marriage in particular as a unit of social cohesion. Time and again, it introduced the palpable reality of a woman challenging the givenness of male authority. By treating male and female adultery on the same legal plane, this innovation undercut long-held assumptions about the greater sanctity of female fidelity. By dividing up marital property, divorce threw a spanner into families' economic strategies and undercut male control over goods. To many this act seemed dangerous to the gender order, even though it left women impoverished more often than it did men.

Post-Thermidorian contestation over divorce, sexuality, gender, and the social order made clear how much divorce crystallized the tension at the heart of the revolutionary attitudes toward marriage. For marriage to be truly regenerative and central to citizenship, it had to be happy, freely chosen, mutually contracted, and fulfilling to each individual: the freedom to sever that bond was fundamental to the very essence of republican marriage. But at the same time, the revolutionaries counted on marriage to stand as the quintessential unit that naturally, morally, and legally underpinned the social unity of the Republic and citizenship. For this reason, divorce seemed simultaneously necessary and deeply threatening.

4. "War between Brothers and Sisters"

Egalitarian Inheritance and Gender Politics

In the spring of 1795 the citoyenne LeFranc of Caen penned an angry warning to the National Convention: "You have only passed one law beneficial to women, the law of 17 nivôse [which guarantees equal partitions of inheritance.] If you destroy this law of equality that has converted to the Republic an infinity of women and girls led astray by the fanaticism of priests, they will say with good reason that you are unjust and that you have taken advantage of the fact that we are not represented at the Convention. . . . They will say to you that men have made the laws and they have made them for themselves." LeFranc was not the only French citizen with strong opinions about the new inheritance laws designed to introduce equality into the family, nor was she the only one to view the reform of the family as, at least in part, a contest over gender dynamics within family and nation. In their petition to the deputies several months earlier, the male citizens Lenoir and Lammarré had argued from the opposite viewpoint, denouncing the new laws that had torn apart the "tranquility of families" and "had depaternalized, defraternized, and desocialized [France]. . . . The social order is entirely overturned. . . . The sister is engaged in open warfare with her brother."[1]

While divorce produced an ample share of litigation, no aspect of family restructuring generated more contention in court or more outbursts of popular approval or anger than the new inheritance laws. As the Revolution grew more radical, successive legislatures passed increasingly egalitarian inheritance laws. After abolishing primogeniture in 1790, the National Assembly decreed in April 1791 that intestate estates must be divided equally among all children, regardless of sex or birth order. By 1793–94 the Convention extended this egalitarian principle to *all* forms of inheritance in both direct and collateral lines: the deputies pronounced that all offspring—including illegitimate ones recognized by their parents—would divide family property evenly. Most controversially, this egalitarian partition was made retroactive to July 1789. Striking at the heart of family structures, property arrangements, and agrarian customs, these reforms provoked intense and acrid controversy. While thousands of men and women called on family tribunals across France to untangle the intricacies of Old Regime practices, revolutionary law, and family relations, many citizens also peppered the various national legislatures with petitions, pamphlets, and individual appeals. Indeed, during the 1790s the French wrote more petitions on inheritance reform than on any other aspect of civil law.[2]

The revision of inheritance law had a profound impact on the relationships among siblings and between parent and child. In certain areas of France, such as the Midi and parts of the North, the new policies undercut the traditional prerogative of the father to direct family strategy by offering preferential legacies to one or more of his children. In northern and western locales that already practiced egalitarian inheritance, fathers still found their control over family goods hampered by the prohibition of entailment, which had allowed a testator to disqualify his or her immediate heir in favor of the heir's successors.[3] In addition to weakening paternal authority, the reforms affected gender relations within households, not only because many regions of France traditionally favored sons over daughters as heirs, but also because marriage arrangements were inextricably bound up with the eventual partitions of estates. Moreover, by offering equal inheritance rights to women as rights-bearing individuals, the reforms threw a wrench into customary allocations of family goods and called into question traditional assumptions about the status and position of women. The revolutionary state was reaching its hand into the family and tampering with intricate webs of mutual obligation, woven on the basis of generational and gendered roles. Especially in regions accustomed to primogeniture, legacy-making by fathers, or customary exclusions based on gender, sisters and/or younger brothers flocked to court to seize the opportunities promised by the new laws.

Out of the various conflicts and possibilities opened up by succession reform, this chapter will focus on its implications for gender dynamics within families and on women's response to the new laws. These legal changes would affect individual women differently: women in certain regions and certain positions in the family were especially likely to embrace the new policies. Inheritance reform gave new legal standing to many women in Normandy, the Midi, and pockets of the North, East, and Center, where daughters generally had no claim on parental legacies beyond their original dowry or their *légitime* (lawful portion). For some families, these changes in women's economic and legal status demanded that parents and siblings rethink the nature of their interpersonal relationships and imagine different family strategies and internal hierarchies.

I will also argue that in these same areas, the demand for inheritance reform became a basic arena of female legal activism and revolutionary politicization, as various women first demanded egalitarian reforms and then fought to enact and defend this newly won right. Keenly aware of their new relationship to property, family, and the state, many women in these regions developed various political and legal means to make their claims known and implemented whenever possible. To examine this activism and to probe the impact of civil reform on internal family dynamics, I will analyze litigation over inheritance law in Normandy through a case study of the family courts in the district of Caen between 1790 and 1796, with some consideration of the ongoing contestation until 1799 under the Civil Tribunal's jurisdiction. I will then set this examination within the broader context of popular petitioning and agitation from across France, paying particular attention to petitioning by women.

PATERNAL AUTHORITY UNDER ASSAULT

As many historians have pointed out, the patriarchal authority of fathers underpinned the absolutist political system of early modern France. Political theory, popular traditions, religious beliefs, and royal law all drew parallels between the political authority of kings and the domestic power of fathers. "To love, to govern, to recompense, and to punish are all duties both of the father and of the king," wrote the moralist François Vincent Toussaint in 1748.[4] Within the household, the father's rule sometimes took on forms that seemed excessively harsh to late eighteenth-century critics. Fathers, for example, requested more than half of all the Old Regime lettres de cachet. They used this mechanism to preserve their families' honor, to keep daughters from unsuitable sexual engagements, and to punish sons for disobedience, dissipation, or delinquency. Much more often, fathers made their authority felt informally. As Rétif de la Bretonne commented about his grandfather, the ultimate patriarch, "The father, so friendly with outsiders, was terrible inside the family: he commanded with a look [whose meaning] you had to guess."[5] By the late Old Regime, however, a new model of sentimental fatherhood had emerged and found expression across a gamut of genres. Novelists, painters, authors of Catholic catechisms, philosophes, and parlementary magistrates all contributed to shaping a new image of more responsive and less autocratic fathers. This questioning of puissance paternelle appears also to have affected family practices. For instance, Yves Castan has discovered that younger sons in Languedoc expressed greater defiance of their fathers' authority in the decades after 1760, while Jeffrey Merrick has traced the escalating expectations of affection among aristocratic sons.[6]

Notwithstanding these hopes for paternal tenderness, everywhere in France fathers held their children's future in their hands: the division of goods was one realm where fathers made their power most manifest. Regional variations in inheritance practices, customary laws, and household structure influenced the nature of patriarchal authority and of parent-child relations. Roughly speaking, France was divided into two broad familial systems.[7] Most provinces south of the Loire River favored a single heir with smaller portions (légitimes) for the other siblings; fathers had the right to grant legacies as they wished. The South also had a higher prevalence of stem families: in a typical stem family, the main heir, usually the eldest son, stayed in the family household and lived with his parents, his in-marrying wife, and their offspring. In the North, egalitarian inheritance, communal marital property, and nuclear households more often held sway. While fathers wielded power over their patrimony, they had to work within customary limits on their testamentary power.

This bold, dualistic portrait immediately needs nuancing to suggest local variations and diversity. In a broad stripe across central France—from Poitou east to Franche-Comté passing through the Limousin, Auvergne, Berry, Nivernais, and Morvan—some families lived in large communitarian households, made up of several generations of nuclear units or of two brothers and their offspring (frérèches) all under one roof. This central section of France included a complicated transition zone of inheritance patterns where the system of preferential legacies mingled with more egalitarian practices. In addition, pockets of primogeniture existed in the North and East as well as the Southwest. Also, within Normandy, the "egalitarian" system was severely limited: only sons took part in the equal division of legacies, and all daughters who had brothers received only a very limited share of their parents' goods.[8] (See Map 2.)

When civil law jurists in the revolutionary legislatures looked on this jumble of diverse laws and practices, they saw legal disunity, inequities among offspring, and, above all, the arbitrary authority of fathers. The Midi came to represent the apotheosis of paternal power and inequity among offspring in general, and sons in particular.[9] Here Roman law allowed fathers not only to divide their patrimony as they saw fit, but also to wait until their sons were well into adulthood before "emancipating" them and granting

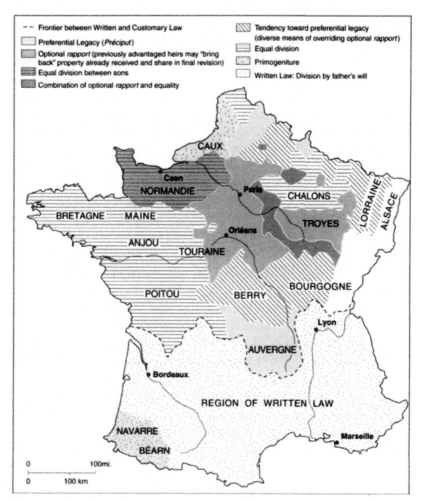

Map 2. Inheritance customs in Old Regime France

them full legal autonomy and the right to manage their own goods. Normandy ran a close second to the Midi as a regional symbol of patriarchal injustice. The Norman custom, with its particular exclusion of daughters, invoked both gender inequity and parental tyranny.[10]

From 1789 on, pamphleteers and petitioners from these areas began to pour forth their suggestions for inheritance reform. They argued that the unequal partition of family goods smacked of favoritism, feudalism, and geographic particularism. These petitioners also tapped into the emerging image of more affectionate, less "tyrannical" fathers.[11] "What cruelty!" lamented one Monsieur Dutemple from Corrèze as he denounced the

Roman law system in favor of a more fraternal sharing of both goods and affection. This campaign found support in political clubs and the press as well. On behalf of the Cercle Social, François Lanthenas led a crusade for a more egalitarian system and then founded a new club, the Société des Amis de l'Union et de l'Egalité dans les Familles, to lobby against primogeniture. This club counted prominent patriots among its members, including Brissot, Bonneville, Jean-Henri Bancal, and Louis-Sébastien Mercier. From a different quarter, the Parisian popular journal *Lettres bougrement patriotiques de la Mère Duchêne* offered its gritty and voluble support, especially on behalf of the female sex. As she consigned to the devil the Norman custom "and all those that resemble it," the Mère Duchêne indicted those succession practices that left women propertyless "in the dust" and forced them "to scratch the earth in order to live."[12]

Even as the press and petitions condemned inequality within families, the National Assembly had begun to take steps to lessen paternal authority. Following the abolition of the nobility, the lawmakers outlawed primogeniture in March 1790. In that same month, in response to vocal criticism and debate, the deputies eradicated the lettres de cachet that had allowed fathers to imprison their children at will. That summer the Assembly assigned the task of disciplining children to family arbitration courts, rather than fathers.[13]

But it was the issue of equal inheritance that provoked the most prolonged debate within the successive assemblies. Within hours after Mirabeau's death on 2 April 1791, Talleyrand rose in the National Assembly to read a speech just penned by the dying man. In support of Merlin de Douai's proposal for a more egalitarian division of legacies, Mirabeau launched an angry attack on the power of fathers "not just to disinherit their children, but to sell them." He also argued forcefully that the right to leave a legacy was not a natural right, but rather a civil one, which the nation should regulate for the social good. This one-time victim of a lettre de cachet flagellated paternal despotism, allied inegalitarian inheritance with feudalism and privilege, and painted a glowing portrait of the emotional and economic benefits of a more egalitarian system. He touched on the major motives and arguments that would resurface repeatedly as the successive legislatures gradually dismantled the inheritance customs of the Old Regime.[14]

Popular petitioning and left-wing political lobbying dovetailed to reinforce the arguments set forth by Mirabeau and his allies. In this same April 1791 debate, the deputy Pétion foregrounded the natural equality of children and sketched an even darker image of "denatured fathers," whose ambitions and cynical maneuvers could not be trusted. Equally intent on curtailing puissance paternelle, Robespierre suggested that filial piety should stem from "the nature, care, tenderness, and virtue of fathers." He debunked a familial system built on excessive patriarchal power, hierarchy, greed, and manipulation that tore apart both fraternal and father-child relations. Eloquently positioning equality as "the basis of social happiness," he also evoked the need to unify French legal customs and make one code, one people.[15]

Not surprisingly, deputies from the Midi and Normandy emerged as the most vocal opponents of inheritance reform. The southern ex-nobleman, Cazalès, defended the natural liberty of fathers to make wills and praised the social order and economic vitality brought by this system. To force equal partition of land would undermine agricultural productivity and destabilize society. Like Cazalès, the Norman deputies Lambert de Frondeville and Achard de Bonvouloir lauded the agrarian utility of their local customs and invoked Montesquieu's notion that laws should reflect the habits and customs of a people. Cazalès in turn rushed to the defense of his Norman allies and their customary exclusion of daughters from legacies. As Lambert de Frondeville observed, if you ask a cultivateur "whether his land and movable goods should be evenly divided between his daughters and sons, . . . he will respond that his land should belong to his sons after him, because their hands guided the plough that fertilized [this land.] . . . Work is the first title of property." For these deputies, justice lay in fulfilling regional traditions and long-standing patterns of expectation, rooted "in the climate, the soil, the number, the morals, and the spirit of a people." These defenses of local tradition and patriarchal stability met with resistance: legislator Louis-Jean Darnaudat equated prerevolutionary customs with privilege and declared that in the new nation, "There is no more Normandy, there are no more Normans."[16]

The lawmakers of the Constituent Assembly moved cautiously. Despite the strong impetus toward creating unified national law, restraining paternal authority, and recognizing equal rights within the home, numerous moderate deputies remained wary of alienating the Midi and Normandy. They reached a compromise solution in April 1791. They did not abolish fathers' rights to make testaments, but did mandate the equal division of *intestate* estates among all offspring without regard for sex or birth order. This same law explicitly abolished the customary practice of excluding daughters from successions. But it also excepted from its new mandates all those with existing marriage contracts, as well as those widowed with children.[17] Despite the moderation of the new law, a fundamental conceptual threshold had been crossed. As Pierre Murat has pointed out, in these April 1791 debates, the deputies "had dared to think of the transmission of property in terms of political equality and individual rights, and no longer only as the perpetuation of a family line [directed] even beyond death by the temporary head" of household. In August 1792 the Legislative Assembly pushed this logic a bit further by outlawing entailment and by curtailing parental authority over adult children's property and marital arrangements. These policies emerged during the debates over laicizing civil records, discussed in Chapter 2. To define the legal status of the individual, liberate youthful fiancés from parental oversight, and guarantee all children equal access to family goods—these objectives all formed part of the same project.[18]

During 1793, egalitarian fervor increased with the radicalization of republican politics. As internal and external war turned up the political heat, some deputies suspected that fathers' abuse of testamentary power could work against the nation. The political goal of stopping counterrevolutionary behavior added fuel to the social desire to institute domestic equality, favor the young, and spread wealth more evenly. At the same time, Jacobin lawmakers intently embraced the Enlightenment concept that well-crafted laws could regenerate morals and emotions at this crucial moment (see Figure 8). In March 1793, the Jacobin deputy Pénières demanded a law against those antipatriotic and antiegalitarian fathers: "We will attack aristocracy even in the tomb and take away its surest means of destroying our liberty." When Jean-Baptiste Mailhe proposed broadening this goal and denying all fathers the right to make wills, Pierre Philippeaux leaped onto the bandwagon, declaring "A hundred thousand younger brothers await this law before flying to the frontiers." On the spot the Convention decreed in principle that will-making would be abolished and that citizens had to leave their property equally to all offspring. This decree left it to the Committee of Legislation to work out the details of a more democratic inheritance system. With the goal of creating one unified body of civil law for the new republic, that committee spent the summer of 1793 reading some 6,000 family law petitions from across France and drawing up the first draft of the Civil Code. The Code made mandatory the egalitarian division of goods among all children.[19]

Although the entire Civil Code did not become law in the super-heated politics of the fall of 1793, the Convention salvaged the Code's inheritance reforms and passed them as independent laws. By the law of 12 brumaire an II (2 November 1793), illegitimate children were granted an equal share in family legacies, provided that they were recognized by their fathers and were not the product of adultery.[20] (The next two chapters will unpack this

Figure 8. Good laws create the happiness of peoples (between 1793 and 1795). Courtesy of the Bibliothèque nationale de France.

law and explore the complex interaction between illegitimate children, their unwed parents, and revolutionary policies and politics.) Equally controversial and more widespread in their effects were the all-important laws of 5 brumaire an II (26 October 1793) and 17 nivôse an II (6 January 1794). These decrees, retroactive to July 1789, outlined detailed rules for egalitarian partition among direct descendants, and in their absence, among collateral relatives. Testators now had very little freedom to choose heirs: they could dispose of only small portions of their property: one-tenth if they had direct descendants and one-sixth if they had no children.[21] These two laws dramatically overturned long-held family customs and opened the door to litigation by sisters and younger brothers. The attempt to implement the new practices stimulated further popular petitioning on both sides of the issue and provoked more legislative debate and explanatory decrees. Although the retroactive prescriptions of these laws would be overturned in the fall of 1795, their stringent egalitarianism persisted throughout the Revolution and ultimately was partially tempered by the Civil Code.[22]

"DOWERED FOR A BOUQUET OF ROSES": INHERITANCE CONTESTATION IN FAMILY COURTS

These revolutionary revisions in inheritance law had a profound significance for women's civil rights and access to property. But the laws' influence was hardly uniform. The varying geography of Old Regime inheritance law and marital practices played a large role in influencing the specific impact of these reforms on individual women. Daughters were most likely to benefit from these innovations in certain regions: most obviously, in the Midi and Normandy; in regions operating by primogeniture, such as the Boulonnais, Béarn, Navarre, and the Pays de Caux (within Normandy); and in areas slightly north of the written law boundary, such as the Auvergne, Burgundy, and Berry, where customs influenced by Roman law tended to favor preferential legacy *(préciput)*.

Each woman's particular position within the family was a second crucial factor in determining her reaction to the new laws. Some favored daughters without brothers and also the wives of favored sons lost out in property redivisions. Widows in certain marital property regimes could be hurt by the limitations on gifts between spouses and the suppression of customary dowers; some courts also interpreted the 17 nivôse law as having suppressed existing dowers.[23] But the new laws enabled numerous daughters to demand a larger share of legacies. And the abolition of the male prerogative to the lion's share of inheritance implicitly gave women higher status within the family. Many women who petitioned for egalitarian inheritance seemed to share the opinion of an anonymous journalist, who was most likely Madame Roland. She wrote in 1789: "One of the most harmful effects of primogeniture is that it regularly exposes the mother of a family to the contempt and vexations of her husband and the sons preferred by him."[24] In the regions of contestation noted above, traditional resistance to the legal changes was deep-rooted. Yet daughters, wives, and widows wrote petitions asserting their succession rights; widows and sisters, often allied with younger brothers, used the courts to demand equalizing divisions or redivisions of family legacies.

The district of Caen, the judicial heart of Lower Normandy, provides a particularly good region for assessing the impact of the new inheritance laws on family dynamics and on women's legal activism because an explicit gender bias informed Norman inheritance practices, yet litigation shared points in common with other regions of inegalitarian partitions. According to tradition, Norman families sought above all to preserve and promote the family line: the all-important obligation to maintain family property and unity overrode any individual desires or ambitions. A complex system of customary law reinforced and even reified these practices by placing tight limits on the disposition of property.[25] To sustain the lineage system, families favored sons over daughters. Norman law restricted daughters to a small dowry or a légitime portion, paid as an annual pension (*rente*), and then excluded them from further claims on the legacies of their parents, siblings, or collateral relatives. Although the custom required brothers to pay légitimes to their sisters, fathers were under no legal obligation to offer dowries to their daughters. As the old expressions went, "A father can dower his daughter with a bouquet of roses"; "He owes his daughter a husband and nothing more." The law even limited the generosity of parents with sons towards their daughters: regardless of the number of girls in the family, their total inheritance share could not legally surpass one-third of the parents' property, unless that property fell within the limits of certain cities.[26] In contrast, brothers benefited from equal division of the remaining inheritance, except in the Pays de Caux where primogeniture persisted.[27]

Once married, the Norman woman forged an economic unit of survival with her husband: "to make one family . . . and be able to eat bread together more easily," as the gardener Nicolas Labbé put it. On occasion, the young woman would move in with her husband's family, although conjugal families were far more common than stem families in Normandy, and particularly dominated within the town of Caen.[28] Even marriage did not entirely fortify the woman's economic position, since Norman law prohibited communal marital property and gifts between spouses, and since a young woman could expect little financial help from her family of origin. Norman law nonetheless offered widows some minimal protection by tightly limiting the husband's ability to use his wife's dowry and by guaranteeing certain dower rights to widows.[29] Despite their disadvantaged position by law, Norman women had long engaged actively in litigation over family goods and played a prominent role in local market and artisanal economies. Moreover, Zoe Schneider has pointed out a central paradox in the Old Regime Norman custom: although women were not supposed to control property, due to the dotal regime many goods passed through the female line and at various life moments, women would have the possibility of controlling these goods and of engaging in litigation to direct or protect them.[30] The Revolution would widen these opportunities for women to step into court.

Because of the specific nature of Norman customary law, struggles over revolutionary inheritance reforms took on a particular cast as a battle between brothers and sisters. For purposes of analysis, this trend allows the isolation of female litigants more easily than in the Midi. Yet, while the alignment of sisters versus brothers was especially prevalent in Normandy, the nature of the struggle over parental legacies nonetheless had much in common with conflict in the Midi governed by written law, as well as in areas of primogeniture or preferential legacy in parts of the North, East, and Center. As the historian Alain Collomp has commented about familial reactions to the 17 nivôse law in Provence, "It was the revenge of the younger brothers and above all of the younger sisters, sisters of the heir, who claimed substantial légitime increases from their brothers, in order to supplement their dowries and make their shares equal to their brothers'."[31] As in Normandy, in all of these areas, revolutionary reforms raised the salient question of how family strategies based on obligation and sacrifice for the family line would incorporate a new definition of the individual, especially if that individual were female.

In the Old Regime, family conflicts could fall under the varied jurisdiction of seigneurial or ecclesiastical courts, or—increasingly in the 1700s—under the royal jurisdiction of prévôtés (provost's court), bailliages, and ultimately the parlements (high royal courts).[32] But after the National Assembly created family tribunals in August 1790, these temporary arbitration courts dealt with inheritance questions. As in divorce cases, two arbiters represented each litigant. Most often, the four arbiters settled the matter, but sometimes they had to choose a fifth arbiter to break a deadlock.[33] By and large, the family courts dealt with inheritance cases more than any other issue.[34] In my sample of 219 family court cases in the district of Caen between 1791 and 1796, roughly two-thirds (143 cases) dealt with inheritance.[35] These conflicts fell into three main categories. Contests between siblings made up almost 60 percent of the cases (83 out of 143). A little more than a quarter of the cases, 40 out of the 143, involved settling the property rights of widows, or, on rare occasions, widowers.[36] In the remaining 23 cases, collaterals or outsiders made succession claims.

Property-owning men and women from a wide range of classes made use of the family tribunals. Unfortunately, the records for the district of Caen almost never give occupational information on the litigants, but the amounts in contestation illustrate the broad social span of participants. While Marie Angélique Roussel and her husband Philippe Despars won 15,728 livres and 2 sous from her brothers after a five-month dispute over arrears of her légitime, Anne Fontaine and her husband gained a mere 6 livres and 1 sou as a yearly income from her brother Jacques as a result of the 17 nivôse law, and the widow Geneviève Betourné went to court repeatedly to defend her pathetic paraphernalia of a few handkerchiefs and other odds and ends.[37] The lack of precise figures, the variety of complex property types, and the vagaries of the assignat make it unworkable to come up with a reliable average of the amounts in contestation.[38] The majority of cases dealt with small annual rentes of about 50 to 300 livres or with flat sums between 300 and 2,000 livres, together with assorted material goods. As a point of comparison, Olwen Hufton estimates that poor families in nearby Bayeux needed about 300–400 livres a year to subsist; manual laborers typically left only about 40 livres worth of material possessions. In the wealthier city of Paris, Old Regime wage earners left behind an average fortune all told of 1,776 livres, while mistress seamstresses left a median fortune worth 1,880 livres and bakers' inventories had a median worth of 5,129 livres.[39] These comparisons suggest that all but the poorest segments of society made use of the family courts, but that heavy use came from small to middling property holders.

The proceedings of family courts were relatively informal. The four arbiters chosen by the opposing parties generally met at the home of one of the arbiters or at the local inn to hear the presentations of the litigants, review any written materials (such as marriage contracts or short legal briefs), listen to witnesses if necessary, and attempt to resolve differences in an amicable fashion. Since cases could be complex and since litigants and arbiters might stonewall or fail to appear, the family tribunal often met more than once. Of the inheritance cases in the district of Caen, about two-thirds were settled in less than two months, while a sixth took two to six months, and another sixth dragged on for even longer.[40] Over the course of the deliberations, one of the arbiters drew up a record of the proceedings in whatever degree of detail seemed appropriate, and then eventually registered the final decision with the clerk of the district tribunal at Caen. Except for cases involving the 17 nivôse law, these results could in turn be appealed to the district tribunal, which also had the authority to enforce the family tribunals' decisions. It sometimes used process-servers to force delinquent defendants to pay or even auctioned sequestered goods. In appeals cases, the district tribunal also reinforced proper arbitration procedures and overturned only those decisions that clearly flouted revolutionary laws.[41]

Although the creators of the family court system envisioned the arbiters almost exclusively as relatives or neighbors, in the district of Caen, as elsewhere, litigants increasingly chose men with legal training to represent them and decide their cases. In the town of Caen, as in Dijon, Lyon, Montpellier, Rouen, Laon, and Angoulême, a group of hommes de loi gradually earned a reputation as specialists in family arbitration.[42] Tie-breaking surabitres and arbiters named by the justice of the peace when necessary were almost always legally qualified men. Critics of the family court system often fingered this dominance of hommes de loi as a corrupting influence. One antagonist in Lyon called them "reptiles," "ogres," and "birds of prey who dwell inside cadavers to devour their prey all the more easily." Yet their legal training undoubtedly helped them to sort out the complex web of civil law in the 1790s: while the new legislation governed certain matters, tortuous customary law continued to hold sway wherever it had not yet been replaced or revised. In short, arbiters and judges struggled to interpret and enforce an intricate mosaic of Old Regime and revolutionary law, which only the Civil Code of 1804 would codify.[43]

Largely because they implemented controversial inheritance laws, the family courts fell under considerable criticism, provoking their abolition in 1796; in the nineteenth century, historians often condemned their practices. But overall, historians who have studied the family tribunals emphasize that they operated relatively efficiently and fairly. As James Traer notes, the family court "was not bound by old jurisprudence and legal formalities, and hence it could and often did render more flexible justice than could be had in the regular court system."[44] Perhaps local authorities agreed: despite their official suppression early in 1796, family tribunals in the Calvados continued to arbitrate some family conflicts until 1799 under the jurisdiction of the new Civil Tribunal.[45]

This flexible procedural style of the family courts had some striking practical effects for women in civil cases. Notably, the particular structure of these courts combined with the complex mixture of new and old laws to allow certain groups of women, sometimes with the help of their husbands, not only to reawaken and settle Old Regime injustices, but also to make new, unprecedented, and successful claims on family property and to enlist the state on their behalf. Furthermore, the courts became forums for negotiating the impact of revolutionary law and ideology on gender dynamics within the home. To make their decisions, the arbiters drew on a fluid combination of cultural norms, new and old laws, and pragmatic considerations.[46] As arbiters and litigants alike strove to untangle custom, Revolution, and family, the court proceedings reveal a fundamental tension over the changed relationship of women to the family and the state. Most crucially, the family tribunals repeatedly made decisions that called into question traditional gender roles and assumptions.

In many cases, women who entered arbitration were essentially defying deeply embedded practices as well as family unity. Obviously, various women had litigated against family members in the Old Regime, but the revolutionary laws had upped the ante by attempting to institute new family norms and behaviors. Since it was no small matter to pit oneself against habitual lineage strategies, women in certain positions in the family were far more likely to undertake litigation. Most frequently, sisters demanded shares of their patrimony, and widows fought to sort out their dotal rights. To justify their bold actions, litigating women sometimes denounced the inequities of traditional customs and above all, cited financial need and/or allegiance to their new nuclear family.[47]

It is important to recognize that while the new laws aimed at creating equality for individuals within households, they also validated the nuclear unit in opposition to the family line.[48] Within this realignment of kinship relations, women, especially married sisters, could carve out a stronger position for themselves by winning cases on behalf of their new families. By invoking egalitarian rights within the home and by opposing the dominant prerogatives of the extended family, litigating women moved in practice toward redefining their own status within the household.

Widows and women who were unmarried, separated, or divorced most often represented themselves, though a few enlisted a male family member, a proxy *(fondé de pouvoir)*, or a solicitor *(procureur)* to present their cases to the arbiters. As in the Old Regime, married women were usually represented legally by their husbands, though many of these women laid out their own arguments during the tribunal sessions. In sibling inheritance disputes, one brother-in-law often acted on behalf of his wife and her sisters, whether married or unmarried. The new courts did not overturn the prerevolutionary practice and assumption that the husband stood as agent for the couple "in his wife's name." For example, when the plaintiff Eléonore Marie married during the course of the tribunal's deliberations, the family court requested that her new husband François Quesnel approve her choice of arbiters. Women never served as arbiters themselves.[49]

Yet, as in the Old Regime, some married women legally represented their own interests or acted as informal or formal agents *(portresses de pouvoir)* for husbands or brothers under attack. For example, the femme Lebourg represented her husband's concerns in a contest versus his sister and brother-in-law in 1794. And in a reversal of the typical pattern of a son-in-law taking his wife's father to court over unpaid dowry items, the citoyenne Marc represented her husband in a suit against his father.[50] The newness, relative informality, and local nature of family courts may well have made this practice of women representing men more common than before. At other times, however, women fell back on more traditional claims of legal powerlessness to protect their husbands or themselves from the law. In October 1792 Marie Levernieux came to the family court session and argued vociferously on her husband's behalf against his stepmother, but when the tide seemed to turn against them, she suddenly pleaded ignorance and claimed that in his absence, "she could not make any agreements on his behalf."[51] Since the various revolutionary reforms had awakened uncertainty about women's exact legal status, individual women worked this lack of clarity to their own advantage.[52]

Most notably, sisters, with their husbands if they were married, repeatedly defeated their brothers in court, upsetting customary family strategies and encouraging more women to push for legal changes. Of the 83 sibling contests, 58 pitted sisters against brothers; sisters clearly won 45 (78 percent) of these cases, and negotiated a compromise in 6 of the remaining cases. While it is impossible to know how many of them collected their funds, the courts levied serious fines on those who failed to comply and the district court took action against some delinquents. Many widows also made successful use of family arbitration to settle their dotal rights at their husbands' deaths or even to regain their rightful dotal shares uncollected in the Old Regime. The court structure facilitated the collection of widows' pensions and often acted to safeguard widows' customary rights. The 17 nivôse law abolished customary dowers in future marriages by replacing customary arrangements with the communal marital property system, but the statute left open to interpretation the status of dowers of women already married. In fact, in Normandy, both the family tribunals and later the appeals courts consistently allowed widows to use the law to maintain their customary dower shares.[53] In addition, as I will discuss below, Norman widows without children particularly benefited from the 17 nivôse law, which allowed them to receive gifts from their husbands. Yet generally speaking, in Normandy the new laws had a much more striking impact on daughters than on widows.

Early in the Revolution, the family court structure made it relatively simple and inexpensive for sisters to demand arrears on unpaid légitimes or, in a few cases, to reopen procedures left over from the bailliages or parlement of the Old Regime. Sibling tension over unpaid légitimes was endemic in prerevolutionary Normandy, as in other parts of France. As some forty citoyennes from Calvados commented in their petition to the National Convention, many unmarried women "lack the bare necessities of life while their brothers, living in abundance, stubbornly deny them not only humanitarian aid but even the small share that the old custom accorded."[54] Numerous family courts met only once and simply asserted the legal claim of a sister on her brother or brothers, ordering them to pay. In some cases, plaintiffs took advantage of the new institution of the family tribunal to open up very old légitime claims or more complex Old Regime cases. The citoyenne Françoise Eustache veuve Lepeinteur successfully took her maternal uncle to family court to reclaim the légitime that he owed her mother who had passed away, while the unmarried Thérèse Pépin seized the initiative and represented her sister and two brothers in a fruitful claim to regain their father's legacy, "usurped from them twenty-three years ago" by an uncle who now had nothing to say in his own defense.[55]

The laws of 5 brumaire and, above all, 17 nivôse were responsible for many of these contests among siblings, as well as among collateral relatives. Although in most cases the arbiters simply enforced the law without much discussion of its content, the simmering tension over this deeply gendered "trouble in the family" sometimes broke through to the surface as litigants referred to the revolutionary principles underpinning the new inheritance laws. In 1795 the Letourneur sisters argued successfully that "the law of equality without distinction according to sex had been established much earlier" in the Revolution and could not be overturned by later laws revoking retroactive effects. Another triumphant sister taunted her brothers with gleeful reminders of their lost prerogative as sons. In November 1793 when the unmarried Victoire Leprovost led her two widowed sisters Scolastique and Louise in a demand that their brother redivide their paternal inheritance, the brother hedged, dragged his heels, and finally demanded at least to choose his share first. His sisters retorted that "since the new laws had abolished any privileges of the oldest or youngest as well as the privilege of masculinity," the four children should choose their lots by chance; but they taunted him with the offer to choose lots according to birth order. Needless to say, their brother was the youngest. No doubt angered by this last dig, the brother walked out of the arbitration session, refusing to sign, while the arbiters pronounced that the drawing of lots would be done by chance in the presence of the commissioner of the district.[56]

Although most sisters did not tease their brothers as did the Leprevosts, many were persistent. When the widow Langlouard failed in her first attempt to use the 8 April 1791 law to share the inheritance of the curé Guillot with her brother Thomas Guillot, she declared, "I will persevere," and did, in fact, succeed in a second claim according to the 5 brumaire law. On occasion, the family tribunal structure combined with the new laws and the presence of reformist lawyers to encourage the most daring women to make even more radical demands on their brothers. Late in 1794, for example, Angélique Poignaut, recently emboldened or perhaps just impoverished by divorce, requested that the family court force her brother to increase the size of the dowry he had offered her back in 1779. She argued that the annual payment of 130 livres was far less than her légitime of 400 livres a year would have been. The arbiters turned down her proposal and expressed alarm at the concept of other divorced women upsetting "family peace" with requests for higher dowries. "The law cannot admit revisions so unjust and so troubling to the tranquility of families," they concluded.[57]

Especially in redivisions ordered retroactively, brothers were understandably reluctant to surrender land that they had already improved or cultivated. They developed a whole repertoire of moves to delay court decisions: lost inventories, contracts, and deeds, no-show arbiters, no-show defendants, and elaborate excuses and ruses became common. Given the instability of revolutionary politics, some hoped to stonewall long enough that the law would be altered or repealed. These maneuvers in turn forced determined plaintiffs to call repeated court sessions and, in some cases, to hire legal help. The frustrated Rogne sisters Marie and Marie Jeanne denounced the "trickery" of Norman men who deliberately chose their "best and most stubborn friends" as arbiters to drag out court cases. They suggested that the National Convention authorize commissioners to speed up cases by standing in for missing brothers or arbiters. In addition, testators seeking to favor sons over daughters came up with various means of eluding the law through false sales, forced gifts between siblings, légitimes paid in near worthless assignats, new forms of marriage contracts, and so forth. By and large, however, the family courts were remarkably persistent in implementing the new laws. In cases where brothers dilly-dallied too long, most arbiters simply made a decision without the brother(s) ever having appeared.[58]

As they interpreted and carried out the new laws benefiting sisters, the family courts seem to have been keenly aware that restoring legacy rights to daughters as individuals could violate family expectations and disadvantage brothers who had worked on paternal lands. Particularly in settling retroactive 17 nivôse cases, some arbiters mitigated the harshness of the law by assessing the value of brothers' or sons' work on their parents' property and reducing the required payments to sisters or widowed mothers accordingly. Family courts sometimes heard the testimony of neighbors or experts to determine these values and did their best to sort out shares of future and past harvests, locations of threshing, and so on. Justice cut both ways: when the brother Vasnier secretly removed all the manure and animal bedding from a piece of contested land, the arbiters calmly waded in to rescue some of the material for his two sisters.[59]

Since the family courts sought to integrate egalitarian inheritance into an older moral code of mutual obligation, the women who used family arbitration were most often successful if they could make traditional moral and economic arguments in addition to ones based on revolutionary law. Litigating women who made demands backed by the new laws often also sought to prove that they had fulfilled Old Regime expectations of family duty, but had nonetheless been short-changed. In the spring of 1794 the unmarried Françoise Faroux had difficulty convincing the arbiters that the 17 nivôse law increased her inheritance share, but she finally persuaded them to grant her twenty-nine years in légitime arrears by pointing out that she "had lived with her brothers only to increase the goods of the household . . . which she had enabled to flourish through her good housekeeping, thrift, and painstaking, beneficial labor . . . serving as mother and main servant at the same time."[60]

In some cases, women used arbitration sessions to enforce traditional family duties as well. Daughters of widowed or separated fathers in particular used the court structure to demand their share of maternal inheritance as annual food pensions. The Lemoine twins argued successfully that their father "had a widower's right to their mother's whole fortune, but his first duty was to feed, maintain, and educate his children." In 1794 the arbiters had little patience with a divorced father who alleged that the new inheritance law in fact left him totally "free control over his property" and ended customary obligations. Lemasson contended that "no law obliges me to pay [my daughter] a pension; Article 61 of the 17 nivôse decree releases me from even setting aside the customary one-third; . . . if I already let her have 200 livres, it was only due to my good will and friendship for her and due to the repeated insistence of the court." His daughter Augustine retorted that she had cared for her father and "never refused all the help he demanded from her." She asserted that "the place of a daughter is to be with her mother," and boldly demanded an even larger pension of 400 livres. The court concurred with her version of filial duty, noted that the new 17 nivôse law did not relieve a father of his conventional responsibilities, and ordered the father to pay his daughter.[61]

As the family courts sorted delicately through the complex mixture of the customary and the new, they faced the difficult demand of the new legislation that they suspend, or at least temper, the established practice of sacrificing daughters to family strategies. Ultimately, though resistance ran deep, in the majority of the cases the arbiters chose the new version of the family over the old one. In arbitration, litigating women clearly benefited from the reformist leanings of some well-placed lawyers in Caen. These men played a crucial role, for example, in interpreting the 8 April 1791 law, which forbade customary exclusions based on sex or birth order. Initially, this law excluded married offspring from benefiting from its provisions and elicited a confused response about the impact of the law on married daughters in particular.[62] The family courts negotiated in practice an issue that petitions and pamphlets would raise in theory: should the law favor unmarried women and men over married women, the mothers of families? And even more important for juridical implementation, had Norman married women been automatically excluded by custom or had they renounced their inheritance portion via freely made contracts? In effect, the new law raised the broader question of whether daughters were entitled to equal rights as individuals or whether they should subordinate their interests for the good of the family line.

Litigation provoked by the 8 April 1791 law led family courts directly into debates over the legal rights and status of daughters within families. For example, when arbiters met in March 1793 to determine whether the married sisters Marie and Madeleine LeCreps and their husbands could redivide their paternal inheritance with their brother's widow, the debate turned to the heart of the issue regarding women's status: had they contracted freely or not? The arbiters chosen by the brother's widow asserted that a marriage contract could not be broken without overturning societal order: paradoxically, they wanted to maintain that daughters in fact had exercised individual property rights in the Old Regime. In turn, the sisters' arbiters argued vehemently that the law was now restoring lost equal rights to women. Above all, they contended that daughters had not been free to contract: "The heirs who make contractual agreements are free to agree; the daughter in Normandy has no freedom; she is subordinated to the will of her father; he can endow her or not, she is forced to accept what he offers her." These lawyers pointed out that mothers who gave children to the Republic should benefit from its equality and noted that most Old Regime Norman dowries were small—a notably weak argument in the current case, which featured dowries of 43,000 livres for each daughter.[63]

Although the LeCreps sisters lost their case, most others were more successful in a reformist legal climate. Four pro-revolutionary hommes de loi who often served as arbiters in Caen and surrounding communes wrote a 1792 opinion that urged fathers to recognize their daughters' rights to their affection as well as their property:

> We were so accustomed to see our daughters only as a portion, so to speak, of our beings; it was so convenient to send them out of the paternal house with a bouquet of roses, that we cannot resolve without pain to treat them as the equals of their brothers. . . .
> By remembering that *by birthright, all the children of the same father merit his affection and his aid equally,* we will convince ourselves that this disposition of *the new law* does not so much offer daughters an additional benefit, as it *restores a right,* which the old law had taken away from them out of contempt for nature [my emphasis].[64]

Even as they argued on behalf of married daughters, these lawyers' words betrayed the pervasive ambivalence about recognizing the "restored rights" of daughters once seen "as a portion, so to speak, of our beings." As one homme de loi in nearby Condé-sur-Noireau commented, "The old Norman prejudices do not surrender willingly to the authority of the law when it does not serve their personal interests." Nonetheless, by 1793 many lawyers repeatedly made arbitration decisions or published briefs that whittled away at those "Norman prejudices." Citizen Lasseret, a frequently employed arbiter in Caen, wrote, "Daughters . . . should have the same rights as their brothers. The outmoded and barbarous laws had forgotten the rights of nature: the new laws, drawn from the bosom of philosophy and reason, have returned them to this agreeable and useful sex."[65] Revolutionary ideology had entered the courtroom and the family.

The family courts provided the forum for individual women to regain these new rights in practice. Sister after sister used the April 1791 or 17 nivôse laws to their own advantage. The legal historian Françoise Fortunet has uncovered a similar pattern in Burgundy. In addition, some families repartitioned inheritance shares amicably with the help of a notary and without recourse to the family courts.[66]

Moreover, in Normandy, the new inheritance laws and the reformist legal mood also had a side effect that worked to many women's advantage. The 17 nivôse law took the communal marital property system as its model because the deputies believed that this system would most cultivate conjugal togetherness and joint labor; it would also facilitate the flow of capital by making all property open to investment by the couple.[67] Since this change placed the old Norman dowry guarantees into an uncertain legal status, families whose daughters married in 1794 or later struggled to clarify property arrangements. Many chose a legal separation of goods within marriage, granting women extensive control over their own property. Contracts for séparation de biens often stated that the wife would "conserve the entire administration of her goods," even as she contributed a set amount to the joint costs of the household. In addition, from 1795 until almost the fall of Napoleon, a majority of families abandoned the Norman system and stipulated communal property in their sons' and daughters' marriage contracts. The intention of parents and notaries was to find systems more in line with the changing legal structures and to free property from the traditional controls that hampered the investment of dotal goods. But the result was to enlarge many widows' shares and to encourage the solidarity and independence of the married couple, apart from the family line.[68]

In the early nineteenth century, other potential heirs sometimes challenged the right of Norman couples to stipulate communal marital property before the Civil Code had made community into the default system, but local and national courts of appeals repeatedly upheld marriage contracts allowing partial or total community. As one decision by the Cour de Cassation stated: "The law of nivôse simply had as its goal to extend the rights of the wife, by allowing an increase in the repayment accorded to her by the custom for her collaboration in the business of the [marital] community."[69] At least some parts of the Midi witnessed this same shift toward communal property in marriage, for example, among the artisanal classes of Montauban and among the working people and artisans of the coastal regions southeast of Aix-en-Provence.[70]

The 17 nivôse law facilitated yet another crucial transformation in Norman marital property that benefited wives. In keeping with its emphasis on preserving family lines, the Norman custom had forbidden mutual gifts between spouses. The 17 nivôse law overturned this prohibition. In towns such as Caen and Lisieux in the mid 1790s, a flood of couples, many of them childless, expressed their "tender friendship" or "sincere gratitude" by contracting to offer each other mutual gifts as part of their legacies. Most of the couples who made this reciprocal commitment were members of the merchant, professional, and artisanal classes, but a few came from peasant backgrounds. The shepherd François Vastienne and his wife Françoise Lejuif from the village of Fumichon did not have many goods to share, but they came to Lisieux to record their transaction and to formally register their "good friendship, . . . and the gratitude that they should and do have for each other."[71]

Two themes dominated these notarized contracts for mutual gifts. Multifaceted expressions of "equal friendship" *(amitié)*, "reciprocal affection," or "sentiments of attachment" abounded. Second, many couples acknowledged their desire to share the results of their joint labor. For example, Marguerite Estimion and Jean Marc, "weak in body but strong in mind and memory," took advantage of the "new laws" not only because of their friendship, but also because "it was more just for the survivor" to benefit from "the fruit of their economy and their common collaboration."[72] As Julie Hardwick has pointed out in her study of Old Regime Nantes, these mutual gifts gave women control over their own patrimony in ways that superseded traditional familial expectations. Moreover, extended family members often resented these donations because they removed property from customary inheritance patterns. Despite challenges, these new spousal gifts held up in both family tribunals and the district court of Caen. As one arbiter noted in 1794, the lawmakers intended "to favor and to give all the latitude possible to matrimonial arrangements and to gifts and legacies between husband and wife."[73]

By encouraging shifts in marital property arrangements between husband and wife, the new laws challenged the lineage system of Normandy and chose the model that most seemed to promote conjugal complementarity and affection. As André Burguière has suggested, the state played a key role in generating the emerging focus on the conjugal couple in the French imagination of this epoch.[74] Like the daughters seeking legacies in court, these wives and husbands strove to put into practice a more egalitarian vision of familial relations. The courts did their best to sort out these family conflicts and to harmonize traditional family practices with the revolutionary attempt to guarantee and stimulate individual liberty and equality within the home. The court records make little direct mention of revolutionary politics, but they reveal how deeply revolutionary ideology and laws both demanded and facilitated changes in existing conceptions of family structure and gender roles. Nervous about such changes, one arbiter commented that family courts "should not carry the Inquisition into families."[75]

The workings of the family court also illustrate the instability of revolutionary settlements and help us to understand the growing conservatism of the later 1790s. In fact, family tribunals came under attack in the mid 1790s because of their crucial role in trying to administer the divisive and controversial 17 nivôse law. They faced abolition in early 1796, shortly after the Convention overturned the retroactive clauses of the 17 nivôse law. Under the auspices of the departmental Civil Tribunal, some family courts nonetheless continued to operate in the Calvados, to enforce egalitarian divisions, and to handle some redivisions of properties that had been divided retroactively.[76]

Above all, the courts' negotiations of inheritance law reveal the profoundly complex impact of the Revolution on women. Civil law changes affected individual women in diverse ways, depending on their familial positions. Significantly, the same radical leaders who denied full political participation to women simultaneously increased many women's legal leverage within the home and civil society. The new court structure, the influence of reform-minded lawyers, and the new set of laws governing the family created a situation in which many women could step into the legal arena and make unprecedented claims for egalitarian status within the family. Clearly, not all women won in the family courts: some lost their own individual cases; some lost when their husbands, fathers, or children were defeated; some who won retroactive settlements in the family courts would lose them in yet another redivision after 1795. But in inheritance cases, as in many cases involving divorce or paternal authority, the courts and laws allowed women, especially sisters and widows in certain regions, to demand rights that they had not had in the Old Regime. They were able to use the new revolutionary state on their own behalf.

Furthermore, for many women, the act of challenging family practices inspired them to look beyond their individual cases, to rethink the nature of the family, and to question assumptions about gender roles. These women had turned to litigation in a highly politicized climate, in the context of a Revolution that sought to convert women as well as men and stimulated the vocal participation of all its citizens. The political ideology of the Revolution combined with the possibility for greater legal rights within the family to politicize many women and to encourage them to express their demands for family reform. As in the case of divorce and marital reform, many women chose to go beyond the local family tribunals and to petition the national legislature, advocating changes in law and family structure. Analysis of these rich sources complements the examination of litigation in court to provide a more complete view of the political as well as legal contestation over family structure at the grass-roots level.

POPULAR PETITIONING FOR EGALITARIAN INHERITANCE

Petitions to national legislatures, individual deputies, and committees provide a valuable glimpse into how ordinary people perceived and received inheritance reforms and how they related to the new politics and the new state. Unlike lawmakers, the majority of petitioners had been or were engaged in litigation, so their words represent well the concerns, impressions, and varied political opinions of those most directly involved in the attempt to reconfigure the family. Since the petitions were meant to persuade, they need to be read with care: the authors often embraced a hyperbolic and inflammatory rhetoric. Their engagement in contentious litigation could lead them at times to exaggerate or distort the impact of revolutionary laws on family dynamics. Yet even as they wrote about how family, revolution, and law *ought* to interact, their idealized visions enable us to grasp popular political thinking with much greater depth than the leaner court records allow. Moreover, since their audience consisted of deputies rather than lawyers or fellow family members, petitioners generally voiced their political agendas and visions more explicitly than they had in court.[77]

This section will examine petitions from across France that demanded equal inheritance for women early in the Revolution or which defended its implementation, retroactive to 1789, according to the 17 nivôse law. I will include some comparisons with the appeals by the younger sons of the Midi and the Pays de Caux, but my focus here remains primarily on female-authored petitions in favor of new property rights for daughters.

Both men and women petitioned on both sides of the issue, but two points need emphasis. First, female petitioners were much more likely than male petitioners to discuss the gender inequities of Old Regime succession practices and to demand their reform. Younger sons from areas governed by Roman law, primogeniture, or preferential legacy appealed for egalitarian divisions in rhetoric that often paralleled their sisters', yet they made scant reference to their sisters' plight or to gender injustice. Strikingly, even in regions like Normandy where many husbands would clearly benefit via their wives from the abolition of the customary exclusion of daughters from legacies, very few men petitioned on behalf of their wives' fate or defended the new laws. One female petitioner wrote to the National Convention that they should maintain the egalitarian 17 nivôse law because it made even its critics happy: "All the brothers who clamor against this law benefit from it themselves through their wives," she noted in its defense. Numerous Norman husbands sided with their wives' litigation against their brothers on an individual basis, but these men—unlike their wives—rarely made general appeals for gender equity in inheritance. Among men, only the occasional husband or younger brother, some vocal lawyers, and a few popular societies explicitly petitioned to support equal succession rights *for women*.[78]

Second, not all women petitioners favored egalitarian inheritance. Some wives and mothers remonstrated against the laws on behalf of newly disadvantaged husbands or sons, as did some who lost out because of changed rules governing bequests to non-family members, the ordering of collateral successions, gifts to living family members, and so on.[79] Since I seek to probe pro-revolutionary female politicization in particular, I will draw primarily on petitions written by women who favored egalitarian inheritance. I will explore their moral stances, their uses of revolutionary ideology, their expectations of the state, and above all, their visions of family reform.

In any analysis of petitioning, the question of direct authorship is central. Only ten women clearly signed petitions written on their behalf by a lawyer, husband, or other proxy, and I found no evidence of women copying model petitions in favor of female inheritance rights.[80] Overall, the evidence suggests that individual women appealing for equal partition by and large wrote and composed their own petitions. Most petitions by women were poorly written, scribbled in a barely legible hand, and riddled with grammatical errors and spelling mistakes. Some petitioners were woefully misinformed and responded to rumors or false interpretations of the complex new laws. Other barely literate petitioners displayed a strikingly good grasp of new and old laws, and the revolutionary press kept them keenly aware of legislative debates and popular opinion in distant regions. For example, in 1795 a poorly written letter from the "young woman Villiers" of the Saône-et-Loire urged the deputies to open "their souls" to the pro-equality appeals "made by a great number of citizens from the department of the Manche."[81] Groups of women also sent collective petitions, occasionally even printed ones, whose authorship is hard to determine. Many communes, especially in the Midi, sent collective petitions that argued for egalitarian partition more generally and were signed by both men and women. Brothers occasionally made common cause with their sisters. The campaign in the South focusing on egalitarian inheritance for younger sons (and to a lesser extent daughters) produced more collective petitions and more appeals printed in pamphlet style than did the movement for women's inheritance rights.[82]

As women, collectively or individually, demanded the reform of inheritance laws or the maintenance of the 17 nivôse law, they adopted the revolutionary language of equal rights. In 1795 when an anonymous woman of the Calvados argued in favor of maintaining the retroactive power of the 17 nivôse law, she claimed that the law "re-established the *natural and imprescriptible rights* of the [female] sex. . . . The legislative assembly decreed all men equal in rights in 1789, and women and girls were included in this generic expression" (her emphasis). Writing in the same cause, Jeanne Barinçon of the Aude complained that it had taken the deputies "three years, six months, and twenty-two days" to restore equal rights by decreeing egalitarian inheritance. Certainly, these rights should be retroactive to 1789 because "a great people who have done everything possible to break their chains and reestablish their rights should enjoy them from the very moment that they rose up against these usurpations."[83]

Repeatedly, petitioners proclaimed that nature called for equality within the family; both laws and political institutions should work to *restore* this *natural right.* Sisters shared this language of rights with the more numerous inheritance petitions by younger brothers. Both individuals and groups presented their particular juridical circumstances as violations of equality that the deputies must feel compelled to repair. For example, in Normandy, throughout the first half of the 1790s, a series of collective all-women petitions adopted this strategy in their appeals for specific laws protecting or increasing their légitime shares. The "citoyennes du département du Calvados" asserted, "Our claim . . . cannot be rejected by the defenders of Equality," echoing a similar declaration by the "citoyennes" of Coutances in 1792. The "unmarried women of Saint-Lô" warned the Legislative Assembly that the "immortal Constitution . . . will accomplish the happiness of the French people only once the assembly realizes that the *filles légitimaires* (daughters due to receive légitimes) in the former province of Normandy have not yet been the object of your solicitude for the Nation." "At birth nature gave us equal rights to the succession of our fathers," asserted some forty women from the district of Falaise in 1795.[84] Far to the south, a petition from the Lot-et-Garonne, signed by both men and women, grounded its argument particularly eloquently in natural law: they reminded the deputies that the 17 nivôse law was "a restoration of the rights of nature. . . . This sublime law does not belong to you, legislators, it is from nature; she alone has dictated it, you have only been her mouthpiece." Individuals echoed this same emphasis on the restitution of rights to forgotten groups: "Your succession laws have not yet spoken about the fate of widows, which means that sacred equality does not yet reign in our republic," observed the veuve Gingoir.[85]

Even as they appropriated the principles of natural rights and equality, pro-equality petitioners almost invariably imbued their appeals with a moral critique of the family as well. They seemed acutely aware that the new civil laws posed a challenge to customary family practices and, in particular, to the gender hierarchy within the household. Far from preordaining women's subjection within the nuclear family, liberal rights ideology—when put into practice—in fact led directly to questioning women's traditional subjugation to the family line.[86] And yet, the new ethic of individualism and equality stood in tension with an older validation of mutual contributions to the collective good. In a delicate balancing act, petitioners sought to criticize these customs without surrendering moral ground. As they claimed equal rights within the family, they drew on deep-rooted moral language to fortify the ethical rhetoric of rights and natural law, to lay bare customary injustices, and to validate their proposals for change. They perceived revolutionary politics not simply as a philosophical battle over citizens' rights as individuals, but as a moral struggle over definitions of justice within the collectivity, that is, within the family as well as the nation. Finally, as petitioners re-envisioned the family, contrary to what one might expect, they did not simply assimilate republican domesticity and emphasize women's value as mothers. Rousseau's emphasis on maternal softness held no place in their appeals. Rather, they forged a new vision of the family based on egalitarianism and affection, evenly divided "without distinction according to sex."[87]

From the outset, women petitioning for equal inheritance denounced paternal and fraternal despotism within the family. Like the critics of marriage discussed in Chapter 1, they unmasked the routine surrendering of women to the family interest. Two anonymous women in Rouen fired an opening salvo on this theme with their *Remonstrances des mères et filles normandes de l'ordre du tiers* in 1789: "*Why would we remain enslaved by this barbarous Custom which allows the father to sacrifice his daughters* through bad marriages to the puerile ambition of enriching the one who will carry his name? . . . On what grounds would we want to maintain these hateful distinctions between children who have an *equal right to paternal tenderness?*" (my emphasis).[88]

Female petitioners in Normandy and the Midi amplified on these themes by claiming that the law itself, the "barbarous laws" and "tyrannical customs" of the "feudal" Old Regime, had stifled the natural affection and equality within families and had especially hardened the hearts of fathers. It had allowed them "to regard their daughters as if they were not their own children" and "to dower them capriciously." Likewise, the old law had encouraged brothers to grow "deaf to the cries of Nature and to the voice of justice." In petition after petition, women demanding equal inheritance wielded revolutionary terminology to denounce "unnatural brothers," who perpetrated a "long and oppressive despotism" and who benefited from "privileges that wounded common rights and equality."[89] They also mastered the age-old imagery of hunger to condemn the gendered basis of misery. Margaret Briançon warned the Convention matter-of-factly that if they repealed the 17 nivôse law, "My brother will be a fat rich man and I will have no more bread. . . . Representatives, bring about true justice and make equality reign between brothers and sisters." Countless writers contrasted the hardship of sisters with the "opulence," "laziness," and "greed" of (older) brothers, and appealed "in the name of humanity" for a "law which wants all citizens to survive."[90]

Some told individual tales of woe, adopting the heart-wrenching style of novels and printed legal briefs to give particular power to their petitions, to illuminate the unethical nature of prerevolutionary customs, and to move the sensitive hearts of the deputies.[91] The fille Anquetil described how her brother had locked her up, accused her of theft, stolen her possessions, chased her out of their house at midnight, and then stalled during an endless court case. The citoyenne Galot Thiphaine charged the legislators to consider her specific plight on behalf of the "public good. . . . It is by paying attention to a particular case that you can rise to the task of perfecting the general law, for out of the discussion of particular cases are born . . . the codes of civilized nations." Others gave more generalized depictions of injustice to emphasize the universality of the wrong and to clarify its gendered dimension. The "citoyennes du Calvados" claimed that the monster of despotism, "crushed by friends of liberty and equality, . . . had taken refuge in Normandy, . . . for it knew well that it would find almost as many protectors in this region as there are male inhabitants, because they are all interested in keeping the prerogatives that benefited sons to the detriment of daughters."[92]

By explicitly exposing the accepted policy of sacrificing daughters to family lineages, the petitioners clearly articulated in words what their litigation in family courts put into practice: they called into question a whole structure designed to conserve family property, place decision-making in the hands of fathers alone, and facilitate the establishment of one or several sons. As the citoyenne Beaufils veuve Lavallé put it, "It was a mania and a prejudice on the part of our fathers pushed to excess to favor the conservation of family goods ('biens propres et de familles.')" She saluted revolutionary laws that had abolished distinctions between property of different origins and made it more difficult for families to keep property within the paternal or maternal line. The citoyenne Montfreulle offered a matter-of-fact description: "I was married in 1773 'for a bouquet of roses' to use the Norman expression. That was how girls were married then. Greed was in the air and one often sacrificed the daughters for the happiness of one son."[93] A lengthy printed petition made the point explicit:

> Each family (and especially among the class of *cultivateurs*) wanted to see several of their children shine in the Church, Robe, commerce, military, or other arts, and it was the daughters who—out of respect and obedience for their father and mother and out of friendship with their brothers—upheld the work of the father by staying at home and working hard and with care; and their thrift enriched their brothers.[94]

Here their appeals for more democratic inheritance dovetailed with the demand for conjugal reform. Petitioners laid bare not just the submission of daughters, but also the legal subjugation of wives within marriage. Some women proposed new laws to repair these injustices that left widows in a tenuous financial position. For example, the veuve Gouet exposed the lack of legal protection for wives who were "forced by duty and by their state [of marriage] to follow their husbands" into a region governed by a different custom. She demanded legislation to safeguard their property under the new marital regime. Likewise, when the citoyenne LeBalleur sent the Convention a legally complex request to protect women's dowries at a "just price," she exposed the inequity of marital structures that allowed "a husband, or rather a master" to coerce his wife to comply with the sale of her dotal goods. "I raise the veil over marital despotism with regret . . . [but] I claim this natural equity, superior to forms, to texts, to opinions, to circumstances. . . . I am convinced, citizen representatives, that in the name of the French people, you will give my daughters a model of exact justice by decreeing what I demand."[95] By invoking a "just price" and an "equity superior to forms, to texts," LeBalleur tapped into the resonant language of the moral economy even as she reminded the deputies of their duties within the new nation.

In associating customary family practices with tyranny and inequity, female petitioners harped on two themes with strong political and moral resonance: the need to attack egotistical wealth and to restore natural human sentiment. Their protest held particular power because it melded traditional moral judgments with the new revolutionary ethic. In their accounts, they fused popular culture depictions of excessive greed with the Jacobin image of wealth as a crime at once political and immoral. In addition, they adopted the republican ideals of fraternity and sensibilité. Jeanne Côme of the Gironde brandished this discourse in a colorful fashion: "Our brother rolls in money, our deceased father made him a fat procureur in the old royal justice system here, a notary all round and puffed up with pride." But at her father's deathbed, when she "had scarcely closed his eyes and begun to give vent to the tears and cries of Nature," her oldest brother assembled the family in the next room to reveal that he had tricked their father into leaving everything to him alone. The excessive power of fathers and the heartless cupidity of brothers, rather than the radicalism of revolutionary laws, tore the family apart. Catherine Douillat of the Charente-Inférieure accused her brother of being "more attached to money than sensitive to the tenderness that his sister and mother had always shown him." She demanded the maintenance of the "just" 17 nivôse law, which "spread equality in families while maintaining unity and peace."[96]

Beyond simply critiquing the family system, female petitioners also staked out a positive new vision of the affective family and voiced confidence that the law could regenerate human emotions as well as morality. Petition after petition suggested that the revolutionary laws would not just "restore equality within families," they would also encourage kind-hearted ties within households and end "the reign of domination of the weakest by the strongest." Mutual regard within the family was a natural as well as social law, "for, whatever one says about it, it derives from Nature that one father divides all his tenderness, all his cares, the whole product of his work and thrift, among all his children, without distinction according to sex."[97] In the egalitarian family, personal affection and moral behavior would hold more sway than ambition or authority. As the citoyenne Bureau from the Midi argued:

> The less power the laws accord to despotism, the more power sentiment will have. Announce to fathers that their principal influence should rest only in the authority of their virtues, the wisdom of their lessons, and the demonstration of their tenderness. . . . Then they will be more loved, more respected, and more listened to. . . . What domination loses, filial love will gain.[98]

Good laws would cultivate "a just equilibrium" within households. In the words of the Delié sisters: "Here, a kind and virtuous wife receives recompense for her work and cares from her grateful and just husband. There, a self-seeking mother is forced to transmit part of her husband's legacy to her children."[99] Far from promoting a simple individualism, petitioners suggested that laws should foster a sense of equitable responsibility within the home. As a new ethic of equality and mutual esteem between the sexes replaced the old codes of hierarchy and sacrifice, families would be happier as well.

Younger sons in many ways echoed the arguments of their sisters as they too demanded a fair share and made a plea for their moral right to inclusion. But their appeals differed from their sisters' in certain distinct ways. Sons emphasized above all the tyranny of fathers, and rarely paid heed to gendered dynamics of "paternal" or "marital despotism" operating against sisters or wives. Brothers' visions of a more affectionate and just family did not include greater mutual regard between the genders. They complained instead that fathers emasculated younger sons, particularly by preventing them from marrying and by limiting their control over property. Condemned to celibacy, younger brothers found themselves "cruelly" chased from the family home, sometimes pressured into the priesthood, or forced to "desert the region and often even the kingdom," in the words of one incensed citizen. One young man claimed that he had poured the "fire of his youth and all the impatience of his passion" into courting a young woman, only to find himself virtually stiffed of his légitime and given a pathetic marriage contract made by "denatured parents." Sons who were soldiers expressed particular rage at being deprived of their hard-won independence and goods. According to their own moral economy, soldiers had especially earned the right to equitable treatment from fathers and state alike. One group of grenadiers longed for the day "when we know that in fighting for our country, we are also fighting for our own property."[100]

Aware of their newly won political rights as citizens, some brothers pointed out that this infantilization by their fathers had political as well as economic consequences. Without inheritance reform, pro-revolutionary sons could too easily be punished in the wills of vengeful right-wing fathers. Comparing himself to a serf in the Jura region, one son lamented that he could not buy or sell goods, nor could he benefit from the fruits of his own labor; adding insult to injury, his lack of propertied status meant that he could not be "an active citizen" of France.[101] For sons, full male adulthood and political citizenship should be part and parcel of their new equal status within the family.

Although daughters did not see their inheritance claims carrying them into full political citizenship, they were just as likely as male letter writers were to trumpet the broader political significance of social reform. Explicitly drawing links between family and nation, female petitioners asserted that reformed families conformed to the wishes of the sovereign people and would underpin the Republic. Equitable inheritance laws fulfilled "the public interest" and "the wishes of the majority of the sovereign people"; they created "twenty-five happy people for each unnatural brother" and "spread joy within families."[102] Some petitioners even suggested that family structures jibed with political forms of government. For example, the citoyenne Mallet asserted that the kinship practices of the old custom of Normandy were fitting to a monarchy, but the republic should have equal inheritance "without distinction according to sex," retroactive to 10 August 1792. Such parallels could be colorful: "They say loudly that you will give us a king if you give heirs back their old prerogatives," warned one petitioner, adding that she might become another Charlotte Corday and use her example to "embolden the cadets and sisters to take justice into their own hands because the law only cared for them for a moment." Indeed, the interests of nation, nature, and morality were one. The young Adelaide Durand argued forcefully that egalitarian partitions enabled unmarried sisters "to marry and to fill that destiny so much in conformity with the wishes of Nature and the interest of the nation."[103]

Interestingly, petitioners also saw a parallel between affective families led by compassionate fathers and a state governed by transparent and openhearted legislators.[104] Just as petitioners portrayed an idealized world of kind fathers, they importuned the deputies to be morally attuned and sensitive (*sensible*) to all citizens alike and to maintain egalitarian partitions as "a sign of your affection" for all the citizens of the Republic. Declaring their "intimate confidence" in the deputies, some even entreated them as "the fathers of the nation" or as empathetic fathers of families to embrace the egalitarian laws.[105] Some authors added a particular twist: they invited the deputies to step in where their own fathers had failed or gone astray. "Deign to replace our fathers and defend us against the injustice, tyranny, and despotism of the brothers of Normandy," exhorted Jeanne Gallien in 1795; "Don't all your children have an equal right to your tenderness?" Likewise, Josephine Letellier urged the deputies to help her become "wife, mother, and citoyenne. . . . Can't I pass into your hands the power my father has over me?"[106]

Most petitioners did not ask their deputies to step so directly into their families, but on some level, they all appealed to the state to validate their independent criticism of family structures. The Revolution did more than supply a discourse and political context for demanding family reform; it became a rival point of authority, an institutional, legal, and moral ally against the traditional family. To align oneself with the nation in demanding family regeneration, to write *"in the name of all the républicaines of the former province of Normandy,"* as did the self-proclaimed "Julie . . . républicaine," was to find a political lever to balance against the weight of family networks. It also exerted a certain moral pressure on the deputies to live up to their promises and to heed the words of citizens, "or citoyennes," added the veuve Descages.[107]

Positioning themselves between the traditional family and the new state, pro-equality petitioners set forth their demands and ideal visions. Egalitarian inheritance reform would not tear apart the tightly woven fabric of the family; rather, it would soften the hearts of fathers and also foster a more natural and just reciprocity, based on mutual affection and an ethos of equality between the sexes. Such families would remain true to codes of collective justice and would also constitute the moral fiber of the Republic. Indeed, the state's representatives had a responsibility, as well as an interest, in making laws to reform families in this way.

· · ·

This exploration of women petitioning and litigating on behalf of egalitarian inheritance should contribute to our understanding of the nature of female politicization and feminist demand during the Revolution. For most women, to engage in revolutionary politics was not simply to embrace an entirely new set of principles. Rather, it was a complex balancing act between new and old allegiances.[108] They viewed politics above all as a struggle over justice, over the moral economy of the family and nation. In defining this moral economy, petitioners for egalitarian inheritance appropriated the revolutionary language of equal rights guaranteed by nature and by law. But they fused this overly individualistic rights ideology with deep-rooted moral notions in order to voice a sometimes radical critique of existing family relations and gender dynamics, to make an appeal for the centrality of affect and reciprocity within family morality, and to link the legal reform of inheritance to the political and moral regeneration of the family and the state. Good laws, they argued, would bring about these goals. And like their fellow advocates for marital reform, these women asserted that the new nation would become possible only when the rights of women were no longer sacrificed to the family.

This revolutionary challenge to domestic practices took place not just in the cultural and political imagination, but also in the texture of interpersonal relations and in the very partition of family goods. Just as the new practice of divorce upset the permanence of conjugal arrangements and the authority of husbands, so too, the new inheritance policies and court cases contested embedded family strategies and disputed the dominance of fathers and the preeminence of brothers, especially older brothers. In the attempt to remake both family and nation-state, revolutionary laws, institutions, and ideology abruptly transported a new model of individual equality and even gender equity into the home. In Normandy and elsewhere, resistance to these new practices was pervasive and hard fought. Court cases dragged on as reluctant brothers hoped to outwait the law. The vocal outcry against new laws would gain force during the post-Thermidorian backlash and influence the authors of the Napoleonic Code to seek a less controversial, less radically even partition of legacies.

Yet, individual Norman sisters nonetheless successfully won property from their brothers again and again, and may well have gained greater status in their own nuclear families as they brought new goods into their households and conjugal business ventures. The power of fathers to direct patrimony was sharply undercut by the victories of these Norman sisters and of younger brothers and sisters in other regions. Litigation forced open the space for imagining both conjugal and parent-child relations in a different frame. As the historian Jacques Poumarède commented about the role of cadets in inheritance contestation in the Pyrénées, "the wind of equality had risen up, it will never again fade away."[109]

Although the Civil Code would restore fathers' authority in virtually every arena, it did not entirely reinstate their control over succession. In an attempt to balance egalitarianism with patriarchalism, the codifiers enlarged the disposable portion that a father could use to privilege one heir. Fathers in some regions, especially in parts of the South, worked the system to perpetuate customary family strategies favoring one child. In its thrust toward patriarchal power, the Code certainly tempered the transformation begun in the 1790s. But the revolutionary and Napoleonic changes in inheritance policy nonetheless facilitated more egalitarian policies in regions like Normandy and stimulated structural family changes even in resistant pockets of the Midi. In Haute-Provence, for example, fathers continued to privilege one heir in the early nineteenth century, but younger daughters and sons used the law to limit that share. Moreover, marriage contracts moved away from establishing stem families that subordinated son and daughter-in-law to the father's authority within his very household. As Alain Collomp comments, "in their youth these fathers had taken part in the egalitarian turbulence of the revolutionary period."[110]

Revolutionary lawmakers had intended not only to lighten paternal authority and increase equity between offspring, but also to encourage conjugal unity by choosing a communal marital property regime over a dowry system. The Civil Code opted for the same default communal system, although it allowed dotal variations. It is extremely difficult to assess how changes in marital property affected spousal relations, but in the 1790s the new laws clearly stimulated some Norman couples to put their mutual affection into action by establishing reciprocal legacies for each other—a practice not possible under the Old Regime. Revolutionary laws also chipped away at the Norman lineage system by encouraging more fiancés (or their parents) to choose marital community of goods in their marriage contracts. Indeed, among dotal areas, nineteenth-century Normandy showed a marked willingness to let the old system slip away, in part because the region's modernizing economy made the liberation of capital especially appealing. A precipitous decline in birth rates and the paucity of stem family households also added to the readiness of Norman families to transform their family strategies. The communal arrangement did not necessarily increase mutual regard between spouses, but it arguably gave the couple more autonomy from kin networks, increased their joint interest in marital ventures, and granted widows a larger share of inheritance, if the couple had been financially successful. In short, revolutionary changes in property law contributed in multiple ways to nudging Normandy away from its lineage mentality.[111]

Legal innovations of the 1790s formed only one component in the evolution of family practices, and the law's short- and long-term impact varied immensely according to region, family structure, and the position of each individual woman or man within the household. But this exploration of inheritance contestation suggests an alternative to the notion that the Revolution simply created domesticity. Rather, the Revolution called into question the nature of the family and its internal dynamics. It injected politics into interpersonal relations and brought about institutional and legal changes that ruptured familial patterns: for example, inheritance patterns that subordinated daughters to patriarchal family strategies. As I have illustrated in the case of Norman daughters and widows, the revolutionary state and culture created the possibility for women in certain familial positions to take advantage of these opportunities, negotiate new property arrangements, and demand more reciprocity in family relations. The Civil Code curtailed these opportunities and restructured once again the relationship between family, woman, and state, but it did not erase aspirations for a different family model and it facilitated the continuation of certain trends, such as the slow erosion of lineage mentality. By and large, the revolutionary attempt to institute familial equality and individual rights improved many women's civil status within the household, but this was not so for women who gave birth outside of the much-praised structure of marriage. The next two chapters will examine the fate of unwed mothers, fathers, and their illegitimate offspring as the revolutionaries contended with the complex issue of how to bring revolutionary principles into "natural families."

5. Natural Children, Abandoned Mothers, and Emancipated Fathers

Illegitimacy and Unwed Motherhood

In the summer of 1793 in the bocage country of Normandy, an illegitimate, eight-year-old girl lost her father. When a distant cousin of the father came to demand his familial goods, the girl's mother, the citoyenne Eveu, planned for battle in court and fired off a heartfelt plea to the National Convention on behalf of her natural daughter. Painting an image of a natural family bound by love rather than law, Eveu defended her own "free union" with the child's father and, above all, upheld the rights of their illegitimate child. "She is about to be without bread," wrote Eveu, and yet her father had "loved and cherished her tenderly." Didn't the new law promise her father's legacy to the child? Eveu remarked that for the last twelve years she herself had "ignored the prejudices of the time out of my affection" for this man, and now the Convention had pledged to "destroy all prejudices." Would the "ceremonies of a priest have made this child any dearer to us?" she asked pointedly.[1]

With her defiant words, the citoyenne Eveu's questions cut to the heart of issues on the deputies' minds that summer and fall of 1793. As they strove to remake the family according to revolutionary principles and to piece together a secular, state welfare system, the legislators debated the rights of illegitimate children, the fate of unwed mothers, and the nature of fatherhood. Like Eveu, they asked, what did the revolutionary commitment to equal rights and natural law mean for illegitimate children and their parents? How did family ties forged by nature intersect or compete with the bonds built by civil society, law, and custom? What were the boundaries of families? Would recognizing the rights of children born outside of these boundaries destroy the institution of marriage or undercut the security of property? How did one define motherhood and fatherhood? Should society weigh the consequences of male and female sexuality differently?

In the attempt to answer these questions, the National Convention stitched together a new set of policies designed to destigmatize illegitimacy, to grant limited rights to children born out of wedlock, and to offer state-run welfare for *mères célibatrices* (unwed mothers)[2] and their children. More specifically, the poor relief law of 28 June 1793 promised to open homes for unmarried mothers and to welcome abandoned children into hospitals until the age of twelve. A few months later, the stunning and controversial law of 12 brumaire an II (2 November 1793) endowed illegitimate children, *if recognized by their parents,* with inheritance rights equivalent to those of legitimate children. The same law implicitly outlawed the customary right of unwed mothers or their children to pursue paternity suits for their support.[3]

Although the revolutionary state would face difficulty and uncertainty in fully implementing these plans, the deputies imagined and began to put into practice a wholesale reconfiguration of the relationship between the state, natural children, unwed mothers, and putative fathers. Fathers outside of marriage won newfound freedom to choose whether or not to embrace their paternity. Some illegitimate children gained unprecedented inheritance rights. However, most unmarried mothers and many natural children eventually lost out, for the state could not make good on its welfare promises, nor did mother and child retain their customary, legal ability to win child support from alleged fathers. While Chapter 6 will explore the results of these policies, this chapter asks how they came into being and pays particular attention to the genesis of the law of 12 brumaire an II.

I situate the revolutionaries' legal innovations within the broader context of the experiences of unwed mothers and illegitimate children in the early Revolution. Historians most often discover the roots of the 12 brumaire law within the revolutionary jurists' commitment to natural law ideology. In addition, for the most part legal historians sever legislative thinking about illegitimate children's rights from the issue of unwed motherhood and paternity suits.[4] Without a doubt, egalitarian, natural rights ideology stimulated the deputies' choices, but they also responded to specific social and political forces. Moreover, when the deputies chose to grant civil rights to some natural children, they also sought to reshape motherhood and fatherhood according to certain gender ideals. I argue that the attempt to redefine the contours of the natural family grew out of three intertwined elements: anxiety about escalating rates of illegitimacy and child abandonment; vocal popular pressure on the Convention from adult *enfants naturels* (illegitimate children) intent on claiming rights; and the deputies' own deeply gendered interpretation of natural law ideology. As the jurists attempted to imagine a more inclusive, more egalitarian "natural" family, they juggled intersecting images of coerced fathers, wayward but naturally loving mothers, and stigmatized and impoverished children. Altering the legal boundaries of the family, regenerating its moral makeup, and planning to augment state poor relief formed part of the same project for the deputies.

This chapter, then, examines illegitimacy from three viewpoints. A case study of *déclarations de grossesse* (pregnancy declarations) and paternity suits in the Calvados explores the experience of unmarried mothers, probes the impact of the Revolution on courtship practices, and asks why illegitimacy rates continued to rise in the 1790s. I interpret these Norman cases in light of comparative work on unwed motherhood in other Old Regime and revolutionary regions and thus provide a crucial social context for revolutionary reform attempts.[5] Second, I turn to the illegitimate children themselves and investigate their demands for inclusion within the nation and the body social. Third, in examining legislative debates over illegitimacy and paternity, I ask how the deputies navigated a complex course toward transforming illegitimate children into rights-bearing citizens without destabilizing marriage and the legal family. In the process, the lawmakers worked out crucial assumptions about the "natural" differences between motherhood and fatherhood. These notions led them to define the mother's and father's relationships to state and child in distinctly separate and lasting ways.

THE COMPLEX DANCE OF UNWED MOTHERS AND FATHERS

In late October 1794, twenty-five-year-old Marie Mirey made her way to the neighborhood justice of the peace in the Norman town of Lisieux for the second time. Three months earlier, this unmarried seamstress had officially declared that she was five months pregnant. Now she returned, with anger burning beneath the formal language of her second declaration. The first time around, she had declined to name the father, for he had impressed upon her his fear of being named. As she reported to J.P. Jacques-Pierre Langueneur, "But once she had given in to his fear, this citizen [the father] from that moment on abandoned her entirely, which made her decide to add to her declaration that she was pregnant by the work of Louis Boulenger, shoemaker in this commune . . . , who had frequented her for more than six years." As she completed her declaration, perhaps Marie Mirey hoped, as had so many other unmarried pregnant women over the centuries since Henri II's 1556 edict, that her formal naming of the father might enable her to pressure or sue him for some lying-in expenses and child support. In this new revolutionary world where at least some illegitimate children had rights, perhaps she also anticipated that the declaration might one day win her soon-to-be-born child a right to the father's inheritance, however limited that legacy might be.[6]

Like Marie Mirey, most women pressing paternity suits came from humble backgrounds. Servants, seamstresses, and spinners, they sought damages, child support, pregnancy expenses, and aid in educating and establishing the as-yet-unborn child in a profession. As Marie Catherine Gire put it early in the Revolution, she wanted her reluctant lover to "have [the child] baptized and brought up in the principles of the Roman Catholic religion and to make sure he learnt a profession appropriate for his sex."[7] In most cases, the women first made a déclaration de grossesse before the local justice of the peace. Since the 1556 edict of Henri II, these written acts were intended to prevent unwed mothers from concealing their pregnancies and committing infanticide. They also served as a foundation for subsequent paternity cases, pursued in civil or criminal courts. Particularly before the mid 1700s, local officials in some places used the declaration as a *plainte* (legal complaint) to force putative fathers to make an initial payment toward the woman's expenses. Unmarried women could also wave these acts beneath the noses of reluctant fathers, convincing a few to marry and some others to offer recompense toward child support. Many men ignored the declarations, but as one anonymous pamphleteer complained during the Revolution, a named man might ante up just to protect his name. "Back then, a false sense of shame, an unyielding prejudice, a fear of being ridiculed in the courts and in public, caused him to recognize [the child] in order to put an end to any proceedings, avoid all scandal, and ward off what was then called *dishonor*" (his emphasis).[8]

In September 1791, the new penal code protected unmarried women from accusations of infanticide based on simple suspicion. By lessening the presumption of infanticide, it also implicitly ended the need for pregnancy declarations. But women across France continued to make them. Often, local authorities and pregnant women alike assumed that they were still required, and until 1794 or even 1795 they served as an initial step in a possible lawsuit against a recalcitrant father. On occasion, the justice of the peace as mediator used the declaration to pressure the father and negotiate some arrangement between the unmarried partners. Midwives, family members, or neighbors persisted in urging justices of the peace to come quickly and note down the statements of women in labor. In the Calvados as late as 1800, some justices of the peace still recorded the formulaic phrase that these acts were done "to satisfy the law" and held these declarations as evidence that women had not concealed their pregnancies with intent to commit infanticide. In December 1795, citizen LeBailly, the justice of the peace of the Section de l'Egalité of Lisieux, duly registered that Marie Chauvel, twenty-four years old and destitute, had declared her pregnancy at eight months; a month later, moments after she gave birth to a stillborn daughter, "covered in blood . . . folded in half," the same justice of the peace rushed to the scene to examine the child for unnatural bruises. Once the midwife and health officer testified to Marie's agonized labor and the impossible presentation of the child in the womb, LeBailly closed the case, only one in a lengthy register of stillborn births and abandoned children.[9]

In some regions, déclarations de grossesse included detailed narratives of the scenes of seduction leading up to pregnancy.[10] The judges who inscribed the 123 declarations from several communes in the Calvados provided more streamlined information, but they nonetheless sketch a portrait of the vulnerability of unwed mothers.[11] Youth was a characteristic shared by natural mothers in both the city of Lisieux and the rural communes surrounding Honfleur and Fervaques. Women in their early to mid twenties predominated; only a handful were older than thirty-one, while 15 had not yet reached twenty-one. Most were illiterate; only 29 percent of these young women could sign their brief statements. Within the city of Lisieux, 70 of 99 women offered information on their occupations: in this textile town, the registers bear the names of 31 spinners, 17 servants, and 22 other working women, mostly seamstresses and the occasional lace-maker or knitter. Just over a third of them had come from surrounding communes, most to find work, a few to give birth in the relative anonymity of this city of 10,000. None reveal a higher social standing. As in the Old Regime, the daughter of a merchant or businessman might more easily make a private financial arrangement with the father and conceal her unwanted pregnancy within a family anxious to avoid shame. But she would also be less exposed than would a spinner or servant to courtship far from the eyes of parents, to the precarious unions of needy and mobile workers, or to the unequal power relations between a male employer and a female employee. Most often, natural mothers tended to come from roughly the same social background as the alleged fathers, at least in the cases where the father is named. Illegitimacy—in the Calvados as in other regions of late eighteenth-century France—was primarily a phenomenon of the working poor.[12]

To move beyond declaring pregnancy and take the putative father to court was neither cheap nor easy, but in the Calvados it was often successful, even during the Revolution.[13] District tribunals, rather than the family arbitration courts, handled these cases. In my sample of thirty-six paternity suits within the department between 1790 and 1794, I have results for twenty-two cases.[14] In sixteen of these, the woman won recognition of paternity and some form of payment. In one further case, the court denied proof of paternity but nonetheless fined the alleged father for slandering his pregnant accuser. In the five remaining cases, the judges cleared the men of all responsibility.

As the paternity suits articulated in practice, neighbors and abandoned women believed that fatherhood was a biological and social matter whose reality could be established by the *community* as a whole. Judges were less certain that fatherhood could be decisively demonstrated, yet they remained confident that witnesses would help them to establish a clear *presumption* of paternity. The producers of the 12 brumaire law soon would emphasize the mysteries of nature that surrounded paternity, but Old Regime and early revolutionary judges appeared less daunted by this barrier. They questioned a series of witnesses, usually between twelve and twenty individuals, who could testify about the behavior of the man and woman in question. In 1781 Jean-François Fournel, Parisian barrister and jurist, advocated this long-standing system in his influential *Traité de la séduction, considérée dans l'ordre judiciaire.* He readily acknowledged the ambiguities of paternity, but stated definitively, "Each [child] needs a father." "We are initiated enough into the mysteries of nature to know that it [paternity] belongs exclusively to one person. Because the interests of both the public and the child demand that we assign a father who will take care of his upbringing, we can only look among those who have consorted with the mother."[15]

Both public opinion and ongoing jurisprudence considered it just for the reluctant father to be held responsible for his actions and to furnish what support he could for the growing child. During the Revolution, judges in the Calvados generally awarded women damages of several hundred livres, lying-in expenses of 60–150 livres, food pensions averaging 80–150 livres/year, and court costs of around 100–250 livres. In weighing what costs to assess, judges took into account the social status, reputation, and age of the unwed mother. The Tribunal of Bayeux, for example, allotted an exceptionally high damage award of 1,900 livres to Jeanne Marie in 1793, given that "she was of an age that excluded any idea of seduction."[16] Children were rarely placed with fathers, and the meaning and responsibility of fatherhood remained circumscribed.

By allocating partial responsibility to the father, the community and the law lightened the community's own financial burden and in effect restored some of the honor lost by the woman and her family. Here the jurists and the public may have differed in the finer points of their interpretations. Steeped in the contract theory of marriage, the jurist Fournel insisted that a woman could win damages not to repair her lost honor, but rather because the suitor had violated his marriage promise. In contrast, abandoned women and their families, as well as many judges on the bench, focused primarily on the "stain" or "lost reputation" left behind by the seducer's betrayal. So crucial was a young woman's honor to her chances of marriage that Marie Anne Touyon and her widowed mother took Jacques Lesage to court for spreading rumors that Marie Anne had acted like a "whore" and had "taken drugs to let flow away" an unborn child, product of Gilles Noël, local wood-worker. Jacques Lesage ultimately bowed to the weight of judicial urging and the communal pressure of twenty-one witnesses; he settled out of court. Most paternity suits in the Old Regime and the new were instigated by the women themselves, but in a few cases, the father of a pregnant daughter took her seducer to court. These fathers likewise made no bones about the point of honor. As Marie-Madeleine Tautel's father commented in 1792, "There is no doubt that a father of a family has the right to pursue vengeance when his paternal tenderness has been so painfully attacked and his honor so notoriously insulted." This father won his case hands down, for it turned out that his next-door neighbor had seduced and impregnated not just one, but two of his daughters, the second one even as the father initiated a charge of *rapt de séduction* (kidnapping in order to seduce) on behalf of the first.[17]

Despite regional variations in family structure, *recherche de paternité* (paternity suits) had long fit within a broader socioeconomic and cultural system across Old Regime France that placed emphasis on sustaining the family line, excluding illegitimate children from inheritance, and using marriage in order to create alliances and property transfers between families. Succinctly put, only honorable daughters from reputable families could win upstanding suitors. Catholic and Protestant teaching, economic motivation, and social expectations all encouraged individuals to internalize the moral codes that underpinned this system of familial honor and alliance. The double standard ruled in prerevolutionary France, but men nonetheless bore some responsibility for their sexual behavior. As late as 1781, Fournel brushed aside the possibility of fraudulent accusations of paternity far more lightly than the revolutionaries would. A man falsely saddled with paternity charges could only fault himself; "he can only blame his own misconduct and imprudence, in allowing himself to be exposed to this suspicion." In the Old Regime and the first years of the Revolution, the law reinforced this conviction. In addition to facilitating paternity suits by unmarried women, the courts recognized that a father who hoped to arrange a fine match for his daughter could legitimately be angered at the man who damaged her marriage prospects irreparably. A father also had the legal right to pursue the criminal charge of rapt de séduction against any suitor who convinced an underage daughter to fly away with him.[18]

Within this familial system, marriage forged a useful economic union for couples in all classes, but constituted a crucial "hope of economic security" for lower-class women: the combined efforts of the working couple enabled them to survive the harsh economic vicissitudes of city or countryside.[19] Mères célibatrices found themselves and their children abruptly cut off from this family economy as well as its networks of emotional support. Within this culture that defined female honor through sexuality, natural mothers, once abandoned the first time, often had a difficult time marrying. As the unwed mother Madame Grandval noted in 1792, "After the weaknesses that made them mothers, they are rarely in a position to aspire to legitimate unions." In the mid to late eighteenth century, for example, only about 10 percent of unwed mothers in Carcassonne and 8 percent of those in Nantes found husbands. And many women were forced to abandon their infant children in order to survive.[20]

Women in desperate straits traditionally turned to paternity suits as a last resort, anxious to salvage the shreds of their reputations and secure what little financial aid they could. In the seventeenth century and most of the eighteenth, judicial officials by and large gave pregnant women the benefit of the doubt in their naming of the father. According to tradition, a woman who disclosed the father's name in the throes of labor did not lie. Well into the eighteenth century, parish priests, with midwives at their elbows, recorded these alleged fathers' names into the baptismal records of illegitimate children. But the later 1700s witnessed gradually harsher treatment of natural mothers. Neither the naming of the father in labor, nor the earlier déclaration de grossesse carried the same credibility. As Fournel observed about current jurisprudence in 1781, "The declaration, renewed during labor pains, does not constitute a stronger title against the accused; it is only a simple presumption, that needs to be sustained by proof." After 1750 judges in Carcassonne hardened their attitudes toward unwed mothers, granting only four victories in thirty-one paternity cases between 1755 and 1786. In Paris, judges grew more reluctant to trust women's initial declarations as partial proof by 1793. Elsewhere—in the Maine from 1722 to 1794, and in the Calvados during the early Revolution—judges nonetheless continued to favor women's claims at least two-thirds of the time.[21]

Illegitimacy rates remained remarkably low throughout the seventeenth and the first half of the eighteenth century. But over the course of the 1700s illegitimacy rates as well as prenuptial conceptions rose steadily. In France as a whole, the proportion of illegitimate births grew from about 1 percent to at least 2.7 percent by the century's end, with wide regional variations. The village of Cérans in the Sarthe, for example, saw a rise from 2 percent to 13 percent. In urban areas the growth was uniformly marked, rising from 3 percent to 10 percent in Nantes, from 4.5 percent to 12.5 percent in Lille, and reaching as high as 16–20 percent in Paris on the eve of the Revolution. Within the Calvados, illegitimacy rates in Bayeux and Caen climbed to at least 4 percent by the late eighteenth century.[22] In the cities, child abandonment skyrocketed and foundling hospitals found themselves overwhelmed with homeless infants. The 1790s would witness further increases in both illegitimate births and child abandonment.[23]

Inevitably, paternity suits increased as well. The *sénéchaussée* (seneschal's court) of the Maine handled few cases before 1750, roughly one case a year in the third quarter of the century, and four to five cases a year from 1790 to 1795. Strikingly, these suits became more common just as the familial system that produced them began to change dramatically. Particularly after about 1770, not only did young couples experience greater independence in courting sociability, but also many more of them seemed to expect freedom in choice of a marriage partner. Even as the broader climate of opinion challenged parental authority over marriage, across class lines individual couples anticipated a form of marriage that included affectionate as well as economic bonds. At the same time, putative fathers felt freer to abandon their pregnant partners. Anne Fillon has suggested that by the eve of the Revolution codes of male honor had shifted: seducing fathers might respond to communal opprobrium backed by the power of the law, but they felt less internal pressure to " 'clear their consciences' by accepting the consequences of their acts."[24] This changing milieu of rising illegitimacy rates, freer courtship, and greater expectation of marital affection intensified in the 1790s and provides a crucial context for the passage of the 12 brumaire law.

In the Calvados the paternity suits of the 1790s betray a compelling mixture of both deeply traditional and recently evolving attitudes toward family honor, sexual responsibility, paternal authority, and courtship. Above all, the court cases portray young women caught between two worlds. On the one hand, they remained as anxious as ever to marry in order to survive and to maintain their honor. On the other hand, they confronted a world in which male mobility had escalated with war and Revolution, in which shifting courtship practices encouraged earlier capitulation and less parental oversight, and in which the ever more present language of love and affection permeated the expectations and interactions of couples.

The paternity suits of the 1790s fall primarily into two categories of seduction.[25] A small but significant group follow the classic pattern of a servant or female worker seduced by her employer, master, or the master's son. A second much larger group, about two-thirds, of the liaisons took place between more equally situated couples who could well have made a reciprocal marriage choice. Woman after woman called on witnesses to testify to their public courtship and implicit or explicit promise of marriage. Inevitably, uneven power dynamics and the unequal economic potential of men and women informed these seductions, but they nonetheless took place within the framework of open, mutual courtship. Alongside depictions of "tumbling" women onto haystacks or beds, both men and women often spoke explicitly—though not always sincerely—about the friendship or love between them. These cases of the 1790s cap off a pattern noted elsewhere by the 1780s. On the eve of the Revolution in both Nantes and Carcassonne, for example, the number of young women producing marriage promises when they declared pregnancy increased. In Aix and Nantes, more declarations bore testimony to relationships between social equals. In all these cities, the percentage, though not the real numbers, of master-servant liaisons declined. Female servants and employees faced the perennial advances and harassment of employers, but illegitimacy rates grew even more strongly due to precarious unions or courtships between equals gone wrong.[26]

The Calvados in the 1790s witnessed this same trend toward more sexual liaisons between equals. To verify their tales of betrayal, natural mothers in the Calvados called upon witnesses to delineate either the impossible context of imbalanced power relations, or, more commonly, to vouch for their legitimate expectations for an imminent marriage. In these latter episodes, as in the pregnancy declarations, the woman and man generally came from similar social backgrounds. While dressmakers and spinners frequently cited tailors and weavers as putative fathers, Marie-Madeleine Gobille, the seamstress daughter of a stonemason, in turn named a young stonemason from the nearby village of Beauville. Not only would shared neighborhoods and work worlds facilitate meeting, but they also encouraged the woman to believe in the reasonable possibility of marriage. Quite a few of these named fathers were now also soldiers. Leaving town "to serve the Republic" proved an easy way for men to forget whatever murmured commitments they had made in the corner of a workshop or barn to a girlfriend back home.[27]

In both town and country, witnesses depict considerable latitude and freedom in courting sociability. When the seamstress Catherine Colombel of Fourneville accused Jacques Delaunay of authoring her child in 1792, thirteen witnesses offered abundant and typical testimony about the couple's flirtatious encounters: constant teasing, joking, and cavorting; one hand under the handkerchief about her neck and the other up her skirt; visits, kisses, and caresses so constant and so distracting that Catherine's employer sometimes refused to let Jacques in for she lost too much time from work. Even as neighbors, employers, and fellow workers provided plentiful information about contact and courtship, they maintained a certain discretion about sexual details. The fruit merchant Pierre Campry testified that he had seen Jacques Delaunay escort Catherine into the mill and even "lay her on the bed and lie down beside her." Pierre claimed he didn't know what happened next, since he left at exactly that crucial moment! Another witness saw the same incident, but reported—perhaps with regret—that Catherine blew out the candle at this tantalizing juncture.[28]

But for all of the witnesses' delicacy in revealing details, they painted a world in which open wooing and scenes of seduction were taken as a given, permeating daily life in routine ways (see Figure 9). If Jacques romanced Catherine at the shop where she sewed and escorted her to the mill, Michel Letouzé of Etouvy pursued Marie-France Enguehard in the cider press-house and out in the open fields. She duly reported to the district tribunal that when Michel took her into his arms in the meadow and "wanted to tumble her onto the ground, she opposed him by observing that they could be seen." While the comment may not have convinced the judges of the stalwart nature of her resistance, it reveals the public nature of courtship, as well as her awareness of communal judgment. Within households, sexual intrigues were scarcely more private. LePrince dit Dumesnil roundly denied any undue familiarity with Madeleine Petit, but they had been seen playing dress-up, and perhaps LePrince should not have waltzed through the kitchen with her under-drawers in his hand. Likewise, the servant Martin Hemert met with no luck when he tried to rule out his fellow domestics' testimony; after all, reasoned the judge, his amorous endeavors took place in the male servants' common bedroom.[29]

Nor did the participants hesitate to speak about their prospects and pursuits. Unwed fathers often were later caught by comments made in a moment of bravado or swaggering. Jacques Delaunay could not resist boastful allusions to his exciting new love connection. When another apprentice seamstress remarked to him that he seemed to know Catherine rather well, he said, "You haven't seen anything. When we are alone, it's really something else!" Likewise, in 1794, when François Sainte-Croix asked a fellow villager about the newborn child of Jeanne LeRoi, he gave himself away

Figure 9.   Courtship scene (late Old Regime). Courtesy of the Bibliothèque nationale de France.

with the suggestive comment, "Maybe she looked at me more than she looked at others." And after a pause he added, perhaps with a hint of defiance, "She chased after me until she got what she has."[30] How could he know that his casual comments to a neighbor would come back to haunt him in court?

Communal observations about courtship carried weight in part because the witnesses essentially were testifying that the man had courted the woman, had acted as if he meant to marry her, and would or should have married her in the normal course of events. In these Norman villages, as in the teeming neighborhoods of Caen, Paris, or Lyon, the community passed judgment: it named the father and held the power to differentiate between salacious misbehavior and the acceptable escapades of courtship.[31]

Faced with unwanted accusations of paternity, men pursued several strategies of defense. They routinely denied intimacy and marriage promises,[32] attacked witness testimony, and angrily denounced accusations that seemed to jeopardize their independence and impugn their honor within the community. Jacques Groult threatened to beat up the baker who "reproached" him for fathering Marie-France's child, while Jacques Lemoine faced an additional fine for assault after he threw the paternity suit process-server down a set of stairs. Most frequently of all, they strove to shift sexual responsibility onto the natural mother. Men accused of being fathers were keenly aware of the nuanced concepts of female honor and sexuality. One married man vigorously denied any legal responsibility for fatherhood; after all, without a hope or promise of marriage, no honorable girl would engage in passionate acts. Taking a different tack, Pierre Jouvin unsuccessfully tried to escape charges on the grounds that Françoise Eudes was "a widow, older than he, and with much more experience." The judges of the district tribunal candidly acknowledged that a widow could not make powerful claims for damages, but Jouvin's coy attempt to play the innocent, seduced one foundered against ample testimony about his energetic and passionate pursuits.[33]

Predictably, many a man employed the age-old tactic of declaring that his pregnant accuser had run with more than one man. As the jurist Pierre Guyot had confirmed in his 1784 handbook, judges in the eighteenth century routinely decided against women shown to be promiscuous. Some male defendants pointed to an alternate possible father: in 1791 Michel Letouzé claimed that he had been fingered rather than Jacques Groult only because he was richer than Jacques. Others relied on more global allegations of promiscuity. In defense of his own honor, Nicolas Flaust fulminated that his servant Renée Marie should be the defendant; she, rather than he, should be punished for her indiscriminate, loose behavior. Male defendants studded their defenses with counter-accusations of "prostitution," "libertinage," "free conduct," "allowing herself to receive all kinds of touches." "She has even been surprised in the midst of the flagrant act with other individuals," inveighed François Morin against Françoise Busnel in 1793. In these cases, the community weighed in to assess insinuations of female licentiousness. When Françoise called no one in her own defense, witnesses corroborated François's tale and he won back the 30 livres of supplies provisionally levied against him.[34]

In fact, perhaps because they were aware of the power of communal observations, some men denounced as fathers pursued the opposite strategy of proclaiming that they had never heard of any scandalous conduct or inappropriate relations by the woman in question, including of course any liaisons with themselves.[35] In any event, so crucial was communal opinion in defining a woman's honor and attributing paternity that the courts occasionally came down hard on a man who defamed his former lover's reputation with exaggerated accusations of loose living. Catherine Gonfroy ultimately lost her paternity suit against the cultivateur Jean Godefroy: it turned out that several other suitors had been passing silk handkerchiefs and caresses in her direction. But she did win a substantial sum, 900 livres, from Godefroy for slandering her reputation and spreading rumors that she was "a libertine and a whore."[36]

Needless to say, women remembered a quite different version of events. They always depicted the men as the initiators and stressed their own passivity. Above all, they emphasized the alleged father's promises of marriage and his fervent, virtually unstoppable pursuit. Invariably, women portrayed themselves as deceived, betrayed, surprised, or overcome "in one of those fatal moments where the most solid virtue almost always gives way to the sway of inflamed passions." As long as marriage was expected, love had a life of its own, they argued, normalizing their moment of weakness. If the man in question was married, the seduced woman depicted her innocence and gullibility all the louder, and lawyers or fathers defending underage daughters took the depictions of the "weakness of the sex" to flamboyant heights. "Enchained by the laws of nature and honor to the fate as well as the wishes of her lover, she was absolutely incapable of thwarting him, and on the contrary, a blind submission was from then on her only remaining resource to stave off the hideous wolf who threatened her," argued one lawyer in 1792.[37]

Women's accounts of their own passivity need to be read on multiple levels. Dominant ideas about male and female sexuality and psychology virtually demanded that women play up their own credulity and innocence. Across early modern Europe, women in various situations could sometimes gain legal advantage through accentuating their own powerlessness. For example, in the Old Regime, some women participated in their own kidnapping (rapt de séduction) by an inappropriate lover as a marital strategy and then attempted to use the judicial system to engineer a marriage that violated social expectations. (Judges sometimes offered the male seducer the option of marrying the victim of his rapt in order to restore her honor.) In the 1790s, some of these unwed mothers may have held similar hopes. Even when they could not anticipate marriage as a possible outcome of their court cases, they no doubt underscored their own passivity partly as a strategy for winning in court.[38] According to her account, the youthful Marie Anne Sicot appeared to take the prize for naïveté. Her would-be suitor Jacques Lemoine brought her to the larger town of Vire to conceal her pregnancy; once there he promised to marry her, if only she would sign a notarized act denying his paternity. Bent on the marriage promise, she signed, only to be abandoned. However, she also won her court case. The District Tribunal of Vire promptly penalized him for this "too presumptuous act."[39]

In recounting their own surrenders, young women alluded often to male persistence and force. With understated phrases, such as "he tumbled me" or "he lifted me," some women intimated that physical coercion brought about their fateful surrender. But interestingly, they did not emphasize their seducers' violence or aggressiveness nearly so much as the words of affection and promises of marriage that accompanied the teasing games of courtship. Witnesses repeatedly depicted the couple's interactions with the verbs "fréquenter" (to go out with) and "badiner" and "folâtrer" (to joke around, flirt, tease, frisk about); these were the habitual diversions of courtship. They also referred to the power of emotions over the participants engaged in the ritual dance of sexual attraction. Love could captivate both men and women. "If Rabecq could not have her, he would be sick from this, and if she had to say no to him, he would not want to see her ever again," testified the laboureur Louis Lechevallier. Suzanne Massieu admitted that Jean Dethan had "been seen alone with her day and night and that during this time he captivated her, caressing her and allowing himself familiarities that cemented his mastery over her heart and person . . . as he leaned toward her saying 'It's no risk, we will marry.' "[40]

For their part, the women represented their lovers' language and behavior as evidence of sincere affection and apparently serious intentions. "We went together. . . . He showed me a great deal of friendship [*amitié*]," remarked Catherine Bourguiard, newly pregnant and stunned to learn that Jacques Prestatoire "had told various other people that he wanted to have done with it." In tracing the increasing expectations of heterosexual love and companionship within marriage over the course of the eighteenth century, historians Marie-Claude Phan and Anne Fillon have noted the frequent and multivalent use of the word "amitié" among the popular classes. As in the novels read by more literate members of society, "amitié" could imply affection, friendship, and also love, standing in for the less often used word "amour" that carried more controversial connotations of sexual passion, of "fol amour" (crazy love).[41]

Natural mothers during the Revolution shared these language patterns.

Jeanne Marie Leinis commented in 1794 about the "very rich young man" who sometimes visited her master, and herself: "his *amour* simultaneously left its fruit in my womb." Hers was a tale of orphanage, domestic servitude, and victimization by a *ravisseur* (ravisher). A more long-term relationship produced a different narrative. The Revolution's validation of romantic love had granted added legitimacy to the languages of love. In the spring of 1794 one serving girl reported that when she had gone to work in the fields of a local widower almost three years before, he "didn't wait long before letting her see that he had amitié for her and he showed her all the signs." Convinced by his repeated promises of marriage, for the last two years she had "acted as if she were the mistress [of his home]" and now she carried his child. In her view, signs of "amitié" legitimized their sexual liaison, for marriage should have ensued in the normal course of events. Some men no doubt used the current romanticization of affection to their own advantage. Marie Madeleine Tautel now realized that she had given way to the "dangers . . . of the most sincere love" ("amour") when she misinterpreted Jean Baptiste Delacroix's small acts of attention and devotion. For his part, Jean Baptiste disavowed any "inclination of the heart" toward her as vigorously as he denied having flirted or bantered with her, as if his lack of heartfelt attraction prevented him from being the father.[42]

According to the abandoned women, the behavior of their male companions had reinforced ordinary expectations of sentimental affinity, as man and woman played out the roles appropriate to lovers on the verge of marriage. The hope for a convivial relationship did not lessen women's awareness that men and women played complementary economic roles within marriage. Françoise Eudes related that Pierre Jouvin "had a great deal of kindness ["complaisance"] for her, that he took her day and night to his friends and family, that he had her lie down with him in his bed and lay down with her, . . . and that finally, they acted together like husband and wife, and that even since she gave birth, Jouvin had made every effort to enjoy her, and that he had provided linens for her child." In her account, signs of fondness and attachment blend with sexual acts, naturalizing and justifying their relationship and revealing her assumption that sex and sentiment, responsibility and companionship went hand-in-hand for a couple en route to marriage.[43]

The seductions of the 1790s took place within a cultural context that not only increasingly validated conjugal affection, but also explicitly challenged parents' authority over adult children. The revolutionaries abolished lettres de cachet and established family courts in 1790, lowered the legal age of majority and curtailed parental authority over marriage in 1792, and severely diminished paternal control over testaments in 1793–94. Together with the cultural climate that contested paternal power and deference to tradition, these legal changes encouraged some young men and women to defy their parents' suggestions more boldly or to have greater confidence in their own judgment. It is difficult to assess the indirect impact of these laws on behavior. The average age of marriage declined slightly over the 1790s.[44] No doubt, the attempt of men to escape conscription through marriage was the primary force fueling this decline, but newly emancipated young couples could also more easily choose on their own to marry young, assuming they could afford it.

In any event, a few intrepid youths, male or female, took advantage of new laws and the new family tribunal system to demand the right to marry according to their hearts against their parents' wishes. In the small number of cases within the district of Caen, these young couples were always successful, although bitter battles and appeals sometimes ensued.[45] As parents and children faced off, their arguments echoed some of the themes voiced by inheritance petitioners. They pitted the traditional wisdom of fathers versus the liberty and love pangs of the young. In 1791 Thérèse Manchon and Sébastien Roger of Notre-Dame-des-Estrées near Pont-l'Evêque had been courting for two years. When her father's grudging acceptance erupted into blunt opposition and then abusive treatment by both father and brothers, Thérèse moved out and convinced the nearby justice of the peace of Cambremer to call a family council to approve her marriage. In the words of the justice of the peace, "the frequency of [Sébastien's] visits had the effect of awakening an invincible inclination for him in her heart, . . . so much so that it was impossible for her to surmount it and no one in the future could replace him in her heart." As the local judge spoke with such romantic overtones, he validated the affective choices of the young.[46]

Steeped in the confidence of the early Revolution, the couple claimed—erroneously but convincingly—that the 24 August 1790 law had lowered the age of majority to twenty-one. At a subsequent conciliation meeting, Sébastien declared boldly that Thérèse was legally "an unmarried adult woman, twenty-one years old, and according to the new laws, she has become independent and mistress of her own actions." The courting couple blended traditional methods of persuasion with revolutionary ones. Sébastien provided evidence of his financial standing and promised his "respect and submission" to his future parents-in-law. Following an Old Regime legal custom, Thérèse sent her parents three "sommations," official notifications of her intent to marry, in the attempt to gain their approval. When all efforts failed, the couple used the family council's permission to marry secretly in a neighboring parish, only to face a *rapt de séduction* charge against Sébastien by Thérèse Manchon's father. Nicolas Manchon accused Sébastien of "taking advantage of the changing times" to kidnap, seduce, and ravish his daughter. Invoking the authority of "natural and positive law . . . and the ancient ordinances on marriage," Nicolas succeeded in having his new son-in-law thrown into prison in early 1792. This imprisonment was only temporary, however, for the revolutionary tide had turned against authoritarian fathers.[47]

Most young lovers did not face so bitter a fight with their parents as did Thérèse and Sébastien; and many of the natural mothers filing paternity suits would gladly have traded the caprice of their now-reluctant lovers for the loyalty of Sébastien. Yet, the challenge to *puissance paternelle* in its various forms bears relevance for the plight of natural mothers and the growing number of illegitimate infants. As both political and legal culture undermined parental as well as religious authority, wooing couples—especially men—might well have felt fewer constraints than before. Migration to the cities and the displacement brought by war and revolution also lessened parental oversight and increased male mobility. The Revolution even provided new lines of seduction. Pierre Raimbaud seduced Magdeleine Masson with the promise that he would divorce his wife and marry Magdeleine should she become pregnant. Alongside the most blatant audacity of men who convinced underage girls to leave home, hints of milder defiance of parental authority pepper the scenarios of courtship. Moreover, young women as well as men tasted the possibility of youthful independence from parental authority. Catherine Gonfroy commented to a friend that she went out with Jean Godefroy, though "her parents did not want to let her marry him." (Perhaps their opposition had some logic: Catherine herself admitted that "she would rather marry a richer man than Godefroy, who has nothing.") Likewise, Marie Longuet reported that Jacques Lascéré came around at night and also snuck in when her mother went out to Sunday high mass, "to enjoy her during the time that she was alone."[48] While young lovers had long spurned their elders' advice, the political and legal context of the 1790s offered new validation for this behavior.

Although both men and women felt emboldened by the changes in courtship patterns, parental authority, and sentimental expression, these transformations affected men and women differently. For women, the Revolution changed nothing about the biological reality of pregnancy, nor did it alter entrenched notions about female sexual honor, despite the optimistic pronouncements by the deputies Oudot and Théophile Berlier that *mères célibatrices* who produced children for the nation should not feel ashamed. Philippe Petit ranted against the hairdresser who had impregnated his daughter Madeleine in 1791: he had "stained" her honor and cast the young girl into despair and ignominy by "depriving her of that precious holding, her virginal purity."[49]

During the Revolution, as before, women balanced the perennial fear of pregnancy and dishonor against their own desires and against the pressures of a persuasive suitor or an overbearing master. Illegitimacy rates rose during the Revolution not so much because women felt sexually emancipated, as Edward Shorter has suggested for this era as a whole. Rather, they faced a diverse set of circumstances that had changed the rules of the game: an increase in male mobility, a decrease in parental and religious authority, a political and cultural mentality validating affective attachment, and freedom in the sociability of courtship.[50] These changes had begun in the late Old Regime and were intensified by the early Revolution.

In the early 1790s, as the natural mothers of the Calvados pressed their fragile claims in court, the deputies in Paris anxiously turned their attention to the growing numbers of unwed mothers and their illegitimate offspring. The Revolution's attack on the Church, especially its dismantling of the convents, decimated Old Regime mechanisms of poor relief and made the problem of illegitimacy all the more pressing.[51] The Committee on Poor Relief and the Committee of Legislation addressed these social questions from different angles. Overcome with the extent of child abandonment and indigent natural mothers, the architects of revolutionary poor relief developed plans that engaged the state ever more deeply in trying to ameliorate the difficult position of both these groups. For its part, the Committee of Legislation wrestled with the civil status of illegitimate children. How could the law endow them with rights but also safeguard the liberty of alleged fathers and maintain the sacrosanct status of marriage and the prized conjugal family? Before disentangling the complex legislative interplay between these lawmakers and their visions for change, let us turn to the natural children themselves. For some of them also demanded a voice in the matter.

THE NATURAL CHILD: "ATTACHED TO HIS MOTHER'S DESTINY, INNOCENT VICTIM OF PREJUDICE"

In the late 1700s the children born of these unwed mothers experienced varied fates. Very few grew up in their fathers' households. Some women attempted to raise the newborns on their own, but more often than not were forced to abandon them in order to survive and return to work. Some deposited their infants anonymously on a church step or convinced a local foundling hospital to accept them. With scant resources to care for the growing number of abandoned children, some foundling homes systematically sent the children to Paris, while others shipped them out to wet-nurses or "baby farms" in the countryside where their odds of survival were slim at best. In the Calvados, for example, the Hôtel Dieu of Caen tried to nurse some babies locally, dispatched others to Paris, and sent most to the wet-nurses in the Bocage Virois who had long welcomed this industry. Across France mortality rates ran astonishingly high for these infants: they often exceeded 50 percent, and reached as high as 85–90 percent in large cities, such as Rouen. Only one out of every ten children carted to Paris from the provinces survived the first three months of life.[52]

Obviously, given the precarious household economy of the 1700s, some of these children came from destitute married parents. Perhaps only 70–80 percent of foundlings were illegitimate, but all were "reputed to be bastards" in the Old Regime.[53] To be classified a "bastard" was to hold outcast status in the eyes of society and the law. Illegitimate children carried the legal and moral stigma of their parents' transgression. Within the framework of a Christian morality that indicted sex outside of marriage and underpinned the economic cohesion of families, the very blood that ran within their veins carried the taint of dishonor. Natural children were widely viewed as inherently impure and shameful, although various Enlightenment works, such as Diderot's *Le fils naturel* and *La religieuse,* had widely denounced this prejudice against illegitimate children. In practice, the legal treatment of "bastards" seems to have grown less harsh in the eighteenth century, but their technical legal status still reflected a deep stigma. Certain professions, such as the clergy or royal officeholding, remained closed to them without special permission. Although they themselves could marry, own property, and pass on goods to their offspring, natural children essentially were excluded from their parents' families. A few exceptional regions allowed them to inherit from their mothers, and either parent could will them small amounts as "particular heirs." But in no part of France could illegitimate children become the primary ("universal") heirs of their fathers, nor could they inherit from fathers who died intestate. As one anonymous woman lamented to the National Assembly, when her mother died suddenly, her "hard and inhumane relatives snatched and took away my [goods], . . . and with no right whatsoever to claim anything back, here I am at twenty-five-years-old, reduced to serving people one thousand times more base in soul and sentiment than I."[54]

Excluded from familial property rights, natural children held only tenuous civil status. Their very names bore witness to this marginality. Most often denied their fathers' names, illegitimate children came by their sur-names in a catch-as-catch-can fashion. In Normandy, as in some other re-gions, the mother traditionally gave her first name to the child; "Marie" be-came a remarkably common last name. Children of unknown descent who wound up in foundling homes or were placed with charitable families some-times existed in a nameless limbo for years. As one adult natural son wrote to Cambacérès, he experienced "surprise mixed with the sharpest bitter-ness" to discover as an adolescent that his baptismal record bore only his first name. Like him, other abandoned children were rapidly christened with only a saint's name and then waited for the community to identify them ac-cording to their characteristics, as "Lepetit, Legros, Legrand, Legras, Lenoir, Leblanc, Leroux, Leclair, Lebrun, Lebeau, Lebon, Ledoux, Lesage or other vulgar names of this type. . . . Honor is a prejudice," concluded this disillu-sioned indicter of the Old Regime system.[55]

For adult natural children the Revolution awakened new expectations and the potential for improved status. The prevalent ideology of equal rights and the early reforms of inheritance laws raised the possibility of granting civil rights to illegitimate children as well. In July 1790, the *Moniteur universel* printed a proposal by M. Peuchet to end "these senseless and barbarous dis-tinctions . . . as if some men were more legitimate than others."[56] Within a revolutionary political culture validating popular expression, as early as 1790–91 some intrepid individuals began to petition the legislature to endow illegitimate offspring with full equality. Illegitimacy petitioners were never as numerous as their fellow inheritance petitioners born within mar-riage: I found only about forty petitions received before the 12 brumaire law, although comments in the Committee of Legislation records suggest that more petitions existed. In any event, while these letter writers and pamphleteers do not seem to have formed a large lobby, their use of natural law ideology and their indictment of social inequity nonetheless struck a powerful chord with the Committee of Legislation. Not only did legislators mention the "accumulating" petitions in their speeches, but minutes of the committee as well as the marginal comments and drafts of reply letters all bore testimony to the jurists' attentive reading of these petitions. As Cambacérès commented in reply to one proud father of a newborn natural son in June 1793: "I congratulate the young citizen who owes his birth to you, for he will not be the victim of our old errors and atrocious prejudices." Petitioners had an especially strong opportunity for influence in the summer and fall of 1793 as the committee strove to give specific shape to the Convention's 4 June 1793 promise to grant inheritance rights to illegitimate offspring.[57] If the petitions illustrate popular pressure on legislative thinking, they also offer insights into the status and thinking of some of the most politicized natural children.

Some natural parents petitioned on behalf of their progeny. With the notable exception of Olympe de Gouges's defense of the mother's right to name her child in *The Declaration of the Rights of Woman,* few women penned critiques of the paternity suit system before its dismantling in the mid 1790s.[58] More often, literate unwed mothers leaped to the defense of their children's rights. Most petitioners had themselves been born out of wedlock. Although many letter writers complained of their poverty or low social standing, they offer little concrete information about their social backgrounds. A few had been foundlings, but many had not been, for they described relationships with mothers or fathers and expressed the hope of receiving inheritance and being integrated into known families. Scattered across France, the petitioners often remained anonymous, especially if they published their work in pamphlet form. Although lawmakers and many pamphleteers imagined the natural child as male, natural daughters as well as sons offered their comments. In contrast to the collective appeals signed by legitimate siblings in Normandy and the Midi, enfants naturels and their parents usually wrote as individuals. There is scant evidence of lawyers' penning missives in their clients' names before the 12 brumaire law, and none whatsoever of model petitions. The fragmented and spontaneous nature of these petitions reflects the social marginality of illegitimate offspring. After the passage of the 12 brumaire law, the number of petitions increased as individuals grappled with interpreting the ambiguous law, but for the moment I will draw primarily on the early petitions.[59]

Most petitioners demanded the right to full inheritance. Like the legitimate sons and daughters of the Midi and Normandy, they appropriated the language of equality and natural rights and indicted the "barbarous" or "feudal" customs of old, but they gave this language several particular twists. For illegitimate children, to gain equality would mean not just to win inheritance rights, but also to purge public opinion of the "deep-rooted prejudice" against them. Natural children repeatedly decried their humiliating "stain," that "odious difference," that "shame" that nothing could erase. How could it be just to punish children for the sins or weaknesses of their parents, demanded letter after letter? Moreover, just as Norman daughters struggled to prove their worthy contributions to household and family, natural sons stressed their honorable service in the armies of the nation. Implicitly, they suggested that their actions and devotion exposed long-standing bigotry as all the more reprehensible.[60]

For children born out of wedlock, equality also meant unprecedented inclusion within the political and social body. "All France blesses the moment that transformed a multitude of men into a people of brothers," proclaimed one anonymous pamphleteer, as he demanded that one last forgotten "class of men" be incorporated within the fraternal, national bond. While legitimate sisters and younger brothers stressed that they had been cut off from family fairness, natural children portrayed their banishment from the "social body" more globally. They continually asserted that they, too, merited inclusion within the new nation "because they have sealed with their blood this oath common to all the French." Insisting on the "immense number" of natural children, another anonymous petitioner pleaded for the same treatment as his legitimate siblings: "Like them, [enfants naturels] are children of the patrie; like them, they are called to become citizens and fathers of families; like them, they have the right to the same favors and benefits of the law." Likewise, when a group of fifty-five "natural children brought up in the countryside" requested the right to take part in the division of communal lands, they emphasized that they too paid taxes, they too provided services and produce, they too anticipated caring for their adoptive parents when they grew old. The very appeal that illegitimate children be given the name "enfants de la patrie" resonated with this desire for inclusion within the "body social."[61]

If "equality" carried special connotations of redemption, purification, and inclusion for illegitimate petitioners, "nature" also took on additional meanings. "Shouldn't these puerile distinctions disappear before the sacred rights of nature?" insisted one group of enfants naturels. No set of claimants referred more frequently to "nature" and "natural law." For these petitioners, nature implied not just an immutable, moral code of law and equal rights, it also stood opposed to the injustice of institutional practices. But many of these conventional practices, most notably marriage, were ones highly valued by the revolutionaries. Thus, the petitioners worked hard to validate the natural, emotional bonds between parent and child or man and woman outside the strictures of marriage and family. On occasion, illegitimate children distanced themselves from their parents' errors. According to the embittered Perrié Dumummier writing in 1791, natural children were "unhappy beings who did not ask for existence"; their parents had created them out of "immodest corruption" and the pursuit of pleasure, only to "scorn them and abandon them to the mercy of their misfortunes."[62] More often petitioners pursued the opposite tack: they justified their parents' unorthodox behavior by arguing that heterosexual attraction and parental bonds were natural and heartfelt. Faced with difficult circumstances, their parents had done the right thing to defy convention and follow their hearts.

This claim could take humorous form. "I used natural law with her," explained one petitioner about the fertile governess who had comforted him after his own wife had lost her mind and been placed in a convent. In 1789, the *Assemblée de tous les bâtards du royaume; avec leur demande à l'Assemblée nationale* (Assembly of all the bastards in the kingdom; with their demand to the National Assembly) playfully trumpeted that bastard children born of love were far superior "in wit and intelligence" to legitimate children, born of boredom and indifference. Listing off notable bastards, the pamphlet proposed elevating love children and rewarding their mothers who, by "obeying nature's will, had fulfilled their duty toward society, and had given . . . a citizen to the state."[63]

Many petitioners suggested that illegitimacy grew out of the inflexible and harsh conditions governing Old Regime family arrangements. Forced into indissoluble marriages dictated by authoritarian fathers, young men could not fulfill their obligations to the "first penchant of their hearts" for they feared losing their inheritance, argued one citizen G. Within that system, the illegitimate child was "attached to his mother's destiny, innocent victim of prejudice and the laws, he had to be stigmatized and abandoned, like her." Granting rights to natural children was only fair, for they were the hapless products of impossible alliances in harsher times. Nor would giving them succession rights threaten the stability of future marriages, claimed citizen G. The newly granted right to divorce would make extramarital affairs rarer, and the weakening of paternal authority would make it easier for a son to "listen to the soft voice of nature." Once everyone could seek "happiness only in the pure affection born of nature," men who became fathers outside of the law would rush to marry and embrace fatherhood. Public opinion would urge along those few men whose turbulent hearts made them hesitate. In short, citizen G., like other petitioners, strove to associate the exclusion of natural children with the rigidity and inequity of the Old Regime patriarchal family and to ally their equal status with the regenerated, freer, more affectionate family. He nonetheless walked a fine line in condoning natural love alliances. After singing the praises of the new family, he admitted that, since the social order had an interest in establishing a distinction between free unions and unions sanctioned by the law, perhaps illegitimate children should have full rights only to their ascendants' legacies, and but a half-share of collaterals' estates.[64]

In 1793 when deputies Oudot and Berlier threw all their powers of oratory behind granting full inheritance rights to illegitimate children, they argued that couples who produced natural children had come together in a "private marriage" as legitimate as any conjugal bond.[65] These deputies clearly shared the convictions of those petitioners who also defended the natural, reciprocal commitment of couples bound in "free unions," "secret marriages," or "private marriages." In toned-down form, they echoed the opinions of letter writers like the citizen Meunier, who poured scorn on the hypocrisy of legal sanctions: "Is marriage a maleficent god to whom we must heartlessly sacrifice the rights and honor of citizens? . . . Now that divorce is established, what is [marriage] but a union between two beings who want to live together and have children. A simple union without any act can last longer than one certified by an act of marriage." In the new reign of equality, all natural children, abandoned children, even children born of adultery or incest should be freed from callous distinctions: "all children are natural, legitimate, and children of the patrie."[66]

Many petitioners were less defiant but equally intent. Early in 1793 Antoine Dupront complained that the local municipal official had refused to record him as father of his newborn natural daughter, and now he feared that she would be deprived of the "feeble product of my labors after my death." Hoping to elicit sympathy, he urged the deputies to be moved by "the innocence of a child who should not suffer from my error, supposing that following Nature's path is indeed an error." Others took pains to explain why circumstances had led them or their parents into unusual arrangements; they sometimes cited tacit communal acceptance of these unions, especially if parental opposition had prevented the young couple from marrying. The citizen Besarnac had a particularly colorful scenario to report and defend. Over twenty years ago, he had married, but could not consummate his marriage because of his wife's "narrow" physiology. He insisted that they therefore were not really married, but he and his companion [wife] lived together like brother and sister and grew close in friendship. All of this is "certain fact, well known in my region." For the last four years, another woman had lived with them also and, to Besarnac's great joy, had borne him a son. "I named him Liberté." Valiantly defending his ménage à trois, he described his lover as "an excellent mother, an ardent patriot. The child is superb, he is generally loved, and we know that he is not the fruit of a crime. My companion [the legal wife] loves him as a mother would; if he is not her son, he is the son of her friend. . . . She smothers him with caresses and gifts." Fearful that baby Liberté would be classified as the product of adultery, Besarnac appealed for a special law allowing those locked in un-consummated marriages to leave legacies to their natural children.[67]

Just as they defended the deep bonds between unmarried mothers and fathers, petitioners praised natural parental and filial affection. "I have a son who is no less dear to me for having been born out of wedlock," wrote one mother. Descriptions of maternal care, whether written by mother or child, almost always emphasized the hardship, sacrifices, and disgrace endured by tender mothers. "She was a real mother . . . a sensitive mother, victim of an unfortunate inclination . . . she overcame all the opprobrium brought about by a miserable prejudice," recounted one anonymous daughter. In situations of adultery, illegitimate offspring worked all the harder—and with less success—to convince the legislators that the bonds between parent and child legitimized their relationship. One son recounted that his well-off, married father had not only bestowed his name and care upon him, but had even helped to arrange a marriage and dowry for the boy's mother. But after his father's death, relatives had stripped the son of both his father's wealth and his surname.[68]

To make their appeals more compelling, some petitioners moved beyond their personal tales of natural affection and unwarranted misery to suggest the broader social ramifications of reform for poor relief. Especially aware of the "many children without resources" in his own commune, one justice of the peace from the Orléanais contended that it would more equitable and more pragmatic to let enfants naturels inherit whatever meager sums their mothers or fathers might leave behind. "Will you do nothing for a crowd of orphans in this agonizing position?" demanded one pamphleteer on be-half of *enfants adultérins* (children born of adultery) who lost their fathers. A fellow anonymous petitioner claimed it would "lighten the burden of the state" to grant rights to illegitimate children. "How many unhappy and abandoned mothers, how many families just being born, will bless the Citizen Cambacérès . . ." promised yet another enfant naturel, already liti-gating against his collateral relatives.[69]

These appeals suggested that destigmatizing illegitimacy could help state and society as a whole. Those who petitioned on behalf of illegitimate chil-dren strove to balance civil order with their request for unprecedented rights. But theirs was a difficult task, for they aimed to stretch the bound-aries of the family. Their appeals cut to the core of the lineage family as a so-cial and economic construct, as they pushed the word "natural" toward the radical inclusion of children born out of wedlock.

LEGISLATIVE CHOICES

"I am a mother," began Madame Grandval as she stood at the bar of the Legislative Assembly in the spring of 1792. "Sinister prejudices reduce natural children to the most wretched isolation: they hold to their families only by the bonds of nature; and these bonds, oh shameful civil laws! these sacred bonds bring opprobrium. The tender mother dare not press this child to her breast." Decrying these feudal laws, she beseeched the deputies to allow illegitimate children to become universal heirs of their mothers' legacies.[70] With her tangible presence, as well as her words, Madame Grandval embodied both the pressing problem of unwed motherhood and the inequitable treatment of illegitimate children. Her vibrant appeal spurred the Committee of Legislation to produce its first study on the legal status of natural children.

These jurists carried a keen awareness of these children's tenuous position, as well as of growing rates of illegitimacy, paternity suits, and child abandonment. "What have our social morality *(mœurs)* and severe laws on bastardy done up to this day?" demanded the deputy Léonard Robin on 20 September 1792, as he introduced the Committee of Legislation's initial bill on illegitimacy. "We have more abandoned children, and more at the charge of the State; infinitely more scandal and libertinage: one could even say that our bad laws and prejudices that stigmatize the father, the mother, and the natural child have brought about more vice and countless crimes." As he indicted the Old Regime system, Robin invoked public opinion, voiced by the "crowd of petitions on this important matter." Robin argued that natural law bound all parents to their offspring, natural or legitimate. Anxious to recognize their rights without attacking the significance of marriage, he proposed that recognized illegitimate children should share parental legacies with legitimate siblings, though they should receive only a half-share.[71] Robin's proposed law saw no debate and certainly no action on 20 September 1792, this busy, final day of the Legislative Assembly. But when the Convention subsequently considered childbirth outside of marriage, it shared his concern with child abandonment and with the tricky matter of balancing the natural rights of illegitimate children with the sanctity of marriage and property. Moreover, how should morality, law, and opinion shape the intimate behavior of men and women, and the differing responsibilities of mothers and fathers?

Although a few deputies and petitioners at the bar had called for action on behalf of illegitimate children in the early 1790s, it was not until 1793 that the Committees of Legislation and of Poor Relief both convinced the legislature to take decisive action.[72] On 4 June the deputies decreed in principle that illegitimate children would have a share in parental legacies, "according to the form that will be determined." On 28 June, the Convention passed a poor relief bill to aid unwed mothers and their children. A few days later, a group of abandoned children from the Faubourg Saint-Antoine paraded before the National Convention to commend the deputies for having "made them members of the body social" and to urge them to make good on their 4 June promise to give succession rights to natural children. The Convention triumphantly decided to rename "foundlings" as "enfants naturels de la patrie." Within weeks, Cambacérès proposed the first Civil Code, which included both the abolition of paternity suits and the granting of rights to natural children recognized by their parents. In August 1793, deputies Berlier and Oudot, fellow members of the Committee of Legislation, became the major champions of this policy. Impossibly bogged down by the divisive politics of the early Terror, the Convention abandoned the Civil Code, but salvaged these policies on paternity and illegitimacy in slightly different form as the law of the 12 brumaire an II (2 November 1793). This law accorded inheritance rights to natural children whose parents died after 14 July 1789, provided that their parents had recognized them as their own.[73]

Several points about the 12 brumaire law need highlighting. This poorly written law lacked juridical clarity and inadvertently left the courts a great deal of room for varied interpretations, but it nonetheless established the revolutionary principle that illegitimate offspring should have the same natural rights as other children. However, the law's authors acted like jugglers struggling to keep three concepts in the air at once: they wanted simultaneously to recognize the natural rights of individual children, to preserve the primacy of legal marriage over free unions, and to guarantee a new liberty for fathers out of wedlock to recognize their own children without the coercion of a paternity suit. To pull off this juggling act, the deputies limited the far-reaching implications of their equality principle: they curtailed these new civil rights to offspring with ample proof of paternity. Only a father's public or private written acknowledgment of paternity or evidence of his continual care would do.[74] This demand for strict evidence of voluntary fatherhood also implicitly undercut the legal basis for paternity suits by unwed mothers. As they decoded the laws of nature, the deputies tapped into "natural" distinctions between male and female sexuality and between motherhood and fatherhood. They relied both on the apparently natural bond between mother and child and on a newly imagined relationship between unwed mothers, their children, and the idealized welfare state.

A particular interpretation of natural law ideology formed the bedrock of the jurists' logic. In moving toward the 12 brumaire law, the deputies strove to carry natural rights into the controversial realm of illicit sexuality and to weigh natural equality against social conventions. Again and again, they foregrounded the argument that natural law designated all children as equal, even those born out of wedlock. "Nature . . . has not made it a crime to be born," declared Cambacérès in 1793. Like the petitioners, he pitted the "incorruptible force of nature" against the "the tyranny of habit." Just as ardently, the deputies Berlier and Oudot too invoked nature as they ranted against the "monstrous practices," the injustices of violating natural equality and penalizing innocent children at birth. Nature, not the religious ceremony of marriage, endowed the child with his civil status *(état)*, argued Berlier.[75]

At the same time, Cambacérès, Berlier, and Oudot were intent on positing that new rights for illegitimate children would not threaten the institutions of marriage and family. In order to justify granting rights to children born out of wedlock, the deputies essentially created two categories of natural children. They imagined an ideal natural child, born of free parents who had made an unofficial, mutual marriage contract and who recognized their child. The jurists concentrated their arguments in defense of this first category of children: these natural children would win full rights. Into the second category fell all those born of adultery or incest and all those whose fathers—and sometimes even their mothers—did not acknowledge them. The deputies counted on mothers and, ultimately, on the state to provide for this second, much larger group of "children of the nation." Although the jurists spoke less often and less grandly of this second category, it is crucial to recognize that their assumptions about maternal commitment and state poor relief underpinned the plan of endowing certain natural children with rights and emancipating natural fathers to choose paternity without judicial constraint.

In depicting the conception of the ideal natural child, the deputies claimed that the very act of choosing to conceive a child created an implicit marriage, a "private marriage," between the couple. Oudot asserted, "Each time that a child is born, the law should presume that the father and mother had the intention of fulfilling the will of nature and the attendant obligations, and that consequently, a marriage has occurred, unless a contrary intention is proven."[76] Oudot and Berlier built on the recent definition of legal marriage as a voluntary contract to imply parallels between natural, private unions and formal, civil marriage. They stressed that the purpose of marriage was to procreate, and that the will of the couple, not the force of the law, made marriage real. A child born of a private union had every bit as much right to parental care, love, and legacy.

Not only did private marriage parallel legal marriage, but it also dovetailed neatly with the revolutionaries' emphasis on personal liberty and affect. Here the deputies echoed the language of petitioners who suggested that constrictive Old Regime practices had led them to form free unions and give birth out of wedlock. Oudot explicitly indicted the Old Regime familial system: the combination of indissoluble, arranged marriage, the glorification of celibacy, and excessive paternal authority had led to a "multitude of clandestine unions" and encouraged unwed mothers to commit infanticide or to abandon their children as bastards condemned by all. By destigmatizing natural unions and their offspring, the Convention could solve myriad social ills and move toward that liberty so crucial for forming strong and affectionate personal relationships.[77]

Advocates of the 12 brumaire law argued that freeing natural children and their parents from a debilitating prejudice would also introduce equality into the family and into society at large. Like the more general egalitarian inheritance passed only a week earlier on 5 brumaire an II (26 October 1793), granting inheritance rights to natural children would help to redistribute the fortunes of the wealthy. At the Paris Jacobin Society a few weeks earlier, the speaker Chabot highlighted this point and berated existing laws for condemning the offspring of "pure and tender sentiment" to "poverty and opprobrium." In late October, picking up the baton from Berlier, Oudot, and Chabot, the deputy Cambacérès seconded this equalizing principle, trumpeted the indubitable claims of nature, and especially worked hard to assure skeptics that the new law did not undermine marriage or encourage immorality. Because of "the respect for social morality (mœurs), faith in marriage, and social conventions," the law would exclude children of adultery from equal inheritance rights, promised Cambacérès. Just as he pledged, the 12 brumaire law limited enfants adultérins to a food pension, amounting to just one-third of what legitimate children could receive.[78]

To legislate equal civil status for certain natural children was a bold and unprecedented move: it demanded that licit families incorporate these formerly outcast relatives into new property arrangements. Crafting the law also required the deputies to clarify which illegitimate children would benefit and to address the delicate task of defining the child's relationship to his or her parents. Once again they turned to nature and to the concept of private marriage. Although they spoke of private marriages as freely chosen mutual contracts, Berlier and Oudot in fact envisaged men's and women's situations within the contract quite differently, especially once pregnancy occurred. Nature placed men and women into disparate positions, theorized the jurists. They did not simply equate women and nature. Rather, nature revealed to women what it concealed from men: the certainty of parenthood. And from that anxiety-producing difference flowed a whole line of reasoning. In that very certainty of motherhood lay the mother's natural love for her child as well as her responsibility toward him or her. As Oudot stated, "If a man abandons the woman that he has made into a mother, it is up to her, to whom nature has made manifest the proof of maternity, to feed and raise her child and to replace the cowardly father whom she trusted too imprudently."[79] In contrast, especially outside the protected realm of marriage, a man never knew definitively whether or not he was the father. Within this doubt lay a certain freedom, for the jurists reasoned that fatherhood could not be forced upon a man. Only if a man fully acknowledged his paternity could his illegitimate child gain full civil and inheritance rights.

Building upon this logic about nature, Oudot and Berlier also effectively reversed the Old Regime juridical assumption that children had a natural right to food from their alleged fathers and that natural mothers could use the courts to prove paternal responsibility. In 1781 Fournel had written, "The civil stain, imprinted on these children by their illegitimate birth, does not deprive them of the rights they derive from nature: the first of these is the right to obtain the means of subsistence from their fathers." Fournel remained confident in the power of judges to penetrate the mysteries of nature and attribute paternity—or at least the presumption of paternity—with reasonable accuracy and justice. Paradoxically, for the revolutionary jurists, nature, normally so bountiful in distributing rights, concealed fatherhood and curtailed the child's right to press a paternity suit to demand food. "These are the very secrets of nature, which in this case, restrains the exercise of rights," commented Berlier. At the same time, the deputies remained confident that true fathers would *voluntarily* fulfill their natural obligations to provide food and upbringing to their offspring.[80]

The authors of the 12 brumaire law forged a new definition of fatherhood made up of two key components. Republican fatherhood demanded greater masculine sensitivity and responsibility than in the Old Regime. But outside of marriage, fatherhood could not stem from coercion. According to the first principle, every father owed his offspring affection, tender care, and material support. The revolutionaries expected far more from *all* fathers than the Old Regime had. As Lynn Hunt has demonstrated, the political culture of the radical Revolution worked hard to replace authoritarian patriarchs with a new model of willing, sensitive, and responsive fathers. As the citizen Dulaurent proclaimed in his speech on the "Good Father" that fall of 1793, "You would not be a father if you did not shed tears for your son."[81] In discussing fatherhood outside of marriage, Berlier, Oudot, and Cambacérès espoused this republican validation of affectionate, engaged fathers. As they defended private marriages and the filial rights of natural children, the jurists imagined that nature forged bonds of paternal responsibility as strong, indeed stronger, than those determined by the law. "In effect, when any honorable man, any sensitive and delicate man, has become a father and has had a natural child with a free [unmarried] woman, hasn't he contracted an engagement? . . . This man is bound to all the duties of fatherhood" whether or not he had carried out religious or civil formalities of marriage, insisted Cambacérès. Oudot even suggested that a natural father who failed to provide food and education to a child *whom he had recognized* should be deprived of his rights as a citizen. Fathers as well as mothers had a profound and natural obligation to their progeny. Certainly they owed all their children a legacy after death.[82]

Yet in that phrase "whom he had recognized" lay the quintessential core of the deputies' second innovation regarding paternity. As historian Jacques Mulliez has illustrated, they believed that true fatherhood derived from a man's voluntary choice to be a father. The legislators imagined the putative father in the Old Regime as a young man, in need of liberation from his own authoritarian father. Rather, every son should be free to choose love and contract marriage. Individual liberty was sacrosanct. To become an ideal sentimental father, to experience love for one's child born *outside of marriage*, a man must embrace fatherhood freely. Just as conjugal love was rooted in the autonomous choice of a marriage partner, paternal affection outside the security of faithful marriage could only develop as an unconstrained emotion. Berlier ranted against the absurdity of imposing this relationship onto a man against his will. "I ask what bonds can ever be established between a child who enters a family only through the wretched auspices of a court case and the man who will be his father only because a tribunal has said so?" Nature concealed paternity—thus Berlier advised the Convention to "stop where nature herself has established limits."[83] No longer could communal witnesses be trusted to attribute biological paternity as best they could, based on circumstantial evidence.

The uncertainty of fatherhood outside of marriage contrasted with married paternity. Within the ideal republican marriage of companionship and trust, a woman's fidelity guaranteed her husband the secure knowledge of his fatherhood. "The principal goal of legal marriage is to assure with the greatest certainty that the children will have the affection, care, and protection of their father and mother; and for the father, this affection and care rests on the assurance of his paternity," asserted Oudot. For this reason, the wife's "fidelity is the essence of marriage." It allowed a man to truly love his children. Outside of legal marriage, paternity remained elusive, but all the more important because of the greater expectations from attentive and sensitive fathers and because of the greater rights now accorded to enfants naturels recognized by their fathers. As Berlier commented "It is no longer a question today of a small sum of money paid to relieve oneself of an onerous title."[84] For the revolutionaries, republican natural fatherhood carried meaning and responsibility far beyond the mere child support payments levied by Old Regime courts. And yet in an ironic twist, precisely because so much more was at stake, the revolutionaries made it easier for natural fathers to escape their obligations.

The deputies' new vision for sentimental and liberated fatherhood rested on corollary expectations about motherhood and the state. For Oudot, Berlier, and Cambacérès, nature manifested and generated a powerful and useful bond of love and duty between mother and child (see Figure 10). Like other republicans, they believed in the political possibilities of maternal kindness. Aware of the rising rates of unwed motherhood and child abandonment, these civil law jurists ranted against the Old Regime for stigmatizing and dishonoring this natural tie between mother and child outside of marriage. Berlier indicted the "shame and misery" that caused women to commit infanticide or abandon their children, while Oudot waxed poetic about enabling natural mothers to experience the "ineffable joys of maternity without blushing." Republican mothers, even unwed ones, should be encouraged to nurse their children without shame and to raise citizens for the Republic.[85]

But even as they praised natural motherhood free from shame, the deputies' new system in fact was rooted in the traditional concept that a young woman's honor lay in guarding her virginity. Without a doubt, their recurrent assertions that abolishing paternity searches would improve morals and reduce scandalous behavior relied on the unproblematized and naïve assumption that unmarried women would develop formidable powers of resistance once they knew that they could no longer trap men through paternity searches. The deputies held a rather ambivalent and bifurcated view of female nature and sexuality. After birth, the mother's moral force and breast milk would nurture the natural child and regenerate society; before birth, this same young woman was most often portrayed as a wanton seductress. In his attack on paternity suits, Berlier indicted women (along

Figure 10.   To Maternal Tenderness, from the *Manuel des autorités constituées de la République française* (1797). Courtesy of the Bibliothèque nationale de France.

with Old Regime courts) for scheming and falsely inculpating innocent men as fathers: "a real commerce, calculated prostitution," the old laws "allowed more than one immodest girl to transform her fecundity into financial speculation." As Berlier's comments suggest, the jurists imagined natural mothers as lower-class women, who might use their sexuality to rob wealthier men of property. Oudot likewise incriminated unwed mothers for garnering "a salary for their weakness and vices."[86] In 1793, the jurists emphasized these women's acts of seduction more than their theft of familial property. Immersed in the egalitarian discourse of 1793, the lawmakers did not push the point that these women had transgressed class lines. But these metaphors hint at the deputies' class-based assumptions about the nature of paternity suits and suggest yet another logic for depriving natural mothers of the right to press charges. In the conservative backlash after Thermidor, attacks on unwed mothers more explicitly positioned them as violators of family property, as well as sexual transgressors.

The deputies worried far less about the possibility of irresponsible sexual behavior by men, even though they tacitly recognized that a young man might evade his obligations. In stipulating that men should have the right to acknowledge paternity later in life, Berlier commented, "Often, only after the torrent of youth in the calm of mature age does a man, meditating on his past life, recognize his duties and make a vow to fulfill them."[87] In any event, women, not men, were the seducers. Here the deputies were also influenced by the late Old Regime judicial trend toward questioning the credibility of unwed, pregnant women. Moreover, as historian Marie-Claude Phan has pointed out, the deputies needed this contradictory depiction of female sexuality because they sought simultaneously to defend the morality of legitimate marriage and to attack the unjust stigma against illegitimate children.[88] For this balancing act to work, women still had to bear the ethical burden of pregnancy.

With the maternal role came certain moral duties to both the child and the Republic. Mothers, whether married or not, owed it to the state to use their regenerative, maternal capacity on behalf of the new politics. In turn, the new state, deeply invested in this potent, natural bond, should both support and oversee *(surveiller)* the material necessities and moral development of women and children who slipped through the cracks of the family structure. Here Oudot and Berlier tapped into and reinforced recent reformulations of the relationship between mother and state.

In late June 1793, when the deputy Etienne Maignet presented a report by the Committee on Poor Relief, he laid out crucial portions of a new social and political alliance between family and state, and among state, mother, and child. Maignet believed that legally formed families acted as forces of regeneration and reproduction for the nation-state; whenever possible, the state should help fathers to support large families within their homes. But he also tackled the pressing problem of abandoned children and impoverished *mères célibatrices*, invoking images of homeless women and children (see Figure 11). According to Maignet, the patriotic state and society owed poor children and abandoned mothers care and solicitude. After all, unwed mothers, however they might differ from married mothers, "had nonetheless also borne citizens for the State." And they might, through breast-feeding and patriotic education, like all mothers, help to fashion the moral fiber of France. He fervently embraced the Rousseauian vision of nursing and maternal education as political acts. According to his 26 June 1793 proposal, which would become law a few days later, the state would offer aid to unwed mothers who nursed their offspring, pay their lying-in expenses, and even build homes for unwed mothers in every district of France. Maignet's

Figure 11.   "Ah! But the times are hard." Impoverished mother and children (c. 1789), detail. Courtesy of the Bibliothèque nationale de France.

poor relief report simultaneously called for cleansing natural mothers of humiliation and promised to let them give birth in secret. Since extramarital childbearing still carried dishonor, Maignet envisioned motherhood as a form of republican redemption for the unmarried mothers' earlier moments of weakness. Their illegitimate offspring would then become children of the nation, eligible for welfare pensions or upbringing in state homes. Adoption of indigent children would complement this system.[89]

Boldly shifting onto the state those responsibilities that communities and the law had traditionally placed on the shoulders of fathers, Maignet scarcely mentioned unwed fathers at all. He certainly did not condemn their acts of seduction or abandonment, though he expressed the optimistic belief that once a hesitant father saw the mother nurse and tend to their child with such dedication, "it will be impossible for him . . . to refuse to return to this woman." Echoing Jean-Jacques Rousseau, Maignet stated, "Once women become mothers again, soon men will become fathers and husbands again." Although he indicted déclarations de grossesse for encouraging women to conceal their pregnancies or even commit infanticide, Maignet did not directly address paternity suits.[90] But his vision of maternal and state responsibility informed the arguments of Oudot and Berlier.

Like Maignet, these jurists called on the state to aid the most poverty-stricken mères célibatrices and illegitimate children. Like him, they envisioned the overhaul of family and morals as a total system that would bring about the decline in unwed motherhood. Already, in his initial appeal to endow natural children with rights in June 1792, Oudot had called for state-run asylums where unwed mothers could nurse their babies in privacy.[91] Legalizing adoption would help to remove some children from the state's charge. Berlier and Oudot reiterated these plans more thoroughly in August 1793. Both supported adoption, which the deputy François de La Roche-foucauld-Liancourt had initially advocated on behalf of the Committee on Poor Relief in 1790 as a means of alleviating poverty. As various deputies argued, adoption would not only contribute to redistributing wealth, but this practice also fit well with the notion that family ties were rooted in sentiment and liberty. As Figure 12 suggests, revolutionary adoption rested on the father's free embrace of paternity and the mother's natural tenderness. Adoption had been legalized in principle on 18 January 1792, and the proposed Civil Code now strove in the summer of 1793 to give this practice a real frame. (In fact, some adoptions took place with state approval during the 1790s, but its legal status was not clearly delineated in the 1790s. The Napoleonic Code outlined a very limited form of adoption of adults by childless individuals over the age of fifty for inheritance purposes.) In the summer of 1793, the deputies viewed adoption as an integral part of their attempt to reduce poverty and restructure family boundaries. Oudot argued that adoption would comfort the childless and make them more useful, "but adoption should be instituted less to console them than to come to the aid of those who have lost their natural protectors."[92]

Most important, the civil jurists called for public homes for both natural mothers and their offspring. Berlier, for example, proposed that the father of an unwed mother pay for his grandchild's upbringing; if he and his wayward

*Ma bonne amie nous n'avions que 7 enfans;
celui-là fera le huitieme*
Le 29 9bre 1789 . V·S·

Figure 12.   Adoption scene: "My good friend, we had only seven children; this one will make the eighth one" (1789). Courtesy of the Bibliothèque nationale de France.

daughter were too indigent, she and her child should have access to state-run establishments, financed by an additional tax on bachelors.[93] As they seconded new welfare plans and republican roles for unwed mothers and their children, the crafters of the 12 brumaire law also facilitated their goals of endowing *recognized* natural children with civil rights and liberating putative fathers from coercive paternity. The natural maternal bond and the generous, responsible state could be counted on to provide for one set of fatherless children. The other set of more fortunate natural children would gain full rights to the love and legacies of emancipated fathers and devoted mothers.

In sum, the jurists presented a coherent if problematic vision of the triad of natural child, mother, and father. This idealized conception wove together rights ideology, gendered assumptions about sexuality and parenthood, and new expectations from a secular poor relief system. Invoking natural law and validating the bonds of affection that produced progeny outside of marriage, the deputies hoped to restore the natural child's dignity and equality. As they imagined it, in the regenerated new republic, the natural father would be freed from coercive Old Regime family practices and would feel the strength of paternal tenderness, honor, and love and embrace the joys and duties of fatherhood. Once recognized, this child had a legal right to his or her father's goods and a moral right to his love. Likewise, nature ordained the mother to love her child without hesitation and to do everything within her power to raise the child as a true republican. Should she find herself destitute and abandoned, the state would step in with support and, ideally, enable the mother to nurse and then raise the child herself. In fact, the revolutionary state would far fall short of adequately funding this welfare system.[94] But in 1793, the deputies optimistically imagined that the burden on the state should not be excessive, for the deputies reasoned confidently that illegitimacy would become less frequent, since divorce would reduce adultery and young couples now had greater liberty to choose their own marriage partners. As always, the revolutionary jurists envisioned their bundle of family reforms working together to regenerate France.

. . .

The revolutionaries' attempt to transform bastards into citizens fit part and parcel within the broader familial and social reforms of the Convention. When the deputies chose to endow at least some illegitimate children with natural rights, they responded to the social pressure of rising rates of illegitimacy and child abandonment as well as to the revolutionary logic expressed by petitioners on behalf of natural children. As in other aspects of family law reform, the deputies were profoundly influenced by the ideology of natural rights and equality, but they interpreted their mandate from natural law in light of other republican goals and assumptions. Integrally connected to the imagined possibilities of moral regeneration and state aid to the poor, the 12 brumaire law articulated distinct gender roles within the natural family: it reconfigured the legal and familial identity of natural mothers and fathers and their relationship to the state and the natural child. Specifically, the 12 brumaire law stepped up expectations from those men who voluntarily acknowledged their fatherhood outside of marriage. It sought to destigmatize illegitimacy and granted full civil status to natural children recognized by their parents.

But by implicitly outlawing paternity suits by both mother and child, the law also intended to create a new alliance between mothers and the state that enabled unmarried fathers to choose liberty over fatherhood. As I will discuss in the next chapter, in practice in the mid 1790s, unwed mothers, local communities, and regional judges resisted the imperative to let putative fathers off the hook; although the jurists' intention to suppress paternity cases had been clear, the law was markedly vague. Only repeated clarifications from the legislature and various administrative committees would bring this traditional practice to a close in 1795. The Civil Code abolished paternity suits more explicitly, and the nineteenth-century courts still struggled to find limited ways to attribute paternal responsibility.[95] But the fundamental premise and practice of maternal responsibility and paternal choice and liberty would stand firm until the 1912 law reestablishing paternity suits.

In addition, this reliance on the "natural" bond between mothers and children illustrates paradoxical and crucial elements of the revolutionary leaders' thinking about gender, nature, the state, and civil rights. The natural qualities of motherhood, especially motherhood outside of marriage, constituted a stumbling block for the revolutionaries in conceiving of women as equal citizens. Revolutionary jurists were surprisingly capable of imagining daughters, sisters, wives, and even mothers within marriage, as citizens with civil rights. By earlier laws on divorce and parental authority, a woman facing marriage should have almost the same freedom as a man, to make—or break—the voluntary contract of love. And within ten days of indirectly depriving unwed mothers of access to paternity suits, the deputies granted egalitarian inheritance rights to sisters and approved the Civil Code's provision to grant equal and shared control over communal marital property to wives. Although it never became law, the proposed Civil Code of 1793 stipulated that married mothers and fathers had the same authority over their children and that they jointly shared in the administration of their offspring's goods.[96] But mothers were nonetheless envisaged less as rights-bearing citizens than as the natural caretakers of the social body. For the jurists, *unwed* mothers, as lower-class interlopers, also threatened the property and sanctity of families. This theme of familial property, muted in 1793, would become prominent later in the Revolution. When it came to dealing with mothers at their "most natural," as mothers outside of marriage, even those revolutionaries most bent on creating an egalitarian family lowered the boom of honor and responsibility—both moral and financial—onto their shoulders.

The law of 12 brumaire also reveals fundamental tensions within revolutionary definitions of masculinity and fatherhood. On the one hand, various new family laws had undercut the power of married fathers, envisioned as older men whose authority needed tempering and whose hearts might well be in need of regeneration. On the other hand, by implicitly abolishing paternity suits, the 12 brumaire law certified the liberty of putative, unmarried fathers, imagined as young men whose manhood lay in independence and who should be free to embrace their natural paternity as they saw fit. The Revolution cultivated an ideal of sentimental paternity for *all* fathers, but it simultaneously introduced an implicit generational divide into the image of masculinity. In the view of some critics, the Revolution validated the liberty of young men at the expense of older men's authority.[97] The liberty of fathers outside marriage seemed to fit poorly with their loss of authority within marriage. In reaction, some jurists and pamphleteers, foreshadowing the Civil Code, began to promote another definition of masculinity, rooted in the father of the family as honorable defender of family name and property.

Moreover, the new law accentuated another contradiction difficult to resolve in practice: how could the courts simultaneously recognize each man's freedom to choose his own paternity but also require him to fulfill his natural obligations to his progeny? Should a natural father's responsibilities to offspring born outside of marriage be allowed to infringe upon his commitments to his legitimate children and wife? As the next chapter will explore, the courts wrestled with these questions and in the process chipped away at the revolutionaries' attempt to construct a new form of natural, sentimental, and freely chosen fatherhood.

Finally, the 12 brumaire law brought remarkable opportunities to some illegitimate children. The state had articulated the undeniable and daring principle of their civil equality and inclusion within the social and political body of both nation and family. As illegitimate children began to enter the courts in pursuit of inheritance rights, the difficulty of implementing this bold challenge to family customs and property quickly became apparent. The law provoked intense resistance from families intent on preserving their patrimony, it created complex legal subcategories of natural children, and, above all, "voluntary fatherhood" proved to be a seriously difficult matter to determine and define.

6. What Makes a Father?

Illegitimacy and Paternity from the Year II to the Civil Code

"Let the name 'illegitimate child' disappear," asserted the deputy Berlier in the summer of 1793. As he proclaimed the rights of enfants naturels, his imagery echoed Cambacérès' memorable statement from two months earlier: "Nature . . . has not made it a crime to be born." When the legislators set out to destigmatize illegitimacy and endow natural children with civil rights, they spoke with bold strokes. They passed the controversial law of 12 brumaire an II (2 November 1793), which granted illegitimate children, if recognized by their parents, full inheritance rights equivalent to those of legitimate children. At the same time, the law hedged against attributing filiation too lightly. Wary of forcing fatherhood on a man against his will, the legislators stipulated that paternity could be proven only by a father's written word or by evidence of his "continuous care." The law would have an impact both on the inheritance possibilities of illegitimate children and on the paternity suits initiated by unwed mothers.[1]

From its very outset the law generated dissension and criticism. Like the decrees mandating egalitarian inheritance among legitimate siblings, the 12 brumaire law seemed to disrupt traditional family property arrangements in the name of equality and natural law. It pitted the rights of newly recognized individuals against customary practices designed to promote and protect the family line. Moreover, in the eyes of some observers especially after Thermidor, this law carried the taint of immorality: not only did it threaten marriage by validating illegitimacy, but it also formed part and parcel of the devastating social program of the Terror. "All families are trembling," warned the lawyer who was defending the Dupin-Rochefort family legacy against an enfant naturel in July 1795. Moving beyond the simple defense of his clients' property, he demanded the repeal of this 12 brumaire law, associated with the Terror and other "laws from the Year II, some tyrannical, others bloodthirsty, all disorganized, made and promulgated under the blade of the executioner."[2]

We still know too little about the attempt to implement the law across France.[3] Most scholars have focused on the genesis of this law.[4] This chapter builds upon the last one by exploring grassroots litigation over both halves of the 12 brumaire law: first, its tacit abolition of paternity suits and then its granting of legacies to recognized natural children. Many of these contestations over paternity, child support, and inheritance also took place within the attempt to restore and redefine the social order in the aftermath of the Terror. In the mid to late 1790s, a groundswell of conservative opinion challenged family innovations that seemed to tear apart the trustworthy bonds of custom, law, and mutual obligation. The next chapter will analyze this mood of backlash more fully.

In its pursuit of social stability after the Terror, Thermidorian culture often questioned the abrupt attempt to inject equal rights into domestic relationships. This chapter will begin to suggest the power of these changes in politics and social philosophy by asking how the political and cultural climate of Thermidor and the Directory informed litigants' arguments and influenced courts' adjudication of the 12 brumaire law. The inheritance rights of illegitimate children were especially vulnerable to political shifts for two reasons. First, the statute itself was ambiguously worded and left ample room for conflicting interpretations. Second, for some critics, the move to include natural children more fully within the body social epitomized the destructive quality of the new family policies and their threat to property. Court cases became an arena for debating the meaning of fatherhood and reassessing the legitimate boundaries of families.

The 12 brumaire law was difficult to interpret and put into practice. It lacked legal clarity. Notably, the law's abolition of paternity suits was markedly vague. It did *not* directly address unwed mothers' traditional use of the courts to claim lying-in expenses and child support. Rather, in the context of discussing the inheritance rights of natural children, the law placed tight limits on proving paternity: article 8 stipulated that only the father's written acknowledgment or evidence of his continuous fatherly care could legally prove his paternity. Over the years 1793 to 1795, the Convention and other authorities reinterpreted this article to mean the abolition of paternity suits by natural mothers as well as their offspring. Both unwed mothers and local judges resisted this reading of the law and persisted in following the customary practice of paternity suits until the Convention clarified and enforced the abolition of *recherche de paternité*.

In addition, the law contained numerous ambiguities for inheritance cases. Even though the deputies' express purpose was to grant rights to illegitimate offspring, they tempered the radicalism of their own law, created complicated subcategories of natural children, and left various provisions open to confusion and dispute. Uneasy about encouraging illicit unions, the deputies denied full rights to children born of adultery. These children could claim only one-third of a full share of their parents' legacies. To benefit fully from the law, natural children had to be born of *parents libres*, that is, unmarried parents, who voluntarily recognized them and whose estates had entered probate after 14 July 1789. While conflicts over maternal recognition were rare, proving "voluntary" paternity often turned out to be difficult. How to do so was particularly unclear for those children whose parents had died after the promulgation of the 12 brumaire law. For the decree specified that their cases fell under the aegis of the Civil Code, yet that code would not be completed until 1804. Despite all its legal ambiguities and limitations, for certain children the 12 brumaire law opened the door to unexpected opportunities.

In the first section of this chapter, I will draw on my case study of the Calvados to explore the persistent attempts of unwed mothers to press paternity suits. The chapter then turns to the issue of natural children seeking their inheritance. In contrast to the flood of cases initiated by legitimate siblings, only a handful of enfants naturels made their way to the various tribunals of the department of the Calvados to solicit a share of the family patrimony. Nor did other regions witness a much larger outpouring of succession claims by natural children.[5] To analyze inheritance demands, then, I broaden my source base and use both local suits from around France and the decisions made by the Tribunal de Cassation between 1794 and 1804. During the Directory and Consulate, this national-level court of appeals gradually expanded its juridical authority and increased its influence on jurisprudence across France.[6]

I will argue that, paradoxically, the 12 brumaire law inadvertently did more to harm illegitimate children than to help them. Many were deprived of child support because their mothers gradually lost the capacity to pursue paternity suits, but only a few could take advantage of the law's unprecedented promise of egalitarian inheritance rights. Yet these judicial contests over paternity and natural children's rights also had significance beyond their immediate impact on individual natural children and their relatives. For as magistrates, lawyers, and citizens battled over legacies and child support in the courts, they set forth competing models of the social and familial order. Several pivotal issues gripped the popular, judicial, and legislative imagination and would in turn influence the crafting of the Civil Code. First, how should family laws and practices balance the natural rights of individuals with the integrity of family property? Second, what did it mean to be a father? How did his liberty or authority intersect with the natural duties or claims of the mother and with the child's right to affection, care, and goods? Third, in building a society to shore up the fragile Republic after the Terror, how should lawmakers and judges weigh the needs of the civil order against the claims of nature?

PATERNITY SEARCHES: "THIS ODIOUS INQUISITION . . . IS FOREVER OUTLAWED"

In January 1794 in the Norman village of Saint-Germain-de-Livet, Marie-Rose Marais initiated a paternity suit against Nicolas Dutacq. By Old Regime standards, her case was both classic and strong. She had gone to work as a seamstress for this widowed cultivateur two-and-a-half years earlier. She recounted that amid his promises of marriage, she "succumbed to his caresses, . . . and Dutacq let her run his home as if she were his wife." Servants and other workers offered ample testimony that he treated her differently, kissed her in the garden, and "held her in his arms and caressed her." Above all, he had been seen in the master bedroom with her between the 8th and 12th of the previous August, the crucial dates for conception. By all accounts, by the judgment of the community, this case was clear: he was the father. Not surprisingly, Nicolas Dutacq, the alleged father, had a different tale to tell. Like many a man in his shoes, he swiftly denied being the father, but then his defense took a new tack. Cloaking himself in the rhetoric of equality, he abruptly changed the topic to the fate of illegitimate children and their new civil and inheritance rights by the 12 brumaire law. But, he announced accurately, the legislators did not want to give out this right too lightly, nor attribute paternity and a share in paternal inheritance without proof. Far too often, magistrates had "charged a man for a girl's lack of restraint." Echoing the deputies' invocations of the unknowable mysteries of nature, Dutacq set forth a new definition of paternity: "Oral testimony no longer establishes paternity," he asserted. "A tempting and seductive girl can no longer slanderously accuse [a man] because one or several witnesses have seen the young woman and the young man give in to the innocent games of their age, frolic together, and embrace each other." Never taking up the details of the account provided by Marie-Rose and the host of witnesses, he quoted boldly from the 12 brumaire law about written proof of paternity.[7]

The judges of the District Tribunal of Lisieux were thrown into a quandary, for the 12 brumaire law was by no means clear. Article 8 declared that only the father's written word or his continual actions of parental care could legally establish fatherhood. Yet these stipulations of article 8 referred to proving paternity in succession cases. Although the lawmakers had certainly spoken as if they intended their law to outlaw paternity suits by unwed mothers, the law itself made this point only through analogy. The magistrates of Lisieux split evenly on whether the law also forbade the traditional right of natural mothers to make claims based on witness testimony. The tie-breaker judge covered sheets of paper with his scribbled indecision about whether paternity could be differently proven and construed at the moment of conception than at the time of inheritance. Could there be two kinds of fatherhood?[8]

Ultimately Dutacq won his case, and gradually, other men named as fathers would increasingly cite this law and boldly claim their right to choose whether or not to embrace fatherhood. But for well over a year after the fall 1793 promulgation of the 12 brumaire law, local officials and judges proved reluctant to deny women the right to press paternity suits. Unwed mothers continued to register déclarations de grossesse with local justices of the peace or police commissioners. These declarations in turn still served as the basis for paternity claims, and district tribunals welcomed the long-standing practice and clung to the Old Regime tradition of placing the financial burden of fatherhood onto the man's shoulders.[9] Indeed, in some instances, women clearly hoped that the new law would actually widen paternal responsibility and bring greater benefits to their illegitimate offspring. In May 1794 when Marie Longuet of the Bocage Virois initiated a paternity suit against Jacques Lascéré, she demanded not only that he pay the traditional child support and reparations to her honor, but also that he clearly acknowledge his paternity so that their newborn "would take part in his legacy." Likewise, in the spring of 1795 when Marie Morin formally declared her pregnancy to the justice of the peace at Rochefort, she recorded that Jacques Roy had promised that their enfant naturel would be their only heir; in an uncommon twist, this father was present and signed in recognition of his paternity and promise of care.[10]

But fairly soon, alleged fathers such as Dutacq began to question the legality of the traditional practice of recherche de paternité. Other putative fathers pursued strategies similar to Dutacq's. In August 1794 Jean Morin even stood before the District Tribunal of Pont-Châlier (Pont-l'Evêque), brandishing a letter from the Committee of Legislation stating that the law had abrogated paternity suits. Most often, recalcitrant fathers fused invocations of the Convention's decree with more customary forms of defense. Pierre Angot combined a classic attack on his lover's witnesses with reference to the 12 brumaire law. Pierre Jouvin of Proissy denounced the boldness and promiscuity of the widow who cited him in court. Then he added, "Only if a man formally recognizes his paternity can he be charged with the feeding and care of a child." Moreover, alleged fathers played upon the uncertain mood in the aftermath of the Terror and the lack of clarity in the 12 brumaire law. When the Parisian Geoffroy Lafreté was sued by the newly divorced Victoire-Marie Maillard for lying-in expenses late in 1794, he successfully accused her of seducing him and plotting with her divorced husband to win Geoffroy's wealth for the child. The tiebreaker judge granted victory to Geoffroy, for how could an adulterous woman be granted a monetary reward for a child illicitly conceived during her very own marriage?[11]

Neighboring courts enforced conflicting policies, and the same court interpreted the law differently from time to time. For example, the District Tribunal of Lisieux, which had denied Marie-Rose Marais's case in April 1794, subsequently decided in favor of other women's claims. As late as November 1794 they favored Thérèse Lefranc, perhaps because she was a minor and the accused father was a former priest. As magistrates, justices of the peace, and commissioners from across France queried the Committee of Legislation on whether paternity suits truly had been outlawed, tribunals did their best to make policy in uncertain times, sometimes with inventive results. In January 1794, the court in Bayeux overturned one woman's successful claims for child support on the grounds that the *divorce law* decreed that parents should split child-care costs equally.[12]

Faced with these shifting policies, unwed mothers urged local courts as well as the Convention to hold fathers responsible for their progeny. As Jeanne Marie Leinis told the deputies, her lover, "a very rich young man," had died while serving the Republic. Now she found herself blocked from pressing a claim for child support, let alone inheritance, because her "child, through the prejudice of the law, cannot claim his father's recognition; nevertheless he had a real one who left a great deal of property." Outraged, she demanded a change in the law, for "real fathers" should pay. Likewise, when Rose Grandin was denied her paternity suit on the basis of the 12 brumaire law, she denounced the judge at Falaise as an "aristocrat" and penned an angry letter to the National Convention: "It is not fair for the nation to support children who have fathers."[13] Rose Grandin's comments cut to the heart of the issue, for in the summer of 1793 the Convention had promised that state-run poor relief would step in to replace wayward fathers and provide pensions or homes for natural mothers and abandoned children as children of the nation. Yet the national state could not fulfill its welfare promises in the war-weary and impoverished France of 1794–95, particularly after it had just dismantled the religious networks of charity.[14]

All too aware of the social burden of destitute mothers and abandoned children, district tribunals in Normandy and other parts of France did not easily and directly surrender the traditional policy of demanding child support and reparations from putative fathers. To let them off scot-free seemed to validate libertine morality and, above all, could well throw the child and perhaps the mother onto local poor relief. When the District Tribunal of Pont-Châlier (Pont-l'Evêque) allotted Jeanne Vaugeon a small food pension and lying-in expenses for her newborn child in August 1794, they commented defensively, "The law wants the nation to support abandoned children whose fathers are unknown, but the law did not mean to provide support for children with known fathers, nor did it mean to crown the treachery of an unnatural father."[15]

Some regional judges did their best to justify clinging to the old jurisprudence. As they continued to routinely grant child support to unwed mothers in the winter and spring of 1794, the judges at Vire explicitly noted in several suits that the new laws had not reformed the "very old and established jurisprudence" that awarded damages to the mother and upkeep to the child. Even the Tribunal de Cassation initially ruled in April 1795 that the 12 brumaire law had not abrogated paternity suits. Judges found themselves puzzled by a policy that intended to benefit enfants naturels yet seemed to make it impossible to establish their civil status or secure their economic survival. "Often the uncertainty about their status will subject children born out of wedlock to irreparable and painful prejudice," warned one court commissioner from Louviers in 1795, for he had trouble believing that the Convention had truly intended to impose silence on natural children and their mothers.[16]

While provincial judges wrestled with 12 brumaire's equivocal implications for paternity suits in 1794–95, most members of the Committee of Legislation suffered no such doubts. "This odious inquisition . . . is forever outlawed from French jurisprudence," remarked the committee categorically in its drafted reply to this commissioner's query, as to many others. In fact, as it dealt with stacks of petitions requesting all kinds of clarification of the 12 brumaire law, the Committee of Legislation replied more definitively on the intent to suppress paternity suits than on other aspects of the law.[17] Within the halls of the Convention the jurists stood by the logic that had supported their initial move to abolish paternity suits in the fall of 1793. In September 1794, in his proposed project for elucidating the 12 brumaire law's ambiguities, Oudot once again clarified the law's intention to "outlaw scandalous court procedures . . . that are always inadequate for establishing paternity." In December 1794, the Convention seconded this interpretation when it passed the article of the newly proposed Civil Code that explicitly forbade the "pursuit of unrecognized paternity [*la recherche de paternité non avouée*]."[18]

In the debate over this article, Pons de Verdun warned the Convention that allowing fathers to embrace or deny their own paternity would over-burden mothers unjustly. Several deputies dismissed his worries by invoking marital morality and denouncing the "inquisitorial" and "ruinous" trials that wrongly imposed paternity on a man. As Cambacérès commented:

> Everyone knows how easy it is to spread the presumption of a paternity that never existed. . . . It is necessary for all women to know well that every time they give themselves up to a man without having taken the necessary precautions to assure the status of the child who could be born from their commerce, that they will be exposing themselves to being solely responsible for that child.[19]

As he omitted any promises of aid to *mères célibatrices* and their children, Cambacérès made clearer than before that women bore the sole moral and economic liability for offspring born out of wedlock. His comments also resonated with a class-based defense of putative fathers' property against impoverished seductresses: he insisted that the "benevolence" of a man who paid lying-in expenses and child support should not be misinterpreted as an avowal of paternity. Only his "writing" and not his "acts" could prove fatherhood. Cambacérès' clear denial of recherche de paternité had difficulty penetrating judicial opinion and practice in the provinces, for in April and June 1795 the Committee of Legislation and the Commission des administrations civiles, police et tribunaux both issued circulars that directed justices of the peace and district courts to put an end to these customary court cases.[20]

By 1795, after repeated instructions from the center, departmental courts gradually stopped hearing paternity suits, with scattered exceptions here and there.[21] From 1798 on, the Tribunal de Cassation reinforced the legislative policy by consistently overturning regional court decisions allowing paternity suits, unless they had been initiated before 12 brumaire an II (2 November 1793) or unless the father was reneging on an earlier acknowledgment of his paternity. For example, in 1801 the unwed mother Desforges had successfully won child support. Attempting to defend her initial victory, she strove to balance older practices with the new law by drawing a distinction between the natural and civil implications of paternity. The 12 brumaire law "was only made in order to improve the condition of natural children. . . . A father's obligation to provide food for his child born out of wedlock is based on natural law; [this obligation] is independent of civil effects. Food can be granted, and the right to inherit refused; one does not lead to the other." Although the Tribunal d'appel de Liège bought her reasoning, the Tribunal de Cassation overturned this judgment in 1803, ruling that "paternity is indivisible." Fatherhood was an all-or-nothing affair: a man found to be a father and thus responsible for his daughter's food would surely owe her his legacy as well.[22]

The drive to unify fatherhood and to root it in the will of the father worked against natural children and their mothers. In 1803, Article 340 of the Civil Code would make explicit what the 12 brumaire law had left implicit but had worked out in practice: "Paternity searches are forbidden," except in cases of abduction. Ironically, this abolition of mothers' rights to press paternity suits undoubtedly affected more natural children than did their novel right to make claims on legacies. The majority of natural children in the 1790s, as before the Revolution and after, were born of impoverished mothers who could scarcely provide sustenance for their children, especially once deprived of the assistance of putative fathers. During the 1790s and into the early 1800s, illegitimacy and child abandonment only continued to grow.[23] Even conservative critics were keenly aware that the 12 brumaire law had a detrimental impact on vast numbers of illegitimate children. In 1795 the lawyer Bellart satirized the 12 brumaire law and its unrealistic goal of granting legacies to enfants naturels. He made a rare call for a return to the paternity suits of old: "With too much munificence, the law, in defiance of nature and truth, condemns [natural children] to die of misery and hunger. . . . They do not need grand inaccessible rights and great hopes, difficult to ever realize. They need bread and sure sustenance."[24]

Although the abolition of paternity suits provoked its share of contention and resistance at the local level, by and large legislators and the Ministry of Justice formed a united front and enforced this policy from the center out to the provinces. It was relatively easy to discern a man's will to espouse fatherhood at the moment of the natural child's birth. As the next sections will show, to assess a father's commitment after his death proved more problematic. Judges faced the tricky task of disentangling a man's intentions from a complex web of behaviors and expressions. Beyond the essential difficulty of attributing paternity, controversial cases over the inheritance rights of illegitimate children exposed broader tensions within the revolutionary redefinition of fatherhood. How could the courts preserve a father's freedom to embrace paternity but enforce his natural obligations to the paternal bond? How should judges weigh a father's commitment to a natural child against his social and economic responsibility to his legitimate family? And finally, wasn't there a contradiction between his loss of authority within marriage and his newfound liberty outside of marriage?

PROVING PATERNITY: NATURAL CHILDREN ENTER COURT

Initially, natural children with ample proof of their father's freely chosen paternity and extensive care met with success in seeking their new inheritance rights. When Pierre Avenel died in the winter of 1795, his natural son produced a baptismal certificate from 1766 bearing his father's signature and, better yet, a notarized statement that he had been brought up in his father's home in Caen since birth.[25] But few cases were this clear-cut. The courts quickly found themselves struggling to interpret a law that lacked technical clarity and created multiple subcategories of natural children, all with slightly different rights or means of proving paternity. Moreover, the legislators provided little guidance: they repeatedly debated various aspects of the law, but passed little in the way of clarification.

Natural children did not flood the courts with demands for inheritance. For the myriad illegitimate children who came from poverty-stricken backgrounds or who had been abandoned without parental recognition, no legacies loomed on the horizon. Hesitations about revealing the stigma of illegitimacy, and, above all, the difficulty of proving paternity kept others from trying their luck in the courts. In addition, only certain categories of natural children could initiate suits. The initial law applied to those whose parents' legacies entered probate after 14 July 1789, but on 15 thermidor an IV (2 August 1796) the Councils moved this date up to 4 June 1793. The law left the situation particularly unclear for those whose parents died after 12 brumaire an II (2 November 1793), because it referred their fate to the Civil Code that had not yet been successfully completed. Did their fathers have to acknowledge them formally before a public official, or was care or the father's written statement enough to prove filiation? As a result, recognized children whose parents died in the five-month interval between 4 June and 2 November 1793 could benefit most easily from the law. Despite these limitations, some natural children nonetheless made claims, which in turn often generated lengthy contestations in the courts and frequent appeals to the legislature for aid in interpreting or reforming the law. Because of the scattered nature of local claims, I will weave together diverse local and national cases with petitions and pamphlets in order to analyze the grassroots contest between illegitimate children and their opponents.

As the courts wrestled with the technical details of the law, judges, lawyers, natural children, and their relatives strove on a broader scale to define the meaning of fatherhood and to assess the relationship between customary social conventions on the one hand and natural bonds on the other. The law allowed natural children or their guardians to demonstrate paternity by presenting their father's public or private written acknowledgment or by illustrating his "care without interruption." But, as court case after case made clear, in practice, men performed fatherhood without a script. Their behavior varied. A natural father, for example, might ignore his duties, marry another woman and produce legitimate offspring, only to remember his illegitimate child late in life. Or he might tend to the child's needs erratically, only under court orders, or out of fear of dishonor. As one anonymous petitioner wondered, how long must a man feed his child to demonstrate paternity by "continuous care"? Seven years, fourteen years, or longer still? When Anne Dubernet's natural grandfather took her into his home after the death of his son, Anne's alleged father, did that certify paternity? "Non, non" wrote the Committee of Legislation in the margin of this query. Did it prove fatherhood when a man placed his daughter in a convent and set up an annuity for her? Or when, like Bernard Haitze, he signed his daughter's marriage contract, but had sent only a proxy to her baptism? Regional courts varied in their rulings, but the Tribunal de Cassation ruled against the natural child in both these cases.[26]

This uncertainty over how to prove fatherhood left considerable room for natural children and their opponents to carve out differing visions of the parent-child bond. Each side drew on certain elements from the logic laid out by the authors of the law. But in delineating paternity, while the illegitimate children tapped into the Old Regime's emphasis on communal responsibility and honor, their opponents evoked the Thermidorian validation of social cohesion. In fact, these contests were very much shaped by the Thermidorian and Directorial climate and its fear that family ties and property arrangements had been undercut by policies associated with the Terror. Pivotal to this cultural moment was the attempt to redefine the boundaries of the family and to rethink the relationship between the natural and the civil order.

A pamphlet skirmish between enfant naturel Auguste and fifty-odd members of the Boulogne family highlights this battle over defining paternity within the natural and civil order. In their *Adresse à la Convention nationale, au nom d'une infinité des pères et mères chargés des familles* (Address to the National Convention, in the name of an infinite number of fathers and mothers responsible for families), the Boulogne family attacked the rights of children born out of wedlock. The pamphleteers represented nature as a brutal and Hobbesian space: men and women mated without affection, brothers competed violently for goods, property did not exist, and "a father owes nothing to his son." Only stable laws and the secure custom of marriage could rescue humanity from this world of passions run rampant: "It is the law that establishes the husband vis-à-vis the wife, by attributing to him the status and rights of the head of household. It is the law that imposes on him the duty to live with her, despite the sterility of daily life and his aversion, often too well founded, to domestic society. . . . It is the law that obliges the man to recognize the children that his wife gives him during their marriage, . . . and obliges him to bring up these children, watch over their education, and assure their subsistence."[27]

Absent were the early revolutionaries' optimistic visions of the regenerative power of conjugal love, of natural parental devotion, fraternal bonds, or filial love. Absent also was any pretext of companionate or egalitarian relationship between the sexes, as the pamphleteers proposed that a return to male authority within the home would compensate men for having to rein in their wayward passions. As in other attacks on the 12 brumaire law, in this account, "bastards" became intruders, isolated and wealthy individuals, selfish bachelors who built no social bonds of their own. The collaterals, in contrast, were a tight-knit family of citizens, soldiers who fought for the Republic, and poor younger sons who had only just won back their own legitimate inheritance rights.[28]

In a scathing reply, citoyen Auguste defended the newly won rights and status of natural children. In a two-column pamphlet, he set out his point-by-point rebuttals against the Boulogne family's sketch. Steeped in the natural law fervor of the year II, Auguste painted a state of nature in which sons united with their father to fight off ferocious beasts, cared for him in old age, and in turn naturally inherited from him. Auguste prized filial devotion as a natural component of human morality and masculine identity (see Figure 13). He satirized his opponents for their harsh depiction of man as patriarch and master. In Constantinople, no doubt, the law forced wives to submit to husbands, but not in France where divorce put an end to marital tyranny. Nor did the law need to prevail upon fathers and mothers to feed their offspring, for "nature, tenderness make this a need, a pleasure, and never a duty." In an earlier pamphlet, Auguste bemoaned the denigration of

Figure 13. To Filial Piety, from *Manuel des autorités constituées de la République française* (1797). Courtesy of the Bibliothèque nationale de France.

nature: "The code of nature, this eternal book that should be the regulator of social man has become an object of scorn and derision." As natural successors of their parents, illegitimate children had also earned rights by their contributions to the French army and republican society. Hardly rich, hardly egotistical, they were "almost always the children of poverty seduced," who had at last been restored their rights and incorporated into the social fabric of France.[29]

These pamphlets suggest the parameters of the battle over the father-child relationship. While opponents of illegitimate children praised the strongly bounded patriarchal family, secured by law for the social good, natural children embraced the more fluid, natural family, bound by affection and altruistic participation in the Republic. Court cases would amplify this clash over family and fatherhood, contrasting the reliability of married paternity with the natural strength of paternal bonds, and pitting the certainty of lineage property against the freedom of human sentiment and the promise of natural rights to every individual. I turn first to examine the viewpoints and rhetoric of natural children.

NATURAL CHILDREN SEEK THEIR RIGHTS

In 1794 the natural daughter Marie-Catherine Dampville startled her alleged half-siblings with a claim on the legacy of their father, Jean Gondouin of Heurtevent near Livarot. To support her case, she presented a baptismal act from 1755 bearing her father's name and even brought along the old curé to vouch for its validity. Witnesses testified that Jean Gondouin and the mother, Catherine Dampville, had been on the verge of marriage at Marie-Catherine's birth. Jean had taken the baby to a wet nurse, paid for her care, rented a home for her mother, and had also made "an act bearing a promise of marriage and the recognition of the child." He and Catherine had published marriage banns, but then his parents had stepped in to forbid their union. Under this pressure, Jean underwent a change of heart and compelled Catherine to return his marriage promise and recognition of paternity by threatening to kidnap the baby and abandon her at a foundling home.[30]

In her attempt to win her alleged father's inheritance almost forty years later, Marie-Catherine Dampville fused traditional and revolutionary meanings of paternity. On the one hand, she wanted to follow the Old Regime practice of using communal judgment to establish her filiation via the witness testimony of neighbors; as always, the village or neighborhood should collectively assign paternal responsibility. On the other hand, her case fit exactly the scenario that the jurists had had in mind when they lobbied for the 12 brumaire law. Anxious to defend the liberty of young couples to make love matches, Oudot and Berlier in particular imagined granting rights to natural children as part of a broader refashioning of conjugal bonds freed from parental constraint. Marie-Catherine Dampville and her parents were victims of an Old Regime marital system: her father had been denied the opportunity to embrace his natural paternity. His attempts at care and his promise to marry certified paternity by either Old Regime or revolutionary standards. However, the District Tribunal of Lisieux ultimately decided in July 1795 against Marie-Catherine, natural daughter, for she could not produce the written marriage promise, which had been stolen, nor could she show care "without interruption" to illustrate her father's freely chosen paternity.[31]

Other natural children made the customary claim that the community had named the father while simultaneously invoking the newer, revolutionary validation of love that defied constraint. Antoine Valbe-Monteval's father and mother, locally "treated in society as husband and wife," had lived together in "secret marriage" only because grandfather Monteval would have disinherited his defiant son had the marriage become official. Antoine defended his parents' unorthodox behavior and announced that his own natural father had "paternal love" for him. But now the machinations of his aunt and uncle, suspected of counterrevolution, blocked his inheritance claims.[32]

Like Monteval, natural children, their guardians, and mothers foregrounded evidence of paternal affection. True fatherhood, true family, lay not solely within marriage, but in the affinity, the natural bonds between parent and child, between father and mother. Here, illegitimate children built both on the prominent revolutionary image of the sentimental father and on the specific logic of the 12 brumaire law. The radical revolutionaries had worked hard to replace the model of the authoritarian patriarch with a new validation of the willing, sensitive, and responsible father (see Figure 14). The crafters of the 12 brumaire law shared the belief that nature endowed fathers with both affection and responsibility for their children, as long as they were certain of their paternity. The jurists drew on the republican concept that manhood lay in sensibilité, as well as in political dedication to the nation. In defending the rights of illegitimate offspring, Cambacérès stated: "Here our hearts are the tablets of the law." When any "honorable man" became a father, he contracted an "engagement, . . . and what an engagement is this one, which is simultaneously under the safeguard of the two first sentiments of nature, honor and love!" The Convention had promised to offer natural children their succession rights as well as parental tenderness and care, remarked Oudot. With their avid faith in regeneration and in natural law, the authors of the 12 brumaire law had confidently assumed that true fathers would behave as fathers should: in other words, they would follow their natural duties and transparently voice their natural love for the child through their actions. Fatherly responsibility would encompass political and moral guidance. Their care during the child's lifetime expressed their devoted embrace of fatherhood and also constituted proof of paternity.[33]

In this vein, children born out of wedlock presented themselves as the offspring of love rather than of weakness or libertinage and identified various actions as evidence of paternal attachment. Echoing the language of the petitioners who had called for egalitarian treatment, in court natural chil-

Figure 14. Father with son, from the *Chansonnier de la montagne* (1794–95). Courtesy of the Bibliothèque nationale de France.

dren and their lawyers painted a world in which human bonds and behavior mattered more than the formalities of social convention. As one lawyer claimed on behalf of natural daughter Sellons, by favoring her in his will her father "left the most precious rights to a child of love and nature, whom he had cared for with the solicitude of a real father before his death." One son reported that he had lived with his mother, a servant in his father's household; he had been offered "the most tender care" by his father and even his father's wife, only to find himself thrown out by greedy collaterals after his father's death.[34] In court, only active, consistent care provided evidence of paternal affection. In a complex cause célèbre involving the illegitimate grandson of Chancellor René de Maupeou, Marguerite Trouillet la Roche demonstrated that her lover Charles-Victor-René Maupeou had not only paid handsomely for their natural son's upbringing, but had also visited him at the wet nurse and "had presented the child as his son to his friends and his late brother." While Marguerite Trouillet submitted that their son had been well cared for and even incorporated into the family, her opponents countered that she and her son were "strangers to the family," which they had "invaded" to devour its patrimony.[35]

Some situations made it particularly difficult for children or unwed mothers to prove paternity by care and affection. For example, fathers who died while their children were still in infancy or even still in the womb had little time to express fatherly impulses, so their natural children emphasized the mutual commitment of their parents. They presented their fathers' fond and responsible actions to their natural mothers as evidence of paternal recognition. Mère célibatrice Lepeigneux produced a letter from Antoine Banès, addressing her as his "good friend [*bonne amie*]" and urging her "to take care of what she was carrying." But the letter of the law said nothing about a man's affection or care for an unmarried woman as proof of paternity. So in 1799 the Tribunal de Cassation overturned the lenient treatment of natural mother Lepeigneux by the Civil Tribunal of Eure-et-Loir. In a similar case, Elisabeth R. furnished witnesses who vouched that the presumed father had demonstrated his devotion to her and on his deathbed had verbally acknowledged the soon-to-be-born Etienne Pierre as his child. The District Tribunal of Montpellier hesitated before this compelling evidence, but overturned the family court's earlier decision in Etienne's favor. After all, "it is clear enough that this declaration, these signs of paternal tenderness are ineffectual in the eyes of the law for proving possession of status [as son]."[36]

When natural children and their guardians presented their cases, they strove to stretch the definition of voluntary, natural fatherhood. In the face of judges and opponents who probed the validity of their written or testimonial evidence, natural children emphasized the many ways of expressing natural fatherhood and pinned their hopes on all kinds of proof. Refuge and care by grandparents, a father's belated recognition in a holographic will, child support sent all the way from Saint Domingue, adoption under the shaky and uncertain revolutionary law, an imprisoned father's listing of annual payments "for Rosalie, my natural daughter" on his tax account.[37] Few of these expressions of paternity would pass muster, for the law stated that care had to be continuous and a man had to acknowledge his fatherhood without coercion. Moreover, as I will argue below, in the cautious conservatism of the Directory, courts would increasingly interpret the law narrowly as they opted for social certainty and the defense of property and legitimate families.

Natural children in court tried to enact in practice what petitioners and pamphleteers articulated more explicitly: the *grande famille* of the Revolution should not exclude any of its children, "fortified by the rights that they hold from nature and the social order; stronger even than those that they hold from you, citizen representatives," in the words of one polemicist. Natural children hastened to offer reasons for their inclusion. My own sons serve the Republic. I languish in poverty. My collateral opponents are enemies of the Revolution. "What did the legislator promise me when he had me swear to maintain equality? That I would participate in it just as you would." A few even echoed the attacks on wealth and aristocracy of the days before Thermidor and identified natural children as "children of the people."[38]

Given the stringency of the 12 brumaire law, natural children also lobbied for accepting weaker forms of evidence, for some natural fathers faced difficulty expressing their paternity. In the Old Regime "prejudices, religion, and pride" encouraged men to camouflage their paternity. Proof could be hard to come by, especially for the offspring of the cavalier and wealthy "privileged castes." Alternatively, revolutionary turmoil could prohibit a man from making a formal declaration before a municipal official. One pamphleteer posed the point in dramatic terms: what if in the depths of a dungeon, a father heard the cries of nature urging him to care for his forgotten natural child? If he fell below the blade of the guillotine too soon, he would have no time to recognize this child.[39] Some flesh-and-blood fathers did worry about the kinds of proof required. One Frenchman from Saint Domingue reported that he had brought up five natural children of color "with that tender solicitude that nature has placed in the heart of man." Fathers in the colonies should be able to recognize their children without the mother's consent, given the distance from France and the perilous insurrections of Saint Domingue. This exception would favor equality and aid citizens of color in this tumultuous time, he argued.[40]

In a particularly perilous position, enfants adultérins or their parents repeatedly petitioned the legislatures to include them more fully within the contours of the 12 brumaire law. The citoyenne Loudios of Montauban had read the new law with high anticipation until she learned of its "awful dividing line" between children born of adultery and all others. This self-proclaimed republican mother narrated her great pride at raising a fine citizen, but now her collaterals claimed that he could not inherit from her, let alone from his married father. Enfants adultérins and their parents made no headway with their pleas. With the single exception of Oudot, the deputies were too wary of jeopardizing marriage to advocate full rights for the offspring of adultery. Because of the extreme difficulty of proving voluntary paternal recognition, children of adultery initiated court cases by the 12 brumaire law even more rarely, and with even less success, than did natural children born of free, unmarried parents.[41]

In presenting their cases, illegitimate children or their guardians stressed the power of sentiment and the natural father-child bond. In court, the language of natural rights, so prominent in pamphlets, took a backseat to the multifaceted depiction of fatherhood, made manifest in a series of actions from care of the mother before birth to belated recognition on the edge of death. While illegitimate children clearly furnished these details to provide legal proof of paternity, they simultaneously bore testimony to a new vision of the family: inclusive and permeable, marked by the fluidity and complexity of human relationships, peopled by wayward fathers who either had acted on their natural ties or had been prevented by Old Regime prejudice from recognizing their own. This image of the family drew strongly on the revolutionary validation of equality, affective freedom, and natural bonds. At the same time, natural children evoked a deeply traditional definition of fatherhood as biological and social. As in the Old Regime, the community of witnesses judged and certified this physiological tie and attributed paternal responsibility. Nature, community, the new law, and the force of human emotion and attachment all testified on behalf of the restored rights of the natural child.

THE LEGITIMATE FAMILY FIGHTS BACK

Legitimate siblings and collateral heirs painted a very different image of family and fatherhood. They emphasized the tenuous nature of relationships and portrayed illegitimate children as a profound threat to property and family unity. After the Terror, they built on the pervasive mood of unease about social disorder. They suggested that the new civil laws, and especially the 12 brumaire law, imperiled family property arrangements and shattered the emotional bonds and harmony of families across France. Like the Boulogne pamphleteers above, legitimate siblings, collaterals, and their lawyers voiced deep mistrust of both nature and human sentiment, for neither seemed capable of holding the family together. They made their arguments within the Thermidorian political climate that valued social order, legal certainty, and the protection of property over innovation, natural affection, and social inclusion.[42] More specifically, they countered natural children's image of malleable fatherhood in action by demanding proof of the father's extensive care and formal recognition. Marriage, not nature, made true fathers. Outside of marriage, paternity lay encased in mystery and uncertainty: only a man's most explicit acknowledgment made him into a father. The legal opponents of natural children represented putative fathers as rather fragile and in need of protection, for the property and validity of the legitimate family lay in the balance. The rights of man protected family property rather than the claims of intruding individuals. Alleged fathers could easily become victims of manipulative women, the social pressure of honor, or the vicissitudes of revolutionary politics.

For example, in 1794, mère célibatrice Laborde had approached the deputies on mission in Bordeaux and elicited their assistance in urging Philippe de Richon to acknowledge his three natural children and offer her a payment of 60,000 livres. Within two months, Richon had sent his wife as his official proxy to recognize his sons and had written a *"testament mystique"*—a signed will, held by a notary in a sealed envelope—naming them as his natural sons and universal heirs along with his legitimate son. By midsummer 1794 he had died. His legitimate son argued vehemently, and successfully, that only "entirely free contracts" manifested the father's unfettered acknowledgment of his paternity. The deputies on mission, the Terror, and its impact on Richon's will lurked powerfully in the background of the legitimate son's case.[43]

According to opponents of natural children, if politics, especially the politics of the Terror, could hamper a man's liberty, the tyranny of honor and the fear of being forced into a scandalous paternity suit could also have coerced him into acknowledging paternity in the Old Regime. An anonymous pamphleteer captured this logic dramatically as he decried Old Regime settlements and their impact on the accused father: "A false sense of shame, an invincible prejudice from the time, the fear of being trumpeted in the courts, in the public, caused him to acknowledge his paternity, which put an end to any court case, avoided all scandal, and warded off what was then called *dishonor*. . . . Where is the liberty to act in such a situation?" Following this line of reasoning, collaterals and legitimate offspring successfully argued that local courts should not allow a natural child to demonstrate filiation by relying on a paternity suit or the father's subsequent payments. In 1758 Claude Gaujoux had dodged a rapt de séduction case by agreeing out of court to pay child support. Almost forty years later his legitimate son fended off the inheritance claims of Marguerite Euzières, Gaujoux's natural daughter, by pointing out that his avowal of paternity had been "extorted out of fear" in order to escape a demeaning trial. Collaterals soon developed a litany of accusations characterizing child support as "extorted despite resistance," and depicting each putative father as "threatened by a vexatious court case," and only seeking to "avoid public scandal."[44] Following this logic, from 1795 on, the Tribunal de Cassation repeatedly overturned local judgments that established paternity by some combination of lying-in expenses, food pensions, or reparations to the mother.[45]

If a father's liberty seemed tenuous and threatened, so too, apparently, were the bonds that held the family together. Collateral relatives and their lawyers chipped away at the "naïve" assumptions of the year II that human feelings within the family would naturally follow a moral and unifying path. Far from being a reliable, natural act, fatherhood was cloaked in uncertainty. Even fraternity, the familial wellspring of revolutionary unity and fervor, had lost its mooring and resonance in the aftermath of the Terror. As one set of collaterals argued before the Paris Tribunal in the year IX (1800–01): "Fathers only recognize their children based on confidence, and children only recognize their siblings because of the habit of having been fed and brought up together, having been called brothers and treated as such. All men finally found their relations of kinship and consanguinity on presumed titles, but never on definitive proof. It is in this position, always vague and undetermined, that the legislators came to establish the immutability of their principles." The law had to step in to provide certainty and stake out the boundaries of the family. Scornful of their opponent's heart-wrenching tale of mistaken identity and unwavering parental devotion, the collaterals commented, "You want a father and a mother, eh! You forget what the law, the titles give you."[46]

Opponents of natural children relied on the legal premise that marriage determined fatherhood, at times regardless of the opinion of the mother. On 19 floréal an II (8 May 1794), the Convention had decreed that a married woman could not deny her husband's paternity of a child born to her during their marriage.[47] The principle that "pater is est quem nuptiae demonstrant [the father is he whom marriage indicates]" dated back before the Revolution. But in the mid 1790s the laicization of the état civil, the long absences of husbands away at war, the legalization of divorce, and the granting of rights to illegitimate offspring all focused renewed attention and anxiety on adultery as a threat to family honor and property.

In 1799 an acrimonious court dispute over the état civil and paternity of a child born of adultery highlighted this flashpoint issue. Late in 1796, at her father's insistence, Marie-Catherine Pénicaud, only twenty years old, had married a doctor, Jean-Baptiste Lanefranque in Mérignac near Bordeaux. But her heart remained tied to another: André-Théophile Racle, a local printer. As her legal brief testified, "Love was my only guide; it led me to citizen Racle, my ecstasy on seeing him is easier to feel than to express. . . . My person and my property were delivered to the most vile of men . . . citizen Lanefranque." Within a month after the wedding Marie-Catherine had begun her unsuccessful attempt to win a divorce. Nine months and fifteen days after the marriage, she gave birth to a son, whose birth certificate in Bordeaux named André-Théophile Racle as father. Husband Jean-Baptiste Lanefranque demanded custody and legal paternity of the boy and charged his wife with slandering her own husband in a publicly circulated court brief. In that brief, Marie-Catherine used a language that had resonated strongly in the early 1790s: she denounced her own victimization by arranged marriage, glorified the power of heartfelt love, and presented her son as a product of nature. He is "the work of love, . . . nature has printed on his face all the features of the beloved one who gave him life." In contrast, her husband's case embodied the integrity and honor of the family line and the authority and esteem of the legal husband and father. Both law and state should support the masculine identity of fathers as guardians of the legitimate family.[48]

By 1799 the cultural and juridical climate had turned against star-crossed lovers like André-Théophile Racle and Marie-Catherine Pénicaud. The Paris Tribunal suppressed her brief for slandering her lawful husband, validated her arranged marriage as legal, and ruled that the child's birth act be legally revised to name Jean-Baptiste Lanefranque as father. He also won the right to take back the child. In a prelude to the logic of the Civil Code, this decision restored the power of husband and father and defined marriage as an institution built to contain female sexuality and transmit family goods. In the words of one opponent of natural children's rights, "the civil status of children is the principal purpose of marriage." Behind this statement lay the crucial assumption that a wife's fidelity guaranteed paternity and maintained the integrity of family property.[49]

In defendants' accounts, if law, social morality, and the convention of marriage staked out the safe boundaries of family, then illegitimate children became intruders, virtual thieves who corrupted civilized practices and upset the property arrangements of large and deserving families. As the lawyer of the Loiseau-Monny family argued in 1797, to put "bastards" into families "seems to chase man out of civil society and push him back into a state of savagery." In this logic, natural children once again became "bastards," associated with their parents' criminal and immoral flouting of marital practices, rather than with nature or the right to love freely. Above all, opponents identified natural children with the apparent duplicity, greed, and profligacy of their unmarried mothers. Why should illegitimate children benefit from their mother's intrigues? "A few courtesans . . . cry out and have it proclaimed from the rooftops that it is counter-revolutionary not to let them place their children into any family that they choose, *on the simple presumption of paternity,*" commented one pamphleteer (his emphasis).[50]

In this same vein, numerous collateral heirs of David Morisse accused citoyenne Raimbaud, Morisse's cook and the mother of his natural child, of deviously tricking them out of Morisse's inheritance. Associating Raimbaud with other unwed mothers "without morals . . . without good behavior . . . without principles," the collaterals inculpated her for winning over supporters at the Le Havre Jacobin club by exaggerating her son's poverty. In fact, not only had he already received 200,000 livres, but this money would also have benefited some eighteen heirs and their more than thirty children. In their defense of passing on property within the legitimate family line, they did not hesitate to invoke the revolutionary principle of distributing wealth, albeit within the parameters they saw as valid. In their view, the certainty of property transfers preserved social harmony.[51]

In 1795 as he defended one Parisian family's goods against an enfant naturel, the lawyer Bellart also tapped into the current post-Terror fear of unstable relationships, property, and passion. Aligning his defense with the reestablishment of social and political order, he commented "They say that sensibilité and nature have acclaimed this law [of 12 brumaire]. . . . It is not sensibilité that should dictate laws. It is reason, political interest, and the interest of morals and families. Nature, that's a mistake." In distinct contrast to natural children and to the deputies of the year II, Bellart drew a clear-cut line between the laws of nature and the laws of civil society. Nature had nothing to say about successions, for that was a question of civil society and civil law. Faced with the 12 brumaire law, "nature is silent," asserted Bellart. "But society speaks, and it speaks against this law." Whether compelled by Bellart's social theory or by the relatively weak case of his opponent, this Paris Tribunal decided against Madeleine Moret, guardian and mother of the natural child Marie-Claude Sophie.[52]

Natural children whose fathers died between the promulgation of the 12 brumaire law and the Civil Code held a particularly controversial position. The 12 brumaire law stipulated that the Civil Code would govern their fate. While awaiting the code, most local courts simply followed the rules in article 8 for proof based on care or paternal writings.[53] However, some opponents of natural children began to argue that plaintiffs had to produce an *official public act* by their fathers, a formal entry in the état civil recognizing paternity before the local municipal official, confirmed by the mother. Not only did article 11 of the law propose this method as a possible means of recognizing fatherhood, but fathers still alive after brumaire an II (November 1793) would have had the opportunity to acknowledge their own paternity clearly and freely. Yet, the "legislation was incoherent, uncertain, and obscure," in the words of one lawyer seeking to defend several illegitimate daughters whose father had *adopted* them in the spring of 1794 in the attempt to illustrate his paternity. A month later, he had officially recognized them before the Paris Tribunal as his natural offspring, but their opponents argued powerfully in 1797 that his adoption implied that they were not in fact his children. In an equally complex case, in October 1800 in Lille, Catherine Deledecque initially won part of Augustin Laloi's legacy for her natural son, for Augustin had given the boy his name and continual care and had even sponsored his apprenticeship. But on appeal in 1802, the Laloi family convincingly argued that Augustin Laloi had made no "formal recognition," and that Catherine and son were instituting an illegal paternity search, effectively violating Augustin's liberty.[54]

The demand that the father officially recognize his paternity crowned the defendants' insistent apology for the father's free will, to the detriment of natural children and their mothers. As one pamphleteer commented, conveniently forgetting the mother's presence at conception, "the father is the only competent judge of this important matter."[55] Opponents of natural children positioned themselves as guardians of the father's independence outside of marriage in order to reincorporate his economic responsibility to the family line within marriage. Furthermore, in contrast to natural children plaintiffs, they redefined the individual rights of the natural child and mother as dangerous and immoral invasions of the moral and economic order. Refuting the revolutionary confidence in natural bonds and the power of human affection, collaterals and legitimate siblings stressed the need to reassert the secure boundaries of marriage and to ally masculine liberty with the defense of property and family. For them, social convention and law, rather than nature and affect, forged the most powerful bonds of kinship.

THE COURTS WEIGH THE EVIDENCE

Faced with this battle over the meaning of fatherhood and family between natural children and their opponents, family tribunals and the courts did their best to sort out the complexities of the law and to read the nuances of each father's will and attachment within his varied acts or writings. Uncertainty in interpreting the law clearly plagued tribunals across France. Arbiters, local magistrates, lawyers, notaries, and the commissioners attached to district and civil tribunals sent frequent queries to the Ministry of Justice, the legislature, and its committees soliciting help in interpreting the law. One notary from the Drôme urged the deputies in 1797 to clarify and unify the laws governing natural children's legacies "so that citizens in the countryside are not hindered by the application [of the law], and so that you can put an end to uncertainty at the same time."[56]

In family courts and district and civil tribunals across France, natural children met with mixed success. Their chances of victory decreased after the year III (1794–95). Not only did social and judicial conservatism reemerge after Thermidor, but specific legislative changes also lessened their odds. In 1795 the legislature took their cases out of the hands of local family courts in favor first of the district tribunals and then of the more distant, department-wide civil tribunals. In 1796 the window of retroactive appeals narrowed to cases opened after 4 June 1793.

Furthermore, at the national level, the Tribunal de Cassation provided increasingly conservative leadership in interpreting the law. Most notably, this court's initial endorsement of judicial independence and leeway in interpreting this problematic law gave way to a distinct hardening of jurisprudence against natural children, especially by 1797. Early in 1796, the Tribunal de Cassation acknowledged that the 12 brumaire law had not elucidated how to establish adequate care; nor had it been specific about the nature of written evidence by the father. Thus the law left it "up to the arbitration and the conscience of the judges to decide on the merits of either the father's writings or his care, which the natural child attempts to prove." Second, even for succession cases that fell into the period of limbo between the 12 brumaire law and the promulgation of the Civil Code, the Tribunal at first ruled in the summer of 1796 that local judges could follow article 8. In other words, they should exercise their own discretion in interpreting paternal writings and care-taking practices as legal proofs of paternity.[57]

But this early flexibility in assessing paternity was quickly curtailed. From the very outset the Tribunal de Cassation reinforced the notion that the father's voluntary, free, and spontaneous recognition was the sine qua non of any natural child's case. Beginning in 1795, this court overturned any attributions of filiation based on Old Regime paternity suits and scrutinized each case to be sure that paternal acknowledgment had definitively "emanated from the free will of the father."[58] Moreover, in its conservative turn before being purged in fructidor an V (September 1797), the Tribunal gradually constructed a high standard of proof of paternity by care or writings. After striking down several equivocal claims by natural children, the court ruled in 1797 that it was not enough to document a paternal contribution to upbringing and education: "One has to discover paternal solicitude with all its characteristics, both [during the upbringing] and over the whole life of the father; otherwise, [his contributions] can only be considered to be simple acts of generosity." In the Directorial climate so mistrustful of emotional bonds, demonstrating adequate "paternal solicitude" was no easy matter. Later decisions would only reinforce this trend toward ratcheting up the definition of a true father's "care" and free choice of his own paternity.[59]

The Tribunal de Cassation used its decisions to reinforce the boundaries of legal marriage and to narrow the definition of paternity outside of marriage. For example, in 1800 in the interest of discouraging divorce and adultery, it chose to classify a child born during her father's divorce as "adultérine," depriving her unwed mother of the inheritance already won for this natural daughter.[60] Above all, the court played a pivotal role in transforming the juridical practices governing natural children whose parents died in the interval between the 12 brumaire law and the Civil Code. From 1799 on, the Tribunal de Cassation consistently decided that these natural children did in fact have to present their fathers' formal declarations of recognition. This interpretation effectively reduced once again the number of illegitimate offspring who could file claims.[61]

It also shows that, even before jurists began to write the Civil Code, the Tribunal de Cassation moved in practice toward the stringent definition of natural paternity that would soon become the letter of the law. To stipulate that the filiation of a natural child could be established only by formal paternal recognition in the état civil allied the will of the father with the power of the state to determine the contours of the family and the fate of marginal family members. In effect, this move strengthened the premise that marriage above all determined paternity. Outside of marriage, once state-controlled declarations of filiation replaced maternal declarations and the more nebulous proofs of paternity by care or the father's writings, both the Old Regime and the revolutionary models of paternity outside of marriage were discarded. Not only could mother and community no longer name the father and demand reparation from him, but the child born out of wedlock lost all claim to the father's natural bond of affect and obligation. No longer did law attempt to mirror nature; rather the civic order, positive law, and social utility would quietly but powerfully fill the void that nature had vacated. The Civil Code would take this logic a step further by stating that even if a father had acknowledged his paternity before a municipal official, a natural child had no status as an heir within the family, although he or she could receive a limited share of the succession as a creditor.[62]

. . .

The 12 brumaire law possessed a potent combination of characteristics: it initiated a controversial new policy but lacked precision and force, leaving extensive room for reinterpretation at every level. The attempt to destigmatize illegitimacy was transformed in practice as new aspirations collided with Old Regime customs and with the increasingly conservative politics of the later 1790s. Law is always forged in practice rather than on paper, but the implementation of the 12 brumaire law undercut both the spirit and loosely worded letter of the law in an especially striking fashion. The new policy toward illegitimate children was far less successful than the revolutionary decrees favoring divorce or egalitarian inheritance among legitimate siblings. In trying to guard marriage and protect the alleged father's freedom, the jurists of the year II had already limited the law's benefits to natural children: they had built a tension into the law between the father's natural responsibility to his offspring on the one hand and his voluntary right to embrace or reject fatherhood on the other. "Voluntary paternity" turned out to be exceptionally difficult to prove. Especially after the Terror, as confidence in radical family reform gave way to a strong thrust toward strengthening family and property, judges exploited this tension to redraw the boundaries of legitimate families. Between 1797 and the Civil Code, the Tribunal de Cassation crucially transformed the meaning of the 12 brumaire law, in effect subverting the original intention of the lawmakers. These judicial actions took advantage of the technical ambiguities within the 12 brumaire law to vitiate its attempt to endow certain natural children with civil rights. Their actions also show how profoundly the political climate influenced the courts as they interpreted the laws and goals of the radical revolutionaries.

Some natural children nonetheless did win legacies, particularly in the middle years of the 1790s. Their success bore testimony to the power of revolutionary law to undercut Old Regime exclusions. Yet, by and large, natural children lost out in this struggle to interpret and reshape the contours of fatherhood and families. The law fell short of its aims. The deputies' interlocking vision of state welfare, the free embrace of natural motherhood and fatherhood, and egalitarian access to the family proved unworkable in practice. As illegitimacy rates continued to grow in the 1790s and early 1800s, thousands of natural children were especially disadvantaged by their mothers' loss of the right to sue for child support. As the royalist deputy Joseph-Jérôme Siméon commented in 1797 about the suppression of paternity suits, "The Convention is accused of having favored natural children too much, and yet it has crushed them with a rigor unheard of before now."[63] Although the revolutionary state *envisioned* far-reaching, state-run welfare and endeavored to put ambitious pension programs into effect, actual poor relief did not match the optimistic promises and predictions of the deputies. The state was far from being able to provide for these needy unwed mothers and their offspring.[64]

The court cases over paternity and illegitimacy could not definitively answer the question "What makes a father?" But they highlighted the centrality of this question for resolving the new social order and galvanized legislative debate over paternity and illegitimacy. Individual causes célèbres,[65] confusion in judicial practice, and continual queries to the legislature captured the deputies' attention and provoked repeated controversies over retroactivity, proof of paternity, and the mother's right to name the father. For jurists and legislators still seeking to formulate a successful Civil Code and sort out the revolutionary transformation of the family, to debate the bond between natural children and their fathers became a means of discussing critical matters such as the nature of fatherhood and masculinity in general, the dangers of female sexuality, and the need to secure property and reinforce the boundaries of families. At least fifty-eight different deputies participated in these debates between 1794 and 1801.[66]

The deputies drew upon portrayals of paternity forged in court as two opposing visions of fatherhood and family squared off. On the one hand stood the image of the loving father, bound to his offspring by a powerful natural bond that should not be denied. Unlike mothers, the father should be free to embrace or reject this natural bond. On the other hand stood the notion that only marriage made the father: the civil order rested on the secure boundaries of families, and while fathers should be free, their liberty should not disrupt the legal boundaries of families nor threaten the property of legitimate children and wives. This vision of fatherhood found further underpinning in a particular definition of masculinity: manhood lay not so much in independence and sensibilité, but rather in personal ambition on behalf of the family and, above all, in the patriarch's honorable defense of family property and reputation. Ultimately, the deputies, like the

judges in court, edged toward this second model of fatherhood and family—
a model that would profoundly inform the Civil Code. The Civil Code of
1804 formalized the abolition of paternity suits by unwed mothers or adult
illegitimate children. And it finally did away with the effort to grant inheritance rights to some illegitimate children. It put an end to the revolutionaries' bold but flawed attempt to put into effect their slogan: "There are no
bastards in France!"[67]

7. Reconstituting the Social after the Terror

The Backlash against Family Innovations

In the aftermath of the Terror, hundreds of French citizens deluged the legislature with petitions bemoaning the "social disorder" of their country. Marriages torn by divorce; elderly parents deserted by their children; brothers and sisters at each other's throats over family fortunes; illegitimate, grasping offspring who suddenly appeared to demand their share in the name of equality. "Listen to the sorrowful voices of an infinite number of desolate families," lamented one petitioner as he recounted his typical tale of woe. According to these petitioners, behind all this anarchy and heartbreak lay the Terror of 1793–94 and its attempt to overhaul the family with reforms that "plundered property, were subversive of the foundation of society, destructive of the moral and political order, disruptive of all legislation, deadly for some, alarming to all."[1]

Hardly limiting themselves to the laws passed during the Terror, in fact these plaintiffs called into question the entire body of revolutionary family reform, including divorce, egalitarian inheritance, the weakening of paternal authority, and the granting of civil rights to illegitimate children. While some letter writers defended the reforms or even pushed for their expansion, by 1795 a mood of backlash permeated popular political outcry on the family. This outpouring of complaints about new family practices coincided with the rightward swing in politics after the fall of Robespierre. The conservative context of the Thermidorian reaction lent power and credence to this upswell of dissatisfaction, even as court cases continued apace and many family members continued to support the changes. This chapter shifts the focus from proponents of family innovation to its opponents.

For their part, revolutionary leaders during Thermidor and the Directory were keenly aware of the social discontent over family reform: they debated family laws repeatedly and discussed—yet again—two more unsuccessful versions of the Civil Code. They peppered their speeches with references to the provincial reception of reforms, often based on impressions gleaned from petitions supporting or opposing the laws. Between 1795 and 1799, the representatives changed only the most radical aspects of the existing laws: they abolished the retroactive clauses of inheritance laws, dismantled the family courts, and made divorce slightly harder to attain. In many ways, the deputies moved haltingly, hesitant to disassemble wholesale the egalitarian and individualist thrust of family reform. Yet through their recurrent debates in this era, they formulated key conceptual foundations for the eventual Civil Code. Finally, with the coming of Napoleon, French lawmakers fundamentally altered the family reforms of the Revolution and produced a unified Civil Code—one whose family laws bore a remarkable resemblance to many of the demands made by the angry petitioners of the mid 1790s.

An examination of how popular and legislative attitudes together transformed notions about family, law, and state can help us to understand the route to the Civil Code as well as the nature of the social and political reordering of Thermidor and the Directory. Although conservative petitioners exaggerated the destructive and invasive impact of revolutionary laws, their dramatic depictions posed crucial questions about the tensions between individual rights and social stability, and highlighted the difficulty of putting revolutionary ideals into practice within the home. Petitioners conceived of this "trouble within families" in two interconnected ways. They argued that revolutionary legislation and court cases had wreaked emotional havoc within families. Conjugal love, bonds of filial affection, and sibling relationships lay in tatters. Second, petitioners cried just as loudly that the new laws had undermined the web of mutual obligation within the family as an economic unit. They had sown chaos into property arrangements, conventional strategies, and long-standing expectations.

This chapter argues that in appealing for the repair of both the affective and economic well-being of the family, as the underpinning of social, political, and moral order, the petitioners portrayed family turmoil along certain gendered and generational lines in ways that would fuel the Thermidorian search for order and eventually would influence the writers of the Civil Code. Rather than simply demanding a return to past practices, the appellants sought to integrate their traditional customs and family practices with some aspects of republican ideology and an expanded role for the state. Reformulating revolutionary principles to fit customary family interests, they grounded their defense of the family and property in a constitutional order of limited civil equality, a tempered rule of law, and the protection of certain rights, based on social position.

Analysis of this pervasive criticism and rethinking of family structure in the aftermath of the Terror can also offer insights into the reconstruction of the social during the Thermidorian and Directorial periods. Historians have shown how the complex politics of the late 1790s profoundly informed the drive to stabilize the family, but they tend to focus on legislative or literary sources rather than on the popular outcry born of litigation and grassroots legal practice. The crucial dialogue between deputies and their provincial constituents remains for the most part under-examined.[2] Moreover, despite the widespread assumption that Thermidor marked a "return" or "revenge of the social" after the political intensity of the Terror, historians have left this category of the "social" remarkably under-explored. Most commonly, the "re-emergence of the social" implies both a certain fatigue with politics and a willingness to accept politics based on the propertied interest of the bourgeois class—or in the revisionist version—of property-owners and notables.[3] The most insightful recent analyses of Thermidor have focused on political culture without adequately problematizing the link between the social and political order. For example, Bronislaw Baczko's brilliant exploration of the Thermidorian "counter-imaginary" defines the problem of "ending the Terror" as primarily political and to a lesser extent cultural; he acknowledges "social conflicts" between rich and poor mainly as a backdrop to political instability and the problem of representation.[4] His work reflects the tendency in recent work on political culture to downplay social questions.

Yet, in order to end the Terror and reestablish political order, reconstituting civil society was crucial, in the eyes of both the deputies and the vocal French population. Ultimately, for moderate and conservative legislators, to reconstruct social stability as the basis of politics would come to mean the affirmation of the propertied classes' control over politics, but that reformulation of the republic was fundamentally intertwined with a new emerging vision of the relationship between the family, law, and the state. As conservative petitioners appealed for the rebuilding of trust and certainty throughout the social tissue, their concerns cut across class lines and formed part of a broader search for moral and political order based on the family, a need also expressed in journalistic, literary, and political writings. Integral to this reconstitution of civil society was the role of law: the law should work to establish stability rather than moral regeneration and social transformation. Implicitly, the petitioners appealed for positive over natural law: an informed state should make laws beneficial to its citizens.

In addition, disenchanted petitioners pointed angrily at the contradiction between universal, individual rights and a social order based on unified families. As I argued in Chapter 2, the early revolutionaries had hoped that families and marriage could sustain the social fabric, but they had worked above all to guard individual rights and liberties within the household. Now, this earlier attempt to incorporate individual rights into a new social unity came under assault. Particularly problematic to the familial order were the rights of women, illegitimate children, and defiant adult sons and daughters. As they recommended that individual rights be redefined within the framework of family and social utility, petitioners in effect advocated a return to a gendered patriarchal order and contributed to transforming the social and political priorities of the republic. I will suggest that widespread popular demand for securing lineage property through law, limited rights, and strong families would work to help the Thermidorian leadership's reaffirmation of the propertied classes' power. Debate over family needs would also enable centrist and right-wing deputies to shift political focus away from the issues of representation, natural law, and universal rights in the name of "social interest" and the rule of positive law.

These developments emerged in dialogue between the nervous legislature and a disillusioned sector of the populace, as they stimulated each other's social imagination and political rethinking. To probe this dynamic, this chapter begins by analyzing those conservative petitions that solicited the reform or repeal of revolutionary innovations in family law in the mid to late 1790s: I will explore their depiction of emotional and economic chaos and their appeal for a constitutional politics of certainty and social stability. Then, I ask why the petitioners' formulation of issues struck such a responsive chord among Thermidorian and Directorial leaders and illustrate how they built upon the petitioners' logic to redefine the social underpinnings of the republic.

THE PROCESS OF PETITIONING

Thermidorian questioning of revolutionary family policy formed part of a groundswell of conservative reaction beginning in late 1794.[5] In the wake of the Terror, social matters ranging from agrarian reform to religious policy to Jacobin styles of dress came up for public scrutiny, both serious and satirical. Family law, too, entered the public spotlight. Divorce gripped the popular imagination most compellingly, while egalitarian inheritance, the loss of paternal authority, and the status of illegitimate children received public attention as well. Royalist pamphlets and newspapers stirred up anti-divorce sentiment most flamboyantly by pouring forth dramatic scenes of marriages broken by libertine husbands or calculating, seductress wives. These exaggerated scenarios betrayed anxiety and hostility about the overturning of class as well as gender hierarchies. For example, in the spring of 1797 the *Miroir* satirized the "regeneration" and "patriotism" of the former wife of the governor of Saint Domingue for initiating divorce after forty years of marriage. This countess, descendant of "marshals, generals, dukes, counts, and marquis, . . . she has hooked up with a wigmaker, an inn-keeper, and a saddler."[6]

Other, less explicitly reactionary authors also whittled away at public opinion and positioned divorce as just one facet of a wider social disintegration. Social theorists Charles Guiraudet and J. Girard proclaimed that only the reestablishment of patriarchal authority could save the republic.[7] Novels and the new theatrical genre of melodrama likewise expressed more generalized trepidation about family lineage and internal family dynamics. Plays, such as Beaumarchais's *La Mère coupable* and P. Barré and N. Bourgueil's *Le mur mitoyen, ou le divorce manqué*, gained great popularity through celebrating the virtues of constancy over the scandal of divorce. Even songs and satirical poetry joined in the general free-for-all. The Muscadins allegedly chanted, "Why should we marry / When other men's wives, / To become our wives also / Put up so little resistance? Why should we marry?"[8]

Yet, even as the journalistic and literary public sphere began to encourage a critical stance toward family reforms, the experience of litigation—bitter contention in family tribunals across France—had already placed family issues at the center of many people's political consciousness. Thousands of court cases had challenged existing property arrangements as well as cultural expectations about gender, generation, and filiation. Although individuals and groups had poured forth petitions on family matters since the early years of Revolution, the attempt to implement the radical laws of the year II led to a dramatic increase in appeals to the legislature from 1794 to 1797.[9] Divorce and the egalitarian inheritance laws provoked by far the loudest outcry after the Terror.

Obviously, petitioners proffered opinions on both sides of family reform. While earlier chapters have explored proponents of innovation, this one focuses on the conservative petitioners who fostered the increasingly dominant backlash. On the issue of inheritance, opinion was most evenly divided between partisans and detractors of the new laws. On divorce, especially easy access to divorce for incompatibility, critics distinctly outnumbered supporters after Thermidor. These plaintiffs did not always demand the total repeal of the recent innovations. Often, they concentrated on a softening of the law, especially when rumors or the press pointed to a revision under debate by the Convention or the Council of Five Hundred. For example, from 1795 to 1797 many letter writers demanded that legislators end divorce for incompatibility, without necessarily attacking other forms of divorce. Likewise, a massive petition campaign soon after Thermidor denounced the *retroactive* implementation of the 17 nivôse and 12 brumaire laws on egalitarian inheritance and the rights of illegitimate children, without questioning their aptness for current and future cases.

This body of family law petitions shares many characteristics with those appeals that solicited divorce, egalitarian inheritance, adoption, or civil rights for illegitimate children. Like their political opponents, the defenders of Old Regime family customs had varying degrees of literacy and expertise. Although most petitioners simply wrote out their own thoughts in their own hand, a few collective petitions were printed.[10] In the petition warfare over the retroactive divisions of inheritance, some individuals copied model letters,[11] but most often authors drew their inspiration from their own litigation of cases or from rumors or newspapers.[12] The geography of petitioning followed a marked pattern. Petitions about divorce and illegitimacy came from all across France, though attacks on divorce originated disproportionately in larger communes or cities, like the practice of divorce itself. In contrast, protests about egalitarian inheritance and the downfall of paternal authority flowed from rural as well as urban pens. Notably, they came overwhelmingly from the Midi and Normandy, regions where the new laws most affected Old Regime systems of inheritance and patriarchal authority. Inheritance petitioners were most likely to offer clues about their class backgrounds: clearly they came from families with at least a minimum of property to pass on and the sums mentioned in inheritance cases suggest that many appellants were small peasant proprietors. In general, letter writers spanned the class spectrum from well-off, highly educated individuals to those scarcely able to pen a phrase.

Most authors were male, although women also wrote individual petitions, signed collective petitions, or appealed jointly with their husbands, siblings, or offspring. An individual's specific position in the family played a key role in influencing attitudes toward the egalitarian family. Women had an especially ambivalent relationship to family reform. Their petitions underscore the extent to which a woman's position within the family influenced her reaction to legal changes. While younger sisters wrote to defend the new egalitarian inheritance, daughters-in-law whose husbands' inheritance had been reduced became fervent attackers of the new social order. Among female divorce petitioners, more women defended divorce, but others inveighed against this law that had allowed a divorcing husband to abandon them and leave them destitute. Like the petitions lobbying in favor of innovation, the majority of these critiques were the individual and original creations of people directly involved in family litigation. Despite their spelling errors, hyperbole, and spontaneous forms of expressions, their anger, anxieties, and visions of reform fairly leap from the page and provide important access to grassroots concerns about family, property, and the law.

THE TERROR WITHIN THE FAMILY: EMOTIONAL TREACHERY AND CHAOS BY LAW

"The social order is entirely overturned," commented two vocal opponents of France's new inheritance laws. "You do not have to be profoundly politically sensitive to sense the truth of this claim," they wrote as if uttering an ominous warning to the deputies. In this world turned upside down, three themes lay at the center of the petitioners' discourse: how to strengthen affective bonds within the family; how to restore faith in property, especially lineage property, as the basis of social order; and how to endow the law and political structures once again with certainty and with a justice at once particular and universal. "Pitiful victim of an abuse authorized by the law, it is with tears of blood and a heart broken with grief that I implore you in the name of suffering humanity," wrote one critic of divorce. "My pains and woes are not unique. . . . You are the fathers of a great family, you should hasten to heal the wounds of your children."[13]

The petitioners' melodramatic presentation echoed a style of argument dating from the Old Regime and early Revolution.[14] But significantly, this discourse of emotional disorder and betrayal took on particular overtones within the broader "counter-imaginary" of Thermidor. As Bronislaw Baczko has illustrated, Thermidor unleashed an overwhelming political and psychological need to pour out the tragedies of the Terror, to recount personal sufferings and deceptions in Manichaean and vivid language. Political speeches and pamphlets, plays, the press, and personal accounts all raced to expose the torment and treachery of the Terror, as if this catharsis of self-expression could somehow wash away its atrocity and make way for a new purity and stability. Only by revealing the horror of the Terror could France prevent its return.[15] While the direct victims of the Terror, emerging from prison, had the most powerful claim to this language of victimization, the family petitioners spoke in the same register. Their personal stories of familial betrayal, broken marriages, and stolen legacies flowed together with even darker depictions of political backstabbing, imprisonment, and execution. The Terror had wrought chaos at once intimate and public, social and political.

The Terror lurked behind these family tragedies like a haunting specter; it figured in several different ways. Sometimes its arbitrary cruelty merely intensified personal dramas: the widow Cousin had lost her husband to Antoine Fouquier-Tinville's icy justice; she now found her inheritance under threat from a stranger—an illegitimate daughter of her late and beloved husband. Political conniving could invade domestic happiness: divorced husbands blamed their political enemies for seducing their wives or enticing them into initiating divorce. In other cases, the grotesque violence of the Terror seemed to unleash within the petitioners' imaginations the most barbaric and surreal scenarios that the laws could conceivably allow: several petitioners depicted in gory detail the vicious torture of a husband and wife by brigands, and accused the relatives who found the dying couple of deliberately allowing the husband to die first so that the wife's family would benefit from her new mutual property agreement.[16]

As these letter writers evoked the treachery of the Terror invading the family, their writings neatly inverted the tendency to imagine the worst political purges of the Terror in familial terms. In the winter of 1794–95 perhaps the most forceful conception of the Terror was the image of "republican marriages," carried out by the Jacobin deputy Jean-Baptiste Carrier in Nantes. According to testimony offered at his trial, men and women had been stripped naked, bound together, and forced into the Loire River to drown a cruel death. Prints circulated that emphasized the innocence and suffering of these stricken, youthful couples, whose nudity and innocence stood in stark contrast to the heartlessness of their executioners (see Figure 15). Terrorists at Nantes were said to have taken a special oath to "renounce parenthood, fraternity, the tenderness of a father or son."[17] That the Terror in Nantes should be etched into the collective memory as a perversion of "civic marriage" and an inversion of familial affection made morbid sense at this moment when the wreckage of human intimacy gripped the social and political imagination.

A new disillusionment about the role of the law echoed throughout these appeals. Petitioners assaulted certain laws as disorderly and destructive because they were enacted by "tyrants" and "drinkers of blood" during the year II. Victim of political passions and factionalism, the law itself no longer held any claim to impartiality. Sharing this popular indictment of family reform as "laws of passion and circumstance," the deputies Jean-Baptiste Mailhe and Merlin de Douai made key speeches in the spring and summer

Figure 15.   Drownings at Nantes: A "republican marriage" (between 1794 and 1799). Courtesy of the Bibliothèque nationale de France.

of 1795, holding the Terror responsible for easy divorce and the retroactive clauses of egalitarian inheritance legislation.[18]

According to this discourse, if the Terror had injected perverse partiality into the legal system and heart-wrenching disorder into families, it had also transformed widespread assumptions about the relationship between law and the emotions. In the early 1790s reformist petitioners, journalists, and deputies alike had voiced an optimistic faith that laws could promote sentiments that in turn had regenerative moral power. In the discourse of the radical revolution, the transparent power of sensibilité and the redemptive power of natural law stood at the center of political and moral renewal.[19] But in the aftermath of the Terror, both the law and sensibilité as regenerating forces had become deeply suspect. Rather, affect and the passions, as well as the law itself, could no longer be so easily trusted. How easily the emotions could be led astray. How fragile were the "sacred bonds" of marriage, family, and society. How powerfully the law could wreak havoc and carelessly make victims of its citizens.

As they demanded the reforging of civil society and social trust, the petitioners had clear-cut ideas about what the relationship should be between laws, emotions, and family. The best emotions were not those that promoted political regeneration or even patriotism. Rather, at the pinnacle of sentiment stood that unwavering loyalty and duty that cemented family unity and that bound husband and wife, father and son, brother and sister. The new laws placed these "natural" and enduring bonds between family members under constant threat from frivolity, inconstancy, and the duplicitous manipulation of the passions. Loftier feelings of reciprocal obligation were corrupted or curtailed. Without the freedom to leave legacies as they wished, fathers and mothers, aunts and uncles could not express gratitude to thoughtful, care-taking offspring. "This equality detaches children from their fathers and mothers," declared the anonymous B.B.B. in late 1796. Tender emotions and budding relationships could also be sabotaged by the new inheritance policies. One young woman wrote plaintively to the Convention that because of the 17 nivôse law, her true love had suddenly stopped visiting her, claiming that "he was no longer rich enough. I don't esteem him any less for that; I demand the suppression of this vile decree, so that my friend will return and we will be able to marry." Casting a broader net, a printed petition from "the mothers and fathers of divorcés" enumerated a series of divorces that had upset the honor and property of whole families, and had turned marriage into "a cold and sterile calculation."[20]

Depictions of wayward emotions, immoral relationships, and manipulation often explicitly faulted gender disorder and were couched in sexualized terms. If divorce for incompatibility had facilitated the abuse of the passions for political, financial, or other nefarious reasons, according to many petitioners, the liberal divorce laws also encouraged that peculiarly female susceptibility to credulity, wanton sexuality, and fickleness.[21] Divorce came under attack for "seeming to authorize women in particular to engage in libertinage," in the words of one petitioner in 1796. Another claimed it had transformed this sex, "once so timid, once so protective of its honor." Now women demanded divorce with one central goal: "To throw off the yoke, . . . to escape the severe observation of a husband." As petitioner after petitioner evoked the "leonine fury" of "women led astray," they framed marriage as an institution in which women's volatility and sexuality had to be kept under control.[22] They simultaneously defined Thermidorian disorder as the subversion of sexual and gender roles within the family and evoked problems that the crafters of the Civil Code would seek to resolve with patriarchal authoritarianism.

Not surprisingly, critics of egalitarian inheritance assailed women's unexpected access to property more than their unbridled sexuality. Yet they too painted images of female weakness in their arguments that women should not control property. The self-proclaimed deist republican Duval wrote late in 1794, "God having given weakness to women as their share as it were, . . . it is quite clear that his first intention was not that they become owners of land. Therefore to return civil laws to the purity of deism, we must lay down as a legislative principle their exclusion in this regard and their submission to males." Falling prey to the control and duplicity of women was disastrous for men, warned the soldier Jean Dumont as he urged the legislators to negate the 17 nivôse law: "Will you allow men to be debased by women? No. No doubt man is endowed by nature to be the master of woman. Today, by the law, he becomes her slave. Woman acquires control over him rather than being his equal. She becomes unequal by her shrewdness and bad faith."[23]

Tempestuous times, personal betrayals, disastrous laws, unruly passions, gender disorder . . . all these allusions paved the way for the petitioners' recurrent appeal that the sensitive deputies forge new equitable and stable laws above the fervor and partisanship of the radical revolution. Law and passion must be disentangled, and the relationship between the particular and the general must be rethought. "You will weigh everyone's interests, and you will measure their motives with the scales of equality and justice," commented Jeanne Aumont to the Committee of Legislation in 1795 as she added her own saga of injustice to the mountain of stories.[24]

PROPERTY, LAW, AND THE STATE

Thus far, I have argued that the petitioners' narrative of emotional wreckage within the home helped to forge the broader post-Thermidorian mistrust of sensibilité and the law, and vocalized the need to reestablish social trust within the home as within politics. But closely linked to these tales of affective betrayal and moral chaos was a second equally strong narrative about the *economic and structural* destruction of the family. The "disorder of families" also referred to the disruption of family strategies, property allocations, and mutual obligations.

At the core of the complainants' portrait of the network of family were three notions that combined customary family concerns with specific expectations of the revolutionary state. First, embedded within the family structure were gendered and generational roles that merited recompense; revolutionary egalitarianism within the home was a worthy goal but clearly it had to remain within certain limits set by these traditional practices. Second, the right to transfer property in certain ways formed the core of this system; this right had to be protected as had been promised in 1789 by the Declaration of the Rights of Man. Rights, undergirded by state law, served less to guarantee individual liberty endowed by nature than to preserve socially defined positions. Third, particular customs, contracts, and the rule of law had to join together to underpin existing regional expectations and arrangements. Even as they spoke the language of the "general good" and portrayed the state as a central force of uniformity, stability, and law, these petitioners exhorted lawmakers to validate particularistic traditions and to place certainty and the defense of property over the universalism of the radical revolution.

The petitioners were virtually unanimous in their premise that strong, hierarchical families formed the basis of social as well as political order, and that property—embedded within family structures and guaranteed by contract, blood ties, and law—forged the strength of this social pact. "The peace within families lays the foundation for the happiness of society . . . [and] it is on the respect for property that the social contract is founded," declared one self-proclaimed "tender and virtuous mother," as she decried an illegitimate child's intrusion into her marital property arrangements.[25]

In depicting the family and its destruction by family reform, petitioners repeatedly voiced the assumption that the family, its lineage, and marriage alliances formed a web of identity, expectation, duty, and justice, ideally reinforced by affective bonds. Envisioning position within the family as the basis of identity, these plaintiffs welcomed and fortified the post-Thermidorian definition of citizenship as based not on individual natural rights, but on social position and duty. Reformulating a phrase from the newly approved Constitution of the Year III, the anti-divorce schoolteacher Arthon commented in 1796, "The duty of a good citizen, isn't it to be a good son, good husband, and good father?" Shouldn't the state produce laws that protected citizens according to their interdependent family positions? Especially prevalent was the assumption that women's appeals for rights and property had upset familial order. As the petitioners of Friardel in the Calvados commented, "On the pretext of equality, we must not ruin brothers in order to enrich sisters: everyone must submit to the lot that the law has ordered."[26]

Presenting as a given that one's role and opportunities were defined by gender, generation, marital status, legitimacy, and birth order within the family web, petitioners argued that fair customs provided recompense in exchange for meritorious work. Neither individual liberty nor strict equality was at issue as values within the family, but rather unity, justice, mutual obligation, and devotion. In the moral economy of these petitions, closely related to the emotional disorder depicted above was an economic disorder of recompense denied. Many a divorced husband told tales of monetary deceptions and protested that he had been "a good friend to my wife and two children," only to become "the victim of a rich woman's caprices." For their part, inheritance disputes allowed by the egalitarian laws often aroused resentment about work and duty unrewarded. In Agen, Marie Tourme had lost her mother's legacy to greedy siblings, despite the endless "care, labor . . . and fruits of their industry" that she and her husband had devoted to her dying, partially paralyzed mother. Eldest sons of the Midi, along with Norman sons, complained that their useless younger brothers or ungrateful sisters, "dowried twenty, thirty, or forty years ago" now returned to steal away the "goods which are the fruit of my sweat." Model petitions circulated in Normandy, allowing each unhappy brother to flesh out in detail his own diligent contributions to a father's fortune or lands, now tragically threatened by sister(s) who had doubled their own dowries long ago.[27] Downgrading the value of sisters' work, these petitioners argued that each sibling should receive from the family according to his or her position, fulfillment of family obligation, or natural status.

Property lay at the crux of this discourse about family structure. It becomes crucial to ask how conservative petitioners defended this right "so sacred and so inviolable." A few defined property as a natural right, which some argued was conferred "at the moment of birth." For some citizens, the concept of natural rights blended with the notion that the natural order preordained certain kinship principles regarding property. One asserted that for collateral relatives ever to inherit before parents was "an offense against nature." Another asked, if a woman controlled communal property within marriage, "wouldn't that be a kind of contravention of the natural law which makes the husband the master of the association and the protector of the wife?"[28]

Far more common was a defense of property based on its social usefulness and its guarantee by the state and law. Enlightenment thinkers and revolutionary leaders across the political spectrum had at times based property on social utility and civil law, rather than natural rights.[29] But their definitions of social utility varied widely from the redistribution of goods to the maintenance of the status quo. In their defense of property, petitioners emphasized first that it must serve as the bedrock of social order and certainty, and second, that family lineage properties were the building blocks of the social structure. It was not necessary to own much property to leap to its defense in this form. Even petitioners who owned but little articulated in various ways the stipulation in the Constitution of the Year III, "On the maintenance of property rests . . . all social order."[30] In an outraged eight-page scribble on the dangerous abuses of divorce, Arnold du Bois ranted that the divorce law "violates property," and poured forth abundant and vitriolic examples of divorces for incompatibility that left whole families in financial ruin. He berated various initiators of divorce as "denatured people" seeking "to double their wealth, while depriving heirs of their legacy and robbing companions of the fruit of their marriage contract."[31] Like other critics of divorce, du Bois focused on marriages and liaisons between couples mismatched in age or fortune, as if to spotlight the world out of kilter.

If divorce law disrupted conjugal and lineage systems, the retroactive effect of the egalitarian inheritance law was even more to blame. Petitioners argued that retroactive redivisions trampled on the right to property and introduced countless contradictions into the law, contestation into the courts, and paralysis into the workings of agriculture, business, and family. Proclaiming that property was "the first basis of society," Monfreuille demanded the suspension of court cases over inheritance that turned "the most sacred contracts into insignificant rags," and "established a juridical war between brothers and sisters. Are there [any laws] that attack the bases of social order more than those which institute permanent confusion over properties and a continual uncertainty about the titles which guarantee them?" Only by repealing the retroactive provisions of the law could the legislators restore faith in contracts, property, and family structure and "set the first stone of the social edifice in eternal cement."[32]

Petitioners championing private property did not adopt the language of liberal individualism, nor did they advocate unlimited free use of goods. For example, in defending contracts, they did not share the conviction of early revolutionaries who endorsed the freedom to contract as an expression of individual liberty and proclaimed marriage to be a civil contract. Rather, contracts formed a legal scaffolding that guaranteed the "public faith" in the broader network of family blood ties and business alliances. Thirteen oldest sons from the Pays de Caux made the distinction explicitly: "If marriage itself is based simply on the will of two people, it is not the same for the marriage contract. . . . Here two families together stipulate the reciprocal advantages of two spouses."[33]

Within this social pact of family, property, and law, certain individuals held precarious positions. Three groups were especially perceived as threats to the family line: overly independent married women, illegitimate offspring, and adult children who defied marital and succession plans. In a reference to Old Regime practices and a prelude to the logic of the Civil Code, petitioners endorsed legal limitations on these individuals' right to control property or challenge existing arrangements. Louis Goulé of Normandy warned against disruptive family members: "Here it is a sister, married twenty years ago, . . . who comes to dispute her inheritance at the price of the sweat and work of her brothers. Or there it is a bastard who makes an incursion against legitimate children. Everywhere property is uncertain."[34]

Women in particular should not be allowed to control family property, not only because they were weak by nature, but also because they could disrupt kinship strategies through remarriage or the introduction of illegitimate children. An anonymous author worried that a debauched woman who bore a child through adultery could gain control over her late husband's property, "after having caused him to die of sorrow and having induced or accelerated the death of the child."[35] In a petition about the possible effects of divorce on the property of offspring, one anonymous individual argued that the divorced father should maintain control over his ex-wife's goods for the sake of their offspring:

> The Roman Law . . . , copied by our own laws, . . . and based on the knowledge of nature and on the experience of centuries, has placed woman into continual dependence on her husband so that within the civic order, the weakness of one sex was effectively secured by the wisdom of the other. . . . What can happen if the divorced woman is neither constrained nor supervised in managing the patrimony of the children born of the dissolved marriage, and if the father is a stranger to the conservation of their rights?[36]

To reaffirm a more traditional gender order would set civil society and property on a more secure footing.

The petitioners repeatedly stressed the need to reestablish social trust, but this was fundamentally a political and legal question. Here, their expectations of the revolutionary state, its laws, and its ideology become clear. Rather than denying the legitimacy of the Revolution, they merged traditional notions of family property with redefined concepts of equality and the law. They embraced a limited definition of civil equality, in tension with liberty and existing rights. And above all, they endorsed the idea that the rule of law, the Declaration of Rights, and the Constitutional position of the state should forge social stability and public faith. Abandoning any notion of natural law as a redemptive moral force, they spoke the language of the Civil Code rather than of 1792–94. In other words, they saw the state as a source of positive laws that underpinned the social order; laws gave the state legitimacy and force. The law owed the people certainty rather than transformation.

But the Terror had left this role of the state and its laws in doubt and had made imperative a joint refashioning of society and politics. Petitioners argued that the political order was dependent on the just reconstitution of the social, just as the restoration of social order depended on political equilibrium. In this world of disorder, family law reform had defiled the political principles and constitutional promises of the Revolution. Citizen Cahuac told the sad tale of how his wealthy sister had deprived him of his hard-earned parental legacy, and then asked the deputies how such injustice was possible:

> What will happen to the principles consecrated in the constitutional act?
> . . . And if you don't repeal this tyrannical law, how can you reconcile it
> with the Declaration of the Rights of Man, which expressly says in article 14 that giving a retroactive effect to a law is a crime. But no, citizen
> representatives, you will not reject the reclamations of such a large
> number of oppressed and dispossessed ones, because virtue triumphs and
> it is therefore the moment to make justice triumph.[37]

Like Cahuac, petitioner after petitioner invoked justice and the Constitution, as well as various articles of the Rights of Man, especially Article 17 guaranteeing property and Article 14 against the retroactive effects of laws.[38]

If the family reform laws contravened the letter and principles of constitutional law, they also violated the revolutionary allegiances of the French people. Time and again, conservative petitioners portrayed themselves as more republican and patriotic than their opponents. Many emphasized their military service to the Republic. "I am French, I serve my country, I like justice. And it is under these claims that I am concerned with the maintenance and the strengthening of the Republic," wrote the soldier Armand Mame.

Older sons of the Midi claimed their undeserving younger brothers had not been old enough to fight for the Republic, and one petitioner even argued that brothers deserved larger estates than their sisters who never shed blood for France! Another divorced husband who had lost control over his ex-wife's dowry declared angrily that the new regime meant to protect the rights of man "as much from woman as from despotism."[39]

In articulating the relationship between the new state and older customs, petitioners reinterpreted the revolutionary ideals of equality, liberty, and rights in ways that supported customary practices. For example, critics of the retroactive effect of the inheritance laws routinely voiced their support for the egalitarian thrust behind the laws and agreed that it should be followed for future divisions. However, the same petitions pointed out that to redivide goods essentially already parceled out by marriage contracts and légitime arrangements long ago was to "overturn the principle of equality itself." Such inequitable division would "injure the equality of partitions," violate existing rights, and be "opposed to the essence of a free government." Fathers complained that the new laws favored daughters over sons, bastards over legitimate offspring, or younger sons over the eldest. In other words, they suggested that perhaps the new laws were less egalitarian than the old. More to the point, they implied that civil equality could only be defined in the context of the family. Furthermore, petitioners had a tendency to conflate the question of "equality" with that of "justice." They slid easily from an emphasis on "equality" to the language of *équité* (equity) instead. Their arguments repeatedly highlighted the complexity of implementing new principles in their entirety: what was good in principle might be inequitable in practice. The words "équité" and "justice" were often paired and pitted against the moment of the Terror when "the legislators . . . did not dare to defend the principles of justice." Now that calamity had passed, the legislature should restore existing rights.[40]

As they threaded their way between revolutionary principles and Old Regime practices in the name of justice, letter writers put their finger on the critical problem of property in the 1790s: the tension between equality on the one hand and liberty and existing rights on the other.[41] Two Norman brothers commented, "However advantageous the law of equality may be, was its execution so urgent that we had to annihilate rights which had already been acquired?" Another anonymous critic claimed that the laws should not "destroy liberty" and work toward "the leveling of fortunes" in the name of equality.[42] Like the crafters of the Civil Code, these petitioners resolved the tension by limiting both equality and liberty to take into account obligations and hierarchy within the kinship network. Certainly, male heads of households must benefit more directly from these qualities. Rights became redefined as existing rights acquired by virtue of family position, geographic location, or social status. In other words, social utility rather than natural law defined rights as well as equality. And it was the role of the Law to reinforce and cement these definitions, and to form the pragmatic and trusty link between social and political order.

This emphasis on justice, law, and limited equality took the petitioners full circle back to the issues of emotional disorder and the relationship between individual interests and the general good. In their exaggerated depictions of familial justice denied, petitioners contended with panache that the law somehow needed to take into account the complexity and variety of particular interests. Some made the abstract problem explicit: one citoyenne legitimized her specific story of wrangling over marital property with the comment that it was "by paying attention to a particular case that you can rise to the task of perfecting the general law, for out of the discussion of particular cases are born . . . the codes of civilized nations." Petitioners were anxious to speak the language of the general good and even to advocate a unified law, but they demanded a rearticulation of the relationship between localized practices and the universalism of the year II. The veuve Boudeau insisted that she did not speak out of personal "sordid interest" and advocated "one Law for all," but the malicious and inequitable impact of the 17 nivôse law in the custom of the Marche forced her to speak: "for the sake of the happiness of several particular individuals, you should not create general unhappiness," she argued, turning the rhetoric of general good on its head.[43]

Conservative family law petitioners wrote out of the anger born of litigation and conflict within families. Their words resonated with the bitterness of expectations denied, and they clung vocally to traditional assumptions about gender, generation, and obligation. The most literate petitioners were keenly aware of every move of the legislators as they debated these contentious family issues: appellants pounced on rumors of legal changes or wording from the new Constitution as they strove to bring their personal outrage to bear in the broader political arena of the state. In their acrimony, they exaggerated the impact of revolutionary legislation on families. But their articulations of social and familial turmoil, their mistrust of law and emotions, and their search for moral and economic certainty would find a receptive ear in the particular political climate of Thermidor and the Directory. Especially influential was their struggle to merge traditional notions about property, gender, and obligation with the new constitutional order, the rule of law, and a limited defense of socially useful rights.

LEGISLATIVE RESPONSES:
FAMILY, PROPERTY, AND THE SOCIAL ORDER

The popular backlash energized legislative discussion about family order throughout Thermidor and the Directory. Overall, the legislators moved with some hesitation in refurbishing revolutionary family law. But although they would leave it to the crafters of the Civil Code to turn the family definitively toward a patriarchal structure, the Thermidorian and Directorial deputies took some legislative steps in that direction and developed crucial ideological formulations about the relationship between family, law, property, and the political order. At specific moments the flood of petitions on key topics both spurred and legitimized debates over family law in the legislature. Most notably, in the reactionary spring and summer of 1795 the outpouring of petitions attacking egalitarian inheritance and the rights of enfants naturels stimulated the Convention's decision to end retroactive application of the 17 nivôse law on egalitarian inheritance and, temporarily, of the 12 brumaire law on illegitimate children's succession rights as well. In that same summer, the Convention abolished the 4 floréal an II (23 April 1794) law, which had allowed divorce on six-months de facto separation. The following winter the legislature disbanded the family courts, which seemed to allow or even promote so much "trouble within families." Finally, antidivorce petitions combined with pamphlet, press, and literary attacks to have a cumulative effect by late 1796 and 1797: the deputies endlessly debated the fate of divorce for incompatibility and finally added a six-month delay to the procedure. The conservative petitioners made their mark at moments when the political pendulum swung to the right and facilitated challenges to the most controversial laws.[44]

Family law petitions could both legitimate and influence the legislators' positions. In a general sense, the appeals evoked existing concerns and flowed together with broader public debate about social and familial order in the theater, journalism, and political writings. More specifically, the two committees that dealt with civil law under the successive legislatures clearly took the petitions seriously. The Committee of Legislation during the Convention and the Committee on the Classification of Laws during the Directory generated civil law reforms and helped the jurist Cambacérès to produce drafts of the civil code. These committees kept their finger on the pulse of public opinion; they regularly read from individual petitions to launch legislative debate, replied on occasion to some lay appeals, and wrote comments on the margins of others. While some petitions received the summary comment "au carton," others merited a more serious read, earned scribbled reflections, or even provoked a bill or an outline for a decree. "Well done," commented Merlin de Douai in the margin of the citoyenne Galot Thiphaine's petition attacking egalitarian inheritance.[45]

In some cases the line of influence was strikingly direct: when Cambacérès presented his third unsuccessful civil code in July 1796, he directly borrowed language (without acknowledgment) from an anonymous petition to argue that wives should not share in the administration of communal marital property. In other cases, deputies used an emblematic or powerful petition as the spearhead for initiating legislative debate on specific laws. As the historian François Olivier-Martin has suggested, individual petitions may have directly provoked deputies to action.[46] Or, perhaps more plausibly, they introduced these petitions into the legislature because they so neatly embodied dominant concerns, had rhetorical power, and offered validation from "the people." Roughly twenty petitions dealing with the retroactive effects of inheritance laws were read aloud at the bar of the Convention in the winter and spring of 1795. Eighteen months later, multiple individual complaints about flagrant divorces became the advance guard in the legislative battle to tighten the marital bond. For example, in late 1796 the deputy Guillaume Favart prefaced his indictment of divorce for incompatibility by reading a petition from an angry dragoon captain who wrote that his wife, the greedy mother of his four children, was attempting to divorce him for incompatibility and win control of the family possessions, even as he marched valiantly toward Italy. How could this loaded example fail to touch the anxiety stirred up by the prolonged absence of so many young men, some of them leaving wives and children without adequate supervision? When it denounced divorce a few months later, the right-wing newspaper *Le Censeur des journaux* would reiterate this trope of soldiers rejected by callous and avaricious wives back at home.[47]

The mode of petition warfare was peculiarly characteristic of the Thermidorian period. Thermidorian leaders shared and had helped to create the unique political psychology in which personal narratives of victimization and betrayal had become a potent means of exorcising the past and of choosing what to forget, remember, or rebuild.[48] Even as these petitions influenced legislative debate, they also legitimized the deputies' own goals. Just as the wave of antiterrorist addresses from across France fueled the lawmakers' purging of former terrorists from their midst,[49] the onslaught of petitions attacking or defending the retroactive enforcement of egalitarian inheritance laws supported the plans of Thermidorians anxious to associate disorder with the darkest days of the Terror and to build a new social order on limited equality, the rule of law, and the defense of property. "Cross-examine your Committee of Legislation about the numerous reclamations that have come from all corners of the Republic," cried the legislator Jacques-Henri Laurenceot in his 1795 assault on the 17 nivôse law. Interestingly, leftist defenders of the year II laws were often less anxious to invoke the petitioners' voices: "Are we still, will we always be reduced to the servile condition of dragging ourselves from example to example? Reason, principles—do they mean nothing then for us?" commented François Darracq in his defense of the rights of illegitimate children in 1796.[50]

The legislators' most forceful speeches unmasking the "system of Terror" had always included their own revelations of its familial and emotional disorder. "The Terror breaks all bonds, extinguishes all affections; it defraternizes, desocializes, demoralizes. . . . And above all, what changes it has brought about in the relations between the sexes!" commented Jean-Lambert Tallien, a leading Thermidorian, in his crucial speech of September 1794 outlining the "system of the Terror."[51] The deputies' early disclosures about the Terror nonetheless necessarily foregrounded political imprisonment, intrigue, and executions. But after the Thermidorians accomplished the first urgent political tasks of opening the prisons, beginning to allot responsibility, trying Carrier, and reintegrating the Girondins into the Convention, they in effect also cleared space for the generalized social horrors of the Terror to take on more importance.

By the spring of 1795, Thermidorians began to put new emphasis on the need to resolve political turmoil with social stability. In early 1795 the political revelations continued to snowball, but the corollary focus on social chaos grew proportionately stronger. In the year III, the deputy Boissy d'Anglas seemed to have a knack for framing and articulating conservative Thermidorian stances on pivotal issues.[52] In his influential speech on 21 ventôse an III (11 March 1795), he helped to redirect the social goals of the Revolution. As he unveiled the social destruction wrought by the terrorists against the people, he made a crucial maneuver: he moved from unmasking the terrorists' hypocritical claim to speak for the people to arguing that the role of government was to establish social order, soothe emotional discord, and placate conflicts between the rich and the poor. He posed a social solution to France's troubled past: the Republic would choose stability over strict equality. For while men could be "equal in rights, [they] could never be equal in virtue, talent and fortune."

> The mass of men born on the soil of France, this is the people. Part of the people have acquired property by inheritance, acquisition, or their own industry; a second part of this same people is working to acquire some or to gain more. Imperceptible gradations of comfort or poverty exist be-

tween these two groups of people, called the rich and the poor; they serve each other . . . their union is their force, and on their misunderstandings or harmony depend the unhappiness or the prosperity of the State.[53]

Boissy d'Anglas forthrightly allied the defense of property with the will of the people, and based the Republic on the acceptance of class difference. The legislators must use the law to protect property and maintain emotional harmony. The Parisian uprisings of germinal and prairial that same spring of 1795 would only accentuate his point. It quickly became apparent that reform of family law offered a key arena for defining the new social underpinning of political stability. In this climate, conservative and moderate deputies willingly listened to petitioners' graphic storytelling about shattered emotional bonds and threats to property. In dialogue, petitioners and deputies developed the discourse on how to reconstitute the social order.

Shortly after Boissy d'Anglas's speech and the germinal riot, a group of petitioners arrived at the bar of the Convention to denounce the corrosive impact of the 17 nivôse law on property and contracts. They found a receptive response for the first time. In their support, the deputy Jean-Baptiste Quirot commented, "It doesn't matter to the Republic that this one or that one is richer or poorer, but it matters that property be certain and that tranquility be assured." The Convention commissioned the Committee of Legislation to study the issue. And indeed, in his subsequent reports proposing the repeal of the retroactive clause of 17 nivôse, Lanjuinais clearly delineated the pivotal position of positive, civil law in protecting property to safeguard the social order. He argued cogently that "civil law creates property and only civil law can regulate the mode and order of its transmission." Debunking the mythologized, rhetorical power of nature or equality, he pointed out that nature distributed property unequally, while state-made laws would operate "according to social interest. . . . Why are we talking about *equality, reason, or nature?* These vague and undefined words—if we apply them to private property, there would be no more property, there would be no more society" (emphasis in original). As he laid out the critical role of law in defining society, he invoked justice to override the rights of individuals such as younger sons or "daughters married outside the paternal household." "Justice . . . should be blind; she does not recognize the eldest or youngest; she protects the property of all equally."[54]

In effect, he repositioned equality and the law to sustain property in the interest of the family and social order, rather than in the interest of the individual. He simultaneously reinforced the shift away from faith in natural or regenerative law: by defining the social order, positive law would be both product and protector of the state. Other speakers would expand upon his line of argument in future debates over inheritance, illegitimacy, and divorce.[55] Later, the Civil Code would rest on the same notion of state-made laws rooting property in the family, albeit a more explicitly patriarchal one.

In the short term, Lanjuinais faced opposition from more liberal deputies. Alexandre Villetard and Pierre Paganel, for example, called vehemently for equality as the basis of the social order, claimed that the law must protect the property rights of the weaker sex and weaker family members, and warned against a return to the tyrannical regime of old. As Paganel indicted the "barbarous customs that created a proud tyrant in the bosom of families," he powerfully warned the Convention against a return to the abuse of patriarchal power. For all of their desire to restore order, Thermidorians remained wary of endowing paternal authority with its Old Regime strength.[56] The left forestalled any serious attempt to dismantle egalitarian inheritance altogether. But the retroactive clauses were fair game as the Convention in its last months sought to distance itself from the most radical policies of the year II. The tide was turning in Lanjuinais's direction. By September 1795, his logic had led directly to suspending the retroactive clauses of the egalitarian inheritance laws of 17 nivôse and 12 brumaire an II.[57]

THE POLITICS OF REPRESENTATION, RIGHTS, AND THE SOCIAL INTEREST

The struggle to reconstitute the social basis of family and property had profound political implications for the Thermidorians and Directorials. The debates over family structure served as a forum for wrestling with the quintessential political problems of representation, particular interests, and individual rights defined by natural law. Petition after petition, with saga after saga of family tragedy, illuminated the difficulty of guaranteeing individual rights and pressed the deputies to both represent and conciliate the varying interests of individuals, families, and regions. In seeking solutions, the deputies moved somewhat haltingly: the Terror had left them wary of seeming to promote a specific interest or faction and also wary of speaking unquestioningly in the register of the general will. Moreover, the ever-shifting politics of Thermidor and the Directory required constant compromises between the left and the right. Leftist representatives continued to evoke the "natural rights" of all family members as fundamental to the sociopolitical order, but even they increasingly complemented rights ideology with their own attempt to define a stable social order and a politics that did not overturn the law or Constitution.[58]

Most tellingly, the conservative and moderate deputies gradually developed a discourse on justice, the social interest, and the good of the family that allowed them simultaneously to downplay or even dismiss issues of rights and liberty within the home and to set aside their responsibility to political representation in favor of their duty to shore up the social order. Faced with this explosion of the personal—this torrent of stories elaborating personal interests and trumpeting the violation of existing rights— Thermidorian legislators most often did not respond by calling upon the general will, the people's voice, or popular sovereignty. Rather, they emphasized the need for "justice," "principles," and the "interest of society." In other words, they circumvented the loaded question of political representation and shifted the focus to social order and a disembodied "justice." Increasingly, "justice" and "social interest" replaced the "general will" as the opposite of "particular interests."[59] In August 1795 when Mailhe, one of the leading critics of radical family laws, censured the retroactive provision of equal inheritance law, he pitted particular interests against justice in a typical fashion:

> Your discussion about the 17 nivôse law has put into motion an infinity of personal interests. Those dispossessed by it claim its repeal; those favored by it demand its maintenance. Whatever your decision, it will make some discontent; this is the fate of all laws; but if it is just, no one will have the right to complain, and the entire Nation will applaud [the law]. . . . *Justice! That is the true general interest.* Without it, neither social bonds nor government exist [my emphasis].[60]

The constant invocation of justice allowed the Thermidorians to claim that they operated without regard to passion, favor, or faction, but rather followed the rule of law. "It is not a question here of favor, but of justice," commented Edmond Dubois-Crancé in his attack on egalitarian inheritance, "and the National Convention should not make its decision based on the number [of people] who win or lose, but only based on what is supremely just, and what most benefits the social order."[61]

If Thermidorians could make laws based on the principles of justice and social order, it freed them from the tyranny of popular sovereignty and the responsibility of direct representation. In the summer of 1795, deputies often invoked the support of the conservative petitioners, but at the same time brushed aside their need to respond to popular demand. When Lanjuinais delivered his attack on the retroactive redivisions of inheritance, he claimed the support of the "general will which has made itself heard against the 17 nivôse law"; but then he immediately noted that the "reclamations have become too numerous; many have also been sent to you to maintain the law." As a result, the committee had placed itself above the war of petitions, "this fight between opposing interests, this conflict of claims. . . . Your committee has seen only justice, has consulted only principles."[62] Despite his apparent confidence, his words betrayed an underlying uncertainty about how the legislature should deal with this outpouring of conflicting stories about the impact of the law on families. In addition, at this political point he dared to wield the discourse of justice to attack only the *retroactive* implementation of inheritance laws.

But, above all, the rhetoric equating justice and social order with the general interest would enable centrist and conservative Thermidorians and Directorials to forget or occlude the issues of individual rights and equality within the family. Individual rights became increasingly positioned as particular interests that undercut the social interest of the family. For example, the rights of illegitimate children now came to be seen as "particular interests" that "invaded" or "intruded" upon the family, and upon social order more generally. Echoing the language of the most distraught of petitioners, the legislator Charles Blutel painted the sufferings of "a virtuous family . . . chased piteously from their humble home" by a "stranger's act of tyranny, subversive of all principles. What will become of these sad victims, if you smother their cries!" The 12 brumaire law, which had restored civil rights to at least some illegitimate offspring, was re-envisioned as one that "favored enfants naturels much more than children born within marriage." Even Cambacérès, who often fought to retain the innovations of 1792–94, surrendered these rights rather easily to the need to outlaw paternity searches that might violate the social order. "What difference does it make if a few individuals are deprived of their familial rights and are raised at the State's expense, if by this sacrifice, libertinage is proscribed, domestic tranquility is assured, and legitimate unions are encouraged?" he asked in the speech introducing his third and most conservative Civil Code in the summer of 1796.[63]

By downplaying individual rights and equality within the family, the deputies allegedly sought to cleanse the family of the conflicts enkindled by revolutionary politics—those conflicts so violently depicted by petitioners and court cases alike. Crucially, in claiming to depoliticize the family, they did not so much turn it into a private sphere separate from politics as make it into an interest group whose claims were not "particular," but universal. In Directorial discourse, the family became the moral, affective, and economic bedrock: "the bonds of families are the element, the basis, the guarantee of the body social," stated the ever representative Mailhe in 1797.[64] At times, right-wing deputies ruefully reminded their colleagues that religion no longer melded the family into a holy unit. Opponents of divorce, for example, alluded to the transformation of marriage from "a sacred bond," "the most holy of obligations," into a "mere" contract, "a market of human flesh," a "fraud," or even "prostitution." The religious politics of the Directory made it impossible for them to demand a return to sacramental marriage, but by evoking the flight of the sacred, they touched a chord of anxiety and strengthened their appeal for fortifying families on behalf of the collective good.[65]

Once family interest became conflated with the interest of social order and justice that underpinned the republic, it became much more difficult for individuals to make claims against the family and its collective needs. Among men, illegitimate children, obstreperous sons, and in-marrying foreigners would be expected to surrender their interests. In contrast, certain other men—above all soldiers, followed by fathers of families—had a more sacred claim to rights and property. Women's rights above all would be sacrificed for the good of the group. In debating the rights of dowried daughters customarily excluded from further inheritance, the jurist Durand de Maillane asserted that the old dowry system had brought happiness to couples as well as justice and peace to families; why encourage daughters' greed and quest for a larger share?[66]

In the debates over divorce for incompatibility, this shift away from guarding women's rights became particularly marked. The anti-divorce deputies unveiled the callow and libertine behavior of both male and female divorcés, but focused with particular intensity on the erosion of feminine submissiveness and modesty. Right-wing legislators accused women of abusing the divorce laws to allow their passions free rein and to escape domestic responsibilities to husband and children. Nicolas Golzart claimed that it was "women above all, [who] forgetting the natural shyness of their sex, and the modesty which is their most beautiful ornament, have abused this too lenient law." Likewise, the deputy Henri Bancal contended that divorce had "legally armed" women against their husbands. It enabled the "frivolous woman . . . to disobey [her husband] with impunity . . . and spread war within the family." Inverting the language of 1792, Bancal stated that divorce violated "individual liberty, and property, because the man and woman, . . . united for their entire life, are no longer masters in their home, when a strange man or woman, . . . can trouble the interior of their family, can soon chase them from this sacred asylum, and take their possessions." Bancal's denunciation of female insubordination and his slippage equating individual liberty with the defense of home and property both prefigured the Civil Code: like the Code, he validated male authority and domestic unity over individual rights, especially the rights of women.[67]

The disgruntled deputies faulted wives for upsetting family harmony. Conversely, they also contended that the divorce laws often worked against women, depicted this time in a position of fragility. Reversing the 1792 argument that divorce laws prevented the domestic slavery of women, many suggested that the abolition of divorce (at least for incompatibility) would protect vulnerable women from being seduced or fooled out of their dowries and would guarantee male fidelity to this "sex which has already lost one of its main attractions as soon as it is surrendered, the sex which sees its beauty fade daily and its fertility age prematurely." In the words of Pierre-Louis Duprat, "Who formulated most of these demands? Women, young wives, some of whom are nursing their babies while others are just about to become mothers. Their weakness and sensibilité have been abused: most often [they are] the dupes of some ambitious man or libertine, their greatest error is their charm or their fortune." In a nutshell, opponents of easy divorce seized on the two problematic characteristics purported to be at the heart of female nature: the dangerous and seductive quality of female sexuality on the one hand, and the susceptible character of the flighty feminine on the other, for women were so seductive and yet so easily seduced. Women needed protection—from their own sexuality as well as that of audacious men. To guard women from adultery took precedence over guaranteeing them rights.[68]

In the name of justice and social order, the discourse on liberty within the family became as suspect as that of equality and natural rights. In the winter of 1797, the royalist Siméon argued that it was absurd to discuss marriage and divorce in terms of protecting individual liberty: "As if spouses were slaves; as if the mutual gift of their faith was an alienation; as if the natural contract by which the two spouses become one . . . could be compared to that abuse of force which introduced servitude against the rights of nature and equality." These political issues played no role within marriage; like the petitioners, Siméon emphasized instead the familial bonds of mutual aid, "these perpetual relationships, sentiments, moralities, almost needs, " that bound husband, wife, and children alike.[69]

The Thermidorian discourse on the social gradually shifted the definition of individual rights away from its 1789 basis in natural law toward a new basis in social utility. Within the vision of conservative Thermidorians and Directorials, the expanse of rights governed and guaranteed by nature shrank. Notably, the right to inherit familial property was no longer based on the natural right to equality; divorce was no longer grounded in the natural right to liberty. Likewise, according to this discourse, the illegitimate child could no longer invoke nature to claim anything beyond food.[70] Yet, without a doubt, this undermining of natural rights met opposition from the left that starkly limited the ability of conservative legislators to repeal family law innovations. The assault of these deputies on natural rights cut to the heart of the revolutionary project. Their attempt to rebalance the relationship between the individual and the social found viable expression owing to the reactionary climate of Thermidor and the Directory. But the political vacillations of the Directory and the continuing voices lifted in defense of revolutionary reforms made it impossible to carry the reaction through to its completion—at least until the coming of Napoleon.

THE VACILLATIONS OF THE DIRECTORY

Strikingly, in the legislative debates over the family in the mid to late 1790s, much was said to attack the new family laws, but little was done to change them. I have been arguing here that Thermidorian and Directorial deputies paved the way for the Civil Code not so much by specific legal actions as by discursive work that significantly reconceptualized the relationship between individual rights, family, and social interest. But why were the Councils so hesitant to make changes? In answering this question, I would like not only to briefly highlight the resilience of natural rights arguments, but also to suggest that left-wing and moderate legislators protected family law innovations from abolition by appropriating the discourse of moral order, political stability, and legal certainty. In the seesaw politics of the Directory, both sides sought to commandeer the discourse of moderation, for it held tremendous appeal.

Leftist supporters of the recent family reforms continued to draw on the principle of equality rooted in nature. For example, in his 1796 defense of the retroactive gains of illegitimate children, François Riou noted the timeless distinction between "natural and positive" law. Because of the "imprescriptible rights of nature" that had also abolished feudal dues and slavery, the natural child had a claim, running within his very veins, to the property of his father. Civil law had every authority to recognize this claim retroactively. Likewise, Louis-Joseph Charlier straightforwardly argued that the retroactive clauses of the 17 nivôse law were just because "the inequality of succession goes against the laws of nature." In the divorce debates, Cambacérès more pointedly and eloquently put his finger on the central question: "Moral needs should not serve as a pretext for attacking individual liberty," nor should "the right to property . . . do harm to the equality that is the basis of our social organization."[71]

In this same vein, in 1797 defenders of divorce for incompatibility resurrected the language of liberty and love from the early 1790s. Darracq aligned divorce with the natural right to personal freedom as well as happiness when he warned that marriage without divorce would constitute "the mutual *alienation of their persons*" (his emphasis). He caused a ripple of laughter in the Council of Five Hundred with his observation that one could not "contract a pledge to love eternally, to love all one's life." Several deputies also chastised their right-wing opponents for trying to reinstate "sacerdotal errors" and stir up retrograde religious sentiments about marital indissolubility, just as nonjuror priests were starting to agitate in the countryside. This anticlerical argument still held power and there was little support for returning family matters to ecclesiastical hands.[72]

However, above all, left-wing deputies succeeded in limiting changes in divorce and inheritance law by coopting two key Thermidorian discourses and turning them to their own purposes. Like their opponents, they positioned themselves as champions of moral order and legal stability in the aftermath of the Terror. For example, the defenders of divorce claimed to guard domestic tranquility and honor. In their accounts, far from instigating domestic chaos, divorce for incompatibility in fact protected the honor and privacy of families. Rather than forcing couples to "reveal shameful secrets and dishonor themselves," this form of divorce draped a morally healthy "official veil" over a multitude of private causes for unhappiness, ranging from "adultery and impotence" to "shameful diseases" to a wife's forced prostitution at the hands of her "wasteful and cowardly" husband, in Oudot's words. Advocates of divorce matched their opponents' flamboyant narratives with their own dramatic tales of families forced to endure wretched lives together or to reveal their gut-wrenching secrets at the moral expense of the whole nation. The Terror, too, figured in their stories. In a telling example, Lecointe-Puyraveau concluded his 1797 defense of divorce with a vivid portrait of a young woman forced to remain married to the man who had denounced her father during the Terror. If she were not allowed to divorce she would face the executioner of her father daily. "When he approaches her, she envisions in his hand a bloody head suspended by its white hair. She cries out to you: he is the one who has killed my father; he cannot be my husband." "Good enough to figure in a novel," was the phrase chosen by the anti-divorce Joseph-Vincent Dumolard to debunk these scenarios.[73]

Within the debates over the 17 nivôse and 12 brumaire laws, the left also depicted these laws as stewards of harmony and justice. Jean-Baptiste Desmolin vigorously inveighed against depriving an enfant naturel of the rights, family, and honor that he had just refound. To an imagined natural child, Desmolin cried out, "You will no longer be the acknowledged son of your father; the caresses he has given you, these tender outpourings of kindness from your parents, I tear them away from you." Likewise, in the 1795 debates over the retroactive clauses of inheritance, Villetard explicitly defined the desirable society as an egalitarian one. If the legislators abandoned the defense of every citizen's equal right to property, they would be "troubling the social order." Interestingly, Villetard vindicated women's equal rights to inheritance by invoking their "weakness" and need for protection. Waxing poetic about women's role as nurturers and consolers of men, he claimed that since this sex "is less favored by nature with the means to assure subsistence, it [the female sex] has a greater need for property."[74] As he couched his defense of women's inheritance in female frailty rather than in natural rights, Villetard wielded powerful imagery but also contributed to the Directorial trend toward abandoning rights discourse and emphasizing women's vulnerability and dependency.

Just as they portrayed egalitarian inheritance and divorce as sources of *social* order and domestic equity, left-wing legislators also defended innovative practices by warning against introducing a new round of *legal and political* turmoil. To overturn inheritance divisions already accomplished was to undermine faith in contracts and vitiate legal authority—hardly wise at this moment when the Revolution needed to be brought to completion, admonished François Lanthenas in his speech on behalf of natural children. To suspend the law allowing divorce by incompatibility was an unconstitutional and anarchical political act, playing with the laws and stability of the land. Deliberately summoning up memories of the Terror, the pro-divorce deputies insinuated that this "political anarchy" would only worsen the social situation. Pons de Verdun captured the spirit of the position well when he stated: "Every day men who call themselves the best friends of the constitution, and the farthest away from revolutionary ideas, talk to you about anarchy; I am astonished to hear them make an anarchical proposition themselves: because what is anarchy, if it isn't an interregnum of the laws?"[75]

The political strength of this discourse of legal certainty and moderation stands out in the debates over divorce for incompatibility. In the summer of 1797, Félix Faulcon wielded these arguments with particular power when he negotiated a compromise to these endless debates. Rather than doing away with divorce by incompatibility in its entirety, why not simply add a six-month waiting period to deprive this form of separation of its flighty character? Faulcon worked hard to position himself as the ultimate moderate, an impartial figure who presented this compromise for the collective good of a divided nation. Master of the discourse of social and legal chaos, Faulcon imbued his speech with a sense of urgency, as if to come to a viable compromise on this one issue would save France and the legislature from further divisiveness. "Hélas! we have only *revolutionized* too much in France; I would like to believe, Citizens, that you do not want to *revolutionize* divorce" (his emphasis).[76] In the end, this six-month delay as a compromise solution found backing from a coalition of leftists and moderates who were wary of the growing royalist presence in the legislature, for the left had just been soundly defeated in the elections of germinal an V (April 1797). His project was unanimously adopted by the Council of Five Hundred in June 1797 and passed through the Council of Ancients three months later, despite the vocal opposition of the conservative Jean-Etienne-Marie Portalis, future architect of the Napoleonic Civil Code.[77]

In this successful move to forestall serious changes in the divorce law, several points stand out and find parallels in the debates over illegitimacy and inheritance. The political vacillations, the continual balancing acts of left and right, made major reform politically impossible. The Terror had left the representatives wary of making legal changes that would "revolutionize" the family once again. Given their need to "stand above factionalism," the overwhelming flood of particular stories about trouble in the family left the deputies cautious about choosing sides too decisively. Vacillating between protecting liberty and equality in the home and shoring up the social order, they were hesitant to abandon innovations too quickly or absolutely. As long as France retained its goal of being a republic, legislators could still viably evoke the correlation between political liberty and individual rights. As one anonymous deputy commented in defense of the divorce compromise in June 1797, "in its wise and brilliant discussions," the Legislative Assembly "had recognized the necessity for divorce in a free state." Finally, despite the rise in royalist sentiment, the majority of legislators remained reluctant to restore authority to fathers in ways that seemed to smack of Old Regime patriarchalism or domestic monarchy. As I will discuss in the next chapter, only as the Directory gave way to the Consulate did the jurists finally agree on reconstituting paternal authority.[78]

Most striking in these debates, however, is the left wing's appropriation of the language of social and legal order. Leftist deputies still spoke the language of natural rights. But so powerful was the conservative evolution in political culture and the nationwide desire for an end to turmoil that even the left found it politically necessary to foreground certainty, stability, and defense of the status quo. They won over moderates by forging their own vision of domesticity: perhaps the ideals of the early revolution could be made compatible with post-terror social tranquility. As they argued against creating political anarchy, disrupting laws, and fomenting doubt among a populace weary of upheaval, the defenders of divorce both tapped into and helped to create the prevalent Directorial discourse validating order above innovation.

The tenor of these debates also had significance for thinking about the role of law. The emphasis on continuity and the gradual shrinking of natural law allowed the Directorials to restore—albeit only partially—the tarnished role of law by emphasizing its stabilizing, social purpose. The majority of leaders shared popular mistrust for the law as a force of regeneration in the aftermath of the Terror; they no longer were so willing to rely on legal pronouncements to produce social and moral reform. In part because of the Ideologues' emphasis on the imagination, they would come to place increased stress on education and festivals as forces of cultural conversion.[79] In contrast, the law itself should no longer be a dynamic force of transformation, nor a catalyst for change in this world that had changed too much. Rather, for Thermidorians and Directorials, the law must regain authority; it must provide a scaffolding of certainty in economic affairs, government, and personal relations. It must shed its apparent saturation in politics and factionalism, and appear to be nonpartisan and egalitarian. Above all, the law's "first goal is to maintain social harmony."[80] By relieving the law of its former responsibility to bestow natural equality and regenerate France, the Thermidorians and Directorials distanced themselves from the year II and moved gradually toward the Napoleonic solution of uniform, positive laws underpinning society and state. By relegating the regeneration of the citizen to the didactic realm of festivals and education rather than the coercive realm of the law, they took a step toward disentangling the state and its legal framework from the work of personal transformation.

• • •

Although their revisions of the laws remained very modest, I have argued here that the Thermidorians and Directorials did much ideological work that paved the way for the Civil Code. Their debates on family and property were crucial in renegotiating the social and political goals of the Republic. They whittled away at the natural law premise underlying rights ideology and reinstated the unified family as a natural unit whose internal structure defined public citizenship and private obligation. In this spirit, the Constitution of the Year III declared that "No one is a good citizen if he is not a good son, good father, good brother, good friend, good husband." In 1797 the pamphleteer Charles Guiraudet took this logic one step closer to the Civil Code when he argued that since the republic essentially "represented the families which compose it," only heads of families should be active citizens. Brushing aside the loss of many people's rights, he concluded, "You will see that the only *rights* of man are the rights of the *father, husband, son, wife*. . . . The real rights of man are those of the elementary society called the family" (his emphasis).[81] In the name of family interest and social utility, rights came increasingly to be defined according to one's social position.

As Thermidorian leaders responded to conservative petitioners' fears about familial property, their debates held importance for understanding the gender dynamics of the Revolution. It is worth highlighting the fact that anxiety over gender in the mid and late 1790s no doubt stemmed from woman's more legally powerful position within the family, as well as from her public presence in the streets, clubs, and legislative galleries. Paradoxically, the Jacobins, who had curtailed women's public political role in 1793–94, had also granted them various civil and property rights. The Jacobin legacy for women was ambivalent. So was the legacy of Thermidor and the Directory, but less so: revolutionary leaders hesitated to dismantle women's legal gains entirely, but nonetheless moved in that direction. According to the developing logic, because of women's crucial position in transmitting lineage property legitimately, their civil rights, property, and sexuality needed to be subsumed to the familial and social interest.

Finally, the Thermidorian reconstruction of the social had profound political significance for France. Even as they built upon the vocal popular backlash to refurbish the family as the social foundation, conservative legislators used this same defense of the social order to deprive popular politics of its voice and legitimacy. For the discourse on the troubled family enabled deputies to set aside the question of how to represent and conciliate the varied interests of individuals. Invoking family unity as a universal interest, they could claim to stand above the politics of particular interests and distance themselves from the responsibility of political representation. On behalf of the family and moral order, they foregrounded a disembodied justice and social interest—as defined by the legislature and its laws—to displace the politics of social transformation and popular sovereignty. They increasingly drained the law of its regenerative role. In effect, Thermidorian and Directorial elites appropriated the conservative petitioners' defense of traditional forms of property in order to legitimize a political order based on class, initially set into place by the Constitution of the Year III. This reconstitution of society and politics on the basis of property was in part possible because a family-based discourse of property also validated the need to reestablish faith in contracts and to solidify the social order at the expense of some individuals' rights.[82] The architects of the Napoleonic regime built upon Thermidorian scaffolding. Further abandoning the politics of representation and regeneration, they placed the bulwark of the family, property, and the law at the center of the Napoleonic state.

8. The Genesis of the Civil Code

In exile on Saint Helena, Napoleon commented, "My glory is not to have won forty battles, for Waterloo's defeat will destroy the memory of as many victories. But what nothing will destroy, what will live eternally, is my Civil Code." Promulgated in March 1804, this *Code civil des Français* consisted of 2,281 articles of civil law, unified into three books governing Persons, Property, and the Means of Acquiring Property. In much modified form, the Civil Code continues to operate in France today. Given its lasting character and fundamental importance, the prominent legal scholar Jean Carbonnier has dubbed the Code "the most authentic constitution of the nation."[1] Although the revolutionaries had been trying throughout the 1790s to enact a unified civil code, the fast-moving currents of revolutionary politics had made it impossible to consolidate support for any of the three drafts presented by Cambacérès in the mid 1790s. Nor could a fourth draft by Jean-Ignace Jacqueminot gain momentum right after Napoleon's coup in 1799. Napoleon was finally able to forge unanimity and accomplish what the revolutionaries could not—but only after a strategic restructuring and purge of the Tribunate in 1802.[2]

Written during the first months of the Consulate, reformed in sessions of the Council of State between 1800 and 1803, voted into law over the course of 1803–04, the Civil Code bore the political marks of the Napoleonic consolidation. It retained certain precepts from the Revolution, but overturned or vitiated the most egalitarian and controversial aspects of family reform. The Code fulfilled revolutionary goals in creating unified law, establishing private property and freedom of contracts, cementing the end of feudalism and privilege, and codifying the secularization of marriage and the état civil. Some of its family laws grew out of the 1790s: notably, the Code maintained certain aspects of egalitarian inheritance for legitimate offspring and it allowed a much-curtailed version of divorce. But more often than not, the authors of the Code reacted against revolutionary innovations in family law.[3] Above all, they reasserted the patriarchal authority of fathers over children and husbands over wives, and attempted to secure the boundaries of legitimate families.

Historians have amply debated the origins and significance of the Civil Code. In trying to account for its longevity, some scholars emphasize the codifiers' ability to enact a "transaction" or act of compromise between the Roman law of the South and the customs of the North, as well as between Old Regime law and revolutionary innovations. Certainly these compromises were crucial, but at times these interpretations glorify the Code by accentuating its apparent ability to rise above politics and create enduring law.[4] Some historians stress Napoleon's integral role in forging the Code, while others assert that the Code, by clarifying the workings of property, facilitated the central role of the bourgeoisie in nineteenth-century French economy and society. Opponents of this interpretation underscore the malleability of the Code and point out that agrarian patriarchs in many regions of France worked around and within the Code to maintain their traditional inegalitarian inheritance practices. The Code could favor agrarian as well as commercial capital. These historians are also responding to an older historiographic tradition, dating back to Frédéric Le Play, that faulted the Code for destabilizing rural society by demanding the egalitarian subdivision of farmland.[5] Yet another debate hinges on the Code's relationship to the Revolution and its political promises. Where some see a reaction against revolutionary policies, others situate the Code as heir to the republican laicization of civil law and its validation of "juridical individualism."[6]

Interestingly, because of the trend in recent gender historiography to see the Revolution as a promoter of domesticity, numerous feminist historians also read the Code as a culmination and continuation of the Revolution; they suggest that it simply codified the Jacobins' emphasis on female domesticity.[7] This assumption, however, is not grounded in close examination of the Code's genesis and of the relationship between its new statutes and the revolutionary ones. I argue here that notwithstanding certain important influences from revolutionary family law, the codifiers reacted strongly against the revolutionaries' attempts to introduce individual rights and equality into the home. Strikingly, the most stringent moves to tighten the contours of the family, to establish its patriarchal character, and to control the sexuality and domestic rights of women did not occur during the radical Republic of the year II, but rather just as the Republic was dying. The legal underpinnings of nineteenth-century domesticity did not stem from republican pens, but from Napoleonic ones.

Second, I stress the Code's creation in the particular political and cultural climate of the Consulate, as the codifiers responded anxiously to what they saw as disturbing social practices and destructive family conflicts in the 1790s. In grappling for a gender order that could more securely underpin the liberal goals of juridical individualism and private property, the jurists often turned back to familial conceptions from Old Regime and customary family law, read through the filter of the disorderly 1790s. When Portalis promised that the Code would replace "vain speculations with the lessons of experience," his "lessons" were drawn both from the "spirit of centuries" and from the tumult of the last decade.[8]

The writing of the Civil Code was inextricably bound up with reconceptualizing the triangular relationship between each citizen, the family, and the nation-state. Where the revolutionaries had wrestled in complex and contradictory ways with the rights of offspring, wives, siblings, natural children, and their parents, the Napoleonic jurists strove for a more clear-cut and less controversial definition of the juridical individual. They chose to limit citizenship and legal equality to male heads of households and to curtail the newly won rights of women and adult children. But at the same time, they attempted to channel male sexuality and male honor toward the defense of the legitimate family. If men were to exercise greater authority within the home, they should serve a certain vision of social stability. As the drafters patched together the elements of this family vision, they often sought to answer the questions posed in the late 1790s. If both human emotions and property were uncertain, how could France restore strength and stability to the family as the building block of the state? How should the dynamics of gender and generation be reimagined in the name of family unity rather than political transformation? What was the role of the law in crafting family bonds?

In fact, the codifiers' answers to these questions did not end contradictions and controversy. Nineteenth-century families and legal authorities invariably transformed the Code in practice, at times tempering its harshest limitations on women's power. By focusing on the writing of the law without exploring its implementation, this chapter inevitably depicts the Code's gender order too neatly. My point here is not to sketch out a patriarchal order that rigidly became reality, but rather to explore how this legal construction emerged out of the collision between Old Regime legal thinking, revolutionary family laws and practices, the post-revolutionary pursuit of social order, and the liberal attempt to protect private property and define legal individualism. In reacting against revolutionary destabilization, the Code created a forceful new set of gender ideals.

THE CIVIL CODE AND THE POLITICAL CULTURE
OF THE NAPOLEONIC CONSULATE

From the very outset, the Napoleonic jurists strove to position their Code in contrast to the passions and partisanship of the Revolution. As Portalis gave his "Preliminary Discourse," laying out the draft of the Civil Code early in 1801, he announced that laws made in the midst of revolution were "necessarily hostile, partial, and destructive. . . . But now France breathes. . . . The laws are not pure acts of power; they are acts of wisdom, justice, and reason." These same themes echoed in the ongoing discussion of the Code. For example, in March 1803, when Honoré Duveyrier introduced the articles on paternity and filiation to the Legislative Chamber *(Corps Législatif)*, he presented this bill as part of an "immortal work" created to overcome adversity and division: although its authors had been "placed between the uncertainties of nature and the necessities of politics, between the severity of reason and the illusion of sentiment, between the errors of their predecessors and the passions of their contemporaries, they succeeded in building this monument of national stability and wisdom."[9]

Although they continually portrayed their project as above politics, the Code's authors in fact wrote within the political and cultural frame of the Consulate. Hallmark elements of this political culture included the pervasive and urgent quest for stability, backlash against innovation, and skepticism about both human nature and natural law. At the forefront of everyone's mind was how to manage, tame, and sort out the Revolution, how to "finish with the romance of the Revolution . . . and see what is realistic and possible in its principles," in Napoleon's oft-quoted words. Above all, the early 1800s were characterized by Bonaparte's deliberate depoliticization of opinion among both national leaders and the populace at large. (In fact, the codifiers' self-positioning above the passions of politics was a quintessential move for this political moment.)

In consolidating his leadership, Napoleon could not erase the vibrant sentiments that gripped the hearts of Jacobins and royalists alike, but he did succeed in damping down their expression. In early January 1800, the Consulate shut down sixty out of seventy-three Parisian newspapers. Muzzling the press, forbidding political clubs, and moving quickly against vocal attacks from either the left or right all contributed to sapping popular politics of its voice.[10] When the four primary drafters of the Code sent their Project of the Year VIII to the courts of appeal for commentary, few pamphleteers offered their criticisms and suggestions. In place of the explosion of popular opinion in the petition, press, and pamphlet literature of the 1790s, the early 1800s witnessed a decline in public discussion, a shift toward more conservative views, and increased domination by official culture. The most prominent spokesmen on family matters denounced recent reforms as devastating in their results and naïve in their principles. Notably, the Catholic conservative Louis de Bonald and the jurist André Nougarède both indicted divorce as a destructive holdover from the Revolution.[11]

As the Consulate drained public political culture of its oppositional elements, among the nation's leaders Napoleon also pursued strategies aimed at forging a new consensus. Designed to pave over the ideological animosities of the last decade, the new consensus was defined above all by fidelity to Napoleon and his political order. He struck out at extremists on the left and right, but simultaneously called upon both proponents and opponents of the Revolution to become his partisans and advisors. At the meetings of his Council of State, backers and victims of the antiroyalist fructidorean coup of 1797 sat side-by-side. As Napoleonic minister François-Nicolas Mollien later observed in his memoirs, Napoleon dissipated dissension by placing loyalty to himself above the bitter political wars of the 1790s. Among his supporters, former revolutionaries "were astonished to regain a kind of security that they had not known when they themselves governed," in Mollien's words.[12]

The authors of the Code reflected this new political amalgamation. Certain leftist lawmakers, such as Oudot, Pons de Verdun, Lecointe-Puyraveau, and Darracq, had either withdrawn from public life or had been sidelined to more peripheral judicial positions. Other former crafters of revolutionary laws, most notably Cambacérès, had altered their opinions in line with the times. Even Berlier, the lone voice on the Council of State defending revolutionary reforms, surrendered many of his earlier ideals, such as the civil rights of natural children. Regicides Berlier and Thibaudeau, quasi-regicides Cambacérès and Jean-Baptiste Treilhard, as well as Pierre-François Réal, procureur-syndic of Pierre-Gaspard Chaumette's hébertiste Commune, all worked together with jurists who had never favored radical family transformations and had experienced exile, arrest, or harassment during the Terror. This group included Siméon, Jean-Louis Emmery, Duveyrier, and Antoine Boulay de la Meurthe. Indeed, the four primary authors of the Code—Portalis, Jacques Maleville, Félix Bigot de Préameneu, and François-

Denis Tronchet—had all faced imprisonment or gone into hiding during the year II, although all but Portalis had supported the earliest phases of Revolution.[13]

In consolidating support overall and in working toward the Civil Code, Napoleon did not hesitate to override opposition. The Code was initially drafted by four appointed jurists, commented upon by the courts of appeal, debated and rewritten by the Council of State, and then sent on piece by piece to the Tribunate and Legislative Chamber.[14] In 1801 when the Tribunate vigorously debated the first few sections of the proposed Code and advised the Legislative Chamber to reject them, Napoleon simply suspended discussion of the Code for six months while he purged the Tribunate of opposition. Already annoyed at some Tribunes for their oratorical displays against other laws, he also restructured this body so that only a limited legislative section would discuss future bills. Subsequent articles of the Code underwent energetic deliberation and revision in the Council of State but sailed through the two legislative bodies without difficulty or dispute. Napoleon himself presided over 55 of these 107 sessions of the Council of State and pressed avidly for his own goals, such as restoring male authority and retaining certain forms of divorce. In sum, Napoleon and his closest collaborators were responsible for getting the Code "voted by authoritarian means," and the jurists no longer felt the same popular pressure as in the 1790s.[15]

At the same time, these men negotiated an effective compromise, a workable response to a widespread desire among populace, judges, and leaders for a more secure familial order. Napoleon's constriction of democracy and his concentration of political authority within his own hands in a sense opened the way for imagining a more patriarchal family as the essence of social order. But the specifics of that vision did not follow automatically from the new politics. As the jurists made choices about how to remold social and legal relations, they disputed how to fuse the notions of uniform law and male juridical equality with various legal elements from Roman law, Old Regime customs, and theorists such as Pothier. With their disparate political backgrounds and with geographic roots in different Old Regime legal systems, the men who hammered out the Civil Code in the Council of State often disagreed about what statutes would work best to reknit the social fabric of France.

But they loosely shared a set of cultural assumptions framed by the experience of Revolution. They often expressed a mistrust of human emotions as well as a keen anxiety about the domestic chaos, born of having gone "too fast . . . and too far" in overhauling the family. Associating loose female sexuality and the impetuosity of the young with the disorders of the Revolution, they agreed on the need to reassert male authority over women and children as a key step toward soothing domestic discord. In articulating their philosophy of society, they built on the tentative lead of the Thermidorians and Directorials: social cohesion, secure private property, and tranquility took precedence over the former drive toward equality and individual rights. Also like these forerunners, the drafters endlessly lamented the precariousness of family bonds and repeatedly indicted laws written within a "whirlwind of intrigue." Even more than in the late 1790s, they voiced the need to *purify* the family, to "restore the dignity of marriage," and save it from profanation by shameless laws and practices. Michel-Louis-Etienne Regnaud de Saint-Jean-d'Angély made clear this desire to cleanse away revolutionary corruption, as he called for "expiatory reactions" against civil law excesses, such as egalitarian inheritance. Intent on producing social stability, they had no desire to innovate, but rather picked and chose among old and new customs and practices. Portalis claimed that the crafters had chosen "to conserve all that it was not necessary to destroy."[16]

In the aftermath of the Revolution, most of these jurists remained highly skeptical about the reformist possibilities of the law. Following the cultural relativism of Montesquieu rather than the universalism of natural law theory, many argued that laws could create order only if they matched the customs and morals of a people.[17] Abandoning the heady promise to write natural laws onto the souls of citizens, the jurists strove instead to produce positive laws to guide and frame the contours of civil relations and economic exchange. Figure 16, "The Laws create their security," evokes a belief prevalent at the end of the Revolution: lawmakers needed to bring both civilization and security to the shaky realm of nature.

Despite their differences, the codifiers held a collective willingness to generate pragmatic compromises that would reassure heads of household and property-holders in the different regions of France. Defining the parameters of property stood foremost in their minds. As the Tribune Jacques Lahary commented, "The most precious maxim of the Civil Code, the first, the most important of its dispositions, is the one that consecrates the right to property; all the others are only results and consequences of this first one." The drafters embraced the Revolution's goal of defending private property. Also, disputes over family legacies, communal lands, the transfer of national lands (biens nationaux), and the status of slavery had made contracts and property seem perilously uncertain across France and the colonies. The negotiation of the Concordat in 1801–02 had validated the sale

Figure 16.   The Laws create their security (1799). Courtesy of the Bibliothèque
nationale de France.

of biens nationaux, while Napoleon's restoration of slavery in the Caribbean
had most strikingly chosen to validate the right to property over the universality of individual liberty. The authors of the Code were intent on creating a juridical and familial framework that would further reinforce the security of property in France.[18]

The politics of the Consulate made it possible for Counselors of State and
Tribunes to distance themselves more definitively from republican disorders and to inculpate certain revolutionary family laws more extensively.
But even as they reacted against the Revolution, they preserved the belief
that the internal dynamics, structures, and mores of the family should
match and maintain the political and social structure of France. Portalis concluded his "Preliminary Discourse" by praising the ability of the "esprit de
famille" to underpin the "esprit de cité": "*It is through the little patrie, that
is, the family, that we are attached to the great one*" (his emphasis).[19]

In choosing how to best attach each citizen to the state via the family, the
Napoleonic jurists conserved the revolutionary goals of uniform civil law
and legal equality. But they endowed these terms with fundamentally
different meanings than had their revolutionary predecessors. Most no-

tably, they chose to confine their definition of the juridical individual to the male head of household and to endow him with extensive rights over property and other family members. Other members of the family, including his children and above all his wife, would be joined to the nation-state and to the law via this head of household. Furthermore, in framing the contours of the family, the codifiers placed their faith in the law, legal marriage, and legitimate lineage. Whenever possible they dismantled those pieces of republican civil law that based the family in voluntary choice, affection, or those ever-slippery bonds of nature. Adoption, the civil rights of natural children, the father's right to recognize and freely reward his natural offspring, and the freedom to make or break the conjugal bond—all of these innovations would find themselves sharply curtailed in the patriarchal family of the Napoleonic Code.

THE NEW PATRIARCH: EMBODIMENT OF FAMILY UNITY, HONOR, AND PROPERTY

The redactors of the Civil Code placed the authority of the father at the heart of familial unity, honor, and survival strategies. Dubbing the father the "first magistrate" and the "legislator" of the family, the codifiers anxiously reinvested married fathers with considerable power.[20] Lawmakers had taken an initial step in this direction within months after Napoleon's brumaire coup. By the law of 4 germinal an VIII (25 March 1800), they weakened egalitarian inheritance and increased parents' command over their legacies. Fathers or mothers could now reward one or more children with a larger portion of their goods—up to one-fourth if they had one to four children, one-fifth if they had five, and so on. The Code would enlarge the disposable portion further: a parent with one child could dispose of half of his or her estate by will or gift. For parents with two children, this disposable portion shrank to one-third, and to one-fourth for those with three or more children.[21]

The Tribunate's debates over the 4 germinal law reveal that even this partial restoration of paternal authority still met with resistance in 1800. Not only did 40 percent of the Tribunes and a fifth of the Legislative Chamber vote against the law, but also the Tribunes' vociferous discussion made clear what was at stake. For opponents of the reform, led by François-Guillaume Andrieux, to overturn the 17 nivôse law was to "institutionalize inequality" and reestablish the "patriarchal throne." It was "dangerous, immoral, and *anti-republican*" (my emphasis). It enabled fathers "to imagine that their

children are their property." In contrast, for supporters of the law, the vilifi-
cation of puissance paternelle stood at the core of the moral and domestic
chaos of France. "The irreverence of children reaches revolt," complained
Duveyrier. "Obedience and even filial respect provoke only scorn and sar-
casm." If one spoke in favor of the dignity of marriage or the authority of
fathers, one was "laughingly classified among the *faction of fathers of families*" (his emphasis). And yet, as Boulay de la Meurthe asserted, paternal
authority is "so sacred, so legitimate, so closely tied to the interest of good
morals that the legislator cannot surround it with too much confidence, consideration, and force."[22]

In this clash between deputies, the principle of equality and political dedication to the Republic squared off against the Napoleonic commitment
to restoring order and unity, embodied in fathers of families and ultimately in
Napoleon himself. Before the 18 brumaire coup, conservative Thermidorians
and Directorials had indeed identified the rights of women and overly independent children as problematic, but they had hesitated to propose reestablishing paternal authority as the solution. Now Duveyrier, Boulay de la
Meurthe, and others took the Thermidorian defense of family solidarity into
a new realm: they aligned the universal position and authority of fathers—
hardly a faction after all—with the broader social interest and order. Several
months later, the National Institute of Sciences and Arts announced an essay
contest on the "extent and limits of the power of the father." Hoping to steer
a middle course between revolutionary egalitarianism and Roman law patriarchalism, the Institute chose not to crown a clear winner, but nonetheless
gave "honorable mention" to the conservative Nougarède, who favored increasing paternal control over legacies and posited that fathers should act
as auxiliaries of the state to control the morality of women and the passions
of the young. In the Napoleonic imagination, the sentimental father was
steadily losing ground to the disciplinarian, at least in intellectual and juridical circles.[23]

Two years later, as the Council of State debated the Civil Code, all participants agreed that social order rested in the hands of the father, although
they hemmed and hawed about where to limit his parameters.[24] Ultimately,
although the Code did not grant him full control over his legacy, it dismantled one-by-one the Revolution's other primary restraints on the father's
power. In 1790, the revolutionaries had abolished the lettres de cachet as a
premier emblem of the tyranny of father and king alike. The Code reinstated a father's right to imprison a delinquent or disobedient child under
the age of sixteen for up to one month. Explicitly creating a new alliance between father and state, the Code empowered fathers to incarcerate older

children for up to six months, with the permission of a local judge. Only fathers held this right and only they could exercise puissance paternelle, stated Article 373. As Réal argued, "If nature has given this power (puissance) to the father and the mother, it is easy to recognize that reason demands that the father alone exercise it, and that the mother enjoy this power only from the time that she becomes a widow." However, the Code insisted on the child's deferential relationship to both mother and father and specified that, in the absence of the father, a mother could wield paternal authority. As Sylvia Schafer points out, paternal power was a gendered legal principle that sometimes included space for mothers as guardians to exercise parental power, as "a matter of masculine power deferred." Widowed mothers held the crucial right to manage their children's property, although they required the formal consent of two relatives to confine a child.[25]

The early revolutionaries had denounced parental control over marriage, lowered the age of majority to twenty-one, and allowed children to turn to family courts to demand protection from abusive fathers or solicit the right to marry. The codifiers rejected these family tribunals: allegedly, they had deprived fathers of their natural authority, sown hatred within families, and "created court trials between fathers and sons." Young adults would no longer have access to family councils or courts to step in against their father's will, and the Code revoked the Old Regime right of daughters and sons to sue their fathers for a dowry or légitime. Nor would illegitimate children have the capacity to pursue paternity suits or demand legacies; fathers were free to disavow their natural children. The Code retained twenty-one as the age of majority, but vitiated the legal meaning of majority, at least for sons: fathers maintained control over their sons' marriages until age twenty-five. If the father and mother disagreed about granting permission to marry, the father's opinion held sway. For children over the age of majority, the statutes demanded that they notify their parents of their conjugal plans with "respectful acts," as in the Old Regime. Although these acts were a formality, they signaled the new legal tone, for they presumed that offspring were subject to parental oversight and that family strategies took precedence over individual liberty. Finally, children under the age of eighteen had no license to leave the paternal household without their father's consent, except to volunteer for the army. As Peter McPhee notes, this renewed emphasis on patriarchal authority found parallels outside the family: Napoleonic laws reasserted employers' right to demand that wage-earners carry passbooks *(livrets)* and strengthened the Le Chapelier law of 1791 against workers' associations.[26]

Although the Code gave fathers extensive authority, it had distinct limits. The codifiers made clear that they did not intend to reinvent the *patria potestas* of Roman law. Gone were the days when fathers, especially in the Midi, brandished unlimited testamentary powers and held eternal control over the goods of their unemancipated adult children. Fathers could no longer disinherit their offspring. Parents could garner income from their offspring's goods only until age eighteen, and clearly the inheritance provisions of the Code limited fathers' prerogatives over their legacies. The Code maintained one crucial provision of the revolutionary vision of egalitarian families: by default, goods would be divided equally between children. Fathers retained control only over a "disposable portion" of one-fourth to one-half their goods, which they could use to favor one or more children. Moreover, the law worked to protect the property of wife and children within legitimate marriage: no father could recognize an adultérin illegitimate child, nor could he privilege any natural child to the disadvantage of his legitimate family. Finally, fathers and mothers could use adoption only if they were over fifty years old and childless; the adopted child had to be at least twenty-five years of age. In other words, even as the Code fortified paternal power, this prerogative was neither undivided nor complete. The law subsumed and directed masculine authority to the broader social goal of assuring the legitimacy, continuity, and stability of families.

As the Napoleonic jurists squabbled their way toward the final wording of these statutes, they balanced and rebalanced customary differences in patriarchal power in the various regions of France. They threaded their way through historical laws and theories from ancient Rome to Jean Domat and Robert-Joseph Pothier to the revolutionary decade. These informed debates over Roman law, regional customs, and jurisprudence were also permeated with a palpable frustration and anxiety about the tenuous position of fathers in the aftermath of Revolution. While they discussed legal technicalities with learning, the Counselors of State were prey to continual, sometimes fantastic visions of familial chaos; the Thermidorian rhetoric of the Terror had not yet been quieted.

Fathers seemed in need of protection—from unwed mothers exposing their peccadilloes past and present, from family courts or councils eager to usurp their authority, from public opinion denigrating their motives and sense of justice, and last but not least, from their own children, ready to pursue them in court and abandon them in old age. The Code made explicit the belief that laws had to make up for the moral failures of the last years. The very first article on puissance paternelle enunciated a "moral precept" as law: "A child of any age owes honor and respect to his father and mother." The Tribune Jean Albisson felt compelled to justify this strange inclusion of a moral precept as a statute: at this moment when turmoil had so threatened filial subordination, this guiding principle was needed to remind children of their duties and offer judges a "point of support." The codifiers anticipated that judges and fathers needed mutual support in forming a united front against the chaos born of disrespect, the excess of freedom, and the uncertainty of property and familial lines. As Xavier Martin has stressed, the Code was written within a mood of deep philosophical pessimism about human moral capacity.[27]

The need to compensate for the fragility of fathers and build a new association between father, conjugal family, and the state pervaded all the debates touching on paternal authority. This theme popped up in unexpected places, for example, in the Tribunate debates over proposed Article 60 on the état civil. According to this proposed article, which never became law, an unwed mother would be allowed to record the alleged father's name onto the birth certificate of her illegitimate baby. No legal right would flow from this naming, since other articles in the Code outlawed both the prerevolutionary practice of paternity suits for child support and the revolutionary attempt to institute equal inheritance rights for recognized natural children. Article 60 nonetheless provoked a furor of debate when it reached the Tribunate before the 1802 purge. On the surface, Article 60 had no direct bearing on paternal authority. Its substance was most closely allied with the question of whether alleged fathers should bear responsibility for natural children. During the Revolution, republican lawmakers had abolished paternity suits on the grounds that nature concealed paternity and that young men had to be free to make their own love matches and voluntarily embrace (or reject) their own paternity. But in the debates over Article 60, the putative father came to be represented not as a young man in need of liberation from his own father and from Old Regime prejudices, but rather as a married man, whose integrity and property were under threat from an unwed mother or her offspring.

At the heart of the debates over Article 60 lay the integrity of the legitimate family, embodied in the honor of the father. Benjamin Constant rose first to decry the article. Imagine a scenario in which a venerable *père de famille* (father of the family) suddenly finds his reputation sullied by the son of a prostitute who "appears, birth certificate in hand." Twenty-odd years ago, she named this père de famille as the alleged father of her son. Although this young man's accusation carries no legal consequences, the results are dire nonetheless: the old man's family life crumbles as his wife loses faith in him, his legitimate children "become disobedient and reproach him for his past conduct, adventurers slander him, and opinion is wavering, undecided, and necessarily malevolent." Even death cannot erase the family's stigma as his legitimate heirs face accusation as "unnatural brothers."[28]

The revolutionaries had imagined fathers as tyrants in need of taming, but tyrants with potential: more egalitarian laws would lead them to cultivate their innate love and care for their children. So powerful and natural was the desire to embrace fatherhood that men would raise their children with patriotic affection, recognize their illegitimate children, and even choose adoption to construct new families. In contrast, Constant and others played upon the vulnerability, the unmanning of the father by the Revolution and by the wayward freedoms of women. Sédillez cautioned that to permit an unwed mother to name her child's father would "weaken paternal authority" and "give women a pretext for engaging in misconduct, insulting the sanctity of marriage, and provoking divorce." "We must not debase [puissance paternelle] after having weakened it," declared Portalis as he lobbied successfully against endowing the daughters of the Midi with their Old Regime right to sue their fathers for dowries.[29]

For the codifiers, paternity needed to be ensconced by the legitimate family and upheld by both law and honor. As the debates over Article 60 made clear, it was in the interest of the tightly bounded family to protect the father—his reputation as well as his property—from slander or threat. As the embodiment and caretaker of family unity, he needed defending from insiders and outsiders alike, but the family also needed protection from excessive male freedoms. The married father, or the unmarried son for that matter, was sexually free to pursue his desire outside the boundaries of marriage, as long as his behavior had no detrimental impact on the transfer of family property and was not allowed to besmirch the family name. In contrast to the revolutionary ideal of "voluntary paternity," men were no longer free to embrace or reject natural fatherhood at will. The father lost his right to offer full inheritance benefits to a natural child, and even patriarchs had no right to introduce illegitimate children or concubines into the family home. Nor, according to the Code, did fathers exercise clear-cut puissance paternelle over natural children, for only marriage truly made the father. Within marriage the father gained great authority and liberty; in exchange, the law enlisted him as the custodian of order, legitimacy, honor, and familial unity. "From the viewpoint of the State's true interests, paternal authority ought to be extended . . . and the father is to society what the son is to the family, he owes obedience and respect to the laws," commented one of the contestants in the Institute's essay contest on paternal power.[30] Fathers owed order and lawful obedience to society.

Moreover, just as the patriarchal family was meant to support the French

social order, the civil rights of the père de famille were fundamentally intertwined with his national rights as a French citizen. Nationality passed
through the male head of household to his offspring and wife alike.
Conversely, for foreigners, the full rights of fatherhood came only with
French citizenship. Foreign fathers within France had no right, for example,
to bequeath property to their offspring. Furthermore, in contrast to both
Old Regime and revolutionary France, if a man was convicted of a crime that
resulted in "civil death" (the loss of French citizenship), he also lost his familial rights. His marriage was automatically dissolved, for, as Jennifer
Heuer points out, "exclusion from the 'grande famille' of the nation and lit-
eral families went hand in hand." Napoleonic statutes and judicial decisions
reinforced this bond between fatherhood and national civil rights. As the
Tribune Jean-Claude Gillet succinctly stated, "The rights of paternal authority blend with those of society."[31]

In sum, the Code articulated a new alliance between state, father, and
conjugal family. As guardian of family honor, the father should act as a
magistrate of internal order and as manager of property and family strategy.
The state stood behind the father as he imprisoned wayward offspring, negotiated their conjugal choices, and used his control over legacies, within
distinct limits, to influence his children's roles within family strategy. But at
the same time, the Code pressed men to marry and stay married and to invest their honor and goods in the defense of legitimate families and social
stability. The jurists chose this model in contrast to the egalitarian families
of the 1790s with their messy family courts, uncertain boundaries, and
overprotection of the rights of women and children. But neither did they
seek to return to other Old Regime options, such as the rambling, extended
families of the Center or the excessively authoritarian patriarchal stem families of the Midi. As Jean-François Vesin stated, "Public authority comes to
join with paternal magistracy, but with a prudence compatible with the interest of the family."[32] The codifiers enlisted fathers as allies in the
Napoleonic national project of stabilizing property, politics, and the passions.

RESTORING THE HONOR AND DIGNITY OF MARRIAGE

The alliance between father, state, and conjugal family was rooted in the
legal institution of marriage. Like the revolutionaries, the crafters of the
Civil Code believed that marriage as a legal and moral institution could bind
each individual to the nation-state and to the social good. Also like the rev-

olutionaries, the codifiers had no desire to reinvest the Church with jurisdiction over marriage. Although some jurists felt the powerful influence of
right-wing, Catholic thinkers like Bonald, they retained the revolutionary
decade's laicization of marriage, as well as the expectation that marriage
should underpin the state. Despite these points of agreement, leading lawmakers in the two epochs imagined and defined marriage in fundamentally
different ways. For the revolutionaries, two aspects of marriage were para-
mount. First, marriage was a civil contract, freely chosen, between two individuals. Second, ideally, marriage, grounded in gender complementarity,
held the power to regenerate France through the natural affection between
the sexes and the particular moral power of women. In contrast, although
the codifiers plainly recognized contractual elements within marriage, two
other characteristics dominated the Napoleonic conception of marriage: its
hierarchical, even feudal character and its role as the natural origin of families and the perpetuation of society.

When Portalis delivered his "Preliminary Discourse" in 1801, he devoted
well over a quarter of his time to analyzing the history and character of
marriage, for he recognized its centrality to the whole project of the Code.
As Christian Biet and Irène Théry have illustrated, Portalis worked hard to
drain the contractual definition of marriage of its legal clarity and force. He
depicted marriage not as a contract between two individuals, but as a romanticized coming together of man and woman in a natural realm.
"Marriage is neither a civil act, nor a religious act, but a natural act that fixes
the attention of legislators, and that religion has sanctified," he stated. In
later speeches, he reiterated this discursive move, effectively displacing the
issue of individual liberty and consent within marriage: "Marriage is not a
pact, but a fact; it is the result of nature."[33]

In Biet's and Théry's words, once Portalis had repositioned marriage "as
the source of the family, and not the union of two individuals or a contract
made between two free wills, it became legitimate for the government to
regulate it in the name of the general interest." Former liberties now became suspect, including the free choice of a marriage partner by the young
and easy access to divorce by wives and husbands alike. Portalis begrudg-
ingly admitted that the Code had to allow a limited form of divorce, not as a
contractual liberty, but rather because the freedom of religion made divorce
legally necessary. For Portalis, the marriage contract was "essentially perpetual." Bigot de Préameneu, Treilhard, Tronchet, and others echoed his reasoning that the conjugal bond was no "ordinary contract." It "does not belong only to the spouses, and cannot be destroyed by them: children, society
are interested parties."[34]

In addition to diluting marriage's contractual essence, the drafters resurrected an essentially feudal definition of marriage and were particularly influenced by the writings of the customary law theorist Pothier. As Jacques Mulliez notes, prerevolutionary jurists, such as Pothier, defined marriage simultaneously as a sacrament, a contract, and a feudal relationship in which wives owed fidelity, aid and advice, and obedience to husbands. In turn, husbands were bound to furnish their wives with necessities according to their status. With their emphasis on contract and individual liberty, the revolutionaries had deliberately abandoned this feudal definition of marriage. The Code now rearticulated the "duties and rights" of husband and wife as reciprocal yet hierarchical, and fused this customary definition of marriage with the liberal concept of the man's juridical rights before the law. From Roman law, the crafters drew an emphasis on the *fragilitas* of women in need of protection, just as minors were. The Code's statute highlighted male protection and female submission. "The spouses mutually owe each other fidelity, aid, and assistance. The husband owes protection to his wife, the wife owes obedience to her husband," stated Articles 212 and 213.[35] In defending this understanding of marriage, Portalis turned to the natural difference of the sexes:

> It is not law but nature that has determined the lot of each of the two sexes. Woman needs protection because she is weaker; man is freer because he is stronger.
>
> The preeminence of man is demonstrated by the very constitution of his being, which does not subject him to as many needs, and which guarantees him more independence for the use of his time and the exercise of his faculties . . .
>
> *The obedience of the wife is homage offered to the power who protects her;* and is a necessary result of conjugal society, which can only exist if one spouse is subordinate to the other [my emphasis].[36]

Portalis adopted this model of gender relations in express reaction to the revolutionaries' debates over how to form a more egalitarian form of marriage. Revolutionary laws had never actually deprived husbands of their prerogative over communal marital property, although the first two drafts of the Civil Code in 1793 and 1794 had proposed this reform, and the Convention had voted in favor of women's equal control in October 1793. The Napoleonic jurists reacted strongly to the very act of this issue being raised. They responded as well to the outpouring of feminist demands and the critique of marital tyranny. Portalis deliberately dismissed these polemics over "the equality of the two sexes. Nothing is more futile than these disputes."[37] Also weighing heavily on the codifiers' minds were women's successes as litigants in court, and, above all, their role in promoting the deeply threatening act of divorce. Divorce, especially divorce by incompatibility, "ruined the husband's authority," observed Portalis. "A family needs an authority; the preeminence of his sex gives this [authority] to the man; if he does not exercise it, anarchy rules; if he exercises it, divorce is demanded." As Boulay de la Meurthe summarized it neatly, "Revolutionary laws have broken up families."[38]

Like the revolutionaries, the redactors imagined marriage as a force for social cohesion, but they rejected the revolutionary emphasis on the unifying power of companionship and freely chosen sentiment. The Napoleonic jurists relied instead on investing legal and domestic authority in one figure to guarantee household solidarity. In her study on the *Décade philosophique* during the Directory and Consulate, Elizabeth Colwill highlights the male contributors' unease with women's influence or authority within marriage: "the bonds of marriage like the bonds of love sat uneasily with the ideals of male autonomy and individualism." As they grappled with the relationship between love, male citizenship, and male autonomy in the late 1790s, the literary and medical authors of the *Décade* increasingly rooted masculine identity in self-sufficiency and self-control, and in individualism freed from the "empires of superstition, despotism, and even love." For this same time period, William Reddy has also suggested a decline in the cultural validation of male sentiment, as the passions of the heart became increasingly associated with the feminine.[39] These broader cultural shifts resonated for lawmakers who decried the disorder produced by republican family law and voiced skepticism about the unifying and redemptive power of natural bonds. The codifiers picked and chose among revolutionary notions of gender complementarity and essentially remolded them to emphasize man's natural superiority rather than his need or capacity for sensibilité. The unity of the family would rest not in the regenerative force of love but in the unified legal will of the husband.

Just as the father embodied family honor, the husband would speak with one voice to make the couple's legal decisions and manage their property. As the Counselors of State debated various marital property arrangements, they voiced their preoccupation with conjugal unity. The wife's relationship to property seemed problematic, for she was central to transmitting and gaining goods, yet she was tangential to their management. Contention arose over the relative merits of the dotal system versus the communal one. Although the redactors eventually agreed to allow couples to opt for a dowry mechanism in line with the traditions of the Midi or Normandy, the

Code stipulated communal marital property as the default system in part because—as Berlier, Treilhard, and Tronchet insisted—this merging of goods encouraged the unity of the household and invested women in the joint economic project of the marriage. This choice also validated the conjugal couple over the lineage family as the primary familial unit: less tied to their families of origin than in the dotal system, wives as well as husbands would ideally focus their energies on creating wealth for a new household and line of descendants. The drafters maintained the republican privileging of communal marital property and the conjugal unit, but the revolutionary notion of *joint administration* of goods did not come anywhere near the table. Rather, Berlier had to work hard to convince some of his colleagues that artisanal and peasant wives indeed contributed substantially to the marital economy and deserved to share in its benefits. His opponent from the Midi, Maleville, warned that the communal system "accumulated riches on women's heads" and certainly did not encourage them to be respectful of their husbands.[40]

But even as the Counselors pitted the two systems one against the other, all agreed on the vital need to invest all authority over property in the hands of the husbands. "It is necessary, in the regions of both customary law and written law, to give authority to the husband," commented Bigot de Préameneu. "Without it, there will be neither order nor morals in families." In fact, the Code stipulated that in dotal regimes, even the paraphernalia (non-dotal goods traditionally managed by the wife in the Midi) would now fall entirely under the husband's purview. As Gillet argued, to let the wife manage goods "wounds this unity, this invisible communication . . . that is one of the principal elements of marriage: the bond of affection can weaken because it is only supported by the bond of property." Echoing Portalis's feudal language, Gillet asked how a man's protection of his wife would be "entire and effective, if he could not prevent his wife from losing her fortune through imprudent arrangements?"[41]

The logic of conjugal unity and the natural supremacy of men justified repeated limitations on married woman's rights and civil status within marriage. In exchange for the husband's obligation to furnish his wife with necessary goods, she was required to follow him to his place of residence, even if he left the country. In contrast to the revolutionaries' fluid treatment of marriage and national identity, under the Code a married woman always took on her husband's nationality. During the Revolution the government had frequently ruled that French women who married foreigners retained the duties and rights allied with French citizenship, and marriage to a French woman became one form of legal evidence that a foreign man could use to claim French citizenship during the 1790s. Moreover, in the treatment of wives of émigrés, the revolutionary government had acted in contradictory ways, sometimes holding wives responsible for their husband's emigration, and in other instances letting divorcées, widows, and some other wives off the hook by recognizing that their loyalty to the nation superseded their ties to aristocratic or émigré husbands. The Civil Code ended this possibility of recognizing a wife's national status separate from her husband's; his nationality became hers.[42]

If she had no nationality of her own, neither did she have goods of her own. A married woman had no right to her own earnings, nor could she administer, sell, or mortgage marital or dotal goods. This exclusion of women from economic affairs was tempered in practice: many wives would continue informally to manage the goods of households or businesses. Moreover, a husband could grant his wife, as a *femme marchande*, the right to run her own business. However, any wife required her husband's permission to appear in court, sue, or press legal charges, even if she had legally separated her property or held femme marchande status. Gone were the family courts that granted equal access to husbands and wives, mothers and fathers. All women also lost the right, gained in 1792, to act as legal witnesses to the état civil. Unlike the revolutionary era, within marriage, the husband as father also held more authority over the children's marriages, property, and delinquent behavior than did the mother. In a small window of liberty, a wife nonetheless could make a will without her husband's authorization.[43]

The Code had far less to say about women who did not marry. It deprived them of the right to be members of family councils, sue their fathers for dowries, serve as guardians, or officially witness legal acts. But as Cécile Dauphin notes, "outside marriage a woman became, in the eyes of the law, a responsible adult, competent to deal with her own affairs and property. Unlike a married woman, a *feme sole* enjoyed the same rights as a man, except that she was not considered a citizen." Although she might have difficulty procuring certain loans or underwriting letters of exchange, a single woman nonetheless held legal independence and financial rights that contrasted strongly with her married sister's dependent status.[44]

Central to the Code's redefinition of marriage were its new policies on divorce. The statutes resurrected the option of séparation de corps and created a much more limited form of divorce. Having discarded the notion that marriage was based in the contractual liberty of the individual, the drafters placed divorce into an entirely different category than had the revolutionaries. Divorce became, in Napoleon's words, "an extreme remedy" for marriage gone wrong; it was no longer a natural right. The Napoleonic jurists also flatly rejected the argument of the early 1790s that divorce would fortify the bonds of love by making them all the more freely embraced. In contrast, Portalis, for example, argued that surrounding divorce with difficulty would strengthen the conjugal tie by encouraging those traits so necessary for marriage: "patience, forgiveness, support, indulgence."[45] This less romantic vision of gender relations only reinforced the legal thinking.

As in early nineteenth-century America, conceptualizing divorce as a public remedy for an extreme wrong rather than as a private, individual right led to curtailing the grounds for divorce and to building gender differences into the divorce law.[46] Either spouse could seek divorce on three different grounds: adultery; cruelty or harsh treatment; or the condemnation of one's spouse to infamous punishment. As I will discuss below, the codifiers inscribed the disparate treatment of male and female sexuality into law: a husband's adultery had to be far more egregious and blatant for his wife to successfully divorce him on this ground. The Code also allowed divorce by mutual consent, but placed such a complex set of restrictions on this mode that it became almost impossible to use.[47] Given the limited motives and the abolition of family courts, all forms of divorce became much more expensive and legally complex. Not surprisingly, divorce rates plummeted across France.[48] In 1816 after the Restoration of King Louis XVIII, the Chamber of Deputies outlawed the practice entirely. So onerous to obtain had divorce become under the Civil Code that legal historian Xavier Martin has argued that the 1816 abolition of divorce marked the code's "completion," rather than an "infringement on the intentions of the Napoleonic Code." Not until 1884 would divorce once again become legal in France. Not until 1975 would divorce become as accessible as it had been in the 1790s.[49]

The Civil Code made it especially difficult for women to file for divorce. The statutes institutionalized a double standard for adultery: a wife could use this motive only if her husband maintained his mistress within the conjugal household. In contrast, a man was entitled to divorce based on a single act of infidelity by his wife; he also won back his Old Regime ability to imprison her for adultery, now for a period of three months to two years. The revolutionary Penal Code of 1791 had decriminalized adultery and the 1792 divorce law had made the grounds of adultery equally open to husband or wife.[50] In 1810 the Napoleonic Penal Code reintroduced adultery as a crime and reinforced the Civil Code's double standard by allowing a husband to incarcerate his unfaithful wife. Moreover, Article 324 absolved the husband of responsibility if he killed either his wife or her lover when he caught them *en flagrant délit* in the home. This Code treated male adultery much more lightly: an adulterous man could be fined between 100 and 2,000 francs for bringing his mistress into the home.[51]

The authority of the state became invested in confining female sexuality within marriage. As they built a Code dedicated to transferring property securely down through the legitimate family line, the drafters explicitly defended their view that female sexual liberty had different meanings and consequences than did the freedom of men. In presenting the divorce statutes to the Tribunate, Jacques-Fortunat Savoie-Rollin justified the article that allowed a wife to charge her husband with adultery only if he kept his mistress within their very home: "The reason for this limitation lies in the different obligations imposed on the two sexes by the very nature of the marriage contract. The wife's adultery dissolves the family," he declared matter-of-factly. Following the same line of logic, he warned that easy access to divorce by the 1792 law had too often deprived a husband "of the most sacred property of man, the property of his family." Other jurists restated the undisputed point that adultery's "effects are indeed different in the case of the husband and the wife" and that "all nations" had always judged "the man less severely." As Napoleon himself commented, husbands should have "absolute power" over their wives' behavior to prevent them from introducing "foreign children" into the family. The succession laws, too, shored up the recognition that a wife's infidelity could misdirect property. The statutes excluded all natural children from equal inheritance and deprived *adultérin* children of even a claim to sustenance from their married parent(s). They also penalized wives who seemed capable of infidelity. Any wife who abandoned her husband or won a *séparation de corps* against him was deprived of her share of communal marital property. Tronchet pointed out in vain that most wives who won separations would be victims of abuse and should not be doubly punished.[52]

Female infidelity put into jeopardy not just the family property, but also the principle of male honor that bound the family together. As many historians have noted, Napoleon played a pivotal role in defending divorce by mutual consent. He also argued powerfully for creating divorce mechanisms that would defend the privacy and reputation of husband and family at the expense of women's freedom and civil rights. Perhaps already contemplating the possibility of divorcing the unfaithful Josephine who never bore him a son, the First Consul developed a logic that linked the honor of cuckolded men to the moral health of both nation and family. Once a man knew that his wife was an adulteress, "he will not be able to live with her. Out of pity for her, he does not want to divorce her on the grounds of adultery; for himself, he does not want to use [this motive] due to the ridicule that rebounds onto the husband according to our customs; nor does he want to use it for his children, who would be dishonored by their mother's bad conduct." By Napoleon's reasoning, the law should provide means for the married man to guard the boundaries of domestic privacy. Raising the issue of familial privacy and female fidelity to a matter of national pride, two days later he remarked, "It would be scandalous, and contrary to the honor of the nation to reveal what happens in a certain number of households; people would conclude, albeit wrongly, that these are morals of the French." The Code engraved into law a gender ideology that made the double standard a principle of Frenchness and that rooted masculinity in the repression, or at least the concealment, of female sexuality outside of marriage.[53]

"SOCIETY HAS NO INTEREST IN RECOGNIZING BASTARDS" . . . OR THEIR MOTHERS

In the eyes of the codifiers, unwed mothers and their children, like adulterous wives, constituted a threat to the sanctity of marriage. The Napoleonic jurists formalized the abolition of paternity suits that had been implicit in the law of 12 brumaire an II and had been worked out in practice from late 1794 on. According to Article 340, neither mothers nor illegitimate children could seek to prove the father's identity. Legal claims for child support were impossible. Likewise, the proposed Article 60, which would have allowed mothers the right to record putative fathers' names in the état civil, never became part of the Code. Illegitimate children were granted the right to conduct maternity searches, but could only launch a suit by providing some initial form of written proof. Tarred once again with the "crimes of their parents," illegitimate children, even if recognized, lost their new right to share equally in inheritance. Even those children recognized by their fathers could not become heirs, but only creditors on their fathers' estates. They could receive no more than a third if legitimate descendants existed, a half in the presence of siblings or ascendants, and no more than three-fourths even if no ascendants or descendants remained. A married man could not recognize an adultérin child conceived during his marriage, nor could an adultérin child make any claims on a married mother or father.

In definitively abolishing paternity searches, the Napoleonic lawmakers echoed certain arguments made by the authors of the 12 brumaire law: they noted that nature concealed paternity even as it revealed maternity and they reiterated the republicans' wariness of women's seductive nature.

Certainly, the drafters shared the revolutionaries' assumption that mothers were more responsible for the conception and care of the child. However, the Napoleonic indictment of unwed motherhood fit within a new social logic. Notably, the abolition of paternity suits was no longer tied to granting rights to recognized illegitimate children as it had been in 1793. Nor was it tied to the republicans' attempt—albeit naïve and deeply problematic—to destigmatize unwed motherhood and provide for these women and children through (inadequate) state welfare. No longer did the jurists idealize voluntary, sentimental paternity and wrestle with the issue of how to recognize that families could legitimately be united by the bonds of nature rather than law. For the Napoleonic jurists, to outlaw paternity suits and to exclude illegitimate children from inheritance rights fit part and parcel with the broader "social interest" of resanctifying marriage, clarifying its legal boundaries, safeguarding family property, and privileging male heads of household in order to secure order. "Society has no interest in recognizing bastards," Napoleon put it in a nutshell.[54]

This harsh treatment of mères célibatrices and their children did not prevail without opposition. In the Tribunate debates over Article 60 in 1801, the Tribune Andrieux went to bat for both groups. As a lone voice, he asserted that the unwed mother's capacity to press a paternity suit was a "sacred" and "natural" right, designed to save mother and child from misery. Excoriating the Code for allowing men who had "no heart and no guts" to "do whatever they want with their victims," he asked his colleagues to remember that women were their mothers, wives, and sisters, and that they too should be able "to love the laws." While no other deputies called for a return to the paternity suits of old, some were plainly nervous about rendering men irresponsible for their sexual acts. Several argued that at least allowing the mother to record the alleged father's name would put a brake on the passions of libertines and seducers. Others hoped that such declarations would help natural children and fathers to reunite after the death of the mother.[55] Ultimately, the jurists chose to handle anxiety about the male libido not by demanding that men take responsibility for their illegitimate offspring, but rather by validating only legal familial bonds and by ostracizing both unwed mothers and their children.

Far outweighing the expressions of concern about male abandonment and libertinage were the repeated indictments of natural children and their mothers as the ultimate violators of familial property, honor, and unity. During the Thermidorian and Directorial periods, conservatives had gradually redefined natural children as "offshoots of criminal love," drained them of natural rights, and associated them once more with the loose morality and speculative greed attributed to *mères célibatrices*.[56] By the time of the early Consulate, so threatening a figure had the illegitimate child become that Counselors of State severely curtailed the rights of married fathers to recognize or reward their natural offspring. As they spun scenarios about fathers damaging their legitimate families or about multiple fathers fraudulently claiming the same child, the jurists distanced themselves further and further from revolutionary acclaim for the powerful father-child bond. They made clear that families needed protection against their own members, even fathers. Brushing aside the needs of illegitimate children, especially *adultérins*, the debaters reassured one other that the natural children who would be deprived of civil status or sustenance claims would be far less numerous than those who had "unjustly troubled the rest of families." In their zeal to defend the boundaries of upstanding families, the Counselors of State even came close to outlawing maternity searches aimed at *married* mothers, for those suits too threatened the domestic realm with shame, fury, and regret. Ultimately, however, the codifiers chose not to protect the reputation of any mother, who had "sacrificed her child and duped her husband." As in the laws governing adultery, the Code once again held women rather than men responsible for extramarital sexuality.[57]

Throughout discussions of illegitimacy in both Tribunate and Council of State, lawmakers were keenly aware that they were piecing together an entire *familial system*, rooted in marriage and secured by civil law. As he justified the Code's statutes severely limiting the claims of natural children, Bigot de Préameneu commented, "It is to maintain the honor of marriage that we reduced the claims of natural children to a simple credit. We could not lessen this severity without unhinging this system." The system found its strength, its source of legitimacy not in nature but in the law itself. Only the law, via the legal institution of marriage, could designate families. In an 1803 speech presenting the completed articles governing paternity and filiation to the Tribunate, Lahary laid out the quintessential role of law in assuring the civil status, tranquility, and property of families. Contrasting the promise of stability to the turmoil of the recent past, he proclaimed, "The family is a sacred property. And one can only be admitted when one has a legitimate title or a possession equivalent to this title." In a clear-cut reversal of the revolutionaries' invocation of natural affection and natural bonds, he argued that the law had to "break the bonds that have not been able to be legally formed" and to exclude "foreigners" from families.[58] Just as the Code enlisted fathers as guardians of domestic order and honor, the law strove to demarcate clear and legitimate family boundaries in the name of unity and the defense of property.

. . .

The Civil Code of 1804, officially renamed the Napoleonic Code in 1807, embraced a fundamentally different family model than had the revolutionaries. In one comment during the divorce debates, Tronchet voiced the new spirit: "Civil law . . . can nonetheless establish all that the public interest requires; and in this connection, its power includes restricting individual liberty."[59] The Civil Code reflected a profound shift in the meaning of "public interest" in the early 1800s. It also helped to create this shift as its statutes validated stability over regeneration, opted for patriarchal family solidarity over the rights of wives and children, and redefined civil equality to refer only to male heads of households. The codifiers placed great stake in the ability of the Code to resolve the contradictions and controversies of revolutionary familial practices and to institute a new social order.

The Code did not emerge seamlessly out of any single ideology: notably, it is not simply a "liberal" law code. Rather, the drafters cobbled together a powerful body of statutes that built on several key sources. In terms of family law, the jurists most often took inspiration from Old Regime Roman and customary law, as they compromised and negotiated between regional differences. The Code incorporated certain elements of revolutionary innovation in less radical form, most markedly in decreeing a watered-down version of egalitarian inheritance. At the same time, the codifiers drew on the liberal attempt to define juridical individualism and equality before the law: they demarcated the rights-bearing legal individual as male. They did not make this choice because liberal ideology preordained a masculine definition of the rights-bearing individual.[60] On the contrary, the interpretation of liberal rights is malleable and is deeply influenced by particular social and political contexts. The drafters reacted against the perceived gender turmoil and "trouble within families" that both liberal and republican revolutionaries had stirred up by granting unprecedented legal rights to women, adult children, and natural children. The codifiers wrote within a moment marked by the depoliticization of society and a deep desire for social stability, rooted in a more secure gender order.

The Civil Code reinforced the domestic power of husbands and fathers. Just when ordinary male citizens were losing their voice in public politics, they regained greater authority at home. Moreover, the Code had tremendous endurance, as well as international significance. It was introduced into Belgium, Luxembourg, Switzerland, Bavaria, the Rhineland, and parts of

Italy during the Empire; it inspired imitation over the course of the nineteenth century in diverse locales, including the Netherlands, Romania, Portugal, the Dominican Republic, and Louisiana. One particularly powerful notion within the Code—the concept that a woman's nationality follows her husband's—took hold even in nations that did not institute other aspects of the Code, in Great Britain and the United States, for example. As Anne McClintock has written, "Women were incorporated into the nation-state not directly as citizens, but only indirectly, through men, as dependent members of the family in private and public law."[61]

By so often reacting against the Revolution, the Civil Code framed a new set of gender ideals. In this book, I have attempted to illustrate the complexity of republican ideas and practices surrounding gender in the 1790s: the Revolution simultaneously reinforced notions of natural, maternal responsibility, encouraged women to embrace their domestic influence, and also offered women new rights within the family and created spaces for them to challenge the hierarchies of gender and generation. By suppressing the most egalitarian elements in republican family ideology and law, by denying female citizens direct access to the state, and by depriving them of civil rights, the Code essentially spun the legacy of Revolution toward reinforcing domesticity. Its statutes rendered women dependent on men. At least by the letter of the law, the relationship of women to law, politics, and citizenship would be mediated through the family and especially through marriage. Nineteenth-century feminism defined itself in part by its attack on this set of family laws that so patently deprived married women of legal autonomy and economic independence. The Code naturalized the authority of husbands and fathers and forwarded the notion that true masculinity lay in the ideal of honorable "fathers of families" who served the nation as guardians of family property and reputation.[62]

Like any set of laws, these too were transformed in practice, provoking Napoleon to exclaim, "My Code is lost."[63] Especially in the Midi, families often succeeded in skirting or manipulating the inheritance provisions of the Code in order to maintain their customary systems, which had typically benefited the eldest son and held family land together.[64] The nineteenth century witnessed an ongoing negotiation between fathers and the state over the extent and nature of paternal authority.[65] Likewise, at times, judges and families chose to temper the harshest elements of the Code's treatment of women. Couples could insert holdovers from Old Regime law into marriage contracts to secure greater protection for married women's property and greater female control over property than the Code technically allowed. On the borders of France, local authorities, anxious to entice foreign male workers, sometimes ignored the Code and decided that mixed marriages granted civil rights to foreign husbands rather than resulting in French wives' loss of nationality. Some pregnant unwed mothers managed, within limits, to circumvent the law's abolition of paternity suits by suing putative fathers for damages *(dommages-intérêts)*.[66] In short, without a doubt the Code forged a strongly patriarchal set of family ideals and curtailed the independence and property rights of women and children, but its laws could be tempered in practice in ways that we have only begun to explore.

One final point about the Code merits emphasis: its contribution to French national identity. The Code promoted a new sense of national, legal unity and valorized, even mythologized the notion that France had one equal law for all adult French men. Over the course of the nineteenth century, although the Code was attacked from various angles and modified in juridical practice and in law, its staying power as a law code gradually earned it remarkable status as an emblem of legal orderliness, mythologized equality, and even French rationality. When the modern jurist Jean Carbonnier called the Civil Code the "veritable constitution," a "sociological" constitution of the French, he not only implicitly praised its socially stabilizing effect, but also highlighted the assumption that a unified body of civil law guaranteeing "universal equality" and the security of property was foundational to modern France's sense of itself.[67] The meaning of "universal equality" would provoke contestation for generations to come.

Conclusion

"Yes, I was carried away. Who wasn't during the Revolution? . . . Yes, passion burns within my breast; I am intoxicated with the idea of liberty." As he reflected on the radicalism of the Terror, this sansculotte captured the raw energy of the Revolution. In its attempts to remake the family, the French Revolution burned with transformative power, injected fierce demands for change into the most intimate relationships, and insisted that citizens rethink the ordinary. In the spaces created by new political and legal practices, thousands of women and men rushed to reimagine their domestic lives. As lawmakers battled over critical legal reforms, citizens bombarded them with visions of ideal families, couples severed marriages devoid of affection, and young adults embraced the "intoxicating" languages of liberty and equality to defy their parents and make new claims to independence, love, or property. At the same time, many individuals struggled to defend customary rights now lost. "All the ties that existed between [family members] are broken," lamented the widow Boudeau of Angoulême. Indeed, the new policies undercut various traditional strategies and could not help but infuriate some family members.[1]

I have argued in this book that the family became a crucial arena for working out the practical meaning of the most fundamental revolutionary goals. The family served as the core institution for defining the legal individual, fashioning patriotism, and testing out the daily meaning of equality. While revolutionary politics provoked many citizens to try to create a more just and affectionate family, the very issue of how to reform gender and domestic dynamics also became integral to inventing a new nation of regenerated citizens and a new state of rights-bearing individuals. The fate of family reform was bound up not just with each family's complex negotiation of customary and innovative practices, but also with the shifting currents of revolutionary politics. Each attempt to remake the politics of state intersected with local renegotiations of personal relationships. Contestation over the family formed a microcosm of the elemental struggle of the 1790s, as the revolutionaries strove to integrate the new individualism, rights, and liberty with their simultaneous drive for social and political unity. Ultimately, just as republicanism sparked a political backlash, so too its bold drive to refashion the family provoked a social reaction, crowned by the Napoleonic Civil Code that endowed only male heads of household with individual rights.

The Revolution infused politics into the most intimate relationships and wrenched many families away from the patriarchal practices of the Old Regime. Over the course of the 1790s, individual family members were able to forge vital, if uneven, opportunities to enact revolutions within their own homes. Two transformations stand out as particularly striking: first, the decline of parental, especially paternal, authority; and second, the challenge to marital indissolubility and to male authority within marriage. Both political culture and legal innovations encouraged this pervasive questioning of the practical logic that underpinned family life. When revolutionary deputies lowered the age of majority, mandated egalitarian inheritance, and abolished lettres de cachet, fathers lost the legal right to manage the property, inheritance, marriages, and personal freedom of their offspring. The revolutionary emphasis on sentimental bonds and youthful liberty facilitated the questioning of puissance paternelle, as did changes in the judicial system. Likewise, in hopes of making marriage into a terrain of individual liberty and political conversion, the revolutionaries legalized divorce, reduced parental authority, and valorized conjugal affection as a political and cultural ideal. While divorce enabled some women and men to escape heartless marriages, the Revolution spurred an avid debate on gender practices within marriage and fostered an explicit political critique of the puissance maritale of husbands. At every turn, individual family members seized the initiative in remaking their private lives within the cauldron of politics.

This book overturns the assumption that the Revolution's primary impact on women was to create domesticity and requires us to rethink the connections between gender and republicanism. In fact, French revolutionary republicanism left conflicting legacies regarding women's position within households and their relationship to the state and politics. The Revolution certainly fostered strong rhetoric urging women toward domestic roles, but it also enacted laws giving women new civil rights as individuals, granted them new forms of legal and political access to the state, and generated languages and practices for criticizing gender inequities. Although women did not gain full rights to political participation during the Revolution, no simple sexual contract or inclusive private sphere underpinned democratic republicanism. Nor was the abstract individual necessarily imagined as male.[2] While powerful beliefs in female inferiority and dependency remained, they were nonetheless sharply undercut in law, discourse, and social practice during the Revolution.

In the process of attempting to alter their familial positions, female family members became engaged in a wide range of political activities: they petitioned the state, went to court, created familial festivals, asserted moral authority over the politics of daily life, spoke out at political clubs, produced pamphlets and placards, demanded that political ideologies affect their personal lives, and served as legal witnesses for births, deaths, divorces, and marriages. At the same time, the republican attempt to create rights-bearing citizens and to enact equality enabled women in certain family positions to claim greater autonomy, property, or authority within their households.

These momentous changes in women's political and familial lives had tremendous significance for the nineteenth century. I would argue that the gradual construction of domesticity drew on the revolutionary validation of women's moral role, but also developed as a *reaction* against the gender instability and the political and legal power of women forged during the Revolution. Moreover, nineteenth-century feminists of various political leanings appropriated, reworked, and transformed arguments about woman's moral nature and individual rights that had been so powerfully articulated in law, language, and day-to-day practice during the 1790s.[3]

Admittedly, during the Revolution itself, resistance to reforming family and gender dynamics ran deep and, as I have tried to sort out, numerous factors, from geography to politics to class to family position, informed the ability of individual women and men to reshape or defend their domestic experiences. Access to the legal and political opportunities created by the Revolution was markedly uneven. Notably, urban dwellers, especially women of middle-class or artisanal background, were far more likely to initiate divorce than were other social groups, while inheritance reform and the assault on paternal authority had a much stronger impact on some daughters and sons in certain parts of Normandy and the Midi. In some cases, the revolutionary reformers fell far short of their goals. The case of natural children and their mothers makes a noteworthy example of the limitations of republican policies: the post-Thermidorian conservative backlash, the ambiguous wording of the 12 brumaire law, and the deputies' own gendered desire to prioritize the rights of putative fathers over those of natural mothers and children all contributed to limiting the number of illegitimate offspring who fully benefited from the new inheritance laws. Unwed mothers suffered under a new set of policies that gradually deprived them of their traditional right to paternity suits but failed to replace this loss with the promised poor relief from the state.

Yet, acknowledging the halting, uneven quality of revolutionary family reform should not undermine our recognition of its radicalism, nor its profundity. Not until 1975 would divorce be so easy to obtain for French women and men. Not until 1972 would illegitimate children regain the full right to appeal for inheritance.[4] When the authors of the Civil Code dismantled many controversial aspects of revolutionary family law with such anxious intensity, they bore testimony to how profoundly the Revolution had disrupted the social practices and gender dynamics of lineage families. The codifiers attempted to restore social order by guaranteeing private property, curtailing the rights of women and children, and allowing for certain regional variations within unified law: the Code tempered, transformed, and in some cases sharply reversed the thrust of revolutionary family innovations. The drafters reacted against the revolutionaries' idealization of a more egalitarian and affectionate family and sought to promote an honor-based, patriarchal family, rooted in male authority and the defense of family property.

The Revolution and Civil Code left French families in the early 1800s scrambling to realign their strategies and expectations. Despite some superb work, French family history for the early nineteenth century remains under-examined. From what we know so far, two general patterns stand out against the backdrop of immense regional and class variation. First, families in the early nineteenth century innovated and strategized by combining elements of Old Regime custom, revolutionary practices, and the new parameters of the Civil Code. To take but one example, Norman couples frequently pieced together new marital property arrangements that incorporated elements of communal marital property (promoted by Code and Revolution) with customary dotal protection of certain lineage goods.[5] Second, some of the family policies emerging from both Revolution and Code—most notably, the thrust toward egalitarian inheritance and the choice of communal marital property as the default system—nudged families in certain regions and classes toward adopting new practices that privileged conjugal unity and reduced the influence of the lineage family of origin.[6] As part of a much longer-term trajectory, the revolutionary era encouraged the shift toward conjugal families and amplified what André Burguière has called "the invention of the couple." As couples reinvented their relationships in the early nineteenth century, they not only developed new codes of domesticity, merit, and honor, but also negotiated the gendered laws of the Civil Code in ways that are not yet fully explored.[7]

If the revolutionary era demanded that the early nineteenth-century family engage in a dynamic act of social reconstruction, it also endowed citizens with a heightened awareness of the political centrality of the family. The family and gender ideology had certainly been intertwined with politics in the Old Regime.[8] My intent is not to downplay the rich work of familial imagery and gender politics in the Old Regime, but rather to highlight and problematize how the Revolution reconfigured the relationship among the family, individual, politics, and state.

The Revolution had decisively altered the frame for experiencing and thinking about family and politics. At the most basic level, the Revolution and its aftermath led to the multiplication of political ideologies, each articulated around a particular vision of the familial and social order.[9] By striving to endow individuals with rights, equal status, and political agency within the family, the Revolution exploded the possibility of simply imagining the family as an organic whole. Once models of individual liberty and contract had so directly entered the family and had granted civil rights to wives, younger sons, daughters, and even natural children, no one, least of all the conservatives, could take the makeup of the family and the sacrifice of individuals as givens. As the royalist Louis de Bonald commented during his campaign against divorce, "The question of the indissolubility of the conjugal tie is the first of all social questions after the existence of God."[10]

As part and parcel of its attempt to construct individual citizens, the Revolution also transformed the position of the family by tearing away at the fundamental religious and cultural underpinnings of the state and social relations. As the revolutionaries did away with Old Regime sources of corporate cohesion, they hoped that the conjugal family would act as an affective and cultural force of regeneration and social unity. When they sought to transfer sacrality from God, Church, and King to the social body of the nation,[11] the revolutionaries engaged the family in their all-encompassing endeavor to recreate and sacralize the foundations of the secular nation-state and society. They wove their heightened expectations of the family into the cultural practices of politics and into the very constitution of the republican state. More than one hundred years later, Jean Jaurès spotlighted the fact that the revolutionaries had rooted the family in the state and put a decisive end to the Church's potent legal authority over domestic affairs (although the clergy maintained a powerful informal influence over intimate relations into the modern era). He wrote that the secularization of the état civil "was one of the most profoundly revolutionary measures. . . . It reached into the foundation of social life. It changed, if I may say so, the very basis of life." Laicizing marriage and civil law contributed to the Revolution's long-term secularizing influence and paved the way for the gradual escalation of state authority over familial matters.[12] At the same time, it formed part of a broader revolutionary vision, in which the family was enlisted by the secular nation-state to serve as both legal matrix and cultural cement, bonding each individual to the uncertain new nation.

In a nutshell, the Revolution simultaneously destabilized the internal workings of the family, loaded it with immense political significance, and left the nineteenth century with the pressing question of how to harmonize the new individual with the social whole. The family as a political unit seemed to hold all the more importance in a post-revolutionary world in which no political regime could endure more than two decades (until the Third Republic), Catholicism could no longer provide full cultural cohesion, and a powerful but often disturbing new social code valorized economic competition over corporate systems and prioritized "merit" and money over privilege and birthright.[13]

Our attempts to understand the "emergence of domesticity" in this troubled moment need to take into account the extent to which the family remained a site of political and social contestation in the early 1800s. Family members, political thinkers, and social commentators at the time held an acute sense of both the fragility and the political possibility of the family. As Michelle Perrot has pointed out, with their endless configuring of familial visions of social harmony, the early nineteenth-century socialists placed much greater emphasis on a familial solution to social discord than did their later counterparts. At the other end of the political spectrum, conservatives wrestled with the gender disorder generated by republican politics: "In order to keep the state out of the hands of the people, it is necessary to keep the family out of the hands of wives and children," stated Bonald. And, as Jo Burr Margadant has recently argued, the Bourbon and Orléanist constitutional monarchies floundered in their efforts to forge successful "family romances" in a world that emphasized individual merit and familial sentiment over hereditary rule. In this context, rather than assuming a smooth turn toward uniform domesticity that severed politics from the home, it makes more sense to ask how domesticity was promoted, challenged, and reconfigured within an ongoing political contestation over gender, sentiment, family, and social practice.[14]

Nineteenth-century republicans inherited an especially complicated set of gender messages from the Revolution. In fact, the Revolution had endowed republicanism with three competing elements regarding family dynamics: first, a powerful discourse on woman's moral power and her ability to shape citizenship; second, a potent set of political practices, ideologies, and legal precedents for attacking gender hierarchy or other forms of inequality in the family; and third, a deep wariness about social disorder and a tendency to see both family and politics through the lens of the Terror and gender chaos. Over the course of the nineteenth century, republicans juggled and weighed these three different components in complex ways, and individuals could draw on republican ideology to argue for divergent visions of the ideal gender order. For example, using republican ideology, Emile Acollas proclaimed the "autonomy of individuals" and excoriated the patriarchalism of the Civil Code on behalf of women and children; Jules Michelet pronounced that women should subsume their rights and identity to a maternalist devotion to family and patrie; and republican feminists, such as Jenny P. d'Héricourt, denounced his misogyny and the nation's failure to recognize women as political and legal individuals: "Our rights have the same foundation as yours: in denying the former, you deny the latter in principle."[15]

Nevertheless, it is true that leading republicans, especially male republicans, put women's claims to civil and political rights on the back burner for decades. In the years between the Revolution and the Third Republic, many elements affected republicans as they recrafted gender ideals and so often chose to emphasize woman's domestic, moral role at the expense of her rights. Among other factors, republicans were influenced by the Civil Code's patriarchal reconfiguration of "individual rights" and "equality," the feminization of religion, the development of utopian socialism on the left, the social transformations and anxieties of early industrialization, and the need to distance republicanism from any association with the Terror.

Once the Third Republic was created, the relationship between republicanism and women's rights remained a point of continual contestation.[16] Republican lawmakers focused their attention on domestic, legal reforms first produced by the revolutionaries of the 1790s, as well as on a host of new family issues. The late nineteenth-century context had transformed debates over family dynamics in myriad ways, but memories of the Revolution still formed one element in this complex mix. Nervousness about recreating the turmoil of the 1790s meant that reformers negotiated the legacy of republican family reform with great care. To take a prominent example, lawmaker Alfred Naquet succeeded in restoring divorce in 1884 by aligning divorce with the republican tradition of personal freedom and anticlericalism. Yet, even as he defended divorce as the social policy most emblematic of republicanism, he ultimately presented a version of the law that bore more re-semblance to its Napoleonic than its revolutionary forerunner. After attacking those who sought to undermine the "principles of the Revolution," he commented, "Divorce will have the same effect on the family that political liberty has in the nation; it will be a *factor for order* in the family, as political liberty is the element of order in the nation" (my emphasis). His colleague Louis de Marcère rushed to reassure the Senate that France would not revert to the sexual and social anarchy of the Terror: "None of us want a return to the law of 1792." The proponents of divorce threaded their way between varying interpretations of republican priorities in the tangled moral politics of the 1880s.[17]

Little wonder that these reformers regarded the revolutionary family as both touchstone and taboo. For, just as the revolutionaries had recast the nature of public politics and had left behind competing models for the nineteenth century to make anew, so too, the revolutionaries had reframed the nature of the family and generated wrenching debates over the ideal gender order, domestic social practices, and the relationship between gender and politics. As in so many other arenas, the French Revolution left behind bitterly contested questions. But it had also created a dynamic repertoire of political practices, legal innovations, and potent ideologies of liberty, equality, and self-fashioning. The Revolution had made it impossible to remake state and citizenship without also debating and reshaping gender dynamics, the meaning of intimacy, and the rights of individual women and men.

Communes in the Calvados Studied for Cases of Divorce

This appendix lists the names of the seventy-eight communes in the department of the Calvados whose état civil records were examined for divorce cases. The "film numbers" refer to the microfilm numbers used by the Church of Jesus Christ of Latter-day Saints, whose members have filmed the original registers in Caen as part of their larger genealogy project. My research assistants and I used these microfilms at the Church of Jesus Christ of Latter-day Saints in Madison, Wisconsin. The Archives départementales du Calvados classifies these same films under the archival code "ADC 5mi 1." The Napoleonic divorce law was promulgated in germinal an XI (March 1803), but local officials tended to implement the old divorce law into the year XII (1803–04), so we examined films for most communes through 1803 or year XII, as available. For Caen, we also examined divorces under the Civil Code until the 1816 abolition.

COMMUNE NAME	LDS MICROFILM NUMBER	DATES EXAMINED
Amayé-sur-Seulles	0659813	1793–1802
Argences	0659646	1793–1803
Aunay-sur-Odon	0601299	1793–Year X
"	0601300	Year XI–XII
Balleroy	1119886	1793–Year XIII
Bavent	0659664	1793–1803
Bayeux	1119785	1793–Year IV
"	1119786	1793–Year V
"	1119787	Years VI–VIII
"	1119788	Years IX–X

COMMUNE NAME	LDS MICROFILM NUMBER	DATES EXAMINED
"	1119789	Year XI
Beaumont-en-Auge	0671625	1793–Year XII
Bény-Bocage	0691210	1793–1803
Bény-sur-Mer	0665790	1793–Year XII
Beuvron-en-Auge	1122365	1793–Year XII
Blangy-le-Château	1122274	1793–Year XII
Bonnebosq	1122371	1793–Year XII
Bretteville-l'Orgueilleuse	0659520	1793–1803
Bretteville-sur-Laize	0662735	1793–Year X
Caen	0658421	1793
"	0658422	Year II
"	0658422+	Year II
"	0658426	Year III
"	0658427	Year IV
"	0658430	Year V
"	0658432	Year VI
"	0658434	Year VII
"	0658436	Year VIII
"	0658438	Year IX
"	0658440	Year X
"	0658444	Year XI
"	0658449	Year XII
"	0658453	Year XIII
"	0658456	1806
"	0658458	1806
"	0658461	1807
"	0658465	1808
"	0658469	1809
"	0658473	1810
"	0658476	1811
"	0658479	1812
"	0658484	1813
"	0658488	1814

COMMUNE NAME	LDS MICROFILM NUMBER	DATES EXAMINED
"	0658495	1815
"	0658499	1816
Cahagnes	0687430	1793–Year XII
Cambe (La)	1120093	1793–Year XII
Cambremer	1122352	1793–1803
Caumont-l'Eventé	1119948	1793–Year XII
Cheux	0659537	1793–1803
Clécy	0660491	1793–Year X
Condé-sur-Noireau	0692722	1793–Year IV
"	0692723	Year V
"	0692724	Year VI–X
"	0692725	1802–1805
Courson	0602204	1793–Year XIII
Courtonne-la-Ville	0670379	1793–Year XIII
Crépon	0653327	1793–Year XII
Cresserons	0656396	1793–1803
Creully	0665763	1793–Year XII
Crèvecœur-en-Auge	0669145	1793–Year XII
Crocy	0660383	1793–1803
Danvou	0687449	Year V–1803
Dives-sur-Mer	1122476	1793–Year XII
Epinay-sur-Odon	1119665	1793–1803
Evrecy	0656489	1793–1803
Falaise	0660168	1793–Year VIII
"	0660169	1793–Year VIII
"	0660170	1793–Year IV
"	0660171	Years V–VIII
"	0660172	Years IX–X
"	0660173	Year XI
"	0660174	Year XII
Ferrière-au-Doyen (La)	0687451	1793–Year XII
Fervaques	0679256	1793–Year IX
"	0679257	Years XI–XII

COMMUNE NAME	LDS MICROFILM NUMBER	DATES EXAMINED
Hamars	0660050	1793–1803
Honfleur	1123768	1793–Year IV
"	1123769	Years V–VI
"	1123767	1793–Year VI
"	1123770	Years VII–X
"	1123771	Years XI–XII
Isigny-sur-Mer	1120079	1793–1802
Juaye-Mondaye	1119922	Years VI–XII
Lion-sur-Mer	0656429	1793–1803
Lisieux	0607069	1793–Year V
"	0607070	1793–Year II
"	0607071	Years III–IV
"	0607072	Years V–VI
"	0607074	Years VII–VIII
"	0607076	Years IX–X
"	0607078	Years XI–XII
"	1122237	1793–Year VII
"	1122238	Years VIII–X
Livarot	0679030	1793–Year XIII
Locheur (Le)	1119676	1793–1803
Maltot	0660060	1793–1803
Martragny	0656298	1793–Year X
"	0656299	Years XI–XII
Mathieu	0656452	1793–Year XII
Mézidon	0667668	1793–1803
Mondeville	0662971	1793–1803
Mouen	0659577	1793–1803
Moult	0665107	1793–1803
Moyaux	1121122	1793–Year X
Norrey-en-Auge	0660424	1793–1803
Notre-Dame-de-Fresnay	0684626	1793–Year XIII
Ouilly-le-Basset	0660258	1793–1803
"	0660262	1793–Year XII

COMMUNE NAME	LDS MICROFILM NUMBER	DATES EXAMINED
Orbec-en-Auge	0671587	1793–Year X
"	0671588	Years XI–XII
Pont	0660439	1793–1803
Pont-Farcy	0701239	1793–Year XIII
Pont-l'Evêque	0671612	1793–Year X
"	0671613	1802–1804
Potigny	0660272	1793–1803
Quilley	0662736	1793–Year X
Ranville	0659755	1793–1803
Saint-Aubin	0656486	1793–1803
Saint-Benin	0660461 item 2	1793–1802
Saint-Marguerite-d'Elle (Baynes)	0653285	1793–1803
Saint-Martin	0662722	1793–1803
Saint-Pierre-sur-Dives	0680170	1793–Year IV
"	0681563	Years V–XI
Saint-Sever	0696688	1793–Year XIII
Saint-Sylvain	0665741	1793–Year X
Thury-Harcourt	0660459	1793–1802
Tilly-sur-Seulles	0659505	1793–1803
Touques	0686778	1793–Year XII
Tour-en-Bessin	0662322	1793–1803
Trévières	0653470	1793–1803
Troarn	0659627	1793–Year XII
Vassy	0606260	1793–Year V
"	0606261	Years VI–XI
Villers-Bocage	0659806	1793–1803
Vire	0685974	1793–Year IV
"	0685975	Year IV
"	0685976	Years V–VIII
"	0685977	Years IX–X
"	0685978	Year XI
"	0685979	Years XII–XIII
"	0685980	Year XIII

Chronology of Revolutionary Family Laws and Decrees

15 March 1790	Abolition of primogeniture (in conjunction with abolishing feudal rights), with exception for preexisting contracts, widows or widowers with children; abolition of distinction between noble and non-noble goods.
16–26 March 1790	Abolition of lettres de cachet (that had allowed families to imprison their own members).
16 August 1790	Establishment of family tribunals to handle various family matters, including disputes between parents and children to age twenty.
8–13 April 1791	Establishment of equal division of intestate inheritance properties; Exception made for marriage contracts and widows with children; Abolished uneven division of goods by principle of exclusion of daughters.
27 August 1791	Assembly adopts (for Article 7, Title II of Constitution of 1791) statement that "the law considers marriage only as a civil contract." This article directs the legislature to establish a uniform mode of registering the civil records of all inhabitants.
25 September 1791	Penal code protects unmarried women from accusations of infanticide based on "simple suspicion," implicitly ending the requirement for pregnancy declarations, although women continue to make them.
18 January 1792	Adoption legalized in principle; Committee of Legislation is given job of studying more thoroughly; adoption will be included in the proposed Civil Codes, but its legal status will not be

	resolved until the passage of the Napoleonic Civil Code; during Revolution mothers as well as fathers could adopt.
25 August 1792	Abolition of entailment in principle; valid for future only.
28 August 1792	Abolition of parental authority over children on reaching majority (twenty-five; reduced to twenty-one for both sexes in September 1792).
20 September 1792	Divorce granted. Both sexes have equal right to file on grounds of insanity, conviction of criminal offense, abuse or cruelty, immoral behavior, absence for five years without news, desertion for two years, immigration; can convert previous séparation de corps into divorce; can also file based on mutual consent or incompatibility; one-year wait for remarriage; custody of children under age seven to be granted to mother, boys over age seven to father, although other arrangements can be made.
20 September 1792	Laicization of civil record-keeping (état civil). For marriage, the law clarifies that adult children of twenty-one or older can marry without parental permission. Children under twenty-one need father's consent; mother's consent if father is dead; consent of five closest maternal and paternal relatives in case of orphan; if no relatives, then neighbors assemble and vote on marriage. No marriage before age thirteen for girls, fifteen for boys. No bigamy. Canon law obstacles to marriage are in effect abolished. Women are explicitly granted the right to witness acts in the état civil.
14 November 1792	Abolition of entailment except those already open; retroactive to 1789.
4 January 1793	Revision of the laws of 15 March 1790 (abolition of primogeniture) and 8 April 1791 (equal division of intestate estates) to remove the exceptions for married people, existing contracts, and widows with children.
7 March 1793	Abolition in principle of the freedom to will goods; all descendants to have an equal right to the goods of their ascendants.
4 June 1793	Establishment in principle of the right of illegitimate children to inherit from their parents "ac-

	cording to the mode to be determined"; assigns Committee of Legislation the task of determining this mode.
28 June 1793	Law on aid to poor: promises aid to children from poor families; nation will support abandoned children; any unwed mother who promises to breastfeed her child has right to aid and lying-in expenses; promotes establishment of homes for unwed mothers.
4 July 1793	Convention decrees that foundling children be given the name "enfants naturels de la patrie."
9 August 1793	Cambacérès presents the first draft of the Civil Code.
5 brumaire an II/ 26 October 1793	Establishment of equal inheritance in both direct and collateral lines; made retroactive to 14 July 1789; at time of execution of will children must return to the pool *(rapporter)* any previous gifts or advantages from parents, including all post–July 1789 gifts whether they participate in inheritance allotments or not. Parent can freely dispose of only one-tenth of property if she or he has direct descendants, one-sixth if there are collaterals; spouse to have usufruct of one-half deceased's property, with one-half to children immediately.
6 brumaire an II/ 27 October 1793	Convention approves the proposed article of the Civil Code stipulating equal administration of communal marital property by both husband and wife; neither husband nor wife could sell or mortgage goods without the other's consent. This adoption in principle of equal control over property never becomes law owing to the adjournment of the first draft of the Civil Code.
9 brumaire an II/ 30 October 1793	Closing of Jacobin women's clubs.
12 brumaire an II/ 2 November 1793	Illegitimate children, if recognized by parents, are granted equal shares of inheritance. Recognition of paternity is voluntary by father, but children can prove paternity by presenting written records by father or by showing care without interruption if parent died between 14 July 1789 and November 1793; leaves it to Civil Code to determine mode of proof for offspring whose parents die after the promulgation of the law; children born of adultery are entitled to re-

ceive only one-third of an equal share. Implicitly outlaws paternity suits, but interpretation varies, and paternity suits continue into 1795.

15 brumaire an II/
5 November 1793

Convention "adopts" young children whose parents have had their property confiscated by the state.

29 frimaire an II/
19 December 1793

Establishment in principle of primary schools with mandatory attendance; extended by later laws, especially the Lakanal Law of 27 brumaire an III (17 November 1794) committing the Republic to providing schoolteachers for voluntary primary schooling.

8 nivôse an II/
28 December 1793

Divorce law modified to allow men to remarry immediately; women must wait ten months.

17 nivôse an II/
6 January 1794

Amplification of laws mandating equal division of inheritance and limiting the freedom of will-making. Equal division among offspring. If no descendants, then property goes first to ascendants, then to collaterals, but always descendants over ascendants in every category. Retroactive to 14 July 1789. Disposable property equals up to one-sixth if no children, one-tenth if children exist; this *portion disponible* (disposable property) must be left to someone outside line of family succession (e.g., charity); donation or legacy cannot surpass 10,000 livres and recipient must have less wealth than that. Family tribunals to hear disputes without appeal. Spouses may give each other usufruct of half of goods if children exist, all goods if they have no children; pre-1789 spousal mutual gifts are to be recognized; post-1789 reduced to usufruct of one-half of property if children exist. All other donations with recipient still living or dead since 1789 are abolished. Donations in wills from pre-1789: recipients have choice of whether to keep or to return to pool (rapporter) and enter succession; post-1789 donations must be returned to succession pool (even if recipient wants to renounce succession). Calls clergy, nuns, and monks to succession also, but they have to return dowry to the pool. No distinction between goods of family line *(propres)* and goods earned by new conjugal unit *(acquets)*, in the spirit of reducing power of lineage system, increasing equality, and favoring the circulation of goods.

22 ventôse an II/ 12 March 1794	Decree answering sixty questions, clarifying 17 nivôse an II law.
4 floréal an II/ 23 April 1794	Divorce permitted on basis of *de facto* separation of six months or more.
19 floréal an II/ 8 May 1794	Decree that a child born to a married woman should get name of husband and he should be listed on état civil as father, even if woman insists that he is not the biological father; marriage makes the father; refuses woman the right to list another father. In practice, father can disavow paternity by notary later if he wishes.
9 fructidor an II/ 26 August 1794	Decree clarifying thirty-six points on 17 nivôse an II law; allowed justices of peace to name arbiters when necessary.
23 fructidor an II/ 9 September 1794	Cambacérès presents second draft of Civil Code.
16 frimaire an III/ 6 December 1794	Decree confirming recognition of adoption without defining details; affirmation that adopted children are to be recognized as legitimate heirs.
19 frimaire an III/ 9 December 1794	Convention passes the article of proposed Civil Code definitively outlawing paternity searches; although this Code does not become law, in April and June 1795 circulars from the Committee of Legislation and the Commission des administrations civiles, police et tribunaux tell local district courts and justices of the peace to put an end to paternity searches by unwed mothers.
25 nivôse an III/ 14 January 1795	Questions regarding natural children's inheritance rights are to be judged by district tribunals, rather than family tribunals.
5 floréal an III/ 24 April 1795	Provisional suspension of court cases based on retroactive effect of 17 nivôse an II law; not a definitive change in law.
15 thermidor an III/ 2 August 1795	Suspension of 4 floréal an II law allowing divorce based on six months de facto separation.
9 fructidor an III/ 26 August 1795	Retroactivity of most radical inheritance laws removed in principle; in early vendémiaire, this will become full law.
1 vendémiaire an IV/ 23 September 1795	Proclamation of Constitution of Year III, which replaces district tribunals with one civil tribunal per department.

3 vendémiaire an IV/ 25 September 1795	Definitive overturning of retroactivity of 17 nivôse an II law to 1789. Also revokes retroactivity of 12 brumaire an II law on illegitimate children, but retroactivity is restored on 26 vendémiaire an IV (18 October 1795), then re-revoked on 15 thermidor an IV (2 August 1796). Gave specific mechanism on annulling acts and took matters out of the hands of family tribunals.
19 vendémiaire an IV/ 11 October 1795	Decree suppressing district tribunals, as in Constitution.
26 vendémiaire an IV/ 18 October 1795	Restoration of retroactive clause of 12 brumaire an II law.
3 brumaire an IV/ 25 October 1795	Daunou law on education: Republic will no longer pay schoolteachers in attempt to guarantee universal, free primary education; voluntary parental choice on primary school; separation between girls' and boys' primary schooling; establishment of a boys' secondary school in each department.
3 brumaire an IV/ 25 October 1795	Introduction of seven national festivals, in cluding a marriage festival *(Fête des époux)* on 10 floréal by Executive Directory decree; the fête is most promoted in years VI–VII.
9 ventôse an IV/ 28 February 1796	Suppression of family courts.
messidor an IV/ July 1796	Cambacérès presents third draft of Civil Code.
15 thermidor an IV/ 2 August 1796	Revocation of retroactivity to 1789 of inheritance rights of illegitimate children; but new retroactivity established based on 4 June 1793, not 14 July 1789. Maintains principle of equal inheritance for all children.
27 frimaire an V/ 18 December 1796	Abandoned newborns will be received free in civil hospitals, but one who brings them in will be sanctioned with three *décades* (thirty days) of detention.
18 pluviôse an V/ 6 February 1797	Partial return to retroactive effects of 17 nivôse an II law; complex law but with little effect; mainly upheld April 1791 law outlawing exclusion of offspring based on sex.
1er jour complémentaire an V/ 17 September 1797	Law extends waiting period for divorce based on incompatibility by an additional six months;

	this compromise is reached after lengthy divorce debates.
30 frimaire an VIII/ 21 December 1799	Jacqueminot presents draft of Civil Code to Legislative Commission of the Council of Five Hundred in the name of the Legislative Section.
4 germinal an VIII/ 25 March 1800	Inheritance law revised, increasing size of disposable portion, allowing larger share for one child; limited to one-fourth if there are one to four children, one-fifth if five children, etc. May leave this disposable portion to own offspring. If no descendants exist, disposable portion is raised to one-half of goods.
24 thermidor an VIII/ 13 August 1800	Portalis presents first Napoleonic draft of the Civil Code; written by Portalis from Provence; Tronchet from Paris; Bigot de Préameneu from Brittany; Maleville from Périgord. Their proposed "Projet de l'an VIII" is sent to departmental tribunals and to courts of appeal for commentary. It is rewritten and discussed in the Council of State starting in thermidor an IX (July 1801), and presented to Tribunate beginning in frimaire an X (November 1801).
nivôse an X/ December 1801	Tribunate debates civil records portion of Code and argues extensively only over Article 60, which allows an unmarried mother to name the father; great controversy even though this declaration will have no apparent legal value without father's subsequent recognition. The Tribunate has earlier urged the Legislative Corps to reject two initial sections of Code.
germinal an X/ April 1802	Napoleon purges Tribunate and alters its structure; future portions of Civil Code, as revised by the Council of State, will pass through the Tribunate without debate or opposition.
1802–03	Council of State debates and revises further portions of the Civil Code, and these are step-by-step passed by the Tribunate and Legislative Corps as individual laws.
30 ventôse an XII/ 21 March 1804	Promulgation of Civil Code in its entirety.

Note on Archival Sources

The core primary source information for this study came from archival documents, printed pamphlets and newspapers, and legislative debates. Below I offer a brief list of the central archival sources; this listing also serves as a reference point for the archival citations in the notes. The endnotes in effect operate as a thematic bibliography of both primary and secondary printed sources.

ARCHIVES NATIONALES

ADII	Printed papers of the Legislature. Materials to do with civil legislation.
ADXVIIIb	Procès-verbaux of Convention.
ADXVIIIc	Printed papers of the Legislatures. Supplements to the debates. Cartons related to civil justice, family, festivals, and the revolutionary calendar.
BB16	Correspondence of the Ministry of Justice. Cartons related to the Calvados.
C	Letters, addresses, and petitions sent to the legislatures.
DIII	National Convention. Committee of Legislation. Numerous cartons containing petitions and projects related to family law.
DIV	National Assembly. Committee of the Constitution.
DIV bis	Population reports.
DXXXIX	Directory. Committee of the Classification of Laws.
DXXXIX bis	National Assembly. Committee of Research.

F20   Statistics. Population reports.

W   Revolutionary Tribunal. Carton 76.

ARCHIVES DÉPARTEMENTALES DU CALVADOS

1B   Bailliage de Caen. Cartons on civil separations, Old Regime family councils, and selected Old Regime civil court cases.

2L   Population records for the Revolution.

3L   Series on Civil Justice during the Revolution. Most important series for the local case studies. Cartons for the district tribunals of all the districts; family tribunals as available for all districts, with most intensive focus on the district of Caen; the department-wide Civil Tribunal; records of justices of the peace; registers of pregnancy declarations, civil separations, arbitration sessions, inheritance divisions, etc. For the état civil records, I used the films made by the Church of Jesus Christ of Latter-day Saints. (See Appendix I.)

3Q   Tables of successions and inheritance divisions.

8E   Notarial acts.

BIBLIOTHÈQUE MUNICIPALE DE CAEN

Fonds normand   Revolutionary pamphlets and speeches.

OTHER PROVINCIAL ARCHIVES AND LIBRARIES

For the material on women's clubs, I used the *Archives municipales* of Bordeaux, Dijon, and Lyon (D series: municipal council deliberations; I series: police and popular societies); the *Bibliothèques municipales* of Dijon and Lyon; the *Archives départementales* of the Côte-d'Or, the Doubs, the Gironde, and the Rhône (L series, French Revolution).

Abbreviations

AD	Archives départementales
ADC	Archives départementales du Calvados
AN	Archives nationales
AP	J. Mavidal and E. Laurent, eds., *Archives parlémentaires de 1787 à 1860. Recueil complet des débats législatifs et politiques des chambres françaises* (Paris, 1879–), première série
Dalloz	D. Dalloz, *Répertoire méthodique et alphabétique de doctrine et de jurisprudence*, 44 vols. (Paris, 1845–70)
Douarche	A. Douarche, *Les tribunaux civils de Paris pendant la Révolution (1791–1800)*, 2 vols. (Paris, 1905)
Duvergier	J. B. Duvergier, *Collection complète des lois, ordonnances, réglemens*, 30 vols. (Paris, 1834–38)
Enfant	*L'enfant, la famille et la Révolution française*, ed. Marie-Françoise Lévy (Paris, 1990)
Fenet	P. A. Fenet, ed. *Recueil complet des travaux préparatoires du Code civil*, 15 vols. (Paris, 1936)
FLE	*La famille, la loi, l'Etat de la Révolution au Code civil*, ed. Irène Théry and Christian Biet (Paris, 1989)
JDP	*Journal du Palais: Recueil le plus ancien et le plus complet de la jurisprudence française*, ed. Alexandre Ledru-Rollin, 3d ed. (Paris, 1858)
RévJur	*La Révolution et l'ordre juridique privé: rationalité ou scandale. Actes du colloque d'Orléans, 11–13 septembre 1986*, ed. Jean Bart et al., 2 vols. (Orléans, 1988)

SA   Sentences arbitrales

Sirey   *Recueil général des lois et des arrêts*, ed. J. B. Sirey (Paris,
               1800–01)

Sirey N.   *Recueil général des lois et des arrêts, avec notes et commen-
               taires . . . , fondé par M. Sirey*, 10 vols., rev. and completed
               by L. M. Devilleneuve and A. A. Carette (Paris, 1840–43)

TDD   Tribunal du district

Notes

1. Archives nationales (hereafter AN) AD XVIIIc 164, *Adresse des Cadets du tiers état de Provence et d'autres pays de droit écrit au roi* (n.p., 1789), 8, 21–22.

2. Jean Bodin, *Six livres de la république* (Paris, 1576); Jacques-Bénigne Bossuet, *Politique tirée des propres paroles de l'Ecriture sainte* (Paris, 1709); Natalie Zemon Davis and Arlette Farge, eds., *A History of Women*, vol. 3, *Renaissance and Enlightenment Paradoxes* (Cambridge, Mass., 1993), 1; Jean-Louis Flandrin, *Families in Former Times: Kinship, Household, and Sexuality*, trans. Richard Southern (Cambridge, 1979).

3. Sarah Hanley, "Engendering the State: Family Formation and State Building in Early Modern France," *French Historical Studies* 16 (1989): 4–27; Jeffrey Merrick, "Fathers and Kings: Patriarchalism and Absolutism in Eighteenth-Century French Politics," *Studies on Voltaire and the Eighteenth Century* 308 (1993): 281–303; Jeffrey Merrick, "Sexual Politics and Public Order in Late Eighteenth-Century France: The *Mémoires secrets* and the *Correspondance secrète*," *Journal of the History of Sexuality* 1 (1990): 68–84; Arlette Farge and Michel Foucault, eds., *Le désordre des familles: Lettres de cachet des Archives de la Bastille au XVIIIe siècle* (Paris, 1982). On other European areas, see Julia Adams, "The Familial State: Elite Family Practices and State-Making in Early Modern Netherlands," *Theory and Society* 23 (1994): 505–539; Susan Amussen, *An Ordered Society: Class and Gender in Early Modern England* (London, 1988).

4. For a sampling of approaches to cultural contestation over gender in early modern Europe, see Davis and Farge, eds., *History of Women*, vol. 3. Historians looking at local legal practices frequently emphasize the fluidity of the law and complexity of familial dynamics, noting, for example, that married women exercised more control over property than expected and that eighteenth-century policies regarding inheritance by illegitimate children were not as exclusionary

as anticipated. See Barbara Diefendorf, "Women and Property in Ancien Régime France: Theory and Practice in Dauphiné and Paris," in *Early Modern Conceptions of Property*, ed. John Brewer and Susan Staves (London, 1994), 170–93; Julie Hardwick, *The Practice of Patriarchy: Gender and the Politics of Household Authority in Early Modern France* (University Park, Penn., 1998); Matthew Gerber, "The End of Bastardy: Illegitimacy in France from the Reformation through the Revolution" (Ph.D. diss., University of California at Berkeley, 2003). For analysis highlighting women's economic and legal power, see Clare Haru Crowston, *Fabricating Women: The Seamstresses of Old Regime France, 1675–1791* (Durham, N.C., 2001). On the intersection between law and practice, see Bernard Dérouet, "Les pratiques familiales, le droit et la construction des différences (15e–19e siècles)," *Annales: Histoire. Sciences sociales* (1997): 369–91; James Farr, *Authority and Sexuality in Early Modern Burgundy (1550–1730)* (New York, 1995); Jean Hilaire, *La vie du droit* (Paris, 1994).

5. Lynn Hunt, *The Family Romance of the French Revolution* (Berkeley, 1992); Sarah Maza, *Private Lives and Public Affairs: The Causes Célèbres of Prerevolutionary France* (Berkeley, 1993); Jeffrey Merrick, "Domestic Politics: Divorce and Despotism in Late Eigtheenth-Century France," in *The Past as Prologue: Essays to Celebrate the Twenty-Fifth Anniversary of ASECS*, ed. Carla H. Hay and Syndy Conger (New York, 1994); Nancy Miller, *French Dressing: Women, Men, and Ancien Régime Fiction* (New York, 1991); James F. Traer, *Marriage and the Family in Eighteenth-Century France* (Ithaca, N.Y., 1980).

6. *Remonstrances des mères et filles normandes de l'ordre du tiers* (Rouen, 1789).

7. Among the many works on gender construction, see esp. "Gender: A Useful Category of Analysis," in Joan Wallach Scott, *Gender and the Politics of History* (New York, 1988). Cf. Kathleen Canning, "Feminist History after the Linguistic Turn: Historicizing Discourse and Experience," *Signs: Journal of Women in Culture and Society* 19 (1993): 368–404; Mary Louise Roberts, *Civilization without Sexes: Reconstructing Gender in Postwar France, 1917–1927* (Chicago, 1994). Works on the history of political culture include: Keith Michael Baker, *Inventing the French Revolution: Essays on French Political Culture in the Eighteenth Century* (New York, 1990); François Furet, *Interpreting the French Revolution*, trans. Elborg Forster (Cambridge, Eng., 1981); Lynn Hunt, *Politics, Culture, and Class in the French Revolution* (Berkeley, 1984) and *Family Romance*.

8. My approach to legal history has been influenced by diverse methodologies. E.g., Pierre Bourdieu, *The Logic of Practice*, trans. Richard Nice (Palo Alto, 1990); André Burguière, "Les fondements d'une culture familiale," in *Histoire de la France: Les formes de la culture*, ed. André Burguière (Paris, 1993), 25–118; Robert Gordon, "Critical Legal Histories," *Stanford Law Review* 36 (1983–84): 57–125. Nancy Cott drew my attention to Gordon's work. See her "Giving

Character to Our Whole Civic Polity: Marriage and the Public Order in the Late Nineteenth Century," in *U.S. History as Women's History: New Feminist Essays*, ed. Linda Kerber, Alice Kessler-Harris, and Kathryn Kish Sklar (Chapel Hill, 1995), 107–121; Hendrik Hartog, *Man and Wife in America* (Cambridge, Mass., 2000); Sherry Ortner, *Making Gender: The Politics and Erotics of Culture* (Boston, 1996), chap. 1. In legal anthropology, see John Comaroff and Simon Roberts, *Rules and Processes: The Cultural Logic of Dispute in an African Context* (Chicago, 1981); Olivia Harris, ed., *Inside and Outside the Law: Anthropological Studies of Authority and Ambiguity* (London, 1996); Francis G. Snyder, "Anthropology, Dispute Processes and Law: A Critical Introduction," *British Journal of Law and Society* 8 (1981): 141–80; Sally Falk Moore, *Law as Process: An Anthropological Approach* (London, 1978); Thomas Kuehn, *Law, Family, and Women: Toward a Legal Anthropology of Renaissance Italy* (Chicago, 1991). On the narrative power of plaintiffs, see Peter Brooks and Paul Gewirtz, eds., *Law's Stories: Narrative and Rhetoric in the Law* (New Haven, 1996); Natalie Zemon Davis, *Fiction in the Archives: Pardon Tales and Their Tellers in Sixteenth-Century France* (Stanford, Calif., 1987); Maza, *Private Lives and Public Affairs*. On the making of French revolutionary family law, see esp. *L'enfant, la famille et la Révolution française*, ed. Marie-Françoise Lévy (Paris, 1990) (hereafter *Enfant*); *La famille, la loi, l'Etat de la Révolution au Code Civil* (hereafter *FLE*), ed. Irène Théry and Christian Biet (Paris, 1989); *La Révolution et l'ordre juridique privé: Rationalité ou scandale. Actes du colloque d'Orléans, 11–13 septembre 1986*, ed. Jean Bart et al., 2 vols. (Orléans, 1988) (hereafter *RévJur*); Jean-Louis Halpérin, *L'impossible Code civil* (Paris, 1994). On family practice during the 1790s, see Dominique Dessertine, *Divorcer à Lyon sous la Révolution et l'Empire* (Lyon, 1981); Roderick Phillips, *Family Breakdown in Late Eighteenth-Century France* (Ithaca, N.Y., 1980); Margaret Darrow, *Revolution in the House: Family, Class, and Inheritance in Southern France, 1775–1825* (Princeton, 1989).

9. Although the creators of the family court envisioned the arbiters as relatives or friends, litigants increasingly chose men with legal training to represent them and decide their cases. See Chapter 4. Also, James F. Traer, "The French Family Court," *History* 59 (1974): 211–28; Jean-Louis Halpérin, "La composition des tribunaux de famille sous la Révolution, ou les juristes, comment s'en débarrasser?" in *FLE*, 292–304.

10. On popular practices shaping the state, see Florencia Mallon, *Peasant and Nation: The Making of Postcolonial Mexico and Peru* (Berkeley, 1995); Gilbert Joseph and Daniel Nugent, eds., *Everyday Forms of State Formation: Revolution and Negotiations of Rule in Modern Mexico* (Durham, N.C., 1994); Timothy Mitchell, "The Limits of the State: Beyond Statist Approaches and Their Critics," *American Political Science Review* 85 (1991): 77–96; Isser Woloch, *The New Regime: Transformations of the French Civic Order, 1789–1820s* (New York, 1994).

11. AN DIII 338, Pétition des héritiers rappellés par la loi [du 17 nivôse an

II], au Comité de législation, n.d., c. winter–spring 1795, from Lot-et-Garonne with c. 100 signers. Some of the female signers added, "tant pour moi que pour mes frères xx et xx à l'armée."

12. Lynn Hunt's *The Family Romance of the French Revolution* also explores the interconnections between revolutionary politics and family models. She asks how gender models interacted with the political imagination. I argue that it is also necessary to ask how social practices within families, popular activism, and state-building played an integral role in generating gender models to underpin the political order.

13. Joan B. Landes, *Women and the Public Sphere in the Age of the French Revolution* (Ithaca, N.Y., 1988); Madelyn Gutwirth, *The Twilight of the Goddesses: Women and Representation in the French Revolutionary Era* (New Brunswick, N.J., 1992); Dorinda Outram, *The Body and the French Revolution* (New Haven, 1989), and " 'Le langage mâle de la vertu': Women and the Discourse of the French Revolution," in *The Social History of Language*, ed. Peter Burke and Roy Porter (Cambridge, Eng., 1987), 120–135. The French legal historian Michèle Bordeaux argues that the Revolution curtailed women's opportunities, not by dividing public and private, but by including women as legal subordinates within "a new social liberal project." See "L'universalisme juridique et l'impasse de l'égalité," in *Les femmes et la Révolution française: Actes du colloque international, 1989, Université de Toulouse*, ed. Marie-France Brive, 3 vols. (Toulouse, 1989), 1:427–40. Cf. Vida Azimi, " 'L'exhédération politique' de la femme par la Révolution," *Revue historique de droit français et étranger* 69 (1991): 177–216.

14. Hunt, *Family Romance*; Carole Pateman, *The Sexual Contract* (Stanford, Calif., 1988); Joan Wallach Scott, *Only Paradoxes to Offer: French Feminists and the Rights of Man* (Cambridge, Mass., 1996), chaps. 1–2; Geneviève Fraisse, *Muse de la Raison: La démocratie exclusive et la différence des sexes* (Aix-en-Provence, 1989); Christine Fauré, *La démocratie sans les femmes: Essai sur le libéralisme en France* (Paris, 1985); Jean Elshtain, *Public Man, Private Woman* (Princeton, N.J., 1981); Maza, *Private Lives and Public Affairs;* Sara E. Melzer and Leslie W. Rabine, eds., *Rebel Daughters: Women and the French Revolution* (New York, 1992). I also used the public/private dichotomy in my chapter " 'Constitutional Amazons': Jacobin Women's Clubs in the French Revolution," in *Re-Creating Authority in Revolutionary France*, ed. Bryant T. Ragan and Elizabeth Williams (New Brunswick, N.J., 1992), 11–35. My own inability to better understand and conceptualize the "private" spurred the initial research for this book. For a discusssion of Pateman's role in French revolutionary historiography, see Rachel Weil, *Political Passions: Gender, the Family and Political Argument in England, 1680–1714* (Manchester, Eng., 1999), 7–11. As Weil points out, there are multiple versions of "the anti-liberal feminist narrative." On prerevolutionary origins of domesticity, work on Rousseau is especially prominent: Mary Trouille, *Sexual Politics in the Enlightenment: Women Writers Read Rousseau* (Albany, N.Y., 1997); Nicole

Fermon, *Domesticating Passions: Rousseau, Woman, and Nation* (Hanover, N.H., 1997).

15. Hilda L. Smith, *All Men and Both Sexes: Gender, Politics, and the False Universal in England, 1640–1832* (University Park, Penn., 2002). For Smith, the exclusionary "false universal" emerges generally from seventeenth-century liberalism and from a definition of modern individualism rooted in "male maturation." Linda Kerber, *No Constitutional Right to be Ladies: Women and the Obligations of Citizenship* (New York, 1998); Isabell Hull, *Sexuality, State, and Civil Society in Germany, 1700–1815* (Ithaca, N.Y., 1996); Christine Hunefeldt, *Liberalism in the Bedroom: Quarreling Spouses in Nineteenth-Century Lima* (University Park, Pa., 2000). Historians, such as Kerber and Hunefeldt, who emphasize the gender constrictions of republicanism and liberalism also stress women's agency in working these systems. For a critique of Kerber's notion of republican motherhood, see Jeanne Boydston, "Making Gender in the Early Republic: Judith Sargent Murray and the Revolution of 1800," in *The Revolution of 1800: Democracy, Race, and the New Republic,* ed. James Horn, Jan Lewis, and Peter Onuf (Charlottesville, Va., 2002), 240–66.

16. Landes' work has particularly faced criticism. See Dena Goodman, "Public Sphere and Private Life: Toward a Synthesis of Current Historiographical Approaches to the Old Regime," *History and Theory* (1992): 1–20; Keith Baker, "Defining the Public Sphere in Eighteenth-Century France," in *Habermas and the Public Sphere,* ed. Craig Calhoun (Cambridge, Mass., 1992), 181–211; Daniel Gordon, "Philosophy, Sociology, and Gender in the Enlightenment Conception of Public Opinion," *French Historical Studies* 17 (1992): 882–911. For criticism of the public-private dichotomy more generally, see Nancy Fraser, "Rethinking the Public Sphere: A Contribution to the Critique of Actually Existing Democracy," in *Habermas and the Public Sphere,* 109–42, and "What's Critical about Critical Theory? The Case of Habermas and Gender," in her *Unruly Practices: Power, Discourse, and Gender in Contemporary Social Theory* (Minneapolis, 1989), 113–143; Linda Kerber, "Separate Spheres, Female Worlds, Women's Place: The Rhetoric of Women's History," *Journal of American History* 75 (1988): 9–39; Carole Pateman, "Feminist Critiques of the Public-Private Dichotomy," in her *The Disorder of Women: Democracy, Feminism, and Political Theory* (Oxford, 1989), 118–40; Amanda Vickery, "Golden Age to Separate Spheres? A Review of the Categories and Chronology of English Women's History," *Historical Journal* 36 (1993): 383–414; Jeff Weintraub, "The Theory and Politics of the Public/Private Distinction," in *Public and Private in Thought and Practice: Perspectives on a Grand Dichotomy,* ed. Jeff Weintraub and Krishan Kumar (Chicago, 1997), 1–42. For a discussion of recent approaches to women's political engagement in the Revolution, see Suzanne Desan, "What's after Political Culture? Recent French Revolutionary Historiography," *French Historical Studies* 23 (2000): 163–96. Diverse approaches to women's political engagement include Brive, ed., *Les femmes et la Révolution française;* Dominique Godineau, *The Women of*

Paris and Their French Revolution, trans. Katherine Streip (Berkeley, 1998); Carla Hesse, *The Other Enlightenment: How French Women Became Modern* (Princeton, 2001); Jennifer Heuer, "Foreigners, Families, and Citizens: Contradictions of National Citizenship in France, 1789–1830" (Ph.D. diss. University of Chicago, 1998); Darline Gay Levy and Harriet B. Applewhite, "A Political Revolution for Women? The Case of Paris," in *Becoming Visible: Women in European History*, ed. Renate Bridenthal, Susan Mosher Stuard, and Merry E. Wiesner (Boston, 1998), 265–92; Mona Ozouf, *Women's Words: Essay on French Singularity*, trans. Jane Marie Todd (Chicago, 1997), 229–83. Lynn Hunt—whose *Family Romance of the French Revolution* highlighted the centrality of female domesticity—has more recently questioned the pervasiveness of republican motherhood and portrayed the Revolution as a source of women's rights, rather than restraints. See "Male Virtue and Republican Motherhood," in *The French Revolution and the Creation of Modern Political Culture*, vol. 4, *The Terror*, ed. Keith Baker (Oxford, 1994), 195–208; Lynn Hunt, "Forgetting and Remembering: The French Revolution Now and Then," *American Historical Review* 100 (1995): 1119–1135, esp. 1130–1132.

17. On the problematic tendency to see the Revolution as having an overall "good or bad" impact for women, see Karen Offen, "The New Sexual Politics of French Revolutionary Historiography," *French Historical Studies* 16 (1990): 909–922.

18. On the need to bring together family history and gender history, see Megan Doolittle, "Close Relations? Bringing Together Gender and Family in English History," *Gender and History* 11 (1999): 542–54; Louise A. Tilly, "Women's History and Family History: Fruitful Collaboration or Missed Connection?" *Journal of Family History* 12 (1987): 303–315.

19. On the need to study masculinity with regard to gender hierarchies and in domestic settings, see Doolittle, "Close Relations?" 544; Lynn Hunt, "The Challenge of Gender: Deconstruction of Categories and Reconstruction of Narratives in Gender History," in *Geschlechtergeschichte und Allgemeine Geschichte: Herausforderungen und Perspektiven*, ed. Hans Medick and Anne-Charlotte Trepp (Göttingen, 1998), 59–97. For works looking at various aspects of domesticity and masculinity, see Anna Clark, *Struggle for the Breeches: Gender and the Making of the English Working Class* (Berkeley, 1995); Leonore Davidoff and Catherine Hall, *Family Fortunes: Men and Women of the English Middle Class, 1780–1850* (Chicago, 1987); Susan Lee Johnson, *Roaring Camp: The Social World of the California Gold Rush* (New York, 2000), chap. 2; Stephanie McCurry, *Masters of Small Worlds: Yeoman Households, Gender Relations, and the Political Culture of the Antebellum South Carolina Low Country* (New York, 1995); William Reddy, *The Invisible Code: Honor and Sentiment in Postrevolutionary France, 1814–1848* (Berkeley, 1997), chap. 3; Steve J. Stern, *The Secret History of Gender: Women, Men, and Power in Late Colonial Mexico* (Chapel Hill, N.C., 1995).

20. Archives départementales du Calvados (hereafter ADC), 3L 616,

Sentences arbitrales du district de Caen (hereafter SA Caen), 8 prairial an III (27 May 1795).

21. On female publishing during the Revolution, see Hesse, *Other Enlightenment.*

22. E.g., Elsa Barkley Brown, "Negotiating and Transforming the Public Sphere: African American Political Life in the Transition from Slavery to Freedom," in *Jumpin' Jim Crow: Southern Politics from Civil War to Civil Rights,* ed. Jane Dailey, Glenda Elizabeth Gilmore, and Bryant Simon (Princeton, 2000), 28–66; Nan Enstad, "Fashioning Political Identities: Cultural Studies and the Historical Construction of Political Subjects," *American Quarterly* 50 (1998): 745–82; Laura McEnaney, *Civil Defense Begins at Home: Militarization Meets Everyday Life in the Fifties* (Princeton, N.J., 2000); Iris Marion Young, *Justice and the Politics of Difference* (Princeton, N.J., 1990).

23. Hunt, *Politics, Culture, and Class,* 56.

24. Zoe A. Schneider, "Women before the Bench: Female Litigants in Early Modern Normandy," *French Historical Studies* 23 (2000): 1–32; Clare Crowston, "Engendering the Guilds: Seamstresses, Tailors, and the Clash of Corporate Identities in Old Regime France," *French Historical Studies* 23 (2000): 339–71, and *Fabricating Women;* Daryl Hafter, "Female Masters in the Ribbonmaking Guild of Eighteenth-Century Rouen," *French Historical Studies* 20 (1997): 1–14; Olwen Hufton, *Bayeux in the Late Eighteenth-Century: A Social Study* (Oxford, 1967), 83–85.

25. Burguière, "Fondements d'une culture familiale," 37–47.

26. Paul Hanson, *Provincial Politics in the French Revolution: Caen and Limoges, 1789–1794* (Baton Rouge, La., 1989); Jean Lethuillier, *Le Calvados dans la Révolution: L'esprit public d'un département* (Condé-sur-Noireau, 1990); Christine Peyrard, *Les Jacobins de l'Ouest: Sociabilité révolutionnaire et formes de politisation dans le Maine et la Basse-Normandie (1789–1799)* (Paris, 1996); Serge Bonin and Claude Langlois, eds., *Atlas de la Révolution française,* vol. 6, *Les sociétés politiques,* ed. Jean Boutier et al. (Paris, 1992), 80; Hunt, *Politics, Culture, and Class,* 131.

CHAPTER 1

1. Comte d'Antraigues, *Observations sur le divorce* (Paris, 1789), 1, 11–12.

2. For an overview, see James F. Traer, *Marriage and the Family in Eighteenth-Century France* (Ithaca, N.Y., 1980), chap. 2. Cf. David Denby, *Sentimental Narrative and the Social Order in France, 1760–1820* (Cambridge, Eng., and New York, 1994); Joan DeJean, "Notorious Women: Marriage and the Novel in Crisis in France (1690–1715)," *Yale Journal of Criticism* 4 (1991): 67–85; Dominique Dessertine, *Divorcer à Lyon sous la Révolution et l'Empire* (Lyon, 1981), 25–31; Paul Hoffmann, *La femme dans la pensée des lumières* (Paris, 1977), 281–86; Sarah Maza, *Private Lives and Public Affairs: The Causes Célèbres of Prerevolutionary France* (Berkeley, 1993), 264–71; Roderick

Phillips, *Putting Asunder: A History of Divorce in Western Society* (Cambridge, Eng., 1988), 163–72; Francis Ronsin, *Le contrat sentimental: Débats sur le mariage, l'amour, le divorce de l'Ancien Régime à la Restauration* (Paris, 1990), 39–51; Joan Hinde Stewart, *Gynographs: French Novels by Women of the Late Eighteenth Century* (Lincoln, Neb., 1993).

3. M.C.D., *Essai sur les Mœurs, ou Point de constitution durable sans mœurs* (Paris, 1790), as presented to the National Assembly and reviewed in *Moniteur universel*, 28 Jan. 1790.

4. Lynn Hunt, *The Family Romance of the French Revolution* (Berkeley, 1992). Hunt does not analyze the role of marriage within the family romance.

5. On marriage and legal status, see Jacques Mulliez, "Droit et morale conjugale: Essai sur l'histoire des relations personnelles entre époux," *Revue historique* 278 (1987): 35–106.

6. For overviews, see Roger Chartier, *The Cultural Origins of the French Revolution*, trans. Lydia G. Cochrane (Durham, N.C., 1991); Dorinda Outram, *The Enlightenment* (Cambridge, Eng., 1995), chap. 2. On literacy, see François Furet and Jacques Ozouf, *Reading and Writing: Literacy in France from Calvin to Jules Ferry* (Cambridge, Eng., 1982). On print culture and the public sphere, see Jack Censer, *The French Press in the Age of the Enlightenment* (London, 1994); Roger Chartier, *The Cultural Uses of Print in Early Modern France*, trans. Lydia G. Cochrane (Princeton, N.J., 1987); Robert Darnton, *The Forbidden Bestsellers of Pre-revolutionary France* (New York, 1996), and *The Literary Underground of the Old Regime* (Cambridge, Mass., 1982); Dena Goodman, *The Republic of Letters: A Cultural History of the Enlightenment* (Ithaca, N.Y., 1994); Margaret C. Jacob, *Living the Enlightenment: Freemasonry and Politics in Eighteenth-Century Europe* (New York, 1991); Michael Lynn, "Enlightenment in the Public Sphere: The Musée de Monsieur and Scientific Culture in Late-Eighteenth-Century Paris," *Eighteenth-Century Studies* 32 (1999): 463–76; Maza, *Private Lives and Public Affairs*; Daniel Roche, *Le siècle des lumières en province: Académies et académiciens provinciaux, 1680–1789*, 2 vols. (Paris, 1989).

7. Michael Kennedy, *The Jacobin Clubs in the French Revolution: The First Years* (Princeton, N.J., 1982), and *The Jacobin Clubs in the French Revolution: The Middle Years* (Princeton, N.J., 1988), 3; Carla Hesse, "Economic Upheavals in Publishing," in *Revolution in Print: The Press in France, 1775–1800*, ed. Robert Darnton and Daniel Roche (Berkeley, 1989), 69–97, p. 92; Lynn Hunt, *Politics, Culture, and Class in the French Revolution* (Berkeley, 1984), esp. 19–20; Jeremy Popkin, *Revolutionary News: The Press in France, 1789–1799* (Durham, N.C., 1990); Emmet Kennedy et al., eds., *Theatre, Opera, and Audience in Revolutionary Paris, Analysis and Repertory* (Westport, Conn., 1996).

8. Dozens of *cahiers de doléances* (petitions of grievances) appealed for the abolition of lettres de cachet, the simplification of civil procedure, or the unification of customary, civil law. But only a few critiqued parental authority over marriage age or even mentioned divorce: three apparently to support it and four

to oppose it. Dessertine, *Divorcer à Lyon*, 47; Ronsin, *Contrat sentimental*, 50–51; Jean-Louis Halpérin, *L'Impossible Code civil* (Paris, 1994), 46–49; Traer, *Marriage and the Family*, 82–83, 110, 140–42.

9. *Il est temps de donner aux époux qui ne peuvent vivre ensemble la liberté de former des nouveaux liens* (Paris, n.d., c. 1790), 1.

10. [Hubert de Matigny], *Traité philosophique, théologique, et politique de la loi du divorce, demandée aux Etats-généraux par S.A.S. Mgr. Louis-Philippe-Joseph d'Orléans, prince du Sang* (n.p., June 1789). For examples of the varied cahiers format on many subjects, see listings in André Monglod, *La France révolutionnaire et impériale: Annales de bibilographie méthodique et description de livres illustrés*, 9 vols. (Grenoble, 1930), 1:63–87.

11. *Principes généraux des protestants de la Confession d'Augsbourg et leur incompatibilité avec la Constitution civile du clergé* (n.p., n.d.); *Très humble et très respectueuse adresse présentée à l'Assemblée nationale par les citoyens de la Confession d'Augsbourg des villes de Strasbourg, Colmar, Wissembourg, et Munster en Alsace* (Paris, n.d.).

12. Albert-Joseph Hennet, *Du divorce* (Paris, 1789). Hennet himself lists seven different journals' reviews of his own *Du divorce* in his anonymous *Pétition à l'Assemblée nationale par Montaigne, Charron, Montesquieu, et Voltaire* (Paris, 1791), 34. Most prominent was the review in the *Moniteur universel* 1: 1 Jan. 1790. J. Mavidal and E. Laurent, eds., *Archives parlémentaires de 1787 à 1860. Recueil complet des débats législatifs et politiques des chambres françaises* (hereafter *AP*) (Paris, 1879–), première série, 38: 583, 17 Feb. 1792.

13. Abbé Barruel, *Lettres sur le divorce à un député de l'assemblée nationale, ou bien, réfutation d'un ouvrage ayant pour titre "Du Divorce"* (Paris, 1789); Abbé de Chapt de Rastignac, *Accord de la Révélation et de la raison contre le divorce* (Paris, 1790); *L'homme mal marié, ou Questions à l'auteur du Divorce* (Paris, n.d.); Robert Darnton, "Readers Respond to Rousseau: The Fabrication of Romantic Sensitivity," in his *The Great Cat Massacre and Other Episodes in French Cultural History* (New York, 1985), 215–256.

14. Two women made pro-divorce arguments explicitly in response to Marmontel's attack on divorce in the *Mercure de France*, 6 Feb. 1790: [Madame Cailly], *La nécessité du divorce* (Paris, 1790); Mademoiselle Jodin, *Vues législatives pour les femmes, adressées à l'Assemblée nationale* (Angers, 1790), 72–86. Prominent and diverse examples of reviews include *Moniteur universel* 95: 25 Nov. 1789, Review and partial reproduction of *Réflexions d'un bon citoyen en faveur du divorce* (Paris, 1789); *Moniteur* 1, 1 Jan. 1790, Review of Hennet, *Du divorce; Spectateur national*, 1 Jan. 1790, Review of *L'art de rendre les ménages heureux; Courrier de l'Hymen*, no. 6, 10 Mar. 1791, Review of Bouchotte, *Observations sur l'accord de la raison et de la religion pour le rétablissement du Divorce, l'anéantissement des séparations entre les époux et la réformation des loix relatives à l'adultère* (Paris, 1790). See also Pierre Damas, *Les origines du divorce en France* (Bordeaux, 1897), 93–95; Maurice d'Auteville, "Le divorce pendant la Révolution," *Revue de la Révolution* 2 (1883): 206–13, 311–16, 473–78, esp. 207–8. In mid 1791, in an anonymous pamphlet, Hennet enumer-

ated nineteen different newspapers that had printed articles, reviews, or letters on divorce between Nov. 1789 and June 1791: *Pétition à l'Assemblée nationale*, 28–35.

15. *Journal de Paris* 193: 12 July 1791, Review of Charles Demoustier, *Le divorce.*

16. *Lettre du Marquis de C——— au Comte de F——— contre le divorce* (Paris, 1790); M. Thiébault, *Adresse aux membres honorables de l'Assemblée nationale sur la liberté du divorce, et sur le célibat* (Metz, 1790); *Appel au bon sens contre le divorce en réponse au Paradoxe de M. Hennet* (Paris, n.d., pre-Sept. 1792).

17. Ronsin, *Contrat sentimental*, 53. The two most prominent women to write entire pamphlets dedicated to divorce were [Madame Cailly], *Griefs et plaintes des femmes mal mariées* (n.p., n.d.), *La nécessité du divorce* (Paris, 1790), and *L'ami des enfants, ou motion en faveur du divorce* (Paris, n.d.); and [Madame Fumelh], *Mémoire sur le divorce* (n.p., n.d.). M. Tapin, *Lettre sur le mariage, au rédacteur du journal du club des observateurs* (n.p., n.d.), 1 and 6.

18. [Matigny], *Traité philosophique*, 21–36. Matigny's work was typical in that he fused anticlerical sentiment with the attempt to claim religious support for divorce. Marquis de Villette, *Mes cahiers* (Senlis, 1789), 11–15; *Le divorce, par le meilleur ami des femmes, suivi d'une adresse au clergé* (Paris, 1790); M.C.D., *Essai sur les Mœurs, ou Point de constitution durable sans mœurs* (Paris, 1790). Opponents of divorce sometimes also defended clerical celibacy. Thiébault, *Adresse aux membres honorables.* Conversely, on occasion, attackers of clerical celibacy favored indissoluble marriage and opposed divorce: Jacques Gaudin, *Les inconvéniens du célibat des prêtres, prouvés par des recherches historiques* (Genève, 1781).

19. Varied examples include *Le mariage des prêtres, ou le célibat détruit, par un citoyen de B———* (n.p., 1790); *Le masque levé, ou Pétition de deux curés constitutionnels à l'évêque de leur département, pour obtenir son agrément aux mariages des prêtres* (n.p., 1790); *Observations sur le célibat des prêtres, la perpétuité des vœux monastiques et le sort qu'on veut faire aux curés* (Paris, 1789); *Sur le mariage des prêtres* (n.p., n.d.); M. l'abbé Liger, *Dissertation sur le célibat ecclésiastique, ou Réponse aux assertions fausses et calomnieuses, erronées, etc. du Journal ecclésiastique des mois de septembre et octobre 1790* (Paris, 1790); M. Le Fèvre, *Lettres sur le célibat des prêtres par un jeune homme à qui cette institution a fait quitter l'état ecclésiastique* (n.p., 1789); *Du mariage des prêtres et des religieuses* (Paris, 1790); *Sermon capucino-philosophique par M——— ci-devant cordelier* (Paris, 1791). See Roderick Phillips, "The Attack on Celibacy," *Proceedings of the Annual Meeting of the Western Society for French History* 17 (1990): 165–71.

20. Marked at "6 sols" were the 8-page *Adresse à l'Assemblée nationale, Concernant le mariage des prêtres* (n.p., n.d. c. 1790), and the 15-page *Projet de loi sur le clergé, et utilité du mariage des prêtres* (n.p. [Paris], n.d.). The anonymous *Réflexions impartiales sur l'ouvrage intitulé: Les inconvéniens du célibat*

des prêtres; Sur la conservation ou suppression des Congrégations de l'Oratoire, de la Doctrine chrétienne, etc.; Sur les décrets relatifs à l'élection des Evêques; sur le Divorce, suivies de quelques réflexions sur l'élection du Pape, etc. (Paris, 1790), 4, reported that the much-acclaimed 439-page book by Gaudin, *Les inconvéniens du célibat,* had cost as much as 18 livres in its out-of-print 1781 version, and now cost 3 livres, 12 sous in its new 1790 edition (republished with a brief new "Avertissement" by the Parisian printer J. L. Pellet).

21. Carol Blum, *Strength in Numbers: Population, Reproduction, and Power in Eighteenth-Century France* (Baltimore, 2002); Jacqueline Hecht, "Célibat, stratégies familiales et essor du capitalisme au XVIIIe siècle: Réalités et représentations," in *Ménages, familles, parentèles et solidarités dans les populations méditerranéennes* (Paris, 1996), 257–84; Jean-Claude Perrot, "Les économistes, les philosophes et la population," in *Histoire de la population française,* vol. 2, *De la Renaissance à 1789,* ed. Jacques Dupâquier (Paris, 1988), 499–551; Leslie Tuttle, " 'Sacred and Politic Unions': Natalism, Families, and the State in Old Regime France, 1666–1789" (Ph.D. diss., Princeton University, 2000), chap. 6.

22. *Le mariage des prêtres, ou Recit de ce qui s'est passé à trois séances des assemblées générales du District de Saint-Etienne-du-Mont, où l'on a agité la question du mariage des prêtres; avec la motion prinicipale, et les opinions des honorables membres qui ont appuyé la motion; publié au profit des pauvres ménages du District de Saint-Etienne-du-Mont* (n.p., 1790); *Motion faite dans l'Assemblée générale du District de Saint-Etienne-du-Mont, pour le mariage des prêtres* (Paris, 1789). Works by figures present include François Bernet de Boislorette, *Pétition à l'Assemblée nationale, faite par François-Etienne Bernet de Boislorette, l'un des Aumonniers de l'Armée parisienne, marié constitutionellement à une Anglaise protestante* (Paris, 1791), and *Réclamation du droit le plus cher à l'homme;* [Abbé Antoine de Cournaud], *Le mariage des prêtres* (Paris, 1790). On the early civil marriage of this professor at the Collège de France, see John McManners, *The French Revolution and the Church* (New York, 1969), 114.

23. Defenders of clerical celibacy included *Entretien d'un acolythe [sic] avec son directeur sur le célibat ecclésiastique* (n.p., n.d.); M. Samary, *Examen sur le projet de décret concernant le mariage des prêtres* (n.p., n.d. c. 1791); [Thiébault], *Adresse aux membres honorables,* and *Seconde adresse aux membres honorables de l'Assemblée nationale sur la loi particulière du célibat religieux* (Metz, 1790); *Le vrai mariage des prêtres, Par l'ex-premier vicaire d'Auch, curé de Saint-Jean-Poutge* (n.p., 1792). In the context of the struggle over the Civil Constitution and the independence of the Church from the state, some clergymen defended clerical celibacy as part of a larger defense of ecclesiastical autonomy. See *Distinctions et bornes des deux puissances, par rapport à la Constitution de la clergé, avec deux corollaires sur le divorce, et sur le célibat religieux* (Paris, 1790); *Instruction pastorale de Monsieur l'Evêque d'Amiens* (Paris, 1790).

24. For useful reprints, see *1789 Cahiers de doléances des femmes et autres textes* (Paris, 1981); *Les femmes dans la Révolution française*, 3 vols. (Paris, 1982); *Réclamations des femmes 1789* (Paris, 1989).

25. E.g., Madame de Coicy, *Demande des femmes aux Etats-Généraux, par l'auteur des femmes comme il convient de les voir* (n.p., n.d., c. 1789); M.L.P.P.D. St. L., *Remonstrances, plaintes et doléances des dames françaises, à l'occasion de l'Assemblée des Etats-Généraux* (Paris, 1789). On the Old Regime "querelle des femmes," see Léon Abensour, *La femme et le féminisme avant la révolution* (Paris, 1923), part 2; Maïté Albistur and Daniel Armogathe, *Histoire du féminisme français*, 2 vols. (Paris, 1978), 1:265–303; Elisabeth Badinter, ed., *Qu'est-ce qu'une femme?* (Paris, 1988); Nina Gelbart, *Feminine and Opposition Journalism in Old Regime France: Le Journal des Dames* (Berkeley, 1987); Carolyn Lougee, *Le paradis des femmes: Women, Salons, and Social Stratification in Seventeenth-Century France* (Princeton, N.J., 1976); Karen Offen, "Reclaiming the European Enlightenment for Feminism, or Prolegomena to Any Future History of Eighteenth-Century Europe," in *Perspectives on Feminist Political Thought in European History from the Middle Ages to the Present*, ed. Tjitske Akkerman and Siep Stuurman (London, 1998), 85–103; Candace Proctor, *Women, Equality, and the French Revolution* (Westport, Conn., 1990), chaps. 1–2.

26. Madame B—— B——, *Cahier des doléances et réclamations des femmes* (n.p., 1789), 3–4, 10–11.

27. *Requête des femmes pour leur admission aux Etats-Généraux: Aux Messieurs composant l'Assemblée des notables* (n.p., n.d. 1788?). Other examples include *Délibérations et protestations de l'assemblée des honnêtes citoyennes compromises dans le procès-verbal de celle de l'ordre le plus nombreux de France* (Paris, 1789); *Requête des Dames à l'Assemblée nationale* (n.p., n.d.); *Réclamation de toutes les poissardes* (Paris, n.d.); and *Cahier des plaintes et doléances des Dames de la halle et des marchés de Paris, rédigé au grand salon des Porcherons, le premier dimanche de Mai, pour être présenté à Messieurs les Etats-Généraux* (n.p., 1789).

28. Pamphlets, such as *Requête des dames à l'Assemblée nationale* and *Motion de la pauvre Javotte, députée des pauvres femmes* (Paris, 1790), have been classified as serious feminist works by some authors and as mockeries by others. For helpful classifications, see Jacqueline de Bouët du Portal, "Apperçu sur la condition de la femme pendant la Révolution française (1789–1804)," (Thèse de droit, Université de Paris, 1955), 74; Paule-Marie Duhet, *Les femmes et la Révolution 1789–1794* (Paris, 1971), chap. 2; Ouzi Elyada, *Presse populaire et feuilles volantes de la Révolution à Paris, 1789–1792: Inventaire méthodique et critique* (Paris, 1991). On humor, see Antoine de Baecque, *Les éclats du rire: La culture des rieurs au XVIIIe siècle* (Paris, 2000). On the *poissard* genre, see Carla Hesse, *The Other Enlightenment: How French Women Became Modern* (Princeton, 2001), chap. 1; Rene Marion, "The Dames de la Halle: Community and Authority in Early Modern Paris" (Ph.D. diss., Johns Hopkins University,

1994), chap. 4; A. P. Moore, *The Genre Poissard and the French Stage of the Eighteenth Century* (New York, 1935).

29. Hesse, *Other Enlightenment*, 53–54.

30. Marie de Vuignerias, *Cahier des doléances et réclamations des femmes de la Charente* (n.p., 1789). See the commentary by Léonce Grasilier in her republished edition of Vuignerias's cahier in "Le féminisme en 1790," *Nouvelle Revue rétrospective* (Paris, 1890). Cf. Mme B—— B——, *Cahier des doléances*.

31. On the problem of female authorship, publicity, and anonymity, see Joan DeJean, "Lafayette's Ellipses: The Privileges of Anonymity," *PMLA* 99 (1984): 884–902; Elizabeth C. Goldsmith and Dena Goodman, eds., *Going Public: Women and Publishing in Early Modern France* (Ithaca, 1995); Carla Hesse, "Reading Signatures: Female Authorship and Revolutionary Law in France, 1750–1850," *Eighteenth-Century Studies* 22 (1989): 469–87.

32. [Olympe de Gouges], "Le bon sens du français" (Paris, 1792), reprinted in *Les femmes dans la Révolution française*, vol. 3: *Affiches*. This volume reprints other examples of this genre.

33. *Observateur féminin*, renamed *L'étoile du matin, ou Les petits mots de Madame de Verte Allure, ex- religieuse*, 15–31 March 1790, 6 issues; *Courrier de l'Hymen, ou Journal des Dames*, Feb.–July 1791 and "Prospectus d'un nouveau journal." Cf. *Etrennes nationales des Dames; Annales de l'Education du Sexe* (esp. no. 2); *Lettres bougrement patriotiques de la Mère Duchêne*, Feb.–April 1791, esp. the fifth letter on women's moral influence on the Revolution, and the seventh and fifteenth letters on egalitarian inheritance. "Lettre de Seline," *Bouche de fer* 34 (December 1790): 532, as cited in Gary Kates, " 'The Powers of Husband and Wife Must be Equal and Separate': The Cercle Social and the Rights of Women, 1790–91," in *Women and Politics in an Age of Democratic Revolution*, ed. Harriet B. Applewhite and Darline G. Levy (Ann Arbor, 1990), 163–180, p. 166; Letters from two anonymous women appeared in *Feuille du Jour*, 17 and 22 June 1791, as cited in Damas, *Origines du divorce en France*, 93–94. On the feminine press, see Duhet, *Femmes et la Révolution*, 92–99; Ouzi Elyada, "Préface: La presse patriotique pour les femmes du peuple de Paris," in *Lettres bougrement patriotiques de la Mère Duchêne, suivi du Journal des Femmes*, ed. Elyada (Paris, 1989), 5–14; Evelyne Sullerot, *Histoire de la presse féminine en France, des origines à 1848* (Paris, 1966), chap. 3.

34. Works written by members or printed by the Cercle Social press include Nicolas de Bonneville, *Le nouveau code conjugal* (Paris, 1792); [Madame de Cambis], *Du sort actuel des femmes* (Paris, n.d., c. Sept. 1791); Jean-Antoine-Nicolas Caritat de Condorcet, "Sur l'admission des femmes au droit de cité," *Journal de la Société de 1789*, 5 (3 July 1790); Gabriel Feydel, *Sur la loi du divorce et le système de l'adoption* (Paris, 1793); François Lanthenas, *Inconvéniens du droit d'aînesse . . .* (Paris, 1789); *Pétition adressée à l'Assemblée nationale* (Paris, n.d., c. 1791) [a pro-divorce pamphlet]. On the Cercle Social, see Gary Kates, *The Cercle Social, the Girondins and the French*

Revolution (Princeton, 1985), esp. pp. 118–27, and his " 'Powers of Husband and Wife' "; Judith Vega, "Feminist Republicanism: Etta Palm-Aelders on Justice, Virtue and Men," *History of European Ideas* 10 (1989): 333–51.

35. Many of Etta Palm d'Aelders's works are printed together in *Appel aux françaises sur la régénération des mœurs, et nécessité de l'influence des femmes dans un gouvernement libre* (Paris, n.d., c. May 1791); *Prospectus pour le Cercle patriotique des Amies de la Vérité* (Paris, 1791); *AP,* 41:63–64, 1 Apr. 1792.

36. Suzanne Desan, " 'Constitutional Amazons': Jacobin Women's Clubs in the French Revolution," in *Re-Creating Authority in Revolutionary France,* ed. Bryant T. Ragan and Elizabeth Williams (New Brunswick, N.J., 1992), 11–35.

37. Kennedy, *Jacobin Clubs: The Middle Years,* 206–10; Paul Nicolle, *Histoire de Vire pendant la Révolution française (1789–1800)* (Vire, 1923), 173. Speeches given at Jacobin clubs were sometimes published as pamphlets: M. Gastrez, *Discours sur l'utilité du divorce, prouvée par divers auteurs, prononcé dans la Société des amis de la Constitution, séante à Saint-Germain-en-Laye* (Saint-Germain-en-Laye, 1791); *Réfutation d'une Instruction pastorale de Monsieur l'évêque d'Amiens, par la Société des Amis de la Constitution d'Amiens* [apparently written by the juror M. Mesurole], (Paris, 1790). On female participation at male clubs, see Kennedy, *Jacobin Clubs: The First Years,* 89–93; Marc Villiers, *Histoire des clubs de femmes et légions d'amazones* (Paris, 1910), 109–110 and chap. 5. Françoise Sanson, *Discours fait et prononcé par Françoise Sanson Veuve Duval, dans la séance publique des Amis de la Constitution le 15 avril 1791: Avis aux dames portées pour la Contre-Révolution* (Caen, n.d.). Elisabeth Lafaurie, *Discours sur l'état de nullité dans lequel on tient les femmes relativement à la politique . . . Prononcé le 16 mai 1791, dans la salle des séances de la Société des Amis de la Constitution, séante à Saint-Sever-Cap* (Dax, 1791).

38. See AN DIII 361 for the largest collection of divorce petitions. A. H. Huussen appears to have found the earliest pro-divorce petition from Mar. 1790 in AN DIII 13. See his "Le droit du mariage au cours de la Révolution française," *Tijdshrift voor Rechtgeschiedenis* 47 (1979): 9–51, 99–127, 46. On divorce petitions, see also François Olivier-Martin, *La crise du mariage dans la législation intermédiaire, 1789–1804* (Paris, 1901), 69–74 and his appendix, 221–25; Ronsin, *Contrat sentimental,* 94–103; Gérard Thibault-Laurent, *La première introduction du divorce en France sous la Révolution et l'Empire (1792–1816)* (Clermont-Ferrand, 1938), 87–93. I will look at post-1792 divorce petitions in Chapters 3 and 7.

39. AN DIII 33, Pétition d'un citoyen de Caen aux dignes représentants d'un peuple libre et égal, 8 Sept. 1792.

40. Tapin, *Lettre sur le mariage,* 2.

41. Halpérin, *Impossible Code civil,* 53–67; Jacques Mulliez, "Droit et morale conjugale"; Traer, *Marriage and the Family,* chaps. 1 and 2.

42. Pierre Le Ridant, *Examen de deux questions importantes sur le mariage* (Paris, 1753); François Bourjon, *Le droit commun de France et la cou-*

tume de Paris réduits en principes (Paris, 1747); Robert-Joseph Pothier, *Traité du contrat de mariage* (Orléans, 1771), as quoted in Mulliez, "Droit et morale conjugale," 42.

43. Halpérin (*Impossible Code civil,* 64–66) and Mulliez ("Droit et morale conjugale," 40–48) argue that virtually all jurists endorsed the concept of contractual marriage by the late eighteenth century, but maintained an essential conservatism regarding its possible implications for divorce, marital authority, or arranged marriages. As Traer notes, an exception was Nicolas Lemoyne Desessarts, who advocates divorce for Jews and Protestants in his entry "Divorce" in Joseph Nicolas Guyot, *Répertoire universel et raisonné de jurisprudence,* 2nd ed. (Paris, 1784), 5:734–50, as cited in Traer, *Marriage and the Family,* 39.

44. See note 2. While some authors confined their comments to the West, the philosophes' imaginary explorations of non-Christian marital customs also fueled this line of argumentation. Denis Diderot, *Supplément au voyage de Bougainville* (Geneva, 1955); Charles de Secondat de Montesquieu [1721], *Lettres Persanes* (Paris, 1929).

45. Cerfvol authored five works on marriage and divorce between 1768 and 1771: e.g., [Cerfvol], *Cri d'une honnête femme qui réclame le divorce, conformément aux loix de la primitive église, à l'usage actuel du royaume catholique de Pologne, et à celui de tous les peuples de la Terre qui existe ou qui ont existé, excepté nous* (London, 1773), esp. Lettre 3, pp. 33–36, on natural law. [Philibert], *Cri d'un honnête homme qui se croit fondé en droit naturel et divin à représenter à la législation française les motifs de justice tant ecclésiastique que civile et les vues d'utilité tant morale que politique qui militeraient pour la dissolution du mariage dans de certaines circonstances données* (n.p., 1768); Jacques Le Scène Desmaisons, *Le contrat conjugal ou loix du mariage, de la répudiation, et du divorce* (n.p., 1781).

46. Chrétien de Lamoignon de Malesherbes, *Mémoire sur le mariage des Protestants, et sur l'état civil qu'on doit leur donner en France* (n.p., 1785); *Second mémoire sur le mariage des Protestants* (London, 1787); and *Sur les mariages des chrétiens* (n.p., 1788). See also Geoffrey Adams, *The Huguenots and French Opinion, 1685–1787: The Enlightenment Debate on Toleration* (Waterloo, Can., 1991), part 3; Burdette C. Poland, *French Protestantism and the French Revolution: A Study in Church and State, Thought and Religion, 1685–1815* (Princeton, 1957), 75–82. For the edict, see Lynn Hunt, ed., *The French Revolution and Human Rights* (Boston, 1996), 40–43.

47. On the intersecting discourses on religious minorities and actors, see Hunt, ed., *The French Revolution and Human Rights,* 20–23, 88–90. Pierre-Toussaint Durand de Maillane, *Projet de loi proposé par le Comité ecclésiastique sur le mariage et sur les actes et registres qui doivent constater l'état civil des personnes* (Paris, 1790), and *Rapport sur le projet de décret des comités ecclésiastiques et de constitution, concernant les empêchements, les dispenses et la forme des mariages* (Paris, 1790). Like Hennet, Durand de Maillane faced the barbs of the Abbé Barruel, *Les vrais principes sur le mariage, opposés au rapport*

de M. Durand de Maillane et servant de suite aux Lettres sur le divorce (Paris, 1790).

48. Hennet, *Du divorce* and *Pétition à l'Assemblée nationale;* [Matigny], *Traité philosophique,* 70–74; Bouchotte, *Observations.* In the Old Regime, pro-divorce arguments had included anticlerical elements, although illustrations of historical, biblical, or theological compatibility between divorce and religion dominated.

49. Hennet, *Du divorce,* 61 and 63; *Moniteur universel* 1 (1 Jan. 1790), Review of Hennet, *Du divorce;* [Bergier], *Observations sur le divorce,* 47–48; Chapt de Rastignac, *Accord; Indissolubilité du mariage vengée, Lettre à M——, Député à l'assemblée nationale* (Paris, 31 Dec. 1789), 6–7. *Appel au bon sens contre le divorce* (p. 49) noted that if God had thought divorce were a natural part of happiness, he would have made two Adams or two Eves.

50. *Sur le mariage des prêtres* (n.p., n.d.), 8; *Un mot sur le divorce, suivi d'un projet de loi, et d'un tableau des usages de tous les pays de la terre sur le mariage* (Paris, 1791), 12–30; [Pierre Bruguière], *Réflexions d'un curé constitutionnel sur le décret de l'Assemblée nationale concernant le mariage* (Paris, 1791).

51. [Cailly], *La nécessité du divorce;* [Cambis], *Du sort actuel; Courrier de l'Hymen,* no. 2, 24 Feb. 1791; no. 4, 3 Mar. 1791; *Un mot sur le divorce,* 7–12. In February 1790, the National Assembly officially abolished monastic vows, although convents in particular were slow to disband.

52. [Cailly], *Griefs et plaintes,* 41; *Lettre à Madame —— sur le divorce* (n.p., 1790), 5; Bonneville, *Nouveau code conjugal.*

53. *Du divorce, adresse à un grand prince qui s'est fait homme* (n.p., 1789), 4–6.

54. *Le divorce, ou l'art de rendre les ménages heureux* (Paris, 1790), 1–4, 11, 16; *Lettre à Madame ——,* 5–8; M. P. Juge de Brives, *Les mariages heureux ou empire du divorce, suivi d'une réfutation des ouvrages contre le divorce* (Paris, n.d.); *Réflexions d'un bon citoyen; Remonstrances des mères et filles normandes de l'ordre du tiers* (Rouen, 1789), 6–10. AN DIII 361, Pétition anonyme à l'Assemblée législative, received 4 Oct., no year, probably 1791.

55. Hecht, "Célibat, stratégies familiales"; Blum, *Strength in Numbers;* Maza, *Private Lives and Public Affairs,* 283–86.

56. Antraigues, *Observations sur le divorce,* 36, 11–23. On the novel *Emilie de Varmont* by Louvet de Couvrai, see Traer, *Marriage and the Family,* 115–16.

57. AN DIV 13, Pétition anonyme à nos seigneurs les députés de l'Assemblée nationale, 6 Mar. 1790; *Offrande d'un nouveau genre, et supplique adressée à l'Assemblée nationale, par des religieuses de Paris, tendante à obtenir leur réstitution au siècle, et la faculté de se marier* (Paris, 1789). Cf. *Voltaire sorcier, ou Accomplissement de la prophétie du mariage des prêtres, et de la suppression des moines* (n.p. [Paris], n.d. c. 1791). AN DIII 361, Pétition du citoyen Fleurant à la Convention nationale, 10 frimaire an II (30 Nov. 1793); *L'indignation du Père Duchesne contre l'indissolubricité du mariage, et sa Motion pour le Divorce* 25: 6 Dec. 1790.

58. *Pétition des femmes du Tiers Etat au Roi* (n.p., 1 Jan. 1789); Olympe de Gouges, *Le Couvent ou les Vœux forcés* (1790), performed in Paris forty-two times according to Kennedy et al., eds., *Theatre, Opera, and Audience,* 168; or "over eighty performances," according to Gabrielle Verdier, "From Reform to Revolution: The Social Theater of Olympe de Gouges," in *Literate Women and the French Revolution of 1789,* ed. Catherine R. Montfort (Birmingham, Ala., 1994), 189–221. Cf. Jacques Boutet de Monvel, *Les victimes cloîtrés* (1791, 109 performances); Joseph Fiévée and Henri Berton, *Les rigeurs du cloître* (1790, 71 performances); Jean François La Harpe, *Mélanie, ou la religieuse* (orig. 1768, 82 performances from 1791). Performance figures are from Kennedy et al., eds., *Theatre, Opera, and Audience,* 118, 160, 180. See also Marvin Carlson, *The Theater of the French Revolution* (Ithaca, N.Y., 1966), 21, 56–57, 76–78, and 103. Etta Palm d'Aelders, *Appel aux françaises,* 29–30; [Cailly], *Griefs et plaintes,* 39–41.

59. [Cournaud], *Le mariage des prêtres,* 61; *Motion faite dans l'Assemblée générale du district de Saint-Etienne-du-Mont,* 15–16.

60. *Le divorce, par le meilleur ami des femmes, suivi d'une adresse au clergé;* [Cournaud], *Le mariage des prêtres; Le mariage des prêtres, ou le célibat détruit,* esp. 3–4, 67; MM——, ancien Curé de D., *Le célibat ecclésiastique, ou vues d'un Citoyen pour le rétablissement des mœurs* (n.p., n.d., c. 1790), 7; [Matigny], *Traité philosophique,* 28–35. For the most dramatic account of the physical and mental tortures of celibacy, see *Les funestes effets de la vertu de la chasteté dans les prêtres, ou Mémoire de M. Blanchet, curé de Cours, près la Réole en Guyenne, avec observations médicales, suivi d'une adresse envoyée à l'Assemblée nationale* (Paris, 1791).

61. Julie Hardwick, "Seeking Separations: Gender, Marriages, and Household Economies in Early Modern France," *French Historical Studies* 21 (1998): 157–180; Alain Lottin, *La Désunion du couple sous l'ancien régime, L'exemple du Nord* (Paris, 1975); Jacqueline Musset, *Le régime des biens entre époux en droit normand du XVIe siècle à la Révolution française* (Caen, 1997); Roderick Phillips, *Family Breakdown in Late Eighteenth-Century France: Divorces in Rouen, 1792–1803* (Oxford, 1980), 4–11; Ronsin, *Contrat sentimental,* 26–37. To give one further indication of rarity: the family tribunals of seventy-eight communes across the Calvados converted only nine Old Regime separations into divorces early in the Revolution, seven of these from the city of Caen. See Appendix 1 for sources on divorce cases in the Calvados.

62. [Hennet], *Pétition à l'Assemblée nationale,* 30; Tapin, *Lettre sur le mariage,* 2–7.

63. *Réflexions d'un bon citoyen;* Charles Rousseau, *Essai sur l'éducation et l'existence civile et politique des femmes dans la constitution française* (Paris, 1790), 31; Gastrez, *Discours sur l'utilité,* 13–14; Citoyen Garnier, *Code du divorce, contenant l'explication familière des moyens et de la manière d'exécuter la Loi du Divorce, dans tous les cas où le divorce est permis, et les formules des actes relatifs à la pratique* (Paris, 1792), 18; Hennet, *Du divorce,* 88–90; [Matigny], *Traité philosophique,* 49–50, 110–13; *Il est temps de donner aux époux . . . la liberté,* 2; *Le divorce, par le meilleur ami des femmes,* 5.

64. Simon-Nicolas-Henri Linguet, *Légitimité du divorce justifiée par les Saintes Ecritures, par les Conciles, etc., aux Etats-Généraux de 1789* (Brussels, 1789); *Lettre du Marquis de C——— au comte de F———*, 14; *Le divorce ou l'art de rendre les ménages heureux*, 11–13.

65. Bouchotte, *Observations*, 7–8.

66. M. Gastrez quoted Montesquieu's passage on love from the *Esprit des Lois* at length in his 1791 work *Discours sur l'utilité du divorce*, 4–9. On Old Regime concepts of conjugal happiness, see DeJean, "Notorious Women"; Maza, *Private Lives and Public Affairs*, chap. 6; Offen, "Reclaiming the Enlightenment for Feminism," 86–88; Stewart, *Gynographs*; Traer, *Marriage and the Family*, 70–78.

67. *Loi du divorce* (n.p., n.d.), 8; *Le divorce, par le meilleur ami des femmes*, 6. Olympe de Gouges's unpublished play *La nécessité du divorce* (1790) also suggested that the possibility of divorce would cause a couple to reconcile.

68. *Appel au bon sens*; Barruel, *Lettres sur le divorce*; [Abbé Nicolas-Sylvestre Bergier], *Observations sur le divorce* (Paris, 1790); Chapt de Rastignac, *Accord*; Thiébault, *Adresse aux membres honorables*.

69. Juge de Brives, *Mariages heureux*, 23–25; Antraigues, *Observations sur le divorce*; *Lettre à Madame ———*, 24.

70. Antraigues, *Observations sur le divorce*, 23; AN DIII 361, Lettre du citoyen Matigny à l'Assemblée nationale, 15 Mar. 1792. With his petition he offered the Assembly two pamphlets entitled, *Droit essentiel de l'homme libre, négligé, et totalement oublié dans la déclaration des droits de l'homme en société à la séance du 17 avril 1789* (sic) and *Un nouveau Code civil*.

71. *Courrier de l'Hymen*, Prospectus d'un nouveau journal, nos. 1 and 2, 20 and 24 Feb. 1791; *Bureau de confiance pour les mariages, ses bases et son organisation* (n.p., March 1790).

72. [Matigny], *Traité philosophique*, 67, 80–81, 112–13.

73. Juge de Brives, *Mariages heureux*, 3, 20–24; *Du divorce, ou adresse à un grand prince*, 4–5; Rousseau, *Essai sur l'éducation*, , 8–9, 16–17.

74. AN DIII 361, Mémoire de William Williams, jurisconsulte anglais, 19 Mar. 1792.

75. Nancy F. Cott offers a useful, broad definition of feminism made up of three core components: opposition to sex hierarchy, female self-consciousness of women as a social grouping, and the presupposition that women's condition is socially constructed. See *The Grounding of Modern Feminism* (New Haven, Conn., 1987), 4–5.

76. AN DIII 361, Pétition d'Anne Catherine Waterlot Bagot à l'Assemblée nationale en faveur d'une femme délaissée depuis 12 ans par son mari, received 31 Jan. 1792; AN DIII 361, Pétition de la femme Berlin au Président de l'Assemblée nationale, 27 Sept. 1792.

77. Jeffrey Merrick, "Domestic Politics: Divorce and Despotism in Late Eighteenth-Century France," in *Past as Prologue: Essays to Celebrate the Twenty-Fifth Anniversary of ASECS*, ed. Carla Hay and Sydney Conger (New York, 1994), 373–86; Karen Offen, "Disrupting the Anglophone Narrative: How

(and Why) the Analogy of Marriage with Slavery Provided the Springboard for Women's Rights Demands in France (1640–1848)," in *Sisterhood and Slavery: Transatlantic Antislavery and Women's Rights,* ed. Kathryn Kish Sklar and Jim Stewart (New Haven, Conn., forthcoming).

78. *Etrennes nationales des Dames,* I (30 November 1789).

79. *Lettre d'une citoyenne à son amie sur les avantages que procurerait à la Nation le patriotisme des dames* (Grenoble, 1789), 7–8; Madame B―― B――, *Cahier des doléances,* 8–9; [Madame de Coicy], *Demande des femmes aux Etats-Généraux,* 1. Cf. Mary Seidman Trouille, *Sexual Politics in the Enlightenment: Women Writers Read Rousseau* (Albany, 1997); Mary Wollstonecraft, *Vindication of the Rights of Woman* (New York, 1983, orig. 1792). On Wollstonecraft and Rousseau, see Virginia Sapiro, *A Vindication of Political Virtue: The Political Theory of Mary Wollstonecraft* (Chicago, 1992).

80. Jodin, *Vues législatives,* iii–iv, 25–26, 34–44, 54–86.

81. [Cambis], *Du sort actuel,* 7–11.

82. "Avis aux mères de famille," late 1789, poster reproduced in *Révolution et les femmes,* vol. 3; [Cailly], *Griefs et plaintes,* 19–20; Cf. *Lettres d'une citoyenne à son amie.* On the concept of women's "empire," see Elizabeth Colwill, "Transforming Women's Empire: Representations of Women in French Political Culture, 1770–1807" (Ph.D. diss., State University of New York at Binghamton, 1990).

83. [Madame Fumelh], *Mémoire sur le divorce; Annales de l'éducation du sexe,* no. 1 (n.p., n.d., c. March 1790); *Remonstrances des mères et filles normandes,* 13–15; M.L.P.P.D. St. L., *Remonstrances, plaintes et doléances des dames françaises,* 4–5.

84. "Avis aux mères de familles," c. 1789, and [Olympe de Gouges], "Le bon sens du français," 7 Feb. 1792, both in *La Révolution et les femmes,* vol. 3; [Cailly], *Griefs et plaintes,* 20–25.

85. *Un mot sur le divorce,* 4–5.

86. André Burguière, "Les fondements d'une culture familiale," in *Histoire de la France. Les formes de la culture,* ed. A. Burguière (Paris, 1993), 27–118; Paul Ourliac and Jean-Louis Gazzaniga, *Histoire du droit privé français de l'An mille au Code civil* (Paris, 1985), chap. 5; Adrienne Rogers, "Women and the Law," in *French Women and the Enlightenment,* ed. Samia Spencer (Bloomington, 1984), 33–48. A multitude of factors influenced how regional differences played out in practice. As Burguière suggests, contrary to appearances, the communal marital property system could be less favorable for a woman than the dotal systems of the Midi and Normandy because it protected her dowry less (73–74).

87. [Cailly], *Griefs et plaintes,* 22–24, 39–41 and her *Ami des Enfants; Remonstrances de mères et filles normandes,* 1–10; Madame B―― B――. *Cahiers des doléances,* 9–10. Denouncing the feudal structure of marriage, Cailly quoted Art. 225 and 233 of the Coutume de Paris, making the husband "seigneur" over various forms of marital property. [Fumelh], *Mémoire sur le divorce,* 10–25.

88. *Doléances des femmes de Franche-Comté* (Besançon, 27 April 1789), p. 25, as cited by Traer, *Marriage and the Family*, 83; [Madame Bastille], *Motions adressées à l'Assemblée nationale en faveur du sexe* (Paris, 1789), 3–4.

89. *Opinion d'un citoyen sur le mariage et sur la dot* (Vienne, 1781); *Avis intéressant concernant les jolies filles à marier ou de l'abus des dots dans le mariage* (Paris, 1789); *Procès-verbal et protestations de l'Assemblée de l'Ordre le plus nombreux du Royaume* (n.p., 1789), 11–14, as cited by Traer, *Marriage and the Family*, 107–8; AN ADXVIIIc 165, Lanthenas, *Adresse présentée à l'Assemblée nationale, pour demander que l'égalité des partages entre les enfants soit rétablie par un décret constitutionnel, qu'une émancipation légale soit fixée, et que la faculté d'adopter soit rendue à ceux qui sont sans postérité* (Paris, 1790).

90. Olympe de Gouges, *Le Couvent ou les Vœux forcés* (1790); *La Nécessité du divorce* (never performed, written 1790); *Le Philosophe corrigé, ou le Cocu supposé* (1787); *L'Entrée de Dumourier à Bruxelles ou Les vivandiers* (1793). On her plays, see Gisela Thiele-Knoblach, "Préfaces" in both volumes of Olympe de Gouges, *Théâtre politique*, 2 vols. (Paris, 1991–93); Elke Harten and Hans-Christian Harten, *Femmes, culture, et Révolution* (Paris, 1989), 56–59; Verdier, "From Reform to Revolution: The Social Theater of Olympe de Gouges"; [Olympe de Gouges], "Le bon sens du français." Cf. Joan Wallach Scott, *Only Paradoxes to Offer: French Feminists and the Rights of Man* (Cambridge, Mass., 1996), chap. 2.

91. Olympe de Gouges, *Les droits de la femme*, reprinted in *Ecrits politiques, 1788–1791*, ed. Oliver Blanc (Paris, 1993), esp. 208–12.

92. Palm d'Aelders, *Adresse des citoyennes françaises à l'assemblée nationale*, reprinted in her *Appel aux françaises*, 37–40; AP 41:63–64, 1 Apr. 1792; [Cambis], *Du sort actuel*; *Pétition adressée à l'Assemblée nationale* (Paris, n.d., c. 1791).

93. "Avis aux mères de familles"; Etta Palm d'Aelders, *Discours de Madame Palm d'Aelders, hollandaise, lu à la Confédération des Amis de la Vérité* (Caen, 1791), 4.

94. Dena Goodman, "Women and the Enlightenment," in *Becoming Visible: Women in European History*, ed. Renate Bridenthal, Susan Stuard, and Merry Wiesner (Boston, 1998), 233–62.

95. *Mot sur le divorce*, 3; Juge de Brives, *Mariages heureux*, 1–4, 20–24; *Du divorce, ou adresse à un grand prince*, 15–16; *Lettre du Marquis*, 6, 14. On the revolutionary leaders' desire to win women's support, see Elyada, "Préface: La presse patriotique pour les femmes."

96. Karen Offen, "Defining Feminism: A Comparative Historical Approach," *Signs: Journal of Women in Culture and Society* 14 (1988): 119–157; Scott, *Only Paradoxes to Offer*, esp. chap. 3; Whitney Walton, *Eve's Proud Descendants: Four Women Writers and Republican Politics in Nineteenth-Century France* (Stanford, Calif., 2000).

97. Bonneville, *Nouveau code conjugal*, 6.

CHAPTER 2

1. *Courrier de l'Hymen, ou Journal des dames,* no.1, 20 Feb. 1791, and no.4, 3 Mar. 1791.

2. Gail Bossenga, "Rights and Citizens in the Old Regime," *French Historical Studies* 20 (1997): 219–43, esp. 221–22; Roger Brubaker, "The French Revolution and the Invention of Modern Citizenship," *French Politics and Society* 7 (1989): 30–49; Michael Fitzsimmons, "The National Assembly and the Invention of Citizenship," and Pierre Rétat, "The Evolution of the Citizen from the Ancien Régime to the Revolution," both in *The French Revolution and the Meaning of Citizenship,* ed. Renée Waldinger, Philip Dawson, and Isser Woloch (Westport, Conn., 1993), 29–41 and 3–15; Olivier Le Cour Grandmaison, *Les citoyennetés en Révolution (1789–1794)* (Paris, 1992); Bryan Turner, *Citizenship and Capitalism: The Debate over Reformism* (London, 1986).

3. Jacques Mulliez, "Droit et morale conjugale: Essai sur l'histoire des relations personnelles entre époux," *Revue historique* 278 (1987): 35–106, 44–46, 86; Robert Pothier, *Traité du contrat de mariage* (Paris, 1771), articles 379–83. Cf. the Napoleonic Civil Code, Articles 212, 213, *Code civil des français* in *Manuel de droit français,* ed. J.B.J. Paillet (Paris, n.d.).

4. François Bourjon, *Le droit commun de la France et la coutume de Paris réduit en principes* (1747), as cited in Mulliez, "Droit et morale conjugale," 54; Jennifer Heuer, "Foreigners, Families, and Citizens: Contradictions of National Citizenship in France, 1789–1830" (Ph.D. diss., University of Chicago, 1998); Sophie Wahnich, *L'impossible citoyen: L'étranger dans le discours de la Révolution française* (Paris, 1997).

5. See the previous chapter. Also, A. H. Huussen, "Le droit du mariage au cours de la Révolution française," *Tijdshrift voor Rechtgeschedenis* 47 (1979): 9–51, 99–127; François Olivier-Martin, *La crise du mariage dans la législation intermédiaire, 1789–1804* (Paris, 1901), 68–73; Francis Ronsin, *Le contrat sentimental: Débats sur le mariage, l'amour, le divorce de l'Ancien Régime à la Restauration* (Paris, 1990); Gérard Thibault-Laurent, *La première introduction du divorce en France sous la Révolution et l'Empire (1792–1816)* (Clermont-Ferrand, 1938), 83–92.

6. Gossin, *AP* 17: 616–18, 5 Aug. 1790. Gossin proposed an initial divorce law during the debates over judicial organization.

7. *AP* 18: 126–127, 17 Aug. 1790; M. Bouchotte, *Observations sur l'accord de la Raison et de la Religion pour le rétablissement du Divorce, l'anéantissement des Séparations entre époux, et la réformation des loix relatives à l'Adultère* (Paris, 1790), 88; *Réflexions d'un curé constitutionnel sur le décret de l'Assemblée concernant le mariage* (Paris, 1791); AN ADXVIIIb 22, 8 Apr. 1790; *AP* 38: 583, 17 Feb. 1792; *AP* 38: 466, 13 Feb. 1792; *AP* 40: 39, 16 Mar. 1792, and 40: 138, 19 Mar. 1792; *AP* 41: 63–64, 1 Apr. 1792; *AP* 48: 400, 20 Aug. 1792. Among those presented at the bar: AN DIII 361, Lettre du citoyen Matigny à l'Assemblée législative, 15 Mar. 1792 with pamphlets *Droit essentiel de l'homme libre, négligé, et totalement oublié dans la déclaration des droits de*

l'homme and *Un nouveau Code civil;* Mémoire de William Williams, jurisconsulte anglais, 19 Mar. 1792; Albert-Joseph Hennet, *Du divorce* (Paris, 1789);
James F. Traer, *Marriage and the Family in Eighteenth-Century France* (Ithaca,
1980), 111–12.

8. See AN DIII 361 for multiple divorce petitions. Pétition du Sieur Benoît-
LaMothe à l'Assemblée nationale, Nov. 1791, and Rapport du Comité des pétitions au Comité du législation; Pétition de 40 citoyens aux citoyens représentants, 22 June 1792; Pétition du Sieur Grémion, *AP* 48: 400, 20 Aug. 1792. Cf.
Olivier-Martin, *Crise du mariage,* 69–74, 221–225; Ronsin, *Contrat sentimental,* 94–103; Thibault-Laurent, *Première introduction du divorce,* 87–93.

9. Geoffrey Adams, *The Huguenots and French Opinion, 1685–1787: The
Enlightenment Debate on Toleration* (Waterloo, Can., 1991), part 3. Jews could
divorce more easily in Old Regime France because of their juridical autonomy,
but their civil status remained shakily subject to the French monarachy's definition of this autonomy. The 1787 edict did not apply to Jewish marriage.

10. *AP* 17: 50, 12 July 1790. Marvin Carlson, *The Theater of the French
Revolution* (Ithaca, N.Y., 1966), 22–30; Traer, *Marriage and the Family,* 84–88.
On the rights of actors and religious minorities, see Lynn Hunt, *The French
Revolution and Human Rights* (Boston, 1996), 20–23, 84–101.

11. Carlson, *Theater,* 80.

12. Durand de Maillane initially presented this report in Nov. 1790, and
again in May 1791: *Rapport sur le projet de décret des comités ecclésiastique et
de Constitution, concernant les empêchements, les dispenses, et la forme des
mariages* (Paris, 1790). Among his opponents, see Abbé Barruel, *Les vrais
principes sur le mariage opposés au rapport de M. Durand de Maillane* (Paris,
1790); *Lettre à Monsieur Durand de Maillane sur le rapport . . . concernant le
mariage* (Paris, 1791); *Ouvrez encore les yeux sur les nouvelles erreurs du
Comité ecclésiastique* (Paris, n.d., c. 1791); Abbé Philippe Samary, *Examen du
rapport sur le projet de décret concernant les mariages* (Paris, n.d., c. 1791).

13. Ronsin, *Contrat sentimental,* 89–93; Treilhard, *AP,* 26: 160, 17 May 1791;
Lettre des officiers municipaux de Strasbourg à l'Assemblée, *AP* 39: 529, 10 Mar.
1792; Courtot, *AP* 42: 167–168, 19 April 1792; Bailly, *AP* 25: 720, 10 May 1791,
and *AP* 26: 77–78, 14 May 1791; Mulliez, "Droit et morale conjugale," 69–70.

14. Lanjuinais, *AP* 26: 159–60, 17 May 1791; Durand de Maillane, *AP* 26:
166–72, 17 May 1791. Constitution de 1791, Titre II, Article 7: "La loi ne con-
sidère le mariage que comme contrat civil." *Les constitutions de la France depuis
1789,* ed. Jacques Godechot (Paris, 1970), 38.

15. Jules Basdevant, *Des rapports de l'église et de l'état dans la législation
du mariage du Concile de Trente au Code civil* (Paris, 1900); Traer, *Marriage and
the Family,* chap. 1.

16. Durand de Maillane, *AP* 26: 166–72, 17 May 1791, *Rapport sur le projet
de décret,* quote 169. In a second speech, Durand de Maillane continued to address the relative roles of Church and State: *AP* 26: 175–86, 17 Apr. 1791, *Suite
et défense du rapport sur les empêchements, les dispenses, et la forme des
mariages,* 180.

17. Muraire, *AP*, 38: 531–37, 15 Feb. 1792, *Rapport sur le mode à employer pour constater les naissances, mariages et décès.* Gohier, *AP* 45: 388, 19 June 1792.

18. Muraire, *AP*, 38: 531–33, 15 Feb. 1792.

19. Diderot, "Célibat" in *Encylopédie, ou dictionnaire raisonné des sciences, des arts et des métiers* (1751–72), ARTFL *Encyclopédie* Project; Carol Blum, *Strength in Numbers: Population, Reproduction, and Power in Eighteenth-Century France* (Baltimore, 2002); Jacqueline Hecht, "Célibat, stratégies familiales et essor du capitalisme au XVIIIe siècle: réalités et représentations," in *Ménages, familles, parentèles et solidarités dans les populations méditerranéennes* (Paris, 1996), 257–84; Mulliez, "Droit et morale conjugale," 48–55; Jean-Claude Perrot, "Les économistes, les philosophes et la population," in *Histoire de la population française*, vol. 2, *De la Renaissance à 1789*, ed. Jacques Dupâquier (Paris, 1988), 499–551. Late Old Regime proponents of divorce often lauded its reproductive ramifications: eg. Cerfvol, *Mémoire sur la population* (London, 1768); [Philibert], *Cri d'un honnête homme* (Paris, 1769).

20. Simon Schama, *Citizens: A Chronicle of the French Revolution* (New York, 1989), 522; Jacques Godechot, *Les Institutions de la France sous la Révolution et l'Empire* (Paris, 1968), 167; Slogan quoted in Marcel Reinhard, André Armengaud, and Jacques Dupâquier, *Histoire générale de la population mondiale* (Paris, 1968), 289; Jacques Gélis, "L'Enfant et l'évolution de la conception de la vie sous la Révolution," in *Enfant*, 69–77; Blum, *Strength in Numbers*, chap. 7.

21. *Plaintes et doléances de M. l'abbé T——, Ch. du. C. de B., concernant le célibat ecclésiastique, adressées à MM. les Députés composant l'assemblée des Etats-Généraux* (n.p., 1789), 29–32; *Observations sur le célibat des prêtres, la perpétuité des vœux monastiques, et le sort qu'on veut faire aux curés* (Paris, 1789), 62–85; *Le mariage des prêtres* (Paris, 1790), 97–99; *Projet de loi sur le clergé et utilité du mariage des prêtres* (n.p., n.d., c. 1790), 8–15; *Voltaire sorcier, ou Accomplissements de la prophétie du mariage des prêtres, et de la suppression des moines* (n.p., 1791), 1–2; *Du mariage des ministres de la religion* (Paris, n.d.), 8–12; Etienne Bernet, *Réclamation du droit le plus cher à l'homme, adressée à l'Assemblée nationale* (Paris, 1791), 4–7. On the concept of civil death seen as the opposite of citizenship, see Heuer, "Foreigners, Families, and Citizens," 24–25, and chap. 3.

22. Vergniaud, *AP* 41: 419, 10 Apr. 1792.

23. Quote from Gohier, *AP* 45: 389, 19 June 1792; Vergniaud, *AP* 41: 418–22, 10 Apr. 1792.

24. Vergniaud, *AP* 41: 418–22, 10 Apr. 1792; Adam, *AP* 45: 380, 19 June 1792. On the "transfer of sacrality" from religion to the nation and society, see Mona Ozouf, *Festivals of the French Revolution*, trans. Alan Sheridan (Cambridge, Mass., 1988, orig. ed. 1976).

25. Gohier, *AP* 45: 390, 19 June 1792.

26. Traer, *Marriage and the Family*, chap. 3; Nicolas de Bonneville, *Nouveau code conjugal, établi sur les bases de la Constitution, et d'après les principes et*

les considérations de la loi déja faite et sanctionée, qui a préparé et ordonné ce nouveau code (Paris, 1792). Bonneville produced the pamphlet in response to Muraire's proposal for a secular état civil and the law of 20 Sept. 1792 outlining the basic function of public officials in overseeing civil marriages.

27. Gohier, *AP* 45: 389, 19 June 1792; Jollivet, *AP* 41: 422–24, 432–47, quote 436, 10 Apr. 1792, *Projet de décret sur le mode de constater les naissances, mariages et décès*. As Irène Théry notes, the deputies debated and abandoned numerous legal definitions of marriage; Jollivet's was one of seven proposed: *Le démariage: Justice et vie privée* (Paris, 1993), 48–53.

28. Théry, *Démariage*, 56–59; Pastoret, *AP* 45: 384–85, 19 June 1792; Oudot, *AP* 45: 556–61, 25 June 1792; Lemontey, *AP* 41: 417, 7 Apr. 1792.

29. François de Neufchâteau, *AP* 40: 71, 17 Mar. 1792. See also the warnings of Guadet, *AP* 40: 74–75, 17 Mar. 1792; Courtot, *AP* 42: 167–68, 19 Apr. 1792. For attempts to isolate the état civil from other reform issues, see Adam, *AP* 42: 168–69, 19 Apr. 1792 and *AP* 45: 379–82, 19 June 1792; Vergniaud, *AP* 41: 421, 7 Apr. 1792; Vergniaud and Beugnot, *AP* 45: 651, 28 June 1792. Jean-Louis Halpérin, *L'impossible Code civil* (Paris, 1994), 100–101.

30. See Chapter 4. For pamphlets, see esp. AN ADXVIIIc 164 and AN ADXVIIIc 165. For handwritten petitions, see esp. AN DIII 382. On fatherhood, see Jacques Mulliez, "La volonté d'un homme," in *Histoire des pères et de la paternité*, ed. Jean Delumeau and Daniel Roche (Paris, 1990), 279–312.

31. *AP* 24: 505–515, 2 Apr. 1791; *AP* 24: 562–77, 5 Apr. 1791. Lynn Hunt, *The Family Romance of the French Revolution* (Berkeley, 1992), chap. 2.

32. For debate by mulitiple deputies, see *AP* 46: 213–17, 7 July 1792; *AP* 48: 288, 16 Aug. 1792. Lasource, *AP* 46: 214 and 216, 7 July 1792; Gohier, *AP* 45: 677–79, 29 June 1792.

33. *AP* 48: 564–65, 21 Aug. 1792; *AP* 49: 55, 28 Aug. 1792, and 49: 481–82, 8 Sep. 1792; Loi du 20 septembre 1792, J. B. Duvergier, *Collection complète des lois, ordonnances, réglemens*, 30 vols. (Paris, 1834–38) (hereafter Duvergier), 4: 482–88. On the use of entailment as family strategy, see David Garrioch, *The Formation of the Parisian Bourgeoisie, 1690–1830* (Cambridge, Mass., 1996), 71–73, 165–66.

34. Halpérin, *Impossible Code civil*, 104–7. He also notes that many of the more conservative deputies deserted the Assembly by Aug.–Sept. 1792.

35. On 26 Aug. 1792 the legislature decreed the deportation of refractory clergy, and on 3 Sept. 1792 demanded a new oath to the nation, liberty, and equality from all clergy. On 25 Aug. 1792, it stepped up its attack on feudalism, abolishing seigneurial dues without reimbursement. On kingship and paternal authority, see Hunt, *Family Romance*, chap. 2.

36. Loi du 20 septembre 1792, Duvergier, 4: 477–82. See Chapter 3 for a fuller explanation of the law and its use.

37. Aubert-Dubayet and Cambon, *AP* 49: 117–18, 30 Aug. 1792. Aubert-Dubayet's speech followed on the heels of a 20 Aug. 1792 petition from Citoyen Grémion demanding divorce and provoking the Committee on Petitions to demand the law. *AP* 48: 400, 20 Aug. 1792; Ronsin, *Contrat sentimental*, 103–4.

38. Marcel Garaud and Romuald Szramkiewicz, *La Révolution française et la famille* (Paris, 1978), 67–78; Halpérin, *Impossible Code civil*, 102–7; Huussen, "Droit du mariage," 45–51; Olivier-Martin, *Crise du mariage*, 68–78; Ronsin, *Contrat sentimental*, 103–9; Thibault-Laurent, *Première introduction du divorce*, 86–110; Traer, *Marriage and the Family*, 118–22. These authors give varying weight to public opinion, the ideology of liberty, and the juridical significance of contract theory.

39. Mulliez, "Droit et morale conjugale," 78–83.

40. Cambon, *AP* 49: 118, 30 Aug. 1792; Halpérin, *Impossible Code civil*, 106; Sédillez, *AP* 49: 609–12, 13 Sept. 1792; Mademoiselle Jodin, *Vues législatives pour les femmes, adressées à l'Assemblée nationale, par Mademoiselle Jodin, fille d'un citoyen de Génève* (Angers, 1790), iii–iv, 34–44, 54–86; Bibliothèque municipale de Poitiers S22, Elisabeth-Bonaventure Lafaurie, *Discours sur l'état de nullité dans lequel on tient les femmes, relativement à la Politique*, 16 May 1791 (Dax, 1791); *Lettre d'une dame aux dames de son département* (n.p., n.d., c. 1790).

41. Robin, *AP* 49: 432–33, 7 Sept. 1792; Sédillez, *AP* 49: 610, 13 Sep. 1792.

42. On the marital property debates, see Jacqueline Brisset, *L'adoption de la communauté comme régime légal dans le code civil* (Paris, 1967), 23–40; Halpérin, *Impossible Code civil*, 123–25, 134; Bernard Schnapper, "Liberté, Egalité, Autorité: La famille devant les assemblées révolutionnaires (1790–1800)," in *Enfant*, 325–40, and "L'autorité domestique et les hommes politiques de la Révolution," in *FLE*, 221–33. See the "Premier projet du Code civil," in P. A. Fenet, ed. *Recueil complet des travaux préparatoires du Code civil*, 15 vols. (Paris, 1936) (hereafter Fenet), 1: 17–98, Livre I, Titres II and III, esp. III, Arts. 8, 10, 11 (pp. 18–20).

43. Cambacérès, *Rapport fait à la Convention nationale sur le premier projet de Code civil*, 9 Aug. 1793, in Fenet, 1: 1–16, quote 4–5; Bar, *AP* 70: 636–40, 9 Aug. 1793.

44. *AP* 72: 672–74, 23 Aug. 1793.

45. Lacroix [Delacroix], Danton, Garnier, Desmoulins, Couthon, *AP* 72: 672–74, 23 Aug. 1793; Pons de Verdun, Lecointe-Puyraveau, *AP* 77: 679–80, 6 brumaire an II (27 Oct. 1793). On male revolutionaries' anxiety about female religiosity, see Suzanne Desan, "The Family as a Cultural Battleground: Religion vs. Republic under the Terror," in *The French Revolution and the Creation of Modern Poltical Culture*, vol. 4, *The Terror*, ed. Keith Michael Baker (Oxford, 1994), 177–93; Olwen Hufton, *Women and the Limits of Citizenship in the French Revolution* (Toronto, 1992), chap. 3.

46. Within the same week, the Convention voted to close the women's clubs, to give women in principle an equal right to manage community property, and to grant daughters as well as sons an equal share in inheritance. The timing of these three votes highlights the complexity of the gender politics of the Revolution and undercuts any notion of a unified creation of domesticity with women dependent on men in the private sphere. Different logics governed the three votes. For interpretations setting the club closings within Parisian politics,

see Dominique Godineau, *The Women of Paris and Their French Revolution*, trans. Katherine Streip (Berkeley, 1998, orig. ed., 1988), 158–74; Elizabeth Everton, "A Paradox in Women's Activity: Female Action and the Closing of Women's Clubs in the Terror" (Senior Thesis, University of Chicago, 2002). For the view that closing the clubs played a crucial role in forging domesticity and excluding women from politics, see Joan B. Landes, *Women and the Public Sphere in the Age of the French Revolution* (Ithaca, N.Y., 1988), 142–48. For the Convention debates in English, see Darline Gay Levy, Harriet Branson Applewhite, and Mary Durham Johnson, eds., *Women in Revolutionary Paris, 1789–1795* (Urbana, Ill., 1979), 213–17. For the laws of 9 brumaire an II (30 Oct. 1793) (club-closing) and 5 brumaire an II (26 Oct. 1793) (egalitarian inheritance), see Duvergier 6: 266 and 256–57. See Chapter 4 for women's use of this inheritance law and the law of 17 nivôse an II (6 Jan. 1794) that clarified its stipulations about egalitarian inheritance.

47. *AP* 77: 679–80, 6 brumaire an II (27 Oct. 1793). Halpérin, *Impossible Code civil*, 134–41. The second Civil Code, proposed on 23 fructidor an II (9 Sept. 1794), also stipulated equal control over communal goods by husband and wife.

48. In practice, over the course of the revolutionary and Napoleonic period, an increasing number of couples in Normandy and the Midi chose the communal marital property system or separation of goods within marriage, granting women more control over their own property. See Chapter 4. Also, Charles Alline, *De l'ancien régime matrimonial normand et de sa survivance dans la pratique notariale sous le droit intermédiare et sous le Code civil* (Thèse de droit, Université de Caen, 1908), 94–193; Margaret Darrow, *Revolution in the House: Family, Class, and Inheritance in Southern France, 1775–1825* (Princeton, N.J., 1989), 247. On 1985, see Hugues Fulchiron, "La femme, mère et épouse dans le droit révolutionnaire," in *Les Femmes et la Révolution française*, ed. Marie-France Brive, 3 vols. (Toulouse, 1989), 1: 377–86, 381.

49. Gohier, *AP* 45: 390–92, 19 June 1792.

50. Ibid.

51. David Denby, *Sentimental Narrative and the Social Order in France, 1760–1820* (Cambridge, Eng., and New York, 1994); Joan DeJean, "Notorious Women: Marriage and the Novel in Crisis in France (1690–1715)," *Yale Journal of Criticism* 4 (1991): 67–85; Sarah Maza, *Private Lives and Public Affairs: The Causes Célèbres of Prerevolutionary France* (Berkeley, 1993), chap. 6; Joan Hinde Stewart, *Gynographs: French Novels by Women of the Late Eighteenth Century* (Lincoln, Neb., 1993).

52. Traer, *Marriage and the Family*, 15–21, 192–97. On the modern family thesis, see Sarah Maza, "Only Connect: Family Values in the Age of Sentiment: Introduction," *Eighteenth-Century Studies* 30 (1997): 207–212; Jeffrey R. Watt, *The Making of Modern Marriage: Matrimonial Control and the Rise of Sentiment in Neuchâtel, 1550–1800* (Ithaca, N.Y., 1992), 1–18.

53. *Lettre à Madame —— sur le divorce* (n.p., 1790), 24; Letter from M. J. Lequinio, député de Morbihan in *Moniteur* 48: 17 Feb. 1792. Cf. William Sewell, "Le citoyen/la citoyenne: Activity, Passivity, and the Revolutionary Concept of

Citizenship," in *The French Revolution and the Creation of Modern Political Culture*, vol. 2., *The Political Culture of the French Revolution*, ed. Colin Lucas (Oxford, 1988), 2: 105–123.

54. Comte d'Antraigues, *Observations sur le divorce* (Paris, 1789), 33; *Influence des femmes dans l'ordre civil et politique* (Eleutheropolis, 1789), 3.

55. Madelyn Gutwirth, *The Twilight of the Goddesses: Women and Representation in the French Revolutionary Era* (New Brunswick, N.J., 1992), chaps. 3 and 4; Elke Harten and Hans-Christian Harten, *Femmes, culture et Révolution*, trans. Bella Chabot et al. (Paris, 1989), 37–46 and chap. 5; Hunt, *Family Romance*, chaps. 4 and 6; Landes, *Women and the Public Sphere*, 129–38. More recently, Lynn Hunt has questioned the importance of republican motherhood in the revolutionary imagination: "Male Virtue and Republican Motherhood," in *The French Revolution and the Creation of Modern Poltical Culture*, 4: 195–208.

56. Jean-Louis Carra, "Progrès de l'esprit public chez le beau sexe," in his *Annales patriotiques et littéraires de la France*, no. 736, 8 Oct. 1791.

57. Ibid.

58. *Lettre d'une dame;* Lafaurie, *Discours sur l'état de nullité*, 9–10. Cf. Olympe de Gouges, *Les droits de la femme*, reprinted in *Ecrits politiques, 1788–1791*, ed. Oliver Blanc (Paris, 1993), and in English in *Women in Revolutionary Paris*, ed. Levy et al., 87–96; Jodin, *Vues législatives.*

59. Etta Palm d'Aelders, *Lettre d'une amie de la vérité, Etta Palm, née d'Aelders, hollandaise, sur les démarches des ennemis extérieurs et intérieurs de la France; suivie d'une adresse à toutes les citoyennes patriotes, et d'une motion à leur proposer pour l'assemblée nationale, lue à l'assemblée fédérative des amis de la vérité, le 23 mars 1791*, 25; *Discours sur l'injustice des lois en faveur des hommes, au dépend des femmes*, 6–7; *Adresse de la Société patriotique et de bienfaisance des Amies de la Vérité aux quarante-huit Section* [sic], *rédigée par Etta Palm, née d'Aelders*, 42–43. All of these texts are printed together in her *Appel aux françaises sur la régénération des mœurs et nécessité de l'influence des femmes dans un gouvernement libre* (Paris, n.d.).

60. "Régénération," *Encyclopédie*, vol. 13, 1765, pp. 912–13, as cited in Antoine de Baecque, *The Body Politic: Corporeal Metaphor in Revolutionary France*, trans. Charlotte Mandell (Stanford, Calif., 1997, orig. 1993), 132.

61. Ibid., chap. 3.; Rabaut Saint-Etienne, Speech to the National Assembly, 18 Aug. 1789, as cited in de Baecque, *Body Politic*, 152.

62. Discours de Monestier du Puy-de-Dôme, as quoted in Marc de Villiers, *Histoire des clubs de femmes et légions d'Amazones* (Paris, 1910), 159; Lettre de Catherine Larrieu, née Bordeu, présidente de la Société des Amies de la Constitution à Pau, 12 Aug. 1791, as quoted in Abbé Jean-Baptiste Laborde, *La Société des Amies de la Constitution à Pau* (Pau, 1911), 42.

63. Nicole Villiers, *Barra, ou la Mère républicaine* (an II [1793–94]), in Harten and Harten, *Femmes, culture et Révolution*, 372–429. Archives municipales de (hereafter AM) Bordeaux 174, Projet d'adresse aux épouses et mères de famille par C. Morin, 10 Oct. 1791; Discours du citoyen Moisard, 10 Nov. 1793,

as quoted in Camille Bloch, "Les femmes d'Orléans pendant la Révolution," *La Révolution française* 43 (1902): 49–67, esp. 61.

64. Suzanne Desan, " 'Constitutional Amazons': Jacobin Women's Clubs in the French Revolution," in *Re-Creating Authority in Revolutionary France*, ed. Bryant T. Ragan and Elizabeth Williams (New Brunswick, N.J., 1992), 11–35. For examples of women's role with regard to schools, see Geneviève Langeron, "La Club des femmes de Dijon pendant la Révolution," *La Révolution en Côte-d'Or* 5–7 (1929): 5–71, esp. 47–49; Henriette Perrin, "Le Club de femmes de Besançon," *Annales révolutionnaires* 9 (1917): 629–53 and 10 (1918): 37–63, 505–32, 645–72, esp. 10: 514–19. On pedagogical festivals, see *Journal de Provence*, July 1791, 28: 279, as cited by Yvonne Knibiehler, "Femmes de Provence en Révolution," in *Femmes et la Révolution* , ed. Brive, 1: 149–55, 150; Villiers, *Histoire des clubs de femmes*, 139; Péricaud, *Tablettes chronologiques*, 22 June 1791, as quoted in Albert Metzger and Joseph Vaesen, *Lyon en 1791*, vol. 4 of *Bibliothèque lyonnaise: Révolution française*, 11 vols. (Lyon: 1882–88), 4: 53; *Journal de Lyon*, 9 Jan. 1793.

65. *Discours fait et prononcé par Françoise Sanson, Veuve Duval, dans la séance publique des Amis de la Constitution, le 15 avril: Avis aux dames portées pour la Contre-Révolution* (Caen, n.d.), 7.

66. Pierre Trahard, *La sensibilité révolutionnaire (1789–1794)* (Paris, 1936), 199; "Registre de la société des amies des vrais amis de la Constitution à Ruffec," ed. M. Chauvet, *Révolution française* 46 (1904): 247–78, 248, 258–59 [also published with membership list in *Bulletin historique et philologique* 3 and 4 (1902): 528–30]; "Account of a Session of Revolutionary Republican Women," in *Women in Revolutionary Paris*, ed. Levy et al., 166–71, p. 170; Villiers, *Histoire des clubs de femmes*, 124, 141–42 ("Arrêté des Dames et Demoiselles patriotes de Nancy"); "Chanson de Citoyenne Allain, femme Labertinière, aux défenseurs de la patrie, au nom des femmes," and A. Paséault, "Citoyens législateurs, ma lettre cachetée, mon coeur m'a dicté ces couplets, je me suis permis de vous les présenter," both in Harten and Harten, *Femmes, culture, et Révolution*, 289–90, 306–7. On song culture and fraternity, see Laura Mason, *Singing the French Revolution: Popular Culture and Politics, 1787–1799* (Ithaca, N.Y., 1996), 106–14.

67. *Adresse au beau sexe, rélativement à la Révolution présente, par M.L.C.V.D.V.* (n.p., 1790); Discours de Grosjean à la Société populaire de Baume, 20 Oct. 1791, as quoted in Perrin, "Femmes de Besançon," 9: 640–41.

68. Anne Vila, *Enlightenment and Pathology: Sensibility in the Literature and Medicine of Eighteenth-Century France* (Baltimore, 1998), chap. 7; Antoine de Baecque, "The Citizen in Caricature: Past and Present," in *The French Revolution and the Meaning of Citizenship*, ed. Waldinger et al., 59–80.

69. On stoicism, see Dorinda Outram, *The Body and the French Revolution* (New Haven, Conn., 1989), chaps. 5 and 6. Outram exaggerates the extent to which the drive for stoicism was pitted against sensibilité in a dichotomy of male stoicism versus female sensibilité. On virile fraternity, see De Baecque, *Body Politic*, 140–46; Marcel David, *Fraternité et Révolution française* (Paris,

1987); Hunt, *Family Romance*, chap. 3, esp. 67–70; Jacques-Louis Ménétra, *Journal of My Life*, ed. Daniel Roche (New York, 1986); Albert Soboul, *The Sans-Culottes*, trans. Rémy Inglis Hall (Princeton, N.J., 1980), 144–62.

70. Philippe Contamine, "Mourir pour la patrie," in *Les lieux de mémoire*, Part 2, *La nation*, ed. Pierre Nora, 3 vols. (Paris, 1986), 3: 11–43, 36; *Moyens de rendre le clergé citoyen, ou le Mariage des prêtres* (N.p., n.d., c. 1790–91), 14.

71. Elizabeth Colwill, "Pass as a Woman, Act like a Man: Marie-Antoinette as Tribade in the Pornography of the French Revolution," in *Homosexuality in Modern France*, ed. Jeffrey Merrick and Bryant T. Ragan (New York, 1996), 54–79, 63; Lynn Hunt, "Pornography and the French Revolution," in *The Invention of Pornography: Obscenity and the Origins of Modernity, 1500–1800* (New York, 1993), 301–339.

72. Cited in Trahard, *Sensibilité révolutionnaire*, 125. Although the Constituent Assembly decriminalized sodomy by omitting it from its 1791 penal code, the revolutionary era did not valorize homosexuality. See Michael David Sibalis, "The Regulation of Male Homosexuality in Revolutionary and Napoleonic France, 1789–1815," in *Homosexuality*, ed. Merrick and Ragan, 80–101.

73. Ozouf, *Festivals and the French Revolution*, 187–95, 179–80; Michel Vovelle, *Les métamorphoses de la fête en Provence de 1750 à 1820* (Paris, 1976), 194–206.

74. Gohier, *AP* 45: 390, 19 June 1792; Bonneville, *Nouveau code conjugal*, 30–32; Pierre LeNoble, *Projet de loi pour les mariages, présenté à l'Assemblée nationale* (Paris, 1792), 47–49; Jacques Piron, *Invocation, hymne et autres exercises pour honorer l'Etre suprême et plan de fêtes à l'amour et à la tendresse conjugale, présentés à la Convention nationale* (n.p., n.d.), as cited in Traer, *Marriage and the Family*, 100–101; Ozouf, *Festivals and the French Revolution*, 106–110; Robespierre, *AP* 90: 132–41, 18 floréal an II (7 May 1794); François-Antoine Boissy d'Anglas, *Essai sur les fêtes nationales, suivi de quelques idées sur les arts et sur la nécessité de les encourager* (Paris, an II [1793–94]), 77–80.

75. *AP* 86: 621–22, 28 ventôse an II (18 Mar. 1794); *AP* 87: 373, 6 germinal an II (26 Mar. 1794).

76. Lettre des Amies de la Constitution aux sociétés patriotiques des femmes, *Journal patriotique de la Côte-d'Or*, 20 Sept. 1791; Bibliothèque municipale de Dijon, Fonds Juigné, no. 58, recueil 112, P. Baillot, "Chant de la Côte-d'Or pendant la guerre de la liberté"; *Vedette*, 24 July 1792, as cited in Perrin, "Femmes de Besançon," 9: 641–42. Cf. a very similar letter from "Brutus" to women, printed in the *Vedette*, 13 Jan. 1792 (AD Doubs L2877). Cf. also the women of Bordeaux as they promise to hold returning patriots close to their hearts: AM Bordeaux, I78, Lettre des Amies de la Liberté et de l'Egalité aux Surveillants, 9 Nov. 1792. Joan B. Landes has suggested that revolutionary nationalism for men was rooted in their identifying the nation as female; love of woman blended with love of the nation: *Visualizing the Nation: Gender, Representation, and Revolution in Eighteenth-Century France* (Ithaca, N.Y., 2001), 135–168.

77. Dominique Godineau, "Masculine and Feminine Political Practice during the French Revolution, 1793–Year III," in *Women and Politics in the Age of the Democratic Revolution*, ed. Harriet B. Applewhite and Darline G. Levy (Ann Arbor, 1990), 61–80.

78. *Révolutions de Paris*, 16–23 Feb. 1793, Réponse de la citoyenne Blandin-Desmoulins de Dijon au citoyen Prudhomme, 10 Feb. 1793.

79. AD Doubs L2879, *Vedette*, 7 Aug. 1793; Villiers, *Histoire des clubs de femmes*, 111, 149, 188–89, 203–4; Discours des citoyennes d'Avallon, armées de piques, aux Amis de la Constitution, prononcé par Madame Peutat, Spring 1791, reprinted in *Les Femmes dans la Révolution*, 3 vols. (Paris, 1982), vol. 1. Darline G. Levy and Harriet B. Applewhite, "Women, Radicalization, and the Fall of the French Monarchy," in *Women and Politics*, ed. Applewhite and Levy, 81–107.

80. Citoyenne Desmoulins, *L'héroïne républicaine* (Paris, an II [1793–94]), reprinted in Harten and Harten, *Femmes, culture et Révolution*, 338–71, 362, 369.

81. Thomas Crow, *Emulation: Making Artists for Revolutionary France* (New Haven, Conn., 1994), chaps. 6 and 7; Alex Potts, "Beautiful Bodies and Dying Heroes: Images of Ideal Manhood in the French Revolution," *History Workshop* 30 (1990): 1–21; Lynn Hunt, *Politics, Culture, and Class in the French Revolution* (Berkeley, 1984), chap. 3.

82. Charles Rousseau, *Essai sur l'éducation et l'existence civile et politique des femmes dans la constitution française* (Paris, 1790), 23.

83. On transparency, see Hunt, *Politics, Culture, and Class*, 44–46; Jean Starobinski, *Jean-Jacques Rousseau: La Transparence et l'obstacle* (Paris, 1957). On male sensibilité, see Anne Vincent-Buffault, *Histoire des larmes, XVIIIe–XIXe siècles* (Paris, 1986), chap. 5; Hunt, *Family Romance*, chap. 2.

84. Carla Hesse, "La Preuve par lettre: Pratiques juridiques au tribunal révolutionnaire de Paris (1793–1794)," *Annales: Histoire. Sciences sociales* 51 (1996): 629–42; William Reddy, *The Navigation of Feeling: A Framework for the History of the Emotions* (New York, 2001), 190–99. Cf. Sarah Knott, "Sensibility and the American War for Independence," *American Historical Review* (forthcoming, 2004).

85. Brissot as quoted in Reddy, *Navigation of Feeling*, 187; Denby, *Sentimental Narrative*, 139–45.

86. Oudot, *AP* 45: 559, 28 June 1792; [Madame de Cambis], *Du sort actuel des femmes* (Paris, n.d., c. Sept. 1791), 6.

87. *Les funestes effets de la vertu de la chasteté dans les prêtres, ou Mémoire de M. Blanchet, curé de Cours, près la Réole en Guyenne, avec observations médicales, suivi d'une adresse envoyée à l'Assemblée nationale* (Paris, 1791), 7; *Motion faite dans l'Assemblée générale du district de Saint-Etienne-du-Mont, pour le mariage des Prêtres* (Paris, 1789), 6 and 12; *Plaintes et doléances de M. l'Abbé T——*, 29.

88. [Hubert de Matigny], *Traité philosophique, théologique, et politique de la loi du divorce, demandée aux Etats-généraux par S.A.S. Mrgr. Louis-*

Philippe-Joseph d'Orléans, prince du Sang (n.p., June 1789), 79–81; *Le divorce, par le meilleur ami des femmes, suivi d'une adresse au clergé* (Paris, 1790), 7; *L'homme mal marié, ou Questions à l'auteur du Divorce* (Paris, n.d, c. 1789–90), esp. 6–7; Rousseau, *Essai sur l'éducation,* 23. On paternity, see Hunt, *Family Romance;* Mulliez, "La volonté d'un homme."

89. Etienne Géry Lenglet, *Essai sur la législation du mariage* (Paris, 1792), 5–8.

90. *Histoire de l'établissement du célibat ecclésiastique* (n.p., 1790), 51–53.

91. Dominique Lacombe, curé constitutionnel de la paroisse Saint Paul de Bordeaux, *Discours à l'occasion de la loi qui permet le divorce, prononcé dans l'église de Saint Paul* (Bordeaux, 1793), 24–25. For other divorce pamphleteers who stressed woman's sacrifice, charm, and devotion, see Chapter 1.

92. Plaisant de La Houssaye, *Déclaration des droits des amants* in *La Constitution des Amours* (Paris, 1793), as quoted by Harten and Harten, *Femmes, culture et Révolution,* 165.

93. Lequinio, *Les préjugés détruits* (Paris, 1792), 143–54.

94. Etta Palm d'Aelders, *Discours lu à la Confédération des Amis de la Vérité* (Caen, 1791), 3–4; *Adresse de la société patriotique et de bienfasiance,* 42 in her *Appel aux françaises; Lettre d'une citoyenne à son amie sur les avantages que procurerait à la Nation le Patriotisme des Dames* (Grenoble, 1789), 7–8; [Cambis], *Du sort actuel,* 7–11.

95. *Révolutions de Paris,* 16–23 Feb. 1793, Réponse de la citoyenne Blandin-Desmoulins de Dijon au citoyen Prudhomme, 10 Feb. 1793; "Registre de la société des amies . . . à Ruffec," ed. M. Chauvet, 258.

96. AM Bordeaux I78, Discours de Mlle. Dorbe à la Société des amies de la Constitution pour l'anniversaire du grand homme Mirabeau, 10 Apr. 1792; Lettre de la citoyenne Maugras, c. Mar. 1793, as quoted in Perrin, "Femmes de Besançon," 10: 42–43.

97. Hunt, *Family Romance,* chap. 4; Dorinda Outram, "'Le Langage mâle de la vertu': Women and the Discourse of the French Revolution," in *The Social History of Language,* ed. Peter Burke and Roy Porter (Cambridge, Eng., 1987), 120–35, esp. 124–26; Maza, *Private Lives and Public Affairs,* 283–86. Cf. [Matigny], *Traité philosophique,* 114–29.

98. Gohier, *AP,* 45: 390, 19 June 1792. On tensions within sexualized imagery, see Gutwirth, *Twilight of the Goddesses,* chaps. 6 and 9.

99. AD Doubs L2880, *Vedette,* 4 Jan. 1793; Desan, "'Constitutional Amazons.'"

100. Simon-Nicolas-Henri Linguet, *Légitimité du divorce justifiée par les Saintes Ecritures, par les Conciles, . . . aux Etats-Généraux de 1789* (Brussels, 1789), 37–40;*Lettre à Madame,* 20–21. For a contrast, see Citoyen Garnier, *Code du divorce, contenant l'explication familière des moyens et de la manière d'exécuter la Loi du Divorce, dans tous les cas où le divorce est permis, et les formules des actes relatifs à la pratique du divorce* (Paris, 1792).

101. On the specific politics of women's clubs and the nonjuring clergy, see Desan, "'Constitutional Amazons,'" 15–19; Langeron, "Femmes de Dijon,"

8–16, 41–42; Perrin, "Femmes de Besançon." On male revolutionaries' need for women's allegiance, see Hufton, *Women and the Limits of Citizenship*, chaps. 2–4; Desan, "The Family as Cultural Battleground." On women and the oath, see Timothy Tackett, *Religion, Revolution, and Regional Culture in Eighteenth-Century France: The Ecclesiastical Oath of 1791* (Princeton, 1986), 172–77; and "Women and Men in Counterrevolution: The Sommières Riot of 1791," *Journal of Modern History* 59 (1987): 680–704.

102. Godineau, *Women of Paris*, 97–118; Ouzi Elyada, "Préface: La presse patriotique pour les femmes du peuple," in his edition of *"Lettres bougrement patriotique de la Mère Duchêne," suivi du "Journal des Femmes"* (Paris, 1989), 5–14.

103. *Cinquième lettre bougrement patriotique de la Mère Duchêne, où elle félicite les dames Françaises sur leur amour de la patrie, où elle parle de leur influence sur la révolution* (1791).

104. AM Bordeaux I78, Discours prononcé par veuve Brillat, Amie de la Constitution de Saint André, n.d., c. spring 1792; *Discours . . . par Françoise Sanson . . . , Avis aux dames portées pour la Contre-Révolution;* Discours de Madame Challan, 21 Mar. 1790, as quoted in Villiers, *Histoire des clubs de femmes,* 193.

105. Laborde, *Société des amies de la Constitution de Pau,* 7; AD Gironde 12L19, Lettre des amies de la liberté et de l'égalité aux citoyens frères et président de la section Guillaume Tell, 22 July 1793; Michael Kennedy, *The Jacobin Clubs in the French Revolution: The First Years* (Princeton, N.J., 1982), 96; "Registre de la société des amies . . . à Ruffec," ed. M. Chauvet.

106. In *Women's Words: Essay on French Singularity,* trans. Jane Marie Todd (Chicago, 1997; orig. 1995), Mona Ozouf has interpreted gender complementarity as a social practice, rather than as an ideal that influenced but did not totally determine social practice. Echoing the revolutionaries' own visions, she has argued that unifying gender relations and a liberating state became a social reality in nineteenth- and twentieth-century France, preempting the need to develop a strong feminist movement in France. On the staying power of notions of gender complementarity into the twentieth century, see Michèle Riot-Sarcey, "The Difficulties of Gender in France: Reflections on a Concept," *Gender and History* 11 (1993): 489–98.

107. These ambiguities also explain how the historiography on women and the Revolution can emphasize the winning of rights and discovery of new voices (Levy and Applewhite, "Women, Radicalization, and the Fall of the French Monarchy"; Carla Hesse, *The Other Enlightenment: How French Women Became Modern* (Princeton, N.J., 2001); more recent works by Lynn Hunt, "Forgetting and Remembering: The French Revolution Now and Then," *American Historical Review* 100 (1995): 1119–1135, esp. 1130–1132, and "Male Virtue and Republican Motherhood"); reiterate the revolutionaries' belief in the healing power of gender complementarity (Ozouf, *Women's Words*); or highlight the constricting bonds of domesticity (Landes, *Women and the Public Sphere;* Gutwirth, *Twilight of the Goddesses;* Hunt, *Family Romance*).

CHAPTER 3

1. ADC 5mi 1, Latter Day Saints (hereafter LDS) film 0658421, Acte de divorce entre Pierre Philippe Hommais et Anne Suzanne Delaville, 1 Jan. 1793; ADC 3L 610, Sentences arbitrales du district de Caen (hereafter SA Caen), 27 Oct. 1792. Although arbitration cases often took more than one session, I will list the date of the first session or most relevant session only.

2. Marcel Garaud and Romuald Szramkiewicz, *La Révolution française et la famille* (Paris, 1978), 67–89; Francis Ronsin, *Le contrat sentimental: Débats sur le mariage, l'amour, le divorce de l'Ancien Régime à la Restauration* (Paris, 1990); James F. Traer, *Marriage and the Family in Eighteenth-Century France* (Ithaca, N.Y., 1980), 117–18.

3. AN DIII 361, *Journal et affiches du département de l'Oise,* no. 98, 20 août an II (1793), Lettre du citoyen Acher au rédacteur du journal; Jacques Dupâquier, "Vers une statistique nationale des divorces sous la première République," in *Populations et Cultures: Etudes réunies en l'honneur de François Lebrun* (Rennes, 1989), 31–37.

4. Arlette Farge and Michel Foucault, *Le désordre des familles: Lettres de cachet des Archives de la Bastille au XVIIIe siècle* (Paris, 1982), 28.

5. ADC 5mi 1, LDS film 0658422+, Acte de divorce entre Noel LeGuay et Angélique Elisabeth Poignaut, 5 germinal an II (25 Mar. 1794).

6. The total of 468 divorces includes 422 from the état civil of seventy-eight communes (1792–1804); 13 Napoleonic divorces in Caen; and 33 divorce cases from court records that did not also appear in the état civil registers. Obviously, many other divorces in my court records also appeared among the 422 état civil cases, and are only counted once. Court cases are drawn from the family tribunals of the district of Caen (which had the best records) and of other districts as available, and from the district and civil tribunals. I examined the état civil of all of the district capitals, some randomly selected small communes, and all of the head communes of cantons that had available sources. See Appendix 1 for a list of communes and LDS film codes. By including all cantonal heads, my sample admittedly underrepresents the tiniest villages of the department, but it includes the majority of divorces in the Calvados, since divorces were scarce in small villages. This sample of 422 divorce cases forms the basis of statistical comments on divorce in the department from 1792 to 1804.

7. Dominique Dessertine, *Divorcer à Lyon sous la Révolution et l'Empire* (Lyon, 1981); Elaine Kruse, "Divorce in Paris 1792–1804: Window on a Society in Crisis" (Ph.D. thesis, University of Iowa, 1983); Roderick Phillips, *Family Breakdown in Late Eighteenth-Century France: Divorces in Rouen, 1792–1803* (Oxford, 1980).

8. The divorce law of 31 Mar. 1803 became part of the Civil Code in 1804. In most places, revolutionary divorce law was followed until the fall of 1804, so I have traced divorce through 1804, and to 1816 in Caen.

9. Loi du 20 septembre 1792, Titre 2, Arts. 1–14, as reprinted in Garaud and Szramkiewicz, *Révolution française et la famille,* 198–203.

10. Dessertine, *Divorcer à Lyon*, 171–78, 182–83; Kruse, "Divorce in Paris," 82, 115–16; Jean Lhote, *Le divorce à Metz et en Moselle sous la Révolution et l'Empire* (Metz, 1981), 12–18; Phillips, *Family Breakdown*, 55–58.

11. AN DIII 361, Pétition anonyme aux législateurs, n.d., c. 1793–94.

12. ADC 3L 617, SA Caen, 7 messidor an IV (25 June 1796); AN DIII 272, Pétition du citoyen Beauvais au Comité de législation, 30 thermidor an III (19 July 1795); AN DIII 361, Pétition très importante sur l'état civil d'un enfant aux législateurs, n.d., c. winter 1793; AN DIII 382, Projet de loi par François Belloc, homme de loi près le tribunal du district (hereafter TDD) de Tonneins, aux citoyens membres du Comité de législation de l'Assemblée nationale, 20 Sept. 1793.

13. Loi du 20 septembre 1792, Titre 1, Arts. 4–5; Titre 2, Arts. 15–17, in Garaud and Szramkiewicz, *Révolution française et la famille*, 198–203.

14. The National Assembly took inspiration in part from Old Regime family councils and arbitration systems. Old Regime family councils often dealt primarily with guardianship and emancipation: e.g., ADC 1B 1185, Délibérations de famille, bailliage de Caen, 1788–89; Jean Forcioli, *Une institution révolutionnaire, le tribunal de famille d'après les archives du district de Caen* (Thèse de droit, Université de Caen, 1932), 27. On pre-1789 arbitration, see Nicole Castan, *Justice et répression en Languedoc à l'époque de lumières* (Paris, 1980), chap. 1.

15. In every location studied, litigating individuals increasingly chose hommes de loi, rather than family members or friends, to act as their arbiters in family courts. See Chapter 4. Cf. Jean-Jacques Clère, "L'arbitrage révolutionnaire: Apogée et déclin d'une institution (1790–1806)," *Revue de l'arbitrage* (1981): 3–28; Jean-Louis Halpérin, "La composition des tribunaux de famille sous la Révolution, ou les juristes, comment s'en débarrasser?" in *FLE*, 292–304; Phillips, *Family Breakdown*, 22–28; Paul Viard, "Les tribunaux de famille dans le district de Dijon (1790–1792)," *Nouvelle revue historique de droit français et étranger* 45 (1921): 242–77, esp. 249–56; Olivier Devaux, "Les tribunaux de famille du district de Rieux et l'application de la loi du 17 nivôse an II," *Annales de l'université des sciences sociales de Toulouse* 35 (1987): 135–58; Marc Ferret, *Les tribunaux de famille dans le district de Montpellier (1790–an IV)* (Montpellier, 1926), 103–105; Jean-Louis Debauve, *La justice révolutionnaire dans le Morbihan, 1790–1795* (Paris, 1965), 363–64. Debauve suggests that it cost about 40–100 livres to hire an homme de loi as arbiter in the Morbihan.

16. The law of 15 thermidor an III (2 Aug. 1795) suspended the 4 floréal law allowing divorce based on six-months de facto separation. The law of 1er jour complémentaire an V (17 Sept. 1797) extended the waiting period for divorce for incompatibility to six months or more.

17. For chronological patterns across France, see Dessertine, *Divorcer à Lyon*, 94–109, esp. 97–100 on siege of Lyon; Dupâquier, "Vers une statistique nationale des divorces," 36–37; Kruse, "Divorce in Paris," 75–80; Marie-José Laperche-Fournel, "Les divorcés de l'an II (à Nancy, Metz, et Verdun)," *Annales de l'Est* 45 (1993): 245–63, esp. 246–48; Jean Lhote, *Les divorcés messins sous le*

régime de la loi 20 septembre 1792 (1793–1804) (Sarreguemines, 1996), 88; Phillips, *Family Breakdown*, 43–51.

18. Dessertine, *Divorcer à Lyon*, 161; Geneviève Ducrocq-Mathieu, "Le divorce dans le district de Nancy de 1792 à l'an III," *Annales de l'Est* 6 (1955): 213–27, 217; Lhote, *Divorce à Metz*, 11; Phillips, *Family Breakdown*, 56; Ronsin, *Contrat sentimental*, 271.

19. AN DIII 361, Pétition du citoyen Gauthier aux citoyens législateurs, n.d. (c. 1793–94); Pétition anonyme, n.d. (but after 20 Sept. 1792); AN DIII 361, Copie d'une lettre du citoyen Robin à sa femme, envoyée à l'assemblée, received 21 décembre (no year, c. 1791 or 1792); AN DIII 361, Pétition anonyme à l'Assemblée législative, received 4 Oct. (no year).

20. AN DIII 361, Pétition de la citoyenne Berlin au Monsieur le président de la Convention nationale, 27 Sept. 1792.

21. AN C278, Lettre de la citoyenne Gavot à la Convention nationale, 1e décade brumaire an II (late Oct. 1793).

22. On women negotiating for power within households, see Natalie Zemon Davis, *The Return of Martin Guerre* (Stanford, Calif., 1983); Barbara Diefendorf, "Women and Property in Ancien Régime France: Theory and Practice in Dauphiné and near Paris," in *Early Modern Conceptions of Property*, ed. John Brewer and Susan Staves (London, 1994), 170–93; Julie Hardwick, "Seeking Separations: Gender, Marriages, and Household Economies in Early Modern France," *French Historical Studies* 21 (1998): 157–80, and "Women 'Working' the Law: Gender, Authority, and Legal Process in Early Modern France," *Journal of Women's History* 9 (1997): 28–49; Zoe Schneider, "Women before the Bench: Female Litigants in Early Modern Normandy," *French Historical Studies* 23 (2000): 1–32. On the complexities of male dominance and gender conflict, see Linda Gordon, *Heroes of Their Own Lives: The Politics and History of Family Violence* (New York, 1988), esp. preface and chap. 8.

23. AN DIII 32, Pétition du citoyen Duboulay au Comité de législation, 16 brumaire an II (6 Nov. 1793).

24. Pétition de la citoyenne Th. Van Houten au Comité de législation, n.d., c. 1793.

25. Dessertine, *Divorcer à Lyon*, 188–94; Kruse, "Divorce in Paris," chap. 4; Lhote, *Divorce à Metz*, 11–20; Phillips, *Family Breakdown*, 56–58.

26. AN DIII 34, Pétition de la citoyenne Jacquette au Comité de législation, 17 thermidor an III (4 Aug. 1795).

27. On women's prevalent use of emigration grounds elsewhere, see Joseph Boulaud, *Douze femmes d'émigrés divorcées à Limoges sous la Terreur* (Limoges, 1913); Ducrocq-Mathieu, "Divorce dans le district de Nancy," 223–24; Laperche-Fournel, "Divorcés de l'an II," 253–55; Jean Lhote, *Divorce à Metz*, 12–13; Phillips, *Family Breakdown*, 148–50.

28. AN DIII 273, Pétition de la citoyenne LeBlanc aux citoyens représentants, 4 nivôse an II (24 Dec. 1793).

29. ADC 3L 611, SA Caen, 20 May 1793; AN DIII 33, Pétition de la citoyenne Marie Adelaide Turgot femme Costard dit Saint-Leger aux citoyens composant

le Comité de législation, 12 thermidor an II (30 July 1794). On female honor, see David Garrioch, *Neighbourhood and Community in Paris, 1740–1790* (New York, 1986), 36–42; Laura Gowing, *Domestic Dangers: Women, Words and Sex in Early Modern London* (Oxford, 1996); Clare Haru Crowston, "The Queen and Her 'Minister of Fashion': Gender, Credit, and Politics in Prerevolutionary France," *Gender and History* 14, no. 1 (April 2002): 92–116.

30. AN DXXXIX 4, Pétition de la citoyenne Jeanne Hellequin femme Bernard aux Cinq-Cents, 28 messidor an IV (17 July 1796); AN DIII 361, Pétition de la femme Girard à la Convention nationale, n.d., sent to the Comité de législation, 9 pluviôse an II (28 Jan. 1794); Pétition sans titre et sans signature, n.d., c. 1794; Pétition de la citoyenne Th. Van Houten au Comité de législation, n.d., c. 1793; AN DIII 273, Pétition de la citoyenne Geneviève Lebourdais femme Gras-Soubès au Comité de législation, 10 prairial an II (29 May 1794); AN DIII 363–65, Pétition anonyme, remise par le député de Vienne, questions sur les lois du 12 brumaire an II et 20 septembre 1792, 24 floréal an II? (13 May 1794?). On marriages between French and foreigners, see Jennifer Heuer, "Foreigners, Families, and Citizens: Contradictions of National Citizenship in France, 1789–1830" (Ph.D. diss., University of Chicago, 1998).

31. Cf. Dessertine, *Divorcer à Lyon,* 179–80; Laperche-Fournel, "Divorcés de l'an II," 253; Phillips, *Family Breakdown,* 145–46.

32. Olwen Hufton, *The Poor of Eighteenth-Century France, 1750–1789* (Oxford, 1974), chap. 3; Jean-Claude Perrot, *Genèse d'une ville moderne: Caen au XVIIIe siècle,* 2 vols. (Paris, 1975), 1: 99–176, 301–306.

33. Women married for more than ten years made up 42 percent of female initiators of unilateral divorces, but 55 percent of women filing for abandonment or de facto separation.

34. In cases of mutual consent, the law allowed quicker registration in the état civil for those without children, so I was able to calculate childless couples. Fifty-six percent of couples divorcing by mutual consent in Caen had no children. In areas where the "preliminary divorce acts" have been preserved, historians can get information on children among couples divorcing for a wider array of motives: 63 percent of Rouen's divorcing couples, 62 percent in Paris, and 61 percent in Lyon were childless. Dessertine, *Divorcer à Lyon,* 263–67; Kruse, "Divorce in Paris," 57; Laperche-Fournel, "Divorcés de l'an II," 259; Phillips, *Family Breakdown,* 77–79; Ronsin, *Contrat sentimental,* 281; Germain Sicard and Mireille Sicard, "Le Divorce à Toulouse durant la Révolution française," in *Mélanges dédiés à Gabriel Marty* (Toulouse, 1978), 1051–75, 1072.

35. AN DIII 361, Pétition d'Anne Catherine Bagot à l'Assembleé nationale en faveur d'une femme délaissée depuis douze ans par son mari, received 31 Jan. 1792.

36. Dessertine, *Divorcer à Lyon,* 189; Ducrocq-Mathieu, "Divorce dans le district de Nancy," 224; Kruse, "Divorce in Paris," 82; Lhote, *Divorce à Metz,* 12–20; Ronsin, *Contrat sentimental,* 272; Phillips, *Family Breakdown,* 56–58.

37. ADC 3L 611, SA Caen, 3 Jan. 1793; ADC 5mi 12, LDS film 0659813, Acte de divorce entre Etienne Feron et Marie Françoise Faucon, 3 Apr. 1793.

38. On family violence, see Phillips, *Family Breakdown*, 105–124.

39. ADC 3L 972, Sentences arbitrales du district de Lisieux (hereafter SA Lisieux), 28 brumaire an III (18 Nov. 1794).

40. ADC 3L 612, SA Caen, 15 nivôse an II (4 Jan. 1794); ADC 3L 1334, Sentences arbitrales, an IV–VIII (1795–1800), Tribunal civil du Calvados (hereafter SA Calvados), 24 brumaire an IV (15 Nov. 1795); SA Calvados, 15 brumaire an IV (6 Nov. 1795); SA Calvados, 30 thermidor an IV (17 Aug. 1796); ADC 3L 972, SA Lisieux, 26 Nov. 1792; ADC 3L 1335, SA Calvados, 20 pluviôse an V (8 Feb. 1797).

41. ADC 3L 617, SA Caen, 8 thermidor an III (26 July 1795); ADC 3L 972, SA Lisieux, 10 Dec. 1792; ADC 3L 611, SA Caen, Jugement arbitral du surarbitre Regnault, 28 July 1793; ADC 3L 616, SA Caen, 3 prairial an III (22 May 1795); Lettre du commissaire national de Rouen au Ministre de Justice, 23 frimaire an II (5 Nov. 1793); Aimé Vincenti, *Le Tribunal départemental de Vaucluse de l'an IV à l'an VIII* (Avignon, 1928), 158–61.

42. AN DIII 33, Lettre des juges du TDD de Caen aux représentants du peuple composant le Comité de législation, 2 frimaire an III (22 Nov. 1794); ADC 3L 1004, TDD de Lisieux, 9 Feb. 1793.

43. ADC 3L 972, SA Lisieux, 10 Dec. 1792; SA Lisieux, 28 brumaire an III (18 Nov. 1794); ADC 3L 613, SA Caen, 13 floréal an II (2 May 1794); SA Caen, 19 germinal an II (8 Apr. 1794); ADC 3L 616, SA Caen, 6 messidor an III (24 June 1795); ADC 3L 1335, SA Calvados, 20 pluviôse an V (8 Feb. 1797); SA Calvados, 12 germinal an V (1 Apr. 1797); AN DIII 271, Pétition de la citoyenne Marie-Anne Mindorge, ci-devant femme Duval, au Comité de législation, 24 prairial an II (12 June 1794); AN DIII 33, Pétition, signée Fouque Desmarais, à la Convention nationale, 1 brumaire an III (22 Oct. 1794).

44. AN DIII 361, Pétition du citoyen Vuillerment aux législateurs, 15 frimaire an III (5 Dec. 1794); AN DIII 361, Pétition du citoyen Sullot aux législateurs, 14 pluviôse an II (2 Feb. 1794).

45. Phillips bases this estimate on "preliminary acts of divorce," unavailable for the Calvados: *Family Breakdown*, 59–60. Twenty-two of my divorce cases in the family tribunals never appeared in the état civils of communes or cities examined.

46. AN DIII 273, Pétition du citoyen Genise au citoyen président, 19 messidor an III (7 July 1795).

47. ADC 3L 616, SA Caen, 8 prairial–6 messidor an III (27 May–24 June 1795).

48. AN DIII 273, Pétition de la citoyenne LeMachais au Comité de législation, received 5 brumaire an II (26 Oct. 1793).

49. Men filed 2.1 percent of the 706 petitions for séparation de corps or de biens in Nantes between 1598 and 1710. Thanks to Julie Hardwick for sharing this work in progress and for drawing my attention to this question. See also Hardwick, "Seeking Separations," 162; Zoe Schneider, "The Village and the State: Justice and the Local Courts in Normandy, 1670–1740" (Ph.D. diss., Georgetown University, 1997), 748; Alain Lottin et al., *La Désunion du couple*

sous l'ancien régime: L'exemple du Nord (Paris, 1975), 113–14. While Schneider found no male requests in her Norman study, men filed 15 percent of the unilateral separation requests between 1737 and 1791 in the diocese of Cambrai, where—exceptionally—ecclesiastical courts held jurisdiction over séparation de corps and allowed either spouse to use same grounds.

50. Farge and Foucault, *Désordre des familles;* Brian Strayer, Lettres de cachet *and Social Control in the* Ancien Régime, *1659–1789* (New York, 1992), 17–19. On the Calvados, see Jacqueline Musset, *Le régime des biens entre époux en droit normand du XVIe siècle à la Révolution française* (Caen, 1997), 101–103; Claude Quétel, "Lettres de cachet et correctionnaires dans la généralité de Caen au XVIIIe siècle," *Annales de Normandie* 28 (1978): 127–59; Perrot, *Genèse d'une ville,* 2: 837–39. On occasion, a wife succeeded in imprisoning a violent husband.

51. AN DIII 34, Pétition du citoyen Fortin à la Convention nationale, 25 thermidor an II (12 Aug. 1794); AN DIII 361, Pétition du citoyen Noé aux citoyens représentants, 27 Aug. 1793.

52. AN DIII 361, Pétition du citoyen Sentix à la Convention nationale, n.d. (c. fall 1793); AN DIII 269, Pétition du citoyen Dulac aux citoyens représentatifs, 7 brumaire an II (28 Oct. 1793).

53. ADC 3L 612, SA Caen, 3 brumaire an II (24 Oct. 1793); AN DXXXIX 5, Pétition du citoyen Guérin au citoyen président du conseil des 500, received 13 frimaire an IV (4 Dec. 1795).

54. Robert Pothier, *Traité de la puissance du mari sur la personne et les biens de la femme* (Orléans, 1774); David Houard, *Dictionnaire analytique, historique, étymologique, critique et interprétif de la coutume de Normandie* (Rouen, 1780). ADC 3L 628 and 3L 1391, Actes de séparations civiles, 1791–an III and an V–an VIII (1796–1800). For a husband's failed attempt to overturn a separation of property, see ADC 3L 972, SA Lisieux, 25 vendémiaire–28 messidor an III (16 Oct. 1794–16 July 1795). For alimony, see ADC 3L 1337, SA Calvados, 3 vendémiaire an VII (24 Sept. 1798); ADC 3L 617, SA Caen, 7 messidor an III (25 June 1795); ADC 3L 1146, Sentences arbitrales du district de Pont-l'Evêque (hereafter SA Pont-l'Evêque), 22 nivôse an III (11 Jan. 1795).

55. AN DXXXIX 4, Pétition du citoyen Tardy, officier du santé, Rochefort, au Conseil des 500, 25 thermidor an IV (13 Aug. 1796).

56. Men filed 16 of 18 (89 percent) cases in Lyon; 32 of 49 (65 percent) in Paris; 2 of 2 (100 percent) in Metz; 14 of 26 (54 percent) in Rouen; 10 of 15 (67 percent) in Toulouse. Only in Bordeaux did women use this grounds more often, filing 8 of 11 (73 percent) of the cases. Dessertine, *Divorcer à Lyon,* 189; Kruse, "Divorce in Paris," 109; Lhote, *Divorce à Metz,* 12–20; Phillips, *Family Breakdown,* 57; Ronsin, *Contrat sentimental,* 274; Sicard, "Divorce à Toulouse," 1068.

57. For striking examples of rural family tribunals denying women divorces based on their husband's adultery despite evidence, see ADC 3L 972, SA Lisieux (commune d'Abenon), 26 Nov. 1792; ADC 3L 611, SA Caen (commune de Cresserons), 20 May 1793; ADC 3L 1337, SA Calvados (canton de Crocy), 11

messidor an VII (29 June 1799). Some women eventually won divorces on other grounds.

58. ADC 3L 612, SA Caen, 15 nivôse an II (4 Jan. 1794); ADC 5mi 1, LDS film 0658422, Acte de divorce entre Pierre Bertaux et Séraphine Saint-Pierre, 6 pluviôse an II (25 Jan. 1794).

59. AN DIII 361, Pétition du citoyen Fleurant à la Convention nationale, 10 frimaire an II (30 Nov. 1793); ADC 3L 972, SA Lisieux, 26 Nov.–14 Dec. 1792; ADC 3L 1004, Procédures du TDD Lisieux, 9 Feb. 1793 and 3e décade frimaire an II (Dec. 1793); Ferret, *Tribunaux de famille dans le district de Montpellier*, 290.

60. Phillips, *Family Breakdown*, 130; ADC 3L 972, SA Lisieux, 18 fructidor an III (29 Aug. 1795).

61. This penalty applied to wives divorced on any of the seven grounds (causes déterminées) except insanity. Loi du 20 septembre 1792, Par. 3, Art. 5., as reprinted in Garaud and Szramkiewicz, *Révolution française et la famille*, 201.

62. ADC 3L 614, SA Caen, 4 vendémiaire an III (25 Sept. 1794); ADC 3L 972, SA Lisieux, 10 Dec. 1792; ADC 3L 611, SA Caen, 28 July 1793; ADC 3L 616, SA Caen, 3 prairial an III (22 May 1795); ADC 3L 617, SA Caen, 8 thermidor an III (26 July 1795); ADC 3L 611, SA Caen, 15 May 1793; ADC 5mi 1, LDS film 0658421, Acte de divorce entre André Brunville et Constance Lemarchand, 24 ventôse an II (14 Mar. 1794); ADC 3L 616, SA Caen, 7 germinal an III (27 Mar. 1795); ADC 3L 622, TDD Caen, 16 Jan. 1793.

63. See Chapter 7.

64. AN DIII 361, Pétition anonyme à la législature sur les adultérins, n.d., c. 1793?; Pétition du citoyen Goroy à la Législature sur les adultérins, 21 June 1793; Pétition sur l'adultère, n.d., c. 1793; AN DXXXIX 4, Pétition du citoyen Thomas aux citoyens législateurs, 24 prairial an II (12 June 1794); Pétition sur la loi du divorce dans les cas d'abandon et dérèglement de mœurs notoire par l'épouse (printed, n.d., c. 1793–94).

65. See note 34 above.

66. Loi du 20 septembre 1792, Par. 4. Other historians also found few custody cases. Dessertine, *Divorcer à Lyon*, 271–73; Phillips, *Family Breakdown*, 171–72.

67. AN DIII 74, Mémoire sur la loi du divorce, par un ami des mœurs, citoyen Duran, 15 prairial an III (3 June 1795); AN DIII 361, Demande d'addition à la loi sur le divorce, n.d., c. late 1792–93; AN ADXVIIIb 212, Procès-verbal du Conseil de 500, Pétition du citoyen Lecardonnel aux 500, 24 brumaire an VII (13 Nov. 1798); Dessertine, *Divorcer à Lyon*, 272.

68. ADC 3L 614, SA Caen, 20 frimaire an III (10 Dec. 1794); ADC 3L 612, SA Caen, 15 nivôse an II (4 Jan. 1794); AN DIII 36, Pétition de Préaux, membre du Comité de surveillance de la commune de Molay, au citoyen président de la Convention nationale, 9 floréal an II (28 Apr. 1794).

69. ADC 3L 617, SA Caen, 5 messidor an III (23 June 1795); ADC 3L 614, SA Caen, 12 vendémiaire an III (3 Oct. 1794) .

70. ADC 3L 610, SA Caen, 12 Sept. 1792; ADC 3L 1337, SA Calvados, 3 vendémiaire an VII (24 Sept. 1798); ADC 3L 617, SA Caen, 7 messidor an III (25

June 1795); ADC 3L 1334, SA Calvados, 30 thermidor an IV (17 Aug. 1796); ADC 3L 1334, SA Calvados, 15 brumaire an IV (6 Nov. 1795).

71. AN DIII 361, Pétition de la citoyenne Degay femme Lefebvre aux légis-lateurs, 10 Sept. 1792; Pétition de la citoyenne Berlin au Monsieur le président de la Convention nationale, 27 Sept. 1792; AN DIII 273, Pétition de la citoyenne Félicité Desrogues femme Letellier au Comité de législation, received 23 vendémiaire an III (14 Oct. 1794).

72. AN DXXXIX 4, Pétition de Marie Anne Campion femme Ménouvrier au Conseil des Cinq-Cents, received 29 messidor an IV (18 July 1796); Pétition du citoyen Delespine aux Cinq-Cents, 7 prairial an IV (26 May 1796); Pétition d'Arthon, instituteur de la jeunesse, aux Cinq-Cents, 5 thermidor an IV (24 July 1796); AN DIII 270, Pétition du plus malheureux de vos concitoyens aux citoyens représentatifs, 20 thermidor an III (7 Aug. 1795); AN DIII 363, Projet de loi adressé à la Convention nationale par le Comité de législation, n.d. (c. an IV/1796).

73. AN DIII 361, *Journal et affiches du département de l'Oise*, 98, 28 Aug. an II (1793).

74. AN DIII 361, Lettre du Ministre de la justice, Gohier, au président du Comité de législation, 11 July 1793; ADC 3L 614, SA Caen, 19 vendémiaire an III (10 Oct. 1794); ADC 3L 613, SA Caen, 24 floréal an II (13 May 1794); ADC 3L 613, 21 floréal an II (10 May 1794); ADC 3L 615, SA Caen, 26 pluviôse an III (14 Feb. 1795); ADC 3L 617, SA Caen, 8 thermidor an III (26 July 1795); ADC 3L 1340, Audience du Tribunal civil du Calvados, 4 ventôse an IV (23 Feb. 1796). In some cases, wives used *arrêts de deniers* (acts to impound goods or stop transactions), which husbands then attempted to counter by winning the right *(main-levées)* to get these goods out from impoundment.

75. ADC 3L 617, SA Caen, 5 messidor an III (23 June 1795); ADC 3L 616, SA Caen, 7 germinal an III (27 Mar. 1795). Phillips also deemed property arrangements too complex to determine an "average" settlement: *Family Breakdown,* 166–71.

76. ADC 3L 1337, SA Calvados, 3 vendémiaire an VII (24 Sept. 1798); ADC 3L 611, SA Caen, 15 June 1793; ADC 3L 613, SA Caen, 24 germinal an II (13 Apr. 1794); ADC 3L 1248, TDD Vire, 11 germinal an II (31 Mar. 1794); ADC 3L 613, SA Caen, 19 germinal an II (8 Apr. 1794); ADC 3L 614, SA Caen, 26 brumaire an III (16 Nov. 1794); ADC 3L 624, TDD Caen, 18 prairial an II (6 June 1794).

77. AN DIII 33, Lettres du citoyen Lemoine (arbitre à Caen) aux citoyens législateurs, 15 pluviôse an III (3 Feb. 1795) and 10 ventôse an III (28 Feb. 1795); ADC 3L 611, SA Caen, 17 Apr. 1793; ADC 3L 613, SA Caen, 13 floréal an II (2 May 1794); ADC 3L 614, SA Caen, 12 frimaire an III (2 Dec. 1794); ADC 3L 615, SA Caen, 13 nivôse an III (2 Jan. 1795); ADC 3L 1334, SA Calvados, 1 floréal an IV (20 Apr. 1796); AN DIII 271, Pétition de la citoyenne Marie Anne Mindorge au Comité de législation, 24 prairial an II (12 June 1794); ADC 3L 611, SA Caen, 19 Mar. 1793; ADC 3L 616, 16 floréal an III (5 May 1795).

78. ADC 3L 615, SA Caen, 26 pluviôse an III (14 Feb. 1795); ADC 3L 616, SA Caen, 25 prairial an III (13 June 1795); ADC 3L 1146, SA Pont-l'Evêque, 20 floréal an III (9 May 1795).

79. AN DIII 272, Pétition de la citoyenne R. Andaille au citoyen président de la Convention nationale, 24 frimaire an II (14 Dec. 1793); Pétition de Catherine Boulon aux citoyens législateurs, 26 thermidor an II (13 Aug. 1794); AN DIII 74, Pétition de la citoyenne Boulon aux citoyens représentants, frimaire an III (Dec. 1794). The introduction of paper money or inflation could cause a divorced woman to lose the original value of her dowry: AN DXXXIX 4, Pétition de la citoyenne Susanne Rauly aux députés composant les conseils des 500 et des anciens, received 29 floréal an IV (18 May 1796); AN DIII 361, Effets du divorce par rapport aux époux, règlement de leurs droits, n.d.

80. AN DIII 36, Pétition du citoyen Jacques LeCourt au Comité de législation, 9 prairial an III (28 May 1795); AN DXXXIX 3, Pétition anonyme, envoyée au Comité de classification des lois par les commissaires de la commune de Rouen, received 4 thermidor an II (22 July 1794); AN DIII 361, Pétition anonyme à la Convention nationale, 12 Sept. 1793; Pétition de Mouret d'Anneville au Comité de législation, received 17 pluviôse an II (5 Feb. 1794); AN DXXXIX 4, Pétition du citoyen Joseph Vial au Conseil des 500, received 20 germinal an IV (10 Apr. 1796); AN DIII 382, Pétition de Mathieu Bouché à la Convention nationale, received 21 germinal an II (10 Apr. 1794).

81. AN ADXVIIIc 365, Pétition du citoyen D. de la Grange aux représentants du peuple, 18 nivôse an V (7 Jan. 1797); AN XXXIX 3, Observations sur quelques articles du projet de code civil, n.d., c. brumaire an III (Oct.–Nov. 1794); AN DXXXIX 4, Observations sur le paragraphe de la loi qui règle des effets du divorce par rapport aux enfants, received 3 messidor an IV (21 June 1796); AN DIII 361, Lettre anonyme aux citoyens représentants du peuple composant le Comité de législation, 11 pluviôse an II (30 Jan. 1794).

82. Dupâquier, "Vers une statistique nationale des divorces," 34–36. The divorce/marriage ratio indicates the prevalence of divorce, but does not make any predictions about current marriages.

83. ADC 2L 206, Recensement (1793–an II); *Atlas de la Révolution française*, vol. 8, *Population*, ed. Bernard Lepetit et Maroula Sinarellis (Paris, 1995), 74–75.

84. No extensive study into rural divorce patterns yet exists, but a few authors have counted rural divorces. In the Meuse: 413 of 586 communes had no divorces. In the Moselle: only 16 divorces took place in the canton of Metz-Campagne. Likewise, in the Seine-Inférieure, 31 divorces occurred in the eleven communes surrounding Rouen. In the Haute-Garonne, divorce became increasingly rare the farther one travelled from Toulouse. Laperche-Fournel, "Divorcés de l'an II," 246; Lhote, *Divorce à Metz*, 26; Phillips, *Family Breakdown*, 92–94; Sicard, "Divorce à Toulouse"; and Simone Maraval, "L'introduction du divorce en Haute-Garonne (1792–1816): Etude de mœurs révolutionnaires" (Mémoire de D.E.S., Université de Toulouse, 1951), 47, as cited by Phillips, *Family Breakdown*, 92.

85. On the difficulties of social categorization within the Calvados, see Olwen Hufton, *Bayeux in the Late Eighteenth Century: A Social Study* (Oxford, 1967), 57–59; Perrot, *Genèse d'une ville*, 1: 242–56. The most extensive

exploration of occupation and divorce remains Dessertine, *Divorcer à Lyon*, 113–73. Cf. Ducrocq-Mathieu, "Divorce dans le district de Nancy," 221–22; Kruse, "Divorce in Paris," 47–48; Laperche-Fournel, "Divorcés de l'an II," 249–50; Lhote, *Divorce à Metz*, 11; Phillips, *Family Breakdown*, 89–91; Ronsin, *Contrat sentimental*, 274–78; Sicard, "Divorce à Toulouse," 1073–74. With proportional variations from city to city, the artisans and bourgeoisie dominated divorce everywhere.

86. Comparisons based on Perrot, *Genèse d'une ville*, 1: 256–73, esp. 265–66. See also his Annexe 8 on professional classification, 2: 974–78, which provided the model for categories in this study.

87. These comments on rural divorce and socioeconomic categories must be taken with caution, given recording methods of rural officials in the état civil. My data probably underrepresents divorce among agrarian types: local officials very well may not have recorded the status of various peasants precisely because these occupations were taken as a given. Likewise, they probably were less likely to record professions for the poor and day laborers.

88. Timothy Tackett, *Religion, Revolution, and Regional Culture in Eighteenth-Century France: The Ecclesiastical Oath of 1791* (Princeton, N.J.,1986), 53–54, 315; Emile Sévestre, *Les problèmes religieux de la Révolution et de l'Empire en Normandie, 1787–1815*, 2 vols. (Paris, 1924). Lynn Hunt classifies the Calvados among those departments on the right from 1792 to 1798: Hunt, *Politics, Culture, and Class in the French Revolution* (Berkeley, 1984), 131. For the most detailed discussion of the *esprit public* of the Calvados, see Jean Lethuillier, *Le Calvados dans la Révolution: L'esprit public d'un département* (Condé-sur-Noireau, 1990). For the cities, see Paul Hanson, *Provincial Politics in the French Revolution: Caen and Limoges, 1789–1794* (Baton Rouge, La., 1989); Hufton, *Bayeux in the Late Eighteenth Century*, chap. 3; Paul Germain, *Histoire de Falaise* (Alençon, 1966), 189–210; Christine Peyrard, *Les Jacobins de l'Ouest: Sociabilité révolutionnaire et formes de politisation dans le Maine et la Basse-Normandie (1789–1799)* (Paris, 1996). While Bayeux's republicans and city leadership eventually became Federalist, the city was the least pro-revolutionary of the Calvados. The smaller cities Vire and Condé-sur-Noireau remained more ambivalent vis-à-vis Federalism. On pro-revolutionary Vire and Condé-sur-Noireau surrounded by predominantly counterrevolutionary countryside, see Paul Nicolle, *Histoire de Vire pendant la Révolution (1787–1800)* (Vire, 1923), part 3; Maylis Nadin, *Histoire de Condé-sur-Noireau: Jardins ouverts, jardins sercrets* (Condé-sur-Noireau, 1998), 59–90.

89. AN DIII 273, Pétition de la citoyenne LeBlanc aux citoyens représentants, 4 nivôse an II (24 Dec. 1793); AN DIII 33, Pétition de la citoyenne Marie Anne Angélique Fouque aux citoyens représentants, 24 vendémiaire an III (15 Oct. 1794).

90. Eric Wauters, *Une presse de province pendant la Révolution française: Journaux et journalistes normands (1785–1800)* (Paris, 1993), chaps. 3–8. On the press, pamphlet literature, and bookstore networks within the Calvados, see Peyrard, *Jacobins de l'Ouest*, chaps. 4 and 11, and pp. 78–83, 212–17.

91. Peyrard, *Jacobins de l'Ouest*, 62, 173; J. Charrier, *Claude Fauchet, Evêque constitutionnel du Calvados*, 2 vols. (Paris, 1909), 2: chap. 19.

92. My figures probably slightly exaggerate the literacy levels of divorcing couples, because illiterate spouses (if they had not initiated the divorce) were less likely to be present at the official registration since they could not sign anyway. In general, slightly more than half of husbands and just over one-third of women were not present at the signing, most often because they opposed the divorce initiated by their spouse or because their whereabouts were unknown. On literacy, see Perrot, *Genèse d'une ville*, 1: 308–9. François Furet and Jacques Ozouf, using Maggiolo's figures, estimated that 80–90 percent of spouses in the Calvados signed their marriage acts from 1786 to 1790: *Reading and Writing: Literacy in France from Calvin to Jules Ferry* (Cambridge, Eng., 1982), 49. Parisian divorcés also had above-average literacy: Kruse, "Divorce in Paris," 48. Citoyen Garnier, *Code du divorce, contenant l'explication familière des moyens et de la manière d'exécuter la Loi du Divorce, dans tous les cas où le divorce est permis, et les formules des actes relatifs à la pratique du divorce* (Paris, 1792).

93. On the public reading aloud of newpapers in Caen, see Hanson, *Provincial Politics*, 68. On successive laws mandating public proclamations and postings, see Françoise Fortunet, "Connaissance et conscience juridique à l'époque révolutionnaire en pays de droit coutumier: la législation successorale," in *RévJur* 1: 359–71, esp. 367 n. 5. On rural law bulletins, see Peyrard, *Jacobins de l'Ouest*, 227–28.

94. Almost two-thirds of thirty-four communes in my sample with clubs experienced divorces. The remaining sixteen communes with clubs were not in my sample.

95. *Atlas de la Révolution française*, vol. 6, *Les sociétés politiques*, ed. Jean Boutier et Philippe Boutry (Paris, 1992), 80; Michael Kennedy, *The Jacobin Clubs in the French Revolution: The Middle Years* (Princeton, N.J., 1988), 175–95; Nicolle, *Histoire de Vire*, 172–74. After intense debate, the Vire club initially decided in September 1790 to oppose divorce but appeal for clerical marriage. See also Peyrard, *Jacobins de l'Ouest*, chaps. 3, 4, and 12; Charrier, *Claude Fauchet*, 2: chap. 19. The Amis de la Constitution of Caen and of Lisieux petitioned the National Assembly for egalitarian inheritance between the sexes. AN C125, Pétition des Amis de la Constitution à Caen aux Messieurs, 22 June 1791; Adresse des Amis de la Constitution de la ville de Lisieux à l'Assemblée nationale, n.d., as cited in Françoise de Loisy, "Recherches sur la dévolution successorale légitime et la notion d'égalité en pays de coutume au XVIIIe siècle" (Université de Dijon, Mémoire pour D.E.S. d'histoire du droit, 1970), 45.

96. On legal culture in the Pays d'Auge, see Lethuillier, *Département du Calvados*, 375–76, 389–91. Zoe Schneider reports that in 1704 the Rouen printer Maury published a paper-cover copy of the custom for only 15 sols: "The Village and the State," 655–61; Olwen Hufton, "Le paysan et la loi en France au XVIIIe siècle," *Annales: Economies, Sociétés, Civilisations* (1983): 679–701. ADC 3L 616, SA Caen, 16 germinal an III (5 Apr. 1795).

97. Jean-Pierre Bardet et al., "Labourieux par nécessité: L'économie nor-

mande du XVIe au XVIIIe siècles," in *Histoire de la Normandie,* ed. Michel de Bouard (Toulouse, 1970), 287–318; Mohamed El Kordi, *Bayeux aux XVIIe et XVIIIe siècles* (Paris, 1970); Hufton, *Bayeux in the Late Eighteenth Century;* Bernard Lepetit, *The Pre-Industrial Urban System: France, 1740–1840,* trans. Godfrey Rogers (New York, 1994), 152–74, 255–56; Perrot, *Genèse d'une ville;* Peyrard, *Jacobins de l'Ouest.*

98. Perrot, *Genèse d'une ville,* 1: 162–66; 312–20; 2: 808–881. On French cities and changing sociability, see Daniel Roche, *France in the Enlightenment,* trans. Arthur Goldhammer (Cambridge, Mass., 1998), 174–208.

99. Phillips, *Family Breakdown,* 96–98.

100. Perrot, *Genèse d'une ville,* 1: 312.

101. In the Calvados, women in communes over 2,500 requested 73 percent of unilateral divorces, compared to only 64 percent in the smallest communes. In the neighboring department of Seine-Inférieure, women in the eleven agrarian communes surrounding Rouen initiated only 42 percent of unilateral divorces, in contrast to 71 percent within Rouen. Phillips, *Family Breakdown,* 92–96.

102. Hufton, *Bayeux in the Late Eighteenth Century,* 83–84, 204–48, quote 83. Clare Crowston emphasizes the possible economic independence of mistress seamstresses, of whom 41 percent in Caen and 37 percent to 48 percent in Paris remained unmarried. *Fabricating Women: The Seamstresses of Old Regime France, 1675–1791* (Durham, N.C., 2001), 356–57.

103. Hufton also found this to be true in the 1796 population rolls of Bayeux: *Bayeux in the Late Eighteenth Century,* 83, n. 1.

104. Janine Lanza reports that soft-drink sellers, wine merchants, vinegar-sellers, embroiderers, hosiers, fan-makers, and tanners were the guilds most likely to have widow mistresses, at least in late eighteenth-century Paris. Personal communication to the author, 31 Jan. 2000.

105. ADC 3L 611, SA Caen, 24 Sept. 1793; ADC 5mi 1, LDS film 0658422, Acte de divorce entre Nicolas Bourse dit Lejeune et Marie Anne Robert ditte Coigny, 21 frimaire an II (11 Dec. 1793).

106. Within Caen, the 57 female witnesses made up almost 8 percent of the 724 witnesses; within the department overall, women made up just over 4 percent (73 of 1672 witnesses). The 1701 total signings have been reduced by those witnesses who served multiple times. Six women witnessed mutual consent cases; 60 witnessed female-initiated divorces. Less than 2 percent of witnesses overall could not sign. Both male and female divorcés tended to choose witnesses from their own occupational background, or slightly above. Female witnesses by year: 4 in an I, 27 in an II, 18 in an III, 15 in an IV, 7 in an V, 1 in an VI, and 1 in an X. ADC 3L 1335, SA Calvados, 12 germinal an V (1 Apr. 1797). The case had begun in Aug. 1796 (ADC 3L 1334). ADC 5mi 1, LDS Film 0658430, Acte de divorce entre Charles Vincent et Marguerite Adelaide Paulmier, 6 floréal an V (25 Apr. 1797).

107. ADC 3L 972, SA Lisieux, 26 Nov. 1792; ADC 3L 1004, TDD Lisieux, 3e décade frimaire an II (c. Dec. 1793); ADC 3L 978, TDD Lisieux, 19 frimaire an III (9 Dec. 1794).

108. ADC 3L 611, SA Caen, 15 Oct. 1793.

109. André Burguière, "La Révolution française et la famille," *Annales: Economies, Sociétés, Civilisations* 46 (1991): 151–68.

110. Lisieux, Honfleur, and Orbec totaled 113 divorces among them. The Bessin area around Bayeux had divorce levels distinctly lower than the Pays d'Auge or the area around Caen, and only slightly higher than the districts of Vire and Falaise.

111. Lethuillier, *Département du Calvados*, 321–40, 350–57, 372–77, 386–413, quote p. 390; N. W. Morgensen, "Stratification sociale dans le Pays d'Auge au XVIIIe siècle," *Annales de Normandie* (1973): 212–51; Boutier et al., eds. *Atlas de la Révolution française*, vol. 6, *Les sociétés politiques*, 19 and 80; Peyrard, *Jacobins de l'Ouest*.

112. Lethuillier, *Département du Calvados*, 281–302, 349–72, 399–413; Nicolle, *Histoire de Vire*, part 3; Nadin, *Histoire de Condé-sur-Noireau*, 59–90; Germain, *Histoire de Falaise*, 189–210.

113. Occupational breakdown of Napoleonic divorces in Caen: 5 liberal professionals, 4 rentiers vivant de son bien, 2 merchants, and 1 unknown. Cf. Dessertine, *Divorcer à Lyon*, 94–95, 116–17, 160–62, 176–78; Lhote, *Divorce à Metz*, 21–23. In Lyon divorces dropped from 1,049 (1792–an XII) to 84 (an XIII–1816); in Metz, from 267 (1792–1804) to 20 (1805–16).

114. AN DIII 33, Pétition d'un citoyen de Caen aux dignes représentants du peuple, 8 Sept. 1792.

115. AN ADII 33, Rapport et projet de décret présenté au nom du Comité de législation, par C. F. Oudot, 17 frimaire an III (7 Dec. 1794).

CHAPTER 4

1. AN DIII 33, Pétition de la citoyenne LeFranc à la Convention nationale, 30 germinal an III (22 Mar. 1795); AN DIII 274, Pétition des citoyens Lenoir et Lammarré aux députés du département de la Manche, 1 frimaire an III (21 Nov. 1794).

2. Based on reading hundreds of civil law petitions to revolutionary legislatures and committees, esp. in AN series ADII (Archives imprimées), ADXVIIIc (Suppléments aux Procès-verbaux des Assemblées nationales), C (Adresses à la Convention), DIII (Comité de législation); DXXXIX (Comité de la classification des lois).

3. David Garrioch, *The Formation of the Parisian Bourgeoisie, 1690–1830* (Cambridge, Mass., 1996), 165.

4. François Vincent Toussaint, *Les Mœurs* (Paris, 1748), as quoted in Brian E. Strayer, Lettres de Cachet *and Social Control in the* Ancien Régime, *1659–1789* (New York, 1993), 12. Jean Delumeau and Daniel Roche, eds., *Histoire des pères et de la paternité* (Paris, 1990); Sarah Hanley, "Engendering the State: Family Formation and State Building in Early Modern France," *French Historical Studies* 16 (1989): 4–27; Jeffrey Merrick, "Fathers and Kings: Patriarchalism and Absolutism in Eighteenth-Century French Politics," *Studies on Voltaire and the Eighteenth Century* 308 (1993): 281–303.

5. Strayer, *Lettres de cachet,* 12–13; Jean-Claude Perrot, *Genèse d'une ville moderne: Caen au XVIIIe siècle,* 2 vols. (Paris, 1975), 2: 836–41; Arlette Farge, "The Honor and Secrecy of Families," in *A History of Private Life,* vol. 3, *Passions of the Renaissance,* ed. Roger Chartier, trans. Arthur Goldhammer (Cambridge, Mass., 1989), 3: 571–607; Rétif de la Bretonne, *La vie de mon père,* as cited in Alain Collomp, *La maison du père: Famille et village en Haute-Provence aux XVIIe et XVIIIe siècles* (Paris, 1983), 129.

6. Jean-Claude Bonnet, "De la famille à la patrie," in *Histoire des pères,* 235–58; Jean-Louis Flandrin, *Families in Former Times: Kinship, Household and Sexuality,* trans. Richard Southern (New York, 1979), 158–60; Lynn Hunt, *The Family Romance of the French Revolution* (Berkeley, 1992), 17–40; Jeffrey Merrick, "Patriarchalism and Constitutionalism in Eighteenth-Century Parlementary Discourse," *Studies in Eighteenth-Century Culture* 20 (1990): 317–30, and "The Family Politics of the Marquis de Bombelles," *Journal of Family History* 21 (1996): 503–518; Rebecca Rassier, "History, Literature, and the Representation of Women in Eighteenth-Century France" (Ph.D. diss., University of Wisconsin at Madison, 2000), 74–105; Maurice Daumas, *Le syndrome des Grieux: La relation père/fils au XVIIIe siècle* (Paris, 1990); Yves Castan, "Père et fils en Languedoc à l'époque classique," *XVIIe siècle* 102–3 (1974): 30–44; Thomas Crow, *Painters and Public Life in Eighteenth-Century Paris* (New Haven, Conn., 1985).

7. For an overview, see Alain Collomp, "Families: Habitations and Cohabitations," in *History of Private Life,* 3: 493–529. On household structure, see André Burguière, "Les fondements d'une culture familiale" in *Histoire de la France: Les formes de la culture,* ed. André Burguière (Paris, 1993), 25–188; and "Les transformations de la culture familiale et des structures domestiques autour de la Révolution," *Annales de Bretagne et des pays de l'Ouest* 100 (1993): 395–410; Hervé Le Bras and Emmanuel Todd, *L'Invention de la France* (Paris, 1981).

8. One exceptional region within Normandy, the Pays de Caux, followed primogeniture. In France overall, in the West strict equality prevailed, while custom in the Paris-Orléans region generally allowed heirs to choose between keeping gifts (such as benefits set up in marriage contracts) that they had received during their parents' lifetimes, or returning these gifts and partaking in the final division at the death of the parent (system of "rapport-option"). Emmanuel LeRoy Ladurie, "Système de la coutume: Structures familiales et coutumes d'héritages en France au XVIe siècle," *Annales: Economies, Sociétés, Civilisations* 27 (1972): 825–46. (A translated version of this useful overview appears in *Family and Inheritance: Rural Society in Western Europe, 1200–1800,* ed. Jack Goody et al. [Cambridge, Eng., 1976], 37–70). Jean Yver, *Egalité entre héritiers et exclusion des filles dotées, essai de géographie coutumière* (Paris, 1966). For critiques of Yver's reliance on the letter of the law and tendency to downplay variations in practice, see David Sabean, "Aspects of Kinship Behavior and Property in Western Europe before 1800," in *Family and Inheritance,* 98–110; Bernard Dérouet, "Les pratiques familiales, le droit et la

construction des différences (15e–19e siècles)," *Annales: Histoire. Sciences sociales* (1997): 369–91; Barbara Diefendorf, "Women and Property in *ancien régime* France: Theory and Practice in Dauphiné and Paris," in *Early Modern Conceptions of Property,* ed. John Brewer and Susan Staves (London, 1994), 170–93, 185; Zoe Schneider, "Women before the Bench: Female Litigants in Early Modern Normandy," *French Historical Studies* 23 (2000): 1–32. On women and Old Regime civil law in regions across France, see Paul Ourliac and Jean-Louis Gazzaniga, *Histoire du droit privé français de l'an mille au Code civil* (Paris, 1985).

9. Margaret Darrow, *Revolution in the House: Family, Class, and Inheritance in Southern France, 1775–1825* (Princeton, N.J., 1989), 6–8.

10. Elisabeth Claverie and Pierre Lamaison, *L'impossible mariage: Violence et parenté en Gévaudan, XVIIe, XVIIIe et XIXe siècles* (Paris, 1982); Collomp, *Maison du père;* Antoinette Fauve-Chaumoux, "Mariages sauvages contre mariages-souches: La guerre des cadets," in *Les Cadets,* ed. Georges Ravis-Giordani and Martine Segalen (Paris, 1994), 181–94; Darrow, *Revolution in the House.* On Old Regime noblewomen invoking their victimization by the Norman custom, see Gayle Brunelle, "Dangerous Liaisons: Mésalliance and Early Modern French Noblewomen," *French Historical Studies* 19 (1995): 75–103; Schneider, "Women before the Bench," 28–29.

11. Hunt, *Family Romance;* Jacques Mulliez, "La volonté d'un homme," in *Histoire des pères,* 279–305; and "Révolutionnaires, nouveaux pères? Forcément nouveaux pères! Le droit révolutionnaire de la paternité," in *RévJur,* 1: 373–98; Pierre Murat, "La puissance paternelle et la Révolution française: Essai de régénération de l'autorité des pères," in *FLE,* 390–411.

12. For petitions, see AN DIV 13, AN DIII 379 and 382, AN ADII 48, AN ADXVIIIc 164 and 165. AN DIV 13, Pétition de Dutemple à Monsieur, 25 Dec. 1790. Gary Kates, " 'The Powers of Husband and Wife Must Be Equal and Separate': The Cercle Social and the Rights of Women, 1790–91," in *Women and Politics in the Age of Democratic Revolution,* ed. Harriet B. Applewhite and Darline G. Levy (Ann Arbor, 1990), 163–80; François Lanthenas, *Inconvéniens du droit d'ainesse . . .* (Paris, n.d., c. 1789) and *Adresse présentée à l'Assemblée nationale, pour demander que l'égalité des partages entre les enfans soit rétablie par un décret constitutionnel; qu'une émancipation légale soit fixée, et que la faculté d'adopter soit rendue à ceux qui sont sans postérité* (Paris, 1790). Lanthenas presented his appeal for equal inheritance at the bar of the National Assembly in August 1790. *Septième lettre bougrement patriotique de la Mère Duchêne sur le décret portant égalité des droits aux successions ab intestat* (n.d., c. April 1791).

13. Loi du 15–28 mars 1790, Duvergier, 1: 114–16; Loi du 16 mars 1790, Duvergier, 1: 121–23; Loi du 16 août 1790, Duvergier 1: 326–27. On the debates surrounding the abolition of lettres de cachet, see James F. Traer, *Marriage and the Family in Eighteenth-Century France* (Ithaca, N.Y., 1980), 139–45. Mirabeau, author of *Des lettres de cachet et des prisons d'état* (Hamburg, 1782), served on the committee that orchestrated their abolition.

14. Mirabeau (read by Talleyrand), *AP,* 24: 511–15, 2 Apr. 1791; Philippe-Antoine Merlin de Douai, *Rapport sur les successions ab intestat* (Paris, 1791), delivered 21 Nov. 1790. On this April 1791 debate, see Jean-Louis Halpérin, *L'impossible Code civil* (Paris, 1992), 81–97; Bernard Schnapper, "L'autorité domestique et les hommes politiques de la Révolution," in *FLE,* 221–33; Murat, "Puissance paternelle."

15. Pétion, *AP* 24: 612–16, 6 Apr. 1791; Robespierre, *AP* 24: 562–70, 5 Apr. 1791.

16. Cazalès, *AP* 24: 570–77, 5 Apr. 1791; Achard de Bonvouloir, Lambert de Frondeville, and Darnaudat, *AP* 24: 47–49, 12 Mar. 1791.

17. Loi du 8 avril 1791, Duvergier 2: 287–88.

18. Murat, "Puissance paternelle," 403; cf. Halpérin, *Impossible Code civil,* 94–95. The Legislative Assembly outlawed entailment in principle on 25 Aug. 1792; the Convention made this into law on 14 Nov. 1792. Laws passed on 28 Aug. 1792 and 20 Sept. 1792 provided that parental control over property terminated when the child reached twenty-one and allowed children aged twenty-one or older to marry without parental consent: Duvergier, 4: 375–76, 482–88; 5: 44–45.

19. Pénières, Mailhe, and Philippeaux, *AP* 59: 680–83, 7 Mar. 1793; Halpérin, *Impossible Code civil,* 111–21.

20. Duvergier, 6: 269–71.

21. Duvergier, 6: 256–57 and 6: 373–84. The 17 nivôse law ruled that this small disposable portion could go only to heirs outside the direct or collateral lines.

22. The Civil Code reiterated the principle of equal partition among offspring, but increased the disposable portion to one-half in the case of one child or no children; one-third in the case of two children; and one-fourth in the case of three or more children. The testator could privilege one child or more with this additional share. On succession law, see André Dejace, *Les règles de la dévolution successorale sous la Révolution (1789–1794)* (Bruxelles-Liège, 1957); Jacques Poumarède, "La législation successorale de la Révolution entre l'idéologie et la pratique," in *FLE,* 167–82.

23. Poumarède, "Législation successorale." While the law abolished dowers for those married after its promulgation, the status of dowers for widows married before 17 nivôse lay open to diverse interpretation. In Normandy dowers were granted to any widow married pre–17 nivôse. Appeals courts ultimately judged that the law did not suppress existing dowers across France. Duvergier, 16: 381–82. Corinne Bléry, "L'Application du régime matrimonial normand devant la Cour de Cassation au XIXe siècle" (Mémoire de D.E.A., Université de Caen, 1988).

24. Anonymous review of François Lanthenas' *Inconvéniens du droit d'aînesse,* in *Courrier de Lyon* 14 and 15 October 1789, 313–16 and 320–24, as quoted by Kates, "Powers of Husband and Wife," 168. Gary Kates, *The Cercle Social: The Girondins and the French Revolution* (Princeton, N.J., 1985), 115–27.

25. Perrot, *Genèse d'une ville moderne,* 1: 312–19, 364–65; Charles Alline, *De l'ancien régime matrimonial normand et de sa survivance dans la pratique notariale sous le droit intermédiaire et sous le code civil* (Thèse de droit, Université de Caen [Paris, 1908]), 120–30. Given the control of customary law over the disposal of property, marriage contracts were narrower in scope and less frequently used in Normandy than elsewhere in France. Perrot, "Note sur les contrats de mariage normands," annex in A. Daumard and F. Furet, *Structures et relations sociales à Paris au XVIIIe siècle, Cahiers des Annales* 18 (Paris, 1961), 95–97.

26. Real property in certain cities ("bourgs"), including Caen, legally qualified as "bourgages." Daughters could claim an equal share of this property, and widows could claim their dower share of bourgages property outright rather than in usufruct only. Ambroise Colin, "Le droit des gens mariés dans la coutume de Normandie," *Nouvelle revue historique de droit français et étranger* 16 (1892): 427–69, esp. 460–65; Robert Génestal, *La Tenure en bourgage: Etude sur la propriété foncière dans les villes normandes* (Paris, 1900); Perrot, *Genèse d'une ville,* 1: 30–31, 318. On daughters' inheritance, see Robert Besnier, "Les filles dans le droit successoral normand," *Tijdschrift voor Rechtsgeschiedenis: Revue d'histoire du droit* 10 (1930): 488–506; Jacqueline Musset, "Les droits successoraux des filles dans la coutume de Normandie," in *La femme en Normandie: Actes du XIXe Congrès des sociétés historiques et archéologiques de Normandie* (Caen, 1986), 53–60.

27. Claude Mazauric, "Réflexions sur l'efficacité sociale du droit successoral cauchois à la veille de son abolition révolutionnaire," in *RévJur,* 1: 345–58. Even in other parts of Normandy, the system de facto favored the eldest son, who received his inheritance portion earliest and used it the longest before the egalitarian redivision at the parents' death: Sabean, "Aspects of Kinship Behavior," 106–7.

28. Quotation from Jean-Marie Gouesse, "Parenté, famille, et mariage en Normandie aux XVIIe et XVIIIe siècles," *Annales: Economies, Sociétés, Civilisations* 27 (1972): 1139–54, 1153. On regional family structures, see Burguière, "Fondements d'une culture familiale"; Pierre Goubert, *The French Peasantry in the Seventeenth Century,* trans. Ian Patterson (Cambridge, Eng., 1986), 70–81; Perrot, *Genèse d'une ville,* 1: 312–17; Hervé LeBras and Emmanuel Todd, *L'Invention de la France: Atlas anthropologique et politique* (Paris, 1981), 13–88.

29. The husband could not alienate the real estate portion of his wife's dowry without guaranteeing a specific replacement ("remploi"). A widow had the right to her dowry, to the usufruct of up to one-third of her husband's real estate, and to the simple possession of one-third of his movable goods if they had children, one-half if they had none. Alline, *De l'ancien régime matrimonial normand,* 18–90; Pierre Cinquabre, "Le statut juridique de la femme en Normandie aux XVIIe et XVIIIe siècles," in *Femme en Normandie,* 43–51; Charles Lefebvre, "L'ancien droit matrimonial de Normandie," *Nouvelle revue historique de droit français et étranger* 35 (1911): 481–535.

30. Schneider, "Women before the Bench"; "The Village and the State: Justice and the Local Courts in Normandy, 1670–1740" (Ph.D. diss., Georgetown University, 1997), chap. 8; Clare Crowston, "Engendering the Guilds: Seamstresses, Tailors, and the Clash of Corporate Identities in Old Regime France," *French Historical Studies* 23 (2000): 339–71; Daryl Hafter, "Female Masters in the Ribbonmaking Guild of Eighteenth-Century Rouen," *French Historical Studies* 20 (1997): 1–14.

31. Alain Collomp, "Le statut des cadets en Haute-Provence avant et après le Code civil," in *Cadets*, 157–67, 163; Françoise Fortunet, "Connaissance et conscience juridique à l'époque révolutionnaire en pays de droit coutumier: La législation successorale," in *RévJur* 1: 359–71; Jean Bart, "L'égalité entre héritiers dans la région dijonnaise à la fin de l'ancien régime et sous la révolution," *Mémoires de la société pour l'histoire du droit et des institutions des anciens pays bourguignons, comtois, et romands* 29 (1968): 65–78; Paulette Poncet-Crétin, "La pratique testamentaire en Bourgogne et en Franche-Comté de 1770 à 1815" (Thèse de droit, Université de Dijon, 1973), 16–23, 256–71; Darrow, *Revolution in the House*, 167, 240; Olivier Devaux, "Les tribunaux de famille du district de Rieux et l'application de la loi du 17 nivôse an II," *Annales de l'université des sciences sociales à Toulouse*, 35 (1987): 135–58; Marc Ferret, *Les tribunaux de famille dans le district de Montpellier (1790–an IV)* (Montpellier, 1926); Poumarède, "Législation successorale"; James F. Traer, "The French Family Court," *History* 59 (1974): 211–28.

32. Traer, *Marriage and the Family*, 32–47; James Farr, *Authority and Sexuality in Early Modern Burgundy* (Oxford, 1995), 90–123; Roland Mousnier, *Les institutions de la France sous la monarchie absolue*, 2 vols. (Paris, 1974–80), 2: 249–408. On Normandy, Jonathan Dewald, *Pont-Saint-Pierre, 1398–1789: Lordship, Community, and Capitalism in Early Modern France* (Berkeley, 1987), 251–63; Schneider, "Women before the Bench."

33. ADC 1B 1185, Délibérations de famille, bailliage de Caen, 1788–89. On pre-1789 arbitration, see Nicole Castan, *Justice et répression en Languedoc à l'époque de lumières* (Paris, 1980), chap. 1. On family courts, see Traer, "French Family Court"; Isser Woloch, *The New Regime: Transformations of the French Civic Order, 1789–1820s* (New York, 1994), 307–320; Claudine Bloch and Jean Hilaire, "Nouveauté et modernité du droit révolutionnaire: La procédure civile," in *RévJur* 2: 469–82; Jean-Jacques Clère, "L'arbitrage révolutionnaire: Apogée et déclin d'une institution (1790–1806)," *Revue de l'arbitrage* (1981): 3–28; Jean-Louis Halpérin, "La composition des tribunaux de famille sous la Révolution, ou les juristes, comment s'en débarrasser?" in *FLE*, 292–304.

34. Devaux, "Tribunaux de famille du district de Rieux," 146–47; Ferret, *Tribunaux de famille dans le district de Montpellier;* Traer, "French Family Court," 219–20.

35. My sample includes all the family court cases clearly occurring in the town of Caen and a random sample of cases in communes of the surrounding district. ADC 3L 608 through 3L 617, Sentences arbitrales du district de Caen (hereafter SA Caen). Families who returned repeatedly to arbitration are

counted only once. Also on Caen, see Jean Forcioli, *Une institution révolution-naire, le tribunal de famille d'après les archives du district de Caen* (Thèse de droit, Université de Caen [Caen, 1932]).

36. Three cases involved both sibling and dowry disputes. Only four of these widowhood cases involved widowers rather than widows.

37. ADC 3L 616, SA Caen, 17 fructidor an III (3 Sept. 1795); ADC 3L 614, SA Caen, 3 frimaire an III (23 Nov. 1794); ADC 3L 617, SA Caen, 24 thermidor an III (11 Aug. 1795).

38. Devaux comes to this same impasse and also finds frequent contestation over relatively small sums in the family courts in the Haute-Garonne. Devaux, "Tribunaux de famille du district de Rieux," 155.

39. Olwen Hufton, *Bayeux in the Late Eighteenth Century* (Oxford, 1967), 81–84. Inventory counts overrepresent more well-off individuals. Daniel Roche, *The People of Paris: An Essay in the Popular Culture of the 18th Century,* trans. Marie Evans (Berkeley, 1987, orig. ed. 1981), 59–63, 74–90; Clare Haru Crowston, *Fabricating Women: The Seamstress of Old Regime France, 1675–1791* (Durham, N.C., 2001), 366–83; Steven Laurence Kaplan, *The Bakers of Paris and the Bread Question, 1700–1775* (Durham, N.C., 1996), 337–76.

40. I could determine length of case in 122 of the 143 cases: less than two months: 82 cases (67 percent); two to six months: 19 cases (16 percent); six months or more: 21 cases (17 percent).

41. ADC Registres 3L 618 through 3L 626, Tribunal du district de (hereafter TDD) Caen, minutes d'audience, 5 Jan. 1791—23 fructidor an III (9 Sept. 1795). After the abolition of the district court, the Tribunal civil of the department enforced family court decisions. ADC 3L1354, Tribunal civil du Calvados, minutes d'audience, 28 brumaire an IV (19 Nov. 1795).

42. Only in 1791 did the majority of arbiters lack legal training. See also Forcioli, *Institution révolutionnaire,* 39; Halpérin, "Composition des tribunaux," 298–99; Roderick Phillips, *Family Breakdown in Late Eighteenth-Century France* (Ithaca, N.Y., 1980), 22–28; Traer, "French Family Court," 215–19; Paul Viard, "Les tribunaux de famille dans le district de Dijon (1790–1792)," *Nouvelle revue historique de droit français et étranger* 45 (1921): 242–77, esp. 249–56; Devaux, "Tribunaux de famille du district de Rieux"; Ferret, *Tribunaux de famille dans le district de Montpellier,* 103–5.

43. Halpérin, *Impossible Code civil,* 174–99, quote 183.

44. Traer, "French Family Court," 225; Halpérin, "Composition des tribunaux," 300.

45. ADC 3L 1334–3L 1338, Sentences arbitrales, an IV–VIII (1796–1800), registered by the Tribunal civil du Calvados (hereafter SA Calvados). These arbitration sessions finally stopped calling themselves "tribunaux de famille" by late 1797, and gradually dealt with fewer divorce and inheritance cases. See also, Traer, *Marriage and the Family,* 164.

46. For thought-provoking work on how law, cultural norms, and family and individual strategies all affect practice, see Farr, *Authority and Sexuality;* Hendrik Hartog, *Man and Wife in America: A History* (Cambridge, Mass.,

2000); Thomas Kuehn, *Law, Family, and Women: Toward a Legal Anthropology of Renaissance Italy* (Chicago, 1991).

47. ADC 3L 614, SA Caen 28 frimaire an III (18 Dec. 1794); ADC 3L 615, SA Caen 23 ventôse an III (13 Mar. 1795). Litigators repeatedly justify their actions along these lines in petitions. AN DIII 338, Mémoire de la citoyenne Jeanne Rouillaud femme Mouret au Comité de législation, n.d., c. spring 1795; AN DIII 147, Pétition des citoyennes filles en général de la commune de Tourville (Manche) aux représentants du peuple, 30 germinal an III (19 Apr. 1795); AN DIII 35, Mémoire de la citoyenne Françoise Quesnay femme Lefort à la Convention nationale, reçu 26 fructidor an II (12 Sept. 1794).

48. Traer, *Marriage and the Family;* Poumarède, "Législation successorale."

49. ADC 3L 613, SA Caen, 27 floréal an II (16 May 1794). Phillips, *Family Breakdown*, 22.

50. ADC 3L 615, SA Caen, 2 nivôse an III (22 Dec. 1795); ADC 3L 615, SA Caen, 29 ventôse an III (19 Mar. 1795); ADC 3L 611, SA Caen, 11 July 1793; ADC 3L 611, SA Caen, 22 July 1793; ADC 3L 616, SA Caen, 26 floréal an III (15 May 1795); ADC 3L 617, SA Caen, 22 brumaire an IV (13 Nov. 1795); ADC 3L 615, SA Caen, 25 ventôse an III (15 Mar. 1795); ADC 3L 614, SA Caen, 23 brumaire an III (13 Nov. 1794); ADC 3L 611, SA Caen, 24 Sept. 1793; ADC 3L 1336, SA Calvados, 8 ventôse an VI (26 Feb. 1798). Procurations appointing female proxies were often notarized: e.g., in ADC 8E 4393 and 8E 3119, Tabellionage de Caen, Dépôts de Poignaut and Bocave, an IV. Cf. Darrow, *Revolution in the House*, 121.

51. ADC 3L 610, SA Caen, 25 Oct. 1792. On women's uses of legal power-lessness, see Natalie Zemon Davis, *Fiction in the Archives* (Stanford, Calif., 1987); Castan, *Justice et répression*, 233–37, and *Les criminels de Languedoc: Les exigences d'ordre et les voies du ressentiment dans une société pré-révolutionnaire (1750–1790)* (Toulouse, 1980), 25–36; Brunelle, "Dangerous Liaisons"; Yves Castan, "Statuts féminins au XVIIIe siècle d'après les profils exemplaires des plaidoyers en Languedoc," in *Droit, Histoire, Sexualité*, ed. Jacques Poumarède et Jean-Pierre Royer (Lille, 1987), 169–75; Darrow, *Revolution in the House*, 205.

52. For questions about women's ability to witness or make contracts, see AN DIII 194, Lettre des administrateurs du département de l'Orne au Comité de législation, 19 fructidor an II (5 Sept. 1794); AN DIII 147, Lettre du J. B. Fafrin, membre du conseil général de la commune de Valogne (Manche) au Comité de législation, 17 fructidor an II (3 Sept. 1794); ADC 3L 611, SA Caen, 10 Sept. 1793; ADC 3L 615, SA Caen, 8 pluviôse an III (27 Jan. 1795); ADC 3L 610, SA Caen, 23 Oct. 1792.

53. ADC 3L 1334, SA Calvados, 25 frimaire an IV (16 Dec. 1795); ADC 3L 1335, SA Calvados, 3 nivôse an V (23 Dec. 1796); ADC 3L 1336, SA Calvados, 3 thermidor an VI (21 July 1798); ADC 3L 616, SA Caen, 1 prairial an III (20 May 1795); ADC 3L 616, SA Caen, 15 prairial an III (4 June 1795); ADC 3L 615, SA Caen, 23 ventôse an III (13 Mar. 1795); ADC 3L 614, SA Caen, 8 brumaire an III (29 Oct. 1794); ADC 3L 614, SA Caen, 26 brumaire an III (16 Nov. 1794); ADC

3L 610, SA Caen, 25 Oct. 1792. ADC 3Q 2172, Table des successions. Bureau de Caen, 1791–1809 (= Notarized legacy transactions). On appeals cases, see Corinne Bléry, "Les conflits entre la coutume de Normandie et la loi du 17 nivôse an II à propos de la propriété des biens des époux," in *Révolution et mouvements révolutionnaires en Normandie: Actes du XXIVe Congrès des sociétés historiques et archéologiques de Normandie tenu au Havre du 24 au 29 octobre 1989. Recueil de l'Association des Amis du Vieux Havre* (1990): 63–68; and "Application du régime matrimonial normand."

54. On sisters' inability to obtain their légitimes successfully in the Old Regime, see Roger Bataille, *Du droit des filles dans la succession de leurs parents en Normandie, et particulièrement du mariage avenant* (Thèse de droit, Université de Paris [Paris, 1927]), 116–56; Henri Basnage, *Commentaires sur la Coutume de Normandie*, 2 vols. (Rouen, 1776), 1: 394; AN DIII 32, Pétition des citoyennes soussignées du département du Calvados à la Convention nationale, received 3 Mar. 1793, signed by thirty-five women and several X's.

55. ADC 3L 614, SA Caen, 21 frimaire an III (11 Dec. 1794); ADC 3L 617, SA Caen, 6 messidor an III (24 June 1795). For comparable légitime claims in the Pyrénées, see Poumarède, "Législation successorale," 175.

56. ADC 3L 1334, SA Calvados, 23 vendémiaire an IV (15 Oct. 1795); ADC 3L 612, SA Caen, 20 brumaire an II (10 Nov. 1793).

57. ADC 3L 608, SA Caen, 28 Nov. 1791, sent to TDD for final decision; ADC 3L 612, SA Caen, 18 frimaire an II (8 Dec. 1793); ADC 3L 614, SA Caen, 29 brumaire an III (19 Nov. 1794).

58. ADC 3L 610, SA Caen, 3–5 Aug. 1792; ADC 3L 611 and 612, SA Caen, 21 Feb. 1793–5 brumaire an II (26 October 1793); ADC 3L 610 and 611, SA Caen, 12 Aug. 1792–28 Mar. 1793; ADC 3L 615, SA Caen, 17 pluviôse an III (5 Feb. 1795). Quotations from AN DIII 33, Pétition des citoyennes Marie Jeanne et Marie Rogne au Comité de législation, 5 messidor an II (23 June 1794). Cf. Alline, *L'ancien régime matrimonial normand*, 94–173; Devaux, "Tribunaux de famille du district de Rieux," 143–44; Claverie and Lamaison, *Impossible mariage*, 69–71; Joseph Goy, "Transmission successorale et paysannerie pendant la Révolution française: Un grand malentendu," *Etudes rurales* 110 (1988): 45–56, 52; Poumarède, "Législation successorale," 175–76; Darrow, *Revolution in the House*, 86–170, 210–47.

59. ADC 3L 612, SA Caen, 27 floréal an II (16 May 1794); ADC 3L 613, SA Caen, 20 germinal au 26 floréal an II (9 Apr.–15 May 1794); ADC 3L 617, SA Caen, 8 fructidor an III (25 Aug. 1795); ADC 3L 614, SA Caen, 15 frimaire an III (5 Dec. 1794).

60. ADC 3L 613, SA Caen, 14 floréal au 27 thermidor an II (3 May–14 Aug. 1794). Cf. ADC 3L 616, SA Caen, 5 germinal an II (25 Mar. 1794); ADC 3L 611, 614, and 615, SA Caen, 22 Oct. 1793–7 nivôse an III (27 Dec. 1794); ADC 3L 610, SA Caen, 28 Oct. 1792; ADC 3L 614, SA Caen, 28 frimaire an III (18 Dec. 1794).

61. ADC 3L 610 and 611, SA Caen, 3 Dec. 1791–1 June 1793; ADC 3L 613, SA Caen, 11 fructidor an II (28 Aug. 1794).

62. AN ADII 48, AN DIII 339, and the DIII dossiers for Norman depart-

ments contain printed legal briefs and letters from lay citizens, lawyers, and officials regarding the impact of the 8 April 1791 law. Many complain that neighboring district tribunals do not interpret the status of married women in the same way.

63. ADC 3L 611, SA Caen, 26 Mar. 1793.

64. AN DIII 339, *Question de droit. Consultation. De la succession des filles normandes, délibéré à Caen, 22 décembre 1792*, by hommes de loi Thome, Regnault, Pelvey, et Chrétien (Caen, 1792).

65. AN DIII 34, Pétition du citoyen Grandmaison, homme de loi à Condé-sur-Noireau (Calvados), au citoyen président de la Convention nationale, 4 June 1793; AN ADII 48, "Réponse à un mémoire ayant pour titre, mémoire à l'appui de la pétition présentée à la Convention nationale le 24 mai 1793 relative aux décrets rendus sur la succesion *ab intestat*, par Viellard," par Lasseret, membre du bureau de conciliation de Caen (Caen, n.d., c. 1793); AN DIII 33, Pétition du citoyen Lagranche (de Caen) au Citoyen président, 28 May 1793; AN DIII 145, Pétition du citoyen Dellebecque (homme de loi à Falaise, Calvados) aux citoyens législateurs, 13 Aug. 1793; Pétition du citoyen Desclosets (Falaise) aux citoyens législateurs, 9 June 1793. Various *mémoires* printed by the Imprimerie J. L. Poisson in Caen and by the Imprimerie Desenne in Paris supported this interpretation of the April 1791 law and married daughters' legacy rights in general.

66. Fortunet, "Connaissance et conscience juridique"; Collomp, "Statut des cadets," 163–66; Poumarède, "La législation successorale," 177; ADC 3Q 2172, Table des successions, Bureau de Caen (1791–1809). At least one family notarized their decision not to redivide again regardless of changes in law. ADC 8E 3118, Dépôt de Bocave, notaire Pillet, Accord de la famille Mesange, 25 frimaire an IV (16 Dec. 1795).

67. In most dotal regimes, the husband had to guarantee that he could replace his wife's dowry with other mortgaged goods if he chose to invest it. At his death, the wife took her dowry before any other creditors could make claims on his estate. Such controls limited the circulation of capital, especially in Normandy and certain parts of the Midi.

68. Alline, *L'ancien régime matrimonial normand*, 94–193. Under communal marital property, the wife had little legal control over goods, but would be granted half of jointly held goods at her husband's death and usufruct over other portions. The marriage contract could stipulate what kinds of goods would be held in common and what remained separate. After the Civil Code, many Norman couples created contracts that combined dotal and communal features.

69. These court cases apply to marriage contracts made during the uncertain phase between 17 nivose an II (6 Jan. 1794) and the Civil Code of 1804. Corinne Bléry found a shift in jurisprudence after 1841 against allowing community property contracts during the pre-1804 period. Bléry, "Application du régime matrimonial normand," 15–26, quote from Cour de Cassation, 24.

70. Only close regional studies can assess the immense variety in responses to new marital property possibilities. For example, in the region of Montauban, the peasants clung to the dotal regime, while artisans in town increasingly

adopted communal property. In the Bouches-du-Rhône, the propertied classes of Aix-en-Provence largely stuck to the dotal regime well into the mid nineteenth century, while both the artisanal and working inhabitants of the industrializing region Martigues along the coast moved more quickly to the communal system. See Darrow, *Revolution in the House,* esp. 247; Nicole Arnaud-Duc, *Droit, mentalités et changement social en Provence occidentale: Une étude sur les stratégies et la pratique notariale en matière de régime matrimonial, de 1785 à 1855* (Saint-Etienne, 1985), 291–303; Burguière, "Fondements d'une culture familiale," 62–65.

71. The new law allowed childless couples to give all of their property to each other; those with children were limited to giving the usufruct of half of their goods to each other. ADC 3L 601, TDD Caen, Enregistrement des insinuations et des donations entre-vifs, 31 Dec. 1790–an IV (1796); ADC 3L 970, TDD Lisieux, Registre des donations entre vifs et des insinuations, an III (1794–95).

72. Ibid.; ADC 8E 3119, Tabellionage de Caen, Dépôt de Bocave, Notaire à Caen, Jun.–Dec. 1795. Cf. Alline, *L'ancien régime matrimonial normand,* 153–54.

73. Julie Hardwick, *The Practice of Patriarchy: Gender and the Politics of Household Authority in Early Modern France* (University Park, Penn., 1998), 115–20; ADC 3L 614, SA Caen, 26 brumaire an III (16 Nov. 1794); ADC 3L 616, SA Caen, 15 prairial an III (3 June 1795); ADC 3L 626, TDD Caen, 18 fructidor an III (4 Sept. 1795).

74. Burguière, "Fondements d'une culture familiale."

75. ADC 3L 613, SA Caen, 15 germinal an III (4 Apr. 1795).

76. The law of 3 vendémiaire an IV (25 Sept. 1795) reversed the retroactive portions of the 17 nivôse law, allowing for another round of redivisions for estates opened retroactively. Fewer redivisions occurred than one might expect. Halpérin, *Impossible Code civil,* 261. The family courts conducted a few redivisions: ADC 3L 615, SA Caen, 21 vendémiaire an IV (13 Oct. 1795); ADC 3L 1334, SA Calvados, 6 vendémiaire an IV (28 Sept. 1795), SA Calvados, 22 brumaire an IV (13 Nov. 1795), SA Calvados, 9 brumaire an IV (31 Oct. 1795), SA Calvados, 27 nivôse an IV (17 Jan. 1796); ADC 3L 1335, SA Calvados, 25 ventôse an V (15 Mar. 1797), SA Calvados, 15 thermidor an V (2 Aug. 1797). The vast notarial records no doubt contain more redivisions.

77. See note 2.

78. AN DIII 143, Pétition de la citoyenne Jeanne Gallien veuve Barenton aux citoyens représentants, 9 floréal an III (28 Apr. 1795); AN C125, Pétition des Amis de la Constitution à Caen aux Messieurs, 22 June 1791; Adresse des Amis de la Constitution de la ville de Lisieux à l'Assemblée nationale, n.d., as cited in Françoise de Loisy, "Recherches sur la dévolution successorale légitime et la notion d'égalité en pays de coutume au XVIIIe siècle" (Université de Dijon, Mémoire pour D.E.S. d'histoire du droit, 1970), 45.

79. Wives and mothers petitioned far more often on behalf of their husbands and sons than husbands and fathers did on behalf of wives and daughters.

80. Model petitions *attacking* egalitarian inheritance laws circulated widely

in both the Midi and Normandy, at least in the departments of Lot-et-Garonne, Tarn, Calvados, Manche, and Seine-Inférieure. Model petitions favoring egalitarian inheritance were evidently rare: I found only one, from the Tarn, which favored cadet inheritance without reference to gender. AN DIII 338, Adresse des héritiers rappelés de la commune de _____ à la Convention nationale, n.d., c. 1795.

81. AN DIII 338, Pétition de la citoyenne fille Villier aux citoyens législateurs, 16 floréal an III (5 May 1795).

82. E.g., AN ADXVIIIc 164, *Adresse des Cadets du tiers état de Provence et d'autres pays de droit écrit au roi* (n.p., 1789); AN ADXVIIIc 165, M. Arbaud, *Dissertation critique et politique sur nos loix* (Aix, 1790).

83. AN DIII 274, Pétition anonyme à la Convention nationale, signed "par une calvadosienne qui a été victime de la tyrannie et qui, voyageant actuellement dans le pays de Caux, peut assurer que les vœux qu'elle forme pour le maintien de la loi du 17 nivôse sont ceux de son département et celui de la Seine-Inférieure. Elle cache son nom pour être mieux aportée de dire ce qu'elle pense," 12 messidor an III (30 June 1795). AN DIII 338, Pétition de la citoyenne Jeanne Barinçon au citoyen président de la Convention nationale, 26 prairial an III (14 June 1795).

84. AN DIII 32, Pétition des citoyennes du département du Calvados à la Convention nationale, received 31 Jan. 1793, signed by fifteen women on behalf of "a large number of other citoyennes who have declared that they cannot sign and join with us to solicit the same justice." AN DIII 144, Pétition des citoyennes du département de la Manche au citoyen président de la Convention nationale, envoyée de Coutances, 8 Dec. 1792; AN DIII 146, Pétition de plusieurs filles de Saint-Lô, La Manche, au Monsieur le Président de l'assemblée législative, 5 June 1792; AN DIII 338, Réclamation à la Convention nationale par des citoyennes des communes du district de Falaise (Calvados), n.d., c. floréal an III (May 1795).

85. AN DIII 338, Pétition des héritiers rappellés par la loi |du 17 nivôse an II|, au Comité de législation, n.d., c. winter–spring 1795, from Lot-et-Garonne with c. one hundred signers. Some of the female signers added, "tant pour moi que pour mes frères xx et xx à l'armée"; AN DIII 269, Pétition de la veuve Gingoir, 15 fructidor an II (1 Sept. 1794). Among the myriad examples of younger sons' petitions with rights language, see, e.g., AN DIII 339, Pétition de quelques citoyens au nom de la grande majorité du peuple à la Convention nationale, à Aiguillon, département de Lot-et-Garonne, 12 floréal an III (1 May 1795).

86. In contrast to Pateman and Landes, I argue that liberal democratic ideology did not lead by definition to the exclusion of women from politics and to the creation of a separate private sphere. Rather, liberalism caused the issue of women's position within the family to be raised, but left it unresolved. Only through the extensive struggles in practice would the nineteenth-century turn toward domesticity become clear. Cf. Carole Pateman, *The Sexual Contract* (Stanford, Calif., 1988); Joan B. Landes, *Women and the Public Sphere in the Age of the French Revolution* (Ithaca, N.Y., 1988). Cf. also Joan Wallach Scott,

Only Paradoxes to Offer: French Feminists and the Rights of Man (Cambridge, Mass., 1996). For a suggestive critique of Pateman, see Hunt, *Family Romance*, 201–4.

87. Female petitioners were most likely to invoke the value of marriage and motherhood in their appeals to extend the 8 April 1791 law against customary exclusion of daughters to married as well as unmarried women. AN DIII 34, Pétition de la citoyenne Duparc, 17 June 1793; *Les Filles mariées dans la ci-devant province de Normandie, à la Convention nationale* (Paris, 1793). Notably, two other groups were more likely to use maternalist arguments: men favoring egalitarian partition rights for women; and women *attacking* the laws because of the negative effect on their husbands or sons. AN C125, Pétition des Amis de la Constitution à Caen à l'Assemblée nationale, 22 Jan. 1791; AN DIII 338, Pétition de la citoyenne Varin née LeCoustier aux citoyens représentants, reçeived 6 prairial an III (25 May 1795); AN DIII 382, Observations (d'une femme anonyme qui habite dans la ci-devant coutume de Paris) sur le décret du 5 brumaire à la Convention nationale, n.d., c. winter 1794; AN ADXVIIIc 365, Pétition au conseil des Cinq Cents: Représentation d'une mère sur la successibilité d'un enfant naturel aux droits légitimes, n.d., c. 1797; AN DIII 339, Pétition de la citoyenne Delphine Clerc au Comité de législation, 6 floréal an III (25 Apr. 1795); and Pétition de Marguerite Lassave, fournière à Toulouse, aux citoyens membres du Comité de législation, n.d., c. 1795; AN DIII 270, Pétition de la citoyenne Morin, femme de médecin, 15 brumaire an III (5 Nov. 1794).

88. *Remonstrances des mères et filles normandes de l'ordre du tiers* (Rouen, 1789). On the identity of the authors, see Claire LeFoll, "Les femmes et le mouvement révolutionnaire à Rouen (1789–1795)" (Mémoire de maîtrise, Université de Haute-Normandie, 1985), 45–46.

89. AN DIII 75, Pétition de la citoyenne Elisabeth Lamaire veuve Potin, aux citoyens représentants, 1 fructidor an III (18 Aug. 1795); AN DIII 35, Pétition de la citoyenne Marie Marguerite Cordier femme Morin au Comité de législation, 8 floréal an III (27 Apr. 1795); AN DIII 272, Pétition d'Adelaide Dorothée Durand, à la Convention nationale, received 2 ventôse an II (20 Feb. 1794); AN DIII 145, Pétition de la citoyenne Marie Anne Catherine Duquesnoy, fille majeure, au Comité de législation, fructidor an III (Aug.–Sept. 1795); AN DIII 382, Mémoire (par une femme anonyme) au Comité de législation, n.d.; AN DIII 338, Pétition de quatre veuves au Comité de législation, 14 floréal an III (3 May 1795).

90. AN DIII 338, Pétition de la citoyenne Marguerite Briançon aux citoyens représentants, 14 floréal an III (3 May 1795); Pétition de la citoyenne Piard Convers aux citoyens représentants, 12 germinal an III (1 Apr. 1795); AN DIII 144, Pétition des citoyennes du département de la Manche au citoyen président de la Convention nationale, 8 Dec. 1792; AN DIII 75, Pétition des citoyennes Bonnelly (3 sœurs) au Comité de législation, 16 floréal an III (5 May 1795).

91. On "sensibilité", see Hans-Jürgen Lüsebrink, "L'innocence persécutée et ses avocats: Rhétorique et impact public du discours 'sensible' dans la France du XVIIIe siècle," *Revue d'histoire moderne et contemporaine* 40 (1993): 86–101;

Sarah Maza, *Private Lives and Public Affairs: The Causes Célèbres of Prerevolutionary France* (Berkeley, 1993); Hunt, *Family Romance*.

92. AN DIII 274, Pétition de la citoyenne M. M. Anquetil aux citoyens représentants, 29 prairial an III (17 June 1795); AN DIII 147, Lettre de la citoyenne Galot Thiphaine aux citoyens représentants, received 3 messidor an II (21 June 1794). AN DIII 32, Pétition des citoyennes soussignées du département du Calvados à la Convention nationale, received 3 Mar. 1793, signed by thirty-five women and several X's; this is one of several collective petitions from groups calling themselves "citoyennes du Calvados."

93. AN DIII 273, Mémoire par Marie Magdelaine Montfreulle, envoyé au Comité de législation, 14 messidor an III (2 July 1795); AN DIII 34, Pétition de la citoyenne Beaufils veuve Lavallé au Comité de législation, 9 messidor an II (27 June 1794).

94. *Les filles mariées dans la ci-devant province de Normandie au Corps législatif* (Paris, n.d., c. year III [1794–95]).

95. AN DIII 273, Pétition de veuve Gouet à l'Assemblée nationale, 4 Jan. 1792; Pétition de la citoyenne Marguerite Jeanne LeBalleur veuve Fiquet au Comité de législation, 14 fructidor an III (31 Aug. 1795).

96. AN DIII 338, Pétition de la citoyenne Jeanne Côme ainée, aux représentants, pères d'un peuple libre, 14 floréal an III (3 May 1795); Pétition de Catherine Douillot au Comité de législation, received 15 prairial an III (4 June 1795).

97. AN DIII 338, Pétition de Julie Poursent aux citoyens composant le Comité de législation, n.d.; Pétition de la citoyenne Jeanne Françoise Aumont au Comité de législation, 7 messidor an III (25 June 1795); *Remonstrances des mères et filles normandes de l'ordre du tiers*; AN DIII 339, Pétition de la citoyenne Ruette au Comité de législation, 22 ventôse an III (12 Mar. 1795); AN DIII 48, *Question relative au décret du 8 avril 1791 sur les successions* (Paris, n.d., c. year IV [1796–96]).

98. AN DXXXIX 4, Pétition de la citoyenne C. M. H. Bureau au Comité de législation, received 9 pluviôse an III (28 Jan. 1795).

99. AN DIII 271, Pétition des citoyennes Julie, Florence, et Cécile Délié au Comité de législation, 28 messidor an II (16 July 1794). Cf. AN DIII 143, Pétition de la citoyenne Létolé aux vertueux représentants, 29 ventôse an III (19 Mar. 1795); AN DIII 147, Pétitions de la citoyenne Galot Thiphaine aux citoyens représentants, 3 and 10 messidor an II (21 and 28 June 1794).

100. AN DIV 13, Pétition de Dutemple à Monsieur, 25 Dec. 1790; AN DIII 338, Pétition de Fabre, capitaine des grenadiers du 2e bataillon du Lot, aux Comité de législation, 10 prairial an III (29 May 1795); Pétition d'Alexandre Pierre Lecourt et sa sœur Rose Mathurine Lacourt aux citoyens représentants, n.d., c. 1794; AN DIII 32, Pétition des grenadiers et volontaires du premier bataillon du Calvados aux législateurs, received 19 Mar. 1793.

101. AN DIII 382, Pétition du citoyen Cournol à la Convention nationale, 2 nivôse an II (22 Dec. 1793); Idée d'un républicain de campagne sur la loi du 14 nivôse dernier, n.d., c. 1794; Projet de loi par François Belloc, homme de loi près

le TDD Tonneins, aux citoyens membres du Comité de législation de l'Assemblée nationale, 20 Sept. 1793; Pétition du citoyen Chapier à la Convention nationale, n.d.; Pétition anonyme à l'Assemblée nationale, n.d.

102. AN DIII 338, Pétition de Marie Girard femme Leglize aux citoyens représentants, received 29 floréal an III (18 May 1795); AN DIII 338, Pétition de la citoyenne Piard Convers aux citoyens représentants, 12 germinal an III (1 Apr. 1795). AN DIII 33, Pétition des citoyennes Marie Jeanne Rogne et Marie Rogne au Comité de législation, 5 messidor an II (23 June 1794); AN DIII 146, Pétition de la citoyenne Marguerite Letellier femme LeMonnier aux représentants, 7 floréal an III (26 Apr. 1795); AN DIII 338, Pétition de la citoyenne Heringue aux représentants du peuple français, 10 floréal an III (20 Apr. 1795).

103. AN DIII 34, Pétition de la citoyenne Mallet au citoyen président de la Convention nationale, received 11 pluviôse an II (30 Jan. 1794); AN DIII 338, Pétition de la fille Villier aux citoyens législateurs, 16 floréal an III (5 May 1795); AN DIII 272, Pétition d'Adelaide Dorothée Durand, à la Convention nationale, received 2 ventôse an II (20 Feb. 1794).

104. On transparent politics, see Lynn Hunt, *Politics, Culture, and Class in the French Revolution* (Berkeley, 1984), 42–43, 72–74.

105. AN DIII 37, Pétition des citoyennes Levaillant au Comité de législation, 4 prairial an III (23 May 1795); AN DIII 33, Pétition de la citoyenne Marie Françoise LaLoe au Comité des pétitions et de la correspondance, 26 germinal an III (15 Apr. 1795); AN DIII 32, Pétition des citoyennes Alexandre, LeTonneur, et Antine aux citoyens députés, received 2 May 1793; AN DIII 338, Pétition de la citoyenne Varin née LeCoustier aux citoyens représentants; *Remonstrances des mères et filles normandes de l'ordre du tiers;* AN DIII 32, Pétition des citoyennes soussignées du département du Calvados à la Convention nationale, received 3 Mar. 1793, signed by thirty-five women and several X's; AN DIII 272, Pétition d'Adelaide Dorothée Durand, à la Convention nationale, received 2 ventôse an II (20 Feb. 1794). Clearly, multiple different "family romances" co-existed in the 1790s. Colin Jones, "A Fine 'Romance' with No Sisters," *French Historical Studies* 19 (1995): 277–87.

106. AN DIII 143, Pétition de la citoyenne Jeanne Gallien veuve Barenton aux citoyens représentants, 9 floréal an III (28 Apr. 1795); AN DIII 147, Pétition de Josephine Letellier aux citoyens législateurs, 26 pluviôse an II (14 Feb. 1794).

107. AN DIII 382, Pétition de la citoyenne Julie . . . républicaine au citoyen président de la Convention nationale, received 1 Nov. 1793; AN DIII 338, Pétition de la citoyenne Rausan veuve Descages aux citoyens [représentants], 27 floréal an III (16 May 1795).

108. Cf. the attempts of some Catholic women and men to combine pro-revolutionary and religious sentiment. Suzanne Desan, *Reclaiming the Sacred: Lay Religion and Popular Politics in Revolutionary France* (Ithaca, N.Y., 1990), 135–58.

109. Poumarède, "Législation successorale," 177.

110. Collomp, "Statuts des cadets," 165–66. Collomp and Poumarède provide balanced assessments, stressing the resilience of traditional customs, which

were nonetheless partially undercut and transformed by new mentalities and laws. Certain parts of the Midi, such as the isolated Gevaudan, clung with particular intensity to their customary family strategies. Claverie and Lamaison, *Impossible mariage*.

111. How widows fared under communal versus dotal regimes depended on myriad factors, such as the economic success of the couple, the relative wealth of husband and wife before marriage, the size of the woman's remaining dowry, etc. On competition between lineage and nuclear family models in different regions of France, see Burguière, "Fondements d'une culture familiale," 56–74; Garrioch, *Formation of the Parisian Bourgeoisie*, 105–130, 259–63. On Normandy, see Alline, *Ancien régime matrimonial normand*; Jean-Pierre Chaline, *Les Bourgeois de Rouen: Une élite urbaine au XIXe siècle* (Paris, 1973); Perrot, *Génèse d'une ville*.

CHAPTER 5

1. AN DIII 36, Pétition de la citoyenne Eveu au citoyen président, 15 Sept. 1793.

2. I use the terms "unwed mother," "mère célibatrice," and "natural mother" interchangeably.

3. Loi du 28 juin–8 juillet 1793, Duvergier, 5: 362–67; Loi du 12 brumaire an II (2 Nov. 1793), Duvergier, 6: 269–71. The new inheritance rights applied only to natural children whose parents died after 14 July 1789. In addition, they must have been born of "parents libres," i.e., unmarried parents; offspring born of adultery could claim only a one-third share.

4. On natural law ideology, see Crane Brinton, *French Revolutionary Legislation on Illegitimacy, 1789–1804* (Cambridge, Mass., 1936); Laurence Boudouard and Florence Bellivier, "Des droits pour les bâtards, l'enfant naturel dans les débats révolutionnaires," in *FLE*, 122–44. For a critique, see Matthew Gerber, "Popular Pressure and Illegitimacy in the French Revolution," unpublished paper, Annual Meeting of the Western Society for French History, April 2000, Tempe, Arizona. On paternity, see Jacques Mulliez, "La volonté d'un homme," in *Histoire des pères et de la paternité*, ed. Jean Delumeau and Daniel Roche (Paris, 1990), 279–305; and "Révolutionnaires, nouveaux pères? Forcément nouveaux pères! Le droit révolutionnaire de la paternité," in *RévJur*, 1: 373–98. On unwed mothers and the linkage between poor relief policy and the abolition of paternity suits, see Françoise Fortunet, "Qui sont les mères de nos enfants?" in *Les femmes et la Révolution française: Actes du colloque à Toulouse, 12–14 avril 1989*, ed. Marie-France Brive, 3 vols. (Toulouse, 1989), 1: 403–9; and "Sexualité hors mariage à l'époque révolutionnaire: Les mères des enfants de la nature," in *Droit, histoire et sexualité*, ed. Jacques Poumarède and Jean-Pierre Royer (Lille, 1987), 187–200; Marie-Claude Phan, "La séduction impunie, ou La fin des actions en recherche de paternité," in *Les femmes et la Révolution*, 2: 53–64.

5. Jacques Depauw, *Amour illégitime et société à Nantes au 18e siècle* (Paris,

1973); "Illicit Sexual Activity and Society in Eighteenth-Century Nantes," in *Family and Society: Selections from the Annales: Economies, Sociétés, Civilisations,* ed. Robert Forster and Orest Ranum, trans. Elborg Forster and Patricia M. Ranum (Baltimore, 1976), 145–91; Cissie Fairchilds, "Female Sexual Attitudes and the Rise of Illegitimacy: A Case Study," *Journal of Interdisciplinary History* 4 (1978): 627–67; Arlette Farge, *Fragile Lives: Violence, Power and Solidarity in Eighteenth-Century France,* trans. Carol Shelton (Cambridge, Mass., 1993), 26–41; James Farr, *Authority and Sexuality in Early Modern Burgundy (1550–1730)* (New York, 1995), 90–123; Anne Fillon, *Les trois bagues aux doigts: Amours villageoises au XVIIIe siècle* (Paris, 1981), chap. 5; Claude Grimmer, *La femme et le bâtard* (Paris, 1983), 195–214; Olwen Hufton, *The Poor of Eighteenth-Century France, 1750–1789* (Oxford, 1974), 320–29; Alain Lottin, "Naissances illégitimes et filles-mères à Lille au XVIIIe siècle," *Revue d'histoire moderne et contemporaine* 17 (1970): 278–322; Marie-Claude Phan, *Les amours illégitimes: Histoires de séduction en Languedoc (1676–1786)* (Paris, 1986); Richard Cobb, *A Sense of Place* (London, 1975), 79–134; Dominique Godineau, *The Women of Paris and Their French Revolution,* trans. Katherine Streip (Berkeley, 1998; orig. ed. 1988), 46–51.

6. ADC 3L 1716, Registre de déclarations de grossesse, Jacques-Pierre Langueneur, Juge de Paix de la 2e division de Lisieux, 16 mars 1793 au 3e j.c. an V (8 Sept. 1797).

7. ADC 3L 1179, TDD Pont-l'Evêque, 2 Dec. 1791.

8. On the varied levels and use of declarations, see Farge, *Fragile Lives,* 26–41; Phan, *Amours illégitimes,* 5–9, 119–25; Fillon, *Trois bagues aux doigts,* 241–59. On the promulgation of the edict, see Jean-François Fournel, *Traité de la séduction, considérée dans l'ordre judiciaire* (Paris, 1781), 365–86; Alfred Soman, "Anatomy of an Infanticide Trial: The Case of Marie-Jeanne Bartonnet (1742)," in *Changing Identities in Early Modern France,* ed. Michael Wolfe (Durham, N.C., 1997), 248–72. AN ADXVIIIc 325, *Réflexions tranchantes sur les enfans naturels qui ne rapportent que des actes de reconnaissance déterminés par des poursuites judiciaires de l'ancien régime* (n.p., n.d., c. 1794), 2.

9. My latest set of declarations in the Calvados ran until the fall of 1801: ADC 3L 1648, Canton de Fervaques, juge de paix, Jean Sauvage, déclarations de grossesse, an VI–an X (1797–1801). Cf. Fortunet, "Sexualité hors mariage." Fortunet notes a gradual decline in annual declarations in Dijon from 1790 to 1800.

10. Cobb, *Sense of Place,* 79–134; Fairchilds, "Female Sexual Attitudes."

11. This sample includes all the significant collections of declarations available for the Calvados in the 1790s. (More scattered declarations no doubt exist in the papers of communal J.P.s). Sample: the set in note 9 above; ADC 3L 1716, Registre des déclarations de grossesse, Jacques-Pierre Langueneur, Juge de Paix de la 2e division de Lisieux, 16 mars 1793 au 3e j.c. an V (8 Sept. 1797), and Liasse de déclarations de grossesse, Justice de paix, section de Saint-Germain de Lisieux, 1791–92; ADC 3L 1705, Justice de paix, Lisieux, 1ère section, Registre des déclarations de grossesse et procès-verbaux des découvertes d'enfants aban-

donnés, 17 brumaire an IV–30 thermidor an IX (8 Nov. 1795–18 Aug. 1801); ADC 3L 1720, Justice de paix, Lisieux, 4e section (1792–93); ADC 3L 978, Papier déposé au greffe, District de Lisieux, déclaration de grossesse de Louise Angot, faite aux officiers municipaux de Breuil, 13 May 1791; ADC 3L 1675, Justice de paix, Honfleur rural, registre des déclarations de grossesse, 30 May 1792–11 thermidor an III (29 July 1795).

12. Since women of middling or elite standing would be less likely to record professions, some of the women with no professions listed may come from these backgrounds. On the correlation between higher class standing and parental control over courtship and marriage choice, see Olwen Hufton, *The Prospect before Her: A History of Women in Western Europe, 1500–1800* (New York, 1996), chap. 3.

13. E.g., ADC 3L 1179, TDD Pont-l'Evêque, Mémoire des frais faits et adjugés à Marie Catherine Gire contre le Sr. François Martine, n.d. (c. early 1792), lists a total of 223 livres, 6 sous, 3 deniers of court-related expenses for the unsuccessful defendant François Martine to pay, including the travel costs of multiple witnesses from Grangues or Cricqueville to Pont-l'Evêque for the trial.

14. District tribunals handled paternity suits. These cases come from the TDD of Caen, Lisieux, Bayeux, Pont-l'Evêque, and Vire.

15. Fournel, *Traité de la séduction*, 120–21.

16. Each TDD tended to standardize allotments: e.g., TDD Vire routinely gave 80 livres annual pension, 60 livres lying-in expenses, and 200 livres of damages, if applicable. ADC 3L 978, TDD Lisieux, case on appeal from TDD Bayeux, Jeanne Marie contre Thomas Barbey, 5 Aug. 1793. Cf. ADC 3L 1249, TDD Vire, Gilles Sicot, tuteur naturel de Marie Anne Sicot contre Jacques Lemoine, 2 floréal an II (21 Apr. 1794).

17. Fournel, *Traité de la séduction*, 9–10. ADC 3L 1251, TDD Vire, Marie Vaultier veuve Touyon et sa fille Marie Anne Touyon contre Jacques Lesage, 7 Jan. 1791; ADC 3L 1180, TDD Pont-l'Evêque, Marie-Madeleine Tautel contre Jean-Baptiste Delacroix, 17 Jan. 1792; ADC 3L 1178, TDD Pont-l'Evêque, Marie-Anne Victoire Tautel contre Jean-Baptiste Delacroix, 28 June 1790.

18. Fournel, *Traité de la séduction*, 121; James Farr, *Authority and Sexuality*; Jean-Louis Flandrin, *Families in Former Times: Kinship, Household, and Sexuality*, trans. Richard Southern (Cambridge, Eng., 1979). The use of rapt de séduction reinforced paternal authority over marriage: fathers could use it against unsuitable suitors for their daughters, regardless of whether the daughter wished to marry the man in question.

19. Fairchilds, "Female Sexual Attitudes," quote 641; Olwen Hufton, "Women and the Family Economy in Eighteenth-Century France," *French Historical Studies* 9 (1975): 1–22.

20. Madame Grandval, *Pétition à l'assemblée nationale, pour lui demander une loi qui accorde aux enfans naturels le droit d'héritier de leur pères et mères libres* (Paris, n.d.), 13; Phan, *Amours illégitimes*, 181–85; Jacques Depauw, "Les filles-mères se marient-elles? L'exemple de Nantes au XVIIIe siècle," in *Aimer en France, 1760–1860: Actes du Colloque international de Clermont-Ferrand,*

ed. Paul Viallaneix and Jean Ehrard, 2 vols. (Clermont-Ferrand, 1980), 2: 525–31.

21. Depauw, "Illicit Sexual Activity," 146; Fillon, *Trois bagues aux doigts*, 260–313; Fortunet, "Sexualité hors mariage"; Phan, *Amours illégitimes*, 119–36; Lottin, "Naissances illégitimes," 280–81; Fournel, *Traité de la séduction*, 85–88.

22. Jacques Dupâquier, "Les effets démographiques de la croissance," in *Histoire de la population française*, vol. 2, *De la Renaissance à 1789*, ed. Jacques Dupâquier et al. (Paris, 1988), 469–74; Yves Blayo, "La proportion des naissances illégitimes en France de 1740 à 1829," *Population* 30 (1975): 65–70; Depauw, "Illicit Sexual Activity," 189; Jacques Dupâquier, *La Population française aux XVIIe et XVIIIe siècles* (Paris, 1979), 11–13; Fairchilds, "Female Sexual Attitudes," 627; Fillon, *Trois bagues aux doigts*, 241–42; Flandrin, *Families in Former Times*, 180–86; François Lebrun, "Naissances illégitimes et abandons d'enfants en Anjou au XVIIIe siècle," *Annales: Economies, Sociétés, Civilisations* 27 (1972): 1183–89; Lottin, "Naissances illégitimes," 290. On the Calvados, see Mohamed El Kordi, *Bayeux aux XVIIe et XVIIIe siècles* (Paris, 1970), 90–93; Perrot, *Genèse d'une ville*, 2: 841–53.

23. Claude Delaselle, "Les enfants abandonnés à Paris au XVIIIe siècle," *Annales: Economies, Sociétés, Civilisations* 30 (1975): 187–218; Cissie Fairchilds, *Poverty and Charity in Aix-en-Provence, 1640–1789* (Baltimore, 1976), 83–94; Rachel Fuchs, *Abandoned Children: Foundlings and Child Welfare in Nineteenth-Century France* (Albany, 1984), 9–19.

24. Margaret Darrow, "Popular Concepts of Marital Choice in Eighteenth-Century France," *Journal of Social History* 19 (1986): 261–72; Fillon, *Trois bagues aux doigts*, 479; Jean-Louis Flandrin, *Amours paysannes: Amour et sexualité dans les campagnes de l'ancienne France (XVIe–XIXe siècle)* (Paris, 1970), 237–46; Grimmer, *La femme et le bâtard*, 208–214; Phan, *Amours illégitimes*, 111–14, 179. As Martine Segalen has argued, historians should not create a dichotomy between marriages for love and marriages for economic benefit. *Love and Power in the Peasant Family: Rural France in the Nineteenth Century*, trans. Sarah Matthews (Oxford, 1983), 14–25.

25. I found no explicit accusations of rape, but this crime is substantially under-reported throughout early modern France. Since cases of rape or transient sex show up more clearly in déclarations de grossesse than in paternity suits, those scholars using richer déclarations can speak to these incidences more extensively. See Fairchilds, "Female Sexual Attitudes"; Phan, *Amours illégitimes*, 56–61, 163–67.

26. Depauw, *Amour illégitime*, 99–132; Fairchilds, "Female Sexual Attitudes," 648–49; Phan, *Amours illégitimes*, 85–94.

27. ADC 3L 1716, Registre des déclarations de grossesse, Jacques-Pierre Langueneur, Juge de Paix de la 2e division de Lisieux, 16 mars 1793 au 3e j.c. an V (8 Sept. 1797), and Liasse de déclarations de grossesse, Justice de paix, section de Saint-Germain de Lisieux, 1791–92.

28. ADC 3L 1180, TDD Pont-l'Evêque, Catherine Colombel contre Jacques Delaunay fils, 2 Apr. 1792.

29. Ibid.; ADC 3L 1251, TDD Vire, Marie-France Enguehard contre Michel Letouzé, 3 Apr. 1791; ADC 3L 1180, TDD Pont-l'Evêque, Philippe Petit, bourgeois de Pont-l'Evêque (pour sa fille Madeleine Petit) contre Sieur LePrince dit Dumesnil, Interrogatoire de Dumesnil et de plusieurs témoins, Nov.–Dec. 1791, 13 Feb. 1792; ADC 3L 623, TDD Caen, Marguerite Guilbert contre Martin Hemert, 25 nivôse an II (14 Jan. 1794).

30. ADC 3L 1180, TDD Pont-l'Evêque, Catherine Colombel contre Jacques Delaunay fils, 2 Apr. 1792; ADC 3L 665, TDD Caen, Jeanne LeRoi contre François Sainte-Croix, 13 pluviôse an II (1 Feb. 1794). For similar sexual boasting in male popular culture, see Jacques Ménétra, *Journal of My Life*, ed. Daniel Roche (New York, 1986).

31. Cobb, *Sense of Place*, 105–9; Farge, *Fragile Lives*, 32–35.

32. ADC 3L 1238, TDD Vire, Anne Declois contre Nicolas Beaumont, 16 frimaire an II (6 Dec. 1793); TDD Vire, Françoise Marie contre Philippe et Nicolas LeBounois, 10 nivôse an II (30 Dec. 1793); ADC 3L 623, TDD Caen, Fille Guilbert contre Martin Hemert, 25 nivôse an II (14 Jan. 1794); TDD Caen, Fille Chevallier contre Jean LeChavallier (no clear relation), 26 ventôse an II (16 Mar. 1794).

33. ADC 3L 1251, TDD Vire, Marie-France Enguehard contre Michel Letouzé, 3 Apr. 1791; ADC 3L 1249, TDD Vire, Pierre Leminois, huissier, contre Jacques Lemoine, 24 prairial an II (12 June 1794); ADC 3L 665, TDD Caen, Jeanne LeRoi contre François Sainte-Croix, 17 pluviôse an II (5 Feb. 1794). According to Fournel (*Traité de la séduction*, chap. 3), in certain circumstances married men could be held responsible for child support, but never for damages. ADC 3L 1249, TDD Vire, Françoise Eudes contre Pierre Jouvin, 27 floréal an II (16 May 1794).

34. P. J. Guyot, *Répertoire universel et raisonné de jurisprudence civile, criminelle, canonique, et bénéficiale* (Paris, 1775–84), 8: 334 ff., as cited in Phan, *Amours illégitimes*, 125; ADC 3L 1251, TDD Vire, Marie-France Enguehard contre Michel Letouzé, 3 Apr. 1791; ADC 3L 1238, TDD Vire, Renée Marie, à l'adjonction de son père Louis Marie, contre Nicolas Flaust, 7 nivôse an II (27 Dec. 1793); TDD Vire, Anne Doublet contre Charles Madeleine fils Pierre, 14 nivôse an II (3 Jan. 1794); TDD Vire, Françoise Busnel contre François Morin, 7 nivôse an II (27 Dec. 1793); ADC 3L 1249, TDD Vire, Marguerite Guilbert contre Martin Hemert; AN ADII 36, Extraits du registre plumitif du TDD Pont-Chaslier (Pont-l'Evêque), 27 thermidor an II (30 July 1794).

35. ADC 3L 1178, TDD Pont-l'Evêque, Marguerite Leroux contre François Catherine dit Leguillion, 15 Dec. 1790; ADC 3L 1180, TDD Pont-l'Evêque, Philippe Petit, bourgeois de Pont-l'Evêque (pour sa fille Madeleine Petit) contre Sieur LePrince dit Dumesnil, perruquier, Interrogatoire de Dumesnil, 13 Feb. 1792.

36. ADC 3L 1271, Jugement en premier ressort du TDD Coutances, Catherine Louise Gonfroy contre Jean Godefroy, 11 nivôse an II (31 Dec. 1793); TDD Vire, Jean Godefroy contre Catherine Louise Gonfroy, 23 pluviôse an II (11 Feb. 1794); ADC 3L 1248, Minutes d'audiences, TDD Vire, 3 germinal an II (24 Mar. 1794).

37. ADC 3L 666, TDD Caen, Anne Privay contre Citoyen Renouf, 22 messidor an II (10 July 1794); ADC 3L 1180, TDD Pont-l'Evêque, Philippe Petit, bourgeois de Pont-l'Evêque (pour sa fille Madeleine Petit) contre Sieur LePrince dit Dumesnil, Jan. 1792; ADC 3L 1180, TDD Pont-l'Evêque, Marie-Madeleine Tautel contre Jean-Baptiste Delacroix, 17 Jan. 1792.

38. On rapt, see Danielle Haase-Dubosc, *Ravie et enlevée: De l'enlèvement des femmes comme stratégie matrimoniale au XVIIe siècle* (Paris, 1999); Farr, *Authority and Sexuality,* 90–123. On women using powerlessness, see Natalie Zemon Davis, *Fiction in the Archives* (Stanford, Calif., 1987); Yves Castan, "Statuts féminins au XVIIIe siècle d'après les profils exemplaires des plaidoyers en Languedoc," in *Droit, Histoire et Sexualité,* ed. Jacques Poumarède et Jean Pierre-Royer (Lille, 1987), 169–75; Nicole Castan, *Les criminels de Languedoc: Les exigences d'ordre et les voies du ressentiment dans une société prérévolutionnaire (1750–1790)* (Toulouse, 1980), 25–36; David Garrioch, *Neighborhood and Community in Paris, 1740–1790* (Cambridge, Eng., 1986), 86.

39. ADC 3L 1248, TDD Vire, Gilles Sicot, tuteur naturel (père) de Marie Anne Sicot, fille mineure, contre Jacques Lemoine, 3 germinal an II (24 Mar. 1794).

40. ADC 3L 1238, TDD Vire, Anne Doublet contre Charles Madeleine, 14 nivôse an II (3 Jan. 1794); ADC 3L 1271, TDD Coutances, Catherine Louise Gonfroy contre Jean Godefroy, 11 nivôse an II (31 Dec. 1793); ADC 3L 620, TDD Caen, Suzanne Massieu contre Jean Dethan, 7 Mar. 1792.

41. ADC 3L 1238, TDD Vire, Catherine Bourguiard contre Jacques Prestatoire, 21 nivôse an II (10 Jan. 1794). Fillon, *Trois bagues aux doigts,* 127–40; Phan, *Amours illégitimes,* 193–210; Béatrice Didier et al., "Le mot *amour,*" in *Aimer en France,* ed. Viallaneix and Ehrard, 1: 117–29; Jean-Louis Flandrin, "Amour et mariage au XVIIIe siècle," in his *Le sexe et l'Occident: Evolution des attitudes et des comportements* (Paris, 1981), 83–96; Jacques Mulliez, "Droit et morale conjugale: Essai sur l'histoire des relations personnelles entre époux," *Revue historique* 278 (1987): 35–106, esp. 54–57.

42. AN DIII 363, Pétition de Jeanne Marie Leinis au Comité de législation, 13 floréal an II (2 May 1794); ADC 3L 1007, TDD Lisieux, Marie Rose Marais contre Nicolas Dutacq, 28 ventôse an II (18 Mar. 1794); ADC 3L 1180, TDD Pont-l'Evêque, Marie-Madeleine Tautel contre Jean-Baptiste Delacroix, 17 Jan. 1792; ADC 3L 1178, TDD Pont-l'Evêque, Interrogatoire de Jean-Baptiste Delacroix, 24 Mar. 1792

43. ADC 3L 1249, TDD Vire, Françoise Eudes contre Pierre Jouvin, 27 floréal an II (16 May 1794).

44. Jacques Dupâquier, "La population française de 1789 à 1806," in *Histoire de la population française,* vol. 3, *De 1789 à 1914,* ed. Jacques Dupâquier, 3: 64–84.

45. ADC 3L 610, SA Caen, 13 July 1792; SA Caen, 4 Aug. 1792; ADC 3L 612, SA Caen, 14 pluviôse an II (2 Feb. 1794); ADC 3L 623, TDD Caen, 11 ventôse an II (1 Mar. 1794); ADC 3L 613, SA Caen, 12 floréal an II (1 May 1794); ADC 3L 620, TDD Caen, 20 Mar. 1792; TDD Caen, 30 Apr. 1792. In many other cases,

adult children used the family courts to challenge parents on property matters; these property disputes sometimes resulted from parental opposition to a marriage made by an emancipated son or daughter. In addition, younger children used the courts to win food pensions or escape from domestic abuse.

46. ADC 3L 1179, Procès-verbal du juge de paix de Cambremer, 23 Aug. 1791.

47. ADC 3L 1179 and 3L 1180, Procès-verbal du juge de paix de Cambremer, 23 Aug.–21 Nov. 1791; TDD Pont-l'Evêque, Nov. 1791–Feb. 1792. Cf. Fillon, *Trois bagues aux doigts*, 87–103.

48. AD Charente-Maritime L892, déclaration de grossesse de Magdeleine Masson, canton de Rochefort, 1 brumaire an III (22 Oct. 1794). I thank Anthony Crubaugh for this example. ADC 3L 1271, TDD Coutances, Catherine Louise Gonfroy contre Jean Godefroy, 11 nivôse an II (31 Dec. 1793), on appeal at TDD Vire. ADC 3L 1249, TDD Vire, Marie Longuet contre Jacques Lascéré, 27 floréal an II (16 May 1794).

49. ADC 3L 1180, TDD Pont-l'Evêque, Philippe Petit contre Sieur LePrince dit Dumesnil, première requête, 8 Nov. 1791.

50. On women's defense of their honor in changing circumstances, see Fairchilds, "Female Sexual Attitudes." She effectively critiques Edward Shorter, "Illegitimacy, Sexual Revolution, and Social Change in Modern Europe," *Journal of Interdisciplinary History* 2 (1971): 237–72, and his *The Making of the Modern Family* (New York, 1975).

51. Olwen H. Hufton, *Women and the Limits of Citizenship in the French Revolution* (Toronto, 1992), 53–88.

52. Delaselle, "Enfants abandonnés à Paris au XVIIIe siècle"; Alan Forrest, *The French Revolution and the Poor* (New York, 1981), 116–26; Grimmer, *La femme et le bâtard*, 229; Hufton, *Poor of Eighteenth-Century France*, 318–29; Jean-Claude Perrot, *Genèse d'une ville moderne: Caen au XVIIIe siècle*, 2 vols. (Paris, 1975), 2: 852–53; George Sussman, *Selling Mother's Milk: The Wet-Nursing Business in France, 1715–1914* (Urbana, Il., 1982), chap. 3.

53. Delaselle, "Enfants abandonnés à Paris"; Forrest, *French Revolution and the Poor*, 118; Hufton, *Poor of Eighteenth-Century France*, 319–20.

54. AN DIV 13, Pétition d'une femme anonyme au Monsieur (à l'Assemblée nationale), received 29 Apr. (1790 or 1791). Brinton, *French Revolutionary Legislation*, 6–12; Matthew Gerber, "The End of Bastardy: Illegitimacy in France from the Reformation through the Revolution" (Ph.D. diss., University of California at Berkeley, 2003); Ernest Jacquinot, *De la filiation naturelle dans le droit intermédiaire* (Paris, 1913), 31–56; Jean Thomas, *La condition de l'Enfant dans le droit intermédiaire, 1789–1804* (Thèse de droit, Université de Nancy, [Paris, 1923]), xxvii–xxviii.

55. AN DIII 363, Adresse anonyme au Citoyen Cambacérès, n.d.

56. M. Peuchet, Projet de législation sur les bâtards, *Moniteur universel*, 83, 2 July 1790.

57. AN DIII 380, Réponse de Cambacérès à la lettre du Maire de Montbard adressée à Cambacérès, 7 June 1793. For speeches mentioning petitions, see, e.g.,

Robin, *AP* 50: 194–99, 20 Sept. 1792; Cambacérès, *AP* 66: 34–37, 4 June 1793. As Jacquinot notes, the "crowd of petitions" mentioned by Robin has largely disappeared. *De la filiation naturelle*, 94. For marginal comments and replies to petitions, see examples in AN DIII 338, 339, 363, and 382. Cf. AN DIII 380, Comité de Législation, procès-verbaux des séances, 1792–an III (1794–95). E.g., Minutes of session on 5 Jan. 1793: "A host of petitions to the Constituent Assembly, the Legislative Assembly, the National Convention, make claims in favor of granting natural children the rights and effects of civil equality, inseparable from the rights of natural equality." In the summer of 1793, Cambacérès assigned the Committee of Legislation the task of reading some 6,000 petitions on civil law. Halpérin, *Impossible Code civil*, 113.

58. Olympe de Gouges, *Les droits de la femme*, in *Ecrits politiques, 1788–1791*, ed. Olivier Blanc (Paris, 1993), 204–15. As benefits to soldiers' families became established, some mothers also petitioned to establish filiation for their children whose fathers were off at war. Some women also used the courts to certify their children's paternal filiation and were anxious to correct mistakes in parish registers or the état civil. ADC 3L 1238, TDD Vire, 24 pluviôse an II (12 Feb. 1794).

59. See AN DIV (Comité de Constitution) and esp. the DIII (Comité de Législation) series. In a few cases in this section, I cite a petition written after the 12 brumaire law because it provides an excellent example of ongoing reasoning or rhetoric. I will use the post–12 brumaire petitions primarily in the next two chapters to elucidate reactions to this ambiguous and controversial law.

60. *Pétition à la Convention nationale en faveur des enfants naturels* (Paris, 1793); AN DIII 363, Pétition de Sophie Laporte et Angélique Laporte et Laporte, gendarme, aux citoyens représentants, n.d.; AN DIII 363, Adresse anonyme au Citoyen Cambacérès, n.d.; *Pétition en faveur des enfans naturels reconnus, et nés de père et de mère libres* (Paris, 1792), 6; AN DIII 363, Pétition du citoyen Jean-Baptiste Despans à la Convention nationale, 9 nivôse an II (29 Dec. 1793). Even those who wanted to limit illegitimate children's gains sometimes recognized the need to rid them of "that original stain": *Observations importantes, soumises aux législateurs par un républicain* (Paris, 1793), 1.

61. *Pétition en faveur des enfans naturels reconnus, et nés de père et de mère libres* (Paris, 1792), 3–4; [Auguste], *Opinion d'un citoyen, sur la partie du Code civil concernant les enfans naturels en possession d'état et nés de père et mère libres* (n.p., n.d.), 10. (Auguste's subsequent pamphlet refers to this as his "ouvrage publié en 1793": *Réponse d'un enfant naturel à l'adresse présentée à la Convention nationale par cinquante collatéraux de feu Messire de Boulogne* [n.p., n.d., c. year III (1794–95].) AN DIII 382, Pétition anonyme aux législateurs, received 23 Aug. 1793; AN DIII 363, Pétition en faveur des enfans de la patrie élevés dans les campagnes, signée de 55 habitants du district de Noyon (Oise), received 18 nivôse an II (7 Jan. 1794); *AP* 68: 256–57, 4 July 1793, Instituteur et enfants trouvés du Faubourg Saint-Antoine; AN DIII 363, Pétition du citoyen Meunier aux citoyens représentants, n.d., c. summer 1793.

62. AN DIII 382, Pétition anonyme aux législateurs, received 23 Aug. 1793;

AN DIII 363, Pétition de Perrié Dumummier à l'Assemblée nationale, 25 Oct. 1791.

63. AN DIII 363, Pétition du citoyen Cartanée aux représentants, 25 nivôse an II (14 Jan. 1794); *Assemblée de tous les bâtards du royaume; avec leur demande à l'Assemblée nationale* (n.p., 1789), 3–4, 10–11.

64. AN DIII 363, Mémoire par le citoyen. . . . , n.d. Cf. AN DIII 361, Pétition anonyme, c. 1793; Pétition très importante sur l'état civil d'un enfant, aux citoyens législateurs, c. 1793; AN DIII 273, Pétition de Marie-Anne Beaudouin au Comité de législation, c. 1793.

65. Mulliez, "Révolutionnaires, nouveaux pères?" 379–85, and "La volonté d'un homme," 284–86; Berlier, *AP* 70: 654–62, 9 Aug. 1793; Oudot, *AP* 70: 634–36, 9 Aug. 1793; Oudot, *Essai sur les principes de la législation des mariages privés et solennels, du divorce et de l'adoption qui peuvent être déclarés à la suite de l'acte constitutionnel* (Paris, n.d.), 7; Oudot gave this speech on 9 Aug. 1793: *AP* 70: 712–17.

66. AN DIII 363, Pétition du citoyen Meunier à la Convention nationale, n.d.

67. AN DIII 363, Pétition d'Antoine Dupront aux législateurs, 22 Feb. 1793; Antoine Valbe-Monteval, *Mémoire en forme de pétition au Comité de législation de la Convention nationale* (Vienne, n.d., c. Aug. 1793); AN DIII 363, Pétition du citoyen Besarnac au cher citoyen, n.d.

68. AN DIII 363, Pétition de la républicaine Loudios cadette au citoyen représentant, 24 pluviôse an II (12 Feb. 1794); AN DIV 13, Pétition d'une femme anonyme au Monsieur, received 29 Apr. 1790 or 1791; AN DIII 363, Mémoire à consulter, n.d.

69. AN DIII 363, Lettre du citoyen Carrépontaut, juge de paix du canton de Poilly (Loiret), aux citoyens législateurs, 17 frimaire 1793 (7 Dec. 1793); *Pétition à la Convention nationale* (Paris, n.d., c. fall 1793), 4; AN DIII 382, Pétition anonyme aux législateurs, received 23 Aug. 1793; AN DIII 363, Pétition anonyme au Citoyen Cambacérès, n.d. Cf. also ADII 48, *Plaidoyer pour l'héritage du pauvre, et l'apanage de l'homme, à faire valoir par-devant les représentants de la Nation, principalement lorsque sera discuté l'article hérédité* (Paris, 1790); AN DIII 363, Petition from John Bourne, London, to the National Convention, received 8 Jan. 1793.

70. Madame Grandval, *AP* 40: 479–80, 25 Mar. 1792. Cf. her pamphlet: *Pétition à l'assemblée nationale, pour lui demander une loi qui accorde aux enfans naturels le droit d'héritier de leur pères et mères libres* (Paris, n.d.).

71. Robin, *AP* 50: 194–99, 20 Sept. 1792.

72. Peuchet, "Projet de législation sur les bâtards," *Moniteur universel*, 83, 2 July 1790; and Peuchet, "Quelques réflexions sur la bâtardise," *Moniteur* 24, 24 Jan. 1791; Petitions presented at the bar: Madame Grandval, *AP*, 40: 479–80, 25 Mar. 1792; Pierre Faix, *AP* 53: 363, 11 Nov. 1792; Barailon, *AP* 58: 216, 5 Feb. 1793. With no success, the deputy LeChapelier proposed allowing illegitimate children of free unions to prove paternity and maternity and benefit from intestate successions: *AP* 24: 497–98, 1 Apr. 1791.

73. Duvergier, 5: 314, Loi du 4–6 juin 1793; 5: 362–67, Loi du 28 juin au 8

juillet 1793; *AP* 68: 256–57, 4 July 1793; Duvergier, 6: 269–71, Loi du 12 brumaire an II (2 Nov. 1793). On the politics surrounding the first Civil Code, see
Halpérin, *Impossible Code civil,* 131–41.

74. Children whose fathers died between 14 July 1789 and 12 brumaire an II
(2 Nov. 1794) could prove paternity more easily than those whose fathers died
after the new law: by providing written acknowledgment or evidence of care. For
children whose parents died after 12 brumaire, the law left the proof of paternity
to be determined by the (as yet unpromulgated) Civil Code, and many argued
that fathers had to acknowledge paternity in an official act before a civil official.
On the complex contestation over proving paternity, see Chapter 6.

75. Cambacérès, *AP* 66: 34–37, 4 June 1793; Berlier, *AP* 70: 654–62, 9 Aug.
1793; Oudot, *AP* 70: 634–36, 9 Aug. 1793. Oudot even demanded equal rights
for children born of adultery or incest.

76. Oudot, *Essai sur les principes de la législation des mariages privés,* 7.

77. Ibid., 4–5.

78. Discours de Chabot à la séance de la Société des Jacobins, 20 Sept. 1793,
Moniteur universel, 269, 26 Sept. 1793; Cambacérès, *AP* 78: 66–69, 9 brumaire
an II (30 Oct. 1793).

79. Oudot, *Essai sur les principes de la législation des mariages privés,* 8.

80. Fournel, *Traité de la séduction,* 244; Berlier, *AP* 70: 658, 9 Aug. 1793.

81. Mulliez, "Volonté d'un homme"; Lynn Hunt, *The Family Romance of
the French Revolution* (Berkeley, 1992), chap. 2; Citoyen Dulaurent, *Le bon
père: Discours prononcé dans la section des Tuileries, le décadi 20 frimaire à la
fête de la Raison et de la Vérité* (Paris, an II [1793]), 4.

82. Cambacérès, *AP* 66: 634, 4 June 1793; Oudot, *AP* 45: 559, 25 June 1792.

83. Mulliez, "Volonté d'un homme"; Berlier, *AP* 70: 658–59, 9 Aug. 1793.

84. Oudot, *Essai sur les principes de la législation des mariages privés,* 10;
Berlier, *AP* 70: 658, 9 Aug. 1793.

85. Berlier, *AP* 70: 657, 9 Aug. 1793; Oudot, *Essai sur les principes de la législation des mariages privés,* 15.

86. Berlier, *AP* 70: 658 and 661; Oudot, *AP,* 70: 634–36; Cambacérès, *AP,* 70:
553, all on 9 Aug. 1793. On revolutionary advocacy of nursing, see Madelyn
Gutwirth, *The Twilight of the Goddesses: Women and Representation in the
French Revolutionary Era* (New Brunswick, N.J., 1992), 55–66, 341–68.

87. Berlier, *AP* 70: 660, 9 Aug. 1793.

88. Phan, "La séduction impunie," 56–57.

89. Maignet, *AP* 67: 476–96, 26 June 1793. Fortunet, "Qui sont les mères de
nos enfants?" On republican motherhood, see note 55 in Chapter 2.

90. Maignet, *AP* 67: 476–96, 26 June 1793.

91. Oudot, *AP* 45: 560, 25 June 1792.

92. Each of Cambacérès's proposed Civil Codes included provisions for
adoption, and the decree of 16 frimaire an III (6 Dec. 1794) reconfirmed the existence of adoption without outlining how it should occur: Loi du 16 frimaire an
III (6 Dec. 1794), Duvergier, 7: 342. Eric Andrew Goodheart, "Adoption in the
Discourses of the French Revolution" (Ph.D. diss., Harvard University, 1997),

98–140; Traer, *Marriage and the Family,* 152–54; Kristin Elizabeth Gager, *Blood Ties and Fictive Ties: Adoption and Family Life in Early Modern France* (Princeton, N.J., 1996), 157–64. Oudot, *Essai sur les principes de la législation des mariages privés,* 16. On adoption and voluntary fatherhood, see Mulliez, "Révolutionnaires, nouveaux pères?" Cambacérès and Berlier both advocated adoption: Cambacérès, *AP* 70: 551–54, 9 Aug. 1793; Berlier, *AP* 70: 640–41 and 702–12, 9 Aug. 1793.

93. Berlier, *AP* 70: 657–58, 661–62, 9 Aug. 1793.

94. Forrest, *French Revolution and the Poor;* Hufton, *Women and the Limits of Citizenship,* chap. 2.

95. Rachel Fuchs, "Seduction, Paternity, and the Law in Fin-de-Siècle France," *Journal of Modern History* 72 (2000): 944–89.

96. Halpérin, *Impossible Code civil,* 125; Hugues Fulchiron, "La femme, mère et épouse dans le droit révolutionnaire," in *Femmes et la Révolution,* ed. Brive, 1: 377–85. On egalitarian inheritance, see Duvergier, 6: 256–57, Loi du 5 brumaire an II (26 Oct. 1793). On communal marital property, see Projet du Code civil, Titre III, Art. 11, *AP* 70: 557, 9 Aug. 1793; this article passed, *AP* 77: 679–80, 6 brumaire an II (27 Oct. 1793). The second Civil Code, proposed on 23 fructidor an II (9 Sept. 1794), also stipulated equal control over communal goods by husband and wife.

97. On the codifiers' mistrust of youth and validation of older men's paternal power, see Xavier Martin, "A Tout âge? Sur la durée du pouvoir des pères dans le code Napoléon," *Revue d'histoire des facultés de droit et de la science juridique* 13 (1992): 227–301.

CHAPTER 6

1. Berlier, *AP* 70: 654–62, 9 Aug. 1793; Cambacérès, *AP* 66: 34–37, 4 June 1793; Loi du 12 brumaire an II (2 Nov. 1793), Duvergier, 6: 269–71.

2. A. Douarche, *Les tribunaux civils de Paris pendant la Révolution (1791–1800),* 2 vols. (Paris, 1905) (hereafter Douarche), 2: 170–83, Citoyenne Moret contre les héritiers Dupin-Rochefort, 5 thermidor an III (23 July 1795).

3. Several older works include analysis of the reaction of the Tribunal de Cassation to the law. Camille André, *Oeuvre du droit révolutionnaire en matière de filiation naturelle* (Nancy, 1906); Jacques d'Ayrenx, *La Condition juridique de la famille illégitime dans le droit intermédiaire* (Toulouse, 1908); Paul Baret, *Histoire et critique des règles sur la preuve de la filiation naturelle en droit français et étranger* (Paris, 1872); Ernest Jacquinot, *De la filiation naturelle dans le droit intermédiaire* (Paris, 1913). On judicial practice and paternity suits, see Anne Fillon, *Les trois bagues aux doigts: Amours villageoises au XVIIIe siècle* (Paris, 1981), 306–310.

4. In addition to Chapter 5 above, see Laurence Boudouard and Florence Bellivier, "Des droits pour les bâtards, l'enfant naturel dans les débats révolutionnaires," in *FLE,* 122–44; Crane Brinton, *French Revolutionary Legislation on Illegitimacy, 1789–1804* (Cambridge, Mass., 1936); Françoise Fortunet, "Sexualité

hors mariage à l'époque révolutionnaire: Les mères des enfants de la nature," in *Droit, histoire et sexualité,* ed. Jacques Poumarède and Jean-Pierre Royer (Lille, 1987), 187–200; Marcel Garaud et Romuald Szramkiewicz, *La révolution française et la famille* (Paris, 1978), 109–130; Jean-Louis Halpérin, *L'impossible Code civil* (Paris, 1994), chap. 5; Jacques Mulliez, "Révolutionnaires, nouveaux pères? Forcément nouveaux pères! Le droit révolutionnaire de la paternité," in *RévJur,* 1: 373–98; Marie-Claude Phan, "La séduction impunie, ou La fin des actions en recherche de paternité," in *Les femmes et la Révolution française: Actes du colloque à Toulouse, 12–14 avril 1989,* ed. Marie-France Brive, 3 vols. (Toulouse, 1989), 2: 53–64.

5. In local studies of civil law, illegitimacy cases turn up in very small numbers; Ferret recorded the highest number outside of Paris: 18 in the district of Montpellier (an II–an IV [1793–96]): Marc Ferret, *Les tribunaux de famille dans le district de Montpellier (1790–an IV)* (Montpellier, 1926), 334–62, 511–12. Cf. Jean-Louis Debauve, *La justice révolutionnaire dans le Morbihan, 1790–1795* (Paris, 1965), 374–75; Douarche 1: 777; 2: 157, 170, 209, 222, 226, 240, 285, 315, 319, 402, 404, 469, 506, 677, 730; Brigitte Pinelli, *La pratique notariale sous la Révolution: L'effet rétroactif de la loi du 17 nivôse sur les successions* (Thèse de droit, Université de Paris V, 1980), 189–98; Halpérin, *Impossible Code civil,* 197. Cambacérès commented favorably on the low number of cases: séance du 19 frimaire an III (9 Dec. 1794), *Moniteur,* 82, 22 frimaire an III (12 Dec. 1794).

6. Jean-Louis Halpérin, *Le tribunal de cassation et les pouvoirs sous la Révolution (1790–1799)* (Paris, 1987).

7. ADC 3L 1007, 28 nivôse an II (17 Jan. 1794), déclaration de grossesse de Marie-Rose Marais, juge de paix, canton de Fervaques; TDD Lisieux, Marie-Rose Marais contre Nicolas Dutacq, 28 ventôse an II (18 Mar. 1794).

8. TDD Lisieux, Marie-Rose Marais contre Nicolas Dutacq, 28 ventôse an II (18 Mar. 1794).

9. ADC 3L 1648, Canton de Fervaques, juge de paix, Jean Sauvage, déclarations de grossesse, an VI–an X (1797–1801), for declarations through 1801; cf. declarations in ADC 3L 1716, 3L 1705, 3L 1720, 3L 978, 3L 1625. Fortunet, "Sexualité hors mariage"; Fillon, *Trois bagues aux doigts,* 306–310; Dominique Godineau, *The Women of Paris and Their French Revolution,* trans. Katherine Streip (Berkeley, 1998; orig. ed. 1988), 46–51.

10. ADC 3L 1249, TDD Vire, Marie Longuet contre Jacques Lascéré, 27 floréal an II (16 May 1794); AD Charente-Maritime L892, juge de paix, canton de Rochefort, 11 germinal an III (31 Mar. 1795). I thank Anthony Crubaugh for this reference.

11. AN DIII 36, Lettre du commissaire près le tribunal du district de Pont-Chaslier (Pont-l'Evêque) au Comité de législation, 12 fructidor an II (29 Aug. 1794); ADC 3L 705, TDD Caen, Mémoire pour Pierre Angot contre Marie Tirard, n.d.; ADC 3L 1249, TDD Vire, Françoise Eudes contre Pierre Jouvin, 27 floréal an II (16 May 1794); Douarche 2: 73–76, Victoire-Marie Maillard, épouse divorcée de Dominique Colson, contre Geoffroy Lafreté, fils mineur, assisté de son père, 8 nivôse an III (28 Dec. 1794).

12. For queries to the Comité de Législation, see AN DIII 363. ADC 3L 1009, TDD Lisieux, Thérèse Lefranc contre Pierre Deshayes, 13 brumaire an III (3 Nov. 1794); ADC 3L 978, TDD Lisieux, Jeanne Marie contre Thomas Barbey, 13 thermidor an III (31 July 1795) on appeal from TDD Bayeux, 27 nivôse an II (16 Jan. 1794).

13. AN DIII 363, Pétition de Jeanne Marie Leinis au Comité de législation, 13 floréal an II (2 May 1794); AN DIII 34, Pétition de la citoyenne Rose Grandin aux citoyens représentants, 1 prairial an II (20 May 1794).

14. Catherine Duprat, *"Pour l'amour de l'humanité": Le temps des philan- thropes. La philanthropie parisienne des Lumières à la monarchie de Juillet,* 2 vols. (Paris, 1993), 1: chaps. 4 and 5; Alan Forrest, *The French Revolution and the Poor* (New York, 1981), 124–33, 171–76; Olwen Hufton, *Women and the Limits of Citizenship in the French Revolution* (Toronto, 1992), chap. 2.

15. Fillon, *Trois bagues aux doigts,* 306–310; Douarche 1: 642, 669, 679, 720, 721; Phan, "La Séduction impunie." AN DIII 35, Extrait du registre plumitif du tribunal du district de Pont-Châlier, 27 thermidor an II (14 July 1794).

16. ADC 3L 1249, TDD Vire, Minutes d'audiences, floréal an II–fructidor an III (Apr. 1794–Sept. 1795). D. Dalloz, *Répertoire méthodique et alphabétique de doctrine et de jurisprudence,* 44 vols. (Paris, 1845–70) (hereafter cited as Dalloz), 35: 294, Comm. nat. contre . . . , 3 floréal an III (22 Apr. 1795). The Tribunal de Cassation overturned paternity suits from 1798 on. Dalloz 35: 294; *Journal du Palais: Recueil le plus ancien et le plus complet de la jurisprudence française,* ed. Alexandre Ledru-Rollin, 3rd ed. (Paris, 1858) (hereafter JDP) 1: 220; and *Recueil général des lois et des arrêts, avec notes et commentaires . . . , fondé par M. Sirey,* 10 vols., rev. and completed by L. M. Devilleneuve and A. A. Carette (Paris, 1840–43) (hereafter Sirey N.) 1: 1, 168, Garaud contre Jeanne Manton, 19 vendémiaire an VII (10 Oct. 1798). See also Sirey N. 1: 2, 90, Tribunal d'appel de Paris, Blanquet contre Léchalat, 17 thermidor an X (5 Aug. 1802); Sirey N. 1: 1, 762, Sprimont contre Desforges, 3 ventôse an XI (22 Feb. 1803). AN DIII 75, Lettre du commissaire national près le tribunal du district de Louviers au Comité de législation, 2 prairial an III (21 May 1795).

17. AN DIII 75, Brouillon de réponse du Comité de législation au commis- saire national près le tribunal du district de Louviers, 14 messidor an III (2 July 1795). For further replies, see esp AN DIII 363, e.g., Réponse au commissaire national près le tribunal du district de Wissembourg, 29 floréal an II (18 May 1794); AN DIII 75, Réponse au commissaire près le tribunal du district de Pont- l'Evêque, n.d., c. Aug. 1794. In reply to a petition by citoyenne Bertrand about a suit under way, the Convention had decreed on 4 pluviôse an II that the 12 brumaire an II law had no retroactive effect. By allowing suits in process to pro- ceed, they implicitly reiterated the abolition of post–12 brumaire paternity suits. AN ADII 48, Décret de la Convention nationale, 4 pluviôse an II (23 Jan. 1794).

18. AN ADXVIIIc 325, Oudot, *Projet d'articles additionnels et d'ordre du jour, proposés au nom du Comité de Législation, sur diverses pétitions relatives à la loi du 12 brumaire, concernant les enfants nés hors du mariage* (Paris, an III

[1794–95]); Séance du 19 frimaire an III (9 Dec. 1794), *Moniteur*, 82, 22 frimaire an III (12 Dec. 1794). On this second, failed version of the Code, see Halpérin, *Impossible Code civil*, 205–214.

19. Séance du 19 frimaire an III (9 Dec. 1794), *Moniteur*, 82, 22 frimaire an III (12 Dec. 1794).

20. Circulaire de Berlier, 6 floréal an III (25 Apr. 1795), in Fenet, 8: 223; Circulaire de la Commission des administrations civiles, Police et Tribunaux aux tribunaux des districts et aux juges de paix, 15 prairial an III (3 June 1795), as quoted in Ferret, *Tribunaux de famille dans le district de Montpellier*, 346–48.

21. In my case study of the Calvados, the latest case was initiated in Nov. 1794. ADC 3L 1009, TDD Lisieux, Thérèse Lefranc contre Pierre Deshayes, 13 brumaire an III (3 Nov. 1794). Cases disappeared early in 1795 in the Maine: Fillon, *Trois bagues aux doigts*, 260, 306–310. For a failed attempt in 1797, see Aimé Vincenti, *Le tribunal départemental de Vaucluse de l'an IV à l'an VI* (Avignon, 1928), 117–18.

22. Sirey N. 1: 1, 762, Sprimont contre Desforges, 3 ventôse an XI (22 Feb. 1803). Cf. cases after 1798 in note 16 and Dalloz 35: 362, Marthe contre Linstruisseur, 26 Mar. 1806.

23. By the 1810s illegitimacy rates reached 17–18 percent of births in large cities and 5 percent in France overall. Yves Blayo, "La proportion des naissances illégitimes en France de 1740 à 1829," *Population* 30 (1975): 65–70.

24. Douarche 2: 176–77, Plaidoyer de Bellart pour la famille Dupin-Rochefort contre la citoyenne Moret, 5 thermidor an III (23 July 1795).

25. ADC 3L 1340, Tribunal Civil du département du Calvados, Pierre Jacques Avenel contre la veuve Seigneurie et sa fille et la citoyenne Duprat femme Ganne, 16 pluviôse an IV (5 Feb. 1796). Cf. ADC 3L 1339, Tribunal Civil du département du Calvados, Augot et Guiltot contre Gueroult, tuteur de Rose Agathe Liberté, 13 brumaire an IV (14 Nov. 1795).

26. AN DIII 363, Pétition anonyme, remise par le député de la Vienne au Comité de Législation, 24 floréal an II? (13 May 1794?); AN DIII 363, Question sur l'interprétation de la loi du 12 brumaire, n.d.; Dalloz 35: 295, Adélaïde contre Pateau, 24 pluviôse an VIII (13 Feb. 1800); *JDP* 1: 141, Haitze contre Devanceux, 3 pluviôse an V (22 Jan. 1797).

27. *Adresse à la Convention nationale, au nom d'une infinité des pères et mères chargés des familles, et dont plusieurs sont à la veille d'être ruinés par des enfans nés hors mariage* (Paris, n.d.).

28. Ibid. On isolated natural children versus bands of collateral younger sons, see also *Observations importantes, soumises aux législateurs par un républicain* (Paris, 1793); *Un mot sur les enfans naturels, soumis aux législateurs par un ami de la Liberté et de l'Egalité* (Paris, n.d.).

29. Auguste, *Réponse d'un enfant naturel à l'adresse présentée à la Convention nationale par cinquante collatéraux de feu Messire de Boulogne* (n.p., n.d.); *Opinion d'un citoyen, sur la partie du Code civil concernant les enfans naturels en possession d'état et nés de père et mère libres* (n.p., n.d.), 4.

30. ADC 3L 978 and ADC 3L 1007, TDD Lisieux, Marie-Catherine

Dampville femme Aumont et son mari François Aumont contre Pierre Gondouin et Anne Gondouin, sa sœur, 28 messidor an III (16 Jul. 1795).

31. Ibid. On "mariages privés," see Mulliez, "Révolutionnaires, nouveaux pères?" 379–85, and "La volonté d'un homme," in *Histoire des pères et de la paternité,* ed. Jean Delumeau and Daniel Roche (Paris, 1990), 279–305, esp. 284–86; Berlier, *AP* 70: 654–62, 9 Aug. 1793; Oudot, *AP* 45: 556–60, 25 June 1792; Oudot, *AP* 70: 634–36, 9 Aug. 1793; Oudot, *Essai sur les principes de la législation des mariages privés.*

32. AN DIII 363, Antoine Valbe-Monteval, *Mémoire en forme de pétition au Comité de législation de la Convention nationale* (Vienne, n.d.); Pétition d'Antoine Valbe-Monteval au Comité de législation, 19 floréal an II (8 May 1794).

33. Hunt, *Family Romance,* chap. 2; Mulliez, "La volonté d'un homme." Cambacérès, *AP* 66: 34–37, 4 June 1793; Oudot, *AP* 70: 634–36, 9 Aug. 1793.

34. AN ADII 34, R.F.L.C. Sellons, *Résumé pour la citoyenne Sellons, sur la pétition des Suisses, parents collatéraux de Paul Sellons* (Paris, an II, 1794); AN DIII 363, Mémoire à consulter, n.d.

35. Douarche 2: 112–13, Marguerite Trouillet la Roche, mère et tutrice de Antoine-Charles-Victor Maupeou son fils mineur, né hors mariage d'elle et de feu Charles-Victor-René Maupeou, contre les commissaires du Domaine national, 23 ventôse an III (13 Mar. 1795). Also Douarche 2: 157, 210–11, 238, 515; [Anne-Charlotte Dejassaud d'Erlach], *Pétition au Conseil des Cinq Cents, pour les héritiers de René-Ange-Augustin Maupeou, en réponse au rapport fait le 19 frimaire dernier sur celle d'un prétendu enfant naturel Maupeou* (Paris, n.d. [1797]). In the Council of Five Hundred, this case led to two reports on inheritance via representation by Siméon (19 frimaire an V [9 Dec. 1796]) and Favart (4 brumaire an VI [25 Oct. 1797]). The law of 2 ventôse an VI (20 Feb. 1798) finally ruled that in legacies opened between 12 brumaire an II and 15 thermidor an IV, natural children (like Antoine-Charles Maupeou) whose parent(s) died before 4 June 1793 could inherit by representation. See also Jacquinot, *De la filiation naturelle,* 168–70.

36. *JDP* 1: 411 and Sirey N. 1: 1, 213, Banès contre Lepeigneux, 24 prairial an VII (12 June 1799); Ferret, *Tribunaux de famille dans le district de Montpellier,* 358–59. On care of the mother as inadequate proof, cf. Dalloz 35: 295, Couillandeaux contre Dessidoux, 16 nivôse an V (5 Jan. 1797).

37. Dalloz 35: 294, Billod contre Chapuis, 2 floréal an III (21 Apr. 1795); Sirey N. 2: 2, 81, Cour d'appel d'Angers, Cintré contre Jacques-Marie, 25 thermidor an XIII (13 Aug. 1805); AN ADII 34, *Mémoire à consulter et consultation, pour Benjamin Callender, négociant à Boston, et Marie-Jeanne Fauveau, son épouse; et Anne-Elisabeth Fauveau, fille majeure* (Paris, fructidor an IV [Sept. 1796]); Philippe-Antoine Merlin de Douai, *Recueil alphabétique de questions de droit,* 4th ed.,16 vols. (Bruxelles, 1928), 7: 284–86, "Filiation." For a wide variety of types of proof, see esp. Dalloz 35: 294–96.

38. AN ADXVIIIc 325, A.L.B.D., *Les enfans nés hors du mariage, reconnus et en possession d'état, à la Convention nationale* (Paris, n.d., c. Sept. 1794); AN

DIII 363, Pétition du citoyen Jean-Baptiste Despans à la Convention nationale, 9 nivôse an II (29 Dec. 1793); AN DIII 35, Pétition de la citoyenne LeFort à la Convention nationale, received 26 fructidor an II (12 Sept. 1794); AN DIII 32, Pétition des citoyennes Marie, Marguerite, Marie-Anne Huard, filles naturelles, aux citoyens composant la Convention nationale, received 26 thermidor an II (13 Aug. 1794); Auguste, *Réponse d'un enfant naturel*, 5.

39. *Adresse à la Convention nationale au nom des enfans posthumes, nés hors mariage* (Paris, n.d., c. 1795); AN ADII 34, *Observations sur le rapport présenté par Siméon, relativement à la successibilité des enfans naturels* (Paris, n.d., c. an V [1796–97]). Siméon's report (18 messidor an V [6 July 1797]) advocated requiring a father's formal recognition before a civil official if he died after 12 brumaire an II.

40. AN DIII 363, Pétition de Pascal Ecret? au citoyen [Cambacérès], 15 Sept. 1793. Oudot may have been responding to this petition or a similar one when he advocated easier recognition of Creole natural children from the Caribbean. AN ADXVIIIc 325, Oudot, *Projet d'articles additionnels et d'ordre du jour.*

41. AN DIII 363, Pétition de la républicaine Loudios cadette au citoyen représentant, 24 pluviôse an II (12 Feb. 1794). AN DIII 363 contains further appeals by adultérins both before and after the 12 brumaire law. Cf. AN DIII 361, Pétition très importante sur l'état civil d'un enfant, n.d. Oudot, *AP* 70: 634–36, 9 Aug. 1793; Sirey N. 1: 1, 406, Emmery contre Marie Dumas, 5 nivôse an IX (26 Dec. 1800); Douarche 2: 447, veuve Lavalette contre citoyenne Bougueraud, 8 nivôse an VI (28 Dec. 1797). In the Calvados, I turned up no successful use of the 12 brumaire law by adultérins seeking an increased legacy. On adultérins' limited success in court, cf. D'Ayrenx, *Condition juridique*, 195–202; Jacquinot, *De la filiation naturelle*, 193–96, 211–12.

42. AN DXXXIX 5, Pétition du citoyen Monfreuille au Conseil des 500, 18 floréal an V (7 May 1797). On thermidor and the family, see Hunt, *Family Romance*, chap. 6. On the demise of natural law, see Florence Gauthier, *Triomphe et mort du droit naturel en Révolution: 1789 —1795—1802* (Paris, 1992); Xavier Martin, "Politique et droit privé après Thermidor," in *RévJur*, 1 : 173–84.

43. Sirey N. 2: 2, 108, Richon-Grammont et Richon-Brasier contre Richon, Tribunal Civil de Bordeaux, 9 fructidor an X (27 Aug. 1802), and Cassation, 18 floréal an XIII (8 May 1805). On proof of paternity and acts done in prison during the Terror, see Merlin de Douai, *Questions de droit*, 7: 284–86, "Filiation."

44. *Réflexions tranchantes sur les enfans naturels qui ne rapportent que des actes de reconnaissance déterminés par des poursuites judiciaires de l'ancien régime* (n.p., n.d., c. 1795–97), 2. JDP 1: 163 and Sirey N. 1: 1, 78, Euzières contre Gaujoux, 5 thermidor an V (23 July 1797); JDP 1: 22 and Sirey N. 1: 1, 59, Dumesnil contre Leboucher-Dumesnil, 13 vendémiaire an V (4 Oct. 1796); Sirey N. 1: 2, 205, Cour d'Appel de Poitiers, Malroye contre les héritiers Gilbert, 28 messidor an XII (17 July 1804).

45. Dalloz 35: 294–95, Tribunal de Cassation cases on 18 germinal an III (7 Apr. 1795), 2 floréal an III (21 Apr. 1795), 26 germinal an III (15 Apr. 1795), 5

thermidor an V (23 July 1797), 26 germinal an XII (16 Apr. 1804), 2 fructidor an III (19 Aug. 1795), 22 messidor an III (10 July 1795), 1 messidor an XIII (20 June 1805). Courts nonetheless occasionally recognized a "transaction" as legitimate, voluntary proof if no court case had been under way when the father agreed to pay some form of support. Sirey N. 2: 2, 48, Cour d'Appel de Bordeaux, Guérin contre Guérin, 18 floréal an XIII (8 May 1805).

46. *Recueil général des lois et des arrêts*, ed. J. B. Sirey (Paris, 1800–01), (hereafter Sirey), 1: 2, 632, Tribunal d'appel de Paris, Mlle. Ducloson contre Colson, 21 ventôse an IX (12 Mar. 1801).

47. *AP* 90: 159–60 and Duvergier 7: 160, loi du 19 floréal an II (8 May 1794).

48. Douarche 2: 634–37, Marie-Catherine Pénicaud contre Jean-Baptiste-Pascal Lanefranque, 18 germinal an VII (7 Apr. 1799).

49. Ibid.; AN ADXVIIIc 325, *Considérations sur la loi relative aux enfans nés hors mariage* (n.p., n.d.), 1.

50. AN ADII 34, *Consultation pour les citoyens Loiseau-Monny, sur la réclamation d'état de Marie-Jeanne Elisabeth, anonyme, et Anne-Elisabeth, aussi anonyme, fille majeure* (Paris, 27 nivôse an V [16 Jan. 1797]); *Un mot décisif sur la successibilité des enfans nés hors mariage* (n.p., n.d., c. summer 1798). Cf. *Observations sur la résolution du 16 floréal an VI, relative aux enfans nés hors mariage, au Conseil des Anciens* (n.p., n.d., c. summer 1798).

51. AN DIII 363, *Observation pour le citoyen Lartois, représentant les héritiers Morisse du Havre . . . Contre la citoyenne Raibaut, ci-devant cuisinière du décédé et mère de son enfant naturel* (Le Havre, n.d.); Pétiton anonyme au citoyen Oudot, n.d.; AN ADXVIIIc 365, Pétition au conseil des 500: représentation d'une mère sur la successibilité d'un enfant naturel aux droits légitimes, printed, n.d. (c. 1796).

52. Douarche 2: 170–83, Citoyenne Moret contre les héritiers Dupin-Rochefort, 5 thermidor an III (23 July 1795).

53. As one pamphlet observed, the six Paris tribunals and the national appeals court did not demand formal declarations for post–12 brumaire legacies. *Réflexions relatives au sens de la loi du 12 brumaire an II, sur les enfans naturels* (Paris, n.d., c. 1798), 16–17. Paris tribunals initially used Art. 8, and then reversed this policy from mid 1797 on: Douarche 1: 777, 2: 222, 240, 404, 469, 506, 730. Jacquinot, *De la filiation naturelle*, 123–29. Cf. ADC 3L 1339 and 3L 1340, Tribunal Civil du département du Calvados, Plumitif d'audiences (brumaire–pluviôse an IV [Oct. 1795–Jan. 1796]) and (pluviôse–germinal an IV [Feb.–Apr. 1796]). The Tribunal de Cassation initially advocated allowing proof by Art. 8, and then reversed its interpretation in favor of requiring formal declarations from 1799 on. See Dalloz 35: 296, Jollivet et autres contre Mesnard, 7 fructidor an IV (24 Aug. 1796); Sirey N. 1: 1, 213, Banès contre Lepeigneux, 24 prairial an VII (12 June 1799). Given the uncertainty of the law, in January 1797 the Civil Tribunal of Saône-et-Loire suspended its judgment on a post–12 brumaire legacy case and queried the legislature. Merlin de Douai, the Minister of Justice, seized this opportunity to push for a stringent interpretation of enfants naturels' rights and the Directors instructed the legislature to examine the mat-

ter, generating repeated debates. AN ADII 34, *Arrêté du directoire exécutif concernant un référé sur une question relative aux droits successifs des enfants nés hors du mariage, et dont le père est décédé depuis la promulgation de la loi du 12 brumaire an II* (Paris, 12 ventôse an V [2 Mar. 1797]).

54. AN ADII 34, *Mémoire à consulter et consultation, pour Benjamin Callender, négociant à Boston, et Marie-Jeanne Fauveau, son épouse; et Anne-Elisabeth Fauveau, fille majeure* (Paris, fructidor an IV [Sept. 1796]); *Consultation pour les citoyens Loiseau-Monny, sur la réclamation d'état de Marie-Jeanne Elisabeth, anonyme, et Anne-Elisabeth, aussi anonyme, fille majeure* (Paris, 27 nivôse an V [16 Jan. 1797]); Dalloz 35: 295 and Sirey 2: 1, 246, Deledecque Laloi contre les héritiers Laloi, 4 germinal an X (25 Mar. 1802).

55. AN ADXVIIIc 325, *Observations sur la question: "La loi du 12 brumaire an II, prescrit-elle ou ne prescrit-elle pas aux enfans naturels, dont les pères sont morts depuis sa publication, la nécessité d'une reconnaissance devant l'officier public?"* (Paris, n.d., c. 1797–98), 3.

56. AN DXXXIX 5, Pétition du citoyen Faure, notaire au canton de Grignan, département de la Drôme, au corps législatif des 500, 4 germinal an V (24 Mar. 1797). For further queries, see the DIII series, esp. DIII 363, and DXXXIX 5–8.

57. Dalloz 35: 295, Ivonnet contre Créole Ursule, 24 pluviôse an IV (13 Feb. 1796); Dalloz 35: 296, Jollivet et autres contre Mesnard, 7 fructidor an IV (24 Aug. 1796).

58. JDP 1: 22 and Sirey N. 1: 1, 59, Dumesnil contre Leboucher-Dumesnil, 13 vendémiaire an V (4 Oct. 1796). See notes 44 and 45 above.

59. JDP 1: 141, Haitze contre Devanceux, 3 pluviôse an V (22 Jan. 1797); Dalloz 35: 295, Couillandeaux contre Dessidoux, 16 nivôse an V (5 Jan. 1797); and Eymerie contre Elie dit Sansbesoin, 26 prairial an III (14 June 1795); Dalloz 35: 294, Hérici contre Thomas, 13 germinal V (2 Apr. 1797). Cf. Dalloz 35: 295, Adélaïde contre Pateau, 24 pluviôse an VIII (13 Feb. 1800); Belmont contre Briançon-Belmont, 12 ventôse an IX (3 Mar. 1801); Deledecque Laloi contre héritiers Laloi, 4 germinal an X (25 Mar. 1802); Lavarde contre Thoury, 13 frimaire an X (4 Dec. 1801); Fouques contre Gallard, 5 nivose an XII (27 Dec. 1803). On the court's politics, see Halpérin, *Tribunal de cassation.*

60. Sirey N. 1: 1, 406, Emmery contre Marie Dumas, 5 nivôse an IX (26 Dec. 1800).

61. Sirey N. 1: 1, 213, Banès contre Lepeigneux, 24 prairial an VII (12 June 1799); JDP 1: 582 and Sirey N. 1: 1, 296, Olivier contre Joseph, 4 pluviôse an VIII (24 Jan. 1800); Sirey N. 1: 1, 571, Héritiers Brunel contre Florine, 4 nivôse an X (25 Dec. 1801); Dalloz 35: 295 and Sirey 2: 1, 246, Deledecque Laloi contre les héritiers Laloi, 4 germinal an X (25 Mar. 1802); Jacquinot, *De la filiation naturelle,* 199–200.

62. The law of 14 floréal an XI (4 May 1803) stated that legacies entering probate between the promulgation of the 12 brumaire law and of the Code should follow the stipulations laid out by the Code. Articles 334 and 336 of the Code mandated that paternity outside of marriage could be recognized by the father's formal act in the état civil, validated by the acknowledgment of the mother.

Article 757 of the Civil Code allowed recognized natural children to inherit one-third of a legitimate child's share if there were legitimate siblings; a one-half share if the parent left only ascendents or siblings; and a three-fourths share if the parent left no ascendents, descendents, brothers, or sisters.

63. *Rapport fait par Siméon au nom d'une commission spéciale, composée de Cambacérès, Bézard, Oudot, Favart, et Siméon, sur la successibilité des enfans naturels. Conseil des Cinq-Cents. 18 messidor an V* (Paris, messidor an V [July 1797]), 30.

64. Rachel Fuchs, *Abandoned Children: Foundlings and Child Welfare in Nineteenth-Century France* (Albany, 1984), chap. 1; Duprat, *"Pour l'amour de l'humanité"*, 1: chaps. 4 and 5; Forrest, *The French Revolution and the Poor*, 124–33, 171–76; Hufton, *Women and the Limits of Citizenship*, chap. 2.

65. Two especially controversial cases were the Maupeou case and the Leboucher-Dumesnil case, provoking debates, respectively, on inheritance by representation and on proof of paternity using Old Regime judicial cases. See notes 35 and 44.

66. In the year IV (1795–96), the legislature briefly rescinded, then restored, then rescinded the retroactive application of the 12 brumaire law to 1789. In the years V and VI (1796–98), deputies repeatedly debated whether to allow inheritance by representation and above all, discussed proofs of paternity for those whose fathers died between the promulgation of the 12 brumaire law and the Civil Code. Finally, in 1801 during the initial discussions of the Civil Code before Napoleon purged the Tribunate into passive acceptance, one of the few issues to stir heated debate among the Tribunes was Article 60, eventually dropped, allowing an unwed mother to name the father on the birth certificate of her natural child. Fenet 8: 80–320.

67. Legislative slogan quoted by Traer, *Marriage and the Family*, 157.

CHAPTER 7

1. AN DIII 382, Mémoire de Cotelle aux citoyens représentants, c. summer 1794; AN DIII 339, Pétition des citoyens de la commune d'Agen (Lot-et-Garonne) à la Convention nationale, received 10 floréal an III (29 Apr. 1795).

2. On the deputies' debates, with some material on popular opinions, see Jean-Louis Halpérin, *L'impossible Code civil* (Paris, 1992); François Olivier-Martin, *La Crise du mariage dans la législation intermédiaire, 1789–1804* (Paris, 1901), 221–55. On the legislature, see *La Révolution et l'ordre juridique privé: Rationalité ou scandale: Actes du colloque d'Orléans, 1986* (hereafter *RévJur*), 2 vols. (Orléans, 1988); Marcel Garaud and Romuald Szramkiewicz, *La Révolution française et la famille* (Paris, 1978); *La Famille, la loi, l'Etat de la Révolution au Code Civil*, ed. Irène Théry and Christian Biet (Paris, 1989) (hereafter *FLE*); Francis Ronsin, *Le Contrat sentimental: Débats sur le mariage, l'amour, le divorce, de l'ancien régime à la Restauration* (Paris, 1990). For analysis of the desire to "rehabilitate the family" expressed in novels, art, and melodrama, see Lynn Hunt, *The Family Romance of the French Revolution*

(Berkeley, 1992), chap. 5; Ewa Lajer-Burcharth, "David's *Sabine Women:* Body, Gender, and Republican Culture under the Directory," *Art History* 14 (1991): 397–430.

3. François Furet has been influential in arguing that Thermidor "restored independence to society," facilitated "society's revenge on ideology," and ushered in "another Revolution . . . the Revolution of special interests": François Furet, *Interpreting the French Revolution*, trans. Elborg Forster (Cambridge, Eng., 1981), chap. 1, 71, 74. For a critique of Furet's bifurcation of society and politics under Thermidor, see Lynn Hunt, "Review: *Penser la révolution française*," *History and Theory* 20 (1981): 313–23; Keith Baker, *Inventing the French Revolution: Essays on Political Culture in the Eighteenth Century* (Cambridge, Eng., 1990), 7–8. On the revenge or return of the social, cf. Françoise Brunel, *Thermidor: La chute de Robespierre* (Paris, 1989), 125–6; Keith Baker, "Introduction," in *The French Revolution and the Creation of Modern Political Culture*, vol. 4, *The Terror*, ed. Keith Michael Baker, (Oxford, Eng., 1994), 4: xiii–xxviii. The classic historiography of the Revolution defined the Thermidorian Directory as the bourgeois republic: Georges Lefebvre, *Le Directoire* (Paris, 1946); cf. Denis Woronoff, *La République bourgeoise, de Thermidor à Brumaire 1794–1799* (Paris, 1972); Martyn Lyons, *France under the Directory* (Cambridge, Eng., 1975), and "Recent Interpretations of the French Directory," *Australian Journal of Politics and History* 27 (1981): 40–47.

4. "Counter-imaginary" refers to the Thermidorians' attempt to re-envision republican politics in the aftermath of the Terror: Bronislaw Baczko, *Ending the Terror: The French Revolution after Robespierre*, trans. Michel Petherham (Cambridge, Eng., 1994), e.g., 218–22; Françoise Brunel, "Mélanges sur l'historiographie de la réaction thermidorienne: Pour une analyse politique de l'échec de la voie jacobine," *Annales historiques de la Révolution française* 51 (1979): 455–74, and "Bridging the Gulf of the Terror," in *The Terror*, ed. Baker, 327–46; Mona Ozouf, *L'Ecole de la France: Essais sur la Révolution, l'utopie, et l'enseignement* (Paris, 1984), 91–108.

5. François Gendron, *La Jeunesse dorée* (Québec, 1979); Laura Mason, *Singing the French Revolution: Popular Culture and Politics, 1787–1799* (Ithaca, 1996), 130–54; Jeremy Popkin, *The Right-Wing Press in France* (Chapel Hill, 1980), chaps. 4–5.

6. *Le Miroir* 370, 16 floréal an V (5 May 1797). Cf. various spring 1797 issues of *Le Censeur des Journaux; L'Accusateur Public; Le Grondeur;* Jean Pierre Labouisse-Rochefort, *Observations contre le divorce* (Paris, 1797). Günther Lottes, "Le débat sur le divorce et la formation de l'idéologie contre-révolutionnaire," in *RévJur*, 1: 317–33; Olivier-Martin, *Crise du mariage*, 191–97; Ronsin, *Contrat sentimental*, 163–68; Gérard Thibault-Laurent, *La première introduction du divorce en France sous la Révolution et l'Empire (1792–1816)* (Clermont Ferrand, 1938), 137–42; Suzanne Desan, "Marriage, Religion, and Moral Order: The Catholic Critique of Divorce during the Directory," in *The French Revolution and the Meaning of Citizenship*, ed. Renée Waldinger, Philip Dawson, and Isser Woloch (Westport, Conn., 1993), 201–210.

7. J. Girard, *Considérations sur le mariage et sur le divorce* (Paris, 1797); Charles Guiraudet, *La famille considérée comme l'élément des sociétés* (Paris, an V [1797]). Cf. Suzanne Necker, *Réflexions sur le divorce* (Lausanne, 1794).

8. Plays include Pierre Barré and N. Bourgueil, *Le mur mitoyen, ou Le divorce manqué* (Paris, 1796); Pierre Beaumarchais, *L'autre Tartuffe, ou La mère coupable* (Paris, 1794); Dupont de l'Isle, *La double réconciliation* (Paris, 1798). Most popular were *Le mur mitoyen* (105 performances), *La mère coupable* (84 performances), and Charles Demoustier, *Le divorce* (Paris, 1791), (64 performances), according to Emmet Kennedy et al., *Theatre, Opera, and Audience in Revolutionary Paris, Analysis and Repertory* (Westport, Conn., 1996). Even pro-divorce plays almost always ended in reconcilition, although a divorce actually occurs in Nicolas Forgeot, *Le Double divorce, ou Le bienfait de la loi* (Paris, an III [1795]). Francis Ronsin, "Indissolubilité du mariage ou divorce: Essai d'une chronologie des principaux arguments mis en avant par les partisans et les adversaires du divorce au cours de la période révolutionnaire," in *FLE*, 322–34. For the poem, see Henri d'Almeras, *La vie parisienne sous la Révolution et le Directoire* (Paris, 1909), 224, 238–44; "Le Rabâchage du père Lubon," as cited in James F. Traer, *Marriage and the Family in Eighteenth-Century France* (Ithaca, N.Y., 1980), 129–30. On melodrama, see Peter Brooks, *The Melodramatic Imagination: Balzac, Henry James, Melodrama, and the Mode of Excess* (New York, 1985); Hunt, *Family Romance*, 181–91.

9. Based on the reading of hundreds of civil law petitions to revolutionary legislatures and committees, esp. in AN ADII (Archives imprimées), ADXVIIIc (Suppléments aux Procès-verbaux des Assemblées nationales), C (Adresses à la Convention), DIII (Comité de législation); DXXXIX (Comité de la classification des lois).

10. See Chapter 4 for a discussion of petitioners. The issue of inheritance generated many more collective petitions than did divorce. Most divorce petitions were penned by individuals. For representative examples of collective, printed petitions on both sides of the post-Thermidorian war over inheritance law, see *Pétition relative au rapport sollicité de la loi du 17 nivôse an II concernant les donations et les successions, Par des citoyens du Jura à la Convention nationale* (Lons-le-Saunier, n.d., c. 1795); *A la Convention nationale. Pétition des habitants de la commune d'Yvetot* (Paris, n.d., c. 1795); *Adresse des citoyennes de la ci-devant province de Normandie, département du Calvados, sur la loi du 17 nivôse, à la Convention* (Paris, n.d., c. June 1795). See also Halpérin, *Impossible Code civil*, 215–220.

11. On occasion, the signature of the petition is in a clearly different hand than the body of the text: e.g., AN DIII 339, Pétition de la citoyenne Sophie Renoulaux au président de la Convention nationale, received 24 germinal an III (13 Apr. 1795). For examples of model petitions, see AN DXXXIX 5; AN DIII 145; AN DIII 273; AN DIII 143. Taking the notion of model petitions most to heart, Henri Lelaidier of the department of the Manche sent the Committee of Legislation at least twenty-one versions of his copied attack on the 17 nivôse

law. AN DIII 143, Pétition du citoyen Henri Lelaidier au Comité de législation, 28 nivôse an III (17 Jan. 1795).

12. AN DIII 339, Pétition des cultivateurs de la commune de Cassillonés (Seine-Inférieure) à la Convention nationale, 20 ventôse an III (10 Mar. 1795); AN DXXXIX 5, Pétition du citoyen Daubian aux Cinq-Cents, 8 frimaire an V (29 Nov. 1796).

13. AN DIII 274, Pétition des citoyens Lenoir et Lammarré aux députés de la Manche, 1 frimaire an III (21 Nov. 1794); AN DIII 273, Pétition du citoyen Genise au citoyen président de la Convention nationale, 19 messidor an III (7 July 1795).

14. Sarah Maza, *Private Lives and Public Affairs: The Causes Célèbres of Prerevolutionary France* (Berkeley, 1994); Lise Andries, "Récits de survie: Les mémoires d'autodéfense pendant l'an II et l'an III," in *Les Carmagnoles des muses: Hommes de lettres et l'artiste dans la Révolution*, ed. Jean-Claude Bonnet (Paris, 1988), 261–75; Stephanie A. Brown, "Women on Trial: The Revolutionary Tribunal and Gender" (Ph.D. diss., Stanford University, 1996), chaps. 4–5.

15. Baczko, *Ending the Terror*, chaps. 2–3, esp. 78–92, 136–38; Brunel, "Bridging the Gulf," 337–40; Hugh Gough, *The Newspaper Press in the French Revolution* (Chicago, 1988), 119–23; Popkin, *Right-Wing Press*, 96–97, 100–104. On plays, such as *Cange, ou le commissionnaire de Lazare*, which unmasked the Terror, see Marvin Carlson, *The Theater of the French Revolution* (Ithaca, 1966), chap. 7; Marie-Laurence Netter, "The Great Successes of Each Year," in *Theatre, Opera, and Audiences*, ed. Kennedy, 35–50, esp. 47–49.

16. AN DIII 338, Pétition de la veuve Cousin au Comité de législation, 26 prairial an III (14 June 1795); AN DXXXIX 5, Lettre du citoyen Limousin, commissaire du Directoire exécutif près l'administration municipale du canton de Jarnac, au citoyen président (du conseil des 500), 2 frimaire an V (22 Nov. 1796); AN DIII 363–65, Observations pour le citoyen Lartois . . . , adressées aux membres de la Société de la Liberté et de l'Egalité, contre la citoyenne Raibaut, mère de son enfant naturel, n.d. (c. 1794); AN DXXXIX 5, Réclamation du citoyen Duclaire au corps législatif, 3 germinal an V (23 Mar. 1797); Réclamation du citoyen Audin au corps législatif, received 7 prairial an V (26 May 1797).

17. Baczko, *Ending the Terror*, 154–60; Ian Germani, "Les Bêtes féroces: Thermidorian Images of Jacobinism," *Proceedings of the Annual Meeting of the Western Society for French History* 17 (1990): 205–19.

18. AN DIII 338, Pétition des citoyennes Marguerite Chapuret fille, Marguerite Françoise Chapuret épouse de François Faucon, et François Chapuret aux citoyens représentants, received 21 floréal an III (10 May 1795); AN DIII 273, Pétition de Christine Géritault aux représentants, 25 pluviôse an III (13 Feb. 1795); AN DXXXIX 5, Pétition de Jean-Baptiste Thorel aux Cinq-Cents, received 4 fructidor an V (22 Aug. 1797); Pétition des citoyens Jean-Baptiste et François Hué, fréres, aux Cinq-Cents, 17 thermidor an V (4 Aug. 1797); AN DIII 339, Pétition des habitants de la commune de Campes (Var) à la Convention nationale, 25 germinal an III (14 Apr. 1795); Pétition des cultiva-

teurs de la commune de Cassillonnés (Seine-Inférieure) aux membres de la Convention nationale, 20 ventôse an III (10 Mar. 1795); Pétition des habitants de la commune d'Allayrat (Creuse) à la Convention nationale, received 30 ventôse an III (20 Mar. 1795). For the deputies, see Merlin de Douai, 5 floréal an III, *Moniteur Universel* (hereafter *Moniteur*) 219, 9 floréal an III (28 Apr. 1795); Mailhe, 15 thermidor an III, *Moniteur* 321, 21 thermidor an III (8 Aug. 1795). On the legislative debates, see Halpérin, *Impossible Code civil,* 154–57.

19. On natural law, see Crane Brinton, *French Revolutionary Legislation on Illlegitimacy, 1789–1804* (Cambridge, Mass., 1936), chaps. 3–4; Florence Gauthier, *Triomphe et mort du droit naturel en Révolution: 1789—1795—1802* (Paris, 1992); Xavier Martin, "Politique et droit privé après Thermidor," in *RévJur,* 1: 173–84. On transparency and political regeneration, see Lynn Hunt, *Politics, Culture, and Class in the French Revolution* (Berkeley, 1984), chaps. 1–2.

20. AN DXXXIX 5, Pétition anonyme, signée BBB, aux citoyens représentants, n.d., c. late 1796; AN DIII 33, Pétition de la citoyenne Elisabeth LeTellier aux membres de la Convention, 7 nivôse an III (27 Dec. 1794); cf. AN DIII 339, Pétition d'Elisabeth Colombié, fille habitante à Agen, aux citoyens représentants, received 16 floréal an III (5 May 1795), who also complained that the 17 nivôse law prevented her from marrying; AN ADII 33, Les pères et mères des divorcés aux représentants du peuple français, n.d., c. spring 1795.

21. On notions of female susceptibility, see Suzanne Desan, "'Constitutional Amazons': Jacobin Women's Clubs in the French Revolution," in *Re-Creating Authority in Revolutionary France,* ed. Bryant Ragan and Elizabeth Williams (New Brunswick, N.J., 1992), 11–35; Olwen Hufton, *Women and the Limits of Citizenship* (Toronto, 1992), chap. 3; Dorinda Outram, " 'Le Langage mâle de la vertu': Women and the Discourse of the French Revolution," in *The Social History of Language,* ed. Peter Burke and Roy Porter (Cambridge, Eng., 1987), 120–35.

22. AN DXXXIX 4, Pétition du citoyen Asse au Conseil des Cinq-Cents, received 24 prairial an IV (21 June 1796); AN ADXVIIIc 365, Pétition du citoyen D. de la Grange aux représentants du peuple, 18 nivôse an V (7 Jan. 1797); AN DXXXIX 5, Pétition du citoyen Guérin au citoyen président législateur, received 13 frimaire an IV (4 Dec. 1795); AN DIII 270, Pétition du plus malheureux de vos concitoyens aux citoyens représentants, 20 thermidor an III (7 Aug. 1795).

23. AN DXXXIX 3, Pétition du citoyen Duval aux Cinq-Cents, 13 brumaire an III (3 Nov. 1794); AN DIII 272, Pétition du citoyen Jean Dumont, volontaire, à la Convention nationale, 12 vendémiaire an III (3 Oct. 1794).

24. AN DIII 338, Pétition de la citoyenne Jeanne Françoise Aumont au Comité de législation, 7 messidor an III (25 June 1795).

25. AN ADXVIIIc 365, Pétition au conseil des 500: représentation d'une mère sur la successibilité d'un enfant naturel aux droits légitimes, printed, n.d., c. 1796.

26. Article 4 of the Déclaration des devoirs of the Constitution of the Year III pronounced, "No one is a good citizen if he is not a good son, good father, good

brother, good friend, good husband." *Les Constitutions de la France depuis 1789*, ed. Jacques Godechot (Paris, 1970), 103. AN DXXXIX 4, Pétition d'Arthon, instituteur de la jeunesse à Lille, aux Cinq-Cents, 5 thermidor an IV (24 July 1796); AN DIII 35, Pétition de plusieurs citoyens de Friardel (Calvados) au Comité de législation, 21 ventôse an III (11 Mar. 1795).

27. AN DXXXIX 5, Pétition du citoyen Limousin au citoyen président des Cinq-Cents, 2 frimaire an V (22 Nov. 1796); AN DIII 361, Précis pour le citoyen D'Anneville, n.d.; AN DIII 338, Pétition de la citoyenne Marie Tourme née Dupuy au Comité de législation, n.d., c. summer 1795; AN DXXXIX 5, Pétition du citoyen Jean Levasseur aux Cinq-Cents, 28 thermidor an V (15 Aug. 1797); Pétition du citoyen Lamarre aux Cinq-Cents, 28 messidor an V (16 July 1797); Pétition du citoyen Dominique Digeon aux Cinq-Cents, 15 thermidor an V (2 Aug. 1797); Pétition du citoyen P. Montpensier au corps législatif, 6 floréal an V (25 Apr. 1797); AN DIII 338, Pétition du citoyen Dubout à la Convention nationale, 18 floréal an III (7 May 1795); *Pétition . . . par des citoyens du Jura à la Convention nationale*

28. AN DIII 339, Pétition de Cahuac, cultivateur, à la Convention nationale, 25 germinal an III (14 Apr. 1795), echoing the language of Art. 17 of the 1789 Declaration of the Rights of Man and Citizen; AN DIII 382, Observations générales sur les décrets de la Convention nationale concernant les successions au Comité de législation, anonyme, n.d.; AN DXXXIX 5, Pétition du citoyen Louis Alexandre Audouïn au Conseil des 500, 24 thermidor an V (11 Aug. 1797); Pétition des citoyens Jean-Baptiste et François Hué, frères, aux Cinq-Cents, 17 thermidor an V (4 Aug. 1797). Interestingly, their defense of property by natural rights strongly resembled the defense of the right to make wills by Cazalès and other deputies of the Midi in April 1791. On this debate, see Jacques Poumarède, "De la difficulté de penser la propriété (1789–1793)," in *Propriété et Révolution: Actes du colloque de Toulouse, 12–14 octobre 1989*, ed. Geneviève Koubi (Toulouse, 1990). AN DXXXIX 3, Observations anonymes sur quelques articles du projet de code civil, n.d., c. brumaire an III (Oct. 1794); AN DIII 338, Pétition de Julie Moulinneuf Pellisson et Catherine Moulinneuf Savy, 28 floréal an III (17 May 1795).

29. Jean-Jacques Clère, "De la Révolution au Code civil: Les fondements philosophiques et politiques du droit des successions," *Mémoires de la société pour l'histoire du droit et des institutions des anciens pays bourguignons, comtois, et romands* 43 (1986): 7–56, esp. 33–45; Gauthier, *Triomphe et mort du droit naturel*, 41–51; Poumarède, "De la difficulté de penser la propriété."

30. AN DIII 339, Pétition de la citoyenne Delphine Clerc au Comité de législation, 6 floréal an III (25 Apr. 1795); AN DXXXIX 5, Pétition du citoyen Riboult aux Cinq-Cents, 1 fructidor an V (18 Aug. 1797). Petitioners may have exaggerated their poverty, but as I argued about divorce and inheritance disputes in Chapters 3 and 4, although the very poor made little use of courts, those with small fortunes—such as small landholders, small artisans, and textile workers—used them extensively. Poor handwriting and the discussion of low monetary amounts at issue in many petitions reinforces this impression. Cf. Dessertine,

Divorcer à Lyon, 116–21; Phillips, *Family Breakdown in Late Eighteenth-Century France*, 89–91; Darrow, *Revolution in the House*, chaps. 5–7.

31. AN DIII 361, Réflexions sur la loi du divorce par le citoyen Arnold du Bois, 3 messidor an III (21 June 1795).

32. Article 8 of the Declaration of Duties, Constitution of the Year III, *Constitutions*, ed. Godechot, 103; AN DXXXIX 5, Pétitions du citoyen Monfreuille au Conseil des 500, 18 floréal an V (7 May 1797) and 1 prairial an V (20 May 1797); Pétition du citoyen Delalonde aux Cinq-Cents, 11 prairial V (30 May 1797); AN DIII 339, Pétition du citoyen François Obel à la Convention nationale, 3 floréal an III (22 Apr. 1795). Petitions defending the retroactive clauses insisted that most cases had been decided by late 1794.

33. AN DXXXIX 5, Pétition des citoyens soussignés du ci-devant Pays de Caux au Conseil des 500, 2 thermidor an V (20 July 1797).

34. AN DXXXIX 5, Pétition du citoyen L. Goulé au Conseil des 500, 11 prairial an V (30 May 1797).

35. AN DIII 382, Mémoire anonyme aux citoyens représentants, n.d.

36. AN DXXXIX 4, Observations [anonymes] sur le paragraphe de la loi qui règle les effets du divorce par rapport aux enfants, received by the Conseil des 500, 3 messidor an IV (21 June 1796).

37. AN DIII 339, Pétition de Cahuac, cultivateur, à la Convention nationale, 25 germinal an III (14 Apr. 1795)

38. AN DIII 339, Pétition de Foi Charpaut aux citoyens représentants, received 30 germinal an III (19 Apr. 1795); AN DIII 270, Pétition de la citoyenne Morin aux citoyens représentants, 15 brumaire an III (5 Nov. 1794); AN DIII 338, Pétition de la citoyenne Catherine Goyneau, veuve Encouguère et tutrice de leurs enfants, au Comité de législation, n.d., c. summer 1795; AN DIII 33, Pétition d'un négociant anonyme à la Convention nationale, 12 brumaire an III (2 Nov. 1794). In the Constitution of 1793, Article 14 actually forbade the retroactive implementation of criminal, not civil, laws, but that did not deter petitioners who either ignored that fact or demanded that the principle be followed in civil as well as criminal cases. The year III Constitution extended this prohibition to civil law as well. *Constitutions*, ed. Godechot, 81, 102.

39. AN DIII 339, Pétition du citoyen Armand Mame, lieutenant au 2e bataillon de Lot-et-Garonne, aux citoyens représentants, 15 floréal an III (4 May 1795); Halpérin, *Impossible Code civil*, 217; AN DIII 144, Pétition du citoyen Tardif aux citoyens législateurs, 22 brumaire an III (12 Nov. 1794). Younger sons who favored egalitarian inheritance also claimed to be patriotic soldiers.

40. AN DIII 273, Pétition du citoyen Lepeton et six autres aux législateurs, nivôse an III (Jan. 1794); AN DXXXIX 5, Demande en rapport de la loi du 18 pluviôse an V, envoyée par les soussignés habitants des départements de l'Orne et du Calvados aux Cinq-Cents, 7 messidor an V (25 June 1797); AN DIII 32, Pétition du citoyen Robert Gaillard aux membres de la Convention, 11 ventôse an II (1 Mar. 1794); Pétition de plusieurs citoyens agés de la commune de Livry (Calvados) aux citoyens représentants, received 12 frimaire an II (2 Dec. 1793); AN DXXXIX 5, Pétition du citoyen Robert aux Cinq-Cents, 3 fructidor an V (20

Aug. 1797); Pétition du citoyen Jean Lesauvage au corps législatif, 6 floréal an V (25 Apr. 1797); AN DIII 382, Observations anonymes sur le décret qui ordonne l'égalité des partages, n.d.; AN DXXXIX 5, Pétition du citoyen Robert Lesufleur aux Cinq-Cents, received 5 fructidor an V (22 Aug. 1797).

41. Poumarède, "De la difficulté de penser la propriété."

42. AN DXXXIX 5, Pétition des frères Pierre et Louis Petit aux Cinq-Cents, 27 thermidor an V (14 Aug. 1797); AN DIII 382, Observations générales sur les décrets de la Convention nationale concernant les successions au Comité de législation, anonyme, n.d.

43. AN DIII 147, Lettre de la citoyenne Galot Thiphaine aux citoyens représentants, received 3 messidor an II (21 June 1794); AN DIII 339, Adresse [imprimée] de la veuve Boudeau à la Convention, n.d., c. 1795.

44. Garaud and Szramkiewicz, *Révolution française et la famille;* Halpérin, *Impossible Code civil.*

45. See comments in margins of petitions: AN DIII 146, Marie Mathieu aux citoyens représentants, received 11 nivôse an III (31 Dec. 1794); AN DIII 147, Citoyenne Galot Thiphaine aux citoyens représentants, received 3 messidor an II (21 June 1794); AN DIII 382, Mémoire anonyme aux citoyens représentants, n.d., c. 1794–95. Mutliple specific petitions generated reports that might or might not make it out of committee into the legislature. See esp. AN DIII 366–67. A few petitioners were exceptionally successful. Elisabeth Clay gained a decree guaranteeing her community property share in her complex divorce case in Reims: AN ADII 33, Rapport et projet de décret présenté à la Convention nationale au nom du Comité de législation par C.F. Oudot, 17 frimaire an III (7 Dec. 1794). More frequently the committees commented that they could not give responses to specific cases. Examples in AN DIII 382 and AN DIII 33, e.g., Brouillon d'une lettre du Comité de législation à la citoyenne Regnaud, 17 germinal an III (7 Apr. 1795).

46. Cambacérès, "Discours préliminaire en présentant au Conseil des Cinq-Cents le projet de Code civil, au nom de la commission de la classification des lois," in Fenet, 1: 156; AN DXXXIX 3, Observations sur quelques articles du projet de Code civil, anonyme, brumaire an III? (Oct. 1794?); Olivier-Martin, *Crise du mariage,* 125–39; cf. Ronsin, *Contrat sentimental,* 157–62; Thibault-Laurent, *Première introduction du divorce,* 127–32.

47. Halpérin, *Impossible Code civil,* 215; Favart, 5 nivôse an V, *Moniteur* 97, 7 nivôse an V (27 Dec. 1796). For divorce petitions read at the Council of Five Hundred, see AN ADXVIIIb vol. 158: 560, 27 brumaire an V (17 Nov. 1796); vol. 160: 71–72, 5 nivôse an V (25 Dec. 1796); vol. 182: 528, 20 prairial an V (8 June 1797); vol. 212: 502, 24 brumaire an VII (13 Nov. 1798); vol. 237: 107, 7 brumaire an VIII (29 Oct. 1799). *Le Censeur des journaux* 276, 6 messidor an V (24 June 1797).

48. Ozouf, *Ecole de la France,* 91–108.

49. Baczko, *Ending the Terror,* 70–73; Brunel, "Bridging the Gulf," 331–32, 336–40; Halpérin, *Impossible Code civil,* 215–16.

50. Laurenceot, 8 fructidor an III, *Moniteur* 342, 12 fructidor an III (29 Aug.

1795); Darracq, 26 prairial an IV, *Moniteur* 272, 2 messidor an IV (20 June 1796).

51. Tallien, 11 fructidor an II, *Moniteur* 343, 13 fructidor an II (30 Aug. 1794).

52. Several weeks earlier, Boissy d'Anglas's defense of freedom of religious expression had resulted in the 3 ventôse an III (21 Feb. 1795) law allowing more extensive public worship. Fellow Thermidorians credited his composure as President of the Convention during the 1 prairial uprising, and he played a key role in writing the Constitution of the year III.

53. Boissy d'Anglas, 21 ventôse an III, *Moniteur* 173, 23 ventôse an III (13 Mar. 1795).

54. Anonymous citizens and Quirot, 5 floréal an III, *Moniteur* 219, 9 floréal an III (28 Apr. 1795); Lanjuinais, 8 fructidor an III, *Moniteur* 342, 12 fructidor an III (29 Aug. 1795); 14 thermidor an III, *Moniteur* 320, 20 thermidor an III (7 Aug. 1795). On his vision of state and society, see Bruno Nicolle, "Lanjuinais et la constitution de l'an III," in *1795. Pour une République sans Révolution. Colloque international du 29 juin au 1er juillet 1995*, ed. R. Dupuy and M. Morabito (Rennes, 1996), 91–113.

55. Dumolard, 24 prairial an IV, *Moniteur* 270, 30 prairial an IV (18 June 1796); AN ADXVIIIc 365, Jean-Henri Bancal, *Opinion sur le divorce, prononcée au Conseil des 500, 12 pluviôse an V* (Paris, an V [1797]).

56. Villetard, 14 thermidor an III, *Moniteur* 320, 20 thermidor an III (7 Aug. 1795); Paganel, 9 fructidor an III, *Moniteur* 343, 13 fructidor an III (30 Aug. 1795). For defenses of the retroactive, egalitarian laws, see debates of 8–9 fructidor an III, *Moniteur* 342–43, 12–13 fructidor an III (29–30 Aug. 1795). On antipatriarchal sentiment, see Hunt, *Family Romance*, chap. 6; Jacques Mulliez, "La volonté d'un homme," in *Histoire des pères et de la paternité*, ed. Jean Delumeau and Daniel Roche (Paris, 1990), 279–322; Bernard Schnapper, "Liberté, égalité, autorité: La famille devant les assemblées révolutionnaires (1790–1800)," in *Enfant*, 325–40.

57. The suspension of the retroactive effect of the 12 brumaire law on illegitimate children's rights would in turn be overturned, reestablishing retroactivity again by mid October 1795. The following August 1796, the retroactive enforcement of illegitimate inheritance would be modifed to begin on 4 June 1793 rather than on 14 July 1789.

58. The final section of this chapter will discuss these strategies of the Left. For key examples, see Paganel, 9 fructidor an III, *Moniteur* 343, 13 fructidor an III (30 Aug. 1795); Riou, 24 prairial an IV, *Moniteur* 269, 29 prairial an IV (17 June 1796); Darracq, 26 prairial an IV, *Moniteur* 272, 2 messidor an IV (20 June 1796), and 4 pluviôse an V, *Moniteur* 126, 6 pluviôse an V (25 Jan. 1797); Regnier in Council of Ancients, 14 messidor an IV, *Moniteur* 289, 19 messidor an IV (7 July 1796); Pons de Verdun, 28 nivôse an V, *Moniteur* 120, 30 nivôse an V (19 Jan. 1797), and 12 pluviôse an V, *Moniteur* 135, 15 pluviôse an V (3 Feb. 1797).

59. On somewhat different discourses on "justice" and "will" on the eve of the Revolution, see Baker, *Inventing the French Revolution*, esp. 25–27.

60. Mailhe, 9 fructidor an III, *Moniteur* 343, 13 fructidor an III (30 Aug. 1795).

61. Dubois-Crancé, 8 fructidor an III, *Moniteur* 342, 12 fructidor an III (29 Aug. 1795).

62. Lanjuinais, 14 thermidor an III, *Moniteur* 320, 20 thermidor an III (7 Aug. 1795).

63. Blutel, 17 prairial an IV, *Moniteur* 263, 23 prairial an IV (11 June 1796); Dumolard and Duprat, 24 prairial an IV, *Moniteur* 270, 30 prairial an IV (18 June 1796); Blutel and Mailhe, 26 prairial an IV, *Moniteur* 272, 2 messidor an IV (20 June 1796); Cambacérès, "Discours préliminaire," in Fenet 1: 148.

64. Mailhe, 4 pluviôse an V, *Moniteur* 125, 5 pluviôse an V (24 Jan. 1797).

65. Philippe-Delleville, 11 frimaire an V, *Moniteur* 73, 13 frimaire an V (3 Dec. 1796); Mailhe, 4 pluviôse an V, *Moniteur* 126, 6 pluviôse an V (25 Jan. 1797); Dumolard, 12 pluviôse an V, *Moniteur* 135, 15 pluviôse an V (3 Feb. 1797); Debonnières, 20 prairial an V, *Moniteur* 267, 27 prairial an V (15 June 1797). AN ADXVIIIc 365, *Rapport fait par Favard sur le divorce, au nom d'une commission spéciale, 20 nivôse an V* (Paris, an V [1797]); Bancal, *Opinion sur le divorce;* Pierre-Louis Duprat, *Opinion sur la suspension du divorce pour cause d'incompatibilité d'humeur et de caractère, 13 pluviôse an V* (Paris, an V[1797]; Siméon, *Opinion sur la suspension du divorce pour incompatibilité, 5 pluviôse an V* (Paris, an V [1797]). On religious critiques of divorce, see Desan, "Marriage, Divorce, and the Moral Order."

66. Durand de Maillane, 14 messidor an IV in Council of Ancients, *Moniteur* 289, 19 messidor an IV (7 July 1796).

67. Golzart, 28 nivôse an V, *Moniteur,* 120, 30 nivôse an V (19 Jan. 1797); Bancal, *Opinion sur le divorce.* Bancal denounced divorce and the evils of the "empire of women" in his three-hundred-page *Du nouvel ordre de la société fondé sur la religion* (Paris, an V [1797]), esp. pp. 230–50.

68. AN ADXVIIIc 365, Duprat, *Opinion sur la suspension du divorce;* Siméon, *Opinion sur la suspension du divorce.*

69. Siméon, *Opinion sur la suspension du divorce.*

70. Ibid.; Lanjuinais, note 54; Mailhe, note 64; Gauthier, *Triomphe et mort du droit naturel.*

71. Riou, 24 prairial an IV, *Moniteur* 269, 29 prairial an IV (17 June 1796); Charlier, 5 floréal an III, *Moniteur* 219, 9 floréal an III (28 Apr. 1795); Cambacérès, 3 pluviôse an V, *Moniteur* 125, 5 pluviôse an V (24 Jan. 1797).

72. Darracq, 4 pluviôse an V, *Moniteur* 126, 6 pluviôse an V (25 Jan. 1797); Pons de Verdun, 12 pluviôse an V, *Moniteur* 135, 15 pluviôse an V (3 Feb. 1797); Lecointe-Puyraveau, *Opinion sur le projet de suspension de la loi du 20 septembre 1792, qui permet le divorce pour cause d'incompatibilité ou de caractère* (Paris, an V [1797]).

73. Oudot, 20 nivôse an V, *Moniteur* 112, 22 nivôse an V (11 Jan. 1797), and 28 nivôse an V, *Moniteur* 120, 30 nivôse an V (19 Jan. 1797); Félix Faulcon, "Sur le divorce, 14 prairial an V," in his *Mélanges législatifs, historiques, et politiques, Pendant la durée de la Constitution de l'an III,* 3 vols. (Paris, 1801, an IX), 1:

208–13, 221–24, 228–29, 244, 249–50; Lecointe-Puyraveau, *Opinion sur le projet;* Dumolard, 12 pluviôse an V, *Moniteur* 135, 15 pluviôse an V (3 Feb. 1797); Desan, "Marriage, Religion, and the Moral Order."

74. Desmolin, 25 prairial an IV, *Moniteur* 271, 1 messidor an IV (19 June 1796); Villetard, 14 thermidor an III, *Moniteur* 320, 20 thermidor an III (7 Aug. 1795).

75. Lanthenas, 24 prairial an IV, *Moniteur* 269, 29 prairial an IV (17 June 1796); Pons de Verdun, 28 nivôse an V, *Moniteur* 120, 30 nivôse an V (19 Jan. 1797). For leftists' invocation of social order and legal stability, see the debates on inheritance, 8–9 fructidor an III (25–26 Aug. 1795) in *Moniteur* 341–42, 11–12 fructidor an III (28–29 Aug. 1795); on illegitimacy, 24–26 prairial an IV (12–14 June 1796) in *Moniteur* 270–73, 30 prairial–3 messidor an IV (18–21 June 1796); on divorce, 28 nivôse–12 pluviôse an V (17–31 Jan. 1797) in *Moniteur* 120, 125–35, 30 nivôse–15 pluviôse an V (19 Jan.–3 Feb. 1797); 20 prairial an V (8 June 1797) in *Moniteur* 266–67, 26–27 prairial an V (14–15 June 1797).

76. Faulcon, *Mélanges législatifs,* 214. Cf. Thibaudeau and Oudot, 20 prairial an V, *Moniteur* 267, 27 prairial an V (15 June 1797); Lecointe-Puyraveau, *Opinion sur le projet.*

77. Faulcon, *Mélanges législatifs,* 230–36; Portalis, *Rapport sur la résolution du 29 prairial dernier, rélative au divorce, séance du 27 thermidor an V* (Paris, fructidor an V [Aug. 1797]).

78. Anonymous deputy, 20 prairial an V, *Moniteur* 267, 27 prairial an V (15 June 1797).

79. Colin Lucas, "The First Directory and the Rule of Law," *French Historical Studies* 10 (1977): 231–60; Xavier Martin, "L'individualisme libéral en France autour de 1800: Essai de spectroscopie," *Revue d'histoire des facultés de droit et de science juridique* 4 (1978): 87–144.

80. Lanjuinais, 14 thermidor an III, *Moniteur* 320, 20 thermidor an III (7 Aug. 1795).

81. Constitution de l'an III, Godechot, ed., *Constitutions,* 103; Guiraudet, *La famille considérée comme l'élément des sociétés,* 194–95.

82. The necessity of defending the status of *biens nationaux* would only make more urgent this need to set property on a sure footing. Halpérin, *Impossible Code civil,* 278.

CHAPTER 8

1. As cited in Bernard Schwartz, ed., *The Code Napoleon and the Common-Law World* (New York, 1956), vii; Jean Carbonnier, *Droit Civil* (Paris, 1958), 48, as cited in Jacques Lafon, "Le Code civil et la restructuration de la société française," *Mémoires de la Société pour l'histoire du droit et des institutions des anciens pays bourguignons, comtois et romands* 42 (1985): 101–7, 105.

2. Jean-Louis Halpérin, *L'impossible Code civil* (Paris, 1994). On the purge of the Tribunate, see Irene Collins, *Napoleon and His Parliaments* (London,

1979), 56–67; Jean-Louis Halpérin, "Tribunat" in *Dictionnaire Napoléon*, ed. Jean Tulard (Paris, 1987), 1655–57; Isser Woloch, *Napoleon and His Collaborators* (New York, 2001), 85–89. The Civil Code was renamed the Napoleonic Code in 1807.

3. As Halpérin notes, the Code's statutes governing contracts, property, and debt resembled the laws in the revolutionary drafts. *Impossible Code civil*, 276–80.

4. On approaches to the Code, see James F. Traer, *Marriage and the Family in Eighteenth-Century France* (Ithaca, N.Y., 1980), 182–85. Halpérin has esp. debunked the view that the Code stood above politics. *Impossible Code civil*, 287–96. Cf. the largely celebratory centennial work *Le code civil, 1804–1904: Livre du centenaire*, 2 vols. (Paris, 1904); Marcel Planiol, *Treatise on the Civil Law*, with collaboration of George Ripert, trans. Louisiana State Law Institute (St. Paul, Minn., 1959). For more recent emphasis on the Code as a compromise between Old Regime and revolutionary law, see Jean Carbonnier, *Droit Civil* (Paris, 1957); Jacques Godechot, *Les institutions de la France sous la Révolution et l'Empire* (Paris, 1968), 691–96; Joseph Goy, "Civil Code," in *A Critical Dictionary of the French Revolution*, ed. François Furet and Mona Ozouf, trans. Arthur Goldhammer (Cambridge, Mass., 1989), 437–48. For emphasis on Old Regime elements within the "transaction," see H. A. L. Fisher, "The Codes," in *The Cambridge Modern History*, vol. 9, *Napoleon* (New York, 1906), 148–79.

5. For stress on Napoleon's role, see Jean-Joseph Perouse, *Napoléon 1er et les lois civiles du Consulat et de l'Empire* (Paris, 1866). For the view that the Code set the "rules of the bourgeois game," see André-Jean Arnaud, *Essai d'analyse structurale du Code civil des français: La règle du jeu dans la paix bourgeoise* (Paris, 1973), and *Les origines doctrinales du Code civil des français* (Paris, 1969). Many authors refer to the Code as a force consolidating the bourgeoisie's position. For criticism of Arnaud's formulation, see Michelle Perrot, "The Family Triumphant," in *A History of Private Life*, ed. Philippe Ariès and Georges Duby, vol. 4, *From the Fires of Revolution to the Great War*, ed. Michelle Perrot, trans. Arthur Goldhammer (Cambridge, Mass., 1990), 99–129, esp. 113–14; Goy, "Civil Code," 445. For the view that the Code destabilized rural society, see Frédéric Le Play, *L'Organisation de la famille selon le vrai modèle signalé par l'histoire de toutes les races et de tous les temps* (Paris, 1871). Some historians argue that the Code promoted both agrarian and commercial capital. See, e.g., the useful overview in Martyn Lyons, *Napoleon Bonaparte and the Legacy of the French Revolution* (New York, 1994), 94–103.

6. On continuity with the Revolution, see Jean Bart, "L'individu et ses droits," in *FLE*, 351–62; and "La famille bourgeoise, héritière de la Révolution?" in *Enfant*, 357–72. See also note 4, esp. Carbonnier, *Droit Civil*. On the Code's "individualism" and atomization, see René Savatier, *Le droit, l'amour et la liberté* (Paris, 1963); Lafon, "Le Code civil." On reaction to the Revolution, see Halpérin, *Impossible Code civil*, 276–86, and *Histoire du droit privé français depuis 1804* (Paris, 1996), 15–24; Xavier Martin, "L'individualisme libéral en France autour de 1800: Essai de spectroscopie," *Revue d'histoire des facultés de*

droit et de science juridique 4 (1978): 87–144; Jacques Mulliez, "La volonté d'un homme," in *Histoire des pères et de la paternité,* ed. Jean Delumeau and Daniel Roche (Paris, 1990), 279–312; Mulliez, " 'Pater is est . . . ' La source juridique de la puissance paternelle du droit révolutionnaire au Code civil," in *FLE,* 412–30; Philippe Sagnac, *La législation civile de la Révolution française (1789–1804)* (Paris, 1898).

7. On gender continuity between the Revolution, especially Jacobinism, and the Code, see Michèle Bordeaux, "L'universalisme juridique et l'impasse de l'égalité," in *Les femmes et la Révolution française,* ed. Marie-France Brive 3 vols. (Toulouse, 1990), 1: 427–40; Madelyn Gutwirth, *The Twilight of the Goddesses: Women and Representation in the French Revolutionary Era* (New Brunswick, N.J., 1992), 371–74; Isabelle V. Hull, *Sexuality, State, and Civil Society in Germany, 1700–1815* (Ithaca, N.Y., 1996), 372–77; Joan B. Landes, *Women and the Public Sphere in the Age of the French Revolution* (Ithaca, N.Y., 1988), 145–46. Gutwirth sees ideological continuity but differences in law.

8. As quoted in Mulliez, "La volonté d'un homme," 280.

9. Delivered by Portalis, signed also by Tronchet, Bigot de Préameneu, Maleville, 1 pluviôse an IX (21 Jan. 1801), in Fenet, 1: 464–66; Duveyrier, 2 germinal an XI (23 Mar. 1803), Fenet 10: 206. Irène Théry and Christian Biet, "Portalis ou l'esprit des siècles, la rhétorique du mariage dans le discours préliminaire au projet du Code civil," in *FLE,* 104–21.

10. Claude Bellanger et al., eds., *Histoire générale de la presse française,* 5 vols. (Paris, 1969), 1: 549–67; Alain Cabanis, *La presse sous le Consulat et l'Empire (1799–1814)* (Paris, 1975), 11–36, 43–59; Woloch, *Napoleon and His Collaborators,* 36–89; Laura Mason, *Singing the French Revolution: Popular Culture and Politics, 1787–1799* (Ithaca, N.Y., 1996), 203–8.

11. Traer, *Marriage and Family,* 167–71.

12. F.-N. Mollien, *Mémoires d'un ministre du trésor public, 1780–1815* (1898), 1: 231, 234–35, as cited in Woloch, *Napoleon and His Collaborators,* 43. On constructing consensus, see Woloch, 36–89.

13. *Dictionnaire Napoléon,* ed. Tulard; A. Kucscinski, *Dictionnaire des Conventionnels* (Paris, 1917); David Jordan, *The King's Trial: Louis XVI vs. the French Revolution* (Berkeley, 1979), 247; Woloch, *Napoleon and His Collaborators,* 123–25.

14. Under the Constitution, the Tribunate held the power to debate legislation drafted by the Council of State and then forwarded its recommendation to the Legislative Chamber. This body in turn voted laws but could not discuss them.

15. Halpérin, *Impossible Code civil,* 275.

16. Boulay de la Meurthe, *AP* 2d series: 1, 19 ventôse an VIII (10 Mar. 1800); Treilhard, 19 ventôse an XI (10 Mar. 1803), Fenet 9: 469; Albisson, 3 germinal an XI (24 Mar. 1803), Fenet 10: 533–43; Savoie-Rollin, 27 ventôse an XI (18 Mar. 1803), Fenet 9: 502; Lahary, 28 ventôse an XI (19 Mar. 1803), Fenet 10: 159; Regnaud de Saint-Jean-d'Angély, *AP,* ser. 2, vol. 1: 513, 3 germinal an VIII (24

Mar. 1800); Portalis, as cited in Don Kelley, *Historians and the Law in Postrevolutionary France* (Princeton, N.J., 1984), 53.

17. Kelley, *Historians and the Law,* 43–55.

18. Lahary, as cited by Xavier Martin, "Approche du droit révolutionnaire et du Code Napoléon: Précautions de méthode," in *FLE,* 237–47, p. 241; Martin, "Politique et droit privé après Thermidor," in *RévJur,* 1: 173–78; Arnaud, *Essai d'analyse structurale;* Halpérin, *Impossible Code civil,* 277–78. On slavery, see Robin Blackburn, *The Overthrow of Colonial Slavery 1776–1848* (London, 1988), 161–264; Elizabeth Colwill, "Women's Empire and the Sovereignty of Man in *La Décade philosophique,* 1794–1807," *Eighteenth-Century Studies* 29 (1996): 265–85, esp. 276–77.

19. Portalis, 1 pluviôse an IX (21 Jan. 1801), Fenet 1: 522.

20. Gillet, 23 ventôse an XI (14 Mar. 1803), Fenet 9: 187; Portalis, 30 nivôse an XI (20 Jan. 1803), Fenet 12: 259.

21. Loi du 4 germinal an VIII (25 Mar. 1800), Duvergier 12: 169–70. Jacqueminot also prefigured the Code by urging a restoration of paternal power. Jacqueminot, 30 frimaire an VIII (21 Dec. 1799), Fenet 1: 327–32; Xavier Martin, "A tout âge? Sur la durée du pouvoir des pères dans le Code Napoléon," *Revue d'histoire des facultés de droit et de la science juridique* 13 (1992): 227–301.

22. *AP,* ser. 2, vol. 1: 335–36, 429–34, 471–82, 484–91, 495–505, 507–513, 19 ventôse au 4 germinal an VIII (10–25 Mar. 1800). At least thirteen legislators participated in this debate. Quoted opponents: Andrieux, Challan, and Legonidec; supporters, Duveyrier, Boulay de la Meurthe. The Tribunate's vote (53 in favor, 35 opposed) was only advisory to the Legislative Chamber's vote (213 in favor, 53 opposed).

23. Martin Staum, "Images of Paternal Power: Intellectuals and Social Change in the French National Institute," *Journal of Canadian History* 17 (1982): 425–45, and *Minerva's Message: Stabilizing the French Revolution* (Montreal, 1996), 70–72, 246–47. Most entries and the Institute judges worried that revolutionary legislation had excessively weakened paternal power. Cambacérès and Bigot de Préameneu served as intermediaries between the Institute and the drafting of the Code.

24. Berlier argued most frequently against over-extending paternal authority: 8 vendémiaire an XI (30 Sept. 1802), Fenet 10: 494; 30 nivôse an XI (20 Jan. 1803), Fenet 12: 257.

25. Réal, 23 ventôse an XI (14 Mar. 1803), Fenet 10: 517; Sylvia Schafer, *Children in Moral Danger and the Problem of Government in Third Republic France* (Princeton, N.J., 1997), 34–35; Françoise Fortunet, "Des mères légitimes et leurs enfants," *Mémoires de la société pour l'histoire du droit et des institutions des anciens pays bourguignons, comtois et romands* (2001): 93–101.

26. Réal, 23 ventôse an XI (14 Mar. 1803), Fenet 10: 519; Peter McPhee, *A Social History of France, 1780–1880* (London, 1992), 84.

27. Albisson, 3 germinal an XI (24 Mar. 1803), Fenet 10: 539; Martin, "Individualisme libéral en France," 91–99.

28. Constant, 4 nivôse an X (25 Dec. 1801), Fenet 8: 137–38.

29. Sédillez, Fenet 8: 191. Cf. Fenet 8: 98–249, esp. Grenier, 199–205, and Parent-Réal, 225–26. Although the Tribunate advised the Legislative Chamber to adopt Article 60, the Council of State removed this statute from its next draft and final version. Constant and Sédillez were both purged from the Tribunate in 1802. Portalis, 16 ventôse an XI (7 Mar. 1803), Fenet 9: 175; cf. Gillet, 23 ventôse an XI (14 Mar. 1803), Fenet 9: 191–93.

30. As quoted in A. Cabantous, "La fin des patriarches," in *Histoire des pères*, 321–48, 335. On the Code's ambiguities regarding the father's control over illegitimate children, see Mulliez, " 'Pater is est . . . ,' " 423–28, and "Volonté d'un homme," 302–5. On familial honor, see William M. Reddy, *The Invisible Code: Honor and Sentiment in Postrevolutionary France, 1814–1848* (Berkeley, 1997).

31. Jennifer Heuer, "Foreigners, Families, and Citizens: The Contradictions of National Citizenship in France, 1789–1830" (Ph.D. diss., University of Chicago, 1998), chap. 5, 190. Gillet, 17 ventôse an XI (8 Mar. 1803), Fenet 9: 187.

32. Vesin, 1 germinal an XI (22 Mar. 1803), Fenet 10: 528.

33. Portalis, 1 pluviôse an IX (21 Jan. 1801), Fenet 1: 463–523; Portalis as cited in Théry and Biet, "Portalis ou l'esprit des siècles," 111.

34. Théry and Biet, "Portalis ou l'esprit des siècles," 117; Portalis, 14 vendémiaire an X (6 Oct. 1801), Fenet 9: 248–58, 265; Bigot de Préameneu, same date, Fenet 9: 271; Treilhard, 19 ventôse an XI (10 Mar. 1803), Fenet 9: 472; Tronchet, 16 vendémiaire an X (8 Oct. 1801), Fenet 9: 282–83.

35. Articles 212, 213, *Code civil des français* in *Manuel de droit français*, ed. J. B. J. Paillet (Paris, n.d.) (hereafter cited as *Code civil*). Jacques Mulliez, "Droit et morale conjugale: Essai sur l'histoire des relations personnelles entre époux," *Revue historique* 278 (1987): 35–106, esp. 38–48, 86; Georges Duby, *The Knight, the Lady, and the Priest: The Making of Modern Marriage in Medieval France* (New York, 1983); Robert Pothier, *Traité du contrat de mariage* (Paris, 1771), Articles 379–83; Nicole Arnaud-Duc, "The Law's Contradictions," in *A History of Women in the West* , ed. Georges Duby and Michelle Perrot, vol. 4, *Emerging Feminism from Revolution to World War*, ed. Geneviève Fraisse and Michelle Perrot, trans. Arthur Goldhammer (Cambridge, Mass., 1993), 80–113, esp. 97–99.

36. Portalis, 16 ventôse an XI (7 Mar. 1803), Fenet 9: 177–78.

37. Ibid., 9: 177.

38. Portalis, 14 vendémiaire an X (6 Oct. 1801), Fenet 9: 255; Boulay de la Meurthe, same date, Fenet 9: 272.

39. Colwill, "Women's Empire and the Sovereignty of Man," 272; William Reddy, "Sentimentalism and Its Erasure: The Role of Emotions in the Era of the French Revolution," *Journal of Modern History* 72 (2000): 109–152.

40. Jacqueline Brisset, *L'adoption de la communauté comme régime légal dans le code civil* (Paris, 1967), 58–85. As Brisset notes, Maleville and Carion-Nisas defended the dotal system vehemently; fellow Southerner Portalis likewise expressed hostility toward the communal system. Fenet 13: 492–832; Berlier, 6 vendémiaire an XII (29 Sept. 1803), Fenet 13: 525; Maleville, 13

vendémiaire an XII (6 Oct. 1803), Fenet 13: 550. See also Nicole Arnaud-Duc, "Le droit et les comportements, la genèse du titre V du livre III du Code civil: Les régimes matrimoniaux," in *FLE*, 183–95.

41. Bigot de Préameneu, 6 vendémiaire an XII (29 Sept. 1803), Fenet 13: 533; Gillet, 16 ventôse an XI (7 Mar. 1803), Fenet 9: 194–95.

42. Heuer, "Foreigners, Families, and Citizens," chaps. 2 and 3; "Adopted Daughter of the French People: Suzanne Lepeletier and Her Father, the National Assembly," *French Politics, Culture and Society* 17 (1999): 31–51.

43. For overviews of the Code and women, see H. D. Lewis, "The Legal Status of Women in Nineteenth-Century France," *Journal of European Studies* 10 (1980): 178–88; Jean-François Tétu, "Remarques sur le statut juridique de la femme au XIXe siècle," *La femme au XIXe siècle: Littérature et idéologie* (Lyon, 1978), 5–17.

44. Cécile Dauphin, "Single Women," in *History of Women*, 4: 427–42, 432; Michèle Bordeaux, "Droits et femmes seules: Les pièges de la discrimination," in *Madame ou Mademoiselle? Itinéraires de la solitude féminine, XVIIIe–XXe siècles*, ed. Arlette Farge and Christiane Klapisch-Zuber (Mayenne, 1984), 19–57; Godechot, *Institutions de la France*, 694.

45. Napoléon, 24 frimaire an X (15 Dec. 1801), Fenet 9: 102; Portalis, 14 vendémiaire an X (6 Oct. 1801), Fenet 9: 258.

46. Hendrik Hartog, *Man and Wife in America: A History* (Cambridge, Mass., 2000), 29–30.

47. The couple had to have been married for at least two years, but not more than twenty; the wife had to be between the ages of twenty-one and forty-five and the husband over twenty-five; the couple needed to obtain the consent of parents or other relatives through a year-long series of formal requests. Spouses who divorced by mutual consent also were forbidden to contract a new marriage for three years. They could not divide their goods until half had been passed onto their children.

48. In Caen, I found only 13 divorces by the Civil Code (1803–16), including four by mutual consent. See Appendix 1 for sources. Lyon and Rouen witnessed a similar decline in divorce (84 in Lyon; 83 in Rouen, including only 6 by mutual consent). Dominique Dessertine, *Divorcer à Lyon sous la Révolution et l'Empire* (Lyon, 1981), 93–95; Roderick Phillips, *Family Breakdown in Late Eighteenth-Century France: Divorces in Rouen, 1792–1803* (Oxford, 1980), 44–60.

49. Martin, "Individualisme libéral en France," 121; Marcel Garaud et Romuald Szramkiewicz, *La Révolution française et la famille* (Paris, 1978), 187.

50. By and large, during the 1790s, husbands had nonetheless used this motive more often than wives had, due no doubt to the embedded double standard within popular opinion. See Chapter 3.

51. The Penal Code granted the husband the right to pursue his adulterous wife in court; the Civil Code listed her punishment as imprisonment for three months to two years. Michèle Bordeaux, "Le maître et l'infidèle: Des relations personnelles entre mari et femme de l'ancien droit au Code civil," in *FLE*, 432–45; Lewis, "Legal Status of Women," 182–84.

52. Savoie-Rollin, 27 ventôse an XI (18 Mar. 1803), Fenet 9: 501–3; Treilhard, 19 ventôse an XI (10 Mar. 1803), Fenet 9: 477; Portalis, 16 ventôse an XI (7 Mar. 1803), Fenet 9: 178; Napoléon, 14 brumaire an X (5 Nov. 1801), Fenet 10: 7; Tronchet et al., 9 nivôse an XI (30 Dec. 1802), Fenet 12: 36–38.

53. For a discussion of the historiography that (over)emphasizes Napoleon's role, see Traer, *Marriage and the Family*, 183–84; Napoléon, 14 vendémiaire an X (6 Oct. 1801), Fenet 9: 262 (note), and 16 vendémiaire an X (8 Oct. 1801), 9: 295. Cf. the similar comments of Boulay de la Meurthe, same date, Fenet 9: 266.

54. Napoléon, 26 brumaire an X (17 Nov. 1801), Fenet 10: 77.

55. See Tribunate debates, 2–7 nivôse an X (23–28 Dec. 1801), Fenet 8: 98–148, esp. Andrieux, 193–98, J. A. Perreau, 149–51, Roujoux, 152–55, Duveyrier, 170–78, and Huguet, 207–210.

56. Between Thermidor in 1794 and 1801, fifty-eight different deputies participated in the endless debates on the juridical technicalities of the 12 brumaire law. Particularly in the late Directory, no other family law matter occupied the Councils as extensively. Pastoret, 24 nivôse an V (13 Jan. 1797), *Moniteur* 117, 27 nivôse an V (16 Jan. 1797).

57. For the debates on filiation, see Fenet 10: 3–246. Bigot de Préameneu, 20 ventôse an XI (11 Mar. 1803), Fenet 10: 148; Berlier, 26 brumaire an X (17 Nov. 1801), Fenet 10: 90.

58. Bigot de Préameneu, 13 brumaire an XI (4 Nov. 1802), Fenet 10: 131; Lahary, 28 ventôse an XI (19 Mar. 1803), Fenet 10: 184.

59. Tronchet, 16 vendémiaire an X (8 Oct. 1801), Fenet 9: 282.

60. On the masculine nature of liberal individualism, see Carole Pateman, *The Sexual Contract* (Stanford, Calif., 1988); Joan Wallach Scott, *Only Paradoxes to Offer: French Feminists and the Rights of Man* (Cambridge, Mass., 1996).

61. Jean Limpens, "Territorial Expansion of the Code," in *Code Napoleon and the Common-Law World*, 92–109; Lyons, *Napoleon Bonaparte*, 102–3; Jean Carbonnier, "Le Code civil," in *Les lieux de mémoire*, Part 2, *La Nation*, ed. Pierre Nora, 3 vols. (Paris, 1986), 2:293–315, 297; Hull, *Sexuality, State, and Civil Society in Germany*, 371–406. On women and citizenship, see Heuer, "Foreigners, Families, and Citizens"; Anne McClintock, *Imperial Leather: Race, Gender and Sexuality in the Colonial Contest* (London, 1995), 358, and "Family Feuds: Gender, Nationalism and the Family," *Feminist Review* 44 (1993): 61–80; Virginia Sapiro, "Women, Citizenship and Nationality: Immigration and Naturalization Policies in the United States," *Politics and Society* 13 (1984): 1–23; Nancy F. Cott, "Marriage and Citizenship in the United States, 1830–1934," *American Historical Review* 103 (1998): 1440–74.

62. On feminist critiques of the Code, see Claire Goldberg Moses, *French Feminism in the Nineteenth Century* (Albany, N.Y., 1984); Steven C. Hause with Anne R. Kenney, *Women's Suffrage and Social Politics in the French Third Republic* (Princeton, N.J., 1984); Scott, *Only Paradoxes to Offer*; Whitney Walton, *Eve's Proud Descendants: Four Women Writers and Republican Politics*

in Nineteenth-Century France (Stanford, Calif., 2000); Susan Groag Bell and Karen M. Offen, eds., *Women, the Family, and Freedom: The Debate in Documents,* 2 vols. (Stanford, Calif., 1983). On paternal power, see Schafer, *Children in Moral Danger,* chap. 2, esp. p. 36.

63. As cited in Kelley, *Historians and the Law,* 43.

64. Pierre Bourdieu, "Célibat et condition paysanne," *Etudes rurales* 5–6 (1962); André Burguière, "Les fondements d'une culture familiale," in *Histoire de la France: Les formes de la culture,* ed. André Burguière (Paris, 1993), 25–118, esp. 61–65; Elisabeth Claverie and Pierre Lamaison, *L'impossible mariage: Violence et parenté en Gévaudan, XVIIe, XVIIIe et XIXe siècles* (Poitiers, 1982); Margaret Darrow, *The Revolution in the House: Family, Class, and Inheritance in Southern France, 1775–1825* (Princeton, N.J., 1989); Michelle Salitot, *Héritage, parenté et propriété en Franche-Comté du XIIIe siècle à nos jours* (Paris, 1988); Rolande Bonnain, "Droit écrit, coutume pyrénéenne et pratiques successorales dans les baronnies, 1769–1836," *Les Baronnies de Pyrénées,* ed. I. Chiva and J. Goy, 2 vols. (Paris, 1986), 2: 157–77; Perrot, "Family Triumphant," 113–14.

65. Cabantous, "Fin des patriarches"; Bernard Schnapper, "La correction paternelle et le mouvement des idées au dix-neuvième siècle (1789–1935)," *Revue historique* 263 (1980): 319–49; Schafer, *Children in Moral Danger.*

66. Adeline Daumard's work on the early-nineteenth-century Parisian bourgeoisie demonstrated that most marriage contracts protected married women's property rights by guaranteeing wives a "gain de survie" (an additional widow's portion) and resurrecting Old Regime mortgage guarantees that surrounded women's dowries. In practice, this meant that wives played a much larger role in deciding the use of their dowries than the Code would seem to allow, while wives, especially in the commercial classes, continued to play a crucial role in managing the couple's business goods. *Les bourgeois de Paris au XIXe siècle* (Paris, 1970), 185–97, and *La bourgeoisie parisienne de 1815 à 1848* (Paris, 1963), 357–74. Cf. Nicole Arnaud-Duc, *Droit, mentalités et changement social en Provence occidentale: Une étude sur les stratégies et la pratique notariale en matière de régime matrimonial de 1785 à 1855* (Saint-Etienne, 1985); Heuer, "Foreigners, Families, and Citizens," chap. 7. Heuer emphasizes the conservative gender impact of the Code, but also notes how it could be tempered in practice. For example, in the judgment of municipal officials in Strasbourg, a marriage between a French woman and a foreign man more often resulted in civil rights and rights of residency and work for the foreign man rather than loss of citizenship for the woman; the city needed workers more than it needed to guard Frenchness by the letter of the law. Rachel G. Fuchs, "Seduction, Paternity, and the Law in Fin de Siècle France," *Journal of Modern History* 72 (2000): 944–89. The woman's damages could include "pregnancy, loss of job, destitution, prostitution, and even loss of value on the marriage market because she was 'damaged goods' " (Fuchs, 971).

67. Carbonnier, "Le Code civil," 309; cf. Carbonnier, *Droit Civil,* 48, as cited in Lafon, "Code civil," 105.

CONCLUSION

1. Albert Soboul, *The Sans-Culottes: The Popular Movement and Revolutionary Government, 1793–1794*, trans. Rémy Inglis Hall (Princeton, N.J., 1972; orig. ed. 1968); AN DIII 339, Adresse à la Convention, signée par la veuve Boudeau, n.d., c. 1795.

2. Cf. Joan B. Landes, *Women and the Public Sphere in the Age of the French Revolution* (Ithaca, N.Y., 1988); Carole Pateman, *The Sexual Contract* (Stanford, Calif., 1988); Joan Wallach Scott, *Only Paradoxes to Offer: French Feminists and the Rights of Man* (Cambridge, Mass., 1996).

3. Claire Goldberg Moses, *French Feminism in the Nineteenth Century* (Albany, N.Y., 1984); Karen Offen, *European Feminisms, 1750–1950* (Stanford, Calif., 2000); Michèle Riot-Sarcey, *La démocratie à l'épreuve des femmes: Trois figures critiques du pouvoir 1830–1848* (Paris, 1994); Scott, *Only Paradoxes to Offer; Femmes dans la Cité, 1815–1871*, ed. Alain Corbin et al. (Crest, 1997); Whitney Walton, *Eve's Proud Descendants: Four Women Writers and Republican Politics in Nineteenth-Century France* (Stanford, Calif., 2000).

4. Marcel Garaud and Romuald Szramkiewicz, *La famille et la Révolution française* (Paris, 1978), 187–91.

5. Jean-Pierre Chaline, *Les bourgeois de Rouen: Une élite urbaine du XIXe siècle* (Paris, 1982); Charles Alline, *De l'ancien régime matrimonial normand et de sa survivance dans la pratique notariale sous le droit intermédiaire et sous le code civil* (Thèse de droit, Université de Caen [Paris, 1908]). Norman families often opted for a system known as "société des acquets" that merged newly acquired marital goods and retained separation of certain hereditary properties. For France as a whole, early nineteenth-century court records and jurists' handbooks bear testimony to the complex juggling between Old Regime, revolutionary, and Napoleonic laws and family models. E.g., *Recueil général des lois et des arrêts, avec notes et commentaires . . . , fondé par M. Sirey*, rev. and completed par L. M. Devilleneuve and A. A. Carette, 10 vols. (Paris, 1840–43); *Journal du Palais: Recueil le plus ancien et le plus complet de la jurisprudence française*, ed. Ledru-Rollin, 3rd ed. (Paris, 1858); D. Dalloz, *Répertoire méthodique et alphabétique de doctrine et de jurisprudence*, 44 vols. (Paris, 1845–70); Philippe Antoine Merlin de Douai, *Recueil alphabétique de questions de droit*, 4th ed., 16 vols. (Bruxelles, 1928). See notes 64–66 in Chapter 8 for further studies on family negotiation. Cf. also work on adaptive families and industrialization: Tessie P. Liu, *The Weaver's Knot: The Contradictions of Class Struggle and Family Solidarity in Western France, 1750–1815* (Ithaca, N.Y., 1994); Katherine A. Lynch, *Family, Class, and Ideology in Early Industrial France: Social Policy and the Working Class Family, 1825- 1848* (Madison, Wisc., 1988); Elinor Accampo, *Industrialization, Family Life, and Class Relations: Saint Chamond, 1815–1914* (Berkeley, 1989).

6. Nicole Arnaud-Duc, *Droit, mentalités et changement social en Provence occidentale: Une étude sur les stratégies et la pratique notariale en matière de régime matrimonial de 1785 à 1855* (Saint-Etienne, 1985); Margaret Darrow,

The Revolution in the House: Family, Class, and Inheritance in Southern France, 1775- 1825 (Princeton, N.J., 1989); Alline, *Ancien régime matrimonial;* Adeline Daumard, *La bourgeoisie parisienne de 1815 à 1848* (Paris, 1963), chap. 4; David Garrioch, *The Formation of the Parisian Bourgeoisie, 1690–1830* (Cambridge, Mass., 1996); Bonnie Smith, *Ladies of the Leisure Class: The Bourgeoises of Northern France in the Nineteenth Century* (Princeton, N.J., 1981), 57–63; Michelle Perrot, "The Family Triumphant," in *A History of Family Life*, vol. 4., *From the Fires of Revolution to the Great War*, ed. Michelle Perrot, trans. Arthur Goldhammer (Cambridge, Mass., 1990), 99–165, pp. 113–15. The revolutionary and Napoleonic legal innovations encouraged the longer-term trend away from dotal regimes and toward communal marital property arrangements, but couples embraced this shift only where local cultures and socioeconomic conditions made new strategies appealing. For example, in Provence, the rentier and professional bourgeoisie of Aix-en-Provence clung to dotal practices, while couples in the industrializing region to the west of Aix embraced the more fluid communal marital property system. Likewise, small family size, a sense of political uncertainty, and a modernizing economy seem to have prompted Norman families to transform their customary dowry arrangements and lineage property divisions into a partially communal system. In Paris, bourgeois families relied less than they had in the eighteenth century on their extended lineages and learned to work the conjugal system to promote the couple's economic and affective needs and those of their immediate offspring. Arranged marriages continued to be the norm among bourgeois and upper-class families across France: even as they imagined the "family line" in a more restricted way than before, husbands and wives continued to devote their resources and social connections to setting up their children well.

7. André Burguière, "Les fondements d'une culture familiale," in *Histoire de la France: Les formes de la culture*, ed. André Burguière (Paris, 1993), 25–118; William Reddy, *The Invisible Code: Honor and Sentiment in Postrevolutionary France, 1814–1848* (Berkeley, 1997).

8. Sarah Hanley, "Engendering the State: Family Formation and State Building in Early Modern France," *French Historical Studies* 16 (1989): 4–27, and "The Monarchic State in Early Modern France: Marital Regime Governance and Male Right," in *Politics, Ideology, and Law in Early Modern Europe*, ed. Adrianna Bakos (Rochester, N.Y., 1994), 107–26; Catherine Crawford, "Regency Government in Early Modern France: Gender Substitution and the Construction of Monarchical Authority" (Ph.D. diss., University of Chicago, 1997); Jeffrey Merrick, "Fathers and Kings: Patriarchalism and Absolutism in Eighteenth-Century French Politics," *Studies on Voltaire and the Eighteenth Century* 308 (1993): 281–303, and "The Cardinal and the Queen: Sexual and Political Disorders in the Mazarinades," *French Historical Studies* 18 (1994): 667–99; Sarah Maza, *Public Lives and Private Affairs: The Causes Célèbres of Prerevolutionary France* (Berkeley, 1993).

9. For an overview, see Perrot, "Family Triumphant," esp. 99–113. Cf. Raymond Deniel, *Une Image de la famille et de la société sous la Restauration*

(1815–1830) (Paris, 1965); Claire Goldberg Moses and Leslie Wahl Rabine, *Feminism, Socialism, and French Romanticism* (Bloomington, Ind., 1993).

10. Louis de Bonald, *Journal des débats,* 4 brumaire an X (26 Oct. 1801), as quoted in Darrin M. McMahon, *Enemies of the Enlightenment: The French Counter-Enlightenment and the Making of Modernity* (N.Y., 2001), 137.

11. Mona Ozouf, *Festivals of the French Revolution,* trans. Alan Sheridan (Cambridge, Mass., 1988; orig. ed. 1976); Lynn Hunt, "The World We Have Gained: The Future of the French Revolution," *American Historical Review* 108 (2003): xvi–19.

12. Jean Jaurès, *Histoire socialiste de la Révolution française,* ed. and annotated by Albert Soboul, 7 vols. (Paris, 1970), 3: 348, as quoted by Jean Bart, "La famille bourgeoise, héritière de la Révolution?" in *Enfant,* 357–72, 366. On family and state, see Alain Cabantous, "La fin des patriarches," in *Histoire des pères et de la paternité,* ed. Jean Delumeau and Daniel Roche (Paris, 1990), 321–48; Sylvia Schafer, *Children in Moral Danger and the Problem of Government in Third Republic France* (Princeton, N.J., 1997); Bernard Schnapper, *Voies nouvelles en histoire du droit: La justice, la famille, la répression pénale (XVIe–XIXe siècles)* (Paris, 1991).

13. Peter McPhee, *A Social History of France, 1780–1880* (London, 1992).

14. Perrot, "Family Triumphant," 108–111; Bonald as quoted in McPhee, *Social History of France,* 110; Jo Burr Margadant, "Gender, Vice, and the Political Imaginary in Postrevolutionary France: Reinterpreting the Failure of the July Monarchy, 1830–1848," *American Historical Review* 104 (1999): 1461–96, and "The Duchesse de Berry and Royalist Political Culture in Postrevolutionary France," in *The New Biography: Performing Femininity in Nineteenth-Century France,* ed. Jo Burr Margadant (Berkeley, 2000), 33–71. For a synopsis of the notion that the Revolution created separate spheres, see James F. McMillan, *France and Women 1789–1914: Gender, Society and Politics* (London, 2000), esp. 41–44; Landes, *Women and the Public Sphere.*

15. Jean-Louis Halpérin, *Histoire du droit privé français depuis 1804* (Paris, 1996), 76–78; Jules Michelet, *Love* (1860) and *Woman* (1860), and Jenny P. d'Héricourt, *A Woman's Philosophy of Woman, or Woman Affranchised: An Answer to Michelet, Proudhon, Girardin, Legouvé, Comte and Other Modern Innovators* (1860), as excerpted in Susan Groag Bell and Karen M. Offen, eds., *Women, the Family, and Freedom: The Debate in Documents,* 2 vols. (Stanford, Calif., 1983), 1: 336–49, 347. On d'Héricourt's self-declared republicanism, see Karen Offen "A Nineteenth-Century French Feminist Rediscovered: Jenny P. d'Héricourt, 1809–1875," *Signs: Journal of Women in Culture and Society* 13 (1987): 144–58. Cf. Walton, *Eve's Proud Descendants.*

16. Elinor A. Accampo, Rachel C. Fuchs, and Mary Lynn Stewart, eds., *Gender and the Politics of Social Reform in France, 1870–1914* (Baltimore, 1995).

17. In 1876 Naquet had initially advocated a version of divorce law resembling the 1792 version. Theresa McBride, "Public Authority and Private Lives: Divorce after the French Revolution," *French Historical Studies* 17 (1992):

747–68, esp. 755–56, 759, and 761, and "Divorce and the Republican Family" in *Gender and the Politics of Social Reform*, 59–81; Francis Ronsin, *Les divorciaires: Affrontements politiques et conceptions du mariage dans la France du XIXe siècle* (Paris, 1992), chaps. 4 and 5. Regarding revolutionary innovations with both fascination and anxiety, Third Republic historians often emphasized the "crisis of the family" or "crisis of marriage" during the Revolution. E.g., François Olivier-Martin, *La Crise du mariage dans la législation intermédiaire, 1789–1804* (Paris, 1901).

Index

STUDIES ON THE HISTORY OF SOCIETY AND CULTURE

Victoria E. Bonnell and Lynn Hunt, Editors

Compositor: Binghamton Valley Composition
Text: Aldus
Display: 10/13 Aldus
Printer/Binder: Edwards Brothers, Inc.

Made in the USA
Coppell, TX
11 October 2021

63842515R00262